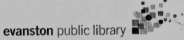
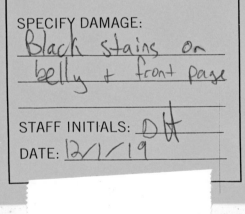

The Rise and Fall of Weimar Democracy

THE RISE AND FALL OF

Weimar Democracy

HANS MOMMSEN

Translated by Elborg Forster & Larry Eugene Jones

The University of North Carolina Press

Chapel Hill & London

© 1989 by Propyläen Verlag im
Verlag Ullstein GmbH
Frankfurt a. Main/Berlin
English translation

© 1996
The University of North Carolina Press
Manufactured in the United States of America

The translation and publication of this book have been aided by
generous grants from the L. J. Skaggs and Mary C. Skaggs Foundation,
the Lynde and Harry Bradley Foundation, and Inter Nationes, Bonn.

The paper in this book meets the guidelines for permanence and
durability of the Committee on Production Guidelines for Book
Longevity of the Council on Library Resources.

Library of Congress Cataloging-in-Publication Data
Mommsen, Hans.
[Verspielte Freiheit. English]
The rise and fall of Weimar democracy / by Hans Mommsen :
translated by Elborg Forster and Larry Eugene Jones.
p.   cm.
Includes bibliographic references and index.
ISBN 0-8078-2249-3 (alk. paper)
1. Germany—History—1918–1933.   I. Title.
DD237.M57   1996
943.085—dc20   95-8902
CIP
00   99   98   97   96   5   4   3   2   1

Contents

Preface

In German historical consciousness, the Weimar Republic has always been associated with the stigma of failure. Even in the deliberations of the Parliamentary Council in Bonn, Weimar was always seen — but particularly by the bourgeois center and Right — as a warning, as a situation whose recurrence was to be avoided at all costs. In the political debates of the western occupation zones, criticism of the liberal foundations of the Weimar Constitution was widespread until the 1950s. It was only with the subsequent success of the democratic regime under Konrad Adenauer that one began to view the Weimar Republic in a somewhat more positive light. Since then, the republic has even been invoked on occasion to highlight the continuity of Germany's democratic and parliamentary traditions with the fateful deliberations at the Paulskirche in 1848–49. Yet despite the increasing willingness of many Germans to recognize the accomplishments of the Weimar Republic, the general disdain they feel for Weimar is unmistakable in the popular claim that "Bonn is not Weimar."

The argument that the rise of Hitler resulted from the "overdemocratization" of the Weimar regime has since given way to a new emphasis on the rupture in continuity that occurred when the Nazis assumed power on 30 January 1933. The stress on the consummate manipulative skills of Hitler and the NSDAP only served to exonerate Hitler's allies and opponents from any real responsibility for his installation as chancellor. The same way of thinking also tended to attribute the collapse of parliamentary democracy to the obstructionist tactics systematically pursued by the parties of the extreme Left and Right, namely, the Communists and National Socialists. According to this view, the Weimar Republic was not only inherently viable, but its demise stemmed from a certain "self-destructiveness" of democracy. And yet, as Arnold Brecht has conclusively argued, it was not the Weimar democrats who were to be held responsible for this demise. Given the bleak conditions facing Germany after 1918, the Weimar regime was able to achieve a remarkable degree of political stability even though it never won the support of Germany's professional and conservative elites. From the very outset, German elites looked on this regime as a makeshift solution, as a transition and nothing more. Still, one should not assume that the descent into a fascist dictatorship was already inevitable at this time.

From the Wilhelmine Empire the Weimar Republic inherited profound social tensions that were temporarily obscured by the war. Rooted in prerevolutionary traditions, these tensions were exacerbated by a process of rapid modernization with which Germany's political institutions were not able to keep pace. It was these antagonisms — and not the much discussed German *Sonderweg*—that, heightened by the German Revolution of 1918–19, did so much to block the development of a pluralist social community and a liberal parliamentary system. The fears and frustrations of an upper class that saw its social privileges threatened by these changes further aggravated traditional class divisions. The frustration of Germany's elites expressed itself in an unexpectedly widespread acceptance of violence as a way of dealing with political opponents. At the same time, it spawned a far-reaching moral indifference that contributed in no small way to the feeble resistance of the bourgeois Right to Adolf Hitler and the Nazi movement. After 1919 significant segments of the industrial labor force found their demands for the democratization and socialization of the workplace almost totally rejected and were pushed to the periphery of German political life by the reactionary military. What remained embedded in the consciousness of this period, then, was not so much the accomplishments of a revolution that had lost its momentum but the counterrevolution and the quasi civil war it helped spawn.

The National Socialists conceived of the founding of the Third Reich as a response to the November Revolution. Echoing notions that surfaced in the immediate postwar period, they labeled their usurpation of power a "national awakening." In doing so, they revealed the patently absurd character of the fantasies long harbored by the bourgeois Right. Political actors of all stripes repeatedly evoked memories of the German defeat and the November Revolution. The collapse of the monarchy and the end of Germany's quest for European hegemony exerted a lasting influence on the political options and decisions of every German from 1918 on. The inner coherence of the period between 1917 and the early years of the Federal Republic was thus inherent in its point of departure in November 1918.

National Socialism represented a phenomenon characteristic of the emotionally overcharged and politically reactionary atmosphere of the first years after the end of the First World War. Originally founded as an offshoot of the Pan-German movement, the NSDAP developed an independent profile of its own under the leadership of Adolf Hitler and quickly moved away from the tutelage of the Pan-Germans. Ideologically it drew from a mixture of nationalist and anti-Semitic ideas that had existed in Germany ever since the founding of the Second Empire. In this respect, the movement could make no claim to originality. What was new, however, even though it was practiced only in a rudimentary manner in the last years of the imperial era, were the party's techniques for mobilizing its followers and for manipulating existing national traditions for its own ends. National Socialism distinguished itself from similar *völkisch* and nationalistic enterprises by a form of organization that pursued action for its own sake. It was this feature that gave the NSDAP its specifically fascist character. Complementing this was a complete lack of scruples in the use of means and a leadership cult that was so completely focused on Hitler's personality that it precluded the emergence of any other organized will within the party.

National Socialism was successful in exploiting the anxieties and resentments of those social groups in Germany that were adversely affected by the process of modernization. At the same time, it greatly intensified the level of national feeling that had been consciously fostered by the bourgeois parties and interest groups extending as far to the left as the democratic camp as a way of countering the threat that modernization posed to domestic political integration. The extreme autism that led the German public to overestimate its own importance rendered it incapable of correctly assessing the interests of neighboring states and lent credence to the National Socialist contention that Germany's potential for political power was solely a matter of the nation's internal cohesion. The mobilization of regressive resentments and the simultaneous satisfaction of the need for mobilization made it possible for National Socialism to establish itself as a sort of negative people's party.

Just as it would be misleading to imagine that National Socialism was a unique phenomenon that destroyed the foundations of the Weimar Republic from the outside, so would it be a mistake to interpret Weimar's external and internal development as a mere prelude to the history of the Third Reich. Most notably in the area of social relations, Weimar undertook a number of important initiatives that, even beyond those of the Third Reich, have left their imprint on the social and institutional fabric of German history since the end of World War II. Still, there is no denying the fact that close ideological affinities existed between the NSDAP and the bourgeois Right and that Adolf Hitler's rise as leader of a "national Germany" could have taken place only against the background of a broader texture of antiliberal and antisocialist currents. The National Socialist conquest of power presupposed the subversion of the parliamentary system and the organized labor movement, something that had already been partially accomplished under the aegis of the bourgeois presidential cabinets.

The transition to a fascist dictatorship, which began with the formation of the cabinet of national concentration in January 1933, presupposed the use of institutional instruments that had been forged and tested during the republican era as a way of strengthening the prerogatives of the executive vis-à-vis the parties and parliament. From a purely political perspective it is impossible to determine just when the break between the republic and the dictatorship took place. The passage of the Enabling Act on 23 March 1933 serves as a convenient dividing line between the Weimar and Nazi eras even though this event demonstrated a high degree of continuity with the general model of conflict resolution that had been established in the Weimar Republic. This account, therefore, ends in February 1933 with a look forward to the Enabling Act as the culminating moment in the break with the constitutional developments of the late Weimar Republic. To be sure, the reorganization of economic and social relationships under the Nazi regime proceeded much more slowly than in the late Weimar Republic, and the methods of the new leadership were fundamentally different from the political style of the bourgeois republic. Yet in many essential respects the aims of National Socialist foreign and domestic policies were identical with those of their bourgeois partners. There was certainly no revolutionary break with the past in the foreign policy arena. And in the domestic arena, the Nazi regime only gradually dissociated itself from the system of government that had been officially coordinated, or *gleichgeschaltet*, by the summer of 1933 until it had become nothing more than an empty shell without ever having been replaced by a new constitution.

The origin and demise of the Weimar Republic have long been a favorite topic of international scholarship. The interest that historians and political scientists have taken in this example of failed political modernization stems in no small measure from the need to answer the question as to how and why Hitler and the National Socialist movement were able to seize power and erect a regime based on terror and violence whose very essence, its claims to legitimacy notwithstanding, was apparent from the outset. Moreover, the Weimar experience represents a model for understanding the obstacles to and the prospects for the democratization of societies marked by autocratic traditions. Few eras of German history have been studied as intensely as that of the Weimar Republic. The plethora of perspectives and questions that has been raised in this context is also to be explained by the fact that Weimar's short history was marked by an unusually rich abundance of creative impulses. This is particularly true in the sphere of art and culture, where the phrase "Golden Twenties" was coined to describe this period, in spite of the inflation, economic stagnation, and increasingly bitter conflicts over the distribution of the social product that characterized it. The intellectual and artistic innovations of the early 1920s had their roots in the late Wilhelmine period. The artistic schools and fashions that followed one after the other, the parallel development of a mass-consumption society, the democratization of cultural life, and the emergence of an artistic avant-garde from Moscow to New York represented a fascinating spectacle that in Germany was limited primarily to Berlin, a city that had only recently emerged as a great metropolis. This new wave of artistic and intellectual modernity, however, did not have much impact upon the political life of the Weimar Republic despite the strong political commitments of many of modernity's advocates. Confined to a largely autonomous segment of German society, the modernist movement was almost completely destroyed with the National Socialist assumption of power in 1933.

By the same token, the 1920s were characterized by a plethora of new impulses in the areas of education, criminal justice, sexuality, ecology, housing, public health, and local cultural policy. Many of these innovations anticipated initiatives undertaken after 1945. The progressive growth of the public welfare state after 1918 has had consequences that have persisted to this very day. The same can be said of innovative bursts in technology, industry, and urbanization, all of which received further stimulus from the war without providing contemporaries with the self-confidence that would have enabled them to overcome their traumatic fixation on the Wilhelmine era.

In many respects, the transformation of the demographic, social, and economic conditions of German life took place independently of the political process. These conditions developed according to a rhythm of their own. I have therefore decided not to undertake a systematic analysis of these areas in the context of the present study, which focuses primarily on the origins and crisis-ridden development of the Weimar Republic. To have done otherwise would have seriously interfered with the goal of describing the political processes between 1917 and 1933, of accounting for the circumstances that gave rise to them, and of illustrating the convergence of different fields of political activity, most notably the interrelationship between domestic and foreign policy. For the same reason, I have tried to discuss economic issues and problems of high finance, both of which were closely related to international politics, in terms of their relationship to the political decision-making process. In some cases, this may have led to oversimplification or to a certain lack of balance. Still, that is the price one has to pay, given the greater disadvantages of a systematic description that might obscure the mutual interpenetration of different arenas of political activity and the structure of social, economic, and political interests. I have also chosen not to disrupt my account with scholarly discussions of issues in the field. The monographs and general studies I have consulted in writing this book are listed in the bibliography. An exhaustive description of the existing body of literature on the history of the Weimar Republic, however, was out of the question.

Abbreviations

ADGB	Allgemeiner Deutscher Gewerkschaftsbund/General German Trade-Union Federation
ADV	Alldeutscher Verband/Pan-German League
AEG	Allgemeine Elektrizitäts-Gesellschaft/General Electric Corporation
AVI	Arbeitsgemeinschaft der eisenverarbeitenden Industrie/Association of Iron-Processing Industry
BVP	Bayerische Volkspartei/Bavarian People's Party
DAF	Deutsche Arbeitsfront/German Labor Front
DAP	Deutsche Arbeiterpartei/German Workers' Party
DDP	Deutsche Demokratische Partei/German Democratic Party
DGB	Deutscher Gewerkschaftsbund/German Trade-Union Federation
DHV	Deutschnationaler Handlungsgehilfen-Verband/German National Union of Commercial Employees
DINTA	Deutsches Institut für technische Arbeitsschulung/German Institute for Technical Labor Training
DMV	Deutscher Metallarbeiter-Verband/German Metalworkers' Federation
DNVP	Deutschnationale Volkspartei/German National People's Party
DVFP	Deutschvölkische Freiheitspartei/German Racist Freedom Party
DVP	Deutsche Volkspartei/German People's Party
FAD	Freiwilliger Arbeitsdienst/Voluntary Labor Service
HJ	Hitlerjugend/Hitler Youth
I.G. Farben	Interessengemeinschaft Farben/I.G. Farben
ISK	Internationaler Sozialistischer Kampfbund/International Socialist Combat League
KAPD	Kommunistische Arbeiterpartei Deutschlands/German Communist Workers' Party
KPD	Kommunistische Partei Deutschlands/Communist Party of Germany

KPO	Kommunistische Partei Deutschlands (Opposition)/ Opposition Communist Party of Germany
Langnam Association	Langnam-Verein or Verein zur Wahrung der gemeinsamen wirtschaftlichen Interessen Rheinland und Westfalen/ Association for the Representation of the Common Economic Interests of the Rhineland and Westphalia
MICUM	Interallierte Mission zur Kontrolle der stahl- und eisenerzeugenden Industrie und des Steinkohlenbergbaus/Interallied Mission for the Control of the Steel and Iron Industry and Anthracite Mining
MSPD	Mehrheitssozialdemokratische Partei Deutschlands/Majority Social Democratic Party of Germany
NLP	Nationalliberale Partei/National Liberal Party
NSBO	Nationalsozialistische Betriebszellenorganisation/National Socialist Factory Cell Organization
NSDAP	Nationalsozialistische Deutsche Arbeiterpartei/National Socialist German Workers' Party
Orgesch	Organisation Escherich/Organization Escherich
RDI	Reichsverband der Deutschen Industrie/National Federation of German Industry
RFB	Roter Frontkämpferbund/Red Front Soldiers' League
RGO	Revolutionäre Gewerkschaftsopposition/Revolutionary Trade-Union Opposition
RjV	Reichsgemeinschaft junger Volksparteiler/Reich Association of Young Populists
RLB	Reichs-Landbund/National Rural League
SA	Sturmabteilungen der NSDAP/Storm Detachments of the NSDAP
SAJ	Sozialistische Arbeiterjugend/Socialist Workers' Youth
SAP, SAPD	Sozialistische Arbeiterpartei Deutschlands/Socialist Workers' Party of Germany
SPD	Sozialdemokratische Partei Deutschlands/Social Democratic Party of Germany
SS	Schutzstaffel der NSDAP/SS
UFA	Universum-Film Aktiengesellschaft/Universal Film Corporation
USPD	Unabhängige Sozialdemokratische Partei Deutschlands/ Independent Social Democratic Party of Germany
VDA	Vereinigung der Deutschen Arbeitgeberverbände/Federation of German Employer Associations
VKPD	Vereinigte Kommunistische Partei Deutschlands/United Communist Party of Germany

VNR	Volksnationale Reichsvereinigung/People's National Reich Association
WTB-Plan	Woytinski-Tarnow-Baade Plan
ZAG	Zentralarbeitsgemeinschaft der industriellen und gewerblichen Arbeitgeber und Arbeitnehmer Deutschlands/Central Association of Industrial and Commercial Employers and Employees of Germany

The Rise and Fall of Weimar Democracy

CHAPTER ONE

The Fall of the German Empire

ON 4 August 1914 the German Empire declared war on czarist Russia, thus setting in motion the inevitable chain of events that culminated in the outbreak of World War I. At the time, few observers had any idea that this war would end with the collapse of the Wilhelmine Empire. Seized by patriotic frenzy, the German masses supported the war enthusiastically. Fears that a war with multiple fronts would prove disastrous for the Central Powers were simply dismissed out of hand. In the face of imminent war, domestic political antagonisms receded into the background. Opponents of militarism on the left wing of the Social Democratic Party (Sozialdemokratische Partei Deutschlands or SPD) suddenly found themselves isolated within the organized labor movement. At the same time, Chancellor Theobald von Bethmann Hollweg brought the hotheads in the military into line by proclaiming a civil truce, or *Burgfriede*, that had been made possible by assurances from the socialist labor unions that they would not obstruct the German war effort. Wilhelm II's statement that he no longer recognized parties but only Germans was greeted with widespread approval. Bourgeois intellectuals rejoiced in the idea that the nation was united as it entered the defensive struggle that had been forced upon it and celebrated the *Burgfriede* as the beginning of Germany's national regeneration.

As the war progressed, the illusion that it might be possible to postpone dealing with the social and political antagonisms within the German nation until some time in the future was effectively shattered. In practical terms, the proclamation of the *Burgfriede* meant that the Reichstag met only sporadically—and then primarily for the purpose of approving military appropriations. At the same time, the parties maintained a low profile and filled vacant seats without the customary political rancor. As a result, the differences that crystallized in the debate over German war aims were initially expressed by special-interest groups and self-styled spokesmen of the people's will. This debate fostered exaggerated expectations that were totally inconsistent with the limited military resources of the Central Powers. Even as it became clear in the fall of 1916 that hopes of a victorious peace, or *Siegfriede*, had receded into the future, it proved extremely difficult to discard the totally unrealistic imperialist ambitions that, in the absence of any public discussion of the issue, had made their way into innumerable memoranda on German war aims.

If, in the long run, appeals to German national unity failed to cover up the domestic cleavages that existed within the nation as a whole, so was it impossible to hide the chronic crisis of Wilhelmine political leadership that had played such an important role in Germany's drift to war in 1914. The crisis was further aggravated by the fact that the status of the military was inadequately defined in the Bismarckian constitution and, as a result, the military was able to push aside civilian political authorities who carried ultimate political responsibility for the conduct of the war. The abandonment of Wilhelm II's "personal regiment" after the *Daily Telegraph* affair had created a leadership vacuum that, under wartime conditions, proved extremely harmful in more than one respect. Major military decisions remained within the competence of the Kaiser, who lacked the necessary political overview and was screened from public sentiment by his civilian advisors. That Bethmann Hollweg was able to engineer the fall of Erich von Falkenhayn and place the Supreme Military Command in the hands of Paul von Hindenburg and his highly talented yet exceedingly ambitious quartermaster general, Erich von Ludendorff, reflected the ineffectiveness of Germany's imperial leadership. After the failure of Falkenhayn's strategy of letting the enemy bleed to death at Verdun became apparent, the chancellor realized that the Central Powers were no longer in a position to win the war. He believed that he could secure public approval for a negotiated peace only if he enjoyed the support of the much celebrated hero of Tannenberg. At the same time, the formation of the third Supreme Military Command under Hindenburg and Ludendorff offered the chancellor a chance to ignore mounting public pressure for a resumption of unrestricted submarine warfare, which, as Bethmann well knew, would draw the United States into the war and thus seal the fate of the Central Powers.

The appointment of Hindenburg and Ludendorff greatly enhanced their already considerable prestige in the eyes of the German public. By the same token, it elevated the Supreme Military Command into a sort of substitute monarchy, or *Ersatzkaisertum*, whereby the monarch himself was effectively removed from the decision-making process. Hindenburg and Ludendorff made full use of the power they now possessed and ignored the prerogatives of the civilian government. From the outset, they intervened peremptorily in both foreign and domestic affairs and began to lay the foundation for a military dictatorship. Bethmann Hollweg's own position was seriously weakened when, in the debate about Prussian electoral reform and the constitutional restructuring of the empire, the Supreme Military Command supported the Prussian conservatives, who wanted to postpone all reforms until at least after the end of the war. At the beginning, the chancellor was able to make certain that the efforts of the new Supreme Military Command to mobilize all the nation's energies for a peace by victory did not violate existing constitutional arrangements. The main goal of the comprehensive armaments program demanded by the

Supreme Military Command was the ruthless exploitation of labor resources at the expense of the civilian production sector. For tactical reasons the Supreme Military Command agreed to the parliamentary ratification of the Patriotic Auxiliary Service bill that was introduced in the Reichstag after protracted negotiations with organized labor in December 1916 and that constituted the nucleus of the so-called Hindenburg Program. Contrary to Ludendorff's initial inclination to enact the required measures by fiat without consulting parliament, both the Defense Ministry and Wilhelm Groener, the head of the War Office, advocated an understanding with the labor unions.

Bethmann Hollweg's hopes of initiating a negotiated peace with the support of Hindenburg and Ludendorff remained unfulfilled. The terms of the peace offer from 12 December 1916 that Bethmann maneuvered through the Reichstag with great difficulty were too vague to be taken seriously by the Western powers. Its brusk rejection by the Allies represented a severe defeat for the chancellor and removed the last political obstacles to the resumption of unrestricted submarine warfare, an expedient the Supreme Military Command demanded in order to reverse the course of the war. Bethmann now stood defenseless against the dictatorial aspirations of the Supreme Military Command without, however, using this as the pretext for submitting his resignation. He did, however, muster enough energy for one more attempt to shake up existing political fronts by calling for a reform of the Prussian voting system and for the implementation of his "politics of the diagonal." In the final analysis, however, this never went beyond Wilhelm II's Easter message of April 1917 that a reform of the suffrage was to take place after the end of the war.

The delaying tactics of the chancellor, who failed to make a clear commitment to the parliamentarization of German political life, created not only with the bourgeois parties but also with the Social Democrats the distinct impression that a change in the lethargy of the imperial government was not to be expected as long as Bethmann Hollweg remained at its helm. Matthias Erzberger thus used classified information about the increasingly desperate military situation of Austria-Hungary to initiate an open polemic against the chancellor. In his speech to the executive committee of the Reichstag on 6 July 1917, Erzberger sought to create the psychological presuppositions for an intensified war effort with the participation of labor by declaring his support for the principle of a negotiated peace. It was against the background of these developments that the Center Party (Deutsche Zentrumspartei), the Progressive People's Party (Fortschrittliche Volkspartei), the Majority Socialists (Mehrheitssozialdemokratische Partei Deutschlands or MSPD), and the National Liberal Party (Nationalliberale Partei) came together to form the Interparty Committee (Interfraktioneller Ausschuß). This committee took the place of the ineffectual Constitutional Committee and functioned until the collapse of the monarchy as an instrument of parliamentary coordination for relaying the concerns of the parliamentary majority to the imperial government and the Supreme Military Command.

The parties represented in the Interparty Committee were held together by their shared opposition to the political Right and their refusal to consider either domestic political reforms or a negotiated peace. Yet this emerging majority lacked the courage of its own convictions and never made the future military appropriations contingent upon a full-fledged parliamentarization of German political life. Even within the Socialist Party, the majority was reluctant to demand that parliament be given its share of responsibility for the conduct of national affairs and therefore refrained from seeking a major leadership role or the presidency of the Interparty Committee. The intermediary position the Majority Socialists took between exerting indirect influence on governmental decisions and remaining in the opposition was rooted in concern over its left wing and the rival Independent Socialists, whom the leaders of the MSPD hoped to keep out of the informal coalition. Nor did the majority parties carry through with the initiative they had taken by voting for the peace resolution. The return to the conditions of the *Burgfrieden* and the defensive war they implied was also motivated by the fact that this made it possible for the SPD to vote for otherwise unacceptable defense appropriations and thereby indirectly strengthen the country's defensive potential. The Socialists reacted with relief to this informal coalition, which in many respects anticipated the creation of the Weimar Coalition. Not only did it rescue them from the political isolation into which they would have been driven had they voted against additional military appropriations, but it also kept them from losing whatever influence they had been able to build up within the governmental structure.

In many ways, the halfhearted policies of the majority parties achieved precisely the opposite of the domestic political liberalization for which they had been struggling. Shortsightedness, coupled with an exaggerated view of the power of the parliamentary majority, brought the Interparty Committee into open conflict with Bethmann Hollweg. For his own part, the chancellor, prompted in part by concern for the crown and in part by his personal political attitudes, was unwilling to identify himself in public with the peace resolution, although objectively he was in agreement with many of its provisions. His continued "policy of the diagonal"—that is, his attempt to strike a balance among the interests of the parliamentary majority, the Supreme Military Command, and the Prussian conservatives—completely fell apart at this particular juncture. The majority parties no longer respected Bethmann Hollweg's efforts to bring about an electoral reform in Prussia, even though the emperor eventually consented to it. On the advice of Erzberger and with the explicit support of the National Liberal Party's Gustav Stresemann, the parliamentary leadership informed the court that the chancellor, who also appeared to have lost the goodwill of the crown prince, could no longer count on a majority in the Reichstag. The decisive action, however, was the ultimatum of the Supreme Military Command, which forced Bethmann Hollweg's resignation by threatening to resign itself.

The chancellor's resignation brought no more than a superficial end to the July crisis. The majority parties had failed to realize that the chancellor's removal would accomplish very little in the absence of an alternative leader. Erzberger's fantasy of seeing Prince Bernhard von Bülow in this position was totally unrealistic, particularly in view of the fact that the prince inspired little confidence in either domestic or foreign affairs. In a surprise move and without the consultation of the Reichstag, the Supreme Military Command therefore chose Georg Michaelis, state secretary in the Office of Wartime Food Supply (Kriegsernährungsamt). To be sure, the change of chancellors led to a reshuffling of personnel in certain governmental ministries and in that sense represented a defeat for the conservative forces that were allied with the Supreme Military Command. As long as the chancellor was not accountable to the Reichstag, however, the parliamentary majority was still not in a position to make him subservient to its policies. At no time was this more apparent than in the disparaging treatment of the peace resolution by the new chancellor, who felt little obligation to accept the formula of peace without negotiations. At the same time, as the peace negotiations in Brest-Litovsk were to show, the Center Party was no longer willing to adhere to the political course that had been charted with the passage of the peace resolution once the fortunes of war seemed to have improved. Michaelis was an outspoken opponent of the transition to a parliamentary system of government to which the majority parties were giving little more than halfhearted support. The formation of a seven-man advisory committee as well as the appointment of several members of the Reichstag to the national cabinet was a highly questionable substitute for full-fledged parliamentarization.

The appointment of Michaelis without consulting the parties of the Interparty Committee represented a severe blow to the committee's prestige. Nevertheless, the reform-minded majority in the Interparty Committee proved to be the only political power that could be counted on to stand up against those on the political Right who, in agreement with the Supreme Military Command, envisaged the creation of an open military dictatorship. Through the founding of the German Fatherland Party (Deutsche Vaterlandspartei), which anticipated fascist methods of organization and agitation, these elements attempted to create a populist basis for their far-reaching domestic and foreign aspirations. The semiparliamentary system that had gradually come into existence prevented the Reichstag majority from bringing the full weight of its influence to bear on the process by which leadership positions were filled. While the parliamentary majority was able to assert its will against Chancellor Michaelis and to force his resignation once the Supreme Military Command also realized that the challenges of the chancellorship greatly exceeded Michaelis's modest capacities, it was unable to determine the choice of his successor. Once again, it was a clear sign of the chronic shortage of qualified political candidates that only the former Centrist politician and Bavarian minister president Georg von Hertling could be persuaded to assume the responsibilities of the chancellorship. As an opponent of parliamentarization, Hertling was reluctant to implement the personnel changes that the Reichstag majority forced upon him. Of the reforms he proposed, only a small part was ever enacted. The modest suffrage reform bill he submitted to the Prussian Landtag was a complete failure despite the fact that the retention of the three-class franchise aroused widespread hostility within the general population.

It is misleading to ask whether the complete parliamentarization of German political life and the enactment of full and equal suffrage in Prussia would have fundamentally strengthened the internal stability of the German Empire. Although the parties of the Interparty Committee could not be appeased with half-measures, they remained unwilling to cut off funds as a means of asserting themselves in the struggle for domestic power. As long as the war was not obviously lost and as long as the Fatherland Party and the Independent Committee for a German Peace (Unabhängiger Ausschuß für einen Deutschen Frieden) continued to harbor illusions of a victorious peace, the position of the Supreme Military Command remained unassailable. Its position, moreover, was greatly strengthened by the inherent weakness of Bethmann Hollweg's successors and by Russia's withdrawal from the war. At no point did the relative weakness of the government and the Reichstag become more apparent than when the Supreme Military Command compelled them to demand the resignation of Richard von Kühlmann, the state secretary in the Foreign Ministry, whose position had become untenable when he publicly declared that the war could no longer be won by military means alone.

The veto power of the Supreme Military Command over all major political decisions remained intact. By the same token, there had been little change in the far-reaching militarization of German social life in spite of the fact that the Prussian Defense Ministry—unlike the staffs of the Supreme Military Command that were engaged in mobilizing the civilian population for the war effort—had ostensibly tried to bring about some degree of social equity. In the absence of applicable constitutional regulations, the district commanders of the army exercised executive power under the terms of a Prussian law on the state of siege that dated back to 1851. All decisions related to censorship, limitations on the right of assembly and the use of surveillance and repression against the civilian population, were left to the discretion of the individual military commanders. In general, the Prussian Defense Ministry was willing to cooperate with the labor unions, which, for their own part, sought to resolve conflicts in the factories and did their loyal best to support the war effort. Not infrequently this led to an implicit alliance against left-wing opposition groups.

The Patriotic Auxiliary Service Law (Vaterländisches Hilfsdienstgesetz) strengthened the position of the labor unions, which were represented in the labor and arbitration committees that the law established. To be sure, this did not come without a price insofar as the unions were expected to provide continued support of the war effort and to help maintain order and prevent strikes in the factories. Nevertheless, the leaders of German heavy industry were still unwilling to recognize the unions as a partner in wage negotiations and continued to press for a revision of the Service Law as late as the fall of 1918. The very fact that the unions were given a major role in dealing with the increasingly severe problems of food distribution made it appear to the labor force that they now shared responsibility for the food shortages. Serious food shortages had occurred as early as the winter of 1916–17, and by the summer of 1917 it was no longer possible to meet the minimal needs of the civilian population. By then, not even the middle classes could afford the horrendous prices that agricultural commodities were bringing on the black market, into which almost a third of Germany's agricultural production was being channeled. Despite rising wages that varied considerably according to region and industrial sector, workers' incomes did not keep pace with a runaway inflation that not even government price controls could contain. After 1917 insufficient bread rations and inadequate deliveries frequently led to strikes, while the theft of produce from the fields and of food from shops and dwellings became increasingly common.

In many respects, the decision to bring the SPD and the unions into the political system was a success. Not only was the strike movement in the first years of the war relatively insignificant, but the food shortages of 1916 led to only local strikes. On the other hand, both the SPD and the unions were caught off guard by the work stoppages that occurred in a number of cities in April 1917 on the initiative of either the newly founded Independent Social Democratic Party of Germany (Unabhängige Sozialdemokratische Partei Deutschlands or USPD) or the Revolutionary Shop Stewards. The spectacular strike by the Berlin munition workers could be brought under control only after the entry of the socialist unions and the SPD leadership into the strike committee. The spontaneous nature of the strike movement made it clear that the SPD and the unions were largely out of touch with the rank-and-file membership of the German labor movement. Despite the efforts of the International Group (Gruppe Internationale) — a faction that thought of itself as a Spartacist League modeled more or less after the Bolsheviks in Russia — revolutionary slogans played a relatively minor role in motivating the workers. What was far more important were demands for improvements in the distribution of food, peace without annexations, and domestic political reforms, not the least of which was the introduction of universal and equal suffrage in the German states and municipalities. Although evidence of increasing bitterness within the work force continued to mount through the summer of 1917, when it culminated in a mutiny of the merchant marine that was brutally repressed, no action was taken to implement the constitutional reforms that had been promised to the workers in recognition of their loyalty to the war effort. At the same time, the government found itself increasingly incapable of alleviating the rapidly deteriorating social conditions throughout the country.

Introduced after numerous delays and initially concerned only with the allocation of raw materials, the German war economy discriminated against middle-class enterprises and small and middle-sized firms at the same time that it favored heavy industry and the defense-related sectors of the chemical industry. It soon became clear, however, that one of the most serious obstacles to the development of the war economy was the availability of labor. During the course of the war, employees in consumer-oriented industries had been shifted to heavy industry, with the result that the unions were able to gain a foothold in this sector of the economy. The mobilization for war, however, had resulted in a sharp drop in union membership, which was not restored to its prewar level until 1917. In the meantime, discontent became increasingly widespread within the commercial middle class and the ranks of the civil service and public employees. It was not the news of the October Revolution in Russia but of Russia's withdrawal from the war that offered a beacon of hope to Germany's civilian population and intensified its longing for peace.

Nevertheless, the Supreme Military Command continued to believe that it could use the victory over Russia to justify the total mobilization of all national energies to force a decision on the western front. Faced with a lack of material resources, the military command mounted an elaborate propaganda campaign that was supported by a special press apparatus. One aspect of this campaign was the introduction of "patriotic instruction" in the public schools in an attempt to boost enthusiasm for the war effort and to counteract the alleged defeatism of the Social Democrats. The mass basis that was necessary for the success of such an action was to be created by the Fatherland Party. Conceived of exclusively as a propaganda instrument for strengthening the domestic war effort, the Fatherland Party constituted a somewhat unorthodox species of extraparliamentary movement that was financed by contributions from heavy industry, the Agrarian League (Bund der Landwirte), and other influential interest groups on the political Right. Its indirect organization rested on the collective membership of parties and interest groups stretching from the German National League of Commercial Employees (Deutschnationaler Handlungsgehilfen-Verband or DHV) to the Christian labor unions and religiously oriented workers' clubs. With a membership of 1.2 million, the Fatherland Party was the largest mass organization in imperial Germany. In many respects, its objectives were similar to those of the Pan-German League (Alldeutscher Verband or ADV), which established a plethora of secondary *völkisch*-oriented associations, among them the Order of Germans (Germanenorden) founded in the late autumn of 1918.

The extreme nationalism that was generated by the agitation of these associations deceived large segments of the population as to the seriousness of Germany's military situation. Reviving the "ideas of 1914," this species of nationalism came to include more and more racist anti-Semitic elements that were part of a conscious effort to drive a wedge between the working class and the Social Democratic movement. Circles close to the Supreme Military Command proposed the compulsory repatriation of Jews of Polish nationality, while plans for the colonization of the East anticipated the subsequent Nazi ideology of *Lebensraum*. It is no coincidence that Anton Drexler, the future founder of the German Workers' Party (Deutsche Arbeiterpartei or DAP), was a member of the Fatherland Party. In comparison to the nationalist Right, countermovements within the bourgeois middle such as the People's League for Freedom and Fatherland (Volksbund für Freiheit und Vaterland) commanded a much smaller following.

The politics of excess and violence espoused by the propaganda of the Fatherland Party found concrete expression in the negotiations that led to the Peace of Brest-Litovsk. The Supreme Military Command adamantly refused to heed the warnings of Richard von Kühlmann, who despite his own expansionist goals was concerned about the political stabilization of eastern Europe. Counting on the political instability of the nascent Bolshevik state, the Supreme Military Command was already anticipating future military interventions. At this point the German side saw nothing improper in invoking Lenin's principle of self-determination but refused to pay serious attention to the independence of newly created entities such as the Baltic border states or the Ukraine. On the contrary, they were destined to play the role of satellites. By the same token, the peace treaty did not prevent the Supreme Military Command from placing vast areas of Russian territory stretching to the Crimea and the Caucasus under military occupation in order to ensure the supply of essential raw materials through the colonial exploitation of these regions.

The majority parties in the Reichstag were fully aware of the fact that Brest-Litovsk and the military actions that were necessary to enforce its military provisions were fundamentally incompatible not only with the peace resolution of July 1917 but also with the Fourteen Points of President Woodrow Wilson. The weakness of the informal party coalition that had come together in the Interparty Committee could be seen in its failure to exercise any influence over the conduct of the peace negotiations on the eastern front. The Majority Socialists were placed in a particularly embarrassing dilemma by the government's breach of its promise not to seek territorial annexations. But in the event that Majority Socialists voted against the eastern treaties in the Reichstag, this would have abruptly terminated the alliance they had just concluded with the more moderate bourgeois parties and would have cast them back into the political isolation they desperately sought to escape. To be sure, there was criticism of Brest-Litovsk within the bourgeois camp as well, but it receded in the face of satisfaction with the greatly overrated German *Machtfrieden*. In the end, the Majority Socialists decided, despite major reservations, to abstain in the vote to ratify the treaty, while the Independent Socialists left no doubt whatsoever about their categorical rejection of what had happened at Brest-Litovsk.

The Russian collapse and the weakness of the Bolsheviks only strengthened the Supreme Military Command in its illusion that victory could be achieved through a tremendous exertion of all national energies. The Bolsheviks had no choice but to accept German peace terms, which became even harsher during the course of the negotiations, and had to acquiesce in subsequent military operations that in the Reichstag were characterized as police actions. This, in turn, only exacerbated the polarization of German domestic politics. Annexationist fever gripped the German public once again, as the slogans of the Fatherland Party fed the wishful thinking that existed within the ranks of Germany's conservative elites. At the same time, however, the food situation of the industrial working class continued to deteriorate. The imports that had been expected from the east did not arrive in time. Moreover, new measures to increase military control over the workers were under consideration. The arrest of several strike leaders after the work stoppage in January 1918 and measures to preempt expected workers' protests created a mood of resignation that continued into the late fall. Finding themselves caught more and more between two hostile fronts, the socialist labor unions warned that unless comprehensive domestic reforms were forthcoming, they would no longer be able to prevent massive protest demonstrations.

While civilian political forces, most notably the parties of the Interparty Committee, were deeply concerned about the arbitrary behavior of the Supreme Military Command, Ludendorff believed that he could end the war by achieving a decisive breakthrough on the western front. The carefully prepared spring offensive of 1918 and a series of subsequent sorties did result in some tactical victories, but they failed to produce the strategically decisive breakthrough on which Ludendorff had been counting. Despite the increasing superiority the Allies enjoyed in the supply of munitions and men, Ludendorff refused to recognize what had become self-evident to his staff officers, namely, that the Central Powers were incapable of conducting anything more than a purely defensive war. The French and British counterattacks on 18 July and 8 August left little doubt that the military situation had changed in favor of the Allies, even though they had not yet used the opportunity created by the defeat of German units on 8 August—the "black day of the German army"—to achieve a strategic breakthrough. Even then, however, the Supreme Military Command failed to inform the government of the dramatic deterioration of the military situation on the western front.

It was not until the successful Allied offensive of 26 September, the simultaneous arrival of news of Bulgaria's capitulation the day before and the virtual collapse of the Romanian front, and the impending dissolution of the Habsburg Empire that the Supreme Military Command drew the obvious conclusions from the existing military situation. Its sudden swing toward support for parliamentarization came as a complete surprise to the majority parties that up to now had only cautiously advocated such a step. On the grounds that he could no longer guarantee the stability of the western front, Ludendorff demanded that the German government immediately offer to conclude an armistice. Ludendorff's intent was transparent. Desperately trying to avert capitulation and the capture of the western army—in short, open military defeat—Ludendorff wanted to saddle the civilian government with responsibility for the loss of the war. Here was the origin of the perpetual lie that it was not the army but the home front that had collapsed and was therefore responsible for Germany's military defeat. With reference to the question of parliamentarization, the quartermaster general cynically remarked that those who had cooked the soup should be the first to dish it up.

Ludendorff's precipitous step, from which he later sought to dissociate himself, coincided with simultaneous endeavors by the majority parties to form a functional government that included the SPD. This entailed the removal of Hertling, whose inability to stand up to the arbitrary conduct of the Supreme Military Command met with universal criticism. The SPD was particularly insistent that Hertling resign, regarding him as incapable of bringing about the negotiated peace in which the Interparty Committee still believed. For the most part, the program of the majority parties adhered to the demands on which they had agreed in principle in July 1917. As before, there was still disagreement between the parties and the government on the modalities of full parliamentarization, particularly insofar as it affected the constitutional relationship between the federal diet, or Bundesrat, and the cabinet. This problem, however, had little bearing on the day-to-day operations of parliament itself.

At this juncture, no candidate for the chancellorship could be found among the leaders of the parliamentary opposition, since neither Friedrich von Payer nor Konstantin Fehrenbach could be persuaded to accept the post. In the end, the parties agreed on Prince Max von Baden. Max's nomination was proposed by Conrad Haußmann and met with the approval of the Supreme Military Command. As a member of one of Germany's ruling dynasties and a politician with an impeccable liberal pedigree, the crown prince of Baden seemed a suitable compromise candidate. Few, however, knew of the extent to which his image and reputation had been manufactured by his personal advisors. By no means was Prince Max an unqualified advocate of parliamentarization. In fact, he had spoken rather disparagingly of "Western democracy" and contrasted it with the murky notion of "German freedom." Paul von Hintze, the new state secretary for foreign affairs, supported the appointment of the prince on the assumption that it would undercut President Wilson's call for the emperor's abdication, a demand against which all of the German parties, including the SPD, had vociferously protested. At the same time, however, Prince Max's appointment was designed to appeal to the solidarity of Germany's dynastic families. Even then, it was not at all certain that the new chancellor had sufficient political experience and will power to provide the nation with the effective leadership it needed in its hour of military and political collapse.

Realizing that Germany would find itself at a serious disadvantage if the armistice offer were to be launched without sufficient diplomatic preparation, the newly appointed chancellor asked the Supreme Military Command for a delay in making such an offer but was turned down. Nor was Max able to obtain from the Supreme Military Command a statement that the military situation demanded an immediate start to armistice negotiations. Under the circumstances, the German armistice offer was dispatched to President Wilson on the night of 3–4 October 1918. The telegram to Wilson was generally interpreted as an admission of defeat and unleashed a sense of profound shock throughout the German public. Deceived not only by unrealistic press reports and censorship but also by the propaganda of the Supreme Military Command and the Fatherland Party, many Germans still clung to their hopes of a German victory in spite of their country's diplomatic situation. The fact that the public was completely unprepared for the possibility of defeat contributed to the paralytic resignation and deep bitterness that spread throughout the country. All of this provided impetus to the forces that now advocated the immediate cessation of hostilities.

When Ludendorff had pressed the government for an immediate armistice, he had not realized that such a step would definitely preclude the possibility of resuming the war if the conditions offered by the enemy should prove unacceptable. Throughout all of this, Ludendorff clung to the illusion that Germany could resume hostilities once it had withdrawn its forces to the Rhine. The economic exploitation of the east would provide Germany with the resources necessary for continuing the war. Without offering much in the way of evidence, the military claimed that the Allies would offer much more favorable peace terms in the spring. When Wilson's reply revealed the consequences of its hasty démarche, the military tried to conceal its responsibility for the desperate situation in which Germany now found itself with the argument that the army threatened to collapse because the home front no longer stood behind it. This, however, did not prevent the Supreme Military Command from rejecting the *levée en mass* proposed by Walter Rathenau—a project that could not possibly have succeeded under existing conditions—on the dubious grounds that it would only lead to the contamination of the army with the revolutionary bacillus. Neither the Supreme Military Command nor the responsible political forces had anticipated the effect of the armistice offer upon the German troops.

The Supreme Military Command was not alone in its thinking. As late as the first half of October 1918, the ruling elites—and that included the parties of the Interparty Committee—were determined to reject peace at all costs. In a telegram to the cabinet, Hindenburg demanded on 14 October that "public manifestations of all kinds" should express the attitude that "for the German people there are only two routes: peace with honor or struggle to the very end." This fictitious alternative had already led to the formation of Max von Baden's cabinet. A more moderate peace offer was seen as the prerequisite for the mobilization of all the nation's energies for one supreme effort. The idea of rallying the nation appealed to the socialist unions and to the right wing of the Social Democrats. There were even informal negotiations between representatives of the Fatherland Party and the General Commission of the Labor Unions (Generalkommission der Gewerkschaften), which nevertheless ended in failure and only strengthened the tendencies in the bourgeois camp toward the formation of a defensive front directed against the Social Democrats. Still, it was not until 26 October that the General Commission and the unions definitively dissociated themselves from such a possibility. Shortly beforehand the cabinet had secured the SPD's cooperation in drafting an appeal for national defense in the event that negotiations with Wilson should fail.

The Social Democratic leadership had decided from the outset to participate in a coalition cabinet despite fears on the part of some party officials that this might contribute to the support of a covert military dictatorship. Most Social Democrats felt that it was a patriotic duty to avert the total collapse of the fatherland and did not want their party to carry the stigma of having failed in the hour of peril. Clearly, the Social Democratic Party was still haunted by the trauma of being accused of unreliability in matters of national interest. The catalog of demands it formulated called not only for the affirmation of the peace resolution, the revision of the eastern treaties, and the restoration of Belgium, Serbia, and Montenegro, but also for the establishment of universal and equal suffrage in the German states and the abolition of all provisions of the imperial constitution that stood in the way of full parliamentarization. It is true that in the ensuing negotiations the SPD backed down on a number of these points, among them any direct mention of the Peace of Brest-Litovsk and the ban on simultaneous membership in the Bundesrat and Reichstag. In the place of the latter, the parties agreed upon an unsatisfactory compromise that members of parliament who were called upon to serve in the cabinet could retain their Reichstag mandate.

The Majority Socialists were still reluctant to assume full political responsibility. This reluctance stemmed in part from concern about the Independent Socialist Party, which accused its sister party of acting as a handmaiden to German imperialism. But above all, the party's reform-minded leadership was loath to become involved in a conflict with the bourgeois parties for fear that this might prejudice the war effort. Although Friedrich Ebert dismissed the idea of a Social Democratic chancellorship as premature, he strenuously objected to Max von Baden's initial tendency to treat the Social Democratic members of his cabinet as a minor nuisance. In point of fact, however, the only socialists associated with his cabinet were Philipp Scheidemann as state secretary without portfolio and labor leader Gustav Bauer as state secretary in charge of the newly created Labor Office. Moreover, since the socialist members of the Reichstag were in the minority vis-à-vis representatives of Germany's traditional ruling elites, the SPD's influence on ministerial decisions remained narrowly circumscribed. After accepting the government's official statement on 5 October, the majority parties voted to adjourn the Reichstag.

The cabinet of Prince Max von Baden did not represent a clear and unequivocal retreat from the semiauthoritarian structure of the imperial constitution. It was supported by the coalition of the Interparty Committee and mixed parliamentary and bureaucratic elements insofar as the chancellor, who was constitutionally responsible to the Kaiser, had been appointed on the initiative of the majority parties. Critics could not help but feel that the government's reforms only went as far as necessary in order to refute the objections contained in Wilson's third note, in which the United States president stated that the German people "still did not have the power to force the Empire's military authorities to heed the will of the people," that "the influence of the King of Prussia on the Empire's policies continued unabated," and that decisions continued to be made by "those who have been Germany's rulers all along." To be sure, outside pressure was not the only factor that moved Wilhelm II's advisors to yield to demands for reform from the Left. Still, this would have been virtually inconceivable without Wilson's conditions on German domestic politics.

In point of fact, the test of wills that Germany's civilian leadership had to undergo in the last weeks of October 1918 only reinforced Wilson's skepticism about the sincerity of Germany's willingness to make peace. The president's third note, received in Berlin on 24 October, shattered once and for all the illusion that it would be possible to resume hostilities after the conclusion of an armistice. The Supreme Military Command responded to this note, without ever consulting the civilian government, by issuing an order of the day, or *Tagesbefehl*, that called upon the army to continue its heroic resistance and declared Wilson's conditions unacceptable. This time Max von Baden threatened to resign and prevailed over Ludendorff, whose threats of resignation had lost their effect, with the argument that the interference of the two generals constituted a threat to the unity of leadership and seriously jeopardized the chances for a negotiated peace. An agreement with Wilson was possible, he insisted, only if the standing system of "double rule" (*Doppelherrschaft*) was ended. In the short run, the crisis was resolved through a compromise that left the underlying problems untouched. While Ludendorff resigned in bitterness, Hindenburg remained in his post at the emperor's insistence, and General Wilhelm Groener, renowned for his excellent work in developing the war economy, was appointed Hindenburg's first quartermaster general.

At the very least, Ludendorff's dismissal meant that the imperial government had once and for all abandoned the idea that the only response to unacceptable armistice conditions would be to call for an all-out war of national defense. There was no alternative to accepting the conditions of the American president, even though they had become even less favorable through the exchange of notes. In the face of obvious military defeat, orders to hold out to the very end were no longer heeded. Disobedience in the reserve army, failure to report to draft boards, and insubordination toward local military authorities became commonplace, while similar occurrences took place behind the lines of the field army. No one wanted to die for a lost cause. Yet at the same time, thousands of workers in the defense industry were ordered to report for military service. As late as 27 October the Majority Socialist party organ *Vorwärts* appealed for contributions to the ninth war loan. Virtually all political groups of the dying empire were overwhelmed by events.

At this point the desire for peace on the part of the broad masses turned into a protest movement that grew more intense by the hour. This occurred more or less spontaneously in the absence of major agitation by the Independent Socialists, the Revolutionary Shop Stewards, or the Spartacus League, whose leaders were just being released from prison. The industrial labor force was inspired by the example of the October Revolution in Russia, where the overthrow of the government had brought an end to the war. By comparison, the rest of the Bolshevik objectives retreated completely into the background. The Majority Socialists, believing in gradual democratization and having joined the cabinet in order to forestall a drift toward a "Russian situation," still believed that they must not question the continued existence of the monarchy and even adopted a wait-and-see attitude on the issue of parliamentarization. It was only under the pressure of Wilson's third note that the Reichstag voted on 26 October to implement the long overdue constitutional reform and transform the German Empire into a parliamentary monarchy. Henceforth the chancellor required the confidence of parliament and was responsible both to it and the Federal Council. Members of parliament could now become ministers without having to relinquish their seats. Decisions concerning war and peace and the Supreme Military Command were no longer in the hands of the emperor but rested in those of a government that was responsible to parliament and in command of the military. The independent position of the Prussian minister of defense was thus abolished. The introduction of universal and equal suffrage in the German states, however, was not included in the provisions for a reform of the imperial constitution. It was only under heavy pressure that the Prussian upper house, or Herrenhaus, went along with the suffrage reform — and then only in the first reading of the bill. Thus, Prussia's hesitant steps in the direction of reform had been overtaken by the tempo of the revolution itself.

Although the new constitutional provisions that went into effect on 28 October 1918 by and large met the demands of the left-liberals and Social Democrats, they failed to address important constitutional questions as a consequence of their improvisational character. Among the most important items omitted from the reforms of 28 October was the question of the monarch's prerogatives and his rights in the absence of a parliamentary majority. A relapse into the "cryptoparliamentarism" of the past, as Majority Socialist Eduard David put it, was still within the realm of possibility. By the same token, it was only at the last moment that the military command structure was shifted in the chancellor's favor. Even then, the hated symbols of the old political system remained intact, while military personnel continued to dominate its political leadership. Conceived of as a "revolution from above," the reforms of October 1918 proved incapable of dispelling the deep-seated distrust of the people, a distrust that now expressed itself in a growing crescendo of calls for the emperor's abdication.

The fact that the parliamentarization of the German political system had taken place begrudgingly and only under the pressure of Wilson's conditions did much to neutralize its intended effect as a political safety valve. It is unlikely that even the abdication of the emperor — an expedient that representatives of the bourgeois middle like the famous social theorist Max Weber had been demanding in the hope that this might save the monarchy — could have changed the course of events. In the eyes of the population, the emperor was first and foremost responsible for the outcome of the war. Not only was Wilhelm II paying a bitter price for having tolerated the interference of Hindenburg's plebiscitarian shadow government, but his refusal to dissociate himself from his military advisors and from the arch-conservative circles that dominated his court only compounded his difficulties. It was an insult to Max von Baden when the Kaiser left Berlin to go to the general headquarters at Spa and thus removed himself from direct contact with the government. His decision to accept Hindenburg's invitation to Spa was politically unconscionable since it underscored the primacy of the military and cast severe doubts on the sincerity of the emperor's consent to the October reforms.

The political and military elites of the Second Empire had reconciled themselves to the parliamentarization of German political life because it offered them the only means of continuing the supremacy of the military and safe-guarding the nucleus of the Prusso-German army. In this respect, there was no psychological motivation for the emperor to take the necessary step of dissociating himself from the military leadership. At the general headquarters, the monarch was virtually unaware of the incipient revolution throughout his country. His immediate entourage completely misunderstood the mood of the troops at the front and never for a moment doubted the legitimacy of using the army as an instrument of domestic power. Courtiers and monarchist officers even went so far as to suggest that Wilhelm II restore order throughout the empire by marching into Berlin at the head of loyal combat troops willing to suppress the various manifestations of revolutionary unrest. Plans to this effect, however, were soon shattered by the bitter realization that it was no longer possible to count on the political reliability of the troops. At a time when the revolutionary upheaval had already started with the mutiny of the sailors in the imperial navy at Kiel, nationalist delusions and monarchist illusions obscured a true understanding of what was happening throughout the country. By now, however, many high-ranking officers had come to regard the emperor's abdication as preferable to Hindenburg's resignation.

The parliamentarization of the German political system could not stem the disintegration of military power. On the contrary, parliamentarization was a consequence of that disintegration. By the same token, the massive protest movement that the Majority Socialists and the labor unions sought to contain within legal bounds could only end in the overthrow of military rule. An early abdication of the emperor would have given the movement even greater impetus. Political and constitutional reforms alone were insufficient to unravel the historical relationship between military rule and the Hohenzollern monarchy. The failure to realize this remains one of the most serious, yet psychologically understandable, miscalculations of Friedrich Ebert and his party associates. Only a categorical and immediate disavowal of Germany's military leadership could have given the transitional cabinet broader popular support. Instead, this transition was used to conceal the military debacle and contributed in no small way to feeding illusory hopes that the public still pinned on a "Wilson peace."

After 4 November the smoldering revolutionary movement came into its own. It was provoked by an unauthorized decision of the naval command to challenge British naval forces to a "final battle." Naval commanders took this step without adequate consultation with the government, arguing that the cessation of unrestricted submarine warfare against their will had made it necessary to reactivate the fleet, which up to this point had done little but protect the submarines. Their true motive, however, was to salvage something of the navy's honor and to rescue it from the stigma of military failure. Nowhere is this intention more clearly elucidated than in a memorandum the naval command wrote in support of such an engagement: "Out of an honorable naval combat, even if in this war it should become a fatal endeavor [*Todeskampf*], will emerge — unless our people fails as a nation — a new navy for the German future." In approving this plan, the naval high command was not interested in providing relief for the hard-pressed German army with an action in the English Channel. On the contrary, it hoped to safeguard the existence of the navy in the face of what it considered an ignominious peace. Not only would the implementation of this plan have meant the pointless sacrifice of innumerable human lives, it would also have placed the peace negotiations in serious jeopardy.

The crews of the naval armada at the Schilling Shipyards in Kiel stood under the impression of rapidly spreading rumors that a last *Todeskampf* of the fleet was planned, which is precisely what the operation would have been. The crews refused to follow orders to set sail for high seas and continued their resistance even after the operation had been called off. The confused orders of the naval command, which ordered the recall of the mutinous third squadron to Kiel, ignited a general revolt by the crews stationed there in which the local garrison and sympathetic industrial workers soon joined. The formation of sailors' councils, or *Matrosenräte*, to carry on negotiations with the naval commander was the signal for a general revolutionary uprising. Even as Gustav Noske, a representative of the Majority Socialists, and state secretary Conrad Haußmann arrived in Kiel to negotiate with the workers on behalf of the imperial government, the spark of revolt had spread to other naval bases and virtually all major German cities. Troops disarmed their officers, and spontaneously formed soldiers' and workers' councils seized political power everywhere. The revolution had become inescapable.

Independent of the question of just how much the naval command had informed the government of its intentions, there is little doubt that mounting a major naval operation immediately prior to the conclusion of an armistice could only be interpreted as an attempt to scuttle the armistice negotiations. Soldiers and workers were deeply — and not altogether unreasonably — suspicious of a military leadership that had lost its moral authority. This, in turn, explains the speed with which the uprising spread throughout the country. Who would have dared to stand in the way of this rapidly accelerating protest movement? After a period of extreme material deprivation and psychological tension, there was an explosion of built-up social animosities that were only intensified by the persistence of class barriers between enlisted men and the officer corps. Hatred of the symbols of military rule explains why so many officers had their emblems of rank ripped from their uniforms. By the same token, workers openly called for fundamental democratic equality in the factories. The struggle against "the obedience of the dead [*Kadavergehorsam*] in the military had its counterpart in the rejection of arbitrary management in the industrial sphere.

The timid social reforms of Max von Baden's government, the formation of workers' committees in key industrial plants, the suspension of legal restrictions on the right of assembly, and amnesty for prisoners detained for political misdemeanors did little to placate politically aroused workers. To be sure, it was still too early to speak of a broadly based revolutionary movement by the industrial proletariat. Still, there were signs that the Majority Socialists were losing ground to the much less equivocal Independent Socialists. The revolutionary forces within the labor movement — namely, the Revolutionary Shop Stewards, the left wing of the Independent Social Democratic Party under Georg Ledebour, and the Spartacus League, which before 8 November had been quasi moribund — gained greater influence only when the authority of the military had been visibly shaken by the course of events.

Blaming the revolutionary Left for precipitating the revolution in the first place was perfectly consistent with the legend that the Supreme Military Command had systematically nurtured since the collapse of early November, namely, that the German defeat had come about because those responsible for securing the home front had turned their back on the troops in the field. As early as the end of November 1918, Ludwig Beck, at that time a major on the general staff, made the following observation: "At the most critical moment of the war we were assaulted from behind by a revolution that — as I now realize without the shadow of a doubt — had been thoroughly prepared beforehand." A few weeks later, the·rumors and deliberate falsifications that circulated within the political Right were reported in the *Neue Zürcher Zeitung* under the heading "Stab in the Back" (*Dolchstoß*). From this point on, the *Dolchstoß* legend became a standard item in the repertoire of the antirepublican Right. In point of fact, however, the collapse of the empire must be attributed primarily to the incompetence of the ruling elites, which not only overestimated the political and economic strength of the Central Powers but also succumbed to the illusion that they could use the war to halt the long overdue modernization of Germany's social and political system that threatened their privileged social position.

The popular movement that swept away the regime in the first days of November 1918 was directed against the usurped authority of the system's military supporters and the social injustice upon which it was founded. This protest was elemental but did not assume the character of unbridled violence and outrageous excesses. The end of the war seemed to signal the beginning of a new era, one that would do away with class justice and mindless obedience, with arbitrariness and social inequality. It soon became clear, however, that there were no political leaders capable of mobilizing these aspirations and their democratic potential for a genuine new beginning.

CHAPTER TWO

The German Revolution

THE reforms of October 1918 had been enacted with the twofold aim of responding to President Wilson's demand for the formation of a democratically legitimated government and of forestalling a revolutionary upheaval from below. The coalition parties were determined to preserve the Hohenzollern monarchy, but only on the basis of the parliamentarization of the Reichstag and the Federal Council, or Bundesrat. It soon became clear, however, that this would be possible only if Wilhelm II renounced the throne in favor of one of the imperial princes or a regent. But once the emperor removed himself to the military headquarters at Spa and came under the influence of military advisors—including, at least in the initial stages, Quartermaster General Wilhelm Groener—who urged him to regain his dominant position in Germany at the head of combat troops erroneously thought to be loyal, such a course of action was no longer possible.

Despite the increasing hesitation of the Majority Socialists, who had demanded the emperor's abdication in an ultimatum of 7 November that was subsequently extended by twenty-four hours, the leaders of the empire still believed that the resignation of the monarch and the appointment of a regency council or a suitable substitute would avert collapse of the only recently modernized Wilhelmine constitutional system. Yet it is by no means certain that a conciliatory gesture on the part of Wilhelm II, who to the very end clung to the implausible idea that he could abdicate as German emperor but still remain king of Prussia, could have stemmed the growing revolutionary tide. After all, the person of the emperor himself was too closely tied to the hated military rule that now stood on the verge of complete collapse.

The equivocation of the monarch obliged Prince Max von Baden to take matters in his own hands and announce the abdication of Wilhelm II on the morning of 9 November without receiving proper authorization from Spa. In doing so, Max hoped to clear the way for the establishment of a regency. By this time, however, a regency was no longer acceptable to the Social Democrats, who around midday issued a ultimatum demanding complete and undivided power. In defense of this demand, Friedrich Ebert stressed that the military units stationed in Berlin had already gone over to the side of the Majority Socialists. In fact, Otto Wels had succeeded in securing the support of these troops in the event of a uprising by the Revolutionary Shop Stewards. The time for the appointment of a regent had indeed passed.

Prince Max von Baden was fully aware of the implications of his decision to ask Friedrich Ebert to assume the chancellorship. To be sure, he realized that in doing so he was exceeding his constitutional prerogatives. At the same time, however, he believed that giving power to the leader of the Majority Socialists was the only way in which the existence of the empire might be salvaged. Even then, Max made Ebert's appointment contingent upon the immediate convocation of a constitutional convention. In this respect, Ebert was no less anxious than Prince Max to avoid revolutionary upheaval insofar as that was still possible and to preserve the October constitution, whereby he envisaged a coalition government that included the bourgeois parties, though with a Social Democratic majority. Ebert was furious with Philipp Scheidemann's spontaneous decision to preempt an anticipated move on the part of the Spartacists' Karl Liebknecht by proclaiming the founding of the German Republic from the balcony of the Reichstag in the early afternoon of 9 November. The fact that Scheidemann promised a purely socialist government only added to Ebert's anger.

In light of the actual political situation, Ebert's contention that a decision on the nature of the future German state could be made only by a constitutional convention was unrealistic. Given the workers' revolutionary mood and the threat of a general strike by the Independent Socialists, Scheidemann had acted properly. For while he may have lacked the strength of conviction that characterized Ebert's position, Scheidemann had a better feel for the mood of the masses and sensed that the Social Democrats had to place themselves at the head of the protest movement if they were not to be drowned in the maelstrom of political upheaval. Thanks to Scheidemann's urgent pleas that the party seize the initiative, the Social Democrats did not lose the confidence of the masses, which saw in Wilhelm II nothing but an obstacle to ending the war.

It is unlikely that even an earlier abdication by the emperor could have prevented the dismantling of a political system that had been thoroughly discredited by the outcome of the war, although not even the Majority Socialists were committed to this course of action. The fate of the German dynasties had already been shaped by parallel experiences in the various German states. In Bavaria revolutionary changes had occurred much more rapidly than elsewhere in spite of the decidedly moderate character of the Bavarian labor movement. On 7 November the two workers' parties issued a joint manifesto in the Theresienwiese calling for an end to hostilities by that afternoon. Kurt Eisner, leader of the Bavarian Independent Socialists and a well-known writer, used this occasion to organize a meeting of workers' and peasants' councils in the Landtag, where he called for the abdication of King Ludwig III and proclaimed the Bavarian Republic.

By this time Erhard Auer, the Majority Socialist leader in Bavaria, no longer rejected the coalition offer from the Independent Socialists and reached an understanding with Eisner, who had been proclaimed provisional prime minister by the assembly of the Bavarian workers', soldiers', and peasants' councils. In an appeal to the citizens of Munich, Eisner promised the convocation of a constitutional convention at the earliest possible opportunity and guaranteed the maintenance of public order by the provisional council of workers, soldiers, and peasants. Eisner's government program of 15 November contained distinctly federalist features and envisaged the dissolution of the empire and the creation of a German Danubian federation. On the issue of nationalization, however, the program was restrained. Ludwig III was thus able to avoid a formal abdication, although he did release the civil servants from their oath of loyalty to him.

Events in the other German states more or less followed the pattern of developments in Bavaria. In one state after another, the princes renounced their thrones and did not stand in the way of the future republic. In most of the states, the Majority and Independent Socialists formed coalition governments, which in a few cases also included parties from the bourgeois Left. In each case the uprising was triggered by spontaneously formed workers' and soldiers' councils, whose initiative forced the two socialist parties to follow their lead. By no means, however, did Berlin assume leadership of the revolutionary movement, although the radical Left did command strong support there. The Revolutionary Shop Stewards and the adherents of the Spartacus League were determined to use the war-weariness of the masses to create a socialist dictatorship. A mass demonstration planned for 4 November was supposed to bring about the collapse of the government. This demonstration was postponed until 11 November, since it did not seem that the situation was ripe for a revolutionary uprising. Both groups were thus caught off guard by the turn of events on the morning of 9 November. This was particularly true of the Independent Socialists, whose chairman was unable to prevent Gustav Noske from assuming the leadership of Kiel's newly constituted workers' and soldiers' council even though he happened to be in Kiel at the time. In the meantime, most of the council's demands — the release of political prisoners, dismissal of the military command, and a promise of democratic reforms — had been essentially fulfilled.

By no means was the revolutionary uprising that took place in November and that led to the spontaneous formation of workers' and soldiers' councils throughout Germany the work of the organized labor movement. The agitation of the radical Left had increased steadily since the middle of October, especially after its leaders, including eventually Karl Liebknecht, had been released from prison under the terms of the amnesty obtained by the majority parties. Before his release, Liebknecht had been widely hailed by his supporters, including segments of the proletarian youth movement, as a martyr to military dictatorship. After all, Liebknecht had been the first Social Democratic deputy to vote consistently against war appropriations and to attack the *Burgfrieden* policy of the Majority Socialists. Although the Spartacus League, with a few thousand members at best, was not sufficiently consolidated to play a major role, the Spartacists, in a climate of rapidly growing anti-Bolshevism, were held primarily responsible for the revolutionary agitation of the subsequent months.

Far more influential than the Spartacus League—a more or less clandestine organization that could only rely on an underground network of communications—were the Revolutionary Shop Stewards. The shop stewards established well-functioning organizational networks in major industrial plants, particularly in Berlin and Bremen, and felt confident that they could ignite the revolution by calling a general strike, even though they scoffed at Liebknecht's "revolutionary gymnastics" and his belief that the masses could be mobilized for spontaneous action. Neither of these groups, however, had a clear-cut program for seizing power. To be sure, the Spartacus League, whose leaders—Karl Liebknecht and Rosa Luxemburg—had just been released from prison, published a number of pamphlets invoking the model of the Russian October Revolution and demanding the transformation of Germany into a republic of socialist soviets. But in the foreseeable future the Spartacus League could hardly hope to exert major influence over the masses of the German proletariat.

In this respect, Rosa Luxemburg was particularly committed to the proposition that the proposed dictatorship of the proletariat must not be based on minority rule and adopted a more consistently democratic position than most of her colleagues. Despite divergent theoretical assumptions, both she and Karl Liebknecht pinned their hopes on the nonorganized sectors of the proletariat. Both believed that a wave of individual revolutionary acts would be followed by a more general revolution of society as a whole. This conviction underlay Luxemburg's biting criticism of the compromises the Majority Socialists had made in the pursuit of their political objectives. Within the Spartacist movement, however, Luxemburg was unable to prevail over either the anarchist tendencies of putschists who advocated terrorist action or the unrealistic idealism of Liebknecht. Nor did more farsighted thinkers such as Paul Levi and Leo Jogiches fare any better. The radical rhetoric with which the Spartacists—at that time still part of the Independent Socialist Party—justified their claims to the leadership of the revolutionary movement drew the newly constituted Communist Party of Germany/Spartacus League (Kommunistische Partei Deutschlands or KPD/Spartakus-Bund) into the whirlpool of violent confrontation that culminated in the bloody days of January 1919.

The majority of the Independent Socialists was hardly any better prepared for the revolutionary turmoil of the immediate postwar period. The fact that the Independent Socialists had consistently opposed the war had earned its

leaders a measure of trust with increasingly large sectors of the industrial working class. Nevertheless the party had to deal with a series of problems that
seriously compromised its political effectiveness. The circumstances of war, as
well as censorship and repressive measures by the government, had made it
impossible for the Independent Socialists to develop an extensive party organization. Moreover, the membership and leadership of the USPD represented
highly divergent political orientations and could never be brought together on
a united political course. Along with the Spartacists, the Revolutionary Shop
Stewards — a group whose influence had grown considerably in the labor conflicts of the last war years — championed a revolutionary-syndicalist course of
action, while the USPD's more moderate wing remained committed to the
basic principles of the Erfurt Program and was unwilling to accept the October
Revolution in Russia as a model for concrete action in the German context.

Although the Independent Socialists were determined to fight for an immediate end to the war, they had no idea what form the necessary revolutionary action should take or what political consequences it might have. In
early November 1918 the USPD leadership still lacked faith in its own ability
to bring about a change in Germany's political system. In the domestic arena,
the USPD's demands were consistent with those of the Erfurt Program and
were limited to calls for comprehensive democratization, the socialization of at
least heavy industry, and the creation of a system of civilian militias. Proclaiming its allegiance to a parliamentary-democratic system, the USPD nonetheless
considered the establishment of workers' and soldiers' councils a welcome opportunity to give proletarian interests a voice in the process of revolutionary
change and thus opposed the Majority Socialists' call for the immediate convocation of a constitutional convention. The Independent Socialists anticipated
that after the councils had revolutionized the social system by removing the
military and industrial magnates from power, democratic elections would yield
a majority for a socialist republic. Only the party's extreme left wing led by the
Revolutionary Shop Stewards thought of the councils as a viable alternative to
representative democracy. A comprehensive theory of government by councils
did not exist before the second phase of revolutionary upheaval in the spring
of 1919.

Given the unforeseen eruption of revolutionary turmoil in the fall of 1918,
the lack of a strategy for gaining power did not necessarily prove disadvanta-
geous for the USPD. A far more serious obstacle was the USPD's own Social
Democratic heritage, namely, the combination of a general lack of experience in wielding power, a rigid adherence to basic principles, and an excessive
concern for the preservation of its party organization and the interests of its
rank-and-file membership. Moreover, the USPD had been so traumatized by
the experience of party schism and interpreted the principle of inner-party
democracy so broadly that it failed time and time again to draw a clear line

between its positions and those of the extreme Left. The fact that the proletarian masses gravitated almost automatically to collaboration with the Majority Socialists proved tactically disastrous for the USPD and made it difficult for the party to ignore Ebert's overtures in the Council of People's Commissars. To be sure, the moderate wing of the USPD possessed outstanding and capable politicians in men like Hugo Haase, Rudolf Breitscheid, Karl Kautsky, Eduard Bernstein, and Rudolf Hilferding. But in the early phases of the revolution they failed to gain the upper hand over radicals such as Richard Müller, Emil Barth, and Ernst Däumig, most of whom enjoyed close ties to the Revolutionary Shop Stewards.

For all intents and purposes, the revolutionary initiative had not come from the socialist parties but from the soldiers' and workers' councils that, with the exception of Berlin, had seized power between 7 and 9 November 1918. Beginning in the coastal cities and naval stations, the council movement spread throughout the rest of the empire. Councils took over the command of garrisons and control of local administrations. In doing so, they filled the political vacuum that had been created by the collapse of military rule. During the general state of emergency that had been proclaimed in the last years of the war, many aspects of civilian administration had become the responsibility of local military commanders. Although military commanders had worked closely with management in the armaments industry, they were reluctant to resort to the ultimate measure of militarizing the plants. The interpenetration of business and military in the war economy helps explain the visceral hostility to the military-industrial complex that manifested itself in the revolution.

The newly formed soldiers' councils focused their energies on improving the treatment of enlisted men and demanded that officers be elected. The envisioned changes included the abolition of obligatory saluting when off duty, equal food rations for officers and enlisted men, the end of the unconditional obedience, or *Kadavergehorsam*, that the ordinary soldier could no longer tolerate, and a ban on carrying symbolic weapons. Frequently soldiers vented their animosity to the officer corps when, in disarming officers, they displayed violence in tearing off insignia and other marks of rank. The army and navy now paid the price for being more patently class-conscious than most other institutions of Wilhelmine society. In this connection, it is worth noting that by no means did radical political groups dominate the soldiers' councils, many of whose members were of bourgeois origin.

Nor did the radical Left, as a rule, dominate the workers' councils. Only in a few strongholds did radical leftist groups succeed in influencing the composition of workers' councils. For the most part, the councils were formed in the hope of healing the split within the Social Democratic movement. Frequently local union leaders, including those from the Christian labor movement, were represented in the councils, except in those cases where they had not been formed spontaneously as a result of public demonstrations. Analogous to the workers' councils were the south German peasant councils, where a conservative influence made itself felt. In any case, a tendency toward regular, organized elections asserted itself. Wherever this was the case—and particularly when it involved multiregional councils—the rivalry between the Majority and Independent Socialists took on much greater importance. In the first phase of the German revolution, the composition of the councils reflected for the most part the political concerns of the workers and soldiers. That the democratic potential represented by the conciliar movement was never fully exploited appears in retrospect to have been one of the most serious failures of the Majority Socialists' leadership.

Although the example of the Russian soviets was present from the very beginning, it was not so much the social revolutionary program of the Bolsheviks—as isolated pamphlets of the Spartacus League might suggest—as the desire for peace that animated the councils in the first phase of the revolution. In this respect, the issues of peace and democratization became inextricably bound to each together. The existence of the councils underscored the profound alienation that had developed between the rank and file of the industrial working class and the official organizations of the Majority Socialists and the socialist labor unions. It is therefore no coincidence that the councils first surfaced as a form of proletarian self-organization during the January strike of 1918, at which time the workers proved reluctant to entrust the leadership of the strike to party and union functionaries who, at the same time, were collaborating with the government.

For the most part, the councils limited themselves to monitoring developments and refrained from interfering in administrative affairs. Only occasionally did the councils claim the right to make changes in personnel—and, even then, they generally consulted with the appropriate central authorities. Their influence thus varied according to local conditions and was predicated on the willingness of municipal authorities to cooperate. To suggest, therefore, that the councils created enormous confusion is—with the exception of the dubious tendency toward bureaucratization on the part of the Berlin central council—a malicious misrepresentation of the actual situation. In point of fact, the councils frequently assumed responsibility for politically charged tasks such as maintaining food supplies, which threatened to collapse altogether under the impact of the Allied blockade, or the social problems of demobilization. The councils thus contributed in no small measure to the maintenance of public order in the face of the agitation of the masses and the erosion of administrative authority. Those who have ridiculed the councils for their Prussian sense of order and have stressed the shortcomings of their improvised activities fail to acknowledge the extent to which the councils demonstrated a genuine capacity for orderly, democratic self-organization.

For their own part, the leaders of the Majority Socialists and the socialist labor unions viewed the councils with distrust and rejection from the beginning. The councils had no place in the political imagination of leading party functionaries, who continued to believe in the principles of tightly centralized cohesiveness and organizational discipline. The long-established aversion to any spontaneous action on the part of the organized workers' movement was now compounded by the fear of falling into "Russian circumstances." Most moderates looked upon the councils as a residue of the October Revolution, at best as an element of disorder that would have to be removed at the earliest possible opportunity. Indeed, the moderates regarded the mobilization of the workers that had begun in early November as superfluous, even harmful, insofar as it only hampered the work of the government, which had proclaimed the end of the revolution just two days after the overthrow of the imperial regime.

When Ebert presented Prince Max von Baden with an ultimatum on the morning of 9 November 1918 demanding he assume control of the government, he still expected the existing coalition cabinet to continue, albeit under Social Democratic leadership. Ebert thus reacted positively to Max's suggestion that a National Assembly be convened immediately as a way of containing the revolutionary movement, particularly insofar as it was clear to him that simply reconvening the Reichstag that had been elected in 1912 — a course of action advocated by the Reichstag president Konstantin Fehrenbach — would encounter sharp opposition from the public. At the same time, Ebert thought it important to keep experienced bourgeois ministers in the cabinet, if only to guarantee its freedom of action in the impending armistice negotiations. It is therefore quite likely that Ebert expected that his offer of governmental participation to the USPD would be rejected. The transition cabinet envisaged by Ebert was designed both to safeguard the authority of the state until the convocation of the National Assembly and to keep the revolution from spinning out of control.

In the final analysis, however, Ebert's well-laid plans for a smooth transfer of government power were thwarted by the revolutionary mobilization of the Berlin workers. This action had the vigorous support of the left wing of the USPD and the Revolutionary Shop Stewards, while the role of the Spartacus League, on the other hand, was negligible. The first two groups exerted massive pressure on the USPD leadership to avoid collaboration with "Ebert's people" under any circumstance, even though they had no idea how a revolutionary left-wing cabinet opposed to the Majority Socialists might appear. On the evening of 9 November the executive committee of the MSPD formally rejected the conditions that the USPD had formulated — at Scheidemann's insistence and under the influence of Liebknecht and the Revolutionary Shop Stewards — for participating in the government. That same night the Revolutionary Shop Stewards held a meeting of the Berlin workers' councils, which adopted a resolution calling for the election of new workers' and soldiers' councils in all factories and military units on the morning of 10 November. Their delegates would then meet later that afternoon in Circus Busch to elect a provisional government.

Faced with this situation and the threat it posed to its precarious hold on power, the leadership of the Majority Social Democrats reacted in a twofold manner. On the one hand, it made a concerted effort to preempt the resolutions it expected to emerge from the next day's meeting by offering to accept the Independent Socialists into the coalition. This explains why on the following day the Majority Socialists immediately accepted the conditions for entering the government that the USPD had set forth under the moderating influence of Hugo Haase, who had just returned from Kiel. These conditions included the stipulation that political power was to be vested in the workers' and soldiers' councils and that the issue of a constitutional convention was to be debated "only after the consolidation of the conditions created by the revolution." On the other hand, the Majority Socialist Party was able, thanks to the vigorous efforts of Otto Wels, to mobilize its network of party operatives and to exert its influence on the elections to the soldiers' councils. As a result, it was already clear on the morning of 10 November that a government without the Majority Socialists, as called for by the Shop Stewards, would not receive a majority in the meeting that was scheduled to take place in the Circus Busch. This episode proved that it was extremely important, particularly in a revolutionary situation, to have access to an effectively functioning party organization. It also underscored the workers' desire to overcome the schism between the two workers' parties.

At the congress of soldiers' and workers' councils at Circus Busch, the representatives of the MSPD succeeded in securing the support of the delegates of the soldiers' councils. This enabled them not only to obtain a clear-cut majority for the newly formed government of the Council of People's Commissars but also to thwart the Shop Stewards' subsequent attempt to subject the People's Commissars to their control through the election of an executive committee that consisted exclusively of representatives of the radical Left. The strategy of Ebert and his party operatives has been called a tactical achievement of the first order. In point of fact, level-headedness and a well-orchestrated plan of action prevailed over the contradictory policies of an internally divided USPD, which ended up as a junior partner relegated to a subordinate position in an already consolidated cabinet.

In addition to Friedrich Ebert, who assumed the role of *primus inter pares* and de facto head of the government, the other members of the Council of People's Commissars included Philipp Scheidemann and Otto Landsberg from the MSPD and party chairman Hugo Haase, Wilhelm Dittmann, and Emil Barth from the USPD. Dittmann had been designated to replace Georg

Ledebour, who categorically refused to collaborate with the MSPD. Highly respected even by the left wing of the USPD, Dittmann came to share Haase's more conciliatory line. Barth, the leader of the Revolutionary Shop Stewards since the spring of 1918 and a member of the German Metalworkers' Union (Deutscher Metallarbeiterverband or DMV), replaced Karl Liebknecht, who had originally been a candidate but had withdrawn his candidacy under pressure from the Spartacus faction. As a result—and this was to have disastrous consequences—the left wing of the USPD was insufficiently committed to the government, particularly since Barth, who encountered a mountain of unwarranted prejudice, was systematically isolated and disavowed by the Majority Socialists. It was not long before Haase and Dittmann, who were willing to engage in constructive collaboration with the Majority Socialists, encountered similar problems. In the meantime, Ebert ruthlessly exploited the advantages of his chairmanship, in large part because the Reich Chancery was staffed with people whom he trusted and because the bourgeois state secretaries, who were closely monitored by deputies from the coalition parties, sided with the MSPD in cases of conflict. It was common knowledge that in the assignment of governmental business the USPD People's Commissars were by and large ignored. Important issues that fell within their purview were frequently sent to Ebert directly or never brought to their attention in the first place.

The leader of the Majority Socialists had thus succeeded in keeping an effective government at the helm of the German Reich and had kept it from being torn apart in the struggles between the two wings of the German Left following the fall of Wilhelm II. The price he had to pay for his success was that the Council of People's Commissars—a name upon which the USPD insisted—rested upon a revolutionary foundation and derived its sovereignty from the workers' and soldiers' councils. As a result, Ebert was more anxious than ever to hold elections for the National Assembly without delay as a way of restoring conditions of legality. This, however, represented a direct breach of the principal condition the Independent Socialists had attached to their entry into the government, namely, that elections to a new National Assembly be held only after the situation created by the revolution had been effectively consolidated.

In the person of Ebert the cabinet of the People's Commissars possessed a dual legitimacy even though his appointment to the chancellorship lacked constitutional sanction. The fact that the various governmental ministries were headed by predominantly bourgeois state secretaries underscored an underlying continuity with the previous cabinet in terms of both its politics and its personnel. This, in turn, made it easier for the Supreme Military Command and the civil bureaucracy to recognize the government of the People's Commissars. Continuity could also be seen in the various state governments, which had been constituted on a parliamentary basis by coalitions between the MSPD, the USPD, and—in a few cases—representatives of the bourgeois parties. Only the

Bavarian cabinet led by Prime Minister Kurt Eisner came into open conflict with the Berlin government.

In light of this constellation, it was not surprising that the Majority Social Democratic leadership should try to thwart every attempt by the Berlin executive committee of the workers' and soldiers' councils to exercise formal control over the decisions of the Council of People's Commissars in spite of the clearcut Majority Socialist majority that existed within that body. Even after the Council of People's Commissars had enlarged its executive committee by adding new delegates from the provinces, the Majority Socialists still rejected it as insufficiently representative and accused it of "dictatorial" tendencies. They leveled the same charges against the Central Council of the German Republic (Zentralrat der Deutschen Republik) that had been elected in December 1918 at the first German Congress of Workers' and Soldiers' Councils. To be sure, practical considerations played a certain role here, for the party did not feel that it should squander its energies on factional disputes in the Central Council, a view shared by Haase and Dittmann from the USPD. By the same token, it was no secret that the left wing of the executive committee tended to favor the establishment of a parallel government, or *Nebenregierung*. Having failed to prevent the formation of the Central Council, Ebert was only willing to grant it the functions formerly assigned to the executive committee (*Hauptausschuß*) of the old Reichstag. Ebert's deep-seated antipathy toward the Central Council and its revolutionary roots could also be seen in his refusal to allow it formally to transfer the reins of power to the National Assembly, even though there was never any doubt of its loyalty to the government's course of action.

Majority Socialist insistence in the Council of People's Commissars that the revolutionary mandate of the workers' and soldiers' councils should not be used to initiate political changes — not even in political personnel as the USPD demanded — is to be seen as a sign of a fundamentally democratic posture. If the MSPD argued that it was improper to anticipate decisions of the National Assembly, this was based more on a formal rather than a participatory understanding of democracy. Hugo Haase and Rudolf Breitscheid, who knew from firsthand experience how decisions at the cabinet level were made, correctly pointed out that the only possible way of creating conditions favorable to a Socialist victory in the forthcoming elections was to change the authoritarian climate that existed in the various government agencies. Rather than heed this advice, the MSPD leadership supported the prerevolutionary administrative apparatus in its endeavors to restrict the role of the local workers' councils with the aim of systematically eliminating them.

There is no question that the government was faced with a number of virtually insoluble problems: demobilization, securing food supplies, settlement of the eastern question, cease-fire negotiations, resumption of economic activity, and public finances. In the disposition of government business under external conditions that can only be described as extremely difficult, Ebert exhibited remarkable circumspection and efficiency. Nonetheless he lacked tactical flexibility in fundamental matters. In some respects, the way in which he conducted government business bore a striking similarity to the behavior the Majority Socialists had exhibited when they joined the wartime strike committee. This is particularly true of the almost incomprehensible rigidity with which his party blocked the initiative of its coalition partners, whether it involved the dismissal of the Prussian minister of war, Heinrich Scheüch, or the formation of the republican people's militia and the dispute over the date for elections to the National Assembly. In this respect, the Majority Socialist members of the People's Commissars showed no inclination whatsoever to bolster the moderate wing of the Independent Socialists against the radical hotheads who remained committed to the tactic of continual mass actions. A conciliatory attitude would have lent support to the endeavors of Eduard Bernstein and Karl Kautsky, who hoped to achieve a clear-cut distinction between the main body of the USPD on the one hand and the Revolutionary Shop Stewards and the Spartacist faction on the other, thereby forestalling a development that by 1920 would drive a considerable part of the USPD into the ranks of the KPD.

One consequence of this policy, which had no other practical means of dealing with left-wing deviationists than expulsion from the party, was the defeat of the moderate wing of the USPD at the national congress of the workers' and soldiers' councils that took place in Berlin on 16 December 1918. To be sure, the success of the left wing's campaign against USPD participation in the Central Council of the Republic stemmed in no small measure from the general ineffectiveness of Haase's leadership of the USPD. Yet in the final analysis it was the intransigence of the MSPD that drove its coalition partner from the government precisely at that moment when the Spartacist faction, an uncompromising opponent of cooperation with the Majority Socialists in any form whatsoever, had reached its own decision to secede from the USPD. The MSPD, which now sent Rudolf Wissell and Gustav Noske to the Council of People's Commissars, did nothing to prevent the resignation of the USPD from the government. Few could have comprehended the consequences of this decision when it took effect on 28 December, for it essentially returned the labor movement to the state of affairs that had existed in 1916. The pressure that the military and other elements of the German state brought to bear on Ebert contributed to this turn of events every bit as much as the widely held suspicion that the USPD was nothing but an instrument for the "Bolshevization" of Germany.

From the very outset relations between the two coalition partners had been severely strained by the military issue. Indeed, the coalition would no doubt have fallen apart earlier had the USPD People's Commissars been aware of the full extent of the contacts that Ebert had maintained with the Supreme Army

Command since Wilhelm Groener had placed the army at the new government's disposal on 10 November 1918. Still headed by Paul von Hindenburg with Groener as his quartermaster general, the Supreme Army Command defended its continued existence by referring to last-minute oral instructions given by Wilhelm II. Its official function was to conduct the orderly retreat of German army units from the occupied areas in the west in accordance with the conditions of the armistice and to avoid the capture of any of these units by Allied forces.

At that point it was still impossible to predict what the disarmament clauses of the peace treaty might demand. In the highest echelons of Germany's military leadership, it was assumed that even a drastically reduced military establishment would remain strong enough for Germany to function as a useful partner in military alliances. Given the unresolved question of the eastern frontiers and the armed clashes between German units and Bolshevist troops and Polish insurgents, it would seem that the continued existence of the German army would be necessary for some time to come. This consideration, along with his profound patriotism, induced Ebert to retain the Supreme Military Command. At the same time, however, Ebert also harbored illusions of military cooperation with the Allies in efforts to contain the spread of Bolshevism.

For all intents and purposes, the military operated on the assumption that in the long run it would be able to bring about Germany's return to military greatness. To the politically conscious workers, on the other hand, it was perfectly obvious that the days of the professional army that had existed in the Second Empire were indeed numbered. To be sure, the SPD's demand in the Erfurt Program for arming the nation as a whole seemed obsolete. Still, it was generally conceded that the Prussian army would have to give way to a people's army based on some sort of civilian militia. Such a goal corresponded to the attitude of the soldiers' councils, which were determined to promote a thorough democratization of the German military by abolishing military status symbols and limiting the areas of military subordination. In a similar vein, many localities had won the consent of the workers' councils for the establishment of socialistic-oriented civil defense militia, or *Volks- und Sicherheitswehren*, for the purpose of maintaining public order and safety.

Temporarily installed in the Wilhelmshöhe castle near Kassel, the Supreme Military Command was by no means willing to limit itself to a narrow definition of its military functions. On the contrary, it was committed to collaborate with the leadership of the Majority Socialists in "preventing the spread of terrorist Bolshevism in Germany," a term that embraced not merely the Communist Spartacus League but the conciliar movement as well. Although the military acted with a certain discretion in public, it was nevertheless obvious that its leaders rejected not just the soldiers' councils but also the workers' councils and in particular the executive organs. This attitude was shared by the leadership of the socialist unions and the MSPD, both of which agreed with the Supreme Military Command that it was imperative to restore normal governmental functions by the immediate convocation of a National Assembly.

The progressive dissolution of the reserve army and the need to organize the orderly retreat of troops returning from the front made it imperative for General Groener and General Heinrich Scheüch, who remained in his post as Prussian minister of war, to reestablish the authority of their command. Not even elaborate propaganda efforts aimed at immunizing combat troops against the revolutionary movement and at limiting the formation of soldiers' councils to the home army could prevent the returning troops from fraternizing with soldiers who sympathized with the revolution. For the time being, therefore, the Supreme Military Command was obliged to tolerate the existence of soldiers' councils while it concentrated its own energies on blocking efforts to curtail its powers of command. With this end in mind, the high command intended to deal in the long run only with delegates who had been duly elected by the troops themselves.

As early as mid-November, the Supreme Military Command drafted a plan based on deliberations in Spa to use the imminent return of combat troops from the front as a pretext for sealing off the capital with reliable army divisions, disarming the civilian population, and isolating the radical Left and those revolutionary army units that sympathized with it. After the Prussian minister of war declined to direct the operation, its the execution, in whose planning General Kurt von Schleicher had been deeply involved, was entrusted to an ad hoc general command under Lieutenant General Arnold Lequis. While Ebert was briefed on the technical aspects of the plan, he remained unaware of its underlying political objectives, which amounted to a "seizure of power" by the command of the field army. Indeed, some of those who were involved in this project intended to provide Ebert with dictatorial powers as provisional president, to convene the Reichstag, and to create a provisional National Assembly. But uncoordinated actions against the executive council on 6 December and the offer of dictatorial powers to Ebert produced a dramatic loss of prestige for the Council of People's Commissars among the more radical elements of the Berlin working class at the same time that it strengthened political resistance to military intervention. To be sure, a handful of military units marched into Berlin on 10 December, but Lequis fell far short of his ultimate goal since most of his own units identified with the Berlin soldiers' councils and simply dispersed.

This episode only fueled popular distrust of the old officer corps. As a result, the so-called Hamburg Points that would have subordinated the Supreme Military Command to the Council of People's Commissars, given the soldiers' councils decisive influence over command decisions, and abolished unconditional subordination along with its symbols met with enthusiastic support from the Majority Socialist deputies to the first congress of workers' and soldiers' councils on 16 December. The adoption of these points over Ebert's strenuous objection provoked an open revolt within the Supreme Military Command, which launched a full-scale protest, replete with threatened resignations by Hindenburg and Groener, against the Council of People's Commissars and publicly proclaimed the impracticality of the Hamburg Points. As a result, the directives the Council of People's Commissars released for the implementation of this program were substantially weakened in the sense that they were not applicable to either the field army or the navy. This, in turn, sparked an angry protest from the radical Left within the Majority Socialist–dominated Central Council of the Republic at the same time that it weakened the position of the USPD People's Commissars in their own party.

By now a lively controversy had developed as to whether or not the Council of People's Commissars should have used all of its influence to create a reliable republican militia for the protection of the government, which in light of the prevailing political climate would have been recruited almost exclusively from working-class elements. Initial efforts in this direction had already been made. Republican units, after all, had dealt with the conflict with the People's Navy that erupted on Christmas Eve before Lequis's troops intervened and seriously aggravated the entire situation. With proper support from the government, some of these republican units, such as the regiment "Reichstag," could have performed important security functions, thus alleviating the need for intervention by so-called regular troops. To be sure, the Council of People's Commissars had promulgated a law for the formation of a volunteer people's militia, but it had not been implemented, although southern Germany and several of the larger cities had positive experiences with the formation of volunteer militias.

In light of the prevailing pacifist sentiments, it would not have been easy to persuade Social Democratic workers to continue serving in the military for the purpose of protecting the republic. But the Majority Socialist wing in the Council of People's Commissars made no—or at best halfhearted—efforts in this direction, in part because of a blind faith in the superiority of the professional military and in part because of the not entirely unfounded fear that proletarian militias might be infiltrated by the militant Left. Moreover, the formation of a proletarian security force to replace the regular army would have presupposed a willingness to reach an understanding with the Independent Socialists. As it was, the leadership of the MSPD lacked the political foresight to realize the dangers inherent in using the service of former imperial officers with outspoken monarchist and conservative views for the purposes of republican self-defense. Warnings against the rise of counterrevolutionary forces fell on deaf ears. The sharp polemics in the USPD press and the vitriolic attacks of Rosa Luxemburg and Karl Liebknecht, who correctly foresaw that the military policy of the People's Commissars would restore the Prusso-German military tradition and create conditions conducive to open counterrevolution, went largely ignored. Social prejudices against the radical Left, which in certain quarters was denounced as "rabble," further strengthened the government in its contention that the increasing militancy of the German working class stemmed almost entirely from the influence of Spartacist ringleaders and elements of the *Lumpenproletariat*.

The conflict with the People's Navy Division would have remained an isolated episode had it not strengthened the resolve of the Supreme Army Command to depend in the future on what it considered "reliable"—that is, antirepublican—volunteer units. In point of fact, it was grotesque that the government failed to respond appropriately when the division first refused to follow orders because it had not been paid and then underscored its position by taking the Social Democratic city commandant Otto Wels hostage and occupying the Reich Chancery for several hours. In the meantime, turbulent negotiations to end the conflict were under way. This prompted Ebert to give in to pressure from Groener to disperse the People's Navy Division by force, although by this time it was clearly prepared to release Wels. Even the leaders of the Independent Socialists were anxious to avoid the impression that they were "soft" on the undisciplined sailors, whose behavior was tantamount to mutiny. The situation was further complicated by the fact that Lequis, who commanded the troops that were brought in to restore order, failed in his attempt to storm the castle and its adjoining stables. The civilian population that witnessed these events was clearly hostile to the military, which left the field of battle with its mission unfulfilled after having caused numerous deaths and injuries with the unwarranted use of heavy weapons. Under heavy pressure from working-class elements that objected to the use of the military, the Independent Socialists, who up to now had gone along with Ebert's questionable military policy, felt obliged to announce their resignation from the Council of People's Commissars on 28 December 1918. In doing so, they acted consistently with the resolutions that the first Council of People's Commissars had adopted two weeks earlier and that severely weakened their own position.

Almost simultaneously the split within the USPD between the majority of the party and those on its radical left wing who favored putschist tactics as a way of radicalizing the workers drew to a climax. At the insistence of the Bremen leftist radicals and with the support of Karl Radek—a Bolshevik emissary who had been denied a visa and was thus illegally in Berlin—the official founding of the KPD/Spartacus League took place shortly before the end of the year. The party congress unconditionally endorsed Lenin's proposition that the revolution should continue and demanded the establishment of a dictatorship of the proletariat based on the conciliar system. Over the objections of Rosa Luxemburg, Leo Jogiches, and the more farsighted party leaders, Karl Liebknecht succeeded in securing the adoption of a resolution that barred the party from participating in the elections to the National Assembly. As in the case of the party's founding, this too was a tactical mistake that drove the KPD, which at this point was not yet integrated into the Leninist system and was still dominated by anarchistic and putschist elements, into political isolation.

The establishment of the extreme Left as an independent force did little to defuse the highly charged domestic political situation created by widespread antigovernment protests against the military for its action against the legendary People's Navy Division. At the same time, the KPD hoped that it could win the support of the USPD's backers by intensifying its attacks against the party. The event that triggered an unexpected escalation of the conflict was the dismissal of Karl Eichhorn, a man with close ties to the Revolutionary Shop Stewards, as head of the Berlin police. From the government's perspective, Eichhorn's dismissal was a logical consequence of the USPD's withdrawal from the Council of People's Commissars at the end of December, particularly since the resignation of the Prussian USPD ministers had met with little, if any, public protest. The unrestrained attacks against Eichhorn in the Majority Socialist press, which pictured him as a putschist financed by the Russians, contributed in no small measure to the emotions that were aroused on both sides of the conflict. With Eichhorn's replacement by a member of the MSPD, the radical Left realized that it was about to lose its last position of power in the capital. In point of fact, the Majority Socialists were determined to exclude the left-wing opposition altogether and to create stable political conditions—even at the price of military intervention—in order not to jeopardize the elections to the National Assembly scheduled to take place on 19 January 1919.

Karl Liebknecht's revolutionary illusions and the putschist activism of the Revolutionary Shop Stewards complemented each other in transforming mass demonstrations against the government into an open civil war. Militant groups had already occupied a number of public buildings and newspaper offices, including those of *Vorwärts*, the leading Majority Socialist organ. A hastily constituted revolutionary committee issued confused resolutions in support of the revolt that was supposed to sweep the government from power. The leaders of the KPD were unable to resist the pull of the revolutionary tide, although the party was totally unprepared for the conquest of power and had to know in advance that such an action would end in a bloodbath.

The cabinet of the People's Commissars accepted the challenge. Initial efforts at mediation by the leadership of the Independent Socialists and the Central Council did little to weaken the cabinet in its resolve to enforce its authority by military means. Gustav Noske, who commanded operations in Berlin and its immediate environment, was not at all reluctant to make use of the recently constituted Free Corps units, among them the *Freiwillige Jägerkorps* under General Georg Maerker, who had refused to take the oath of loyalty to the government, or the mounted rifle guard with Captain Waldemar Pabst as its commanding officer. The recapture of the *Vorwärts* building on the night of 10–11 January with the use of heavy weapons, however, was accomplished by loyalist republican units. By the same token, the security forces formerly commanded by Eichhorn remained loyal to the government, which also received the support of Majority Socialists who were on strike to protest the actions of the radical Left.

The escalation of emotions that characterized this period could only be understood as a reaction to volunteer units, which had declared martial law on 13 January and were now advancing on the inner city and working-class suburbs. The behavior and outward appearance of the Free Corps troops, who did not hesitate to summarily execute anyone with a weapon in his hands, lent credibility to the fear that the counterrevolution was on the march. The civil war that Ebert had hoped to avoid had thus become a reality, and its main thrust was directed against the revolutionary working class.

The military occupation of Berlin triggered off a frantic hunt for the "Spartacist" ringleaders and ended with the violent suppression of any sign of opposition. The savage murder of Rosa Luxemburg and Karl Liebknecht by members of Pabst's mounted rifle guard on 15 January bore dramatic testimony to the intolerance, hatred, and glorification of violence that was dominating the German political scene under the motto of getting even with the Spartacists. On 13 January even the *Vorwärts* had indirectly called for the murders of Rosa Luxemburg and Karl Liebknecht. To be sure, violence had been perpetrated by the Left as well, but the conduct of the Free Corps far outdid anything that had occurred earlier. Friedrich Ebert was deeply shaken by the murder of the two prominent KPD leaders, the details of which became public only gradually. Although the government pressed for prosecution of those responsible, the penalties eventually imposed on the murderers by a military tribunal could only be considered a mocking insult to the idea of justice under law, not to mention the fact that those who had instigated the atrocities went unpunished in any form whatsoever.

Rudolf Hilferding has called the events of January 1919 "the battle of the Marne of the German Revolution." Both the bourgeois and Social Democratic press sought to place sole blame for the tragic course of events upon the Spartacists. To be sure, there is little doubt that the KPD contributed in no small measure to bringing the conflict to a head. However, the KPD was quantitatively insignificant even in Berlin and could have been politically isolated with little or no difficulty. That the Council of People's Commissars would react to the imminent revolt with military means was also inevitable. But the character of the troops it used, as well as the methods they employed, were sufficient to drive even its own adherents into the camp of the opposition. To workers who believed in socialism, the events in Berlin and other German cities in subsequent months appeared to be little more than a return to the conditions of the

First World War. State of emergency and military rule seemed to repeat themselves in the same forms and with the same means. It thus appeared as if the workers' struggle for peace and socialist democracy had ended in failure.

The fighting of January 1919 for control of Berlin initiated the second phase of the German Revolution. This phase was marked by the passionate revolt of large parts of the working population after the realization that the revolutionary developments initiated on 9 November had failed to bring about a true shift in power relations. Such a realization was directly related to an increasing radicalization of the industrial labor force, a radicalization that was not yet apparent in the elections to the National Assembly of 19 January 1919. In this election the MSPD received 37.9 and the USPD only 7.6 percent of the popular vote, so that contrary to their expectations the workers' parties remained a minority vis-à-vis the bourgeois parties. Despite the severe setbacks inflicted on the USPD in its strongholds by government troops in the spring of 1919 and despite its almost total political isolation—after the events of January, cooperation with the MSPD seemed out of the question—the Independent Socialists were able to record substantial gains at the expense of the Majority Socialists. In the Reichstag election of 6 June 1920 the USPD polled 18.0 percent of the popular vote as compared with only 21.6 percent for the MSPD. With only 1.7 percent, the KPD was no more than an insignificant splinter party.

In the elections to the National Assembly, the shift within the industrial working class to the Independent Socialists was not yet fully apparent. Earlier election results in the individual German states already made it unlikely that the two socialist parties would receive an absolute majority. In addition, the lowering of the voting age and the introduction of female suffrage proved detrimental to the socialist parties, as did the low voter turnout of 83 percent. The last of these factors had less to do with the KPD's boycott than with the high percentage of new voters. In agrarian regions that had been previously closed to them, the working-class parties had been able to make some slight inroads as a result of their success in mobilizing the sympathies of rural laborers and occasionally small farmers. In traditional Social Democratic strongholds, however, the MSPD and the USPD increased their share of the vote only rarely and were least successful in those precincts where the Independent Socialists did well, which revealed a high degree of polarization within the socialist camp.

Of the bourgeois parties, the Center Party and the Bavarian People's Party (Bayerische Volkspartei or BVP)—originally united in a parliamentary coalition or *Fraktionsgemeinschaft*—received 19.7 percent of the popular vote. The reason for the remarkably good showing of the German Democratic Party (Deutsche Demokratische Partei or DDP), which received 18.5 percent of all votes cast, was the fact that its principal rival, the German People's Party (Deutsche Volkspartei or DVP), had been founded at a relatively late stage in the campaign and could therefore only enlist the support of those voters who, though they favored a comprehensive democratization of German political life, opposed the abolition of the capitalist economic system. As a result, the DVP received a mere 4.4 percent of the popular vote. Given the apparent strength of those parties pledged to the defense of the republic, the Central Council of the German Republic placed its mandate in the hands of the newly elected National Assembly on 4 February. Demands for the "integration of workers' and soldiers' councils in the future national constitution" evoked widespread protest on the radical Left, which the leaders of the Majority Socialists hoped to silence by convening the second Congress of Councils in Berlin later that April.

As far as the Majority Socialists were concerned, the opening of the National Assembly on 6 February removed the last remaining justification for the continued existence of local workers' and soldiers' councils. Acting as provisional minister of defense, Gustav Noske gave the green light for the elimination of the soldiers' councils. From this point on, they remained active only in strongholds of the radical Left, whereas elsewhere the former chain of command was reestablished with, at best, occasional ombudsmen to safeguard social interests. At the same time, the military intensified its campaign for the formation of Free Corps and civil militias, or *Einwohnerwehren*. Highly controversial from the outset, the compromises that Scheüch's successor, Colonel Walther Reinhardt, had made in the matter of the soldiers' councils in the face of strong objections from the officer corps were now largely countermanded. The law of 6 March 1919 that provided for the preliminary formation of the Reichswehr prompted the majority of the recently formed volunteer units to join the regular army, whereas the few republican units were either dissolved or integrated into more conservative units.

Officially the reorganization of the armed forces in the period before the Versailles peace treaty was undertaken to insure Germany's ability to defend itself against Poland well as against possible encroachments in the west. In point of fact, however, both the Supreme Army Command and the Reichswehr command — which would be placed under the authority of the minister of defense after the adoption of the new constitution — conceived of themselves as instruments of political power. In this respect, they felt that it was their mission to help the state reassert its full authority. This aim involved disarming existing security forces and the population, dissolving unruly workers' councils, and in general suppressing "Spartacism" wherever it might exist. On the other hand, local civilian militias had been organized in the countryside to serve as domestic combat troops and reserve units of the regular army. Members of the educated classes, especially prep school and university students who had not served under the Kaiser, volunteered for private armies that were, in turn, financed by large landlords and industrialists. The extent to which this contributed to the remilitarization of German society can hardly be exaggerated. While wide fluctuations in the strength of these invariably right-wing paramilitary units make precise estimates regarding their membership impossible, it can be safely assumed that more than a million men belonged to this mixed and insufficiently coordinated fighting power. The mobile security police, which would take the place of municipal police forces, were created in close cooperation with local military authorities, a fact that greatly influenced the recruitment of police officers.

The revolutionary elements of the German working class—and not just the leadership of KPD and USPD—regarded these developments as clear evidence that the forces of counterrevolution were indeed on the march. Such a conclusion was justified insofar as members of left-wing parties, including the MSPD, were deliberately excluded on one pretext or another from the paramilitary units that were in the process of being formed. The counterrevolutionary character of these troops was thus established long before the return of the Free Corps units that had been stationed in the Baltic. At first the military was prepared to support the Majority Socialists in their struggle against the radical Left. In return, the Majority Socialists obediently placed themselves at the disposal of the military, as advertisements for Free Corps volunteers in *Vorwärts* clearly demonstrated. Yet there could be no doubt regarding the counterrevolutionary character of the paramilitary formations that emerged in the immediate postwar period. In this respect, anti-Bolshevism became inseparable from antisocialism. The bitterness that not only the extreme Left but also the socialist labor unions and the Majority Socialists felt over these developments prompted them to boycott the recruitment of volunteers for the Free Corps and to take disciplinary action against former Free Corps members in the factories. Once again, party functionaries felt as if they were back in the war years; the only difference was that now the state of emergency had been declared by a socialist government.

How little the growing fear of Bolshevism not only in bourgeois circles but also within the leadership of the MSPD and the socialist labor unions corresponded to reality could be seen in the fact that radical leftist factions were never able to coordinate their actions against the government and the military units under Noske's command. Instead the "Noske boys," as they were contemptuously called, were able to break up centers of resistance in one locality after another. As the more moderate socialists began to distance themselves from the councils, the radical Left gained the upper hand. Frequently the results were nothing less than grotesque, as in the case of the "Independent Socialist Republic of Bremen" that was proclaimed on 10 January 1919. Here dilettantism and romantic revolutionary fervor combined to create a welter of confusion that only intensified bourgeois aversion to socialist politics in any form.

The case of Bremen was typical of Noske's predilection for punitive actions against radical leftist minorities. Conciliar-rule Bremen had already come to an end, and the workers' council had announced its willingness to surrender its arms. Nevertheless, Noske insisted for reasons of prestige on using the Gerstenberg division that had been mobilized for the specific purpose of liberating Bremen. This, in turn, precipitated a series of completely unnecessary, yet bloody confrontations with the Bremen working class. Similar events transpired in a number of other places as well. What had begun as a simple attempt to maintain order and to reestablish normal governmental authority had thus degenerated into a virtual civil war that was to continue for many months. In industrial areas the self-defense of radical leftist positions became closely linked with a mass protest movement on the part of local workers. Virtually all of the major strike movements that took place from January to April 1919 in the Ruhr, central Germany, Upper Silesia, and finally in Berlin occurred without the involvement of the official workers' parties. Not even the KPD was able to channel this protest for its own purposes. The main motive for these strikes was the government's failure to fulfill the social expectations that the end of the war and the subsequent revolution had inspired within the German working class. After the privations of the war, all social groups felt that fundamentally new social configurations would have to replace the Wilhelmine social system. There was a pervasive but unfocused eagerness for a new start, an eagerness that stood in sharp contrast to the seemingly hopeless economic situation and that had more to do with the high degree of political mobilization during the revolution than with the agitation of the radical Left. To the extent that the USPD identified itself with the revolutionary sentiments of the proletarian masses, it fell victim to the political delusions inherent in such a role.

The Council of People's Commissars was reluctant to fulfill the hopes for a comprehensive reorganization of German society that had been encouraged by the Central Council of the German Republic. Aside from promising to introduce the eight-hour day and taking steps to establish unemployment compensation, the Council of People's Commissars refused to intervene in relations between capital and labor. Its principal concern was to facilitate the resumption of industrial production and to expedite the conversion from a war to a peacetime economy, an endeavor hampered both by critical shortages in the raw materials for industry and by difficulties in providing the population with food in the face of the continued Allied blockade. In general the difficulties of demobilization—it was a matter of reintegrating eight and a half million soldiers into the process of production—were overestimated. The preferential treatment that war veterans received in hiring, however, had negative consequences for young workers and women, who were disproportionately affected by the growing unemployment.

During the period of revolutionary upheaval, the labor unions adopted an essentially defensive position. Until the late autumn of 1918, heavy industry refused to acknowledge the strengthened position that organized labor had gained with the adoption of the National Service Law (Vaterländischer

Hilfsdienst) and persisted in its "master-in-the-house" stance. This, however, changed in early October, when management realized that a German defeat was imminent and began to look for allies to ward off the danger of a comprehensive state control of economic life in the event of a general demobilization. At the initiative of Hans von Raumer, executive secretary of the Central Association of the German Electricotechnical Industry (Zentralverband der deutschen Elektrotechnischen Industrie), and with the active support of Hugo Stinnes, Germany's industrial leadership reached an agreement with Karl Legien, chairman of the General German Trade-Union Association (Allgemeiner Deutscher Gewerkschaftsbund or ADGB) on 30 October whereby both parties would cooperate in the establishment of a demobilization agency that would curtail the influence of the Economics Ministry.

Stinnes anticipated that the end of the war would give rise to a tremendous demand for consumer goods that would lead to a far-reaching economic expansion if management could first free the entrepreneurial decision-making process from state interference through a separate understanding with organized labor. The purpose of the Central Association of Industrial and Commercial Employers and Employees of Germany (Zentralarbeitsgemeinschaft der industriellen und gewerblichen Arbeitgeber und Arbeitnehmer Deutschlands or ZAG) that had been established by the agreement of 15 October was to create the social and political presuppositions for this expansion. The price that management had to pay for the cooperation of the unions and to which Ruhr heavy industry assented with great reluctance was to acknowledge organized labor's autonomy in determining wage scales, to terminate support for company unions, and to permit the introduction of the eight-hour day insofar as that was compatible with international conditions. In exchange, the unions — socialist, Christian, and liberal — pledged their positive cooperation in all matters related to demobilization.

While the Stinnes-Legien agreement benefited entrepreneurs by giving them a free hand in such matters as setting prices, stimulating exports, and allocating state subsidies, it left labor's hopes of securing a voice in general economic decision making largely unfulfilled, particularly since the influence of the ZAG was quickly eclipsed by that of the Reich Economics Ministry. To be sure, the formal recognition that heavy industry extended to the unions represented an important turning point in the development of management-labor relations and strengthened labor's prospects for a meaningful role in economic codetermination on a level beyond that of the individual plant. At the same time, however, the alliance with management seriously curtailed the unions' own freedom of action. The revolutionary events had little direct impact on the negotiations that culminated in the formation of the Zentralarbeitsgemeinschaft. From the perspective of the union leadership, the commitment to respect the decisions of the Zentralarbeitsgemeinschaft did not represent a disadvantage insofar as both the unions and management were opposed to economic experiments. In this respect, union leaders agreed with the Majority Socialists that changes in the economic system should be left to the National Assembly.

This was especially relevant in the socialization question. Socialization of the basic raw materials industries was one of the traditional demands of organized labor. By December 1918 even Otto Hue, chairman of the Socialist Miners' Union (Der Alter Verband), dissociated himself from the miners' earlier demand for the socialization of the anthracite coal industry on the grounds that socialism would suffer a severe defeat "if at this time we were to saddle ourselves with the responsibility for totally upsetting the basic conditions governing industrial production." At the same time, however, the representatives of the Mining Association (Zechenverband) looked upon a measure of socialization in the area of anthracite mining as inevitable. At the first Congress of Councils in mid-December 1918, an overwhelming majority of the delegates in attendance advocated the immediate socialization of those plants that were ready for it, including first and foremost the anthracite mines. The Council of People's Commissars treated the problem dilatorily by appointing a socialization commission consisting of representatives of the coalition parties and bourgeois experts. While the commission conceived of socialization as a long-term process that could not be accomplished overnight, it recommended immediate steps aimed at socializing the anthracite mining industry and called for measures that would afford employee representatives "the necessary insight in business operations."

The main arguments against socializing obvious candidates like heavy industry were twofold. Officials not only contended that existing economic conditions were not compatible with further dislocations in the productive process but feared that socialized industries presented a more convenient target for Allied confiscation than privately owned enterprises. The MSPD leadership itself shied away from steps aimed at socialization on the rather vague grounds that it would foster the creation of "Russian conditions." The argument that the government did not have the necessary experts and would therefore have to rely, at least in the initial stages of the process, on the loyalty of the entrepreneurs was also valid. Still, it would have been possible to modify the deeply resented system of personal subordination that existed in the workplace in favor of greater respect for the needs of the work force as a whole and to grant the workers a measure of input into the economic decision-making process. In this respect, even Josef Koeth, director of the demobilization office, suggested that "the workers should be afforded a greater opportunity to form judgments over our economic situation and to gain insight into the management of plants."

In the meantime, the General German Trade-Union Federation remained adamantly opposed to the introduction of autonomous factory councils in individual plants and made every effort to retain control over the workers' committees that had been established in December 1918 under the terms of the Stinnes-Legien agreement. According to the provisions of the Zentralarbeits-gemeinschaft, special committees were to represent workers in individual factories, but their functions would be limited to monitoring violations of working conditions as stipulated in wage contracts. In point of fact, the ADGB greatly overestimated the potential influence the Zentralarbeitsgemeinschaft had given it. Moreover, the general suspicion that surrounded the entire question of factory representation played an important role in the passage of the factory council law in January 1920 by limiting the responsibilities of workers' representatives to matters of social policy within the factories. This, in turn, hampered compromise solutions that might have more effectively secured comprehensive workers' rights in the decision-making process.

Mass strikes in the Ruhr marked the beginning of renewed and widespread labor unrest in virtually all industrialized areas of the country. These strikes began in early January, when the government's break with the USPD made it clear to the workers that the Council of People's Commissars could no longer be expected to undertake a serious move toward socialization. In the Ruhr, miners demanded fundamental improvements in working conditions in the mines and a shortening of the shifts. While constantly rising prices made wage scales a major issue, they were not the primary cause of the strike movement, which at times engulfed the entire Ruhr basin and almost totally shut down the production of coal. The striking miners were also seeking an end to the managers' "master-in-their-own-house," or *Herr im Hause*, principle that had remained in effect in the Ruhr mining industry in spite of the first wage contracts that had been concluded in November 1918.

On 13 January 1919 the Essen Conference of Workers' and Soldiers' Councils from the Ruhr (Essener Konferenz der Arbeiter- und Soldatenräte) established a nine-member commission with equal representation from the MSPD and USPD. This commission submitted a comprehensive proposal for socialization that granted the miners a major role in the management of the mining enterprises, without, however, addressing the question of ownership itself. The promise of socialization and the election of miner's councils brought the general strike to an immediate end. Labor Minister Rudolf Wissell, however, rebuffed the delegation that had been dispatched to Weimar on the grounds that the procedures of the nine-member commission had been illegal. As the Majority Socialists and the leaders of the Alter Verband disassociated themselves from the socialization movement in the Ruhr, the government ordered Free Corps units into the area. Bloody confrontations, in large part provoked by the actions of the Free Corps, proceeded to ignite a general strike in which a majority of the miners participated.

Union representatives blamed the Communist Party for the strike movement and the extreme bitterness that resulted from the April strike. They did not want to admit that union members had been actively involved in organizing the strikes and that the main impetus for the solidarity movement in the mines had resulted from the provocations and violence of the Free Corps. The miners, on the other hand, believed that their actions carried the approval of the government, which seemed to be fulfilling their demands by appointing socialization commissars and distributing posters proclaiming that "Socialization Is on the March!" (*Die Sozialisierung ist auf dem Marsche*) at the very time that it was preparing for military intervention. Only in the last stages of the conflict were Communist elements able to gain appreciable influence, whereas the socialist miners' organizations lost almost a third of their membership to more radical unions.

In central Germany the strike movement followed a similar pattern, except that here it culminated in a general strike in which all industrial sectors participated with the support of the clearly dominant USPD. Government's compromises on the issues of workers' representation in the plant and regional organizations were mainly designed to help it gain time. The outcome of all this was, as it had been in the Ruhr, the violent suppression of the workers' protest movement. Nor was the government's strategy any different in Upper Silesia, where it relied on an even more comprehensive state of emergency to quell an impending general strike on the pretext that the strike had been instigated by Polish provocateurs. Here too, many workers left the socialist labor unions in anger.

Large segments of the work force did not understand why the government opposed their demands for autonomous representation in the plants. The fact is that the government would not accept anything beyond the formation of labor commissions in which management and labor were equally represented. Here officials were fearful that left-wing USPD and KPD labor representatives might transform the factory councils into instruments for establishing a revolutionary dictatorship of the councils. Yet this could only happen if the moderate groups refused to participate. In the meantime, the socialist unions strenuously objected to any form of economic codetermination at the factory level, since this would break the monopoly they enjoyed in representing labor's economic interests. The plan that Max Cohen-Reuss had presented to the Congress of Councils in April 1919 for giving the factory councils sweeping economic rights and establishing industry-wide codetermination thus ran into strong opposition from the ADGB at the MSPD's Nuremberg party congress despite the fact that Majority Socialist deputies to the Congress of Councils had accepted it.

The opposition of the socialist unions to the socialization movement and their rejection of the proposal by Rudolf Wissell and his collaborator Wichard von Moellendorf for a planned economy, or *Gemeinwirtschaft*, modeled after the war economy contributed in no small measure to the dearth of fundamental changes in Germany's economic structure and to the success of German heavy industry, particularly in the Ruhr, in maintaining, if not strengthening, its position relative to the prewar period. The institutional overtures to a planned economy, such as the National Coal Council (Reichskohlenrat) and the Coal and Potassium Syndicate (Kohlen- und Kalisyndikat), soon atrophied for lack of support. With the support of the Zentralarbeitsgemeinschaft, industrialists were by and large able to set their own price levels.

Although the position of the unions seemed to be strengthened by their participation in the ZAG, the revolutionary movements had failed to bring about any fundamental changes in the distribution of economic power. In point of fact, the unions had already lost so much ground that little remained except to fight for a compensatory social policy. Even less spectacular were the achievements of the revolutionary movement in the nonindustrial sector. In its concern for maintaining a continuous supply of food, the MSPD had refrained from demanding far-reaching changes in the structure of German agriculture and settled for promises of cooperation from Germany's landowning classes. The principal casualty of this tactic was a land reform in East Elbia. Similar considerations dissuaded the Majority Socialists from initiating fundamental changes in the civil bureaucracy. All of this can be attributed in large part to an unfortunate tendency to overestimate the possibilities of accomplishing these changes through parliament.

The government's use of military force in the spring of 1919 to crush USPD strongholds in Brunswick, Magdeburg, Mannheim, Halle, Leipzig, and Berlin was tantamount to admitting the political failure of the Majority Socialists. Coercion by the bayonet took the place of endeavors to achieve the political integration of radical workers and to isolate those on the extreme Left who were committed to a policy of putschist terrorism. The notorious unreliability of the Free Corps, which often led to excesses against innocent bystanders, helped create a state of near civil war and sparked feelings of anger and impotence throughout significant segments of the working population. In this respect, the events of March–April 1919 in Berlin and Munich were by no means atypical. Initially called with the approval of the MSPD and over the strenuous objection of the KPD, the general strike in the spring of 1919 did not adhere to the principle of nonviolence as espoused by the strike leadership and involved scattered attacks on police installations. Noske responded by declaring a state of emergency that remained in force for nine months. The armed clashes between radical workers and the Free Corps, which operated ruthlessly and did not shrink from acts of revenge, claimed more than twelve hundred victims and yet failed to restore calm. To the proletarian masses, the Berlin *Blutwoche*, as these events were soon known, only confirmed the class-bound character of the nascent republic.

Events in Munich assumed a somewhat different character, since here the radical Left drew its support more from intellectual circles than from a solid nucleus within the industrial working class. Until the spring of 1919 the socialist coalition government led by Kurt Eisner had been able to ensure relatively stable conditions, even though Eisner's public reputation had suffered severely from his pacifist, if not esoteric, foreign policy and his insufficient mastery of government business. The Landtag elections of January 1919, in which the USPD had suffered a crushing defeat by winning only three seats, had made Eisner's position completely untenable. As a solution to the conflict between the radical and the moderate Left, Eisner envisaged a system of government that sought to combine the principles of parliamentary rule with government by councils. But, as the Austrian example clearly revealed, this compromise might have satisfied party regulars but was politically impractical in view of the hostile attitude of the national government and the growing opposition of influential bourgeois circles.

Eisner's assassination by Count Arco-Valley on 21 February 1919 just as the victim was about to announce his resignation in the Landtag and the subsequent attempt on the life of the Majority Socialist minister of the interior Erhard Auer by one of Eisner's supporters polarized Bavarian society into two mutually antagonistic factions that were fully prepared to wage civil war. The "second revolution" that Arco had wanted to prevent was in fact triggered by his action. Formed under the impact of these events, the new Central Council of Bavarian Soviets (Zentralrat der bayerischen Räte) proceeded under the leadership of Ernst Niekisch to proclaim a Soviet Republic. This would have remained a somewhat theatrical episode had the coalition government formed shortly thereafter by Social Democrat Johannes Hoffmann possessed the energy and political support necessary to hold its own against rival factions in the conciliar movement and security forces loyal to the radical Left. As it was, Hoffmann's government retreated to Bamberg and petitioned the national government for military assistance to strengthen the Free Corps unit that had been formed by retired army colonel Franz von Epp. The proclamation of the Soviet Republic of Bavaria on 7 April 1919 by a coalition of socialist parties was received rather coolly by the KPD, which had just been reorganized under the leadership of Eugen Leviné. It was only when the Munich garrison attempted to overthrow the new Soviet Republic that Leviné and Max Levien decided to assume leadership of the republic, even though they had no realistic hope of stabilizing an autonomous Soviet regime limited to Bavaria alone. The proclamation of a Soviet Republic in Hungary at the end of March fostered the illusion that the Bolshevist revolution was sweeping across central Europe and allowed the leaders of the Bavarian Soviet to forge ahead without concern.

The fourteen days of soviet rule in Munich were little more than a series of disasters. Not only were its economic and fiscal policies a total failure, but the Red Army it had brought into being was pathetically inadequate and could not possibly stand up to the vastly more powerful units mobilized against it.

On 27 April Ernst Toller, the expressionist playwright who had taken a leading role in the initial stages of the soviet experiment, demanded and obtained the resignations of Leviné and Levien who, as Russian citizens, were already quite unpopular. Toller had to watch helplessly as the Free Corps troops that arrived on 2 May, incensed at the slaying of a hostage on the previous day, set up a reign of terror that went far beyond the red terror and claimed the lives of six hundred persons within two days. This episode in the history of the German revolution, which resulted in more than 5,000 court cases against individual participants, laid the basis for the counterrevolutionary and antirepublican climate that helped fertilize the soil in which *völkisch*-nationalist restoration movements could thrive.

The collapse of the Soviet Republic in Munich and the subsequent suppression of the extreme Left by government troops in Leipzig in early May 1919 marked the end of the revolutionary era in Germany. The revolutionary forces saw themselves hopelessly isolated in the face of a remilitarized bourgeois society that was unequivocally committed to the politics of class warfare. For the plethora of defense organizations ranging from civilian militias to the Baltic Free Corps that had declared its autonomy from the national government, all enjoyed close relations with industrial circles and conservative political interests that provided them with the necessary funding. By the same token, connections with the Reichswehr guaranteed them a reliable supply of weapons and equipment. The close cooperation among the Reichswehr, employers' associations, the National Rural League (Reichs-Landbund or RLB), and other right-wing interest groups in the Ruhr and East Elbia made it impossible for the Prussian government and its local administrative agencies to bring the counterrevolutionary movements in these areas under control. Proclaiming the goal of rooting out all forms of "Bolshevism" and socialist internationalism, the Reichswehr Commando I under General Walther von Lüttwitz began as early as the spring of 1919 to cultivate close ties with right-wing bourgeois propaganda organizations such as Eduard Stadtler's Anti-Bolshevist League (Antibolschewistische Liga) and to support *völkisch*-nationalist movements of a decidedly antisocialist character. Adolf Hitler's activities on behalf of the Reichswehr Commando IV, which launched his political career and brought him into contact with Anton Drexler's German Workers' Party (Deutsche Arbeiterpartei), can only be understood against the background of this general context.

The German Revolution of 1918–19 was unique in no small measure because it anticipated a peace whose contours were already discernible in the conditions established for the cease-fire. In this connection, it is important to remember that the continuation of hostilities was not altogether out of the question, that is, except for those who agreed with Haase and Eisner that peace had to be concluded without regard for the conditions that it might impose.

This constellation contributed decisively to the defeated army's ability to restore its powerful position in German domestic politics and to function as an instrument of the counterrevolution under the somewhat spurious pretext of strengthening the government's authority.

The leaders of the MSPD and ADGB went along with this policy on the assumption that, following the establishment of a parliamentary democracy, they would be in a position to rectify any mistakes that had been made along the way. This proved to be a serious mistake, for among other things it alienated the rank-and-file MSPD membership from the party's leaders even more profoundly than had been the case during the First World War. In light of the National Assembly's tolerance for the repressive measures that had been deployed against the working class, it is no surprise that appreciable numbers of proletarian groups preferred the "pure" system of rule by soviets advocated by the KPD to the principle of parliamentary government. Germany's parliamentary democracy thus originated, as it were, on the wrong side of a revolutionary civil war, with the result that from the very outset large segments of the industrial work force adopted a distant and uncommitted, if not altogether hostile, attitude toward the fledgling democracy.

The fury of the strike movements that erupted in Berlin, central Germany, the Ruhr, and numerous large cities in the spring of 1919 caught the leaders of the Majority Social Democrats by surprise, for they had assumed that the convocation of the National Assembly, the establishment of a provisional government, and the dissolution of the Central Council of the Republic had meant the end of the revolution. Convinced that they represented the true labor movement, the leaders of the MSPD saw the strikes primarily as the action of workers led astray by irresponsible radical elements, especially the Spartacists. In reality, this protest movement showed very clearly that the rank-and-file German worker sought to reunite the three working-class parties. None of the three parties, however, was able to subordinate the strikers to their own partisan goals. In addition to protesting the reemergent military rule, the strikers' immediate aim was the improvement of working conditions in the factories. The slogan of socialization had less to do with restructuring property rights than with the desire to eliminate repression and arbitrary rules in the factories and to improve the social conditions of the wage-earning population. For the most part, these were utopian ideas, as exemplified by workers' momentary demands for a six-hour shift in the anthracite coal mines. Putschist actions, which took place with the collaboration of Communist groups acting independently of the party's central headquarters, led to short-lived soviet experiments as in Munich or Bremen and generally lacked the support of the masses.

The Social Democratic leadership identified itself much too closely with the statist tradition of the prewar SPD to benefit from the impulses for greater democratic participation that had inspired the protest movements. The USPD sought to mobilize these impulses with its call for a socialist democracy in its party program from December 1919, but was unable to channel them into a constructive political direction. Following the serious loss of confidence the MSPD experienced in the wake of the January uprisings, the reality of political polarization could no longer be denied. No longer was it possible to resolve conflicts by peaceful political means without taking into consideration the concerns of Social Democracy's bourgeois coalition partners and the revived strength of Germany's armed forces. This proved a severe handicap for Germany's fledgling parliamentary democracy at the very moment of its inception.

Revolutionary upheavals almost invariably involve violence, particularly when they occur in the aftermath of a brutalizing war. The KPD had frequently advocated, albeit in propaganda more than in practice, the use of violence in political conflicts. Moreover, the authoritarian obsession of leading Social Democrats with the need to maintain order also encouraged the use of force. For their part, the protesting workers adhered to older forms of civil strife, such as general strikes and mass demonstrations, which they handled, all things considered, in a remarkably disciplined manner. Only on the fringes of the workers' movement and in response to escalating violence did proletarian groups make conscious use of terrorist means themselves. Rapidly mounting unemployment in the first months of 1919 and increasingly severe food shortages in heavily populated industrial areas contributed in no small measure to the heightened militancy of labor disputes.

With few exceptions, there was no reign of terror in the German Revolution of 1918–19. The terror that did take place was primarily the work of the counterrevolutionary forces unleashed by the MSPD's preoccupation with the restoration of order, and it soon developed a life of its own. The Free Corps epitomized the new style of warfare that idealized violence for the sake of violence. "We certainly were not interested in systems and order, in slogans and programs," wrote Ernst von Salomon about the Free Corps. The cult of male bonding and the erotic glorification of violence melded into a hybrid nationalism and fanatical anti-Bolshevism. The glorification of violence on behalf of the nation survived the end of the German revolution and was to find a lasting place in a culture that systematically failed to deal with the political and social consequences spawned by imperial Germany's military defeat in the Great War of 1914–18.

CHAPTER THREE

Founding a Democracy

IN the unsettled situation that had existed on 9 November 1918, Friedrich Ebert had tried to keep all of his options regarding the future form of the German state open. But when public opinion turned against Wilhelm II, the proclamation of a republic became inevitable. This was done by the Majority Socialist Philipp Scheidemann in an attempt to preempt more radical action by Karl Liebknecht. Contemporary expectations that this would be the first step toward the breakup of the officer corps, however, remained unfulfilled. In the meantime, the political Right accepted the fall of the monarchy as inevitable, at least for the time being. To be sure, both the German National People's Party (Deutschnationale Volkspartei or DNVP) and the German People's Party remained loyal to the principle of a constitutional monarchy. But unlike the arch-conservative *Preußische Kreuz-Zeitung* and the former German Conservative Party (Deutschkonservative Partei), which had been absorbed into the DNVP, these parties did not advocate the immediate restoration of the Hohenzollern dynasty. The "National Manifesto" of the DNVP, for example, only spoke of the formation of a "new imperial monarchy lawfully evolving over time." Nor did it exclude the possibility that at some point in the future a new constellation of political forces might arise in which a majority of the population might demand a return to the monarchy. As a general rule, the parties of the bourgeois Right continued to express their loyalty to the monarchy in order to strengthen their hold on tradition-bound and antirepublican voters.

In the foreseeable future, both foreign and domestic political considerations precluded a restoration of the monarchy. Virtually no one in Germany was prepared even to contemplate such a step, for the reestablishment of the German dynasties would almost certainly have revived the particularism of the individual states. Moreover, the posture of Wilhelm II, who did not formally declare his abdication and that of the two crown princes until 28 November 1919, made it unclear as to which of the two potential pretenders would be entitled to the succession. Thus, although monarchism continued to play a role within the DNVP even in the later years of the Weimar Republic, the notion of restoration reemerged only in the phase immediately before the National Socialist takeover of power. After 1918 the republican form of the state was no longer in doubt.

As a response to the October reforms and Wilson's policies, the process by which a new constitution came into existence following the collapse of 9 November 1918 was heavily weighted in favor of liberal-parliamentary goals. Thrust into a position of political leadership in the transitional revolutionary phase, the Majority and Independent Socialists found themselves unexpectedly faced with the task of providing the Reich with a new constitution. Substantive discussions regarding the most desirable type of constitution, however, had not taken place within the Social Democratic movement since the days of the Erfurt Program. By political tradition the party favored the parliamentary principle, which it had championed vigorously and virtually by itself during the empire. Moreover, its major constitutional demands seemed to have been met by the October reforms of Max von Baden. The USPD's experiences after 1916, on the other hand, caused it to view the parliamentary form of government with definite reservations. It envisaged a system of soviets as a desirable complement to a constitution based on the principle of parliamentary representation, though without any clear idea as to the manner in which these two systems might be linked together.

Under these circumstances, it was only natural that the proposed democratic constitution would reflect the compromises that had been reached by the parties of the future Weimar coalition within the Interparty Committee. By relinquishing their claim to the exclusive responsibility for designing the constitution, the socialist parties uncoupled this process from the revolution itself, although the USPD continued to harbor the illusion that sweeping revolutionary innovations in the civil administration, as well as in society as a whole, would enable it to incorporate concrete socialist features into the constitution. Underlying the attitude of both parties—but especially that of the MSPD—was a constitutional formalism that had lost sight of Lasalle's maxim that constitutional questions were really questions of power and involved far more than the creation of a legal framework for dealing with concrete political issues.

As early as 15 November 1918, the Council of People's Commissars had appointed Hugo Preuß, professor of public law at the University of Berlin, as state secretary in the Ministry of the Interior and assigned him to the task of drafting a new constitution. A former student of Otto von Gierke, a proponent of the cooperative principle, Preuß nonetheless tended to favor the parliamentary principle. In the review *Nation* published by his Left-liberal friend Theodor Barth, Preuß emphatically advocated the parliamentarization of the national constitution. Harking back to the democratic traditions of 1848–49, Preuß had publicly asserted his opposition to the authoritarian Prussian-German state (*Obrigkeitsstaat*) as well as his support for popular democracy as early as 1915. The fact that he had submitted a proposal for a constitution to the Supreme Army Command in July 1917 gave birth to rumors that he already had a complete draft in hand. It was this, more than anything else, that prompted Ebert, who was always inclined to a pragmatic course of action, to assign the preliminary work on Germany's future constitution to Preuß rather than to the Heidelberg sociologist Max Weber, whose name had also been mentioned in this connection.

Weber, however, did participate in the deliberations that took place within the Ministry of the Interior, where he and Preuß were joined by high-ranking departmental officials and two Social Democratic undersecretaries of state in preparing the draft constitution. The first draft, submitted to the Council of People's Commissars on 3 January 1919, clearly bore the mark of Preuß's authorship. Adopting a decidedly unitary perspective, the constitutional draft abandoned the existing structure based on sovereign *Länder* and called for the establishment of sixteen German states. While Ebert approved of the draft in principle, he suggested that the provisions concerning the territorial restructuring be set aside for the moment and that a section on the basic rights of the citizen be included. This modification, he hoped, would alleviate the concern — expressed even within his own party — that the "revolutionary achievements" of 1918 might be nullified. Preuß had not addressed the question of fundamental rights because he did not want to see the debates become bogged down, as they had seventy years earlier at the Paulskirche, on matters of principle. This issue, in his mind, would only delay the constitution-making process.

Ebert had originally hoped to avoid public debate about the constitution until the cabinet had completed a draft. In this respect, however, Ebert was less than successful, for the state governments insisted on being included in the deliberations on the constitutional draft. The Reich Ministry of the Interior thus found itself obliged to hold discussions with a special committee of state representatives, or *Staatenauschuß*, that had been established in November. The most important issue these discussions addressed dealt with relations between the Reich and the states. In this respect, it is significant that Ebert communicated the draft to the Central Council only after it had been modified by the Länder conference that convened on 25 January 1919. He then prevented the Central Council from conducting a thorough review of the draft on the rather spurious grounds that it had to be submitted without delay to the National Assembly, which met for the first time on 6 February. The dissatisfaction the Central Council expressed over this procedure — a sentiment shared by Scheidemann, who characterized the draft as "regressive" — had no practical consequences other than the request that an alternative draft in keeping with socialist tenets be submitted to the National Assembly, a request that was ignored by the MSPD leadership.

Hugo Preuß, who had been obliged to abandon major parts of his original draft, declared in his meeting with the Council of the People's Commissars that it was urgent "to form a regular government as soon as possible, so that we will be in a position to negotiate with foreign powers; this compels us to accept even a bad draft." This statement underscores the extent to which one hoped that peace negotiations could be conducted by a government that had been formed on the basis of a new constitution. For the same reason, Ebert attempted to thwart the debate on the political principles of the constitution in the National Assembly. This explains his readiness to make far-reaching concessions to the particularistic interests of the *Länder*, which were bound to come into play since the Council of People's Commissars refused to acknowledge the Executive Council and the Central Council as provisional guardians of the interests of the national state. Outwardly, this course of action proved remarkably successful. A well-prepared draft was submitted to the National Assembly on 21 February. To be sure, bitter controversies involving issues such as education and religion did arise as the constitutional committee continued its work. Nevertheless, the constitution formally took effect as early as 14 August despite the delay that had been caused in June 1919 by the conflict over the acceptance of the Versailles peace treaty.

In light of Germany's critical political situation, the parliamentary ratification of the proposed constitution was remarkably smooth. This stemmed in large part from the determination of the bourgeois parties and Majority Socialists to put an end to the uncertain legal situation that had been created by the revolution and to eliminate the competing institutions of soviet rule. Moreover, the decision-making powers of the National Assembly had been considerably curtailed. The bill for the Law on Provisional National Power (Gesetz über die vorläufige Reichsgewalt) that had been drafted in cooperation with the state governments and enacted with the votes of the Weimar coalition on 10 February 1919 anticipated important elements of the future constitutional structure, such as the relations between the president, the Reichstag, and an upper house, or *Staatenhaus*, consisting of representatives from the individual German states. In the preliminary negotiations, the states had won an important concession that any bill submitted to the National Assembly by the national government required the prior approval of a majority of state governments. In order to safeguard the formal legality of the procedure, the parties approved the provisional constitution without questioning the legality of the preliminary decisions. In the final analysis, however, the agreement by the Council of People's Commissars to preserve the principle of a professional civil service as well as its regulations for the provisional structure of the Reichswehr had negative consequences for the future constitution.

The decision to give the assembly of states a voice in the national government completely undermined the premise of Preuß's constitutional concept, namely, that the individual states were to be reduced to the status of administrative units within an essentially unitary state. The position of the states was further enhanced by the adoption of a special clause stipulating that territorial reorganization would require the consent of the affected states, thereby eliminating the possibility of unilateral restructuring of the Reich by the central government. In the course of its deliberations, however, the constitutional committee was able to curtail the more extreme expressions of *Länder* particularism by abrogating some of the residual rights to which the south German states had clung with great tenacity and in whose defense Bavaria under Eisner's leadership had played a less than distinguished role. Since a genuine reorganization of the Reich had been blocked, all that could be achieved was the merger of the small Thuringian states and the abolition of the sovereignty of Coburg and Pyrmont.

In his desire to create member states of roughly similar size, Preuß had envisaged the dismemberment of Prussia. This idea, however, encountered vigorous opposition not only from the Prussian leadership of the Majority Socialists but also from Colonel Walther Reinhardt, a native Württemberger who had just been promoted to the position of Prussian minister of war. Eduard David, who doubted that a unitary solution was feasible, advocated subordinating Prussia to the Reich as a *reichsunmittelbares Land* in the hope that this detour would eventually lead to centralization. But this proposal, which anticipated the National Socialist call for the *Verreichlichung Preußens*, fell on deaf ears. Diplomatic considerations and the desire to counteract the trend toward territorial splintering also militated against the dismemberment of Prussia as envisaged by the Reich Ministry of the Interior. Such a step would have encouraged French ambitions to separate the Rhineland from the Reich as well as separatist efforts to form an autonomous Republic of North Rhineland-Westphalia. By the same token, there were preliminary efforts to establish the autonomy of Upper Silesia in a move that would have favored Polish expansionist tendencies even before the terms of the Versailles peace treaty became known.

Since it proved impossible to create a viable federal structure that abolished traditional territorial entities, the preservation of the Prussian state appeared the lesser of two evils. Only by making concessions in this matter was it possible to avoid having the Prussian constitutional convention meet at the same time that the National Assembly met in Weimar. As the experience of 1848 had shown, this would have created additional obstacles to the process of constitution making. In the end, Prussia was prevented from gaining a predominant position in the Federal Council, or Reichsrat, by a provision stipulating that half of Prussia's votes would not be exercised by the government but by representatives of Prussia's provincial parliaments, an expedient that later favored antirepublican forces on the German Right.

All in all, the powers of the Federal Council were considerably weaker than those of its counterpart in the Second Empire. The legislative competencies of the Reich and individual states were readjusted in favor of the former, which greatly expanded its powers in the areas of taxation, finance, education, and transportation and which no longer had to respect the fiscal sovereignty of the states. The reform of national finances, which the Reich finance minister Matthias Erzberger pursued in an energetic, sober, and thoroughly competent manner in the last half of 1919, was based on a modern income tax that distributed the burden of running the government more equitably among the various sectors of German society than the archaic tax system of the Second Empire. Erzberger's reforms represented a milestone on the road to a modern fiscal system. At the same time, however, it produced a fundamental change in relations between the Reich, the states, and the municipalities that henceforth required the states to direct their fiscal claims to the national government.

With the support of the three parties that belonged to the Weimar Coalition, the government's constitutional draft was preserved in an essentially liberal form. In view of the growing strength of Germany's antirepublican forces, this was the most that could be achieved in the summer of 1919. From the outset, the national constitution was consistent with the liberal principle that parliament would determine what was best for the welfare of the nation as a whole through free debates between deputies who were not bound by the instructions of their constituents. According to the prevailing theory of democracy on which the Weimar Constitution was based, the composition of parliament should reflect the various social interest groups that constituted the nation as accurately as possible. Compared with this maxim, the idea that parliament was also responsible for creating viable governmental majorities receded into the background.

The possibility that the constitutional system could be destroyed by manipulation of the democratic process never occurred to the members of the National Assembly, particularly since protection of the constitution seemed to be secured through exceptional powers, such as the right to declare a state of emergency and to assume special executive power, that were granted to the president. At the same time, it proved impossible to reach a consensus on other guarantees, such as the Social Democratic demand for the exclusion of members of dynastic houses from being elected to the presidency. Only on the basis of a purely formalistic interpretation of the constitution could the fundamental opposition between Left and Right be overcome. Those who criticize the republic for having failed to develop a concept of a "combative democracy" (streitbare Demokratie) fail to appreciate the political realities that attended the founding of the Weimar Republic.

The popular election of the Reich president, who, in addition to his normal ceremonial functions, was given the power to dissolve parliament and to appoint and dismiss the chancellor as well as the supreme commander of the Reichswehr, introduced an element into the national constitution that was alien to the basic tenets of classical liberal parliamentarism. By making it possible for the president to appeal directly to the popular will in what amounted to a public referendum, Preuß had hoped to create a counterweight to what he perceived as the danger of "parliamentary absolutism" that would prevent the majority parties from imposing their political will upon the body politic as a whole. In Article 48 of the Weimar Constitution, the president received the right to promulgate legally binding emergency decrees in case of a "clear and present danger," although the Reichstag could revoke these decrees with a simple majority.

Had the German Democratic Party (Deutsche Demokratische Partei or DDP), which came closest to embracing Max Weber's concept of the president as a charismatic personality capable of leading by popular plebiscite, succeeded in gaining approval for its demand that the president exercise his emergency powers without having to obtain the countersignature of the chancellor or the appropriate cabinet minister, the consequence might very well have been the creation of a head of state with virtually unlimited power. This point was raised most emphatically by the Independent Socialists, who countered the dictatorial authority of the president with their own proposal for an executive directorate modeled more or less after the example of Switzerland. In the matter of the countersignature, however, the Social Democrats voted for Preuß's original draft, although as a result of their uncritical sympathy for the principle of direct democracy they indirectly strengthened the power of the president by supporting the incorporation of provisions for plebiscite (*Volksentscheid*) and referendum (*Volksbegehren*) into the new constitution.

The position of the Reich president resembled that of a constitutional monarch to such an extent that one used the term *Ersatzkaisertum* to describe it. In point of fact, however, the president was far more than that, for next to the chancellor he was the authoritative figure in any potential state of emergency. The slide toward the disaster of 1933 that began in the phase of the presidential cabinets had its legal origins in an undue extension of the exceptional powers granted to the president under Article 48 of the Weimar Constitution. These powers were first exercised by the Ebert presidency during the crisis of 1923. At that time many matters subject to normal legislation were handled by legally binding decrees, although from a purely formal perspective the Reichstag was still capable of acting. Far more significant, however, were the negative political and psychological consequences that resulted from the recourse to special presidential powers. For although the chancellor retained ultimate political responsibility by virtue of his right to countersign any presidential decree, the mistaken perception could very easily arise that in a state of crisis such powers rested solely with the president. This was precisely what Carl Schmitt, the most prominent "decisionist" political scientist of the Weimar Republic, had in mind when he said that the sovereign was the "master of the state of emergency." At the very least, this provision encouraged the notion that there was no harm in relying on presidential authority whenever the parties themselves were incapable of reaching a compromise on important governmental matters.

In fact, the special presidential powers did not weaken the Reichstag or the parties represented in it as much as they did the national government. The justification for the creation of these powers was rooted in the traditional distrust of political parties, which were accused of pursuing their own particular interests at the expense of the true will of the people, which, in turn, found expression in a president elected directly by the people. The common welfare was thus seen not as the outcome of partisan political conflict but was identified with the abstract interest of the state. This is why the new constitution mentioned political parties only in a negative sense, namely in Article 21 where it stipulated that a member of the Reichstag was not bound by political instructions and again in Article 130 where it referred to civil servants as "servants of the community as a whole, not of any political party."

The Weimar Constitution has been called — and not without some justification — "the product of an authoritarian frame of mind" (obrigkeitsstaatlichen Denkens). In point of fact, it remained committed to the primacy of the state (Primat der Staatsräson) and in the final analysis denied the unity of state and society. This could be seen in the very origins of the new constitution, which, in a fashion similar to the procedure by which the Second Empire had come into existence, was first prepared by government agencies and then modified by the Reichstag. No one took umbrage at the involvement of high-ranking officials from the national and state governments in the work of the constitutional committee. Moreover, the National Assembly represented the exact opposite of a revolutionary constitutional convention, for in establishing a new system of constitutional law it effectively reestablished the continuity of constitutional practice that had broken down in the confusion of revolutionary upheaval. Nor did the parties exercise a decisive influence upon the process by which the new constitution was drafted. For example, the Majority Socialists, who were entitled to the presidency of the constitutional committee, were perfectly content to relinquish this position to the DDP's Conrad Haußmann.

The only area in which the parties could operate more or less freely was in the question of fundamental human rights, or Grundrechte, an issue of no particular interest to the Reich or state bureaucracies. Friedrich Naumann, widely known outside of his own party for his activities in the National Social Union (National-Sozialer Verein) and for his advocacy of a social monarchy during the last years of the Second Empire, demanded on behalf of the DDP that the natural rights enshrined in classical liberalism should be expanded to include fundamental social rights consistent with the requirements of a modern industrial society. The constitutional provision that "property creates obligations" can be traced to Naumann's influence. Naumann's initiative in the question of an individual's social rights, however, created a situation in which the parties used the expanded section on fundamental rights to codify certain political prerogatives and privileges. This was true not only in the case of the German Center Party, which managed to obtain far-reaching guarantees for special confessional rights, but also in that of the civil service, which secured constitutional sanction for the preservation of its "legitimately acquired rights" (*wohlerworbene Rechte*). Other professional and interest groups were no less successful in making certain that the new constitution accorded them special protection of one sort or another. Given the frequent incompatibility of the rights that various interest groups were able to guarantee in this manner, a *Grundrechtsdrittwirkung* as it exists in the Federal Republic would have had disastrous consequences in the Weimar Republic. The mere fact that ordinary courts continued to have the power to test the constitutionality of laws enacted by parliament was already ominous and left all political decisions open to the prospect of judicial review.

Wherever the fundamental rights provisions of the Weimar Constitution exceeded the civil rights that were already guaranteed by existing law—as, for example, in the case of equal rights "in principle" for men and women or in the efforts to improve the legal status of illegitimate children—they were generally struck down by decisions in the Weimar court system. This was most apparent in the reactionary interpretation of an individual's property rights, which failed to affirm the constitution's commitment to the social responsibilities of ownership. In the area of nationalization, the courts refused for the most part to recognize the principle of confiscation without compensation even though this was possible under the terms of the new constitution. As a result, the basic social rights that found their way into the Weimar Constitution, including the right to employment, were robbed of any real legal substance. Nowhere was this more apparent than in the fate of efforts to incorporate the system of councils into the constitution and thus fulfill a promise that the leaders of the Berlin strike movement had extracted from the Scheidemann government in early March. Article 165 of the Weimar Constitution provided for the creation of the National Economic Council (Reichswirtschaftsrat), which, though its functions were largely advisory, could also initiate legislation. This institution would then be complemented by a multitiered system of factory and district workers' councils (*Betriebs- und Bezirksarbeiterräte*) as well as by a national workers' council (*Reichsarbeiterrat*). These bodies were to be consulted in matters of economic policy and on questions related to socialization without, however, impinging upon the collective bargaining powers of the unions and employers' associations.

Hugo Sinzheimer, the SPD's leading expert on social policy and the co-author of Weimar's labor law, hoped that the creation of the National Economic Council would establish a mechanism for the autonomous regulation of all matters of social and economic relevance. This, in turn, would have provided the unions with a public and legal status that they had originally hoped to secure within the framework of the proposed conciliar structure. The unions objected, however, to having to limit their scope of action to the factory or to a specific industry, particularly insofar as they still believed that their participation in the ZAG accorded them a decisive voice in the formation of the government's economic and social policies. This soon proved to be illusory as a result of the close cooperation between the Economics Ministry and the employers' associations. Moreover, Sinzheimer's proposal presupposed parity between employers and employees in the composition of the economic councils. The Provisional National Economic Council (Vorläufige Reichswirtschaftsrat) established in 1920 quickly assumed the character of a corporatist institution based on the representation of vocational economic interests, although the DNVP's demands for the creation of precisely such an institution had just been rejected by the National Assembly. The other institutions provided for in Article 165 of the Weimar Constitution were never established. Thus, the initial goal of providing the workers' councils with a permanent voice in the formulation of national economic policy was abandoned in favor of a solution that offered the various interest groups little more than the right to be consulted.

The fate of Article 165 is of particular interest because it represented virtually the only instance in which the revolutionary events of 1918–19 had a direct impact upon the drafting of the new constitution. The original goals of the council movement—namely, the democratization of the civil administration and the military—did not find their way into the constitution any more than did the provisions for equal participation of employees in economic decision making. The socialization law, which had been pushed through the Reichstag under the pressure of a series of mass strikes, did little more than provide the national cabinet with special powers that were of no significance whatsoever after Rudolf Wissell's resignation as minister of economics. Although the events surrounding the Kapp Putsch led to the creation of a second socialization commission that addressed the nationalization of Germany's raw materials industries, the outcome of the Reichstag elections of June 1920 effectively destroyed whatever chance there may have been of carrying this initiative to a successful conclusion.

The Council of People's Deputies and the Scheidemann cabinet made only a feeble effort to mobilize the impulses of the revolution on behalf of an intensified social democratization. In the opinion of Walther Rathenau, the new constitution represented a compromise between particularist and liberal elements that failed "to instill a social spirit into the new form of government." When the constitution was finally adopted by a 262–75 margin on 31 July 1919, half of the Majority Socialists' eighty-six deputies abstained. Symptomatic of the inadequate commitment to a genuine new beginning was the fact that there was not even a clear-cut decision about the new national colors, "black-red-gold." Instead, the constitutional commission justified the retention of the imperial black-white-red banner for the military and merchant marine with the stale argument that this flag was easier to see than the new republican standard. Needless to say, this decision set the stage for endless squabbling over the colors of the German flag throughout the Weimar Republic.

The self-conscious appeal to the idealist traditions of Weimar and the revolutionary traditions of 1848–49 did not embody a genuine political commitment even for the parties of the Weimar Coalition. What this suggests is that the instability and eventual demise of the Weimar Republic — Weimar was chosen as the site of the National Assembly for predominantly security reasons, so that even this term carried derogatory overtones — had actually very little to do with the alleged shortcomings of the new constitution. The same can be said for the system of proportional representation (*Verhältniswahlrecht*) that the Council of People's Deputies adopted at the end of November 1918 for the forthcoming elections to the National Assembly. In the years that followed, there was certainly no shortage of attempts to revise the franchise contained in the Weimar Constitution and subsequently codified into law with the voting act of April 1920 in favor of one based on the imperial system of single-member constituencies in which the candidate who received a majority of votes would be declared the winner. The progressive splintering of the German party system in the second half of the 1920s can be attributed to the system of proportional representation only to a limited extent, for in many respects this system was detrimental to the smaller parties. Voting by lists, on the other hand, favored the candidates of representatives of special-interest organizations and intensified the pressure that these organizations were able to bring to bear upon the parties and their parliamentary delegations. Even more problematic was the fact that the parties agreed to preserve the existing electoral districts more or less as they had existed in the Second Empire. For the most part, the system of proportional representation was fully compatible with the widely held view that parliament was an institution in which the diverse interests of modern society were to be represented and whose principal task lay not in the formation of governmental majorities but in adopting legislation that reconciled these interests to each other. The voting system was therefore at most a symptom, but certainly not the cause of what ailed the parties, namely their reluctance to assume full political responsibility.

Caught off guard and politically isolated by the collapse of the monarchy, Germany's bourgeois forces — with the exception of a handful of democratic factions that had managed to secure a measure of influence by virtue of their participation in the council movement or in the formation of citizens' councils (*Bürgerräte*) — recognized the need for a new orientation, if only because the expanded suffrage made it more necessary than ever to seek support among the broad masses of the population. Claiming that they were no longer parties of notables, or *Honoratiorenparteien*, but people's parties that reflected the nation in all of its sociological heterogeneity, the various bourgeois parties that emerged from the collapse of 1918–19 co-opted representatives of the different social groups to serve on their executive committees and nominated them as candidates for election to the National Assembly. The introduction of women's suffrage and the reduction of the voting age to twenty-one only strengthened this trend. With 9.6 percent of the seats in the National Assembly, women were more prominently represented in parliament than at any previous time. This trend, however, was soon to be reversed. In the meantime, salaried secretaries of interest organizations and labor unions became increasingly prominent in positions of leadership. The proportion of professional politicians with no more than a grade school education increased considerably, while the number of academics declined. All of this underscores the extent to which even the liberal and conservative parties had begun to transform themselves into socially heterogeneous integration parties as part of a trend that reflected the general social realignment that had been going on in Germany since the rise of the "new middle class" in the 1890s.

At the same time, the parties found themselves confronted with fundamentally different patterns of voting behavior. While the regional strongholds of the various parties became less and less important, all parties were able to improve their position as a result of the changes in the voting system in areas where previously they had been virtually unrepresented. The Social Democratic Party, for example, recorded heavy losses in large cities at the same time that it scored major gains in rural areas east of the Elbe River. The conservative parties, by contrast, found unexpected support in urban areas but lost votes in the countryside, especially in regions where large-scale agricultural enterprises were prevalent. As the outcome of the 1919 and 1920 elections clearly revealed, these shifts indicated that the social and regional determinants of German voting behavior had begun to break down as a consequence of the war.

This transformation had its greatest impact on the bourgeois parties, whereas in the organized labor movement, where the total number of socialist voters remained approximately the same, there was a shift in favor of the USPD. The changed electoral landscape forced the bourgeois parties to intensify their efforts to forge a core of reliable voters by building organizations that embraced the entire country. This situation also made them more dependent on occupational and special-interest groups, which had become increasingly well organized during the war. The mediation of influential interest groups in the party system, already a characteristic of imperial Germany, greatly curtailed the parties' freedom of movement and their ability to take part in the formation of governmental coalitions.

The pronounced segmentation of the bourgeois parties along the lines of organized economic interests inhibited a fundamental reorientation of the German party system after the revolution of November 1918. The only serious attempt in this direction was the founding of the German Democratic Party.

Aside from the fact that the German People's Party established itself as the successor to what still remained of the prewar National Liberal Party (National-liberale Partei or NLP) and the German National People's Party emerged as a receptacle, or *Sammelbecken*, of the various conservative parties from the imperial era, the changes in the German party system were confined to the fact that those politicians perceived as exponents of the Wilhelmine system had temporarily retreated into the background. In this respect, the early date that had been set for the elections to the National Assembly inadvertently favored representatives of the old party machines, whose experience proved indispensable in preparing for an election that had been made even more complicated by the introduction of proportional representation.

The German Center Party, which under the leadership of Matthias Erzberger had actively supported the October reforms, found itself in the wake of the November Revolution in danger of becoming politically isolated and losing much of its working-class support to the parties of the Left. Should the Center attempt to reconstitute itself as a Christian-democratic people's party and rid itself of its strictly confessional character, as Adam Stegerwald and Heinrich Brauns were so forcefully demanding? Should the Center go along with the Majority Socialists in advocating far-reaching democratic and social reforms? Or should it give in to the demands of its middle-class voters and oppose the trend toward socialism? In the final analysis, however, none of these options prevailed, with the result that there was no change either in the old party name or in the continued dominance of the conservative Cologne faction over reform-minded elements from Mönchen-Gladbach that sought to open the party up both socially and confessionally.

The internal tensions within the Center Party were obscured by its outspoken opposition to the educational and church policies of Adolph Hoffmann, an Independent Socialist who had become the Prussian minister of education. Hoffmann sought not only to remove the last vestiges of clerical authority from the Prussian school system but also to bring about the complete separation of church and state. To be sure, the call for a new *Kulturkampf* by Catholic-ecclesiastical circles was as misguided as the policies of the Prussian government, which insisted on eliminating confessional schools and religious instruction in the public schools. In the final analysis, however, the Prussian government had to back down in the face of increasingly stiff resistance from the Catholic camp and was obliged to rescind large parts of its cultural and educational program. Moreover, by acknowledging the parents' right of choice in the selection of their children's schools, the socialists inadvertently handed confessional groups a way of exercising influence that they could not have otherwise expected.

At the same time, the Center Party found itself under heavy pressure from federalist and particularist forces. The founding of the Bavarian People's Party

(Bayerische Volkspartei or BVP) under the aegis of peasant leader Georg Heim and the end of its parliamentary alliance with the Center in 1922 were to have long-lasting consequences for the internal development of the Weimar Republic. At the same time there were influential elements within the Rhenish Center Party that sympathized with efforts aimed at the establishment of a Rhenish-Westphalian Republic and its separation from Prussia. It was only in 1920 that those elements of the Center that supported the principle of national unity and the continued existence of Prussia were able to gain the upper hand once and for all. This, however, was not so much a victory for Erzberger, whose standing in the national party had reached its nadir in the wake of his unsuccessful libel suit against the DNVP's Karl Helfferich, as it was a result of coalition politics at the national and Prussian level. In March 1919, a cabinet of the Weimar Coalition replaced the rump Majority Socialist cabinet that had governed Germany since January. As one of the government parties, the Center was able to achieve some compromises in educational policy, however controversial these might remain within the party. By invoking the parents' right of choice, the Center Party succeeded in giving confessional schools a secure place within the public school system. On the whole, however, parallel systems remained the rule. When the DDP resigned from the national cabinet in protest against the Versailles peace treaty, the Center not only regained its key position in parliament but also knew how to use this to its best advantage. Nevertheless, there were deep-seated misgivings within the Center's own rank and file about its participation in the Weimar Coalition. Given its sharp criticism of the Social Democrats in the campaign for the January 1919 elections to the National Assembly, this could only have come as something of a surprise to many of those within the party.

The internal divisions within the Center, which stemmed in large part from friction among the divergent social and economic interests — most notably between its agrarian and middle-class constituencies, on the one hand, and its working-class wing, on the other — that constituted its material base, were greatly exacerbated by the domestic political crisis that accompanied the Kapp Putsch and its aftermath. The defection of right-wing Centrists to the DNVP and the formation of nonconfessional splinter parties such as the Christian People's Party (Christliche Volkspartei) inflicted significant, though limited, losses on the Center in the June 1920 Reichstag elections. Still, party leaders were able to stave off an attempt by Adam Stegerwald to enlist the support of the Christian labor unions for a broadly based Christian-socialist people's movement that would initiate a general realignment of the German party system. Speaking before the Essen Congress of the Christian Trade Unions in November 1920, Stegerwald indirectly repudiated the parliamentary system of government by linking the pursuit of republican and social goals to a corporatist agenda. Had Stegerwald and Brauns undertaken this initiative as early as November 1918, it is possible that they might have been able to bring about some fundamental changes in the structure of the German party system. As it was, however, Stegerwald's "Essen Program" only served as a prelude to subsequent appeals for bourgeois unity in the final phase of the Weimar Republic.

The only genuine initiative on behalf of a realignment of the bourgeois party system was taken on 15 November 1918 by Theodor Wolff, editor in chief of the *Berliner Tageblatt*, and Alfred Weber, younger brother of Max Weber, with the founding of the German Democratic Party. This party set as its goal the unification of the progressive elements of the German bourgeoisie with segments of the German working class. While the Progressive People's Party (Fortschrittliche Volkspartei) and the other left-liberal splinter groups wholeheartedly supported this initiative, the National Liberal Party was badly divided in its attitude toward the new party. Gustav Stresemann, chairman of the National Liberal delegation to the Reichstag, had reservations from the very outset about the founding of a new party with an opening to the Left, whereas Robert Friedberg, the party's national chairman, advocated the creation of a united front of the liberal and democratic middle classes.

Even if the new party had not denied Stresemann, an outspoken champion of annexationist war aims, a position in its national leadership on the grounds that it must not be burdened with the legacy of Wilhelmine nationalism, strong differences of both an objective and a personal nature soon would have made the creation of a united party of the liberal bourgeoisie extremely difficult. While Stresemann was forced into founding a separate party by the "coup d'état" of the left-liberals, those National Liberals who went over to the DDP were able to push the original founders of the DDP aside. It was symptomatic of the party's internal development that Theodor Wolff, Alfred Weber, the left-liberal pacifist Hellmuth von Gerlach, and Georg Bernhard, editor of the *Vossische Zeitung*, were soon forced out of the party or became so disgruntled that they abandoned it. Under the leadership of Friedrich Naumann, who was elected to the party chairmanship in July 1919 by the party's national congress against the recommendations of the party organization, the DDP adopted a political course that was primarily concerned with the question of national integration. With Naumann's unexpected death a month later, this tendency was further strengthened under the influence of Hamburg mayor Carl Petersen and Erich Koch-Weser.

With 18.5 percent of the popular vote in the January 1919 elections to the National Assembly, the DDP did unexpectedly well. The main reason for its success was that it was widely regarded as the only party capable of preventing a socialist majority that also seemed to stand for genuine political change. The DDP was destined to play an important role in the drafting of a new constitution, not least because of the influence it exerted through the person of Hugo Preuß. Insofar as the DDP sought to achieve more effective integration of the various elements that constituted its material base by highlighting issues of national interest, it was particularly ominous that it could not even reach a consensus in the matter of the national colors. Nor did the party succeed in maintaining unity between the advocates of a liberal economic policy, who in the cabinet consistently blocked Rudolf Wissell's initiatives on behalf of a planned economy, and those party members who supported a clear policy of social reform. A similar conflict could be seen between the pacifist elements that had congregated on the DDP's left wing and the party's rank-and-file membership, which remained committed to a policy of nationalist protest as espoused by Count Ulrich von Brockdorff-Rantzau, the foreign minister who enjoyed close ties to the DDP.

The inability of the DDP to overcome the antagonisms between its middle-class and industrial constituencies offers only a partial explanation of the heavy losses it suffered in the June 1920 Reichstag elections, when it received a mere 8.4 percent of the popular vote. A far more important reason for the DDP's losses was the widespread disappointment that significant segments of the German population felt with respect to the implicit assurances that President Wilson had made about the benefits of a transition to democracy. Moreover, a trend toward the reemergence of an authoritarian tradition—which was to become evident at the time of the Kapp Putsch—was beginning to take shape within the DDP, which undermined the credibility of its programmatic commitment to the formation of a new "community of the people" (*Volksgemeinschaft*). Even if the party had succeeded in adopting a more forceful stance in the face of the conflicting demands of its various constituencies, it could not have prevented the desertion of the middle classes. Now that the full economic consequences of the war were beginning to be felt, this group defected to the moderate or even extreme Right.

Created by Stresemann from the remnants of the National-Liberal party organization, the German People's Party was to function temporarily as a reservoir, or *Sammelbecken*, for the bourgeois middle class. Because its organizational consolidation began when the campaign was already well under way, the DVP did not receive more than 4.4 percent of the votes in the elections to the National Assembly. Presenting itself as the voice of the moderate bourgeoisie, the new party took full advantage of the fact that the interest groups of the "new" middle class did not feel sufficiently represented in the DDP vis-à-vis the relatively strong influence of academics and the liberal professions. Prominent among the supporters of the new party were most of the civil servants' associations, which had merged in November 1918 to form the German Civil Servants' Association (Deutscher Beamtenbund). Since the wealthy industrial entrepreneurs had maintained a low profile during the revolutionary turmoil of 1918–19, the interest conflicts between them and the DVP's middle-class constituency were slow to take shape. Under Stresemann's energetic and determined leadership, the DVP conveyed the impression that it was more unified than the DDP, whose very program was marked by conflicting values. In the June 1920 Reichstag elections the DVP overtook its left-liberal rival with 14 percent of the vote, the level achieved by the old National Liberal Party in 1912. Yet it soon became clear that the DVP, though profiting from the general drift to the right in 1920, was no more successful than the DDP in building a stable constituency of members and voters with which it could counteract the increasing erosion of moderate liberalism.

Aside from its formal declaration of support for the restoration of the Hohenzollern monarchy, the arguments with which the DVP rejected the Weimar Constitution in the final vote on 31 July 1919 were rather unconvincing, particularly since in almost the same breath the party affirmed its willingness to collaborate loyally within the framework of the new constitution. From a tactical point of view, Stresemann's solicitude for the right wing of the former NLP undercut his hopes of entering the government at the earliest possible opportunity. The odium of having rejected the new republican order was something that clung to him for some time to come. At the same time, Stresemann avoided drawing an early line of demarcation between his party and the DNVP, which was set on a course of unconditional opposition to the Weimar system, without abandoning his own party's fundamentally liberal orientation. Yet this orientation did not keep him from cultivating contacts with the conservative Fronde in the Reichswehr or from attempting to use the Kapp Putsch, in which he had not been involved, for his own purposes. Throughout all of this, Stresemann's primary goal was to lead the DVP out of its political isolation. Yet his tactical alignment with the republic's declared enemies only strengthened the Weimar Coalition's distrust of the DVP and contributed to the parliamentary isolation in which it remained until 1923.

Given the weakness of democratic elements in the bourgeois parties, the hopes that Friedrich Naumann and the left-liberal founders of the DDP had placed in the unification of political liberalism were somewhat unrealistic. Nevertheless, the autonomous existence of the DVP as a party of the liberal center kept the German National People's Party from establishing itself as the strongest bourgeois force in the Weimar party system. The DNVP functioned as the safe haven for the conservative parties from the imperial era and demonstrated an unmistakable continuity with the German Fatherland Party in the personnel of its leadership. Unlike the liberal parties, the DNVP was able to develop relatively stable support from organized economic interests. The party enjoyed particularly close ties to the National Rural League (Reichs-Landbund or RLB), the largest of Germany's agricultural interest organizations and one that was firmly in the hands of the East Elbian estate owners. Further sources of support were the Pan-German League, which had developed a populist ancillary organization called the German Racist Defense and Defiance League

(Deutschvölkischer Schutz- und Trutzbund), and the German National Union of Commercial Employees (Deutschnationaler Handlungsgehilfen-Verband or DHV), which had developed extensive relations, or *Querverbindungen*, with both the neoconservative movement and different *völkisch* groups and therefore occupied a key position in the associational life of Germany's bourgeois Right. By comparison, the DNVP's labor wing remained relatively weak. A few representatives from heavy industry had found their way into the DNVP, but for the most part this sector of German economic life preferred the DVP. One important exception was Alfred Hugenberg, who played a major role in the DNVP at the time of its founding and exerted considerable influence as the administrator of the funds it received from industry. Hugenberg, however, failed in his efforts to bring about a merger of the DNVP with the DVP, largely on account of Stresemann's resistance to such a step. From the very outset, efforts to win the support of the liberal middle classes were never more than a tactical ploy, particularly insofar as the party remained in the control of outspoken conservative nationalist forces at all times.

The DNVP showed no scruple in its polemic against Germany's fledgling democratic republic. In the first place, it did not hesitate to grant radical racist groups a major role in the formulation of its party program, which contained calls for combating "the dominating position of Jewish elements in government and public life." The racist thrust of *völkisch* anti-Semitism met with disapproval from old-line conservatives, who, by no means free of anti-Semitic prejudice themselves, were concerned about the party's social respectability. This conflict led after 1922 to the secession of the DNVP's racist wing, although its close ties to the Pan-German League remained intact. By virtue of its militantly antisocialist and, after the publication of Allied peace conditions, extreme revisionist orientation, the DNVP became a favorite forum for all of the republic's avowed enemies. The DNVP was the first to use the "stab in the back" legend as the main focus of its agitation against the parties of the Left. At the same time, the party openly sympathized with Kapp and Lüttwitz, who for their part endorsed the DNVP's demands for constitutional change. Indeed a virtual identity between the DNVP and the supporters of the putsch of March 1920 could easily be established.

In the elections to the National Assembly the DNVP received 10.3 percent of the votes and thus remained well behind the DDP despite the decision by DNVP national chairman Oskar Hergt to run candidates from the party's moderate wing. As a staunch opponent of the Versailles peace treaty, the DNVP was able to improve its position to 15 percent in the June 1920 Reichstag elections. In this respect, it is noteworthy that the party suffered some losses in its agrarian strongholds—in part as a result of the decline in the number of persons employed in the agrarian sector—but was able to compensate for this by a substantial increase of support in urban areas. This result indicates that the foes of the republic were not only to be found in the residues of the old society but were available for recruitment in the "new middle class" and among upwardly mobile employees.

The German Revolution of 1918–19 had not brought about a fundamental change in the configuration of the German party system. Whatever shifts in electoral behavior one might be able to discern resulted from a long-term transformation of the social system. Given the general mentality of the electorate, the evolution toward a liberal-parliamentary form of government with socialist overtones that had begun with the adoption of the Weimar Constitution was little more than an episode. For even before the elections on 19 January 1919, the voters withdrew their support from the Majority Socialists and DDP, both of which would have fared better had the elections been held earlier. The USPD's demand that elections be postponed until after the reorganization of society had been completed makes little sense in light of these results. On the other hand, a postponement of the elections would have facilitated the realignment of the party system and, in particular, the recruitment of new parliamentary leadership cadres.

The composition of the Scheidemann cabinet shows just how strong continuity between the fledgling German Republic and the interparty committee actually was. Half of the cabinet members had participated in the government of Prince Max von Baden, and the majority had held executive positions in the Council of People's Commissars. With Friedrich Ebert's election to the Reich presidency the personal identity of leadership cadres was most clearly revealed. However one may judge Ebert's role in the revolutionary phase, the fact remains that he was the most forceful and decisive personality within the MSPD, whereas Prime Minister Philipp Scheidemann projected a strangely colorless image as head of the government. Yet Scheidemann's talent for gauging the mood of the country—and not just in the working class—was a valuable corrective to the comparatively rigid priorities that informed Ebert's policies. His career was distinguished more by his conciliatory attitude and his skills as a mediator than by an ability to formulate, pursue, and achieve political goals.

Ebert's remarkably low profile during the critical phase of the republic in the spring of 1919 stood in marked contrast to the energy he had demonstrated as president of the Council of People's Commissars. To some extent, this can be attributed to the personal stress Ebert had experienced since the summer of 1918, but it was also related to his fundamentally legalistic cast of mind, which led him to take a dim view of what still remained of the workers' protest movement. When it came to the decisive questions of the peace treaty, which threatened not only the cabinet but the continued existence of the German state as well, Ebert was once again fully engaged in his capacity as president of the German Republic. In this respect, however, there is considerable evidence to suggest that Ebert overestimated the political power of the presidential office.

As far as the fledgling republic was concerned, it was certainly an advantage that Ebert decided to relinquish his post as chairman of the MSPD. After all, Ebert had earned a great deal of sympathy among conservative civil servants and in the Reichswehr, whereas his own party had turned its back on him. Yet neither the consistently nonpartisan way in which Ebert conducted the affairs of the Reich presidency nor his willingness to grant Noske and the newly created Reichswehr his unqualified support for their suppression of the radical Left prevented the right-wing parties from launching unbridled and highly offensive attacks against him. As early as the late fall of 1919, the DNVP and DVP dragged the presidential office into party politics when they made overtures to Hindenburg and demanded that the president be chosen by popular election. Under these circumstances, it was impossible for the coalition parties to anchor the parliamentary election of the president in the constitution.

On the occasion of the presidential election, Friedrich Ebert had made a ringing declaration of faith in democracy and the rule of law. "Freedom and the rule of law," he had told the National Assembly, "are twin sisters. Freedom can flourish only within a firm order provided by the state." These words suggested that for him the consolidation of the republic was synonymous with the restoration of the state's authority. In a letter to Scheidemann from June 1919 he retrospectively characterized their shared experience of fighting on two fronts "as the time of most pressing danger, both externally and domestically." This assessment of the revolutionary phase made it clear that he saw a direct line of continuity between the newly founded system of government and the legal and political foundations of the nation-state as it existed in imperial Germany. Externally this could be seen in the continued presence of the political leadership cadres from the late imperial era, which, with a few exceptions, had been able to retain their positions of power and influence. By the same token, there was no change in the administrative personnel of the most important Reich and state ministerial bureaucracies. At the same time, many of the essential features of the old party system had remained intact where little in the way of a renewal of elites had taken place.

In light of the immediate economic consequences of the war — above all, the lack of coal and fertilizers, severe food shortages, progressive inflation, and structural unemployment — the leadership of the Majority Socialists felt that more radical modifications of the social constitution would be utterly irresponsible. In countless appeals to the population, the MSPD stressed that the revival of the nation's economic life took precedence over everything else. The bourgeois republic of Weimar thus emerged out of a defensive posture against a twofold danger: the disintegration of national unity and the specter of the

"Bolshevization" of Germany. The MSPD saw the process by which a new constitution had been drafted and ratified as a successful compromise with progressive bourgeois forces. Having to come to terms with the bourgeois parties, however, meant that they had to postpone a fundamental socialist reorganization of society, a goal that seemed equally unrealistic in terms of Germany's foreign policy predicament.

All of this meant that the new republican system of government lacked political self-confidence from the very outset. Even among the left-liberals there was no Gambetta of the bourgeois-democratic republic. In this respect, the former monarchists who accepted the Weimar Republic as the law of the land were not the only *Vernunftrepublikaner*, that is, republicans by reason of necessity but not out of genuine political conviction. It was not just the circumstances of its birth—and particularly its close identification with the stigma of defeat—that made it so difficult for parliamentary democracy to take root in Germany. Even its strongest supporters were ambivalent toward the new political order. With the exception of a few isolated left-liberal publicists like Georg Bernhard and Theodor Wolff, there was hardly anyone to defend it without qualification. And where there was no vision, the pressure of interests gained the upper hand. To some extent, of course, this was inevitable. Still, everyday life in the republic was bound to bring bitter disappointment to the expectations of a new beginning that had flourished in the "dreamland of the armistice period."

The backward-looking character of the Weimar Republic was most clearly demonstrated by its inability to deal with those civilian and military leaders of the former empire who had been responsible for the catastrophe of World War I. While left-wing socialists such as Eisner, Kautsky, and Bernstein advocated a resolute exposure of the role that the German diplomatic and military establishment had played in causing disaster, the Council of People's Commissars, coached by the Foreign Office, refused to cooperate on the grounds that this would weaken the German position in the impending peace negotiations. Indeed, Count von Brockdorff-Rantzau, anticipating the Allies' war-guilt charges, prepared a strategy for denying Germany's unilateral responsibility for the outbreak of the war and urged the government not to dissociate itself from the leaders of imperial Germany. To be sure, there was little likelihood that an unequivocal condemnation of Germany's prewar and wartime imperialism, such as Eisner sought in the spirit of what Lenin had done following the Bolshevik seizure of power, would have had much of an effect upon Allied intransigence. Yet it does stand to reason that this strategy might have made it difficult for French policy makers to cling to their extreme demands with the same degree of tenacity.

Far more important were the domestic political consequences of the peace settlement. Brockdorff-Rantzau and the German Foreign Office based their defense of the German position in the peace negotiations on Wilson's presumed guarantees and were preparing to launch a broadly based protest movement through the use of appropriate propaganda. The German public was thus totally unprepared for the peace conditions that the Allies handed to the German delegation at Versailles on 7 May 1919. To be sure, the progressively harsher conditions imposed with each successive extension of the armistice had made it clear that it was no longer realistic to expect a tolerable peace under the terms of Wilson's Fourteen Points. Matthias Erzberger, the head of the German armistice commission, realized at an early stage in the negotiations that the peace conditions would be harsh and had sought to obtain limited concessions through personal diplomatic contacts with Allied negotiators. He therefore urged the cabinet—without success, as it turned out—to decide in advance how it would react to the forthcoming peace conditions instead of giving Brockdorff-Rantzau and the experts in the German delegation a free hand in deciding how they would respond. The quarrel over procedure that Erzberger initiated led to severe tensions between the cabinet and the peace delegation that, in turn, concealed the absence of clear political options.

It is extremely difficult to give a definitive answer to the question of whether, under the circumstances, Brockdorff-Rantzau's foreign policy tactics were sound or, by the same token, whether Erzberger's unorthodox diplomatic style harmed the German cause by conveying to the Allies the impression that in the end the German government would sign the peace treaty. Initially, of course, virtually no one shared Erzberger's firm belief that this was absolutely unavoidable. Only the USPD was resolved to sign, but since as a party it had committed itself to comprehensive revolutionary change, it was more comfortable with this prospect than the leaders of the MSPD, who still perceived the world in strictly national categories. From the very beginning, the idea of unleashing a broad nationalist protest movement had been part of the strategy pursued by Brockdorff-Rantzau, who was willing to risk the breakdown of negotiations with the Allies. Despite major reservations, the German government went along with Brockdorff-Rantzau's gambit, a fact that accounts for Scheidemann's statement in a special session of the National Assembly at the University of Berlin on 12 May that the hand that lent itself to signing this treaty would wither.

Realistic observers, among them Matthias Erzberger, were convinced that yielding to public opinion was a fateful mistake on the part of the government. After all, active resistance was altogether out of the question, especially since the overwhelming majority of the German population did not show the slightest support for a resumption of hostilities following a German refusal to sign. Those who lived in the border areas in the west were adamantly opposed to any such risk. Nevertheless, Brockdorff-Rantzau clung to the illusion that the neutral powers would oppose military intervention by the Western Allies. This, in turn, would give Germany greater latitude in the peace negotiations.

By publicly declaring in the Great Hall of the University of Berlin that the peace conditions were "unacceptable," the Scheidemann government placed itself in an untenable position. For instead of entering, as expected, into protracted negotiations with the Allies over the terms of the proposed peace, the German side was given barely two weeks to submit its written responses. Having bombarded the Allies with notes that may very well have done more harm than good, the German delegation submitted its counterproposals on 29 May. Contrary to Brockdorff-Rantzau's expectations, they were rejected out of hand. The only concession, made at the suggestion of Lloyd George, concerned the question of Upper Silesia and provided for a plebiscite instead of the immediate surrender of the area. The German government was given only five days to accept the treaty; failure to do so would set in motion the occupation of German territory. The Allies eventually extended this ultimatum by forty-eight hours as a consequence of the government crisis this had caused in Berlin.

Brockdorff-Rantzau and the members of the German peace delegation strongly urged the rejection of the treaty and nurtured the spurious hope that they would be able to sow discord among the Allies. Within the German cabinet, however, opinions were divided. The Democratic ministers and several of the Social Democrats were unwilling to assume political responsibility for signing the treaty. In the meantime, the wave of nationalist indignation that thanks to Brockdorff-Rantzau's defiance had gripped the German public in May had begun to give way to increasing disillusionment and resignation as it became clear that both domestic political and military considerations ruled out open resistance to Allied occupation.

Before the beginning of the official negotiations, the leadership of the Reichswehr had voiced strong objections to a German plan to propose a reduction in German troop strength to 100,000 men as a way of countering expected Allied demands for German territory. But the government, including the minister of defense, dismissed this protest without giving it much thought. Without government approval, Germany's military command had been surveyed in an attempt to determine what the prospects of military resistance were. The result had been uniformly negative. At best, the military felt that it might be possible to build up a center of resistance in the east while it conceded that it would be virtually impossible to protect Germany's western regions against an Allied invasion. Nevertheless, the Prussian minister of war, Colonel Walther Reinhardt, felt compelled to oppose the acceptance of the peace treaty at a meeting between the military leadership and members of the cabinet on 19 June and advocated limited military resistance even if this meant the temporary loss of the western territories. This ran into strong opposition from General Groener, who opposed all military actions that might lead to the disintegration of the state, foster internal unrest, and play into the hands of "Bolshevism." Nor was Hindenburg's written opinion, solicited on 23 June, particularly helpful. Although Hindenburg felt that military operations would be useless, he concluded his remarks with the dubious statement that "as a soldier he was duty bound to prefer annihilation with honor to a dishonorable peace."

This immediately overturned one of the main arguments that had been raised against signing the peace treaty, namely, the claim that the military would never accept it. Nevertheless, the DDP decided to desert the front of potential "signers" that had begun to take shape. The conditions it had attached to its support for the treaty had given rise to considerable controversy within the cabinet but were still included in the draft of a note to be sent to the Allies. It was fortunate that reservations raised by the MSPD board prevented this note from being dispatched the following day, for it would have almost certainly precipitated the breakdown of the negotiations for which Marshal Foch was so fervently hoping. Unable to overcome the dissension within his cabinet, Prime Minister Scheidemann had no choice but to announce his resignation during the night of 19 June. Ebert negotiated feverishly to form a cabinet that would be able to act. In the face of what appeared to be a hopeless situation, both Hermann Müller and Eduard David declined to accept the chancellorship, so that in the end the president found himself with no alternative but to entrust union leader Gustav Bauer with the task of forming a rump cabinet consisting of representatives from the Center and MSPD. In the Reichstag, the DDP insisted on the changes in the treaty it had demanded the day before, whereas the parliamentary delegations of the MSPD and the Center Party—the latter against strong opposition from within its own ranks—reluctantly endorsed a conditional signing of the proposed treaty. Only the fact that the leaders of the state governments were also opposed to the resumption of hostilities made this decision a little easier.

Matthias Erzberger, minister of finance in the new cabinet, had for some time envisaged the possibility of accepting the treaty with the exception of Paragraphs 227 through 231 without ever determining through his French contacts whether this would be acceptable to the Allies. Large segments of the German population, particularly the officer corps, felt that Germany's moral honor could not tolerate the provision that the Kaiser as well as military and civilian officials indicted for war crimes were to be handed over to the victors and that sole legal responsibility for the outbreak of the war was to be assigned to Germany. In the meantime, the Reichswehr command was making preparations to spirit the accused officers out of Allied reach by means of "Operation Holiday Kid" (Aktion Ferienkind).

The exclusive focus of the public debate on questions of prestige indicated that there was an insufficient understanding of the territorial losses and economic burdens that would be imposed by the peace treaty if concern for the "national honor" were allowed to remain in the foreground. Erzberger, whose thinking was not fixed on questions of national prestige, succeeded in persuading the Center Reichstag delegation to go along with a conditional signing of the treaty, whereas the DDP remained overwhelmingly opposed. Just as the ultimatum was about to expire on 22 June, the National Assembly authorized the government to sign the treaty by a vote of 237 to 138 without, however, mentioning the exclusion of those clauses that pertained to extradition and war guilt, which the council of the four Allied powers had already rejected. In order to avoid a new vote, the DVP suggested that the authorization given to the government should also apply to the unconditional signing of the treaty. Although the opposition parties publicly recognized that those who signed the treaty did so out of "patriotic feelings and conviction," this statement did not prevent the DNVP from unleashing a hate campaign against Erzberger and the Social Democrats.

The first real test of the coalition's strength was the task of building a consensus in support of the peace treaty. In this respect, however, the coalition failed and fell apart, with the result that the National Assembly surrendered its parliamentary sovereignty. The DDP and DVP acted on the assumption that even without them a majority for ratifying the treaty would be found and used their vote against ratification to legitimate the bourgeois middle as the defender of Germany's "national future." The retreat from parliamentary responsibility was well under way before the conclusion of peace made it possible to envisage a positive agenda for political reconstruction.

The socialists were becoming increasingly annoyed at having to assume responsibility for unpopular policies time and time again. For the moment, however, this annoyance was outweighed by the self-confidence that stemmed from their position as the "governing party of the republic." But this was not to last. After the elections to the National Assembly on 6 June 1920, the party was eager to leave the government, especially since the USPD once again declined an offer to enter the coalition. According to an editorial in *Vorwärts*, the party had "jumped for joy" at the news that it would go into opposition. In October 1920 the party convention at Kassel passed a resolution stating that the MSPD would join the government only if the "interests of the proletariat" made it absolutely necessary. It was also decided that members of the government could not simultaneously hold leading positions in the party, since this would presumably limit the party's freedom to maneuver. Disillusionment over the Allied peace conditions, which many had hoped to soften by creating a democratic republic, now began to undermine the political foundations of that republic.

The signing of the peace treaty in the Hall of Mirrors at Versailles on 28 June

1919 and its subsequent implementation on 10 January 1920 did nothing to dispel the widespread illusion that Germany could escape its consequences by passive noncompliance. The formal end of the war did not mean that a more pacific attitude and a desire for peace had gained the upper hand. The nation simply refused to face the fact that it had lost the World War. The peace had been forced upon it by the Allies; Germany had nothing to do with it. The ugly word *Diktat* now appeared in Germany's political vocabulary.

In response to nationalist attacks against his role in the passage of the peace resolution, the conclusion of the armistice, and the signing of the peace treaty, Erzberger cited the example of Kerenski, who in Russia in 1917 had not found it in himself to accept an unconditional peace and was therefore swept away by the subsequent force of events. In effect, this was what happened to the Weimar Republic, albeit in a somewhat different sense. The republic came into being during a phase of latent warfare. A parliamentary investigating committee was charged with examining the question of "war guilt," a task that had originally been given to the Constitutional Court. The parliamentary committee soon turned into a forum for indicting the republic. In order not to keep the Allies from collecting evidence that could be used to justify the so-called war-guilt clause contained in Article 231 of the Versailles peace treaty, Brockdorff-Rantzau established a special war-guilt department in the Foreign Office that did its best to prevent a genuine inquiry into the causes of the war. Representatives of the political Left, who sought to document the responsibility of the imperial government for the outbreak and prolongation of the war, encountered a wall of official hostility. The Foreign Office now used the semiofficial propaganda apparatus it had built up during the armistice period in cooperation with the representatives of various nationalist associations for a propaganda campaign against Article 231. Characteristically, this propaganda focused on the Allies' covering note of 19 June 1919, which had sharply outlined the areas of disagreement.

In this form, a manipulation of national sentiments took place that was not so much driven by alleged "patriotic" motives as by the political calculation that the emphasis on shared national goals would integrate a badly fragmented bourgeois party system into a united front capable of ending the predominance of the Social Democrats. The "stab-in-the-back legend," which the nationalist Right henceforth used as the main weapon in its arsenal of attacks against democratic socialism, had, as Paul von Hindenburg's testimony before the parliamentary investigating committee on 18 November 1919 indicated, precisely this function. For instead of helping to explain the events that had led to Germany's defeat and that had forced it to sue for peace, the field marshal read a carefully worded statement that had been prepared with the assistance of the DNVP's Karl Helfferich and lent a semblance of credibility to the cruder forms of the "stab-in-the-back" formula that had been circulating for some time.

In domestic politics the situation after the signing of the peace treaty and the ratification of the constitution was characterized by a broadly based mobilization of extremist nationalism. This created the preconditions for the rise of the *völkisch* movement and for the spread of a psychological climate marked by racial anti-Semitism and anti-Bolshevism in which Adolf Hitler began to make his political way. The reorganization of the German Workers' Party (Deutsche Arbeiterpartei or DAP), originally founded by Anton Drexler as an agent of the Thule Society (Thule-Gesellschaft), served as the foundation on which a fascist party could develop, although for the moment the National Socialist German Workers' Party (Nationalsozialistische Deutsche Arbeiterpartei or NSDAP) was but one of many splinter groups with a *völkisch* orientation. The drift to the right received added impetus from the fiscal reforms of the Bauer government. As a result of Erzberger's energetic work, these reforms not only instituted an across-the-board emergency tax known as the Reich Emergency Levy (Reichsnotopfer), but also imposed higher taxes on the more affluent elements of German society. Karl Helfferich's attacks on Erzberger in the *Preußische Kreuz-Zeitung*, in which he cast doubt on the finance minister's integrity, marked the opening of a systematic smear campaign against the leading politicians of the republic. The finance minister sued Helfferich for libel, but because of the biased attitude of the court the case resulted in Erzberger's virtual condemnation for perjury and embezzlement while the man who had slandered him got off with a slight fine. Helfferich's systematic campaign against the "national corrupter" Erzberger, who resigned his ministerial position following the court decision, opened the gates for a torrent of unrestrained slander and actual violence. By the internal logic of such a situation, one of Germany's most meritorious statesmen in the transition from the Second Empire to the Weimar Republic became the victim of counterrevolutionary terrorism. On 26 August 1921, following five unsuccessful assassination attempts, Erzberger was killed in a cowardly murder plot carried out by members of "Operation Consul."

It would be altogether misleading to assign responsibility for the vitality of nationalist trends to the right-wing parties alone. There was, for instance, the Action Committee of German Leagues (Arbeitsausschuß Deutscher Verbände), whose creation had taken place with encouragement from the DDP. Prominent liberal historians also played a role in preparing the detailed falsifications that were to be perpetuated in the official edition of documents concerning the events that had led up to the outbreak of the war. Finally, the government's Central Office for Home Affairs (Reichszentrale für Heimatdienst) had cooperated with antirepublican organizations on the German Right ever since the conclusion of the armistice. These developments represented successive stages in the emergence of a nationalism promoted by bourgeois-republican circles that obscured an understanding of German imperialism before the war and the conduct of the imperial government during the war. Even the MSPD failed to heed the warnings of Karl Kautsky, Eduard Bernstein, and other maverick left-wing intellectuals and succumbed to the prevailing revisionist mood. Reflecting the growth of a defiant nationalist attitude, the government was distinctly lax in living up to its promise to prosecute war crimes. After all, had not the Allies, acting on the initiative of Lloyd George, already retracted their demand for the extradition of the 900 men accused of war crimes? And had it not become clear that the trial of William II would not take place, since the Dutch government had refused all requests for his extradition? Unresolved until the end of February 1920, the matter of war crimes was an important psychological point of departure for the political mobilization of both the extreme right-wing groups that had sprung up outside the party system and the counterrevolutionary elements in the officer corps. Since the summer of 1919, Captain Waldemar Pabst, subsequently dismissed from the Reichswehr, had used the support of the National Association (Nationale Vereinigung) to make preparations for a "national dictatorship" that in right-wing circles represented the only way in which the extradition of accused war criminals could be prevented.

Different strategies for establishing such a dictatorship were under constant discussion. Some military commanders wanted to wait for an uprising of the Left before "striking with all means at their disposal" (Losschlagen mit allen Mitteln). General Walther von Lüttwitz, on the other hand, demanded the immediate declaration of a national emergency in which he would use the violent suppression of the strike movements that were springing up everywhere as a pretext for proclaiming a national dictatorship, if necessary under the leadership of Noske. Now that the reduction in troop strength stipulated in the peace treaty was actually under way, the military tried to justify its existence by stressing its domestic role in maintaining order, combating the Left, and putting down strikes. Gustav Noske, who did not realize how deeply the Reichswehr was involved in the activities of right-wing military associations and propaganda organizations, unhesitatingly advocated the use of the harshest means available in dealing with troublemakers and strike leaders. At the same time, he publicly criticized the newly founded Republican Leadership Conference (Republikanischer Führerbund), which advocated a democratization of the officer corps. By the same token, Noske failed to do anything to protect officers with Social Democratic sympathies from discrimination and arbitrary disqualification.

Even after the constitution had been adopted, the state of emergency continued, its authorization no longer based on the Prussian law of 1851 but on Articles 48 and 49 of the Weimar Constitution. Even the Prussian state commissar for the maintenance of public order remained obsessed with the exaggerated danger of Bolshevist insurrection and consistently underestimated the influence of the counterrevolutionary forces that had begun to coalesce on the radical Right. Union officials and the Majority Socialists also failed to recognize the largely spontaneous character of the strike movement and subscribed to a general theory of infiltration by the radical Left. In the meantime, the forces of counterrevolution continued to grow, with their strongest support coming from East Elbian agricultural associations and the officer corps.

Suffering from weak leadership, the national government did little to counteract the incipient polarization of German political life. In late fall the DDP had rejoined the cabinet in the hope of preventing the desertion of its voters to the right through a vigorous defense of entrepreneurial interests. In the meantime, Rudolf Wissell's resignation as economics minister spelled the definitive end of efforts to create a centrally planned economy. His successor, union leader Robert Schmidt, endorsed the bourgeois parties' call for greater productivity and increased work discipline. Schmidt was also firmly opposed to labor's increasingly emphatic demands for higher wages and advocated the relaxation of controls on foreign trade, a measure that in the absence of corresponding currency reforms could only intensify upward pressure on prices and wages.

In spite of these economic difficulties, the strike movement had grown noticeably weaker since the summer of 1919. Under the protection of the military, the socialist unions were able to consolidate their position, even though the USPD-led opposition within the labor movement continued to grow and had achieved a majority in the German Metalworkers' Union (Deutscher Metallarbeiterverband or DMV). Still, the Independent Socialists found themselves in a difficult tactical situation, for they could not expect proletarian mass actions to succeed against the opposition of the unions. As a result, attempts to restore the workers' councils and to unite them in a central organization were of limited effectiveness despite the increasing success of agitation by the party's left wing under Ernst Däumig for a "pure" soviet system.

Under the influence of its left wing, the Independent Socialists adopted a radical action program in November 1919 that called for a dictatorship of the proletariat based on the soviet model. In the sphere of political praxis, however, the party remained under the control of its moderate center, which had no use for putschist adventures. The death of Hugo Haase in the fall of 1919 did little to change the situation at the upper echelons of the party leadership. It was no longer possible to paper over the profound philosophical differences that had surfaced within the USPD, most clearly in the question of its relationship to the Comintern. In spite of all this, the party continued to benefit from the significant influx of new members who had become disenchanted with the Majority Socialists after having first supported the MSPD in the period immediately following the end of the war.

The KPD had paid for its defeats in January and March 1919 with a series of further setbacks. The party had been forced underground until the end of 1919, and its publications had been banned. Under the leadership of Paul Levi, the KPD had expelled its putschist wing, which some months later reemerged under the name Communist Workers' Party of Germany (Kommunistische Arbeiterpartei Deutschlands or KAPD). The KPD thus reached the nadir of its public influence with a membership that had dwindled to an estimated 50,000. Nevertheless, the protest potential of the industrial labor force continued to mount as a result of unremitting government repression and the intransigence of management, which worked in close cooperation with the high command of the Reichswehr.

The watershed between the final phase of the German revolution and the beginning phase of economic reconstruction was the Factory Council Law (*Betriebsrätegesetz*). Debate in the National Assembly on the controversial law had been postponed in the wake of the bitter conflict that had accompanied ratification of the Versailles peace treaty. By the time the bill was finally presented for discussion in late 1919, its provisions had been substantially weakened by employer and employee associations cooperating with each other under the auspices of the Zentralarbeitsgemeinschaft. Little remained of the bill's original intent to give the work force a decisive voice in the economic management of individual factories and to establish the factory councils as an intermediary step in the full integration of labor and its interests into the National Economic Council (Reichswirtschaftsrat). Aside from establishing a mechanism for safeguarding workers' interests in the area of plant social policy, the bill provided only for the workers' right to inspect company books—and even then only those balance sheets related to plant operations and the company's profits and losses. The question of employee representation on the board of directors of public corporations was left unresolved pending future legislative action.

The Independent Socialists denounced the Factory Council Law as the "death certificate of the council system." To be sure, there was good reason to see it as the definitive rejection of efforts to infuse the future economy with socialistic elements. Even in its watered-down version, this law, which was to have positive results in the area of social policy, met with bitter opposition from the employers' associations. The DDP, whose social-liberal wing did not want to go back on the existing compromise, eventually accepted the law over the objections of its industrial supporters in order not to jeopardize its place in the coalition government it had just rejoined. The ADGB, which looked upon the factory councils as a source of labor radicalism, did not so much as lift a finger to demand the right of codetermination (*Mitbestimmungsrecht*) on the factory level, a notion it perceived as a direct threat to its own control over wage policies.

It should have come as no surprise that the political Left launched a series of vigorous protests against the proposed Factory Council Law. The severe clashes on the steps of the Reichstag that left forty-two dead and numerous injured resulted primarily from the incompetence of the Prussian minister of the interior, Wolfgang Heine, and secondarily from the activity of putschist minorities. Nor was there any reason to believe, as the anti-Bolshevist hysteria of the security forces seemed to suggest, that the demonstrators intended to storm the Reichstag. The power of the military in the preceding months was simply too awesome for the Communists, their interest in provoking incidents of violence notwithstanding, to have approved plans for an insurrection. Still, the disturbances of 13 January 1920 conveniently provided the government with what a Defense Ministry memorandum called "a desirable justification for severe measures under the state of emergency."

The completely unfounded fears of a "Bolshevist" uprising that had been systematically nurtured by the political Right for the better part of the preceding two years prompted the Bauer cabinet to prolong the newly proclaimed state of emergency in spite of protests from the socialist unions and Majority Socialists. Placing emergency powers in the hands of the military only revived the workers' bad memories of the World War. For weeks on end, the Independent Socialist press was banned, prominent party officials like Ernst Däumig were taken into protective custody, and strikes and protest demonstrations were ruthlessly quelled. This was accompanied by massive interference in the nation's economic and social life that, in its more bizarre manifestations, included bans on street vending and carnival parades. All of this amounted to the virtual usurpation of civilian administrative authority by the military. Not even the mail was free from government tampering. Several high-ranking commanders, on the other hand, were not satisfied with this and demanded a return to justice by court-martial. Within the working class, such high-handedness only evoked outrage and hatred of the military.

Relations between the national government and the Reichswehr became even further strained when the former took steps to accommodate Allied demands for a reduction in the size of the army, whose numerical strength had been greatly inflated by the absorption of the Free Corps, which, in some cases, were reorganized as regular army units. Throughout all of this, the military continued to delude itself into believing that it would be possible to ignore the armament provisions of the Versailles treaty. A special role in these developments fell to the Baltic Free Corps. These units had functioned more or less autonomously in the Baltic and were only withdrawn after the Allies threatened the German government with massive intervention. The government, however, yielded to pressure from the Reichswehr and declared an amnesty that precluded the possibility of disciplinary action against those engaged in open mutiny. When repeated Allied protests made it impossible to delay the dissolution of Captain Hermann Ehrhardt's Navy Brigade II any longer, the government's action provoked an open protest from General Walther von Lüttwitz. When Lüttwitz was subsequently removed from his post as commander of the Reichswehr Battle Group I, he decided to push forward the date of the counterrevolutionary putsch that he had been planning for some time in cooperation with the East Prussian agricultural official Wolfgang Kapp. On 12 March 1920 the Ehrhardt Brigade was ordered to march on Berlin in order to prevent its dissolution. On the previous day, the Defense Ministry's emissary to Döberitz, Admiral Adolf von Trotha, had noticed "nothing suspicious" (*nichts Verdächtiges*). Only at the last moment did Noske inform the cabinet of the putsch that was already under way.

Of the military leaders, only the commander in chief of the army, General Walther Reinhardt, openly declared his willingness to suppress the putsch with the use of armed force. By contrast, Hans von Seeckt, head of the office of general military personnel (Chef des Allgemeinen Truppenamts), declined the Reichswehr minister's request for a mobilization of the army on the grounds that "in view of the impending uprising of the radical Left a split within the Reichswehr had to be avoided at all costs." No statement could have better expressed the way in which the continual state of emergency had increased the arrogance of the military, which now conceived of itself as the true guardian of political stability and did not hesitate to demand that the Reich president relieve Majority Socialist Hermann Müller of his responsibilities as German foreign minister.

The events that resulted from the Reichswehr's refusal to guarantee the protection of the constitutional government cast a revealing light not only on the inadequacies of the chancellor's leadership but also on the unreliable attitude of the bourgeois parties. The cabinet fled, first to Dresden, then to Stuttgart, where it published an appeal to the German people in which it attempted to portray the Kapp-Lüttwitz Putsch attempt as a lightweight farce à la Köpenik. Neither this nor a reminder to the civil service that it owed its allegiance to the legally constituted national government could conceal the helplessness with which the president and cabinet responded to the proclamation of a "national dictatorship" after several months of rumors that such an undertaking was imminent. Left behind in Berlin, the Democratic minister of justice Eugen Schiffer had no qualms about carrying on unauthorized negotiations with the putschists and even went so far as to grant them immunity from prosecution in exchange for their promise to resign in favor of a new right-wing cabinet.

Even Gustav Stresemann acted on the assumption that the Bauer cabinet would not survive. In an appeal published on 13 March, the DVP declared itself to be in essential agreement with the aims of the Kapp government, a fact that it later tried to conceal with mixed success. Stresemann suggested the formation of a cabinet of experts and supported Kapp's demand for the immediate and direct election of the Reich president. Two Prussian ministers, the DVP's Wolfgang Heine and the MSPD's Albert Südekum, also felt that negotiations were the only way to resolve the crisis, but they underestimated the widespread political solidarity that greeted the appeal that was made in the name of the Social Democratic members of the cabinet on the night of 13 March for a general strike. While the KPD hesitated to join the protest, the liberal and Christian trade-union federations, including the German Civil Servants' Association, quickly took their places in the strike front. Even if the strike did not have immediate practical consequences since it was called on a weekend, it represented a powerful demonstration of spontaneous protest by broad segments of the population against the arbitrary and arrogant conduct of the military. The Democratic cabinet members who had remained in Stuttgart and the National Assembly, which had been summoned there, were profoundly impressed by the magnitude of this demonstration and decided to adopt a posture of uncompromising refusal to negotiate with Kapp and Lüttwitz.

Without the general strike it is almost certain that elements within the Reichstag and the groups that had instigated the putsch would have reached a compromise with a strong authoritarian flavor. But the fact that the Bauer cabinet owed its survival to the general strike did not prevent the chancellor from disavowing all responsibility for the strike, which he dismissed as "mystification." In the final analysis, the putsch failed because of the dilettantism of Kapp and his military accomplices, who were incapable of responding to the passive resistance of the ministerial bureaucracy and the Reichsbank and who lacked the political skills necessary for success. The military's habit of placing a civilian figurehead in the foreground was as much an aspect of this dilettantism as the expectation that the quasi-permanent state of emergency would facilitate the smooth transfer of power. To be sure, this is what happened in Bavaria, where a coalition cabinet headed by Johannes Hoffmann was replaced by a right-wing cabinet under Gustav von Kahr that enjoyed the support of the state DDP organization. Other state governments, however, supported the legal government, whose members General Georg Maerker did not arrest in light of the risk this might have posed. Although they sympathized with Kapp, the overwhelming majority of the military commanders adopted a wait-and-see attitude and confined their efforts to suppressing the strike movement on the assumption that a negotiated end to the crisis would make it unnecessary for them to break their oath of loyalty to the duly constituted government.

The conspirators enjoyed the sympathy of heavy industry and large-scale agriculture as well as the open support of the nationalist and *völkisch* Right. They were, however, severely handicapped by the danger that an undisguised violation of the existing constitutional order might lead the French to intervene in the occupied areas and would give new impetus to separatist tendencies. In addition, they were also apprehensive that they might not have sufficient control over the troops in a large-scale conflict that verged on open civil war. This explains why the leading officials in the Defense Ministry refused to take orders from Lüttwitz, who had usurped the supreme command, even though virtually every one of them was in agreement with his political ideas. With the subsequent "pacification" of the military, these essentially tactical disagreements at the upper echelons of the Reichswehr were deemphasized in favor of the common struggle against "Bolshevism."

After the demise of the Kapp government, Bauer and his cabinet believed that they could return to politics as usual. They failed, however, to recognize that the strikes had done much to revive the people's movement that had unleashed the revolutionary upheaval of November 1918. All over Germany, the working class was now trying to heal the rift in the ranks of organized labor by forming action committees in which all factions were equally represented. The newfound sense of solidarity extended to the liberal and Christian labor movements as well and forced the ADGB to abandon its traditional reserve for fear of losing all credibility among the rank and file of the working population. The strikers regarded the Kapp Putsch as a symptom of the revolution's failure to crush the military and bureaucratic machines still hostile to the republic.

Employer associations found themselves obliged not only by pressure from organized labor but also by concern over what might happen in the occupied territories to adopt—at least externally—a neutral attitude toward the Kapp Putsch. In the Ruhr, employer and employee organizations in the mining industry issued a joint declaration against Kapp but avoided joining the general strike. It was only on 17 March 1920 that the ZAG decided to issue a statement denouncing Kapp, though again without giving support to the ongoing strike. In point of fact, significant elements of Germany's entrepreneurial elite sympathized with the attempted coup, and there was particularly close cooperation between the Mining Association (Zechenverband) and the general military command in Münster in suppressing the protest movement by miners from the Ruhr.

Karl Legien realized that he could not go before the striking workers with empty hands and persuade them to end their walkout. The nine-point program the labor unions presented to the government as an ultimatum with their conditions for ending the general strike demanded, in addition to the resignation of the severely compromised defense minister Noske, unequivocal guarantees that those military units that had sympathized with the putsch would be disbanded, that those responsible would be held accountable, and that republican security forces rather than military units would henceforth be entrusted with the maintenance of public order. Beyond that, the unions demanded sweeping social reforms as well as the immediate socialization of the coal industry. The demand for the establishment of a workers' government as insurance that the republicanization of state and society would be carried out was immediately rejected by the DDP as unconstitutional interference by the unions in the process of forming a government, although the party's social-liberal wing—including, among others, Ernst Remmer, chairman of the German Civil Servants' Association—emphatically endorsed the nine-point program.

The rapprochement between the two workers' parties that temporarily seemed to take place in the wake of the Kapp-Lüttwitz Putsch was of short duration. Led by the socialist unions, the strike committee agreed to call off the strike in exchange for the paper assurances from the government. At the same time, Legien declined to assume the chancellorship. His initiative had been motivated exclusively by tactical considerations and was designed to prevent the strike from coming under the influence of the radical Left. The proclamation of 20 March 1920 announcing the end of the strike, however, met with only partial compliance. Particularly in the Ruhr, significant segments of the industrial working class resorted to armed self-help against the reactionary Free Corps units that had marched into the region behind the black, red, and white flag of imperial Germany. By no means was resistance of this sort limited to the syndicalist groups that had become so influential in Hagen and Hamborn. After Kapp's demise the workers were not about to lay down their arms at a time when the Reichswehr, with Chancellor Bauer's full support, seemed to be making preparations for ruthlessly suppressing the movement. The government voted only halfheartedly—and then only for the purpose of isolating the radical Hagen Central Council (Hagener Zentralrat) that had sought to spread the protest movement beyond the Ruhr—to accept the so-called Bielefeld Agreement that Carl Severing, the recently appointed Reich commissar for the Ruhr, had negotiated with representatives of the unions and workers' parties, including the KPD, on 23 March for a political end to the crisis. Although the accord contained the eight points that still remained after Ebert had reluctantly accepted Noske's resignation, the government refused to honor provisions pertaining to the formation of local security forces. Characteristically, the Reichswehr commander of Münster, General Oskar von Watter, protested vehemently against the allegedly unconstitutional Bielefeld Agreement and refused to be bound by it as long as the fighting in the Ruhr continued.

Sabotaged in large measure by his own government, Severing's attempt at pacification failed because numerically significant elements of the Ruhr working class were embittered by the behavior of troops acting under the extended state of siege—particularly irksome in this connection was the reactionary Free Corps Lichtschlag—and continued to wage armed resistance. For the workers it was difficult to understand how the same Reichswehr units that had earlier tried to crush the general strike against Kapp could now present themselves as guardians of the republican order. Only through the mediation of the ADGB's local affiliate and the terrorist intervention of the troops was it possible to put an end to a general strike that had originally enjoyed the support of the overwhelming majority of the Ruhr working class. The formation of the Red Army of the Ruhr, to which more than 50,000 workers belonged, indicated the extent to which official workers' organizations, including the KPD, had lost contact with certain sectors of the industrial working class. The suppression of the armed resistance that had been inspired by the syndicalists was accompanied by atrocities that regular army units committed against the working class. There were repeated incidents of mass shootings and illegal trials before military tribunals. The situation was not materially different in other industrial areas where Reichswehr units suppressed the strike movement with characteristic ruthlessness. From this point on, there could be no talk of fulfilling the promises that had once been made to the labor unions.

The fight of the Red Army of the Ruhr represented the last cry of despair by increasingly discouraged workers who demanded that the social achievements of the November Revolution be honored in full. Their failure, however, was complete. Legien's initiative came to nothing. For if it is true that Noske had to be dismissed, the fact that Seeckt was subsequently appointed chief of staff of the German army with Otto Geßler, a member of the DDP who openly harbored monarchist sympathies, as defense minister underscored the futility of trying to purge the army's personnel. A number of changes in the upper echelons of the military's command structure had been made, but most of those officers who had been involved in the putsch had nothing to fear. By contrast, those officers and troops who in March had expressed their allegiance to the republican government in the presence of their superiors were either demoted or dismissed on the grounds of insubordination.

Criminal prosecution of the conspirators, whose most prominent leaders were able to escape arrest through the help of Justice Minister Eugen Schiffer, was limited to a guilty verdict and a five-year sentence for the Berlin police chief Traugott von Jagow, of which only three were served. Moreover, the general amnesty that was declared soon thereafter drew a veil over the deeds of Kapp's accomplices. These men, in fact, were treated far more leniently than the striking workers, who in some cases were placed in concentration camps for having risen up against Kapp and his followers and for having come out in support of a socialist order. By the same token, the newly formed socialization commission was nothing more than an instrument of pacification. The only thing that the new cabinet headed by the MSPD's Hermann Müller was able to achieve to help pacify the domestic political situation was a directive stipulating that during a state of emergency executive power lay in the hands of the civilian administration and that the use of the military in the event that police power was insufficient could take place only at its discretion. The commanders of the Reichswehr vehemently protested the new regulation, even though it was consistent with Seeckt's desire to keep the army out of the domestic line of fire after its prestige had been seriously damaged by its failure to stand up against Kapp.

In the wake of the crisis caused by the Kapp-Lüttwitz Putsch the elections that had been set to take place later that year were moved ahead to 6 June

1920. As expected, they resulted in a landslide to the right. The parties of the Weimar Coalition lost — as it turned out, permanently — their parliamentary majority. The Majority Socialists suffered particularly severe losses to the USPD in heavily industrialized areas, while the KPD remained an insignificant splinter group. This revealed just how misleading it was to identify the protest movement of the industrial working class with "Bolshevism" and "Spartacism." The social compromises on which the new republican order had been founded were already dead insofar as neither the majority of the politically active workers nor the more progressive elements of the German bourgeoisie, including those who belonged to the DDP, still accepted them. At the same time the German Right had begun to reconstitute, mostly outside of parliament, in a network of neoconservative *Querverbindungen* that included substantial elements of Germany's academic and professional elites. A transformation of German society, on the other hand, had not taken place.

From the very outset, the democracy that had been founded at Weimar was encumbered by heavy foreign and domestic liabilities. The constitution that had taken shape in an essentially preparliamentary environment was designed to counter the twofold threat of "Bolshevization" and national disintegration. As such, it helped prevent a comprehensive social revolution. Herein lay the minimal consensus upon which the civil bureaucracies at the national and state level and the parties of the Weimar Coalition could agree. But this consensus began to fall apart as soon as the realities of Allied peace terms definitively shattered the illusion that a change of constitutions would help Germany secure a peace based upon Wilson's Fourteen Points. The founding of the republic thus took place in the twilight of a psychological state of war that had not yet ended. The struggle against social revolution and Versailles forced the young democracy into greater continuity with the imperial regime than the authors of its new constitution had intended. As long as resistance to the war-guilt clauses and the "infamous peace" (*Schmachfrieden*) of Versailles dominated German political life, it would be impossible for the German people to achieve the necessary political and moral distance from the past. Indeed, the defenders of the old imperial regime did their best to foster the precise opposite of this. Patriotic feeling made it appear as if it was a duty to support the internal and external rearmament of the German people even if this took place under counterrevolutionary or at least antirepublican auspices.

Aside from the fact that during the revolution there were no serious efforts to initiate the necessary democratization of the civil bureaucracy and the military, Weimar democracy possessed an exposed flank that the forces of counterrevolution could attack with impunity, namely, its conscious avoidance of a psychological break with its imperial past. The internal consolidation of Weimar democracy was also endangered as the bourgeois parties of the center and Right began to accommodate themselves to the new power relationships and no longer looked upon the republic as a "ploy" that would help them through a transitional phase that was characterized by the continuation of the war with nonmilitary means. The tendency to revise the constitution in an authoritarian direction began to make itself felt even before it had been ratified. The Kapp Putsch was condemned to failure above all else by the fact that the republic's extreme dependence in the area of foreign policy and its insufficient economic consolidation temporarily precluded open authoritarian experiments. If anything, the events of the Kapp Putsch suggested that the infiltration of the existing political system by authoritarian and bureaucratic elements was more likely than its democratization.

For the political forces that had carried the burden of founding the new democracy—that is, committed democrats and the Majority Socialists—the situation at the end of this process offered little basis for hope. For the industrial workers who had fought in vain for their vision of democratic and social emancipation, the situation was dismal. For Ebert, Noske, Scheidemann, and the leaders of the German labor movement who had stood in the way of proletarian mass movements for the sake of a rigidly enforced policy of law and order and in the name of an almost neurotic fear of Communist anarchy, this was only the price they had to pay for a policy that, to be sure, had performed a great service in securing the continuity of the German nation-state yet, in terms of its broader implications, remained fundamentally flawed.

CHAPTER FOUR

The Inner Rejection of the Peace

FOLLOWING the Reichstag elections of 6 June 1920, lengthy negotiations produced a bourgeois minority cabinet headed by Konstantin Fehrenbach of the German Center Party. The SPD agreed to tolerate the new government until the Spa Conference convened later that summer, but shied away from assuming governmental responsibility. Coalition overtures to the USPD, which had recorded substantial gains in the recent elections, had met with a blunt rebuff and a rehearsal of all the reasons that had led to its break with the Majority Socialists in December 1918. The Majority Socialists, on the other hand, were discouraged by the outcome of the elections and refused to participate in a cabinet that also included ministers from the right-wing German People's Party. After all, that party had shown its true attitude toward the republic at the time of the Kapp Putsch and was much too closely identified with the interests of heavy industry.

It was symptomatic of Weimar's political weakness that the first attempt at the formation of a cabinet—an event that marked the end of the constitutive phase in the republic's history—produced the first in a series of minority governments that accompanied Weimar parliamentarism to its very end. The fact that the parties of the Weimar Coalition had lost their parliamentary majority and the Social Democrats' retreat from governmental responsibility indicated that the internal consolidation of the Weimar's parliamentary system was far from complete. On the other hand, neither the German Nationalists nor the People's Party was prepared to assume political responsibility in the sober realization that this would saddle them with the burden of carrying out the Treaty of Versailles. This, in turn, created a situation of extreme flux in which the decisive influence in governmental affairs was exercised by the Center and DDP with indirect support from the SPD.

The eagerness with which the new cabinet sought to establish its independence from the parliament for the upcoming reparations negotiations with the Allies was reflected in the appointment of Walter Simons as German foreign minister. By virtue of his experience as general council to the German delegation at Versailles, the politically unaffiliated career jurist was regarded as an outstanding expert in the reparations question. After his resignation from the German peace delegation in protest against the signing of the Versailles peace treaty, Simons became a member of the presidium of the National Federation of German Industry. Given the apparently irreconcilable differences that separated the DVP, which had joined the cabinet only with the greatest of reluctance, and the SPD, it was the precarious diplomatic situation in which Germany found itself that kept the parliamentary system of government alive.

German public opinion failed to grasp the full political, economic, and financial implications of the Versailles peace treaty. Simons himself underscored this fact in a speech before the Reichstag: "Only now is the population beginning to understand the enormity of the burden the German people has taken upon itself." Indeed, the near-unanimous rejection of the Versailles peace treaty — only the USPD refused to take this stance — only helped obscure what must have been obvious to any unbiased observer, namely, that the defeat of the Central Powers had brought about a fundamental realignment in the configuration of international power. Under these circumstances, a return to the foreign policy of the imperial era was completely out of the question as long as Germany was not willing to accept the long-term risk of another world war.

The idea that Germany's defeat in World War I was a passing episode and that the peace treaty was an arbitrary construct that would be cast aside in the course of historical change was by no means limited to the extreme Right, where the phrase "a nation born of war" had been coined to help foster the myth of a vigorously regenerated "national community." Oswald Spengler, the prophet of German neoconservatism, had said as early as December 1918 that the peace was only provisional and that the World War "was only now entering its second stage." Even Hans Delbrück, a scholar whose political moderation was usually exemplary, wrote in 1919 in the *Preußischer Jahrbücher*: "The day and hour will come when we will demand everything back." The internal rejection of Versailles also embraced committed pacifists like Ludwig Quidde and Walter Schücking, who protested passionately against Allied peace terms. By contrast, the Independent Socialists continued to believe that the imminent revolutionary overthrow of Europe's capitalist order would make the peace treaty obsolete.

Faced with the necessity of consolidating the nation's economic and diplomatic resources, the relevant political forces (with the exception of the left wing of the USPD and the intransigent extreme Right) regarded the preservation of the parliamentary system to be of paramount importance, an objective they linked to the demands for a revision of the treaty. Based on foreign policy considerations, this consensus concealed an irreconcilable conflict over domestic political goals. The foes of the republic linked their agitation against the "dictated peace" with an attack on the democratic and social achievements of the November Revolution, which they denounced as a consequence of the military debacle the Social Democrats had caused. Their goal was to repeal these achievements as soon as an improvement in Germany's diplomatic situation permitted a return to the traditions of Prussian-German power politics. The parties of the Weimar Coalition, by contrast, were opposed to the treaties of the Paris peace settlement because they seemed to deprive the Germans of the democratic right of self-determination. At first they perceived in the League of Nations a mechanism for creating understanding among the nations of the world and for effecting Germany's reconciliation with the victorious Allied powers. From this perspective, Germany's new republican system represented a new beginning and an opportunity not only to close the gap that separated Germany from the Western democracies but also to free themselves from the diplomatic legacy of the Bismarckian era.

The immediate goals of German foreign policy were to frustrate the French in their demand for sanctions, to secure the unity of the Reich, and to regain national sovereignty. As long as there was relative agreement on these goals, the different motives that lay behind them by and large escaped the attention of contemporary observers. The conflicting social and economic interests that shaped the conduct of German foreign policy were, for the moment at least, obscured by the fiction of a *Notgemeinschaft*, or national community born of necessity. In the final analysis, the viability of the Weimar Republic depended on whether it was sufficiently integrated into the political and economic system of the Paris peace settlement, something that did not necessarily preclude a partial revision of the terms of that settlement. The constraints that limited Germany's freedom of movement in matters of foreign policy therefore did not automatically weaken the prospects for the development of a stable democracy, for the constant diplomatic pressure under which the republic labored during the early years of the Weimar Republic made it difficult to undertake fundamental changes in the governmental and constitutional system and occasionally even obliged avowed foes of the system to identify themselves with it. The lack of maneuvering space in the area of foreign policy was thus an important political vice that facilitated the resolution or postponement of constitutional conflicts that might otherwise have torn the system apart.

The internal rejection of the Paris peace settlement by virtually all political groups in Germany constituted a serious psychological obstacle to recognizing the realities of power in the postwar world and made it difficult for Germany to abandon the political illusions that had, for example, accompanied its precipitous petition for an armistice. It is understandable, of course, that the German public put faith in the promise of a "peace without annexations" contained in Wilson's note of 11 February 1918, especially since the American president had publicly reiterated his basic position on a number of occasions. But government leaders must have realized from the Lansing note of 5 November 1918 that there was no way Germany could escape heavy economic burdens and territorial losses as a result of the lost war.

Many of these illusions should have been shattered, at the very latest, when

Matthias Erzberger signed the armistice in the presence of Marshal Foch and other Allied representatives in the forest of Compiègne not far from Paris on 11 November 1918. For the armistice not only contained provisions for a surprisingly sweeping disarmament of the German Reich that would have made a resumption of hostilities impossible, but it also stipulated far-reaching economic liability for war-related damage that mounted with each day the armistice was not signed and thus greatly affected the eventual shape of the peace treaty. Nonetheless, until the spring of 1919 the German political establishment continued to hope that in the impending peace negotiations it would be possible to preserve Germany's status as a moderately great power, albeit at the price of certain territorial losses and some concessions in the area of national defense. Erzberger, the leader of the German armistice delegation, and a handful of professional diplomats were the only ones who did not share in such an exaggerated estimation of Germany's diplomatic and military position. Such illusions grew out of the wishful thinking of the Wilhelmine diplomatic tradition and the refusal to recognize the enormity of the military defeat Germany had suffered. They were further nourished by the success that German military units had experienced in repelling Bolshevist incursions in the Baltic and by the hopes that even the normally sober General Wilhelm Groener placed in collaboration with the Western Allies for the purpose of a combined action against the Bolsheviks. As late as early summer of 1919, it seemed as if the German military presence in the East—though composed overwhelmingly of Free Corps units and officially disavowed by the German government—was still indispensable to the Allies.

The optimism of Germany's political elites and the concomitant idealization of Wilson were reflected in the tactical line adopted by Count Brockdorff-Rantzau. During the war, the foreign minister and former ambassador to Denmark had advocated a negotiated peace and internal reforms. Enjoying the unconditional support of Ebert and the Majority Socialists, Brockdorff-Rantzau had close ties to the newly founded DDP. Upon his appointment as Wilhelm Solf's successor, Brockdorff-Rantzau demanded the right to prepare for the peace negotiations without interference from the cabinet and expected to take full responsibility for their conduct. His willful and rather unattractive personality, however, was a source of considerable friction within the cabinet. Particularly sharp controversies arose between him and Erzberger who, as head of the armistice delegation, was not willing to have his hands tied by Brockdorff's guidelines. Even though Brockdorff may have been the more experienced diplomat, he failed to understand the domestic constraints that affected the conduct of German foreign policy. Reminiscent of the diplomatic style of the late empire, Brockdorff's demeanor was based on an understanding of foreign policy as a strictly professional pursuit and an inflated view of the success that could be achieved by sheer diplomatic finesse.

In formulating his foreign policy, Brockdorff-Rantzau opted for a strategy that used the Lansing note as the basis for Germany's legal claim to a negotiated peace. More than anyone else, Brockdorff was responsible for the propaganda campaign that provided a one-sided interpretation of Wilson's Fourteen Points as beneficial to Germany's national interests. Partly as a result of this campaign, the public was as surprised by the harshness of the peace conditions that were announced on 7 May 1919 as it had been by the sudden demand for an armistice in October 1918. The German Foreign Office's systematic agitation for a "just peace" provided all the materials needed to portray Versailles as a work of despicable deceit and as an infamous breach of legality and trust. All of this was a conscious attempt to create the impression that the German Reich had entered into the armistice fully believing the assurances of the American president only to fall victim to the ruses and arbitrary machinations of the Western powers.

The German position was prepared by a commission of experts that included respected economists, bankers like Max Warburg and Carl Melchior, and representatives of big industry, as well as established specialists in constitutional and international law, such as the pacifist Walter Schücking. The commission went along with the foreign minister's strategy of responding to the conditions it expected the Allies to present with a forceful restatement of Germany's legal position in the expectation that this would win the sympathies of the neutral powers and thus force the Allies to negotiate individual points of the peace proposal. Individual German claims would then be measured against the standard of Wilson's abstract principles. Such an approach, however, ruled out any flexibility whatsoever and made it difficult to reach a compromise on relatively minor points. The German counterproposals, particularly those contained in the summary that the Germans sent the Allies in their response of 29 May, represented a complete rejection of the Allied peace demands. Such a strategy was hardly designed to bring the victorious powers to the negotiating table.

Brockdorff-Rantzau's diplomatic concept was based on the notion, fueled to a certain extent by the indiscretions of members of the American peace delegation, that President Wilson had reservations of his own about the package that had been put together in Paris conference rooms. However, the German Foreign Office had received inside information about Allied intentions and had come to the conclusion that Wilson's role in the interallied negotiations was by no means as decisive as the German public had been led to think by the Foreign Office's propaganda campaign. Similarly, confidential warnings that it would be useless to play the victorious powers off against each other did not go unnoticed. The net effect of all this, however, was only to make the German attitude even more inflexible, something that could be seen not only in Germany's insistence on the legal correctness of its position but also in its refusal to accept any concessions that might undermine this position. The German counterproposals placed primary stress on the rejection of Articles 227 through 230 as well as the war-guilt clause in Article 231 of the draft treaty. While moral indignation over these allegedly discriminatory clauses was particularly strong within the German delegation and in the German press, Brockdorff-Rantzau hoped to undercut the Allied position on other, more technical issues by refuting the charges of German responsibility for the outbreak of the war.

The German position revealed little sense of the divergent Allied interests that had produced the wording of Article 231 when it lumped this article together with the controversial demands for reparations to characterize the proposed treaty as a "punitive peace." Initially Wilson had intended to limit reparations payments to damages caused by violations of international law, as in the case of the unprovoked attack against Belgium. The use of the term "aggression" in the Lansing note had precisely this in mind. German politicians would have been well advised not to give this formula the sense of a "war of aggression." In the interallied negotiations, in which France and England demanded that Germany be held responsible for the full costs of the war, the scope of reparations was broadened with questionable legality to include pensions for war invalids and the survivors of soldiers killed in the war, although the original provisions only covered damages incurred by the civilian population. This compromise came close to the British position on German reparations payments insofar as Prime Minister David Lloyd George was bound by promises he had made to appease nationalist emotions in the "khaki elections" of November 1918.

The subcommittee at the Paris Peace Conference that was responsible for the reparations question had originally intended to establish the juridical grounds for "integral" compensation in Article 231. Only at the last moment did the subcommittee add the additional demand that Germany acknowledge responsibility for the outbreak of the war. Even then this was not conceived as a fundamental moral condemnation of German policy. It was only in the Allied note and the accompanying memorandum of 16 July—documents signed by Clemenceau but written by a member of the British delegation—that the charges of war guilt were expressed in the exaggerated form that so outraged the German public. In this way, a provision that was initially designed to specify German liability became a battle cry of enormous significance in German domestic politics. Once this had happened, it became impossible, for reasons of prestige, for the Allies to retreat from their position.

To be sure, Brockdorff-Rantzau had not originally intended to invest the war-guilt question with such great rhetorical significance. Yet this was the logical consequence of the German negotiating strategy. Among the Allies there was sufficient reason to assume that the Germans would do everything in their power to renege on their contractual reparations obligations. The scuttling of the German fleet at Scapa Flow was a striking example of this attitude. Nor was the credibility of the German position enhanced by the fact that the new government defended representatives of Germany's imperial regime against Allied accusations for the sole purpose of maintaining a legal position that had been established before the revolutionary turmoil of November 1918. Not only did argumentation of this sort lend a decidedly aggressive tone to the German counterproposals, but to Wilson and Lloyd George, who had gone to great lengths to persuade Clemenceau to mitigate the conditions that were to be imposed on Germany, it only confirmed the view that the founding of the republic had done little, if anything, to change the German mentality.

This impression was only further confirmed by Brockdorff-Rantzau's behavior at Trianon Palace when the Allies handed the German delegation their conditions for concluding peace. In a mixture of social ineptitude and defiance, Brockdorff-Rantzau remained seated as he responded to Clemenceau's address and accused the Allies, among other things, of having caused the death of several hundred thousand noncombatants by continuing the blockade—an accusation that carried an element of truth in that the Allied embargo on food imports had been partially lifted at the urging of Herbert Hoover as late as March 1919. To be sure, the psychological stress on the German delegation, which was cut off from the world in the Hôtel des Reservoirs in Versailles, had much to do with the foreign minister's reaction. But the virtual internment of the German delegation was prompted not so much by continuing feelings of hatred as by the fear that informal conversations with the members of the delegation might destroy the consensus that the Allied powers had labored so hard to achieve. In view of the fact that there had been considerable disagreement within the cabinet over the appropriate negotiating tactics, Brockdorff's address was also designed to mobilize the support of the German public for his position. Although his speech may have contained some positive points of departure on specific issues, it failed completely insofar as it sought to produce a willingness to negotiate on the part of the Allies.

The German foreign minister repeatedly complained that the victors did not seem prepared to grant the republic more favorable terms than the empire would have received. President Wilson was indeed unimpressed by the German transition to a democratic system and was not at all inclined to soften his stance against the Germans as long as they had not proved their democratic reliability and their break with their imperial past by demonstrating their unequivocal willingness to make up for the injury their country had caused. The continuity of Germany's military leadership and the political power these men still wielded in the republic only strengthened Wilson in his resolve to stand firm on the matter of extradition. Not only did the German counterproposals fail to generate much sympathy among the American experts, but they had the further effect of proving to the president that the Germans were "unteachable."

While it is true that a more restrained demeanor that sought to demonstrate a clear break with the style and substance of the Wilhelmine tradition would not have produced any appreciable concessions from the Allies, it would have helped reduce the emotional barriers generated by four years of harsh warfare.

Just how strong distrust of the former military enemy remained in many quarters could be seen at the Bern Conference of the Third Socialist International in February 1919, where only the position taken by the USPD received appreciable applause. It thus became increasingly clear that Germany's hopes for support from the other socialist parties and for intervention by the neutrals would not be realized. Similarly, the constant pleas that Germany must not be driven into the Bolshevist camp by overly harsh peace conditions failed to have much of an effect. Feeling that the internal disintegration of Germany would indeed be in their best interest, the French were not altogether unjustified in rejecting this argument as sheer panic-mongering. For if the Germans themselves took this fear seriously, then the logical course of action would be unconditional acceptance of Allied peace conditions.

Brockdorff-Rantzau was oblivious to the domestic political factors that made a continuation of the armed conflict impossible. In this respect, his views were echoed by Bernhard von Bülow, the future state secretary for foreign affairs, who argued after the peace conditions had become known that the Allied strategy amounted to "one great bluff." If Germany had not fallen for it, he continued, it would have received a "reasonably tolerable" peace and would have had every reason to expect that it would "get back on its feet more quickly than the other European powers." The maxim "keep your nerves" (Nerve behalten) that circulated among Germany's political leaders was sadly reminiscent of the illusions that great-power status had fostered during the war. This attitude, which simply ignored the state of affairs among the common people, contributed in no small measure to the internal divisions that plagued the German attitude toward the peace. It would be a mistake to hold Brockdorff-Rantzau solely responsible.

German policy was based on the premise that the rejection of the peace conditions and the collapse of the Versailles negotiations would, within a few weeks, force the Allies to seek an accommodation. Should this premise prove wrong, the German government would be forced to sign, but this time under evident duress. These assumptions, however, failed to take into account French ambitions, although the German government did envision measures that it would take in the event that the south German states decided to sign the treaty on their own. For all his reluctance to resume the war, Lloyd George was also determined to force German compliance. Only Wilson was in danger of definitively losing the support of the American Congress if his peace mission were to fail. And yet Brockdorff-Rantzau had placed his main hope in the leniency of the United States.

For a time the German peace delegation shared the "all-or-nothing" mentality that was expressed in Brockdorff-Rantzau's attitude and that eventually forced his resignation. The experience of the armistice negotiations raised fears that the Allies might use the treaty to accomplish the long-term economic and financial weakening of Germany. By no means was this apprehension totally unjustified. Fear of German economic potential had above all caused not only French, but also British policy makers to insist on large reparations payments that would limit Germany's ability to compete in international markets. In view of the astronomical financial demands put forth by the French, however, the Allies were unable to agree on the size of the reparations that Germany would have to pay. Under these circumstances, the victorious powers appointed a reparations commission that was to decide on the amount by 1 May 1921, unless in the meantime a satisfactory German proposal had been received. In the interim, Germany was obliged to make payments in kind and cash totaling 20 billion gold marks.

German economic experts insisted that the preservation of Germany's economic potential had to be given priority over disarmament and the possible loss of territory, however desirable it would be to keep the latter to a minimum. This assessment coincided with that of American and British experts. John Maynard Keynes, for example, became extremely popular in Germany through his devastating critique of the effects of the Treaty of Versailles. As early as 1919, he wrote: "The danger for the future has nothing to do with frontiers and territory, and everything with food, coal, and transportation." By this he meant that the economic potential of a state and not its territorial size would define its place in the future constellation of power. Germany's political elites placed great confidence in Germany's economic strength and considered its preservation an essential ingredient of any formula for returning to great-power status. They were also convinced that in the final analysis the Allies were dependent on economic cooperation with Germany and that German participation in the economic reconstruction of Europe was indispensable. This accounted for the high degree of self-confidence that the German political establishment continued to show in the midst of military defeat.

Germany's main objective was the restoration of normal trade and exchange relations — in itself a precondition of Germany's ability to pay reparations — and the protection of its heavy industrial potential. Under these circumstances, German efforts to prevent the loss of the industrial area of Upper Silesia assumed the highest priority, especially since it had become clear that nothing could be done to keep the French from taking over the mining operations of the Saar. These considerations no doubt played a major role in the thinking behind Erzberger's proposal for a program of European reconstruction in which Germany would be directly involved. But such initiatives always remained secondary to Brockdorff-Rantzau's policy of negotiating from established principles.

Only when the peace conditions were finally made public was Carl Melchior able to make some headway with his suggestion that Germany should offer the Allies reparations in the amount of 100 billion gold marks, to be paid off first in goods and after 1 March 1926 in cash. The German Treasury Office (Reichsschatzamt) dismissed this as an intolerably high figure and doubted that it would be possible to encumber public budgets to this extent. Melchior, who obtained Erzberger's hesitant support, pointed out that the Allies were sure to demand even more, having committed themselves to extensive German reparations in order to win public support in their own countries. Max Warburg went a bit further by suggesting that the problem of making these payments could be solved by setting aside a fixed percentage of the national revenue for the purpose of reparations.

Any step in this direction would not only have helped minimize the doubts the Allies justifiably held about Germany's willingness to pay but would also have generated international interest in Germany's economic consolidation. A constructive initiative that would have opened the way for negotiations, it was nevertheless drowned in a mass of legal reservations and counterdemands from the German side. Moreover, Melchior's proposal was tied to the guarantee of territorial integrity, a condition that the Allies adamantly refused to consider. In any event, Brockdorff-Rantzau deliberately prevented any discussion of this proposal by the experts at the Paris Peace Conference, despite Lloyd George's view that such a discussion would be useful. Nonetheless, some of the German counterproposals did attract the attention of American experts, who pointed out to Wilson that the Germans could hardly be expected to make extensive reparations payments unless they were also afforded the means to increase their export trade. But Wilson's proposal that part of Germany's merchant marine be given back was rejected. Had the German delegation been more prompt and more forceful in making limited economic and financial offers, the French negotiating strategy would have been much more difficult to uphold.

From an economic point of view, the Paris peace regulations proved extremely unsatisfactory. The American president had launched the motto "Freedom of the seas" in support of the removal of international trade barriers. Instead, the Paris regulations marked the return to protectionism and the creation of national protective tariffs. War debts and other burdens related to the war also hampered a rapid economic recovery on the part of the victorious powers. Contemporary critics of the treaty were quick to identify its fundamental deficiencies in the economic area. One of these was the absolute unwillingness of the United States to grant easier terms of payment for the war debts owed by France and Britain, even though there were tangible economic reasons for stimulating the European market. This latter fact became clear when Herbert Hoover launched his food-aid program in a move that was not unrelated to his own country's huge agricultural surpluses. In the same manner, the

U.S. Treasury categorically rejected the possibility of guaranteeing the payment of German reparations obligations.

Under these circumstances, France and Great Britain had a compelling financial interest in using German reparations payments to cover either part or all of the interest on the war loans they owed to the United States. There is some reason to believe that the British proposal for a postponement in setting the precise amount of the German reparations burden was in part motivated by the expectation that in a less tense situation rational economic consider-ations might have a better chance of prevailing. On the other hand, the failure to settle the matter of reparations was counterproductive in the sense that Ger-many could hardly be expected to demonstrate its economic capacity if, as a result, it had to count on increased obligations. In addition, the Versailles treaty contained a number of economically discriminatory clauses, including the loss of German property in the victorious countries, the surrender of patents and trademarks, the internationalization of waterways, the validation of German prewar debts, and the granting of most-favored-nation trade status to the Allies.

Even then, French diplomacy did not succeed in realizing its "project heavy industry." Anticipating dramatic cutbacks in Germany's coal, iron, and steel production, this project was designed to provide French heavy industry with a dominant position in the continental market. An important step toward this goal would have been the annexation of the Saar. In this respect, however, France was successful only in having the Saar included in the French customs area as a League of Nations "mandate" and in having the mines in the Saar declared French property. After fifteen years, all of this was to be subject to a referendum, which would ultimately decide the region's national affiliation. The question of Upper Silesia, on the other hand, was left temporarily unre-solved in as much as Lloyd George had persuaded the other Allied powers to agree to a referendum in what was one of the few instances where the Allies re-sponded favorably to a German counterproposal. Determined to pursue their "project heavy industry," the French were therefore obliged to advance this goal by means of the sanctions authorized in the peace treaty.

The new order created by the Paris peace settlement was almost certain to trigger a covert struggle for economic power that would, in time, spell the definitive end of Europe's leadership in the world economy. Europe's inferior economic position had less to do with technological development or the actual political and economic conditions of the individual European countries than with the close connection between heavy industry and the government appa-ratus that had driven the war economy both in France and in Germany. Such a situation was in fact no longer consistent with the interests of an increas-ingly self-confident entrepreneurial elite, while the public at large was much less interested in economic trends than in territorial adjustments. In the final analysis, the old habit of thinking in categories of national self-sufficiency was a major obstacle on the road to a stable new order in Europe.

When the Paris Peace Conference convened on 18 January 1919 with representatives from twenty-seven nations in attendance, the general public may still have believed in Wilson's pledge of a just peace without victors or vanquished and in his vision of a new era in international relations that would make armed conflict unnecessary by submitting disputes between nations to arbitration by the League of Nations. To insiders, however, it was obvious that the multiplicity of conflicting interests that would surface during the peacemaking process could be satisfied only through pragmatic compromise and not on the basis of the abstract principles at the heart of Wilson's program. Almost from the very outset the American president had to deal with the fact that the Western powers had concluded a series of secret treaties that granted the Italians control of the Brenner frontier and that jeopardized a settlement in the Balkans. American contacts with the exile government of Tomáš Masaryk and Eduard Beneš, however, had already prompted the United States to give its consent to the founding of an autonomous Czechoslovakian state that included the Slovak areas formerly under Hungarian rule. Notwithstanding virtually irreversible decisions such as these, the burden of centuries-old historic conflicts severely hampered the search for a fundamental reorganization of the European state system.

President Wilson had proclaimed the fundamental right of "national self-determination" as the basis on which the forthcoming peace settlement should rest. In doing this, Wilson had formulated a democratic counterpart to Lenin's principle of "national self-determination until its supersession" (*nationale Selbstbestimmung bis zur Ablösung*). For the victorious powers, which in March 1919 had invested responsibility for drafting the Treaty of Versailles and the supplemental treaties of Saint-Germain, Trianon, Neuilly, and Sèvres in a decision-making body with executive authority known as the "Council of the Big Four," there was no practical alternative to the principle of the modern nation-state. To be sure, there were modified forms of self-determination such as the principle of "national autonomy" based on the principle of personality as formulated by the Austrian Social Democrat Karl Renner. But ideas such as these found only limited application in the case of Latvia.

The right of self-determination in the sense of a unified nation-state was of limited relevance in east-central and southeastern Europe, where ethnic diversity and the social stratification of the different nationalities made the application of such a principle difficult, if not impossible. Moreover, its very vagueness meant that it could be applied in any number of different ways. Almost without exception, the delegates at Paris thought and operated in the categories of the west European nation-state despite the fact that these categories were not consistent with the realities of the ethnic hodgepodge that existed in east-central and southeastern Europe. To be sure, the statutes of the League of Nations and the various treaties that made up the Paris peace settlement did provide for special agreements that guaranteed the protection of national minorities, which, in the case of Poland, remained in effect until 1939. But such agreements were designed not so much to safeguard the way of life and freedom of action of the newly created national minorities as to facilitate the process of national assimilation.

Any attempt to reorganize the European state system had to take into account the fact that the growing national awareness of even the smallest European nations had received new stimulus from the events of World War I. This was particularly true of the peoples of the multinational entities such as czarist Russia, the Austro-Hungarian monarchy, and the Ottoman Empire that had persisted almost as alien bodies in the predominantly nationalistic milieu of nineteenth-century Europe. Insofar as this had not already been accomplished by the Peace of Brest-Litovsk and the October Revolution, the task of creating a new international order fell to the Paris Peace Conference. The Western powers had long hesitated to go along with Masaryk's demand that the Habsburg monarchy be dismantled. In point of fact, however, the internal disintegration of the Habsburg monarchy was already so far advanced that, following the military collapse of the Central Powers, there was no way to prevent it from happening. The "nationalities manifesto" that Karl I, the last of the Habsburg rulers, issued in October 1918 came too late and was too halfhearted to divert the non-Germanic peoples of the empire from their quest for national independence.

It may very well be that one of the decisive oversights of the Allied powers at Paris was their failure to do anything on behalf of a Danubian Confederation that would have preserved some of the economic advantages that the peoples of the Habsburg Empire enjoyed by virtue of their membership in a large, integrated regional economy. Even then, however, it is likely that the national dynamic would soon have swept away any such attempt in this regard. The only other alternative was partition along national lines. In certain respects it was inevitable that the constitution of the "successor states" should take place at the expense of the previously "dominant" nations. Economic and historical arguments combined with France's tangible interests in winning for itself a reliable ally on Germany's southeastern flank to prevent the predominantly German areas of northern Bohemia and Moravia from becoming part of a German-Austrian republic and to deny the Polish majority in the Duchy of Teschen its right of self-determination. No less momentous was the failure of Masaryk and Beneš to grant autonomy to Slovakia in accordance with the Pittsburgh Agreement of 1917. At the same time, the Allies refused to permit the union of Austria with Germany despite strong support for this idea in the provisional Austrian National Assembly. Although such a union would have been of relatively minor economic and strategic significance, it would nevertheless have provided Germany with a measure of psychological compensation for the territorial losses it had suffered in the east. The Allies' refusal to go along with such a proposal can only be understood against the background of the traumatic reactions that German *Mitteleuropa* schemes since 1915 had elicited, above all in France.

The decisions reached by the statesmen assembled in Paris were shaped in part by nationalist pressures from the successor states and in part by inadequate ethnographic and historical knowledge. This, in turn, made it easier for the Allies to reward their erstwhile ally Romania with the acquisition of the Siebenbürgen, an area settled predominantly by people of German and Magyar descent, and the Banat, while the venerable Kingdom of Hungary was reduced by the Treaty of Trianon of 4 June 1920 to the status of a minor European state with the loss of more than two-thirds of its territory, including Slovakia, Croatia, and an area known as the *Burgenland*. Given these losses, the proclamation of the Hungarian Soviet Republic in March 1919 and the not altogether unrealistic hope of establishing direct contact with the Red Army that had been deployed against Poland can only be understood as an act of desperation in which Bolshevist and nationalist aspirations were intertwined. The fact that in August 1919 Allied troops cooperated with Romanian Free Corps units in installing the authoritarian regime of Admiral Miklos Horthy cast a shadow on the accomplishments of the Paris Peace Conference.

In their efforts to create a stable territorial order in southeast Europe, the statesmen of the Paris Peace Conference found themselves confronted with a task that in many respects simply overwhelmed their capabilities. Neither in Carinthia nor in the Tyrol, neither in Dalmatia nor along the Croatian-Italian frontier was it possible to achieve a peaceful solution to the age-old conflict between the indigenous nationalities. The surprise attack that Gabriele d'Annunzio launched against Fiume on 11 September 1919 — the day after the Allies and the newly founded Austrian Republic signed the Peace of Saint-Germain — underscored Allied impotence to create political stability in this part of Europe. The Kingdom of the Serbs, Croats, and Slovenes — known after 1929 as Yugoslavia — achieved the status of a middle-sized power but revealed serious internal weaknesses that left its long-term stability in doubt. Only by means of a royal dictatorship were the Serbs able to maintain their administrative centralism over the rest of the country. The newly formed states in territory formerly dominated by the Ottoman Empire remained fundamentally unstable. Mustafa Kemal's revolutionary conquest of power effectively nullified the Peace of Sèvres, which the Allies had imposed on Turkey on 10 August 1920 without the support of the United States. Following a lengthy period of military and diplomatic conflict, the Peace of Lausanne in 1923 finally restored a temporary and superficial calm to this region.

Of far greater importance was the question of whether the Allies would

succeed in achieving a stable new order in eastern Europe. It was in the ideological and economic interest of the Western powers to erect a barrier against
Bolshevist Russia—the so-called Cordon Sanitaire—and to contain the contamination of the October Revolution through the creation of a strong and
independent Poland and the formation of the Baltic states of Estonia, Latvia,
and Lithuania. As it became increasingly clear after February 1919 that the
"White Guards" under Admiral Aleksandr Koltshak and then later General
Peter Wrangell were not going to win their civil war against the Bolshevik
regime, the maintenance of such a buffer was more important than ever, particularly insofar as the Western powers—but especially Great Britain—were
intimidated by the prospect of bitter protest by their industrial labor force
from intervening with their own military forces. Lloyd George pleaded in vain
that the Bolshevist government should be invited to take part in the Paris
Peace Conference but did not even have the unqualified support of his own
government.

The exclusion of Soviet Russia from the deliberations of the Paris Peace
Conference proved to be a serious error, particularly insofar as the Allies hoped
to establish a lasting new order in Europe. Having suffered the outright loss
of Poland and the Baltics as well as having been pushed back from the Darda-
nelles, Soviet Russia was clearly among the losers of the war. In the long run,
the Allied refusal to seek the political integration of such a power was bound
to encourage a pro-Russian orientation in the foreign policy of postwar Germany. For the time being, however, this perspective was not yet apparent. As
long as its political activities were subject to the intervention of the Western
powers, Germany refrained from reestablishing the diplomatic ties with the
Soviet government that had been severed in 1918 following the assassination
of the German ambassador to Moscow. In fact, Germany even permitted Józef
Haller's Polish army to pass through its territory in the hope that this might
elicit compensation from the Allies.

For a time the German military command continued to harbor the illusion that it would obtain Allied authorization, if not active Allied support,
for a renewed march on Saint Petersburg. But even this temporary strain in
German-Soviet relations did not prompt the German government to come to
Poland's aid in its struggle against the unexpectedly successful invasion of the
Red Army the following summer, though by doing so it would have, in the
words of Winston Churchill, performed "a most distinguished service to civilization." For its own part, the German government was secretly counting on
the defeat of Poland and the restoration of Germany's prewar eastern boundaries in accordance with promises made by the Soviet commissar for foreign
affairs, Georgi V. Chicherin. But that was before Marshal Józef Piłsudski had
accomplished his famous "miracle on the Vistula." Having forced the retreat
of the Soviet units—though not without the active help of French military ad-

visors under the command of General Maxime Weygand—Piłsudski was in a position to move the Polish frontier considerably to the east of the line proposed by Lord Curzon with the signing of the Peace of Riga on 18 March 1921. The Polish victory in the east led to intensified pressure in Upper Silesia from Polish Free Corps units under the command of Wojciech Korfanty. While the German government was prohibited from taking military measures and was left with no recourse but to encourage the formation of self-defense units (*Selbstschutzverbände*), the occupying powers—and especially the French—did little to prevent an increasingly imminent Polish insurrection. Following the referendum of 1921, this would lead to renewed armed confrontation throughout the area.

The restoration of independence to the Polish Republic—a goal of European democracy ever since the *Vormärz*—was achieved primarily at the expense of Germany. After the collapse of their alliance with Russia, the French staked their security interests primarily on their Polish partner, with whom they enjoyed long-standing cultural and political ties. The creation of the Polish Corridor was inspired by an obsolete dogma that the economic viability of a state depended on its access to the sea. In German public opinion, the loss of this territory and the separation of East Prussia from the rest of Germany represented an act of national humiliation. The fact that it was only as a result of Anglo-Saxon protests that East Prussia remained part of Germany and that Danzig was permitted to retain its primarily German character as a free city under the supervision of the League of Nations went largely unacknowledged. While in southern East Prussia and in the West Prussian areas south of the Vistula the referenda on the future disposition of these areas had by and large favored the German position, the loss of the greater part of the Prussian provinces of West Prussia and Posen as well as the surrender of Memel to Lithuania were denounced by virtually every political faction in Germany as a violation of national honor. The final result, however, would not have been appreciably different had ethnic considerations been given greater weight in drawing the new frontiers.

A feeling of cultural superiority vis-à-vis the Polish, a tendency to forget the ruthless "Germanizing" policy of the imperial era, and the mystique of German settlements and eastward expansion all combined to create the impression of an irreconcilable enmity between Poland and Germany that the former did little to discourage with its incessant nationalist posturing. In February 1920 the chief of the *Truppenamt*, General Hans von Seeckt, remarked: "No German must lift a finger to save Poland—that mortal enemy of Germany, that creature and ally of France, that robber of German soil and destroyer of German culture—from Bolshevism; and if the Devil wants to get Poland, we should help him do it." Friedrich Engels's prophetic words that the freedom of Poland is the "measuring rod for the freedom of Europe" seemed to have been lost on the German Left. For while the German public could reluctantly accept the loss of territory in the west — Alsace-Lorraine and Eupen-Malmedy as well as some territorial adjustments in Schleswig — this was not so in the case of Germany's eastern frontiers. The struggle over the political future of Upper Silesia thus assumed a crucial place in German domestic politics.

The great powers had seen the introduction of parliamentary institutions as a means of forging a greater degree of internal political homogeneity in the hope that this, in turn, would foster the cause of collective security. Yet the new small and middle-sized states of central and eastern Europe were often divided by sharp internal social conflicts, not the least of which was the threat of a Communist takeover. In situations like these, nationalism assumed an indispensable role as an instrument of social and political integration. The net effect of this, however, was to weaken further the position of the insufficiently developed bourgeois-liberal forces vis-à-vis reactionary factions that often commanded the active support of the military. This was one of the major reasons why virtually none of the newly established parliamentary systems in central and eastern Europe proved viable.

After the installation of the Horthy regime in Hungary, the next country to part company with the liberal constitutional states was Italy under the leadership of Benito Mussolini. One by one, the majority of the small and middle-sized states took the path to authoritarian or semifascist systems, whereby the initial impulse generally came from tensions with unassimilable national minorities. In the Polish Republic the bloc of national minorities was effectively isolated and finally broken by electoral manipulations and Piłsudski's unabashed use of terrorist tactics. This signaled the end of the Polish parliamentary system and its replacement by a regime of colonels, which in 1926 secured its power through a constitutional revision that was to serve as a model for Gaullism after World War II. An important exception to this general trend was to be found in Czechoslovakia, where Masaryk and Beneš were able to isolate the radical-nationalist opposition of the German minorities and secure the loyal cooperation of the majority of the German parties until the beginning of the 1930s. At the same time, discrimination against the Slovak People's Party and the Polish population continued unabated. The relative viability of Czechoslovakia's parliamentary system stemmed in no small part from the diplomatic and financial support of the French as well as from the stabilizing effect of its rivalry with Hungary, Poland, and, at least potentially, Germany.

In all of this, the first Austrian Republic constituted a special case. Following the transitional period of radical parliamentary democracy, Austria adopted a constitutional compromise in 1920 that remained more or less intact until 1933–34, notwithstanding amendments in 1929 that were designed to strengthen presidential power. For their own part, the two leading parties — the Social Democrats and the Christian Socialists — either deprecated bourgeois parliamentarism as a transitional stage on the road to socialist rule or were inclined to sacrifice it to corporatist-authoritarian models of order, while the Greater German Party (Großdeutsche Partei) and the Rural League (Landbund) categorically denied the republic's right to exist and agitated for union with Germany. In spite of the latent civil war that threatened to erupt with the burning of the Austrian Palace of Justice in 1927, Austria's continued fiscal dependence on the West, which had begun with the adoption of the Geneva Protocol in 1922, contributed to the stabilization of Austria's parliamentary regime. In all other cases, the democratization process inaugurated by the Allies in 1919 ended in failure, thus creating a situation of permanent political instability that only encouraged aggressors to intervene.

In his Fourteen Points, President Wilson had advocated the founding of a League of Nations for the purpose of "affording large and small States alike mutual guarantees of political independence and territorial integrity." In Wilson' eyes, this was tantamount to the introduction of the democratic principle. Wilson was therefore inclined to deny membership in the League of Nations to autocratically ruled monarchies. The realities of international politics, however, soon put an end to such high expectations. In the face of the continued existence of the Bolshevist regime in Russia, the Western system of collective security came more and more to assume the function of protecting capitalism from radical-socialist experiments. The twofold objective of containing efforts to revise the Paris peace settlement and of holding the threat of communism in check made it impossible for the Allies to pursue a policy based on principles in the grand style of the past.

Even before his arrival in Paris, Wilson had been obliged to modify his objectives to a considerable extent. The first casualty was the principle of open diplomacy. From a preliminary meeting of the major Western governments emerged the official peace conference, which took place without representatives from the Central Powers and Soviet Russia. By the same token, the Western powers were successful in pressing their objections to Germany's immediate admission to the League of Nations. Initially Wilson had envisaged a probationary period during which Germany would demonstrate its democratic reliability. This gave way to an agreement stipulating that Germany could apply for admission to the League of Nations only after it had fulfilled its reparations obligations, a provision that did not necessarily contradict Wilson's commitment to a peace of understanding and equity but conformed to his call for punitive measures against aggressor nations. In the same vein, Wilson supported the conversion of the German colonies into territories ruled by mandates from the League of Nations, a measure that represented the first step toward a more general decolonization of the non-European world.

The fear of "Bolshevization" played only a passing role in the decision to exclude Germany from the League of Nations. A far more important consideration was the fact that Wilson and most of his advisors regarded the Ebert-Scheidemann cabinet as nothing but a continuation of imperial Germany in a different guise. Hopes of bringing to power a government more willing to sign the treaty gave rise to sporadic efforts to support the USPD. But in the final analysis the fear of forcing Germany too obviously to the left was decisive, so that those advisors who advocated a policy of strengthening moderate political forces ultimately prevailed. Wilson, however, had no intention of making concessions to the leaders of the Weimar Republic. In this respect, he failed to recognize that the decision to block Germany's participation in the League of Nations would have the effect of disavowing precisely those groups such as the German Society for the League of Nations (Deutscher Liga für den Völkerbund) that identified themselves with the league's original goals. On the other hand, it is unlikely that Allied concessions on this point would have had much effect on the increasingly nationalistic mood that was sweeping through Germany. It was characteristic of the general climate that when Eduard Bernstein described nine-tenths of the Versailles treaty as inevitable at the Social Democratic party congress in June 1919, he was immediately accused of employing "talmudist" argumentation. Even moderate Social Democrats like Hermann Müller agreed with this characterization despite its clearly anti-Semitic overtones.

Germany's exclusion from the League of Nations saddled this body with the odium of being a forum for the victorious powers. It is unlikely that this fundamental mutation in the League of Nations' character could have been averted had not the U.S. Senate destroyed the very foundation of Wilson's European policy by blocking ratification of the Versailles peace treaty. Without the participation of the United States, the League of Nations was quickly transformed into an instrument of French security policy. The primary objective of this policy was to preserve the constellation of power that had been created by the Paris peace settlement. Under these circumstances, the extremely narrow grounds that Article 19 of the Covenant of the League of Nations recognized for the revision of the treaties seemed irrelevant from the perspective of German policy makers. Furthermore, the League of Nations was unable, even in the early 1920s, to find the means for quelling the violent conflicts that erupted throughout the world and that frequently escalated to the level of extensive military operations. Nor did the League of Nations make the French any less dependent on the bilateral treaties by which they tried to perpetuate the dominating position they had acquired in 1919. On the contrary, many states—but especially those that sought to revise the Paris peace settlement—sought to bypass the institutions of collective security and return to the secret diplomacy of the prewar era. Eventually, even the Soviet Union came to favor this route.

To Wilson, who for the sake of the League of Nations had made far-reaching concessions that in some cases ran counter to his own principles, the distortion of what he had originally envisaged for the League of Nations must have come as a painful blow. Even then, one could still muster some hope that the principle of international cooperation would eventually prevail. A total condemnation of the American president's policy and the Paris peace settlement — and with it the Versailles peace treaty — is therefore unjustified. In the final analysis, the problems facing the Paris Peace Conference were much more complicated than those that confronted the Congress of Vienna. Moreover, the danger that the Bolshevik Revolution might spread throughout central Europe and Wilson's lack of political support at home meant that the Allied powers had to operate under extreme time pressure. In his dealings with the Western powers, the president thus found himself obliged to compromise his principles and goals to a far greater extent than he might have done under more favorable circumstances. Had Wilson given in to his impulses and withdrawn from the negotiations under protest, this would have amounted to little more than an admission of defeat. Such a step, which the German side fully expected Wilson to take, would also have furthered the purposes of the French Right, which preferred a state of cold war similar to what was to emerge from World War II to a formal peace settlement. Yet for the sake of economic reconstruction — a pressing necessity for victors and vanquished alike — even peace agreements with obvious flaws were preferable to an uncertain state between war and peace in which the domestic tranquillity of every nation would have been severely jeopardized.

The Versailles peace treaty was to a large extent dictated by French security interests. Seen in the light of subsequent developments, these concerns cannot be dismissed as irrelevant. It is true, nevertheless, that in this respect Great Britain gave the French only halfhearted support. In his Fontainebleau memorandum of 25 March 1919 British Prime Minister David Lloyd George had pleaded for the fair treatment of Germany as the only way it could be placed in position to fulfill its treaty obligations. This was perfectly consistent with Britain's interests in preserving Germany as a future trading partner, especially since the growing independence movements throughout the Commonwealth would make the British increasingly dependent on the European market. It was for these reasons that Lloyd George had thwarted the French ambitions to acquire a frontier on the Rhine, although he was unable to prevent the demilitarization of a fifty-kilometer buffer on its right bank or the Allied occupation of its left bank for periods of five, ten, and fifteen years.

On the same day that the Versailles peace treaty was signed, Great Britain sought to appease the French obsession with security by concluding an agreement that pledged British support for France should Germany violate the treaty's demilitarization provisions. This agreement, however, was contingent on the ratification of an identical agreement with the United States; its rejection by the U.S. Senate meant that it would not become internationally binding.

Such a stipulation could only intensify French nervousness over the danger of a revival of German power. French foreign policy thus sought to compensate for the lack of formal support France had received from Great Britain and the United States through the political and economic penetration of Austria and Czechoslovakia and the conclusion of close diplomatic and financial ties with Poland, a country whose strengthening had always been a major aim of the Quai d'Orsay's eastern policy.

Germany, of course, presented an insoluble dilemma for French foreign policy. Ideally, France would liked to have seen not only a Rhine frontier and the establishment of Rhenish buffer states but, if possible, the dissolution of German national unity. To this extent, those in Germany who favored accepting the peace treaty were correct in their claim that this had saved the unity of the nation. The minimal goal of French foreign policy was to diminish Germany's economic potential in favor of France, a goal that presupposed — since the direct seizure of German assets was out of the question — an adequate recovery of the German economy. By comparison, the occupation and demilitarization of the Rhineland were no more than temporary expedients that would simply postpone the dreaded revival of German power. It was therefore only logical that French policy insisted on the strictest possible compliance with the treaty's disarmament provisions and on verification by an interallied military commission. At the Spa Conference — the German government's first official meeting with the Entente — the subject of disarmament thus overshadowed the reparations question.

Throughout all of this, General von Seeckt desperately clung to the illusion that domestic social tensions would make it possible for Germany to circumvent the armament provisions of the Versailles peace treaty and maintain an armed force of 200,000 men or, at the very least, postpone demobilization for the near future. In response to this argument, France insisted that neither the security police units, which consisted by and large of former military personnel and were actually housed in barracks, nor the civilian defense forces, or *Einwohnerwehren,* were to be counted as civilian formations. The national government's long-drawn-out struggle with Bavaria, which only in 1923 agreed to dissolve its civilian defense forces, highlighted the tendency of the military and political Right to ignore the threat of sanctions in the hope that it would still be possible to circumvent the stipulations of the Versailles peace treaty. Illegal military formations, secret weapons caches, and frontier patrol units continued to be tolerated. Even then, however, the French were successful in bringing about a reduction in the number of right-wing paramilitary organizations in spite of the fact that Bavaria continued to offer safe haven for the patriotic units that had grown out of the Free Corps.

Even if the decision to restrict Germany to a professional army was problematic from the perspective of the country's democratic integration, it nevertheless represented the only means of averting a rapid regeneration of German armed power. The prohibition against the production and use of modern weaponry served the same purpose. Although the Reichswehr tried as early as 1921 to evade these measures by entering into secret military collaboration with Soviet Russia, their net effect was to severely weaken Germany's military strength until the 1930s. Haunted by the material costs of the recent war, the French military was fully cognizant of the fact that limitations on manpower were of secondary importance to holding the armaments industry in check. It was for this reason, therefore, that the French sought to inflict permanent damage on the productive potential of German heavy industry. This, in the final analysis, was the true purpose of the economic sanctions that had been imposed on Germany since 1919. For the occupation of the Rhineland as well as the foreign trade restrictions on German heavy industry were limited to little more than a half decade. If by then France had not succeeded in breaking the continental dominance of German heavy industry, the fruits of victory—at least from the French perspective—would have been squandered in peace.

At the outset, the situation seemed to favor French aims. Including the losses that Germany would suffer in 1921 through the separation of the industrial areas of Upper Silesia, the Paris peace settlement deprived the German economy of 75 percent of its iron ore reserves, 68 percent of its zinc ores deposits, and 26 percent of its coal production, as well as 44 and 38 percent of its pig iron and steel production, respectively. The appropriation of coal from the Saar, on the other hand, was not sufficient to cover the energy needs of the French economy, particularly pressing since the German occupation of the coal mines in Belgium and northern France had resulted in heavy damage. Moreover, coal mined in the Saar was not suitable for smelting the minette from the newly reacquired region of Lorraine. By requiring Germany to supply 40 million tons of anthracite coal, the French hoped to prevent German heavy industry from resuming full production so that their country might gain the dominant position in continental steel production.

This strategy failed for a variety of reasons. In the first place, German coal deliveries fell short of the quantities anticipated by the French even though these had begun before the treaty took effect. This was to be attributed first and foremost to the overexploitation of German mines during the war. Second, repeated strikes and the total inadequacy of food supplies in the mining areas of the Ruhr had produced a sharp decline in production. At the Spa Conference, which had been postponed until July 1920 as a result of elections to the German Reichstag, the Allies were able to pressure Germany into agreeing to increased coal deliveries that were to be credited to the German reparations account not only at inflated domestic prices, but also with a surcharge of five gold marks per ton. Even then, what the Germans were able to supply still fell far short of French demands. Otto Hue, head of the League of German Mine

Workers (Verband der Bergarbeiter Deutschlands), had convinced the Allies of the need to provide Germany with foreign currency for the purchase of food, while, on the other hand, the inflammatory statements of industrialist Hugo Stinnes, a member of the German delegation at Spa, prompted the Belgian foreign minister to remark: "What would have happened to us if such a man had had the opportunity to come here as a victor?"

In emulating Brockdorff-Rantzau's adamant refusal to compromise, Stinnes clearly revealed the sense of superiority that prevailed within the ranks of west German heavy industry. Industrial circles had prophesied as early as 1918 that the French would be unable to sell their minette. To help this prediction come true, German iron and steel producers used what little foreign currency assets they had at their disposal to liquidate their war debts with Sweden and thus lay the groundwork for the conclusion of long-term supply contracts with that country in 1922. At the same time, the increased use of scrap metal and the widespread adoption of the Bessemer smelting process produced substantial savings in the consumption of coal. By 1922 German steel production in the Ruhr had already reached the production figures of 1913, and systematic efforts to expand capacity in the production of iron and steel undermined French efforts to make Germany's raw material industries dependent on French supplies. As a result of the inflationary boom German heavy industry enjoyed a period of virtually full employment, whereas French iron and steel producers were unable to operate at full capacity because of insufficient coal supplies and concern that its products would not find a suitable market.

By the same token, French expectations with respect to the coal sector also failed to materialize. For while the deliveries that Germany was obliged to make posed serious supply problems at home — though not so much for the steel industry as for the fertilizer and manufacturing industries — they stimulated the widespread rationalization of German industry and prompted new investments that were subsequently passed on to the consumer in the form of indirect public subsidies and domestic price increases. By insisting that Germany fulfill its reparations obligations through the shipment of coal, the French found themselves confronted with the added difficulty that its own heavy industry was anxious not to jeopardize the sale of its minette and therefore preferred to negotiate directly with the German firms rather than wait for the cumbersome state bureaucracy to take its own course. In point of fact, this policy had the effect of creating excess capacities in the heavy industrial sector on both sides of the Rhine, which before long were to become a serious domestic and foreign policy liability.

While the Spa Conference succeeded in producing a compromise on coal that the Germans still had difficulty accepting, the German delegation failed in its efforts to couple the premature establishment of Germany's reparations burden with a reduction of foreign trade restrictions and Allied concessions on the question of Upper Silesia. To be sure, Germany had been able to gain a measure of sympathy for its cash flow problems at several of the conferences of specialists that preceded the meeting in Spa. Still, the Fehrenbach government was unwilling to go beyond its original offer of annual payments of 30 billion gold marks for a period limited to thirty years with the possibility of somewhat larger installments in the event of economic recovery. The cabinet dismissed a temporary solution proposed by the French financial expert Charles Seydoux for annual payments of 3 billion gold marks for a period of five years, at which time Germany's reparations burden would be formally established as unacceptable, and thus lost the initiative to the Allies. This, in turn, proved to be a serious tactical error. For while France chaired the reparations commission and could normally count on the support of Belgium and Italy, it was generally more receptive to the arguments of the financial experts than the conferences of Allied governmental leaders.

At the end of January 1921 the Allied governments fixed the amount of Germany's financial obligations at 226 billion gold marks, payable in forty-two annual installments, in addition to a supplemental transfer amounting to 12 percent of the value of German export trade. This triggered widespread dismay in Berlin, particularly since the note from Paris called for strict control over German financial and monetary policies and thus represented a serious encroachment on German sovereignty. After considerable delay, the German government decided to accept an invitation to attend the conference that was scheduled to take place in London in February 1921, no doubt in the hope that it could win at least partial acceptance for a counterproposal that, for the first time, named a specific sum the Germans were prepared to pay. By proposing to pay a maximum figure of 50 billion gold marks—an amount equal to the nominal value of the forty-two annual payments demanded by the Allies—the German government was actually offering much less, since it placed the value of the payments in cash and kind it had made since the armistice at 20 billion marks. Though subject to verification by a commission of independent experts, this calculation of what Germany had paid aroused widespread indignation among the Allies. At the same time, the German counterproposal reiterated German demands for the retention of Upper Silesia and the removal of all restrictions on foreign trade. Furthermore, the German counterproposal asked for an international loan of 8 billion gold marks that was to be used in liquidating Germany's remaining reparations obligations plus interest accumulating at a rate of 5 percent per year and a 1 percent redemption fee for the settlement of any outstanding obligations.

In the final analysis, however, it was not so much the way in which the German government juggled its figures as its attempt to make compliance with the Versailles peace treaty conditional upon its revision that prompted Lloyd George to adjourn the conference and to threaten Germany with sanctions in case of noncompliance with the Paris resolutions. When the Fehrenbach government did not withdraw its counterproposal, the Allies reacted by occupying Düsseldorf, Duisburg, and Ruhrort on 8 March and by placing the customs administration of the occupied territory in the hands of the International Rhineland Commission. The German government tried in vain to enlist the Vatican and the United States as mediators in its conflict with the Allies at the same time that it tried to avoid a debate in the Reichstag on the impasse over reparations. Nowhere was the government's weakness more apparent than in the way it clung to the illusion that it could pressure the Allies into making concessions on the reparations question by emphasizing the legal correctness of the German position and reviving the campaign against the war-guilt clause. By the time the London payment plan arrived in Berlin on 5 May 1921 with somewhat milder terms than those formulated in Paris, however, the Fehrenbach government had already resigned.

The London Ultimatum, which thanks to Lloyd George's intervention gave Germany six days to respond and which threatened the occupation of the Ruhr in the event of nonacceptance, set the amount of Germany's reparations burden at 132 billion gold marks. The German demand that an upper limit be set was thus fulfilled, though in point of fact only provisionally. For at the outset the German government had only to raise 50 billion marks — 12 million at once in the form of A-bonds and an additional 38 million by November 1921 in the form of B-bonds. The remaining C-bond obligations in the amount of 82 billion marks would come due only when the reparations commission had decided that the German economy was capable of absorbing this burden. Among the experts there was general agreement that this last sum would never be paid. The London payment schedule thus met the German offer of 50 billion marks, though without including the payments in cash and kind that had already been made. More burdensome was the obligation to surrender 26 percent of the value of German exports. This would require annual payments of approximately 3 billion marks, the first of which would come due on 31 August 1921.

In domestic politics, the Allied threat of sanctions had a profound effect. Whereas the Fehrenbach government had done its best to sidestep the question and had made no serious effort to deal with the reparations problem, the parties and the interest groups that stood behind them were now faced with the alternative of either accepting the Allied payment schedule and fulfilling its obligations to the best of their ability or resigning themselves to the occupation of the Ruhr and the dangers this implied for national unity. Under these circumstances, Gustav Stresemann decided to face reality and to accept the terms of the London plan. But the right wing of the DVP with close ties to German heavy industry succeeded in blocking acceptance of the London Ultimatum and thus forced the DVP to resign from the cabinet. Stresemann, who was already in close contact with British Ambassador Edgar Lord d'Abernon, had hoped that acceptance of the ultimatum would clear the way for his appointment as German foreign minister. Instead, another cabinet supported by the parties of the Weimar Coalition came into being. Led by Joseph Wirth from the left wing of the German Center Party, this cabinet did not command a parliamentary majority but could nevertheless count on the toleration of the USPD in matters related to reparations.

The new chancellor had been finance minister in the Fehrenbach government, where he had steadfastly supported the continuation of Erzberger's fiscal reforms. He now coined the expression "fulfillment policy," which was quickly seized by the Right as a term of censure. By making a sincere effort to fulfill the terms of the London payment schedule, which was accepted by a parliamentary majority on 10 May 1921, Wirth hoped to demonstrate the limits of Germany's ability to pay and thus lay the foundation for the conclusion of a politically acceptable compromise on the reparations question. While the government was able to pay its July installment by somewhat unorthodox means, by the end of the year it found itself confronted with virtually insurmountable difficulties in securing credit. Under these circumstances, the cabinet was obliged to ask the reparations commissions for a moratorium — first for the remainder of the year 1922 and then, citing the dramatic fall of the mark, for 1923 and 1924 as well. It also became necessary to intensify its negotiations for an international loan for the purposes of stabilizing the mark, even though the government had not yet fulfilled the mandate of the reparations commission for a balanced budget. When Aristide Briand, who resigned as French premier during the Cannes Conference, was replaced by the less conciliatory Raymond Poincaré, the danger of a Ruhr occupation became more immediate.

That Wirth was even able to move toward a policy of conciliation was closely tied to the situation in Upper Silesia. In the referendum held on 21 May 1921, 60 percent of those who had voted favored remaining with Germany. A considerable portion of those who supported the German position had in fact come to Upper Silesia for the sole purpose of casting a vote. Uncertain as to how the results of the referendum were to be interpreted, the Allied Supreme Council decided to place the decision in the hands of the League of Nations, which in early October recommended that the province be partitioned. When the frontiers were subsequently redrawn at the request of the Allies, the more heavily industrialized parts of the province were assigned to Poland. Here Germany had obtained a clear majority in the cities but had been overwhelmingly outvoted in the surrounding agricultural areas. The Germans bitterly alleged that the Polish insurgents under Korfanty had interfered with the elections but made no mention of the fact that ever since 1918 the province had been governed almost exclusively by emergency decrees and that nothing had been done to reach an understanding with the Polish part of the population.

The setback in the Upper Silesian question spelled the end of Germany's willingness to support to policy of "conditional fulfillment," even though Joseph Wirth and Walther Rathenau, the former minister for reconstruction who was appointed foreign minister in the second Wirth cabinet, continued their efforts in this direction. The Wiesbaden Accord that Rathenau and Louis Loucheur, the French minister for the liberated regions, negotiated in October 1921, represented a serious attempt to achieve economic cooperation through direct negotiations with industry and to further the reconstruction of damaged regions of northern France through the use of German materiel and labor. This agreement was thwarted essentially by the distrust that French industry harbored toward its German competitors as well as by the British feeling that the accord discriminated against its own economic interests since German aid was to be deducted from its general reparations account. By the same token, efforts to persuade German heavy industry to conclude direct agreements with its French counterparts were unsuccessful. For his own person, Hugo Stinnes tended to delay negotiations until he could develop a position of economic superiority from which he could negotiate with French industry.

The policy of fulfillment collapsed first and foremost because the German business community systematically sabotaged the reform of national finances and the payment of reparations. In this respect, it was supported by public opinion, which was virtually unanimous in denouncing Allied demands as illegal or, at the very least, as extremely exaggerated. By the time of the London Conference, it had become clear that the threat to impose sanctions was by no means an empty gesture on the part of the Allies. The German failure to avoid sanctions was as much a matter of vested economic interest as one of ideological posturing. To be sure, Germany's economic situation in 1920 was still critical, partly as a consequence of the accumulated burdens of the war and the strike waves of the revolutionary phase but, more importantly because of the shortage of raw materials and the obstacles to a resumption of foreign trade. Industrial production in the first years after the end of the war were decidedly below the level reached in 1913, although by 1922 it had benefited from the stimulus of inflation to regain three-fourths of the prewar figure. The gross national product had decidedly decreased in comparison with the prewar years, but it was not much lower than that of France or England. Despite the loss of Upper Silesia and the Saar, Germany's economic capacity had remained essentially intact. The steep decline of exports resulted not only from the restrictions of the Versailles peace treaty but also reflected the general state of the world market. Nevertheless, Germany accumulated a foreign trade deficit of considerable proportions. Under these circumstances, the sum of 20 billion marks that was supposed to be paid by 1 May 1921 was simply too high. A further problem for the transfer of reparations payments was the rapid inflation of the German mark, for the recipients were no longer willing to accept German exports in the same amount as before. The shortage of foreign currency also arose from the fact that German firms left their foreign accounts abroad and that the German Reichsbank was reluctant to touch its remaining gold reserves in anticipation of a future currency reform.

Nor was the domestic economy in a position to produce the yearly payments that were due under the London plan, even though public expenditures in relation to the national income had been cut by 20 percent since 1918 and continued to decline. The tax rate rose from 9 to 17 percent between 1913 and 1925, but was much lower during the inflationary phase, at least among the self-employed. The reparations commission was therefore certainly justified in criticizing tax revenues as insufficient. Indeed, effective means to increase tax revenues could have been deployed under Erzberger's fiscal reform. Under these circumstances, the Wirth government responded to increased pressure from the Allies by implementing a new tax policy. While the introduction of the Reich Emergency Levy (Reichsnotopfer) was designed to counter large-scale protests by the Social Democrats and labor unions against increases in indirect taxes, its effects were minimized by the tactics of the bourgeois parties. It is a telling fact that the withholding of income tax—a measure from which the self-employed were exempted—proved far more effective. In other respects as well, the redistributive effects intended by the Erzberger reform were definitely muted, since in the interest of economic "rearmament" the government granted tax breaks to businesses and holders of capital.

Distressed by the growing unfairness of the tax system, the socialist parties demanded that war and postwar profits be taxed under the motto "Taxation of real values" (Erfassung der Sachwerte). However, the proposal of a one-time tax levied on immobile property unleashed such a storm of protest on the part of the agrarian and industrial interest groups that it stood no chance of approval in the Reichstag. Yet this was the only way in which financial stabilization could be achieved, for as long as there was no mechanism for taxing gains resulting from the inflation, taxation itself would never provide the state with the fixed-value assets it needed to meet its reparations obligations. This is precisely why the Wirth government appealed to the major industrial associations to assist in raising the annual payments through a credit action that would involve both mortgaging their physical plants and mobilizing their considerable foreign currency holdings. This proposal led to nothing despite a seemingly endless series of meetings on the subject. The negative outcome of the referendum on Upper Silesia further weakened the willingness of industrial associations to come to the government's aid. Thus industry made its extension of a loan to the state contingent not only on stringent austerity measures in the public sector, but also on the privatization of the national railroad. In this respect, industry's ultimate objective was to dismantle the social and political achievements of the recent revolution, including most of all the eight-hour day.

What began as a loan action to ensure the government's solvency thus ended up, for all practical purposes, as a negotiation for the takeover of the national railroad by big business, a step to which the SPD, USPD, and labor unions were vigorously opposed. The same fate awaited the fiscal reform. By the time the long-overdue tax compromise came into being, inflation had already made its terms meaningless.

The general public erroneously believed that the inflation and German reparations payments to the Allies were inextricably linked. This, however, was not the case before the final phases of the inflation—and then only to a certain extent. The principal cause of the inflation was the excessive national debt that Germany had incurred in financing the war. After the armistice all participants had more or less quietly agreed that carrying out demobilization as smoothly as possible, priming the economic pump, and maintaining social peace assumed priority over balancing the national budget. For its own part, industry knew very well that it could pass on whatever wage concessions it might be obliged to make as a result of the inflation to the consumer. Admittedly, the expense of supporting war victims and surviving dependents, as well as indemnities for private losses resulting from the peace treaty, constituted a heavy drain on the public budgets, which were never able to generate the tax revenues necessary to keep pace with increased expenditures. At the same time, there was a general reluctance to initiate layoffs in the public sector, particularly in the railroad. In the meantime, efforts to maintain liquidity by printing new money and the generous credit policy of the Reichsbank only served to intensify the inflationary pressures that were already at work in the economy. To be sure, there was a relative stabilization of the mark in 1920-21 as a result of investments by foreign speculators. After the summer of 1922, however, the pace of inflation began to accelerate rapidly.

As long as the reparations question remained unsettled, Reichsbank President Rudolf Havenstein and the National Federation of German Industry felt that a currency reform was neither possible nor desirable. In this respect, they were concerned that the mark might be stabilized at too high a level to make German industry competitive in the international market. Moreover, it did not seem to be a particularly good idea to demonstrate the limits of Germany's economic capacity to pay in such a manner. There were, therefore, compelling economic and political factors that made recourse to deflationary measures, such as those that were currently causing widespread unemployment in Great Britain, unacceptable for the time being. The argument that Germany made to the outside world—namely, that a deflationary policy was justified only in the presence of a foreign trade surplus—concealed the vested interests that stood to gain from continued inflation. For the inflation proved to be a genuine benefit to those Germans—and primarily the industrialists—who possessed tangible as opposed to paper-mark assets. If nothing else, the inflation made it possible for companies and plants to pay off their debts with currency that was no longer worth as much as the currency in which those debts had been contracted. Public finances also benefited from the inflation, but not so the agricultural sector. The fact that the value of the mark declined more rapidly on the domestic than on the international market contributed to high profits in foreign trade and, paradoxically, subsidized the financing of imports. Not only did the constant increase in the circulation of money and the resultant erosion of real interest make it possible to obtain cheap credit, but it also caused Germany's capital investors to seek shelter in tangible assets, such as new industrial plants and stock inventories to fill warehouses. And finally, the devaluation of the currency meant that any taxes that were not subject to withholding were worth only a fraction of their original value.

The effect of inflation was most disastrous for persons on fixed incomes or pensions and for those in the service sector. Labor unions and wage earners initially benefited from the inflationary economic policy that permitted industry to respond to demands for higher wages. Hugo Stinnes, who had played a major role in the formation of the Zentralarbeitsgemeinschaft (ZAG), felt that concessions to workers were justified as a way of preventing their radicalization and of countering pressure for nationalization. In the same way, Stinnes also hoped to win the unions' support for the price policies pursued by industry and for the abolition of state economic controls. This, after all, was the real purpose of the Zentralarbeitsgemeinschaft. Whereas the labor unions regarded the ZAG as an opportunity to help shape the country's long-term economic policy, there was a tacit understanding among industrialists that this "historical compromise" would remain in effect only temporarily, that is, until the normalization of the economy, which was expected to take place once reparations had been paid.

As the inflation continued, it began to have an increasingly heavy effect on wage earners as well. Not only did nominal wages fail to keep pace with the inflationary spiral, but wage negotiations resulted in indexed wages and shortened pay periods only when hyperinflation had begun. All of this favored a gradual shift of power within the economy to the employers, whose solidarity increased as the concentration of economic power—exemplified by the economic empire that Hugo Stinnes had created out of thin air—gathered more and more momentum. An impressive reflection of the increased self-confidence of heavy industry was the economic program that Paul Silverberg submitted to the National Federation of German Industry in 1922. This program made industry's cooperation in the efforts to stabilize the German currency contingent upon dismantling the social achievements of 1919, repealing the eight-hour day, and ending the controlled economy. Industry's newly won power expressed itself politically, as it had done on the occasion of the ill-fated industrial credit action in the fall of 1921, in demands that the DVP be brought into the cabinet.

In the eyes of the German business community, governmental participation "would be seen as a tangible sign that Germany's leading industrial sectors had assumed their share of responsibility for the reparations."

The "grand coalition cabinet of national resistance" for which Stresemann had hoped, however, never came into existence, even though Wirth was inclined to bring the DVP into his cabinet because he regarded cooperation with the industrial circles from which the party drew much of its strength as indispensable. For in October 1921 Wirth was forced to resign as chancellor after what Lord d'Abernon sarcastically dismissed as a "contrived international crisis" over the partition of Upper Silesia made it impossible for him to place his cabinet on a firm parliamentary footing. The crisis was precipitated in the first place by the DDP, whose neurotic compulsion to demonstrate its nationalist credentials led it to withdraw from the cabinet as a protest against the SPD's willingness to accept—if necessary, unconditionally—the Geneva ultimatum. The "cabinet of personalities" that Wirth organized in its place, however, remained dependent on transient and unreliable majorities in the Reichstag. Despite the DVP's disappointment with the nomination of Walther Rathenau as Germany's new foreign minister at the end of January 1922, Stresemann supported Wirth's minority government. There was, after all, no valid alternative, for the bourgeois parties were interested in forcing the SPD, which was showing signs of renewed strength as a result of its rapprochement with the USPD, to share responsibility for the unpopular foreign-policy decisions that had become inescapable.

Walther Rathenau, the son and successor of the founder of the General Electric Corporation (Allgemeine Elektrizitäts-Gesellschaft or AEG), one of the most eloquent spokesmen for Germany's political elite, assumed responsibility for the conduct of German foreign policy after having already implemented practical suggestions as minister of reconstruction for the solution of the hopelessly deadlocked reparations question. A well-known writer who after the war had affiliated himself with the DDP and the proponent of highly imaginative proposals for the transition to a "planned economy," Rathenau was a Jewish intellectual who openly acknowledged his Jewishness. This, in turn, had exposed him to unremitting attacks from the *völkisch* Right. At the same time, the fact that he was a representative of the manufacturing sector and an active member of the second Socialization Commission made him anything but persona grata among the Ruhr industrial magnates who dominated the National Federation of German Industry. With Wirth, Rathenau shared an unequivocal commitment to the republic and a profound national loyalty that was tempered by a strict code of ethics and sense of responsibility.

Like Wirth, Rathenau espoused the policy of "conditional fulfillment." Unlike the vast majority of German politicians, however, he did not think in terms of a narrow revisionist policy aimed at restoring Germany's prewar hegemony. Instead he hoped to initiate a program of European reconstruction that would foster economic cooperation and eventually eliminate feelings of hatred among the European nations at the same time that it helped relieve domestic social tensions. In this respect, Rathenau was a kindred spirit to Lloyd George, who since the fall of 1921 had been advocating a comprehensive economic and political consolidation of continental Europe in the hope that this would stimulate Britain's lagging foreign trade and thus bring his country's widespread unemployment under control.

The idea of a European economic conference originated with Lloyd George, who secured Briand's agreement at Cannes in 1922 just prior to Briand's spectacular resignation. For the first time, Germany and Soviet Russia were invited to take part in the conference that was scheduled to convene in mid-April in Genoa. In Berlin this was immediately perceived as a remarkable improvement in the international climate and fueled hopes that it might be possible to raise the issue of reparations, if only on the fringes of the conference itself. For Briand's successor, Raymond Poincaré, had gone to considerable lengths to extract from the British prime minister the reluctant agreement that reparations must not under any circumstances become the subject of formal discussions and that no fundamental questions about the Paris peace settlement were to be addressed. It was no doubt in deference to the French position that Lloyd George clearly stated in a speech before the House of Commons that Genoa was not the place to take up a revision of the Versailles peace treaty. Nevertheless, the British prime minister had to consider himself fortunate that France did not torpedo the plans for the conference when the United States declined to attend. Poincaré, who was prepared to bring the Germans to their knees by occupying the Ruhr if they should fail to give concrete evidence of their willingness to fulfill their reparations obligations, perceived Lloyd George's initiative as a conscious retreat from previous reparations policy. But since he did not want to risk isolating France — a distinct possibility a few weeks earlier at the Washington Disarmament Conference — he felt that he had no alternative but to go along with London.

Against the background of these developments, Lloyd George's efforts to reach an agreement with Soviet Russia about Russia's prewar and wartime debts as the prelude to granting that country urgently needed international loans soon moved to the foreground of the Genoa negotiations. This transaction, known as the "Russian aid program," was to be placed in the hands of an international consortium in which Germany was to be fully involved. Rathenau favored this proposal and expected it to result in a rapprochement with Great Britain and a more open-minded treatment of the financial questions related to reparations. Rathenau thus went to Genoa without great optimism, though he was hopeful that discussions among experts would bring the reparations question closer to a solution. As Rathenau remarked at a meeting of the cabinet, the international climate seemed to have improved so much that Germany must determine just how much the situation would bear.

At this point Rathenau believed that it was possible for Germany to avoid having to take a stand on the Russian question. In the East European section of the German Foreign Office, efforts had been under way for some time to improve relations with Soviet Russia. But relations with the Soviet Union had reached a nadir following the appearance of Grigory Zinoviev at the USPD party congress in Halle and the Soviet instigation of a Communist uprising in central Germany in the spring of 1922. Ago von Maltzahn, the principal proponent of an active pro-Russian policy, fully recognized the tactical advantages of following the British lead for as long as possible. It was for these reasons that the provisional treaty that Germany and Russia had signed at the latter's insistence in May 1921 had had no practical consequences. The invitation to the Genoa Conference only intensified the Soviet Union's interest in a formal accord with their German partner, whereupon it soon became clear that Georgi Chicherin would not be content with a simple economic accord but sought a political agreement. Although Maltzahn urged quick action, Rathenau held back, partly in deference to Germany's pledge to Lloyd George that it would participate in the proposed consortium and partly out of concern that a German-Soviet pact would seriously jeopardize the convocation of a world economic conference. The preliminary talks that Germany and the Soviet Union had conducted just prior to the Genoa Conference and that would have made German participation in the proposed international consortium contingent on Moscow's consent—in other words virtually impossible—thus had to be broken off on a transparent pretext that only aroused the deepest suspicions of Karl Radek.

The contacts that Germany had cultivated with the Soviet Union at various levels since 1920 must be seen in the larger context of the former's strategy for undermining the economic restrictions of the Versailles peace treaty. Germany's booming domestic economy in the midst of the worldwide economic recession of 1920–21 opened the possibility of circumventing Allied trade restrictions through the conclusion of bilateral commercial treaties with the Netherlands, the Scandinavian countries, Hungary, Romania, and Czechoslovakia. The most-favored-nation pact that Germany concluded with Yugoslavia in late 1921 represented a self-conscious step toward a resumption of the policy that Germany had pursued in southeast Europe before and during the war. As early as 1922, the German Foreign Office spoke of "a revival of the *Mitteleuropa* concept in a new form" that sought to reverse French financial and economic penetration of southeastern Europe under the auspices of the Little Entente. At the same time, Germany also hoped to use improved trade relations to overcome its political isolation. This had, after all, been one of the principal goals behind the peace treaty that Germany concluded with the United States in 1921, which, much to the disappointment of German policy makers, had done little to alleviate the country's credit and reparations problems.

It was only natural that German cooperation with the Soviet Union should culminate in an agreement against Poland aimed at restoring Germany's eastern frontier. In this respect, it is significant that cooperation first materialized in the military sphere. With Seeckt's express approval, the Defense Ministry established a "Special Section R," which since 1921 had pursued cooperative armaments ventures and the establishment of training camps in Russia where German soldiers could learn to use weapons forbidden by the Versailles treaty. Even then, the disinterest of German firms—particularly Krupp and Blohm & Voß—in long-term armaments contracts and the construction of industrial installations in Russia could be overcome only very slowly. It was only in November 1922 that the Soviets and the Junkers Company formally concluded an agreement to manufacture aircraft forbidden to Germany under the terms of the Versailles peace treaty.

Only Chancellor Wirth—but neither the Reich president nor the cabinet—was informed of the secret armaments agreements with the Soviet Union. Rathenau, on the other hand, probably knew about the general nature of these agreements even though he may not have been informed about their specific provisions. In any event, German-Soviet military cooperation stood in direct conflict with Germany's possible participation in an international consortium that evoked the specter of prewar imperialism and encountered deep-seated Soviet opposition. To make the proposed consortium more palatable to the Soviets, the West was prepared to honor Russian claims against Germany under Article 116 of the Versailles peace treaty. It was, however, hardly realistic to expect that the Soviet Union would accept such a deal. Since the Germans were in no position to meet their reparations obligations to the Western powers, Soviet reparations claims were little more than a convenient fiction. Moreover, Poincaré could hardly be expected to exchange reparations claims against Germany for promises of debt payment from Soviet Russia in light of the latter's dismal financial situation. Still, this did not deter Maltzahn from making a great deal out of the danger that Article 116 supposedly posed and from letting it become a topic of serious discussion in Berlin.

The reasons why Rathenau allowed himself to be persuaded by the head of the East European section not only to turn his back on the proposed consortium but also to sign at the height of the Genoa Conference a separate treaty with Soviet Russia in Rapallo on 16 April 1922 remain unclear. Coincidence and intrigue no doubt played their part. For one thing, Rathenau was deeply offended by the psychological isolation to which the German delegation was subjected in Genoa as a result of French pressure. Moreover, Rathenau was fearful that separate negotiations between the Western powers and the Soviet delegation would leave Germany caught in the middle. Rumors fueled by the Italians and inflated by Maltzahn that the Western powers might reach an understanding with Soviet Russia behind Germany's back finally prompted Rathenau to sign the treaty without first obtaining the endorsement of either the Reich president or the cabinet and without consulting Lloyd George as he had originally planned. In doing so, Rathenau knew full well that the other powers would most likely perceive this action as a direct affront.

The debate over Rapallo has not abated. Rathenau regarded the treaty as a way of expanding Germany's foreign policy options and in this respect was heartily supported by Wirth. Opinions in the cabinet, however, were divided. Ebert was particularly irritated at having not been informed of the negotiations and feared that the precipitous way in which the treaty had been concluded might turn the SPD's strong support for a Western orientation in the conduct of German foreign policy into its exact opposite. Moreover, the actual benefits of the treaty were far from clear. For in exchange for a Soviet waiver of reparations claims against Germany and vague promises of collaboration against Poland, all that Germany had received was the beginnings of a trade agreement that by and large was to prove unprofitable and long-term damage to relations with the West.

Lloyd George was able to prevent the Treaty of Rapallo from sabotaging the Genoa Conference and thus avoided what would have been a major personal defeat. At the same time, the British prime minister demonstrated a certain willingness to support Germany in its demands that questions related to reparations and international loans be placed on the agenda, while Rathenau offered to mediate with the Soviets and, in an impressive closing address, underscored Germany's commitment to international conciliation. Nevertheless, in the private and public reactions of the participants as well as in the international press Germany was criticized for having done its best to torpedo the conference. In a public speech at Bar-le-Duc on 24 April, Poincaré used the Genoa debacle to warn against an imminent German rapprochement with the Soviet Union and depicted Rapallo as a declaration of war against the international status quo. Renewed threats of military intervention in the event of future German violations of the Versailles peace treaty found widespread support in French public opinion. At the same time, Rapallo severely undermined Lloyd George's political position, even though his government did not fall from power until later that fall in connection with the crisis in the Far East. To be sure, the British prime minister made one last attempt to avert a conflict over the Ruhr by advocating Germany's admission to the League of Nations, a measure that would have made unilateral actions like those envisaged by Poincaré, if not impossible, at least much more difficult to execute. This initiative, however, was doomed from the outset by the conditions the Germans attached to the membership in the League of Nations, the most contentious of which were their demands for a permanent seat on the council and the suspension of military controls.

While in the case of Wirth—as in the case of army commander in chief Hans von Seeckt, who was soon to argue in a memorandum on the "Russian Problem" that the existence of Poland was incompatible with Germany's prerequisites for survival—the east European theme was of paramount importance, Rathenau was primarily interested in using the so-called Russian gambit to pressure the Allies into making concessions on matters related to loan and reparations policy. This, however, turned out to be a major miscalculation, for the style in which the Germans were conducting their foreign policy reminded Great Britain of the *Panther*'s visit to Agadir—Maltzahn was, after all, a disciple of Alfred von Kiderlen-Wächter—and thus had the effect of forcing the British back into the French corner. Moreover, Rapallo was a shot in the arm for those forces within Germany that had called for a hard line toward France and that had hoped to use the moratorium resulting from Germany's deepening fiscal crisis as the pretext for renouncing further reparations payments. In these circles Rapallo was touted as evidence that it was indeed possible to break out of Allied encirclement. Under these circumstances, the conclusion of this pact was bound to nourish the fateful illusion that it would be possible to dismantle Versailles one piece at a time through a policy of defiant noncompliance. At the heart of Germany's effort to break out of the multilateral diplomacy at Genoa lay a fundamental turn away from the Paris peace settlement and a willingness to forgo a gradual rapprochement with France for the sake of an active and unilateral reparations policy for which Germany lacked the necessary material resources.

By supporting the Rapallo policy Wirth only weakened his political position at home. It was against the background of these developments that the chancellor finally broke with the policy of "conditional fulfillment" in the German note of 12 November 1922—even at the risk of inviting French sanctions—after the Allied reparations commission had become increasingly intractable to German demands. To be sure, Wirth was able to mobilize a broad parliamentary majority in support of his position, but the coalition that provided this support soon fell apart over the social conflicts that now began to surface. The first sign of serious trouble came when the Majority Socialists voted against changes in the Grain Levy Bill (Getreideumlage) that would have increased domestic food prices. From a purely formal point of view, the collapse of the cabinet resulted from the SPD's refusal to go along with Wirth and the other government parties in inviting the DVP to join the cabinet. The deeper reason for the crisis, however, was the way in which Wirth's compromises with big business and the Reichsbank threatened to dismantle the sociopolitical system of the postwar era.

The reversal in domestic politics that culminated in the collapse of the Wirth cabinet in the fall of 1922 was last but not least a consequence of the transition to hyperinflation that took place shortly after the Genoa Conference. The assassination of Foreign Minister Walther Rathenau and the refusal of the Morgan banking house to issue an international loan to Germany without prior agreement on the reparations question greatly intensified the inflationary pressures already at work in the German economy. The situation was further complicated by the fact that the influx of speculative capital from abroad—capital that since the beginning of 1922 had made it possible not only to balance the budget but also to secure a surplus for the payment of reparations—came to abrupt end. At the same time, international creditors demonstrated their lack of confidence in the mark when they began to close out their accounts in German banks. Without the help of foreign capital, fiscal stability in Germany was virtually impossible.

If, on one hand, the decision after 1918 not to embark on a course of rigid deflation was correct in light of the loss of income and the deepening of social divisions that this would have almost certainly brought in its wake, the architects of German fiscal policy in the immediate postwar period cannot be acquitted of the charges of gross neglect. The sociopolitical *Burgfriede* that the inflation had made possible was bound to be shattered as soon as the international value of the mark declined more rapidly than its domestic purchasing power. This began to happen in the summer of 1922. Important sectors of the national economy began to keep their accounts in currencies denominated in gold. As a result, the leveling of incomes that had been quietly taking place during the inflation was no longer operative. On the contrary, industry—already suffering from an acute capital shortage—found itself under such pressure to hold its prices in line that it could no longer pass on wage increases to the consumer. This, in turn, triggered a dramatic intensification of the conflict over the division of the social product in which the labor unions, whose financial reserves had been consumed by the inflation, found themselves at a distinct disadvantage.

Wirth proved himself to be a prisoner of these economic constraints. To be sure, it was not simply a question of industrialists and bankers conspiring with each other to ruin the currency so that Germany might be free of reparations. Still, these elements did prefer the inflation to a policy of state regulation that, in their eyes, would have paralyzed the economy without resolving the outstanding social conflicts. As long as it was possible to pass on most of the real costs of the inflation to foreign investors, indirect gains from the inflation gains exceeded German reparations payments, which until 1923 amounted to 2.6 billion gold marks in cash and, according to Allied estimates, about 8 billion in material deliveries. The formula "First bread, then reparations" that Wirth coined to defend his government's decision to reject the London schedule of payments blithely concealed the fact that the collapse of the German currency and the damage this inflicted on Germany's economic and social structure stemmed ultimately from the inadequate pains the German government had taken to achieve fiscal and economic stability. And this was not divorced from the calculation that it still might be possible to avoid reparations payments altogether.

During Wirth's tenure as chancellor the republican system of government appeared to have stabilized itself, although the tendency to circumvent parliament and parties and to deal directly with special-interest groups in the formation of national policy had become indisputably stronger. The primacy of reparations in the formulation of the national agenda meant that fundamental differences over the nature of the economic order had never been addressed. The retention of mechanisms designed during the demobilization phase for the state arbitration of labor disputes and the inflationary price-wage spiral of the early 1920s had kept conflicts between labor and management in check, even if violations of the eight-hour day had become more and more frequent and even if the railway strike in the spring of 1922 could be ended only after bitter internal fighting. In March 1921 the KPD, acting on directions from the Comintern and in total ignorance of the true state of mind of the German proletariat, had instigated a revolt in central Germany. This fatal relapse into putschist and terrorist methods, by which the proletarian adventurer Max Hoelz earned for himself a measure of infamy, handed the KPD a crushing defeat. The so-called Easter Putsch, which outside of Hamburg evoked little support and which was quickly suppressed by Prussian police units, found its sharpest critic in Paul Levi, who was unable to hold his own against the clique of Moscow loyalists who were in the process of marginalizing the KPD.

The true threat to the parliamentary system, however, came not from the Left but from the extreme Right, as Wirth boldly asserted in his famous Reichstag speech following Rathenau's assassination: "This, then, is the enemy; and about one thing there can be no doubt: this enemy stands on the right." The extreme Right enjoyed the propagandistic support of the DNVP, as Karl Helfferich's intemperate attacks against Walther Rathenau clearly revealed. The conspiratorial secret societies, which recruited their members from the now defunct Free Corps and tried to undermine the republic by secret tribunals (*Femegerichte*) and systematic political murder, maintained close ties with the Reichswehr and enjoyed the sympathy of official circles not just in Bavaria. Rathenau's murder on 24 June 1922 by members of the "Organization Consul," a descendant of the Ehrhardt Brigade, constituted a severe challenge to the republic. Under the pressure of public opinion, the government answered with a decree for the protection of the republic and introduced, along with corresponding civil service legislation, a law for the protection of the republic in the Reichstag.

This time, even Stresemann voted "as a matter of national duty" for the enactment of the legislation that had been drafted by the Social Democratic justice minister Gustav Radbruch. Of all the parties in the Reichstag, only the DNVP openly opposed it. In the Reichsrat, however, it encountered vigorous opposition from the Bavarian government, which insisted on and eventually succeeded in getting special treatment under the terms of the bill. Under the influence of the bourgeois parties — not the least of which was the purely formal concept of democracy held by the DDP — the proposed legislation was weakened until it amounted to little more than general provisions for the protection of the state and constitution. As future events would prove, it was a serious mistake for the framers of the Weimar Constitution to have taken over the judicial apparatus of the Second Empire without making fundamental changes of their own. For in the hands of the Weimar judiciary, this weapon for the defense of the republic proved dull when directed against extremism from the right but sharp and merciless when it came to dealing with Communists.

Rathenau's assassination produced widespread solidarity within the German working class. The three working-class parties now felt compelled to act in a concerted manner, and their protest strikes prompted the bourgeois majority in the Reichstag to dissociate itself without equivocation from the public and private foes of the republic. The protests of the workers evoked memories of the mass demonstrations that had led to the collapse of the Kapp Putsch in March 1920 and to the abortive protest movement that followed Erzberger's assassination in August 1921. For a brief moment it seemed as if the democratic republic had experienced an unexpected burst of vitality. An immediate consequence of the workers' protest action was the formation of a parliamentary coalition between the SPD and USPD and the reunification of the two socialist parties at a joint party congress in Nuremberg on 23 November 1922. These developments, in turn, did much to strengthen the parliamentary position of the chancellor, whose vigorous support for the Law for the Protection of the Republic cast him as the leader of a militant left-wing cabinet. In point of fact, however, the reunification brought with it an increased polarization of German party politics. For while the moderate bourgeois parties — namely, the DDP, DVP, and Center — founded the Coalition of the Constitutional Middle (Arbeitsgemeinschaft der verfassungstreuen Mitte), the SPD shied away from including the DVP in the cabinet so as not to jeopardize its hard-fought party unity. What could easily have been a sign of the republic's consolidation, therefore, severely weakened the potential for political compromise between the bourgeois middle parties and organized labor, even if external threats continued to make collaboration between the two inescapable.

With the appointment of Wilhelm Cuno, general director of the Hamburg-America Line, as chancellor in November 1922, a clear shift to the right took place. Reich President Ebert placed great confidence in Cuno's international reputation and passed over Stresemann, of whom he was deeply suspicious. Cuno, who enjoyed friendly relations with Helfferich, was totally unqualified for the position. On the reparations question he adopted a rigid stance in the belief that he could persuade the United States to mediate in Germany's conflict with France. His pledge that Germany would reform its currency without outside help was not taken any more seriously by the French negotiators than the promise that the international loan he sought would be used in part to fulfill Germany's reparations obligations. While in itself correct, Cuno's proposal for a European security pact was launched without any diplomatic preparation, remained without any effect whatsoever, and was quickly dismissed by Poincaré as sleight of hand. Given German fatalism, the British, whose political leadership now lay in the hands of the Conservative Bonar Law, no longer saw any possibility of effectively countering Poincaré's "policy of productive mortgages" (*Politik der produktiven Pfänder*).

The Cuno government underestimated the determination of the French premier, who enjoyed the support of the Bloc National and who had prepared well in advance the Ruhr adventure upon which he now embarked. As a pretext he seized upon Germany's delay in making deliveries of wood and coal. On 11 January 1923 French and Belgian troops marched into the Ruhr. At this point the economic war between France and Germany was transformed into a "policy of national catastrophe" for the latter, casting it back into the situation that had existed in the early summer of 1919. The "primacy of preserving the system," which had led to the relative stabilization of the republic, was abandoned by heavy industrial interest groups once it had become clear that the government was no longer capable of keeping the deepening crisis in check. At the same time, these interests felt sufficiently strengthened not only to risk an open confrontation with France but also to force a domestic political crisis that would permit them to dismantle the social and political compromises on which the founding of the Weimar Republic had been based.

CHAPTER FIVE

Saving the Parliamentary System

JUST why the Franco-Belgian occupation of the Ruhr on 11 January 1923 caught the German government so unprepared is difficult to understand. There had certainly been no shortage of French threats ever since the London Ultimatum in the spring of 1921, and Poincaré had made his intentions perfectly clear as recently as December 1922. Throughout all of this, Cuno clung to the hope that England would intervene on Germany's behalf. Yet while the British cabinet did indeed disapprove of the Ruhr occupation, it was unwilling to obstruct French policy. And if the American secretary of state, Charles E. Hughes, also intimated to Poincaré that it made no sense to solve the reparations question by force, the United States refrained from intervening directly, especially since France had not yet signed the Washington Agreement, and limited its response to withdrawing American troops from the Rhine. For the time being, therefore, Poincaré was free to pursue his policy of force.

The Cuno government risked an open conflict with France in the expectation that this would win for Germany the sympathy of world opinion. For reasons of foreign and domestic politics, military action was out of the question. The German government therefore reacted to the occupation of the Ruhr by calling for passive resistance and tried to create a united front that enlisted the support of all political forces. Such a policy, however, had no real chance of success and revealed an inaccurate assessment of Germany's political possibilities. For aside from confidential and not always authorized declarations of sympathy on the part of Anglo-Saxon diplomats, there was no indication that Germany could sustain an economic contest of strength with France for any length of time or that such a contest stood any reasonable chance of success.

The struggle in the Ruhr seemed—at least in the eyes of the Cuno government—to have recreated the *Burgfrieden* of the First World War. At the end of March 1923 French troops were involved in an incident in the Krupp Steelworks in which a number of workers were killed or injured. As a result, the board of directors, including Gustav Krupp von Bohlen und Halbach, was arrested and convicted by a military court. Journalists immediately used this—as they had in the in the case of Fritz Thyssen's incarceration—as an opportunity to celebrate the cooperation between labor and capital as a sign of national solidarity. The myth of a "national community" that transcended social and

economic divisions, however, only obscured the increasingly antagonistic relationship that had developed between the interests of capital and labor and
that in 1922 had led to the virtual paralysis of the Zentralarbeitsgemeinschaft.
Slogans calling for "perseverance" (*Durchhalten*) and a "national unity front"
were indeed reminiscent of the final years of the war. In the final analysis, this
represented a retreat to the politics of national prestige for which those who
had opposed signing the Versailles peace treaty had clamored in 1919.

Even the Social Democratic and trade-union press revived the nationalist
terminology of the First World War. The experiences of the recent revolution seemed to have been forgotten. Right-wing publicists, in the meantime,
showed no scruple whatsoever in their efforts to foster a sense of nationalism, which in many cases assumed overtly racist overtones. Politicians from all
camps invoked France's Rhineland policy since the days of Louis XIV to prove
that Poincaré too, as Stresemann asserted in a speech before the Reichstag,
was intent on achieving the "annihilation of Germany" and the destruction of
its economic foundations. In point of fact, there was good reason to fear that
the French might very well return to their objective from 1918–19 of trying to
destroy the unity of the Reich.

German public opinion concluded from the occupation of the Ruhr that
reparations had only been a pretext for forcing Germany to its knees. For its
own part, the German government refused to honor its reparations obligations
with respect to the occupying powers and categorically rejected further negotiations with the French. This purely rhetorical stance only fueled the mistaken
belief that France had unilaterally broken the Versailles peace treaty and had
thereby forfeited the right to any future claims under the terms of the treaty.
Resistance would lead, so political journalists apparently believed, to the complete collapse of the Paris peace settlement and to the recovery of Germany's
diplomatic freedom of action.

The Cuno cabinet did little, if anything, to counter illusions of this nature.
On the contrary, it tended to encourage such illusions through the official
propaganda of the Reich Central Office for Home Affairs (Reichszentrale für
Heimatdienst). On the domestic scene, the government's efforts to evoke a
sense of national will sufficiently strong to endure the current crisis played
into the hands of those who opposed a policy of conciliation and encouraged
those who advocated the unconditional refusal of Allied demands. The policy
of limited fulfillment, with which the SPD was closely identified, had fallen
into disrepute and was generally held responsible for the deepening economic
crisis. At the same time, all of this jeopardized the existing constitutional order.
Oswald Spengler, for example, had denounced the republic as "institutional-
ized compliance" with the Versailles peace treaty. Even within the ranks of
the bourgeois center hopes of shedding the chains of Versailles were closely
tied to the goal of replacing the parliamentary system that had been forced on

the nation by the victorious Western powers and was incompatible with Germany's own constitutional traditions emphasizing institutions of a more corporatist and authoritarian character.

Poincaré's pursuit of sanctions provided new impetus to the revisionist movement. By no means were revisionist sentiments limited to the parties of the extreme Right such as the DNVP, the German Racist Freedom Party (Deutschvölkische Freiheitspartei or DVFP), and the National Socialist German Workers' Party (Nationalsozialistische Deutsche Arbeiterpartei or NSDAP). The revisionist movement, for example, received support from Karl Radek, a well-known agent of the Communist International who established contact with the National Bolsheviks and who defended the struggle in the Ruhr in the name of the proletariat. Outside of the parties, revisionism received strong support not only from the Pan-German League and the National Rural League (Reichs-Landbund or RLB), but also from the network of neoconservative associations known as the Ring Movement (Ring-Bewegung) as well as from the press of the Hugenberg concern and the *Deutsche Allgemeine Zeitung*, the mouthpiece of industrialist Hugo Stinnes. It required Germany's defeat in the Ruhr conflict for public opinion to develop a more realistic appraisal of Germany's foreign policy options and to shed the veil of illusions that had mesmerized the leading figures of the German diplomatic establishment.

The declaration of passive resistance in the Ruhr provided the Reichswehr with a pretext for intensifying its efforts to circumvent the armament provisions of the Versailles peace treaty by recruiting temporary volunteers and by cooperating more closely with the various organizations on Germany's paramilitary Right. The Reichswehr leadership was quick to take advantage of the freedom of movement it had gained through the temporary withdrawal of the Interallied Military Control Commission and furnished arms to guerrilla commandos operating in the occupied territory. Bombings of transport installations and surprise attacks on French military posts quickly transformed passive into active resistance. While the national government did nothing to inhibit these activities, the Prussian government had to defend itself against charges of "national treason" as a result of its confiscation of illegal arms and the ban it placed on right-wing paramilitary organizations in the occupied territory. A particularly spectacular case was that of Albert Leo Schlageter, a member of one of these sabotage groups and an early adherent of the NSDAP. When Schlageter was condemned to death by a French military tribunal in Düsseldorf in May 1923, the political Right hailed him as a national martyr, while Radek praised him as a "courageous soldier of the counterrevolution." The net effect of this was to discredit the policy of passive resistance and to prompt the occupation forces to take countermeasures, the brunt of which fell upon an unarmed and defenseless population.

The national government embarked on the policy of passive resistance without properly appreciating its consequences. In the first place, it instructed the state civil service in the occupied territory not to cooperate with the occupation authorities and to impede the transport of merchandise and raw materials. Occupation authorities responded by expelling the striking civil servants, of whom nearly 147,000 were directly affected. At the same time, French and Belgian authorities assumed management of the railway system in the occupied territory and were thus able to undercut whatever effects the policy of passive resistance might have had in this area. Until the middle of 1923, it appeared as if Poincaré's policy of "productive guarantees" was doomed to failure. The fact that just before the beginning of the crisis Hugo Stinnes had persuaded the Rhenish-Westphalian Coal Syndicate (Rheinisch-Westfälische Kohlensyndikat) to move its offices outside of the occupied territory made it difficult for the Interallied Mission for the Control of the Steel and Iron Industry and Anthracite Mining (Interallierte Mission zur Kontrolle der stahl- und eisenerzeugenden Industrie und des Steinkohlenbergbaus or MICUM), a body established by the reparations commission, to seize coal production in the Ruhr. Despite the confiscation of reserves stored above ground, the quantities of coal taken out of the occupied territory were actually less than what Germany had been delivering prior to the occupation of the Ruhr. At the same time, German industry stopped importing minette and French and Belgian pig iron, thereby causing considerable hardship for the heavy industry of Lorraine. The German government's refusal to continue the payment of reparations in kind constituted a considerable financial burden for the French.

Germany sought to strengthen the resolve of those who lived in the Rhine and the Ruhr regions to resist French rule by establishing defense committees outside the occupied area in which management and labor were equally represented, facilitating private assistance to the needy population through programs such as the German People's Aid (Deutsches Volksopfer) and providing foreign currency for the purchase of foodstuffs. At the same time, the national government subsidized heavy industry by providing low-interest loans and compensation for "unproductive wage payments." In order to avoid the mass unemployment that would have resulted from the gradual shutdown of production, industry agreed to keep the work force occupied with the repair and maintenance of equipment. Through the creation of holding companies for the steel and coal industries it was possible to ensure the transfer of capital into the occupied territory. Since the government's financial assistance took place in secret, there was no way for the public to monitor the hefty demands for credit and compensation that firms in the Ruhr frequently made. Moreover, the national government had to pay the costs of the occupation as well as the salaries of those civil servants who refused to work. Eventually, between 60 and 100 percent of all wages in the occupied territory had to paid out of public funds, while tax revenues, on the other hand, declined to virtually nothing.

By no means were the negative effects of the Ruhr occupation limited to the occupied territory. Occupation authorities had responded to the closure of factories in the occupied territory by erecting a toll barrier, charging fees for the exchange of merchandise and preventing the export of Ruhr coal to the unoccupied parts of Germany. These measures created serious bottlenecks for industrial production in the rest of Germany despite the import of larger quantities of coal from Poland, Czechoslovakia, and Great Britain. In the long run this economically absurd situation was simply untenable. Firms in the Ruhr saw themselves severely hurt by the forced shutdown of production, the confiscation of raw materials, and the occupation of their plants and sought to reach some sort of understanding with the MICUM when occupation authorities responded to the termination of reparations deliveries by closing or seizing individual factories. At the same time, the fact that occupation authorities had taken the place of Germany's civil administration meant that they were able to exercise direct power over the general populace. Rising unemployment and inadequate unemployment compensation made the local population all the more vulnerable to pressure of this sort. By spring it was already clear that resistance in the Ruhr could not continue indefinitely and that negotiations on at least some issues were unavoidable.

The main reason for the weakening of passive resistance in the Ruhr was the disastrous collapse in the purchasing power of the German mark. The inflationary effect of Germany's fiscal policy was now compounded by the payment of exceedingly high subsidies to the occupied territory that could be sustained only by increasing the amount of paper money in circulation. In January 1923, the dollar value of the German mark had fallen from 27,000 to 49,000 marks to the dollar. This dismal situation prompted foreign investors to withdraw their remaining mark holdings. Efforts by the Reichsbank to shore up the currency were only temporarily successful in spite of the fact that it could count on the help of English, Dutch, and Swiss credit institutions.

In April 1923 the mark experienced another dramatic decline in value that could have been prevented had the Reichsbank been willing to sacrifice its last gold reserves. The general flight from the mark caused severe economic disturbances. The pressure that labor unions and political parties exercised in light of the deepening economic crisis prompted the government to renew its efforts at stabilizing the mark by raising 500 million gold marks through a domestic bond issue. This step was absolutely essential if the government was to avert a general collapse of the food supply. For not only did the acute shortage of hard currency make it impossible for Germany to import the necessary foodstuffs from abroad, but farmers could hardly be expected to bring their harvest to market if the value of whatever they earned would evaporate within a few weeks. As it turned out, the government's effort to shore up the value of the mark ended in complete failure. By August 1923 the mark was quoted at 5 million to the dollar. The reasons for this are complex. In the first place, heavy industry was much less dependent on the stabilization of the currency than the government since most large firms had already been conducting business in currencies tied to the gold standard and were therefore far less vulnerable to sudden drops in the value of the mark than public agencies or those segments of the population that still had to pay for the necessities of life with paper marks. Big business thus exercised considerable restraint in subscribing to the domestic bond issue.

The National Federation of German Industry made its cooperation in the stabilization of the mark conditional upon an end to the controlled economy, including the suspension of all import-export quotas, and a return to the socio-political conditions of the prewar period. As long as the confrontation with France persisted, however, the federation felt that it would be unwise to force a break with the SPD and the socialist labor unions since this would almost certainly destroy the unity of the national resistance front at home. From this perspective, the link between deflation and a change in social policy that included the abolition of the eight-hour workday and an end to binding arbitration in wage and labor disputes could not be made until after the reparations problem had been solved. To stabilize the mark prematurely would only undercut the argument that Germany lacked the economic resources to meet its reparations obligations.

By the same token, the Ruhr industrial establishment obstructed Cuno's endeavors to draft a schedule for the payment of reparations that contained unequivocal fiscal guarantees, although the British regarded this as an essential precondition for overcoming French opposition to the convocation of an international panel of experts that would assess Germany's capacity to pay and determine the modalities of payment. Just how little room for maneuvering the German government had in this matter could be seen in the fact that at first Foreign Minister Hans von Rosenberg thought it inconceivable that Germany could do anything more than it had already done with its reparations proposal of December 1922.

It was only through persistent pressure from the SPD, the German Center Party, and organized labor that the government was prompted to make a more satisfactory reparations proposal. This proposal, however, met with immediate rejection from the National Federation of German Industry. Industry set virtually unfulfillable conditions, including the demand that the total amount of Germany's reparations obligations be fixed in advance, to its participation in the government's efforts to raise the necessary hard currency. The proposal the government finally submitted after failing to secure the help of German industry had no effect whatsoever. In view of Germany's impending fiscal collapse and Rosenberg's refusal to terminate at least some aspects of passive resistance, hopes that London and Washington might intervene on Germany's behalf never materialized. Nevertheless, this was Germany's first serious reparations offer, which, had it been made earlier, would almost certainly have changed the international climate in Germany's favor. Whether the catastrophic collapse of the German currency in the late summer of 1923 could have been mitigated or even averted by more forceful German leadership is impossible to determine. For while one might argue in support of this thesis that stabilization in November 1923 occurred without outside assistance, it is important to remember that this took place in a vastly more favorable international context. The dependence of the government on powerful economic interest organizations and the Reichsbank made it impossible for it to change course as long as one assumed that Germany could dispose of its reparations obligations to France and the other Allied powers by applying economic pressure. Moreover, the German government still clung to the illusion that, if necessary, it could continue passive resistance in the Ruhr through the coming winter. In the meantime, the crisis had begun to spread throughout the entire German economy, particularly since the economic collapse in the occupied territory and the escalating inflation had combined to produce not only an acute shortage of capital and foreign currency reserves but also a sharp decline in investment activity of all sorts. At the same time, there was a dramatic increase in unemployment because most firms now operated on the basis of hard currencies and could no longer pass the costs of high wages and unused capacities on to the consumer.

When it became increasingly clear in the summer of 1923 that the mark could no longer be saved, retail businesses began to refuse payment in paper marks and to hoard their inventories. Stores would open at first for only two or three days a week, then only on an hourly basis, and even then what they had in stock remained insufficient. Long lines in front of food stores became an everyday occurrence. At the same time, farmers refused to meet the delivery quotas that had been imposed upon them by the postwar economic controls. This, in turn, let to severe food shortages and hunger riots. Trading valuables for food and stealing from fields became increasingly widespread. Instances of looting were no longer rare. In many cases, wages sank so low that working-class families were unable to buy the basic necessities of life. The civil servants, who had initially been shielded from the full effects of the inflation because their salaries had been paid in advance in quarterly installments, now faced similar problems. The hardest hit, however, were pensioners and those who lived off of savings or income from rental property.

Under these circumstances, calls for a "national unity front" were as ineffective as slogans calling for endurance had been at the end of the recent war. Without a doubt one of the principal effects of the hyperinflation had been to close significantly the gap in wages and income between the working class and those segments of the lower middle class who were not economically independent. Psychologically this mattered less than the deep-seated resentment that was aroused by the luxury and ostentatious life-style of those profiteers who, as a rule, had access to hard currencies. The state governments tried to curtail these excesses by enacting largely ineffective ordinances against profiteering, but the revenues generated by these measures were almost immediately consumed by the inflation. Bans on the import of luxury goods and controls over gourmet restaurants and gambling casinos only addressed the symptoms, but not the cause, of the problem. In a situation where the money one had today might be worth half as much tomorrow and in which no one knew what the future might hold, it was only reasonable to live from day to day and to consume as much as possible.

The unimaginably sharp contrast between unearned prosperity and extreme material deprivation was bound to create a fertile environment in which social resentments and criticism of the capitalist economic system could take root and grow. This was the moment of opportunity for radical parties at both ends of the political spectrum, for parties that showed no scruple in exploiting the increasingly hostile mood of the populace for their own partisan ends. Whereas in Munich Adolf Hitler scored one rhetorical success after another with his attacks on the "November criminals," the "indecisiveness of the government," and the "Berlin *Judenrepublik*," the KPD was able to consolidate its position after having more or less recovered from the fiasco of the central German uprisings. With an unusually large increase in membership during this period, the Communists made remarkable gains at the expense of the Social Democrats in a series of local, regional, and factory council elections in the summer of 1923. No longer did the Communist goal of uniting the majority of the industrial proletariat behind its leadership seem an empty dream.

As early as April 1923 Theodor Leipart from the General German Trade-Union Federation (ADGB) had demanded the resignation of the Cuno government on the grounds that it was incapable of coming to an understanding with the Western powers. An indefinite prolongation of passive resistance in the Ruhr was incompatible with the interests of the industrial working class. In spite of the compensation from the national government, mounting unemployment in the occupied areas created intolerable social conditions. The real wages of the industrial worker fell far below their prewar level even after wages had been indexed to inflation in the late fall of 1923. In the meantime, the growing shortage of food supplies caused horrendous price increases. The economic insecurity in the Rhine and Ruhr was further compounded by the repressive policies of the occupation authorities. Syndicalist associations, which were particularly active in the Ruhr mining industry, took advantage of the deteriorating social conditions to call for strikes, which the labor unions could bring under control only with the greatest of difficulty. At the same time, union membership declined dramatically.

For all of this, the SPD executive committee and the leadership of the ADGB were reluctant to take the lead in trying to bring an end to the policy of passive resistance in the Ruhr for fear of being saddled with the odium of betraying the nation. It was not until late July 1923 that the left wing of the SPD took matters in its own hands and called for a reorganization of the national cabinet at a special conference convened at Weimar through the efforts of Arthur Crispien. The immediate background for this turn of events was the indisputable radicalization of influential sectors of the industrial working class that had manifested itself in a series of strikes in both the occupied and unoccupied parts of Germany. For the most part, the wave of strikes from the summer of 1923 had been triggered by the failure of wages to keep pace with the runaway inflation. The KPD was particularly intent on mobilizing the bitterness of the working masses for revolutionary purposes, whereby it pursued an ambivalent strategy that saw it, on the one hand, calling for a national struggle against imperialist exploitation in the Ruhr and, on the other, initiating an antifascist campaign that sought to enlist the masses in a united proletarian front for a period of intensified class warfare.

Particularly in Saxony, the traditional center of the German Left, the agitation for a united front fell on fertile soil in spite of the fact that the national leadership of the SPD sabotaged negotiations that would have brought the Communists into the state government. As in the case of neighboring Thuringia, the Saxon SPD was able to form with Communist toleration a minority government that stood in sharp opposition to the various bourgeois parties. This formed the immediate background to the ultimatum that the left wing of the SPD issued at Weimar for the formation of a Social Democratic minority government at the national level that would be stabilized through a rapprochement with the KPD and the use of extraparliamentary pressure tactics. The national leadership of the SPD rejected this demand, in part because its acceptance would have meant the collapse of Otto Braun's "Great Coalition" cabinet in Prussia. Nevertheless, the SPD now began to press for the replacement of the Cuno cabinet by a government of the Great Coalition in the Reich. The Communists provided the occasion for such a step by introducing a motion of no confidence in the Reichstag.

Friedrich Ebert, who had granted the Cuno cabinet considerable latitude in the use of Article 48 to deal with the inflation and matters related to the stabilization of the mark, now found himself obliged to follow the initiative of parliament and entrust the formation of a new cabinet to Gustav Stresemann. Stresemann, whose appointment as Cuno's successor was endorsed by the SPD, was able to complete this task within twenty-four hours. The return to government by parliamentary majority, however, was flawed by the fact that a substantial minority within the SPD Reichstag delegation as well as the extreme right wing of Stresemann's own German People's Party withheld their approval of the new cabinet. The Social Democratic dissidents, including the deputies from Saxony and a majority of those who had formerly belonged to the USPD, were particularly concerned that the interests of large-scale capitalism would dominate the coalition. Conversely, the minority within the DVP that had voted against Stresemann was closely identified with the representation of big business and heavy industry.

In sharp contrast to the leaders of heavy industry — and in particular to the DVP deputy Hugo Stinnes — Stresemann had felt since the early summer of 1923 that the SPD should be included in any cabinet that tried to resolve the crisis currently facing the German nation. To be sure, Stresemann had toyed with the idea of a dictatorship in July 1923 but only as a contingency should the SPD refuse to go along with the necessary fiscal reforms. Having begun his career as an outspoken nationalist and monarchist, Stresemann had undergone a gradual conversion to a *Vernunftrepublikaner* who supported the republic more out of necessity than conviction. At the same time, Stresemann was well aware that Germany's precarious position in international affairs — it was, after all, by no means certain that the Rhine and Ruhr could be kept from falling into French hands — made the war of attrition between organized labor and the bourgeoisie a serious danger to the long-term health of the country. For tactical considerations, however, Stresemann was reluctant to make concessions in the area of foreign policy unless the Social Democrats agreed to accept a share of the responsibility.

As a defender of liberal parliamentarism, Stresemann was something of an outsider among the politicians of Weimar's bourgeois center. He embodied the traditions of the prewar National Liberal Party to a far greater extent than the leading spokesmen for the DDP and regarded the reconciliation of antagonistic social interests within the framework of the parliamentary system as an indispensable precondition for lasting political stability. It was characteristic of Stresemann that he disposed of his stock portfolio upon assuming the chancellorship. As the controversial, if not constantly maligned leader of the DVP, Stresemann had succeeded in subordinating the representation of special economic interests to the art of parliamentary compromise to the point where his party was prepared to cooperate with the SPD. All of this, needless to say, constituted a severe strain upon his health and no doubt contributed to his premature death in the fall of 1929.

The regeneration of the parliamentary system under Stresemann took place in a situation in which the termination of passive resistance was only a matter of time. The increasingly acute economic crisis forced the parties of the center and moderate Left to accept the burden of political responsibility, while heavy industry and the political Right — whose most influential spokesmen regarded the installation of an authoritarian government as an absolute necessity — planned to leave the liquidation of the struggle in the Ruhr to a parliamentary cabinet so that they could make their move to bring about a change in the political system whenever the appropriate moment presented itself. Stresemann, who had risen to political prominence as chairman of the Reichstag's Committee on Foreign Affairs, had had his eyes on the chancellorship ever since 1921. Still, he continued to support Cuno's foreign policy until the summer of 1923. In a certain sense, Stresemann's restraint was tactical, for by June he had already begun to speak out against a *Katastrophenpolitik* and to advocate negotiations with the French in the sense of Goethe's dictum "tractability with a strong will" (*Nachgiebigkeit bei großem Willen*). Having already come to the reluctant conclusion that there was no alternative to ending passive resistance, Stresemann agreed to accept the chancellorship in the hope that he could close this particular chapter in Germany's postwar history without losing too much face in the process. But preliminary overtures that he initiated with the help of the British ambassador in Berlin, Viscount d'Abernon, yielded largely negative results. In August 1923 Stresemann stated skeptically that one could not wait for England to take the initiative. By 19 September it had become increasingly clear that Stanley Baldwin, the conservative prime minister of Great Britain, was determined to go along with Poincaré's demand for Germany's unconditional capitulation. In light of this position, continuation of passive resistance in the occupied territory could only have played into French hands. In the meantime, the domestic will to resist was beginning to falter. For although the labor unions continued to pledge their support, influential industrial groups from Rhineland-Westphalia were showing signs of wanting to reach an understanding with France behind the back of the national government.

Conditions in the occupied territory, where MICUM was in the process of taking over more and more mines, made further delays impossible. Occupation authorities now began to confiscate funds from the national government that had been earmarked for public relief so that they could either be applied to the costs of the occupation or placed in the reparations account. As a result, these funds had to be funneled through increasingly complicated channels. The lack of legal tender obliged many municipalities to issue temporary scrip. Local bankers and industrialists in the Rhineland were making plans for a Rhenish Gold Discount Bank (Rheinische Golddiskontobank) with its own currency tied to the value of the French franc. Such a step would have been a major step toward the economic separation of the occupied territory from the rest of the Reich. In the meantime, the cabinet's efforts at currency reform were doomed to failure as long as the budget still had to cover the astronomical costs of keeping the Ruhr afloat.

After extensive consultation with the state governments, Stresemann formally declared the termination of passive resistance on 26 September 1923. In an effort to avoid the impression of a total capitulation, however, Stresemann made the fulfillment of Germany's reparations obligations contingent upon the complete restoration of the sovereignty of the Reich in the occupied territory. That the decision to end resistance would encounter sharp opposition from the Right could already be seen in the declaration of the Bavarian envoy to Berlin that his government regarded the termination of passive resistance as tantamount to dissolving the Reich, as a "second Versailles." Hysterical demands in the nationalist and *völkisch* press that Stresemann declare the Versailles peace treaty null and void — to which he responded that it would be foolish for Germany to abandon the legal positions that it had established for itself under the auspices of the treaty — did little to conceal the fact that for all intents and purposes the decision to terminate passive resistance was generally accepted with a sense of relief. Nonetheless, the Bavarian cabinet used the termination of passive resistance as the pretext for declaring a state of emergency in open violation of the Weimar Constitution and for providing Gustav von Kahr with special emergency powers as general state commissar. In an earlier meeting with representatives of the other state governments, Kahr himself had conceded the necessity of ending passing resistance; his action now was motivated solely by internal Bavarian considerations.

From a political point of view, Bavaria's declaration of disloyalty with respect to the national government represented the first step toward the overthrow of the parliamentary system that right-wing circles — and particularly the patriotic associations in Bavaria — had been pursuing for some time. The attempted coup in Küstrin several days later by elements of the "Black Reichswehr" under the command of Major Buchrucker suggested that this was more than a simple matter of "cutting out the festering, pus-filled Marxist boils" in Saxony and Thuringia; it was the first step toward the realization of plans that the leaders of the United Patriotic Leagues (Vereinigte Vaterländische Verbände) had discussed with the Bavarian minister president Eugen von Knilling and units of the Bavarian Reichswehr for a march on Berlin and the forcible removal of the "red government." None of this came as a surprise to the Reichswehr leadership or representatives of the political Right.

General Hans von Seeckt, the commander in chief of the Reichswehr, had established contact with the leaders of Germany's paramilitary Right — most notably with forestry official Georg Escherich, first lieutenant Gerhard Roßbach, and Franz von Epp — as early as the spring of 1923 with an eye toward incorporating their units into the Reichswehr in the event of a military conflict. Seeckt also came into contact — through the good offices of industrialist Hugo Stinnes — with General Erich von Ludendorff, who enjoyed close relations with right-wing nationalist combat leagues. To be sure, Reichswehr Minister Otto Geßler formally prohibited such contacts in February 1923, and in a few cases low-ranking members of the Reichswehr were even discharged for having attended meetings of right-wing extremist organizations. But Reichswehr commanders at the regional level were encouraged by Seeckt to maintain close contact with nationalist associations of all sorts, including the border patrol, or *Grenzschutz*, that worked hand in hand with regional branches of the National Rural League in the eastern provinces and units of the "Black Reichswehr" that had disguised themselves as work commandos.

The military value of the various associations on Germany's paramilitary Right was negligible, particularly since their leaders insisted on complete autonomy in the event of their incorporation into the Reichswehr. From the perspective of domestic politics, however, their mobilization could only mean that the forces of counterrevolution were on the march. This, in turn, led to constant tension with the Prussian government. Without being informed of the full extent of illegal rearmament, the Prussian government had concluded an agreement with Seeckt whereby the Reichswehr would terminate its contacts with private military organizations in return for toleration of border patrol units. In point of fact, however, this pledge was never more than a fiction. When Interior Minister Carl Severing formally dissolved right-wing paramilitary associations and ordered the arrest of Lieutenant Roßbach and other leaders of the Free Corps movement, Seeckt's disgust with the Prussian government mounted to the point where in May 1923 he was preparing for the assumption of executive power by the Reichswehr.

The formation of the Stresemann cabinet elicited profound misgivings within the military leadership. The chancellor, who hoped for the establishment of good relations with the Reichswehr, was informed in no uncertain terms by the commander in chief of the army that the Reichswehr would follow him only if he agreed to go the "German route." After the termination of passive resistance on 26 September 1923, Seeckt found himself under increasingly heavy pressure from his military advisors and representatives of the German Right—among them Oskar Hergt and Count Kuno von Westarp—to assume political power at the head of a three-man directorate. With this in mind, Seeckt drafted a "government program" that, in addition to revising the constitution along corporatist lines, called for the exclusion of the socialist parties, the elimination of the labor unions, and the rescinding of all wage agreements, as well as for merging the offices of the chancellor and the Prussian minister president. By no means were Seeckt's proposals original. They were simply variations of the alternative constitutional model that had been propounded by neoconservative ideologues like Oswald Spengler and by conservative notables such as Ulrich von Hassell and Carl Goerdeler. By early November Seeckt was ready for an open attack and demanded that Ebert dismiss Stresemann as chancellor. Stresemann, he said, was "not the man to lead the fight," for he no longer enjoyed the confidence of the troops.

As Seeckt was preparing his plans for a dictatorship in the early fall of 1923, he received strong encouragement from Friedrich Minoux, executive director the Berlin branch of the Stinnes concern. Minoux was acting on behalf of

Stinnes until he broke with his chief over certain details of the Seeckt plan, above all the proposals to offer the Allies a minority interest in west German industry as part of the reparations package and to maintain the eight-hour workday. In a meeting with the American ambassador Alanson B. Houghton, Stinnes outlined the plans for a directorate and revealed the strategy of the Reichswehr command. At the first sign of a Communist uprising, a military dictatorship would, with Ebert's consent, abolish the parliamentary system and "ruthlessly smash" the Communist movement. This plan, which would mobilize the entire political Right, was predicated upon the assumption that the KPD would indeed attempt to overthrow the system. Stinnes, who earlier in the year had brought Seeckt and Ludendorff together, was concerned that the reaction abroad would be negative if the subversive initiative were to originate in Bavaria. It was with this in mind, therefore, that Seeckt used his close personal relations with Otto Hermann von Lossow and Gustav von Kahr to dissuade them from striking prematurely. Hitler's abortive putsch of 9 November, however, dramatically altered the entire situation.

It was particularly alarming that after the withdrawal of the Social Democrats from the Stresemann cabinet in November 1923 Ebert disregarded the chancellor's emphatic warnings against the establishment of a right-wing dictatorship and gave his tacit approval to Seeckt's contacts with Otto Wiedtfeld, the German ambassador in Washington, about the proposed directorate. Unlike the Bavarian putschists, Seeckt intended to preserve the external appearances of legality in taking over the chancellorship and governing by means of a directorate. It was, after all, not in the interests of the Reichswehr to support a right-wing putsch that might easily lead Germany back to the brink of a civil war. Preparing the German people for a revisionist war against France could not, Seeckt was convinced, be achieved by fighting the authority of the state. This insight, however, did not prevent the Reichswehr command from providing illegal defense associations with weapons and even occasional financial help, for at the very least they seemed indispensable for suppressing socialist activities at home. It is evident that Ebert—who had a totally unjustified confidence in Seeckt that was certainly not reciprocated by the Reichswehr commander in chief—did not fully appreciate the political implications of what Seeckt had in mind. In point of fact, the alliance between the military and heavy industry that had come about by the fall of 1923 sought not just to eliminate the political influence of the KPD but also to abolish the eight-hour workday and to free German management from the constraints of state wage policies, an objective that could be accomplished only if the SPD were forced out of the government.

The industrial offensive against the social legacy of the November Revolution began just three days after the end of passive resistance in the Ruhr. At a conference in Unna-Königsborn on 29 September 1923 the Mining Association (Zechenverband) unilaterally decided to lengthen the shifts from seven to eight-and-a-half hours. In defense of their action, the mineowners cited the need to increase coal production, something that could only be accomplished by lengthening the shifts. This decision reopened an issue that had been hotly contested between the Mining Association and the miners' unions for years. In September 1922 a provisional agreement on supplementary shifts had been reached through the mediation of the Reich Ministry of Labor. While conceding that workers would have to work overtime as they had always done, this agreement reaffirmed the principle of the eight-hour workday. By unilaterally increasing the length of the workday, the employers had set themselves on a collision course with the miners on the regulation of working hours. Moreover, the mineowners' action was incompatible with demobilization decrees that would not expire until 31 October and was designed to bring about the fall of the Stresemann government.

Under pressure from industry and the bourgeois members of the coalition government, Labor Minister Heinrich Brauns found himself obliged to undertake a legal regulation of working hours that went beyond the coal industry itself. In this respect, the entrepreneurs and the bourgeois government parties were firmly convinced that the reparations burden resulting from the MICUM negotiations and the costs of stabilizing the mark could be financed only by significantly increasing the length of the workday. But whereas heavy industry sought a return to the twelve-hour shift and thereby put an end to the three-shift system, Brauns hoped to come up with a less rigid solution. The legislation he introduced provided for the retention of the eight-hour day only for heavy and health-threatening work as well as for the protection of underage and female workers. In all other cases, the length of the workday was to be established through individual collective bargaining agreements. A decree implementing these changes was to be enacted as part of the enabling legislation the government was about to introduce for restoring fiscal and economic stability. Anticipating strong opposition from the labor unions, the Social Democratic members of the Stresemann cabinet pleaded with their colleagues not to include the decree on the length of the workday in the enabling legislation. The DVP, on the other hand, not only insisted that the original procedure be followed but also that the DNVP be brought into the cabinet, a demand with which the Social Democrats could not possibly comply. Efforts to reach a compromise on the working hours legislation that might save the coalition came to nothing because of the rigidity of the bourgeois parties, whereby Ernst Scholz, chairman of the DVP Reichstag delegation, was already making plans for a right-wing coalition from which Stresemann himself would be excluded.

From the outside it appeared as if the Social Democrats had become so fixated on a question of secondary significance that they were incapable of dealing with the life-and-death questions that faced their nation. In point of fact, however, the conflict over the length of the workday was simply another test of strength between heavy industry and the more pliable forces of the German Left. It was symptomatic of the deepening political crisis not only that the DVP went behind the chancellor's back to attach conditions to its support of the enabling legislation that were specifically designed to provoke the Social Democrats into resigning from the cabinet but also that the first casualty of this tactic was Hans von Raumer, a member of the DVP who was forced to resign as economics minister on the day before the collapse of the coalition because of his prolabor attitude. But nothing worked out as planned. Since the DNVP refused to form a right-wing minority government that would have implied indirect acceptance of the parliamentary system and since the SPD did not go along with Stresemann's proposal that it tolerate a cabinet of personalities, the result was the reestablishment of the Great Coalition on 6 October. The major difference between the first and second Stresemann cabinets was that in the latter the Social Democratic minister of finance Rudolf Hilferding had been replaced by the infinitely more dynamic Hans Luther. While a solution to the question of working hours had been postponed by extending the effectiveness of the demobilization decrees, the government gained some room for maneuver by implementing its currency reforms under the auspices of the enabling legislation that now passed the Reichstag by an overwhelming majority.

The stabilization of the German currency through the introduction of the Rentenmark constitutes one of the most remarkable accomplishments of the Stresemann government. That the government did not fall apart under the relentless cross fire of special-interest groups stemmed in no small measure from the fact that the fall of the mark had reached inconceivable proportions. In the fall of 1923 the Reich's floating debt had increased a thousandfold within a month's time. Not only had the simplest budgetary procedures become impossible, but the government no longer had access to the hard currencies that were essential for economic activity. In the meantime, domestic German prices had fallen to the level of the world market. The advantages of the inflation had finally turned into their opposite.

The creation of the Rentenmark rested upon a compromise between the suggestions of Karl Helfferich, who wanted to peg the new currency to the value of rye, and those of Rudolf Hilferding, Hans Luther, and Hjalmar Schacht, who were committed to a return to the gold standard. In the period between the founding of the Rentenbank on 15 October 1923 and the issuance of the Rentenmark a month later, the value of the mark plummeted to the level of 4.2 billion to the dollar. By deliberately postponing the stabilization of the mark for a few days, Luther was able to erase the internal indebtedness of the Reich almost entirely. At the same time, the new government levied taxes on the basis of the gold standard and instituted a rigorous austerity program in the public sector, the first manifestation of which was the decree of 27 October that resulted in the dismissal of more than 300,000 public employees. At the same time, the salaries of civil servants and public employees were reduced on average to 60 percent of their prewar level.

The success of the government's stabilization program ultimately depended on whether it would be possible to close the "hole in the west" (*Loch im Westen*) and put an end to the huge subsidies and other forms of assistance to the occupied territories. Suggestions that all payments be discontinued and that the Ruhr and Rhineland be left to their own devices not only encountered strong opposition in the cabinet but provoked massive protests from Rhineland politicians like Konrad Adenauer, who argued that the Rhine should, if necessary, be worth a second and a third currency crisis. In point of fact, the policy of "letting it all go down the drain" — or *Versackungspolitik*, as it was contemptuously known — would only have strengthened the separatist efforts encouraged by the French. By the end of October separatist groups had proclaimed under the mantle of the occupation authorities the founding of a Rhenish Republic in Aachen and others along the Rhine. The short-lived autonomy of the Palatinate, which came about through the intrigues of Social Democrat Johannes Hoffmann and with the express support of General de Metz, was directed in large part against the dictatorial regime that Kahr had established in Munich.

The Interallied Rhineland Commission under the chairmanship of General Paul Tirard generally overestimated the potential of the separatist movements, which never received the support of more than an insignificant minority. Moreover, Paris lacked the resolve that would have been necessary to separate the Rhineland from the Reich by such means. For while there was strong support at the Quai d'Orsay for the creation of Rhenish buffer states, there was no agreement on whether these should be separated from the Reich or used as leverage by which the French could influence events in Germany. Furthermore, the French interest in the economic exploitation of Germany came into conflict with France's traditional Rhine policy. For his own part, Poincaré tended to vacillate between the two positions, although in the final analysis he was prepared to exploit the capitulation of the Reich to create a Rhenish state whose permanent demilitarization would satisfy the French desire for security. For such purposes the Versailles peace treaty was insufficient inasmuch as it limited the period of occupation and thus provided France with temporary security at best.

To a certain degree, French ambitions regarding the Rhineland converged with Konrad Adenauer's idea of a west German federal state that would be politically separate from Prussia yet part of the Reich itself. Since such a state would be under international supervision, it would satisfy the French obsession with security. As lord mayor of Cologne, Adenauer viewed this solution not only as an opportunity to initiate an era of Franco-German understanding but also, given the collapse of the nation's finances, as the only possible means of charting a middle course between separatism and repudiation of the Versailles peace treaty. The latter alternative was particularly repugnant to Adenauer since it would most likely entail temporary abandonment of the occupied territories, a prospect to which certain elements within the DVP had apparently already resigned themselves. In certain respects, Adenauer's thinking paralleled that of industrialist Hugo Stinnes, who was planning a transfer of industrial stocks that would eventually lead to the merger of French and German heavy industry in a project that was obviously directed against the British. Moreover, Adenauer's idea of a west German federal state coincided with plans the Cologne banker Louis Hagen had broached for the creation of a special Rhenish bank that would be limited to the occupied territories and whose assets would be secured by gold. A majority of the bank's stockholders would be German, although French and British investment would be encouraged as well.

Stresemann, who had coupled the termination of passive resistance with adamant denials that he had any intention of surrendering German soil, had little sympathy for Adenauer's proposal but nevertheless did feel that some sort of administrative agency responsible for the occupied territories would be useful. Since Poincaré had banished representatives of the central government from the area, this agency would assume the functions of the central government and make certain that French political operatives did not pressure regional and local officials into concluding separate agreements of their own. This plan, however, met with strong opposition from the Prussian minister president Otto Braun, who regarded it as a threat to the integrity of the Prussian state. For a moment Stresemann even seems to have considered the temporary surrender of the Rhineland to the French, although he was quick to deny allegations to this effect as categorically as possible. In the final analysis, neither the creation of a separate administrative apparatus for the Rhineland nor the surrender of the territory to the French came to pass. For the success of the Rentenmark made it possible for the central government to fulfill the terms of the compromise by which it agreed to continue paying both unemployment compensation and the costs of the occupation but limited its subsidies to industry. Had Tirard and Poincaré been more flexible, the prospects of translating Adenauer's compromise solution into reality would have been significantly better, although this too would have given rise to a whole gamut of conflicts between French and German heavy industry. For the time being, the Rhineland and Ruhr issue was shelved.

For Stresemann it came as a bitter disappointment that Poincaré avoided all negotiations with the German government following the termination of passive resistance. Attempts to secure the release of prisoners of war, the repatriation of deportees, and the restoration of German administrative sovereignty ended in failure on account of the French premier's fundamental refusal to negotiate with anyone but representatives from the occupied territories. After the Otto

Wolff conglomerate had agreed to fulfill the far-reaching financial demands of MICUM, Stresemann was unable to prevent the Ruhr industrial establishment from entering into direct negotiations with General Jean Degoutte, even though he avoided making financial commitments to the six-member commission that had been formed by the Mining Association.

Efforts to resume coal production were hampered by the onerous levies that had been imposed by MICUM. Not only did the Ruhr mining industry have to agree to large coal deliveries to France and Belgium, but it was also required to make retroactive payments of the coal tax, even though the German government had formally waived payments of this tax as a way of providing financial support for industry in the Ruhr. Stresemann reluctantly went along with this far-reaching encroachment on German sovereignty when it threatened to produce a breakdown of negotiations at the end of October 1923 since the alternative would have been to bring industrial production in the Ruhr to a complete standstill. The compromise that was finally reached stipulated that only the coal tax would be placed into a guaranteed fund, or *Pfänderkasse*, designated for the payment of occupation costs, while the value of the coal deliveries would be credited to Germany's reparations account. Moreover, the German government was obliged to indemnify the Ruhr industry for the expenses it had incurred under the MICUM agreement signed on 24 November 1923. In order not to jeopardize the currency reform, the agreement further stipulated that the industrial concerns were to provide the necessary capital and that these payments would be deducted from their taxes when they became due. Sums that could not be covered in this manner were repaid by the government to the Ruhr industrialists, without, however, ever consulting the Reichstag.

Ruhr heavy industry used the MICUM agreements, which typically had been concluded without the participation of organized labor, to exert heavy pressure not only in the question of working hours but also with respect to wage scales and benefit policies. If Stinnes had stated in the National Economic Council as early as 1922 that German workers would have to work an extra two hours a day, employers now cited the costs of the agreements to justify a return to prewar working hours. No longer did one mention the loyalty that workers had demonstrated during the recent conflict in the Ruhr. On the contrary, the workers were the ones who were being asked to absorb the added costs of Germany's return to fiscal stability. In view of the fact that the inflation had depleted the financial reserves of organized labor, there was little the labor unions could do to resist the management's strategy of direct and indirect lockouts.

With the slogan that "gold wages" (*Goldlohn*) could be paid only for "gold work" (*Goldleistung*) — that is, for work preformed under prewar standards — the Mining Association and the Northwest Employers' Association (Nord-West Arbeitgeberverband) of the iron and steel industry went on the offensive following the expiration of the demobilization ordinances to restore the ten-hour workday through short-time work and massive layoffs. This initiative received the formal blessing of the labor minister in December. Now that German industry had finally come to accept the realities of the lost war, it became increasingly determined to rescind the social and political concessions it had made in 1918 in order to forestall Germany's internal collapse.

It is against the background of these developments that a sharp turn to the left took place first in Saxony, where the Social Democratic minority government under the leadership of Erich Zeigner invited several Communists to join his cabinet on 10 October 1923, and then in Thuringia a short time later. In both cases, the left wing of the SPD, which by no means consisted solely of those who had formerly belonged to the Independent Socialists, was particularly strong. Up until this point, the Social Democratic minority governments had been tolerated by the KPD. The parties of the bourgeois center had to accept a measure of responsibility for this situation since in January 1923 they had helped topple the Saxon cabinet headed by moderate Social Democrat Wilhelm Buch by failing to oppose a Communist motion of no confidence. Dependent upon the toleration of the KPD, the new minister president Erich Zeigner was unable to keep the proletarian control commissions for monitoring usury and price gouging and the auxiliary police units known as the "Proletarian Brigades" (*proletarische Hundertschaften*) from falling under Communist control, although he was successful in blocking Communist calls for a general strike.

Not since the uprising in central Germany was Saxony the source of constant friction between the Reichswehr and the Social Democrats, whose persecution of right-wing extremist groups hampered the illegal rearmament schemes of Germany's military leadership. Geßler and Seeckt were determined to depose the Saxon government by military action at the next opportunity that presented itself. In this respect, they were encouraged by the support of the middle-class parties in Saxony and the League of Saxon Industrialists (Verband sächsischer Industrieller), which recounted tales of horror about the excesses allegedly committed by the control commissions and the proletarian brigades. In August 1923 the military commander of Saxony, General Alfred Müller, prohibited his officers from taking part in ceremonies celebrating the ratification of the Weimar Constitution, while Ziegler's largely accurate revelations about the activities of the Black Reichswehr had led to his denunciation as a national traitor.

It did not take, therefore, Communist preparations for a "German October" under the auspices of the Proletarian Brigades for the Reichswehr to conclude that intervention in Saxony was necessary to restore law and order. In the meantime, the revolutionary agitation of the KPD and its technical preparations for a violent uprising raised tensions to a fever pitch. After the Independent Socialists had split in October 1920 under Comintern pressure over the adoption of Zinoviev's "Twenty-One Points," the party's left wing had merged with the KPD to create the United Communist Party (Vereinigte Kommunistiche Partei Deutschlands or VKPD). Factional strife and repeated splits within the party cost the USPD more than a fifth of its membership, while the KPD, on the other hand, succeeded in transforming itself into a genuine mass party. Paul Levi's efforts to bring about the creation of a united front of all proletarian forces, however, encountered implacable opposition from the socialist parties and labor unions and was eventually disavowed by the Comintern itself in 1921. As a result, Levi's central office — and with it the faction within the KPD that had been most vehemently opposed to revolutionary putschism — folded. Under the influence of Karl Radek, the left wing of the Communist Party headed by August Thalheimer and Heinrich Brandler now threw itself headlong into the fiasco of an insurrection in central Germany.

A shift in Comintern strategy produced not only the first wave of purges in the KPD but also the adoption of a more intensely defensive posture during the course of 1922. Invoking the need to create a "workers' government," the Communists reluctantly supported the Social Democratic governments in Thuringia and Saxony in the hope that this would enable them to consolidate their declining party membership. After the collapse of the national Bolshevist orientation that Radek had tried to impose on the KPD in the face of mounting opposition from its revolutionary left wing, the Comintern's Grigory Zinoviev instructed the party on 15 August 1923 to prepare itself for an impending revolutionary crisis. Influenced by reports from Radek, the Comintern's expert on German affairs, the Politburo of the Soviet Communist Party believed that the revolutionary struggle in Germany was entering its decisive phase. Leon Trotsky was particularly supportive of the new revolutionary offensive to which the KPD chairman Heinrich Brandler had committed himself in Moscow in early September. In this respect, however, both Zinoviev and Trotsky were deluding themselves about the revolutionary potential of the German working masses and the possibility of mobilizing them for the upheaval that had been set for sometime around 9 November 1923.

Communist participation in the Saxon and Thuringian state governments was designed to facilitate the preparations for the planned uprising. One of the most pressing tasks was the procurement of weapons. Brandler, who was originally slated to take over the Ministry of the Interior, was appointed director of the Saxon chancery and in this capacity spent most of his time ferreting out secret weapons deposits. Little of this escaped the attention of the national government, even though it had no advance knowledge of the plans of the Communist International. On 13 October the Proletarian Brigades were declared illegal and the Saxon police force was placed under military command. But this was not the only reason the planned Communist uprising ended in failure. At a workers' conference the KPD held in Chemnitz on 21 October, Brandler's call for an immediate general strike received only minority support. Even in "red" Saxony, the Communists found themselves politically isolated. Why the Hamburg KPD ignored the decision of the party's national leadership to abort the action and incited an insurrection on 23 October that never attracted the support of more than 5,000 workers has never been adequately explained. Communication difficulties and possibly the ambitions of Ernst Thälmann and other local Communist leaders led to this completely isolated uprising of the "German October," which ignominiously collapsed on 25 October.

While the crisis in central Germany drew to a head in October, the conflict between Bavaria and the central government remained temporarily unresolved. On 26 September Stresemann had responded to the Bavarian challenge to the authority of the central government by declaring a military state of emergency and by placing executive power in the hands of the defense minister. In doing this, he rejected demands from the Social Democratic members of his cabinet that he follow this up by forcing the dismissal of State Commissioner Gustav von Kahr. In point of fact, however, Stresemann lacked the means to do that. For Seeckt and Geßler refused to deploy the Reichswehr against the Bavarian government, no doubt with a discrete eye to the proposed directorate. Still, a sharp controversy between Seeckt and the Bavarian government erupted when the commander of the 7th Division, Otto Hermann von Lossow, refused to enforce Geßler's order proscribing the Nazi party organ, the *Völkischer Beobachter*, for having leveled anti-Semitic attacks against the national government in an article entitled "Two Dictators — Stresemann and Seeckt." This conflict revealed that the Bavarian leadership of the Reichswehr was committed to using the so-called fall maneuvers to place the paramilitary patriotic associations under its command in order to carry out the planned march on Berlin, if necessary, without Seeckt. It was therefore not just Lossow's refusal to execute a direct order from the government that accounted for Seeckt's extreme reaction and his request for Lossow's resignation.

Kahr was able to prevent Lossow's dismissal by placing the 7th Division directly under his own command. Seeckt remained firm but tried to minimize the conflict as a personnel dispute, while Kahr, for his part, dispatched the head of the Bavarian police, Colonel Hans Ritter von Seißer, to Berlin to solicit Seeckt's support for a planned putsch by a Lossow-Seißer-Hitler triumvirate. While the head of the armed forces continued to insist that the proposed directorate remain within the bounds of legality, he emphasized in his letter of 2 November 1923 to Kahr: "The Weimar Constitution is not a *noli me tangere* for me; I had no hand in making it, and its basic principles are contrary to my political thinking." A Stresemann government, he continued, was not viable, even if it succeeded in ousting the Social Democrats. Seeckt, on the other hand, wanted to bring about change without precipitating open civil war in which the

Reichswehr would find itself in the uncomfortable position of having to defend the authority of the state on two fronts. Under these circumstances, intervention in Bavaria would not have been possible even if Stresemann had wanted it. The chancellor thus countered the pressure of the Social Democratic ministers for intervention against Kahr with the remark: "I do not want to create the pretext for a right-wing putsch." Indeed, such a step would more likely have prompted Seeckt and the forces that stood behind him to accept the Bavarian offer of an alliance against the Berlin government.

The Reichswehr leadership, however, used the state of emergency to intervene against the Saxon and Thuringian state governments — and at a time when no clear decision in the cabinet had been reached. On 17 October the Reichswehr commander in Saxony censured the Saxon minister president for having failed to clear the text of the new government's declaration of purpose prior to its publication. On 22 October additional Reichswehr units arrived, triggering a series of violent confrontations with protesting workers. This should have been sufficient. Yet the Reichswehr minister urged the chancellor to appoint a civilian state commissar for Saxony. This, however, encountered immediate opposition within the cabinet. Justice Minister Gustav Radbruch pointed out that there was no constitutional provision for the removal of a state's minister president by the central government, but his coalition partners did not agree. In this respect, the Social Democratic members of the cabinet were not fully aware of the pressure the Saxon DVP had brought to bear upon Stresemann. All they achieved was the concession that any military action the central government might undertake would be preceded by a written request from the chancellor for Zeigner's resignation. This the Saxon prime minister rejected as unacceptable and unconstitutional.

It subsequently turned out that Zeigner was willing at this particular point to dismiss the Communist members of his cabinet. The only legal grounds that might have existed for deposing the properly constituted Saxon coalition was Communist agitation against the national constitution. It would therefore have been sufficient to bring about the resignation of the Communist members of the cabinet. Since 21 October a Communist uprising was both politically and, given the increasing control of the military, practically impossible. The appointment of the DVP's Karl Heinze as national commissioner for Saxony proved to be a mistake insofar as he proceeded with the military takeover of the Saxon government on 29 October before such a step had been authorized by the Stresemann cabinet. Stresemann moved quickly to rescind Heinze's ban against the meeting of the Saxon Landtag. In the meantime, the SPD executive committee was able to pressure the party's Saxon Landtag delegation into going along with the election of moderate Social Democrat Karl Fellisch as head of a new minority cabinet that was tolerated by the DDP. This should have brought the state of emergency in Saxony to an end. But shortly thereafter Berlin ordered the military occupation of neighboring Thuringia and forced the coalition government headed by Fröhlich out of office.

The Social Democratic members of the Stresemann cabinet were deeply offended over the fact that Saxony and Thuringia had been treated much more severely than Bavaria. In this respect, they realized that the military action against the Saxon Left was motivated—aside from Seeckt's and Geßler's anger about Zeigner's thwarting of the interests of the Reichswehr—by a twofold aim. A decisive blow against "Marxism" in Saxony would—or so it seemed— confer upon Seeckt, and his circle of sympathizers in the military and industry, leadership in the efforts to revamp the parliamentary system in an authoritarian direction that was predicated above all else upon the exclusion of the Social Democrats. To be sure, the Social Democrats had had their own doubts about the machinations of their Saxon comrades and had sought to exercise a moderating influence. But, as the Prussian interior minister very well knew, the SPD's criticism of the Reichswehr and its role in protecting right-wing extremist organizations was certainly justified even if Zeigner's political posturing had severely strained Saxon resources. The vast majority of the Saxon working class sympathized with efforts to revive the idea of government by councils in an attempt to keep the social and political legacy of the recent revolution from being dismantled and to hold the growing strength of the antirepublican Right in check. But many of the blunders that had been committed during the Noske era were repeated in Saxony. Within the SPD, which found itself the target of incessant Communist agitation, the idea of a military regime that forbade its publications along with those of the KPD rekindled bitter memories of the spring of 1919.

How deeply events in Saxony had divided the SPD could be seen in the reaction of Reichstag president Paul Löbe. An outspoken advocate of reformism, Löbe adopted the slogan "Back to the pure class struggle." Löbe knew full well that the prospects of armed resistance were nil and that his party had its back up against the wall, particularly with respect to its most important priority, social policy. Social Democrats, he declared, could no longer fight for the republic, for the masses felt that a form of government in which capital and the military wielded as much power as they had once wielded in the Second Empire was no longer worthy of being defended. Representatives for the Prussian government, not the least of whom was Carl Severing, responded to this argument by pointing out that the party would only be increasing the dangers of an authoritarian solution if it left the government.

In the end, the executive councils of the SPD made their party's continued participation in the national government contingent on a set of conditions, which took on an ultimatum-like character through their premature publication in *Vorwärts*. Demands for lifting the state of military emergency in Saxony and for censuring the violation of the constitution in Bavaria as well as for establishing effective civilian control over the activities of the Reichswehr in Saxony were little more than face-saving devices that could have been fulfilled with a modicum of goodwill. But the tactically inept fashion in which these conditions were presented made it very easy for the bourgeois parties to saddle the SPD with responsibility for the collapse of the Great Coalition when the Social Democrats withdrew their ministers from the cabinet following the rejection of their demands.

The escalating conflict between the Free State of Bavaria and the national government in the fall of 1923, on the other hand, was much more than a crisis of German federalism. It was a symptom of the far-reaching domestic dangers that faced Weimar's parliamentary system. Ever since the violent suppression of the Munich Soviet Republic in the spring of 1919, Bavaria had become a haven for the forces of the German counterrevolution. The defeat of the Kapp Putsch had resulted in the total isolation of the Bavarian SPD even though its leaders had taken consistently more moderate positions than their Saxon counterparts. At the same time, Bavaria had worked against the stabilization of Germany's new republican institutions. Gustav von Kahr, who had been elected Bavarian minister president in March 1920 on the recommendation of the Bavarian People's Party, was a career civil servant and a convinced monarchist whose base of power was located not so much in the Bavarian Landtag as in the citizens' militias that had emerged in the immediate postwar period as an instrument of the conservative and propertied bourgeoisie. The dissolution of these units at the insistence of the Interallied Military Control Commission led to endless disputes with the national government, which culminated in Kahr's resignation and in the appointment of the considerably less energetic Count Hugo von Lerchenfeld as his successor. Under Lerchenfeld the *Ordnungszelle Bayern* became an El Dorado for competing nationalist cliques and paramilitary combat units that had escaped the control of the state.

In the revolutionary turmoil of the immediate postwar period Bavaria had been the scene of political excess on the Left as well as on the Right. But this brief period of unprecedented experimentation and openness that had witnessed the flowering of all sorts of political utopias from Kurt Tucholsky's "council of spiritual workers" (*Rat der geistigen Arbeiter*) to the Thule Society (Thule-Gesellschaft) had not been so much crushed by the "White Terror" unleashed against the Munich Soviet in the late spring of 1919 as driven into the spectrum of the extreme Right. This spectrum, in turn, stretched from rival monarchist groups such as the Bavarian Royalist Party (Bayerische Königspartei) and the Bavarian Home and King's League (Bayerischer Heimat- und Königsbund) to successor organizations of the Free Corps such as the League for Bavaria and the Reich (Bund Bayern und Reich) founded by public health official Otto Pittinger, the Organization Consul (Organisation Consul)—later known as the Viking League (Wiking-Bund)—under the command of the former Free Corps leader Hermann Ehrhardt, and the League Oberland (Bund Oberland) that had surfaced in Upper Silesia and, under the leadership of Friedrich Weber, had drifted into the "Greater German" camp to more traditionally conservative associations that included not only the Organization Escherich, or Orgesch, under the leadership of the politically deft Georg Escherich but also the Stahlhelm and Young German Order (Jungdeutscher Orden). And on the extreme right of this remarkably heterogeneous spectrum stood the Storm Detachments (Sturmabteilungen or SA) of the NSDAP that had evolved out of the party's gymnastics and sports division founded in 1920.

Whereas the Prussian government was particularly diligent in trying to bring the activities of the extreme Right under its control and invoked the Law for the Protection of the Republic that had been passed in the aftermath of Rathenau's murder to institute organizational bans and legal proceedings against right-wing organizations, the Bavarian government not only refrained from taking any initiative in this regard but defied the central government by declaring the Law for the Protection of the Republic invalid for the state of Bavaria. And whereas Prussia and other federal states outlawed the NSDAP, the German Racist Defense and Defiance League (Deutschvölkischer Schutz-und Trutzbund), the Young German Order, and a host of similar organizations, Bavaria afforded them toleration and sympathy. The fall of the Wirth cabinet in October 1922 meant that the national government no longer provided the impetus for fighting the antirepublican tendencies that had surfaced not just in Bavaria but in other parts of the country as well. With the intensification of the reparations conflict, right-wing extremist organizations and particularly the illegal combat leagues became increasingly active, in part as a consequence of the fact that it was no longer possible to delay a reduction in the troop strength of the Reichswehr.

To those on the extreme Right who were preparing for civil war, the approaching end of passive resistance in the Ruhr meant that the struggle for power that had been suspended for the sake of a united struggle against Versailles could no longer be postponed. In the eyes of the German Right, the Stresemann chancellorship was tantamount to the definitive triumph of Social Democracy and the stabilization of the hated system of defeat and weakness epitomized by the term Weimar. Through the trauma of the Munich Soviet and the disgraceful treatment of the Bavarian royal house, Munich became the home of an overheated political climate in which anti-Semitism and nationalist resentment were inextricably linked and in which the distinction between the blue-white banner of Bavarian particularism and the black-white-red flag of German imperialism lost all meaning. The petty-bourgeois beer-hall culture of the Bavarian capital, whose bourgeoisie was thoroughly disoriented by the course of recent events, nurtured putschist tendencies, which in contrast to their north German counterparts lacked the necessary focus. Deep-seated resentment against Berlin helped bridge the gap between Bavarian particularism and Greater German chauvinism and obscured the fundamentally anarchistic structure of Bavarian right-wing extremism.

The moment of opportunity for the Wittelsbachs came and went on 5 November 1921. The burial of the royal couple in the family vault in Munich had been accompanied by a triumphal funeral procession and by Cardinal Michael von Faulhaber's disparaging commentary on the republican system that "where the people is its own king, it will sooner or later become its own gravedigger." Still, this did not lead, as even Ernst Röhm had wished, to the restoration of Crown Prince Rupprecht to the throne. Nevertheless, the idea of an autonomous Bavarian state, possibly within the framework of a Danubian federation, received more than verbal support from the French and gained in credibility as the separation of the Rhineland and the success of separatist efforts in the occupied territories became increasingly likely.

The driving force behind separatist efforts in Bavaria was Otto Pittinger. Pittinger's first attempt at a coup in July 1922 had collapsed in the face of opposition from the Reichswehr junta around Franz Xaver von Epp and Bund Oberland, which had been hatching their own plans for a strike against Berlin, and eventually "drowned in beer." By the fall of 1922, Pittinger had established contact with Georg Escherich, Captain Hermann Ehrhardt, and other representatives of the conservative-nationalist milieu. What Pittinger had in mind was the establishment of a regency that would, he hoped, attract the support — if necessary, under the threat of violence — of prestigious personalities such as Gustav von Kahr, Munich police president Ernst Pöhner, and Ritter von Epp and that would receive protection from France in the form of money, weapons, and diplomatic support. But this conspiracy, during the course of which several of the participating organizations blatantly made use of French funds, soon exploded with embarrassing disclosures for the forces of Bavarian separatism. In the final analysis, the episode revealed the true nature of the *Ordnungszelle Bayern* and set the stage for the concentration of Bavaria's extraparliamentary Right in the United Patriotic Leagues, which now set their hopes on Kahr and his plans for a conservative renewal of Bavaria.

After the collapse of Pittinger's plot, a rift opened up between those monarchist-separatist associations that were willing to tolerate a Knilling cabinet because of its commitment to the preservation of Bavaria's sovereign rights and those groups that were determined to bring about a fundamental change on the national level. This provided the NSDAP with its first real opportunity to move from the periphery to the center of Bavarian politics. Adolf Hitler had used the occupation of the Ruhr to dissociate himself from the United Patriotic Leagues, whereby he denounced the idea of a national unity front with his new motto, "It is not with France but with the November criminals that we must settle" (*Nicht nieder mit Frankreich, sondern nieder mit den Novemberverbrech-ern*). Through relentless agitation, Hitler hoped to mobilize the support of the masses and thus propel the NSDAP to the leadership of the "national liberation movement." The party's public rallies, at which Hitler vehemently denounced Weimar as the "Republic of the November criminals," attracted unprecedented crowds. Fueled by rumors of an impending putsch and by the actions of rival power groups, the political tension in the Bavarian capital created a fertile environment for the spread of Nazi propaganda and its promises of a "general reckoning with the existing political system."

In the course of 1923 the NSDAP increased its membership from 15,000 to 55,000. For all intents and purposes, however, the party was essentially a Bavarian party and could operate in Prussia, Saxony, and Thuringia only through political surrogates. Eugen von Knilling, the Bavarian prime minister, hoped that he could coax Hitler into a policy of moderation, while Hitler, on the other hand, reassured Knilling that he would abide by a policy of strict legality and had no intention of undertaking a putsch. Knilling was concerned that the use of force against the NSDAP would only provoke a confrontation with the other militant groups on the Bavarian Right. Hitler, after all, not only had close friends in the Bavarian Reichswehr, where Ernst Röhm had brought him into contact with General von Lossow, but could also count on the sympathy of important officials in the Bavarian civil administration, most notably Ernst Pöhner, chief of the Munich police force, and his adjutant, Wilhelm Frick. In 1922, for example, news that the Bavarian government was considering deporting Hitler provoked vigorous protests from the Patriotic Leagues, which did not want to lose the NSDAP's support in the event of a coup, even though neither Crown Prince Rupprecht nor Captain Ehrhardt thought much of Hitler's supposed political talents.

It was only in the extreme counterrevolutionary atmosphere that gripped Bavaria following the suppression of the Soviet Republic that Anton Drexler's fledgling German Workers' Party (Deutsche Arbeiterpartei or DAP) could have become a major political factor in the first place. The founding of the DAP took place in January 1919 on the initiative of the Munich branch of the Thule Society, the successor to the highly secret Order of Germans (Germanenorden) that had surfaced on the fringes of the Pan-German League and that was devoted to the cultivation and practice of Aryan rituals. At the time, the DAP was no more than one of a great number of similar *völkisch*-nationalistic splinter groups that existed without a specific programmatic profile in the steamy back rooms of Bavarian beer halls.

In contrast, the founding in Bamberg of another Pan-German protégé, the German Racist Defense and Defiance League, on the day that the National Assembly convened in Weimar proved somewhat more successful. The Pan-German League's spokesman Konstantin von Gebsattel hoped that an intensified anti-Semitic campaign using "the Jews as a lightning rod for everything that is wrong" (*die Juden als Blitzableiter für alles Unrecht*) would enable his organization to overcome its admittedly patrician character and establish itself as a mass political movement with a broad base of popular support. Heinrich Claß played a critical role as chairman of the Pan-German League in securing the financial and political support that was to transform the German Racist Defense and Defiance League into the most important expression of popular anti-Semitism in postwar Germany. Organized anti-Semitism enjoyed close ties with the Free Corps and right-wing circles in the Reichswehr, in particular with "Organization Consul," the Stahlhelm and other veterans' associations, and the NSDAP, most of whose leaders had been recruited from the ranks of the German Racist Defense and Defiance League. In Bavaria the NSDAP was thus able to establish itself as the league's principal successor after the latter, severely weakened by internal dissension, was officially banned in the wake of Rathenau's murder. Even at the height of its popularity, however, the German Racist Defense and Defiance League never embraced more than 180,000 members. As a mass political movement it remained a conspicuous failure. By the same token, the German Racist Freedom Party that had broken away from the DNVP in December 1922 under the leadership of Albrecht von Graefe and Reinhold Wulle, editor in chief of the *völkisch*-oriented *Deutsche Zeitung*, failed to attract a genuine popular following. The radical anti-Semitism propagated by the Defense and Defiance League was directly responsible for a series of murders that had culminated in Rathenau's assassination and did not hesitate to call for the physical liquidation of German Jewry. By no means was the desire to bring about the collapse of the Berlin *Judenrepublik* confined to the NSDAP, which at this time was still a movement with an essentially Bavarian profile.

As the loudest and most radical of the various groups that made up the *völkisch* movement, the NSDAP recruited the bulk of its membership from the lower middle class and, after 1923, from the rural population as well. At the same time, it was a haven for those war veterans who found it increasingly difficult to adjust to the realities of civilian life and had been active in the Free Corps, the citizens' militias, or the Bavarian security police. Rudolf Heß, Max Amann, Walter Buch, and Wilhelm Brückner were typical of the mostly university-educated former military officers who found their way to the NSDAP in the first years of its existence. After 1921 they were joined by new recruits from the military, including not only Ernst Röhm, who continued to serve as General Ritter von Epp's general staff liaison, and Hermann Göring, a fighter pilot who had been decorated with the Pour le Mérite in World War I and who in 1923 assumed command of the SA, but also Lieutenant Colonel Hermann Kriebel, a man who exercised considerable influence in this phase of the NSDAP's development.

The NSDAP also received support from the Munich Bohemian scene. Among those who found their way to the NSDAP were Hitler's future secretary for the foreign press Ernst Hanfstaengl, the Benedictine father Alban Schachtleiter who made a name for himself by consecrating the banners of the SA, and even Emil Nolde, the famous expressionist painter who later became a target of Rosenberg's campaign against "degenerate art." Arthur Moeller van den Bruck, on the other hand, remained aloof from the movement despite Hitler's visit to his June Club in 1922 and remained convinced that Hitler was incapable of providing National Socialism with any kind of intellectual foundation. The group of *völkisch* ideologues—including Dietrich Eckart, Alfred Rosenberg, and Gottfried Feder, whose thesis on "the breaking of interest bondage" was subsequently incorporated into the program of the NSDAP—remained less influential than the party's military and upper-bourgeois elements.

Originally founded as an organization responsible for maintaining order at party meetings, the SA was transformed at the instigation of Röhm and the regular Reichswehr and with officers recruited from the Organization Consul into a paramilitary association that, until the summer of 1923, stood under the virtual command of Hermann Ehrhardt. The SA's subsequent incorporation into the Alliance of Patriotic Combat Leagues (Arbeitsgemeinschaft der vaterländischen Kampfverbände) that had been founded by Röhm in late January 1923 threatened to wrest the SA from Hitler's control in spite of the fact that it, unlike the other *völkisch* combat leagues, continued to think of itself by virtue of its identification with the NSDAP as a political rather than narrowly military organization. The boundaries between the Reichswehr and the individual combat leagues were extremely fluid, as their dual political and military command clearly indicated. The SA, which received regular military training from Reichswehr officers in October 1923, constituted no more than a minority in the Alliance of Patriotic Combat Leagues. Including the regiment "München," which was recruited almost entirely from university students, the SA consisted of no more than 3,000 men, of whom scarcely more than half could be counted upon in the event of a putsch.

The transformation of the German Workers' Party—in February 1920 it renamed itself the National Socialist German Workers' Party or NSDAP—from a *völkisch* association into a fascist movement is closely connected with the person of Adolf Hitler. During his early years in Vienna and then after his move to Munich in 1913, Hitler had come into repeated contact with racial anti-Semitic and extreme nationalistic ideas. The decisive stage in the formation of his political ideas, however, took place in postwar Munich. He received his initiation into politics at the initiative of the Reichswehr. With the outbreak of the November Revolution Hitler had retreated into the comfortable atmosphere of the Oberwiesenfeld barracks, where he served as a guard and thus survived the turmoil of the Munich Soviet unscathed. Following the comple-

tion of political "training courses"—during which he became acquainted with
Dietrich Eckart, the *völkisch* poet who for a time exercised considerable influence over his intellectual development, and the nationalist historian Karl
Alexander von Müller, who was the first to recognize his oratorical skills—
Hitler was assigned by Reichswehr intelligence to observe and report on the activities of the fledgling German Workers' Party. At one of the DAP's meetings
in September 1919, party chairman Anton Drexler was so impressed by Hitler's
remarks in the general discussion that he subsequently offered him a seat on
the party's executive committee. Hitler accepted, without resigning from the
Reichswehr until March 1920 in spite of the fact that he functioned throughout
this period as a propaganda speaker for the DAP.

The anti-Semitic indoctrination that Hitler had received through his Reichswehr training courses and his personal contacts with Dietrich Eckart and
Alfred Rosenberg—both members of the Thule Society—decisively molded
Hitler's political Weltanschauung and could be seen in the fanatical anti-
Semitism of his earliest public appearances. By no means was the hodgepodge
of *völkisch*-nationalist ressentiment that characterized Hitler's early speeches
the product of an independent mind. While Hitler demonstrated considerable
talent for highly emotional oratory, his opinions were usually derived from
the clichés of contemporary *völkisch* nationalism, to which he was able to give
a semblance of plausibility through schematic simplification and demagogic
overstatement.

In certain respects Hitler's career as a propaganda speaker for the NSDAP
represented a flight from himself. The fascination he exercised over his audience was grounded in a highly developed sensitivity to the emotional needs
of others and compensated for the insecurities that plagued his own efforts at
self-definition. Hitler's almost total identification with the slogans and hate appeals that he repeatedly intoned to the point of physical exhaustion constituted
the key to his undeniable power as a popular agitator. Hitler's effectiveness
as an agitator can only be fully understood in terms of the persona that he
had self-consciously created for himself in an attempt to compensate for an
emotionally impoverished character that left him incapable of forming normal
social relationships. For, in the final analysis, it was not so much the content
of his propaganda as his cult of the will and total commitment that he communicated to the public almost as an act of psychic power that accounted for
his demagogic success and that made it possible for him to outline the most
utopian goals with such conviction that no one could doubt their impending
realization.

Hitler impressed his listeners and followers by portraying himself as a simple
front soldier, as a man of the people, who in his heart of hearts despised politics
and regarded professional politicians as little more than "scoundrels." Yet the
force of circumstances had made it necessary for Hitler to enter the political

arena, which he was perfectly willing to abandon once order had been restored and the political mess had been cleaned up. The imagery of unselfishness
and sacrifice that was carefully cultivated through his style of dress—his fancy
Bohemian life-style was known only to a small circle of party cronies—was an
indispensable aspect of his public persona. The total identification of his person with the fate of the nation and the assertion of personal authenticity that he
conveyed in his propaganda were typical of the way in which Hitler conflated
the private with the public sphere. What this suggests is that Hitler's success
in establishing himself as the most successful demagogue of his time stemmed
not so much from the strength of individual character as from his ability to
absorb the prevailing social resentments and attitudes into his subjective view
of the world. Hitler was primarily a product of the times in which he lived and
could never divorce himself from the roles that they had forced upon him and
that he played with such astounding virtuosity. The collective trauma of the
lost war and the revolution that followed in its wake, the growing awareness
of internal discord, the triumph of moral relativism, widespread status anxiety
compensated by a faith in action for the sake of action and by the glorification
of the hero—all of these formed the indispensable sociopsychological background for the fascination that Hitler was able to exert over those segments of
the German population whose traditional privileges were threatened or whose
social aspirations had been thwarted.

The growth of the NSDAP after 1920 had less to do with its political program
than with the unique political style that Hitler and his clique of supporters
introduced into Germany in the early 1920s. In this respect, it is particularly
revealing that Hitler had far less interest in formulating the famous Twenty-
Five-Point Program—a document with whose contents he could have been in
full agreement—than in the circumstances that surrounded its public promulgation. The eclectic, indeed self-contradictory, party program that Hitler proclaimed at a party rally in Munich in February 1920 coincided by and large with
the ideological positions that had been espoused by the *völkisch* movement and
various groups on the extreme right of Germany's political spectrum, including elements of the neoconservative Ring Movement and the *völkisch* wing of
the German youth movement. Many similarities could even be seen between
the new Nazi party program and the programmatic statements of the decidedly
more conservative DNVP. The major difference lay in the fact that the NSDAP
propagated its brand of *völkisch*-nationalist ressentiment with a radicalism and
an intensity that none of its rivals, whose programs had to accommodate a
variety of different interests, could possibly match.

It was characteristic of Hitler's modus operandi that when he assumed control of the party in the summer of 1921 and began to assert his personal claim
to unlimited power, he did not do this by working through the party executive committee but rather pressured the party leadership into accepting his

demands by means of public demonstrations. Hitler was prompted to seek control of the party by a decision that DAP chairman Anton Drexler had reached in his absence to merge the DAP with Otto Dickel's Völkisch Coalition (Völkische Werkgemeinschaft), a splinter group that was closely identified with the German Socialist Party (Deutschsozialistische Partei). While Drexler had no intention of undercutting Hitler's position within the party, Hitler's reaction was precipitous and lacked any clear plan of action. Still, Hitler's sensational resignation from the party was meant to be taken seriously. In this respect, Hitler seems to have been guided by an instinctual feeling that it was essential to prevent the movement from being recast as an Occidental League (Abendländischer Bund) and from losing its ideological purity by becoming entangled in endless programmatic discussions and campaigns for parliamentary elections. What was most important to Hitler was that the NSDAP remain the only true "German freedom movement" and that it not be submerged into the morass of virtually indistinguishable *völkisch* splinter groups that existed on the German Right. A merger with rival groups, Hitler feared, would force the NSDAP to abandon its claim to uniqueness with the immediate loss of unity and potency.

The real significance of the party conflict in July 1921 was that it forcefully imposed a fascist concept of politics on a peripheral party that up to this point in time had exhausted its energies in the discussion of speculative plans for the improvement of the world. Spurred on by his Munich entourage—particularly Hermann Esser and Rudolf Heß—Hitler persuaded the party to adopt the principle of the leader's absolute responsibility. According to this principle, elections within the party were to be replaced by the delegation of responsibility from the upper to the lower ranks, top down. The leadership principle had long been practiced in the Free Corps and other right-wing associations, but here it became even more stringent when Hitler went beyond merely asserting his absolute power to decide by prohibiting the presentation and discussion of divergent opinions within the party apparatus. From his perspective, such discussions were superfluous, and he sought to dismantle their institutional foundations without delay.

The implementation of the leadership principle within the NSDAP satisfied Hitler's subjective need to avoid debates with rival subordinates and conformed with his life-long aversion to institutional ties of any kind. At the same time, it highlighted his personal aversion to becoming involved in the details of day-to-day party affairs. That the party assumed a largely instrumental function stemmed directly from the concept of politics that Hitler espoused as the self-styled "guardian of the National Socialist idea." A "uniformly organized and directed world view" that could be summarized in a few short phrases, Hitler argued, required a "political party organized along the lines of a storm detachment." Between these two poles—a "world view" that necessarily remained abstract and that could not be compressed into a long-winded party program and a tightly controlled organization designed for the sole purpose of mass mobilization—there was no middle ground on which the integration of divergent social interests and the establishment of national priorities could take place. In short, politics as it was commonly understood and as it had always been practiced was simply beyond Hitler's comprehension. Propaganda was therefore not so much a means to an end as the actual content of politics itself, a politics conducted within the general framework of an abstract world view that was not subject to further discussion. The effectiveness of the party's propaganda was to be measured by the number of adherents it succeeded in mobilizing. If ineffective, it could be appropriately modified.

For Hitler, organizational questions were always subordinate to the party's propaganda objectives. With the founding of local cells, or *Ortsgruppen*, Hitler always felt that this could take place only after there had been sufficient "mass education" in order to avoid failures that might lead to a loss of prestige for the party. By the same token, Hitler always maintained that it was necessary to initiate a broad protest movement before committing the NSDAP to any electoral or organizational alliance. Well into the mid-1920s Hitler considered participation in local, regional, and national elections a liability that served no useful purpose except for that of propaganda. The NSDAP thus concentrated its energy on attracting new supporters and paid little attention to practical political issues. In the intensity of its propaganda, the NSDAP exceeded all its rival parties. In 1923, for example, the NSDAP held forty-six major rallies in Munich alone. It was not the political integration of its constituency but the relentless search for new adherents that effectively defined the NSDAP's political profile.

The decisionism that was so characteristic of fascist politics—and with it, the formalization of subjective values and the resultant reversal of the relationship between means and ends—manifested itself within the NSDAP in the development of external symbols and rituals that served as a surrogate for the missing party program. The swastika banner that had been taken over from the Thule Society, the party insignia, the brown shirt that had made its initial appearance in the Free Corps Roßbach, the SA banners that were introduced at the end of 1922 in imitation of Italian models, and the use of "Heil" as a greeting before it was replaced by "Heil Hitler" at the beginning of the 1930s— all these were examples of the way in which the party leadership consciously sought to introduce an aesthetic dimension into the political arena. As early as 1923 the Nazi party congress, which Hitler managed to hold despite an initial ban and which was accompanied by thirteen public demonstrations in a truly unprecedented display of political propaganda, was highlighted by SA parades, the consecration of flags, and orchestrated outbursts of mass exultation. Although they may not have disappeared altogether, substantive political discussions, which Hitler assiduously avoided, receded into the background.

With a note signed by Dietrich Eckart and the financial help of Franz Ritter von Epp, the NSDAP succeeded in 1920 in acquiring the *Münchener Beobachter* from the Thule Society. Under the new name of *Völkischer Beobachter*, this appeared as a daily newspaper from 1923 on. At the same time, the party received funds from the Anti-Bolshevist Fund of German Industry (Antibolschewisten-fonds der deutschen Wirtschaft) that Hugo Stinnes had launched after the end of the war, as well as from unspecified foreign sources and, for a time at least, the Reichswehr. For the most part, however, the party was—and would continue to be—financed by membership dues and revenues from its public demonstrations. The steady influx of new members, the increasing sympathy of what the Württemberg envoy called the "street-side public of the upper classes" (*Straßenpublikum der höheren Stände*), and the deepening crisis of 1922–23 made it possible for Hitler, now dubbed "the king of Munich," to secure the attention of Bavaria's conservative elites. At the *Deutscher Tag* in Coburg in September 1922, the SA's terrorist manhandling of left-wing counterdemonstrators more than made up for its numerical insignificance vis-à-vis the other patriotic associations.

Although Hitler's leadership position within the party was uncontested, the role that he was to play in the impending national revolution was far from clear. For the time being, Hitler had no interest in assuming the functions of a statesman charged with responsibility for governing the country. On the contrary, Hitler conceived of himself primarily as a "drummer" and propagandist who would work hand in hand with the ruling minister. Even though it was more of a well-staged political melodrama than a popular uprising, Mussolini's March on Rome strengthened Hitler's personal ambitions and gave rise among his supporters to an almost mystical glorification of the leader. While the preparations of the nationalist Right for a march on Berlin were well under way, Hitler continued to think of himself as the "propagandist for the salvation of Germany." Despite efforts by his closest associates to have him included in a directorate led by Lossow and Pöhner, Hitler remained uncertain as to what his own role should be.

In Hitler's opinion, the plans for a military putsch that Captain Ehrhardt had set in motion by moving the Border Patrol North (Grenzschutz Nord) to the Thuringian frontier as a cover for the deployment of the Reichswehr and various national combat leagues, including the SA, were a matter of secondary importance. "The military," Hitler had said after the collapse of the Kapp Putsch in 1920, "can never be the instrument of upheaval, never the bearer of a movement." It is difficult to imagine a sharper contrast to the calculations of the SA leadership. For Ernst Röhm and Erwin Scheubner-Richter were in the process of transforming the SA into a military organization and had made arrangements for it to take part in regular Reichswehr maneuvers in October. At the *Deutscher Tag* in Nuremberg in early September 1923 the SA merged with a number of similar organizations, including the Reich Flag (Reichsflagge) under Captain Adolf Heiß, the Oberland League, and the Munich Patriotic Associations to form the German Combat Alliance (Deutscher Kampfbund). Röhm did this in hopes of reversing the increasing political isolation of the national-revolutionary wing of the paramilitary movement that had occurred under the leadership of Ludendorff and Hitler. This step, however, did not mean the abandonment but rather the intensification of plans for offensive military action against Berlin. Hitler, whose claim to absolute power and "outspoken Napoleonic and messianic posturing" did not sit well with the leadership of the Bavarian Reichswehr and United Patriotic Leagues, was able to establish himself as the Combat Alliance's "political leader" only with great difficulty, while Lieutenant Kriebel was entrusted with its military command. In the final analysis, Hitler was responsible for little more than providing the proposed action with its propaganda cover.

The alliance with General Ludendorff, a favorite of the German Racist Freedom Party who had resurfaced on the political scene at the time of the Kapp Putsch, also turned out to be something of a mixed blessing. The former quartermaster general, who had emerged as a major political figure in northern Germany and who was in the process of organizing a "second front" against Berlin, appeared indispensable for the success of the planned coup. For his own part, however, Ludendorff had no intention of taking his cues from Hitler, particularly since the Nazi party leader had treated the former commander in chief with a deference that bordered on obsequiousness. Ludendorff, whose support for a restoration of the Hohenzollern dynasty had earned him the bitter animosity of the Bavarian monarchists and the ironic criticism of the crown prince, saw himself assuming command of a "German national army," which after the coup in Berlin would proceed to settle scores with France.

Hitler, who struggled desperately to bind the Combat Alliance — by this time elements of the Reich Flag had already seceded from it — to a political program, ran the risk of becoming isolated on two separate fronts. This was all the more true as the newly created General State Commissariat under Kahr threatened to drive a wedge between Hitler and his popular supporters in Munich. Just how little the Reichswehr, its professed sympathies for the NSDAP notwithstanding, was prepared to subordinate itself to the leadership role that Hitler claimed for himself had become abundantly clear during the events of 1 May 1923, when Hitler had to acquiesce in the disarmament of the SA formations, including the Munich Regiment, that he had assembled. As usual, the NSDAP responded to this setback by going into the streets in an attempt to compensate for the tactical mistake it had committed in its response to the Ruhr occupation by intensifying the leadership cult with the claim that from this point on Hitler was the irreplaceable "leader of the German freedom movement."

Amid constant rumors of a putsch and feverish preparations for a military action that was set for 15 November 1923, Hitler was in danger of being pushed completely to the sidelines. In north Germany Hitler was seen as little more than a rabble-rouser. According to Ludendorff, it remained to be seen whether Hitler had the makings of a "German Mussolini." At the same time, Hitler's name had disappeared altogether from the discussions about a directorate. To all of this Hitler reacted with a characteristic mixture of nervousness and indecision. While Röhm and Göring rushed around frantically trying to prepare the units of the Combat Alliance for the prospect of military action, Hitler passed his time in Munich coffeehouses. Eventually, however, Hitler could no longer ignore the need for immediate action, particularly since there was a real danger that in the hyperinflation funds would soon be exhausted and the patriotic leagues would go their separate ways. His vision remained firm. In a meeting with the SA leadership he demanded: "We must unfurl [*aufrollen*] the German question from here in Bavaria. Call for a German army of liberation under a German government in Munich." Hitler immediately jeopardized his own relations with Lossow when he threatened at the end of October to strike out on his own if "things don't get moving," although he knew full well that he lacked the means for doing much of anything on his own. At the same time, Hitler attacked Kahr for his inactivity and portrayed him—perhaps not without an element of truth—as a "Bavarian Cuno" who would have to be swept out of office by a storm of national protest.

In point of fact, the triumvirate of Lossow, Pöhner, and Kahr was reluctant to give the signal for the march on Berlin. Although they entertained little hope of enlisting Seeckt in their project, they still believed that they could trigger a parallel action in Berlin to be undertaken by a directorate under the leadership of Baron Wilhelm von Gayl in which Seeckt's place would be taken by General Richard von Behrendt. Behind the scenes the strings were being pulled by the ADV's Heinrich Claß, who had secured promises of support from the German Racist Freedom Party, the Stahlhelm leadership, the National Rural League, and elements of the DNVP and felt that he could count on the sympathies of officers who stood behind the indecisive Seeckt. For reasons of foreign policy, the conspirators decided to involve Ludendorff only when it became necessary in the second stage of the proposed action to call for the formation of a new national army.

The indecisiveness of the counterrevolutionary conspirators stemmed in part from their fear that the French would indeed follow through with the threat made by the French ambassador in Berlin, François de Margerie, in a conversation with Stresemann to intervene in the event of a right-wing coup. For whatever high-sounding reassurances the leaders of the Reichswehr might have given, the fact remains that a military conflict with France was simply out of the question. Not even Hitler's propaganda slogans could push this fact out of the way. Nor did Hermann Esser's scheme to arrest 500,000 Jews and liquidate them if a single foreign soldier set foot on German soil represent a realistic solution to the dilemma in which the radical Right found itself. Only Hitler did not recognize a problem. For if the nation regained its inner solidarity and shed the yoke of Jewish bondage, he declared, it would necessarily prevail in its struggle against foreign enemies.

The Bavarian Right had originally envisaged a "Turkish solution" after the model of Mustafa Kemal, who had unilaterally smashed the Treaty of Sèvres by undertaking military action from his base in Anatolia. This was precisely the scenario envisaged by Röhm, who wanted to use revolutionized Bavaria as the base from which the rest of Germany could be conquered. Kahr, on the other hand, was more inclined to fight for Bavarian independence, an undertaking for which he had the indirect support of Cardinal Faulhaber, who coupled his plea for moderation to Stresemann with far-reaching demands of dubious constitutionality. For his own part, Lossow remained determined to launch the march on Berlin even if the negotiations with the north Germans over the formation of a "second front" should prove unproductive. To the extent that they both agreed that such an action should not be "a second Kapp Putsch" initiated by irregular troops with the army assigned a secondary role, Lossow enjoyed the support of Ludendorff, who was determined to expunge the infamous events of the fall of 1918 by a heroic act of liberation. Proposals for the creation of a *völkisch* "military state" (*Wehrstaat*) as propagated by Max Erwin von Scheubner-Richter and Theodor von der Pfordten—the latter a casualty of 9 November—thus converged with the ideas that Ludendorff had extracted from the programs of Eduard Stadtler and Oswald Spengler for a "German" or even "Prussian" socialism. None of this had anything to do with Hitler's plans for mobilization through popular plebiscite.

What, then, did Hitler want? Realizing that a military strike without the support of the Reichswehr was doomed to failure, Hitler envisaged for himself a role in which he would provide the initial spark for a "German Revolution" through an "enormous propaganda wave" that would make it impossible for Germany's conservative elites and the patriotic associations to postpone taking action. The leaders of the Combat Alliance set 11 November as the date for the proposed action but only on the condition that they could secure the cooperation of Ludendorff as a guarantee that the Reichswehr would not intervene and crush their movement. To Hitler, however, military preparations were of little, if any, interest. What he had in mind was the deployment of an irresistible, fanaticized mass movement that would simply sweep away all obstacles in its path. After the Bavarian triumvirate of Kahr, Lossow, and Pöhner had let Hitler know that he could take part in the coup but would not be allowed to assume a position of leadership, he decided almost on the spur of the moment to use the rally that was scheduled to take place on the evening of 8 November 1923 in the Bürgerbräukeller, a well-known beer hall in southwestern Munich, to seize leadership of the "German Revolution." In the meantime, preparations for the coup were barely underway in Munich while in the rest of Bavaria virtually nothing had happened. What Hitler and his associates had in mind was not a military putsch, let alone a systematic seizure of power, a fact that helps explain the lack of any concrete plans for a government program or the constitution of an interim government. Once again, Hitler assumed the posture of one who, without ambitions of his own, was bringing the crisis under control. "Until all the criminals who are ruining Germany today have been brought to account," Hitler exclaimed, "I am assuming leadership of the provisional national government." Even then, it was not clear whether Hitler had in mind the chancellorship or some other governmental post.

Later that evening—when Hitler managed to convince the assembled notables of his seriousness with his proclamation that "tomorrow will find Germany with a new German national government or us dead" and succeeded in extorting from Kahr, Lossow, and Seißer the promise to form a provisional national government with Ludendorff, Lossow, and Seißer—he lost the initiative to the former quartermaster general. For it was only at Ludendorff's urging that the Bavarian notables, who could not refuse to follow the "greatest soldier of the world war," agreed to go along with the coup. Ludendorff, who envisaged himself as dictator of the Reich, accepted the promises that Hitler had extorted from Lossow and Seißer at face value and did not order their arrest. As a result, the ill-prepared putsch was doomed to failure as the Reichswehr and Bavarian state police took immediate measures to crush it.

When Hitler realized that his attempted uprising had bogged down, he lost his nerve and in desperation sent a messenger to—of all people—Crown Prince Rupprecht in the hope that he could be persuaded to mediate while the prince's chief advisor and the rest of the Bavarian cabinet were being detained in the villa of Hitler's associate, Ernst Hanfstaengl. At the urging of Kriebel, the military leader of the Combat Alliance, and with the full support of Ludendorff, the conspirators made the fateful decision to mobilize the masses for a protest march to the government district and to demand from the streets the formation of a national dictatorship under Ludendorff and Hitler. Hitler viewed the proposed march with considerable skepticism, but was powerless to do anything except make certain that it was not a military demonstration. Ludendorff, who marched at the head of the parade along with Hitler, was surprised to find the path blocked by armed force. When the march came under fire from the Bavarian state police near the Feldherrnhalle at around noon on 9 November 1923, the result was thirteen dead and an undetermined number wounded. Suddenly Hitler stood before the collapse of his political career.

The trial that took place in the spring of 1924 in the Munich People's Court in what represented a clear breach of the Law for the Protection of the Republic not only afforded the Nazi party leader a public forum from which he could conduct his political rehabilitation with the greatest conceivable success but, more importantly, obscured the extent to which the Bavarian political establishment, the Reichswehr, and the German Right had been responsible for the Munich fiasco and effectively freed Ludendorff from the stigma of high treason. The Ludendorff-Hitler trial thus failed to make contemporaries sufficiently aware of the counterrevolutionary aspirations and activities of significant sectors of Germany's bourgeois Right. These efforts had been undercut by Hitler's premature and ill-prepared action on 9 November. On the following day all of those who had been involved ceased further action against Berlin and did their best to destroy any trace of their complicity in the attempt to overthrow the national government.

The antiparliamentary thrust of the revolution from the Right in the late fall of 1923 enjoyed the support of influential bourgeois circles that, in addition to the DNVP and Bavarian People's Party, extended deep into the ranks of the DVP and even embraced elements from the DDP and the right wing of the German Center Party. Most of Germany's bourgeois interest groups sympathized with such a solution, including, in particular, heavy industry, the National Rural League, the German National Union of Commercial Employees, the National League of Higher Civil Servants (Reichsbund höherer Beamter), most of the German judiciary, influential elements within organized labor, virtually the entire German officer corps, neoconservative intellectuals, a majority of right-wing students and university professors, and, last but not least, a large part of the clergy of both confessions. Public respect for the parliamentary system had reached its nadir. And yet in spite of all this, a change in the system of government failed to materialize. The firm attitude not only of the chancellor but also of the Prussian minister president Otto Braun, who could count upon the support of a stable Great Coalition and did not hesitate to mobilize the Prussian police against the pretensions of the Reichswehr, contributed in no small measure to the sobering process that set in on the German Right after 9 November. In the meantime, the general indecisiveness and the existence of major differences of opinion on the German Right become more and more apparent.

Having received conflicting reports about the Hitler Putsch, President Ebert no longer assigned executive power to Geßler, who favored an accommodation with Bavaria, but to Seeckt, who now found himself reluctantly part of the existing constitutional order. This, however, encountered strong opposition from Braun, who pleaded in vain that one should not depart from the principle established at the time of the Kapp Putsch of subordinating the military to civilian authority. For his own part, Seeckt soon quickly assumed a wide range of administrative functions and, much to the disappointment of the DNVP, abandoned plans for the creation of a directorate. Seeckt was never to revive these plans, particularly after he temporarily considered campaigning for the

Reich presidency. Still, it was only at the insistence of the Prussian government and the republican parties that he eventually agreed in the spring of 1924 to terminate the state of military emergency that, by then, could no longer be justified.

Was the trend toward authoritarianism that had made itself apparent since the fall of 1923 a temporary nightmare that would disappear once the currency had been stabilized? The desperate conditions that had been created by the hyperinflation of 1922–23 did much to undermine the authority of the central government and to encourage a process of extreme political polarization. But the deeper reason for the second major crisis of the Weimar Republic was the catalytic effect of Germany's conflict with France. The illusionary resentments that were rooted in Germany's refusal to acknowledge military defeat and accept the peace were fueled by the activity of irresponsible propagandists and publicists, including university teachers, and created a highly explosive mixture that was prematurely set off by Hitler's impulsive action.

Credit for maintaining the constitutional order rests least of all with the military. To be sure, the army's intervention in Saxony and Thuringia had deprived the counterrevolutionaries in Bavaria of a pretext for an opening attack, but that was also true of the SPD's withdrawal from the Stresemann cabinet. The efforts of DNVP chairman Oskar Hergt to have placed Prussia under the authority of a Reich commissioner were firmly rejected by Ebert and Stresemann, since a Prussian cabinet crisis would have had far-reaching repercussions upon the unresolved situation in the Rhineland. But the decisive factor was the realization that the establishment of a national dictatorship would have provided France with the leverage it needed to intensify its pressure on Germany even further. In the final analysis, the external forms of parliamentary rule were maintained by the simple fact that, as Hugo Stinnes himself had prophesied, the formation of a right-wing dictatorship would have led to the loss of the Rhineland. From this perspective, Poincaré's policy did have some positive benefits, for at the very least it forced the bourgeois parties and the economic interest groups that stood behind them to leave their illusions behind and face at least some of the realities of international power politics.

Although the chancellor had done his best to maintain close ties with the various political parties, the legislative functions of the Reichstag had been by and large usurped during the two Stresemann cabinets through the use of emergency decrees and an enabling act. The conflict with Bavaria had temporarily delayed a vote on the no-confidence motion introduced in early November by the SPD Reichstag delegation. It was finally brought to a vote on 23 November, along with a resolution from the DNVP censuring Stresemann for precisely the opposite reasons. On this occasion Ebert refused to honor the chancellor's request for the dissolution of the Reichstag since he, as Reich president, no longer had faith in parliament's ability to stabilize the situation.

Under pressure from the party apparatus and its rank-and-file membership and in spite of strenuous objections from Ebert, the SPD Reichstag delegation insisted on a vote of no confidence against Stresemann, who, for his own part, was unwilling to make the continuation of his chancellorship contingent on "parliamentary arithmetic." Alluding to the continued existence of Seeckt's plans for a directorate, Ebert warned his party colleagues that they would feel the consequences of their stupidity for the next ten years. Yet for the Social Democrats, it was not so much a matter of hanging on to a certain number of seats in the cabinet as their very identity that made it psychologically impossible for them to share responsibility for the continued erosion of the social and political legacy of the German Revolution.

The defeat of the cabinet "in open battle" prompted Stresemann to utter somewhat sarcastically that this was not so much a crisis of the cabinet as a crisis of the parliamentary system itself. Yet it lay in the mechanics of domestic politics that the acceptance of the status quo by the antiparliamentary Right in the face of severe economic and diplomatic consequences if it had succeeded in overthrowing the system immediately intensified pressure on the SPD and the socialist unions. Moreover, a diplomatic impasse began to take shape when in late October Poincaré reluctantly agreed to the formation of an international committee of experts with American participation and when the MICUM treaties became due for signing. The Great Coalition had come into existence in the late summer of 1923 as the only way in which Germany's political leaders could deal with the foreign policy crisis that had been precipitated by the struggle in the Ruhr. It was only logical that the coalition should collapse once the stabilization of the currency and the conclusion of informal arrangements with the occupying powers signaled an end to the state of emergency that had gripped Germany at home and abroad.

The parliamentary system emerged from its successful struggle with the German Right with severe wounds that were not immediately apparent. Paradoxically the extreme Right regarded the SPD's withdrawal from the national cabinet as a prerequisite for accepting the situation that had been created by the termination of passive resistance in the Ruhr. In this respect, the German Right was willing to come to terms with the fact that the fulfillment of Germany's treaty obligations was unavoidable without, however, ever abandoning its determination to bring about a revision of the Versailles peace treaty at the earliest possible opportunity. The price that Germany had to pay for the return to normalcy at home and abroad was the abandonment of the social and political achievements of the revolution and postwar inflation. The SPD's vote of no confidence in the Stresemann cabinet on 23 November set the stage for its withdrawal from the cabinet, which had become inevitable as the struggle over how the social costs of Germany's lost war were to be distributed throughout

German society as a whole reached a climax. From a tactical point of view, the Social Democrats' vote and their subsequent withdrawal from the Stresemann cabinet may have been a mistake. Still, their decision greatly facilitated the external stabilization of the republican system and thus expedited a process that was already well under way.

CHAPTER SIX

Reconstruction at Home and Abroad

THE crisis of German domestic and foreign policy reached its climax at the turn of 1923–24. Having weathered the storm, the republic now seemed headed toward calmer waters. The collapse of the Hitler-Ludendorff Putsch had done much to clear the air on the domestic political front and had pulled the rug out from under the plans of the conservative Right for overthrowing the republic. The NSDAP, finally banned in Bavaria as well as in the rest of the Reich, continued to exist in the form of rival *völkisch* splinter groups. No one expected that the party would ever recover from the severe blow it had suffered with the failure of its attempt to overthrow the system. In a similar vein, the Communist Party was undergoing a process of internal Bolshevization and found itself in a state of complete political isolation. Within the DNVP a more realistic assessment of Germany's political and diplomatic situation had gained the upper hand, although the party continued to cling to its antiparliamentary orientation and its outspoken revisionist agenda in the area of foreign policy. At the same time, it seemed as if efforts to stabilize the currency had succeeded, at least for the moment. Whether the Rentenmark would continue to enjoy the confidence of the people and whether it would be possible to return to the gold standard, however, depended on the fiscal and economic policies of the national government.

The disastrous effects of the Ruhr crisis and the hyperinflation—and in particular the suffering these had caused for important segments of the lower middle class and the working class—could be relieved only if it proved possible to reach an understanding on the reparations question and to replace the private agreements between the Ruhr industrial establishment and France, scheduled to expire in February 1924, with a more permanent contractual arrangement. For while it is true that the success of the government's currency reforms had averted a catastrophe in the Rhineland, the de facto suspension of German sovereignty in the Ruhr and the continued rule of the French constituted a severe political and economic burden that was bound to compromise Germany's economic revival in a number of different ways.

The German government placed its hopes for relief on a report on the stability and productivity of the German economy that a commission of experts empaneled in January 1924 under the chairmanship of the American bank specialist Charles Rufus Dawes was preparing for the reparations commission. Gustav Stresemann, who continued to serve as German foreign minister in the bourgeois minority cabinet that had been formed in late November 1923 by the Center party chairman Wilhelm Marx, had informed the Allies of Germany's willingness to have its economic capabilities examined by a neutral panel of experts. Although the committee's final vote on the report—soon to be known as the Dawes Plan even though the proposal for a new settlement of the reparations question had been drafted by Owen D. Young—was not yet known, the German government did what it could to temper the experts' overly optimistic assessment of Germany's economic strength. In the final analysis, however, there was little the government could do but await the final report, which was finally released in April 1924.

In point of fact, there was little the German foreign policy establishment could do but follow Stresemann's counsel and accept the experts' report without delay, for any attempt to modify the substance of the report would almost certainly be used by France as a pretext for withdrawing from an international settlement of the reparations question. German acceptance cleared the way for the Dawes Plan, as rough as that road might be. For the most part, German public opinion failed to understand the extent to which the government's own course of action was subject to foreign policy constraints. Nor did it realize that the Dawes Plan represented a qualitatively new stage in the search for a settlement to the reparations problem, which up to this point had been saddled with the odium of constant failure. Poincaré's policy of "productive guarantees" had not only forced Germany to recognize the realities of its diplomatic situation but had also transformed the reparations question into a problem of international indebtedness. Future negotiations could be conducted only on the basis of the Versailles peace treaty, and diplomatic compromise was the only way in which the unity of the Reich could be preserved and the occupation of the Ruhr rescinded.

Poincaré's victory on the Ruhr had been purchased with a substantial erosion of France's economic strength. As a result, the French premier was no longer in a position to pursue a solution of the reparations question on his own terms. It was with considerable misgiving, therefore, that Poincaré gave in to pressure from the United States and Great Britain and agreed to place the entire reparations matter in the hands of a commission of experts dominated by American financial specialists. The general unwillingness of the United States to consider a moratorium on the payment of interallied war debts and the dependence of French industry on foreign loans left Poincaré and Édouard Herriot, the man who succeeded him as premier after his crushing defeat in the 1924 general elections, with no alternative but to follow the American and

British lead. A French rejection of the experts' report, which the German government had accepted on 16 April, would have left France politically isolated and would have meant the definitive collapse of the Entente Cordiale.

During the course of 1924 it became abundantly clear that Europe had lost much of its preeminence in world affairs to the undisputed economic leader of the world, the United States. With the formation of the commission of experts the United States returned to the European negotiating table after the defeat of Wilson's program in 1919 had made it appear as if isolationism had achieved a lasting victory. To be sure, the American government did not formally participate in the London Conference of August 1924, but the decisions of the American experts and the banking consortium for which they were working were carefully synchronized with those of the conference. The low American profile at London was calculated to appease the Republican majority in Congress, which looked upon long-term American involvement on the European continent with great mistrust. By contrast, American business circles were pressing for indirect American intervention in hopes of opening European markets for their own exports. Even before the occupation of the Ruhr, the American secretary of state Charles Hughes had tried to win French approval for an international settlement of the reparations question and the closely related problem of interallied war debts. Once Germany accepted this as the basis on which a settlement of the reparations question was to be found, the diplomatic consideration the United States had shown France became redundant.

Even Cuno had hoped for American intervention on Germany's behalf. The economic consequences of the struggle in the Ruhr and the deteriorating interallied debt structure as a result of the weakness of the French franc made the involvement of the main creditor nation imperative. When this happened, German policy makers moved quickly to capitalize on the political and economic advantages of a close relationship with the United States, whose own business leaders were greatly interested in Germany's undeniable economic potential. The American initiative coincided with the British decision to overcome the deepening social and economic crisis that had been caused by the recession of the early 1920s by increasing its trade with the European continent. From the British perspective, therefore, the German Reich, for years one of Great Britain's most important trade partners and with an economy that had proved remarkably receptive to British industrial products, constituted an essential component of a rejuvenated European economy.

International interest in the reconstruction of the world economic system offered good prospects of breaking out of the hardened and tension-ridden climate of the postwar era. In this respect, however, it was first necessary to liquidate the Ruhr conflict on terms acceptable to both parties and to achieve a settlement of the reparations question that neither hindered Germany's economic recovery nor endangered the German currency by requiring excessive capital transfers. Even then, the commission of experts could not avoid having to cater, at least formally, to the unrealistically high expectations of French public opinion. The commission thus decided to retain the formal modalities of payment that had been adopted at the London Conference. Both the panel charged with the task of ascertaining Germany's economic capacity to pay and the committee working on the problem of capital transfer were careful not to raise the question of suspending Allied sanctions even though it was abundantly clear to everyone who was familiar with the situation that this constituted an indispensable prerequisite for German fulfillment.

Tactical considerations also prompted the commission of experts to leave the total amount of Germany's reparations obligation unspecified. It did, however, establish a schedule that earmarked 800 million marks from the Dawes loan and an additional 200 million marks from the sale of railway bonds for the payment of reparations in 1924–25, while for the following year 1.22 billion marks were to be raised from a variety of sources. By 1927–28 Germany's obligations would have risen to 1.75 billion marks, of which 500 million were to be provided by the federal budget. The first annuity amounting to 2.5 billion marks was due in 1928–29; of this sum, half was to be covered out of the federal budget. The negotiators were careful not to establish a fixed sum, but in any event it would have been less than what had been set by the London payment plan. In return, the German government agreed first to relinquish control of the national railway system, which would be reorganized as a private enterprise under the direction of an international administrative board. The German Railway Corporation (Reichseisenbahngesellschaft) was obliged to issue bonds in the amount of 11 billion marks to generate interest that would be used for the payment of annuities. By the same token, the government agreed to levy certain taxes on consumption whereby the annual reparations payments could be increased if the revenue from these sources exceeded the amounts stipulated in the payment plan.

The experts further proposed that the transfer of reparations payments take place only if Germany had accumulated sufficient foreign currency reserves and if the German balance of payments permitted it. Capital not transferred in this manner was to be invested in the German economy. The special status of transfer capital was designed not only to protect the German currency but also to prevent the balance of payments of the creditor nations from being upset by the influx of excess capital. The difficult task of administering the transfer payments lay in the hands of Parker Gilbert, the reparations agent appointed by the Allies after acceptance of the Dawes Plan and a close associate of American banker J. P. Morgan. Gilbert fulfilled the responsibilities of his office, for which Owen D. Young had originally been slated, with considerable skill and impartiality.

It soon became clear that in the light of Germany's permanent negative trade balance the problem of transfer payments would be insoluble at the very latest by the time the reparations annuities reached the level of 2.5 billion marks. But the experts assumed that German obligations would be reassessed within a few years and granted the German government the right to have its capacity to pay reexamined over the course of the next three years. Although he could not say so in public, Stresemann never expected that Germany would have to pay annuities in what he regarded as the unacceptable amount of 2.5 billion marks.

The international financial experts were above all interested in reaching some sort of agreement on the reparations question that would commit Germany to the fulfillment of its obligations through low initial payments and thus clear the way for an American loan amounting to 800 million marks. This, they correctly surmised, would be followed by further loans running into the billions from American holders of capital eager to find new avenues of investment. By helping to stimulate the European economy as a whole, these investments would relieve pressure on the French franc and thus make it easier to achieve compromises in the reparations question than would have been possible under the impact of the Ruhr crisis. Still, some financial experts were concerned that the French were determined to breathe real life into the "shop-window mannequin" of the Dawes Plan.

The autonomy of the national railroad, the creation of the bank for industrial indebtedness, and the appointment of a reparations agent represented serious encroachments upon German sovereignty. Parker Gilbert, the new reparations agent, was in a position to bring direct influence to bear upon German tax and fiscal policy. Before the termination of passive resistance, similar demands of this nature had been brushed aside in a storm of national protest and had met with almost universal rejection by the leaders of the German business community. This time big business and large-scale agriculture realized that there was no way they could obtain the international loans they so desperately needed but to accept the proposed reparations solution that only a few months earlier they had rejected with such great vehemence. This, however, did not prevent the DNVP and the *völkisch* parties from immediately attacking the Dawes Plan as a new tool for the "enslavement" of the German people.

The architects of German and French foreign policy found themselves confronted with the task of preserving the fictions that had been incorporated into the Dawes Plan for the purpose of appeasing national sentiment in the two nations, while the experts who had been involved in finding a solution to the reparations and related problems were much more aware of the limits this solution imposed upon the principle of national sovereignty. The traditional way of viewing things from the narrow perspective of the nation-state made it difficult, if not impossible, to conceive of financial and economic matters in supranational categories despite the fact that both reparations and war debts were problems that could only be solved through international cooperation. It was typical of the postwar situation that the adoption of the Dawes Plan at the London Conference took place in no small measure because the failure to do so would almost certainly have led to the collapse of the German, British, and French cabinets and would have represented a severe blow to the prestige of the American government.

From this perspective, the deeply divisive question of whether Germany could have actually paid the reparations obligations it assumed with the adoption of the Dawes Plan—in 1924 this amounted to about 7 percent of the gross national product—is of secondary importance. From the economic point of view, long-term reparations obligations of this magnitude were problematic if for no other reason than the fact that they strengthened Germany's industrial potential at the expense of France, England, and other creditor nations at the same time that they intensified the problem of Germany's balance of payments. To some extent, this effect had already happened during the recent inflation. It is, however, more difficult to assess just what the domestic economy could bear, particularly since until 1927 it experienced no appreciable difficulties in raising the required sums. One can therefore assume that under the conditions of sustained economic expansion that would have been created by the Dawes Plan the German economy could have even afforded the large payments foreseen in the final phase but that their transfer would have had negative effects upon the domestic economies of the creditor nations. But, contrary to all expectations, sustained economic growth failed to materialize. What happened instead was a relative stagnation of the economy with a slight recovery in 1925 and then again in 1927–28. The introduction of high protective tariffs by the Western industrial states contributed to a further contraction of the German economy.

The reparations payments envisioned by the London Conference never materialized after the revision of the Dawes Plan in 1929. In the period between 1925 and 1931—that is, until the Hoover Moratorium—Germany paid 11.3 of the 12 billion marks (about 1.7 percent of its gross national product) that had come due under the provisions of the Dawes Plan. At the same time, the influx of large-scale American loans offset the reparations payments that Germany made during this period. Instead of becoming a capital exporting country, Germany became one of the major importers of capital. This, in turn, stimulated an economically irrational circulation of money that prompted American banks to consider ways of cutting the high cost of shipping gold back and forth to Europe. While Germany financed its reparations payments to Western creditor nations with American loans, Great Britain and France used these payments to cover their long-term interest obligations and to retire their wartime debts with the United States.

Although the international financial establishment had long been aware of these problems, it was not until 1932 that the American government decided to create the conditions for an end to reparations by unilaterally canceling the loans it had extended during the recent war. For the American decision to link its loan policy to the reparations problem effectively transformed the latter into an issue of international finance. The French political establishment, however, was slow to draw the appropriate political consequences from this development and fought tenaciously to make certain that the reparations commission retained authority to prosecute possible German noncompliance, while J. Ramsay MacDonald, the new British prime minister, and the Bank of England planned to transfer this function to the finance committee of the League of Nations. In the final analysis, the financial experts were able to accommodate Édouard Herriot, who was particularly concerned about the protest this point was almost certain to provoke on the French Right, by stipulating that the reparations commission could make decisions only in consultation with the reparations agent. For the financial experts who were involved in this decision, a return to the former policy of imposing sanctions was simply inconceivable. If Germany should fail to fulfill its treaty obligations, then the only possible countermeasure would be collective action under the auspices of the League of Nations.

France and Germany were under considerable pressure from the United States to reach an agreement in the reparations question. Their reactions to this pressure were diametrically opposed. Whereas Stresemann sought, in addition to the liquidation of the policy of sanctions, an early end to the occupation of the Rhineland, Herriot made every effort to link the reparations question to that of French security. As late as the London Conference Herriot continued to harbor the illusion that the French evacuation of the Ruhr could be made contingent upon the fulfillment of the German reparations obligations, thereby postponing the end of the French presence in the Ruhr indefinitely. In this respect, however, Herriot encountered strong opposition from Montagu Norman, the governor of the Bank of England, as well as from J. P. Morgan, who flatly stated that under such conditions no American investor would be willing to subscribe to the proposed Dawes loan to Germany, an essential precondition for the resumption of German reparations payments. The leading British and American bankers reluctantly agreed to the proposed annual payments despite the fact that they thought they were too high, but they refused to grant France any kind of economic control over the Ruhr. Indeed, they were generally unwilling to link economic guarantees to the issue of French security. Philip Snowden, the British chancellor of the exchequer who considered the Treaty of Versailles a betrayal of the principles for which the British soldiers had fought during the recent war, rejected the French demands for guarantees in unusually strong terms. The diplomatic skills of the German foreign minister were therefore hardly needed to convince Herriot that the continuation of French rule in the Ruhr could no longer be contemplated.

Ramsay MacDonald, the British prime minister, was far more sympathetic to Herriot's political plight than the consortium of American and British bankers and sought to avoid the collapse of the Cartel des Gauches. As a result, he was prepared to concede to the French the continuation of an "invisible occupation" in the Ruhr, at least for the immediate future, and ended up by acceding to Herriot's request that French forces remain in the Ruhr for another full year. In accord with American policy, Stresemann had insisted on their immediate withdrawal. On the decisive issue of possible sanctions, MacDonald remained firm. He categorically refused to indicate what action might be taken in the event that Germany failed to fulfill the terms of the treaty on the grounds that this would suggest a lack of good faith on the part of his government. For his own part, MacDonald considered France's scarcely concealed determination to leave Germany economically and militarily weakened neither desirable nor feasible.

While Herriot's policy toward Germany was moderate in comparison to that of his predecessors, he too was unable to bridge the fundamental contradiction in a policy that sought, on the one hand, to force Germany to make a substantial contribution to the economic recovery of its neighbors and, on the other, to prevent Germany from regaining its place as the leading economic power on the European continent. At the heart of this lay the nagging doubt as to whether the limitations on German armaments that had been imposed by the Versailles peace treaty could be maintained for any length of time. To be sure, there was no danger at the moment, even though French and British intelligence had become aware of illegal rearmament by the Reichswehr. That in the long run the Interallied Military Control Commission would not be able to prevent Germany's remilitarization was a foregone conclusion as far as MacDonald was concerned. The only alternative, he felt, lay in a bold policy that made a genuine effort to win German cooperation in the political and economic life of Europe. MacDonald therefore rejected French plans to extend the period of the Ruhr occupation in the event that Germany failed to fulfill the terms of the treaty and to make the withdrawal of the troops contingent upon the issuance of reparations bonds. Stresemann responded to Herriot's demand with the persuasive argument that this course of action would have the effect of placing the decision about withdrawing the occupation forces in the hands of the Western central banks, which alone could authorize the sale of reparations bonds on the capital market. It would be a matter in which Germany would have no say whatsoever.

Stresemann, on the other hand, sought to link Germany's acceptance of the Dawes Plan to the termination of Allied occupation of the Ruhr and a revision of the disarmament clauses of the Versailles peace treaty. The tenacity with which the German foreign minister insisted upon the immediate evacuation of the Ruhr and the suspension of Allied military controls was only partly motivated by domestic political considerations, although like his French counterpart, Herriot, he realized that he could not face parliament without signs of tangible success. Heavy industry, large-scale agriculture, and the Reichswehr let it be known that they would not oppose acceptance of the Dawes Plan in spite of the fact that Seeckt sharply criticized the resumption of Allied military controls and dropped his opposition only under massive pressure from Stresemann. A particularly important factor in Stresemann's relentless efforts to exact at least some partial concessions from the Allies was his desire to entice the DNVP into accepting a share of the responsibility for the ratification and implementation of the Dawes Plan. Even then, it is surprising just how much importance the negotiators at London attached to military questions. At one point the London Conference was on the verge of falling apart over the withdrawal of Allied troops from the occupied territories. It was then that the United States, which ascribed merely psychological significance to the problem, intervened to force the acceptance of a compromise that essentially ignored the German point of view by stipulating not only that Allied troops were to be withdrawn from the Ruhr and the "sanction cities" of Düsseldorf and Ruhrort within ten months but also that in the immediate future only a partial evacuation would take place in the area surrounding Dortmund.

For the architects of French foreign policy the issue of evacuating the occupied territory was closely related to the hope that Great Britain could still be persuaded to conclude a defensive alliance against Germany. MacDonald rejected this along with parallel proposals for the conclusion of similar treaties with Poland and Czechoslovakia as well as the idea of a nonaggression pact with Germany that would be guaranteed by the League of Nations. The Labour government was unwilling to go along with French requests that would have obliged Great Britain to increase its armaments. Instead, it hoped to enlist the help of the League of Nations in bringing about a general European disarmament that would put an end to French military supremacy on the continent. At the time of the London Conference Downing Street already had come to the conclusion that Great Britain must not allow itself to be tied to the continent through guarantees of Germany's eastern borders or rule out the possibility of their cautious revision. There were even some who sought to dissuade France from making too strong a commitment to Poland. In this respect, the roots of appeasement may be traced back to the period of the Dawes Plan.

While the results of the London Conference did not meet the sanguine expectations of Stresemann and the German Foreign Office, the net balance as far as Germany was concerned was quite positive. Most important, unilateral sanctions were no longer possible. Reparations were no longer to be exacted under Article 231 of the Treaty of Versailles but were seen as the German contribution to a program of European reconstruction. Placed in the general context of a comprehensive program of European development, these payments were to take place in accord with Germany's economic capacities. At the same time, Germany had received a firm commitment that the remaining French sanctions would soon be lifted and had avoided becoming diplomatically isolated through the conclusion of a new Anglo-French entente. By contrast, France found itself pushed so much to the periphery of events that the major powers tried to portray the accord with Germany as the implementation of French reparations demands.

The new era in European diplomacy that had been ushered in by the adoption of the Dawes Plan contributed in no small measure to the domestic stabilization of the Weimar political system. The restoration of German sovereignty and of Germany's economic rights in the Rhenish-Westphalian industrial area could only have been achieved through international negotiations, which would not have been possible had the abolition or modification of the Weimar constitutional system strengthened French reservations about placing ultimate responsibility for the resolution of the Ruhr crisis in the hands of a committee of specialists. But once the currency had been stabilized and it became clear that Germany could no longer evade its reparations commitments, the domestic political conflict over how the social costs of this was to be distributed throughout Germany as a whole now moved to center stage. This, in turn, prodded the antirepublican opposition—and particularly the DNVP—into seeking a place for itself in the national government. The main impulse behind this strategy was the recognition on the part of Germany's right-wing parties that they would soon find themselves pushed to the periphery of national affairs with no means of representing the interests of their social constituencies if they persisted in their policy of trying to bring about a national catastrophe. The fact that the restrictions that Versailles had placed upon German foreign trade were due to expire in 1925 made it imperative for agriculture and other economic interests that supported the right-wing parties to see to it that their demands were incorporated into future trade treaties.

Within the various interest groups that stood behind the right-wing parties a more sobering assessment of the general political situation became increasingly apparent. Realizing that a sudden change in the existing political system was no longer possible, diverse political and social forces were compelled by the force of circumstances to find for themselves a place in the new republican order. The republic now came under increasingly virulent and radical attacks from its enemies on the extreme Right just as the more moderate elements on the German Right were in the process of transforming it into an instrument for the representation of their social and economic interests. This was true both of organized agriculture and heavy industry. As long as the survival of the state and the unity of the Reich had been at stake, it had been possible to reach political compromises that promised to bridge the gap between capital and labor. The transition to political normalcy that began in the early months of 1924 created a situation in which it was necessary for all actors to look out for their own vested interests. The demand that the National Rural League and DNVP had the minister of agriculture raise directly in the cabinet for the restoration of prewar agricultural tariffs was only a symptom of this general phenomenon.

Operating in the shadow of the forthcoming experts' report, the bourgeois minority cabinet headed by Centrist Wilhelm Marx represented a return to the political constellation that had existed at the time of the Cuno government, even though the chancellorship now rested in the hands of an experienced party politician who was committed to the art of political compromise. Formed in December 1923, the first Marx cabinet thought of itself as a transitional regime whose primary task lay in safeguarding the fiscal and currency reforms that had been introduced under Stresemann. Here the key figure was the highly capable, if not strong-willed, Hans Luther, the former mayor of Essen who was not attached to any political party but almost certainly sympathized with the DVP. By appealing to the SPD's sense of political responsibility, Marx was able to persuade the Social Democrats to agree to a new enabling act that effectively excluded the Reichstag from any sort of meaningful role in the stabilization process. The government then used this authority to promulgate a number of legally binding decrees, many of which went considerably beyond the scope of the enabling legislation. Within a few months the government had succeeded in stabilizing the national budget and in generating large budget surpluses through cuts in public spending that met with strong opposition from special-interest groups on the grounds that this inhibited new investment.

Under Luther's direction, the tax and budgetary reforms of the two Marx cabinets were implemented under signs of a fiscal and economic policy that unambiguously favored the interests of German industry. The first two tax emergency decrees enacted under Marx were deliberately fashioned to provide industry and agriculture with major tax advantages. In part, this policy was motivated by the government's desire to conceal the true extent of Germany's economic recovery so that the international experts who were to assess the country's economic capacity would be encouraged to offer the lowest possible estimate. The assessment of Germany's industrial assets at 29 billion marks for the purposes of a special levy to help pay reparations therefore differed appreciably from the assessment of 47 billion marks that was made shortly thereafter in determining industry's property tax liability. This meant that the liability that German industry had to assume through the issuance of industrial bonds stood at 10 rather than 17 percent of its fixed assets. At the same time, the Ministry of Finance refunded 709 million marks to Ruhr industry without informing the Reichstag or examining the claims of the recipients. Although a parliamentary committee established much later to investigate this matter was prevented from completing its work by the obstruction of the ministerial bureaucracy, there can be little doubt that substantial overpayments were made.

Whatever effect the "Ruhr Aid," or *Ruhr-Spende*, might have had upon existing social tensions was greatly intensified by the national government's persistent refusal to make sufficient funds available for unemployment relief. After having risen to over 10 percent in the preceding year, unemployment fell to approximately 5 percent between April and October 1924. During this period wages and limits on the length of the workday were under intense pressure from management. In October and December 1923 Labor Minister Heinrich Brauns, like Stresemann a mark of personal continuity in the various bourgeois cabinets from 1924 to 1928, found himself forced by rising social tensions to resuscitate a whole array of arbitration measures originally adopted during the period of demobilization in order to insulate Germany's newly stabilized currency from the effects of prolonged and costly labor disputes.

The new arbitration ordinance made it possible for the Ministry of Labor to shape wage agreements fairly extensively by virtue of its ability to appoint state arbitrators who had the right to impose legally binding settlements over and against the objections of the negotiating partners. At first Brauns did not resist pressure from the employer associations to reduce wages and increase the length of the workday since he regarded an increase in productivity as essential and wage increases as incompatible with the cabinet's restrictive fiscal policies. It did not take long for organized labor to recognize the danger that binding arbitration posed to its own freedom of movement in negotiating wage settlements. It soon became clear, however, that without the support of state-sponsored arbitration labor had no recourse whatsoever against the wage offensive of employers in heavy industry. For the inflation had effectively wiped out the unions' strike funds and contributed in no small measure to the fact that membership in the Christian and socialist unions had fallen to about half of what it had been in 1920. It was only with the modest economic recovery of 1926 that the unions were able to reverse this trend. By contrast, management had succeeded in improving the effectiveness of its organizations to a considerable degree. This was particularly true of heavy industry, which was represented by the united and financially potent coalition of the Association of Mining Interests (Verein für die Bergbaulichen Interessen), the Mining Association (Zechenverband), and the Northwestern Group of German Iron and Steel Industrialists (Nordwestliche Gruppe des Vereins der Deutschen Eisen- und Stahlindustrieller), organizations that had no qualms whatsoever about subjecting the government and parliament to sustained pressure. More than one-fourth of the leading officials of the National Federation of German Industry and a good third of the representatives of the so-called Langnam Association (Langnam-Verein or Verein zur Währung der gemeinsamen wirtschaftlichen Interessen in Rheinland und Westfalen) belonged to the DVP, which within the existing party spectrum was the most important advocate of industry's political interests.

Brauns's decision to implement through compulsory arbitration wage cuts in the Ruhr mining industry averaging 25 percent produced widespread anger and resentment among the miners. In the factory council elections of March 1924, the unions that advocated moderation in wage negotiations suffered severe setbacks vis-à-vis the Communist-influenced Union of Manual and Intellectual Workers (Union der Hand- und Kopfarbeiter) and other syndicalist factions. The replacement of the overtime accord of 1923 by the arbitration decision of 29 April 1924 establishing the eight-hour day for work underground—whereas beforehand the eighth hour had been counted as overtime—encountered bitter rejection from the mine workers. Their refusal to perform overtime work that was not covered by the collective bargaining agreement led to widespread lockouts. When the state-appointed arbitrator ruled against the workers, they retaliated in the Ruhr with the so-called May strike in which more than 380,000 mine workers—or 90 percent of the total work force—took part. In spite of personal mediation by Brauns, the conflict ended only after a series of fierce exchanges that left a residue of growing bitterness among the mine workers.

As developments in the mining industry clearly revealed, Germany's economic stabilization in the second half of the 1920s was marked by severe social tensions. This was also true in the public sector, where salary reductions and cuts in staff produced a widespread sense of malaise that was not alleviated by the partial restoration of salary cuts imposed in the spring of 1924. Still, the issue that precipitated the most persistent protests from significant sectors of the German middle class was the revaluation question. The inflation and hyperinflation had triggered an extensive redistribution of wealth that for the most part took place at the expense of the so-called old middle class. The scarcity of money after the currency reforms of 1923–24 hit the artisanry and small family businesses hardest and brought about a dramatic rise in the number of bankruptcies on the part of small and middle-sized firms at the same time that it greatly accelerated the concentration of capital in the hands of an increasingly small number of individuals. This could be seen in the numerical increase of new joint-stock companies, or *Aktiengesellschaften*, and other large-scale enterprises. The middle class saw itself as the victim of the inflation.

Finance Minister Luther had originally planned to forgo the revaluation of paper mark assets that had been destroyed by the inflation in order to relieve the national treasury of liability for prewar and wartime debts that by 1923 amounted to ten times what the government received in tax revenues. Under heavy pressure not only from the general public but, more important, from a decision by the German Supreme Court that reaffirmed the principle of "one mark equals one mark" and threats by the German Judges' Association (Deutscher Richterbund) to initiate a judicial review of the revaluation rates, Luther decided to include in the highly controversial Third Emergency Tax Decree (Dritte Steuernotverordnung) that took effect in April 1924 a provision authorizing the revaluation of old assets and mortgages at 15 percent of their original value. The redemption of private debts was not to take place before 1932, while the repayment of government debts was to be postponed until after Germany had fulfilled its reparations obligations. After a prolonged and heated political conflict, this provision was amended in the summer of 1925 by increasing the revaluation rate for privately held mortgages to 25 percent and introducing a needs test for the holders of public bonds. For different reasons the DNVP and SPD both opposed the Third Emergency Tax Decree and spoke out against an extension of the government's emergency powers.

By dissolving the Reichstag and scheduling early elections for 4 May 1924, the Marx cabinet was able to remain in power long enough to begin negotiations on the report from the committee of experts. Both the Reich president and the cabinet were determined to prevent any changes in the emergency legislation and sought to keep parliament from interfering with the formulation and implementation of the government's stabilization policy. What this reveals is that the erosion of parliamentary control over executive governmental power was already well advanced by the middle of 1924. Subsequent bourgeois minority cabinets also tried to cloak themselves in the mantle of a "national" emergency government that must not be diverted from its appointed mission by the haggling of political parties. It was symptomatic of the deepening crisis of German parliamentarism that formal votes of confidence became increasingly uncommon and were replaced first by "votes of approval" and finally by statements that simply "took cognizance" of the new cabinet. By no means, however, was the tendency to form minority governments from the bourgeois center rooted in the fear of the extremist parties like the KPD and DNVP. On the contrary, it resulted from the refusal of the ministerial bureaucracy and influential bourgeois interest organizations as well as the Reichswehr to pursue stabilization under the auspices of the Great Coalition.

Nor was the outcome of the Reichstag elections of 4 May 1924 particularly conducive to a return to a normal parliamentary government that could function without having to rely upon emergency decrees and constantly changing majorities. The election results did not so much reflect the stabilization that had taken place over the course of the previous six months as the state of latent civil war that had existed in Germany during the previous year. The Social Democrats suffered heavy losses and saw their strength in the Reichstag reduced from 171 to 100 seats, whereas the KPD increased its parliamentary representation from 16 to 62 deputies. These figures reflected not only the social protest of important sectors of the industrial work force but also the fact that many of those who had formerly belonged to the USPD turned their backs on the SPD. That the KPD was able to do so well in spite of constant leadership crises and one abrupt policy change after another was a consequence of the antileftist policy the government had pursued ever since its intervention in Saxony and Thuringia. In the Reichstag elections of 7 December 1924 the SPD recaptured some of the support it had lost to the KPD and rebounded to 131 seats in the Reichstag. The party's losses in the May elections stemmed from the failure of the SPD leadership to integrate the party's left wing and to provide an adequate explanation of its toleration of the Marx cabinet.

Of the more moderate nonsocialist parties, the Center and Bavarian People's Party were able to maintain their positions in the two 1924 campaigns, while the process of erosion seemed well advanced in the case of the liberal parties. In the May 1924 elections, for example, the DVP lost a third of the mandates it had won in 1920, while the DDP could hold on to only twenty-eight of its thirty-nine deputies. The fiasco of the Beer Hall Putsch of the preceding November notwithstanding, the German Racist Freedom Party increased its number of Reichstag seats from three to thirty-two, while the DNVP received ninety-five in addition to the ten seats that regional affiliates of the National Rural League had won in different parts of the country. To be sure, the DVP and DDP were able to improve their position somewhat in the December elections, but this did not prevent the DNVP from recording further gains at the expense of the National Socialist Freedom Movement (Nationalsozialistische Freiheitsbewegung), which saw its number of mandates cut in half. The process of political polarization that had become apparent in the results of the two elections was complemented by a second development that manifested itself in the defection of voters to regional and special-interest parties that had been formed during the period of stabilization and that by 1924 had already attracted close to 10 percent of the electorate. This phenomenon was primarily related to the trauma of inflation that had produced widespread insecurity among Germany's middle-class voters and had prompted them to seek help from parties like the Reconstruction and Revaluation Party (Aufbau- und Aufwertungspartei) and the relatively successful Business Party of the German Middle Class (Wirtschaftspartei des deutschen Mittelstandes) that were committed to the defense of their material interests. The rejection of the more traditional, ideologically oriented parties by a growing number of voters was a symptom of the increasing fragmentation of German political life along lines of social and economic interest, a process that severely weakened the ability of the older parties to form viable governmental coalitions. The government weighed the possibility of halting the proliferation of splinter parties by means of an electoral reform that would be enacted with the use of presidential emergency powers, but it backed away from such a step because of its constitutional implications.

After the Reichstag elections of 4 May 1924 it soon became clear that the

DNVP was not yet ready to share the burden of governmental responsibility in spite of sustained efforts by the DVP to bring the Nationalists into the cabinet. The DVP was hoping that Nationalist participation in the cabinet would oblige the party to go along with Stresemann's foreign policy and thus free the DVP from the threat of competition from the right. DNVP party chairman Oskar Hergt made his party's entry into the government conditional upon the appointment of Alfred von Tirpitz, the one-time head of the Naval Ministry and a spokesman for the Pan-German League, as chancellor, Stresemann's resignation as foreign minister, and the reorganization of the governing coalition in Prussia. Foreign policy considerations alone made the acceptance of these conditions impossible, with the result that the DVP, which encountered strong opposition to the DNVP's entry into the government from the Center and DDP, had to abandon its plans to "break the German Nationalist wave." Now that acceptance of the Dawes Plan appeared inevitable, Ebert pressed for the retention of the Marx government, which received a pledge of support from the Social Democrats in matters related to the conduct of German foreign policy. The DVP, on the other hand, still hoped that it would be possible to bring about a realignment of political forces that would culminate in the formation of an exclusively bourgeois government, or *Bürgerblockregierung*, once the ratification of the Dawes Plan had taken place.

Foreign policy constraints contributed in no small measure to the fact that the election results did not bring about a change in the governing coalition. Although Marx briefly considered the possibility of bringing the Social Democrats into the government, this never materialized because, in light of the momentum toward an exclusively bourgeois government, there was no longer a chance that the SPD might be able to accomplish any of its goals in the area of social and economic policy and thus regain the support of those sectors of the industrial working class whose defection had become apparent in the recent elections. The Social Democrats thus found themselves in the uncomfortable dilemma of being unable to exact concessions in the domestic political arena for their support of the Dawes Plan. On the contrary, the decline in wages was portrayed in the general public as an unavoidable consequence of the government's foreign policy. Moreover, a rejection of the Dawes Plan by the Social Democrats would almost certainly have led to the installation of a cabinet invested with presidential emergency powers and would have seriously jeopardized the continued existence of the Great Coalition in Prussia. The leaders of the SPD still clung to the illusion that they would be able to regain their freedom of action after the Dawes Plan had been ratified. For the time being, however, it had no choice but to follow the "primacy of foreign policy" by tolerating Marx's minority cabinet government.

The relative truce that characterized German domestic politics in the second half of 1924, however, was broken by the DNVP, which demanded through the

Reich minister of agriculture Count Gerhard von Kanitz an immediate return of tariffs to their prewar level. This demand was prompted by the impending expiration of the most-favored-nation status that the Versailles treaty had conferred upon the Allied powers. The DNVP and National Rural League hoped that they could use the position that the SPD had staked out for itself in the area of foreign policy to force it to go along with the reinstatement of protective agricultural tariffs. These tariffs would have meant a substantial rise in the price of foodstuffs that would only have further eroded the living standards of the already hard-pressed working masses. In the final analysis, the proposed tariffs encountered strong opposition from both the Social Democrats and the labor unions, whereby the opposition of the Christian unions was felt deep within the ranks of the governing coalition. Caught in something of a tactical bind, the cabinet waited until the day after the Dawes Plan had been ratified in the Reichstag to introduce its tariff bill on what proved to be the correct assumption that this would destroy the fragile cooperation among the moderate bourgeois parties.

For his own part, Stresemann was hoping that he could bribe the DNVP into abandoning its obstructionist stance in the area of foreign policy by holding out the prospect that the tariff bill could be passed by an exclusively bourgeois cabinet after the Dawes Plan had been ratified. According to the legal opinion provided by the minister of justice, the legislation that would make possible enactment of the Dawes Plan—and particularly the proposed National Railway Law—set aside certain clauses of the Weimar Constitution and therefore required a two-thirds majority in parliament that was attainable only with the assent of the DNVP. Stresemann was determined to force the DNVP to declare its position once and for all and thus showed no interest in trying to circumvent the provisions of the constitution that would be affected by the proposed legislation. To strengthen his hand, Stresemann then arranged a meeting of the Nationalist party leadership with the American ambassador, who reiterated his country's position that without the ratification of the Dawes Plan the desperately needed American credits would not be forthcoming. At the same time, the German government made it clear that the defeat of the Dawes legislation would lead to the dissolution of the Reichstag, thus placing the DNVP in an extremely difficult tactical situation. To make it somewhat easier for the DNVP, Stresemann eventually went along with the DNVP's demand that he formally renounce the war-guilt clause before the Allies. In an effort to exploit his party's key position in the Reichstag as fully as possible, DNVP party chairman Oskar Hergt now demanded the chancellorship for Count Kuno von Westarp, a demand that was unacceptable to both the Center and DDP and that brought Stresemann's foreign policy strategy to the brink of a complete collapse.

The memorable vote on the National Railway Law on 29 August 1924 took place in an apparently hopeless parliamentary deadlock. Quite unexpectedly forty-eight Nationalist deputies broke ranks with the party's leadership and voted for the controversial bill. Just before the decisive vote took place, the DNVP party chairman Oskar Hergt succumbed to pressure from special-interest groups in industry and agriculture and agreed to suspend party discipline that would have required all members of the DNVP Reichstag delegation to support the position of the party leadership. The "Symphony in White," as contemporary observers characterized the collapse of Nationalist unity with reference to the color of the ballots, clearly demonstrated that the crusade of right-wing nationalists against the Versailles peace treaty was primarily for domestic political consumption. In the final analysis, organized economic interests had triumphed over party ideologues and the DNVP party leadership. That this was not simply a carefully staged ploy can be seen from the lengthy debates that the party held in response to demands from the DNVP's right wing that those who had voted for the bill should be expelled from the party. Since this would have destroyed the party's interest structure, the DNVP refrained from following through on these demands.

Under normal parliamentary conditions the debacle of the DNVP in the vote on the National Railway Law should have led to its complete political isolation and to a devastating defeat in the new elections that were soon to take place. The opposite was, however, true. In the aftermath of the vote on 29 August, Stresemann intensified his efforts on behalf of the DNVP's entry into the national government and thus brought about the collapse of the Marx government when, contrary to his expectations, the DDP refused to collaborate with a party that continued to oppose Germany's republican constitution with all the means at its disposal. At the same time, Stresemann ignored overtures from the DDP for a merger of the two liberal parties, no doubt motivated in part by memories of the situation that had existed in the late fall of 1918 but also out of deference to the right wing of his own party and the industrial interests that had come to dominate it. By exceeding the tactical limits of his office and situation, Stresemann had inadvertently precipitated the dissolution of the Reichstag and the call for new elections on 7 December 1924.

In the subsequent election campaign Stresemann assumed an ambivalent position in which, on the one hand, he defended his offer to the DNVP and continued to work for the formation of an exclusively bourgeois cabinet and, on the other, portrayed the DVP as a party of the bourgeois center that did not categorically reject cooperation with the SPD as long as it remained free from the "Marxist" influence of its extreme left wing. Stresemann, however, failed in his efforts to establish the DVP as a *Sammelbecken* for all middle-class voters, who rejected his party's close identification with the policies of big business and remained unimpressed by his accomplishments as German foreign minister. As a result, the DVP could improve its position only marginally in the December 1924 Reichstag elections and was unable to prevent further gains by the DNVP. To be sure, Stresemann's tactical initiative did slow the momentum for a secession on his party's extreme right wing, which in March 1924 had reconstituted itself as the National Liberal Association (Nationalliberale Vereinigung) and was opposed to any opening to the Left. But this did not lead, as Stresemann had hoped, to his appointment as chancellor but rather to the installation after prolonged negotiations of a new bourgeois minority government portraying itself as a "cabinet of personalities."

The deeper cause of the crisis of Germany's parliamentary system in late 1924 lay in the incompatibility of the constantly changing party alliances within the bourgeois political spectrum. With the adoption of the Dawes Plan, the external pressure for unity within the cabinet, which remained in office only through the toleration of the SPD, quickly evaporated. In deference to its own internal constituencies, the Center Party was unwilling to participate in the hard-line right-wing coalition that had begun to take shape during the debate over protective tariffs. At the same time, the formation of a governmental coalition between the political center and Left was also blocked. For whereas the Center was prepared to make concessions to the SPD on the issue of working hours in connection with the pending ratification of the Washington Working Hours Agreement, there was not the slightest chance that the DVP would accept a compromise on social policy that would clear the way for its participation in a coalition in which the Social Democrats were also represented. At the same time, the DNVP, which had emerged from the December elections with 103 seats in the Reichstag, believed that its intransigence in matters of foreign policy had been fully vindicated by the outcome of the elections.

To the outside observer, the Social Democrats were responsible for the collapse of the Great Coalition since they had clearly refused to take part in the negotiations that Marx had initiated in October 1924 for largely tactical reasons. Even then, there was little doubt that the break had been engineered by the industrial wing of the DVP. The tactical inflexibility of the SPD party leadership was directly related to the rigidity of the General German Trade-Union Federation (ADGB), which adamantly refused to place its achievements in social policy on the negotiating table. Still, this does not change the fact that the DVP was determined from the very outset to isolate the Social Democrats in parliament. Even Stresemann emphatically supported the DNVP's inclusion in the governing coalition in spite of its unwavering opposition to his foreign policy and showed little inclination to reach an accommodation with the Left that might have made greater sense in terms of his foreign policy objectives. The DVP lent renewed emphasis to its commitment to form a right-wing government in the Reich when it withdrew its ministers from the Prussian cabinet and effectively destroyed the Great Coalition in Prussia. The party, however, was unable to achieve the same results in the Reichstag in light of the Center's reluctance to participate in a right-wing government from which the DDP had been excluded.

The minority cabinet that Hans Luther formed in the middle of January 1925 after a crisis that lasted for several weeks was indeed a government of personalities and assumed office without formal ties to the parties or their parliamentary delegations only after all other possibilities for forming a governmental coalition had been exhausted. The new cabinet derived its legitimacy ultimately from the authority of the Reich president, notwithstanding the fact that it survived its first test of strength in the Reichstag by a narrow margin made possible by the abstention of the Social Democrats. The DDP, which refused to participate in the new cabinet, had permitted Otto Geßler to stay on as minister of defense on the pretext that this cabinet was a cabinet of civil servants. In terms of its composition, however, the new cabinet represented a return to the *Bürgerblock* that had failed so miserably in matters of foreign policy, an area in which no major decisions were currently pending. Chancellor Hans Luther, the consummate "politician without a party," went on to develop a distinctly self-confident governing style that pointed in the direction of a "strong chancellor democracy" and imposed a heavy cost upon the parliamentary delegations of those parties that supported his government. Although the government managed to survive the debates on the highly controversial tariff bill that was finally adopted in August 1925, conflicts over trade policy and the security pact led to its eventual demise.

The right-wing coalition that assumed responsibility for the conduct of national affairs at the beginning of 1925 did not, however, prove viable in Prussia, particularly since the Prussian Center Party showed little interest in exchanging the proven benefits of its cooperation within the Great Coalition for a *Bürgerblockregierung* that would almost certainly be plagued by strong internal tensions. After a brief interlude in which Wilhelm Marx failed to secure sufficient parliamentary support for a new Prussian cabinet under his leadership, the Weimar Coalition returned to power in April 1925 with the SPD's Otto Braun as the new minister president. In sharp contrast to the situation in the Reich, Prussia's political leaders were able to maintain the viability of the parliamentary system despite occasional relapses into obstructionism by the KPD and DNVP. This was possible not only because the major conflicts between organized economic interests were fought out at the national level but also because the parties of the Weimar Coalition were considerably stronger in the Prussian Landtag than they were in the Reichstag. Moreover, the task of forming a government was much easier in a system where the minister president was directly elected by the Landtag and therefore enjoyed greater personal authority and disciplinary resources. As a result, the Great Coalition in Prussia always represented — except for the crisis of 1925, which was directly related to national political developments—a stabilizing factor in the Weimar parliamentary system, even if here too close ties between the parties and organized economic interests made compromise difficult and encouraged the authoritarian leadership style of Otto Braun.

At the national level, the principle of government by parliamentary majority in the period between 1924 and 1928 remained in effect only in exceptional cases and in limited political contexts. This, in turn, was hardly conducive to extricating Germany's political parties from the subordinate position to which they had been relegated by the pseudoconstitutional system of the Wilhelmine era. The self-image of the political parties as institutions for the protection of necessarily particularist interests and for the representation of specific social groups was only reinforced by this state of affairs. Weimar constitutional law afforded the parties no support whatsoever in the exercise of their various functions and relegated them to the realm of "extraconstitutional entities." The minority of liberal constitutional scholars, among them Gerhard Anschütz and Richard Thoma, were not yet willing to recognize the political parties as indispensable intermediary institutions for the articulation of the popular will. The prevailing constitutional thought of the day thus provided a measure of scholarly legitimation for the widespread resentment and hostility toward the existing party system. In his much-cited Berlin rectoral address of 1927, Heinrich Triepel stressed the necessity of overcoming the role of "irresponsible party organizations" in favor of new "community-forming forces" (gemeinschaftsbildender Kräfte). The ideal of a liberal parliamentarism in which the deputy, bound only by the dictates of his or her conscience and free from ties to party or parliamentary delegation, arrived at a determination of the common good in an atmosphere of free discussion no longer posed a viable alternative to existing modes of parliamentary praxis. This, however, did little to prevent Carl Schmitt, one of the most prominent and sharpest critics of the Weimar parliamentary system, from measuring and condemning the realities of German parliamentary life against the standards of an unrealistic model that had no roots in European parliamentary history.

Constitutional scholarship and conservative professional elites thus shared the conviction that it was vitally important to curtail and, if possible, to eliminate the influence of the various political parties. By no means was this idea espoused only by neoconservative publicists who drew their inspiration from Spengler's criticism of representative institutions as a "glorified beer table" or his characterization of the parties as "swarms of parasites on the body of the Reich." The notion that the "party state"—an intentionally pejorative term coined by contemporary political pundits—had to be overcome if Germany was ever to rise again was a common legacy of virtually all political intellectuals on the margins of the bourgeois party spectrum and stretched from the youth movement through Catholic universalism and Protestant political theology to the old conservatives and the *völkisch* Right and enjoyed increasing popularity among Germany's conservative elites and, last but not least, in the camp of German big business.

The fundamental criticism of the political party system was common to virtually all of the antiliberal forces in German society and occasionally found a certain resonance on the German Left as well. Its corollary was the growing tendency to replace liberal forms of public civic association with a variety of political leagues, which under a variety of labels such as Order, Ring, *Bund*, or Club were reminiscent of preconstitutional structures. Characteristic of this attitude was its stress on the principle of the *Bund*, an idea whose principal advocate, the otherwise brilliant political analyst of the Tat Circle (Tat-Kreis) Hans Zehrer, claimed in 1932 in an article entitled "The End of the Parties": "Today the *Bund* belongs to the future, the party to the past." The almost unimaginable intensity of the polemics against political parties, which were denounced as corrupt, rapacious, and intent upon the destruction of the *Volksgemeinschaft*, could be traced back to a deep-seated antipathy toward political dissent and national fragmentation that was closely related to Germany's experience during the time of its unification as a nation without political cohesion. The belief in a preestablished identity of the welfare of the state with the best interests of the citizen had its origins in the philosophical idealism of the early nineteenth century and was tenaciously upheld throughout the industrial revolution and the subsequent period of intensified industrial development. Such a faith now renewed itself in the myth of a new communal order, or *Gemeinschaftsordnung*, that was free of political conflicts and in which the relationship between the nation and its leadership was no longer corrupted by particularist and selfish interests.

The rejection of political parties and the parliamentary system by influential segments of Germany's intellectual elite was also directly related to the loss of social status they had suffered through the gradual democratization of German social and political life and that had first become apparent with the relative decline of the so-called old middle class. The malaise of Germany's intellectual elite was further compounded by the national humiliation that Germany had supposedly suffered after its military defeat in 1918. By the same token, the parliamentary democracy that Germany had established after the end of the war was perceived as a system alien to Germany's indigenous political traditions that had been forced upon the nation by the victorious Western powers and that represented a logical extension of the ideas of 1789 against which Germany had gone to war in 1914 and whose triumph would mean the permanent dissipation of Germany's national strength. Even the DDP dissociated itself from these "Western" ideas by extolling an independent "German concept of the state" that, with its commitment to the principles of self-administration (*Selbstverwaltung*) and the sovereignty of law, represented a direct line of continuity from the old Germanic concept of a cooperative society, or *Genossenschaft*. It was in this spirit that the ideas of Baron vom Stein, whose political thought was reinterpreted to conform to the national-liberal ethos, became the symbol of Germany's will to preserve its identity in the foreign and domestic arena. In 1932, the one hundredth anniversary of the Prussian reformer's death had served as the occasion for a national Stein renaissance. By the end of the Weimar Republic there was hardly a political faction in the bourgeois spectrum that did not evoke Stein's idealized version of a German constitution as an alternative to the "Western" parliamentary democracy that Germany had adopted after the end of the recent war.

The invocation of a separate "German path" not only made it possible to establish continuity with the traditions of the pre-Bismarckian Reich but also served as the point of departure for a general flight from the ideal of parliamentary democracy now that it had been unmasked as the instrument of special economic interests. The specific alternatives to parliamentary democracy varied according to the special nuances of the antirepublican opposition on the German Right, including groups as diverse as the National Bolsheviks, the National Revolutionaries, neoconservatives, various *bündisch* and *völkisch* factions, German socialists and National Socialists, as well as Catholic defenders of something akin to the Holy Roman Empire and traditional Protestant conservatives. The common denominator that united all of these was the belief that the state must be strengthened in relationship to specific social groups and the political parties through which they pursued their special interests. Greater autonomy of the bureaucratic apparatus from the legislature, the introduction of occupational and corporatist entities, the ennoblement (*Veredelung*) of mass democracy through the creation of a leadership elite, and the dictatorship of the Reich president were all among the panaceas that the antiliberal and nationalistic currents of the day had called forth. All of these proposals represented a radical departure from the conditions of an advanced industrial society and completely lost sight of the fundamental rules of power politics and the need to reconcile pluralistic social interests.

Encumbered by a host of social resentments and irrational longings, this mode of ideological articulation left little room for the indispensable role that political parties had always played in the formation of the national political agenda. This, however, did not keep its leading exponents from seeking influence within the parties or campaigning on their behalf. Notwithstanding how little practical significance Moeller van den Bruck's myth of a "third party" may have had, the prevalence of ideas such as this contributed in no small measure to the delegitimation of the parties of the bourgeois center and moderate Right. Right-wing attacks against the Weimar party system only reinforced the preference that Germany's middle-class voters had shown for special-interest parties over the more traditional, ideologically oriented bourgeois parties and set the stage after 1929 for their defection to the NSDAP as the most resolute opponent of the existing party system. In the final analysis, the systematic weakening of the Weimar party system through incessant journalistic attacks was far more detrimental to the effective reconciliation of conflicting political interests than the parties' reluctance to assume total political responsibility. Yet for all of the increasingly harsh polemics that were directed against the parliamentary system from circles outside of parliament, the parties of the Great Coalition were able to generate a surprising degree of cooperation in specific areas of common interest.

The inadequate understanding of the role that parties in a parliamentary system played in the formation of a government and in the process of political integration accounted only partially for the chronic parliamentary crisis that characterized Germany's political development during the period of the *Bürgerblock* cabinets. With the exception of those extremist parties that were committed to the overthrow of the existing political system, responsible party leaders from the Left to the Right were well aware of the need for political compromise and of the role that political parties in a parliamentary democracy played in sustaining the viability of the state. As the highly respected political economist Gustav Stolper complained in 1928: "What we have today is a coalition of ministers, not a coalition of parties. We don't even have government parties, only opposition parties." Stolper aptly described a more or less permanent state of affairs where compromises reached by party leaders were frequently revoked in the parliamentary delegations but also — and then with more devastating effect — by the parties' grass-roots organizations, even though there was no shortage of institutions, such as party caucuses, leadership conferences, and interparliamentary committees, that were designed to forge a broad political consensus.

The fragmentation of the German party system along lines of social and economic interests was intensified by continued economic stagnation. Conflicts over the distribution of the social product were more detrimental to those bourgeois parties that had not yet developed effective national organizations and were therefore more heavily dependent on contributions from outside sources than to the Social Democrats or the Center, which, from the perspectives of their organization, had become socially diverse "people's parties." But even here spokesmen for special-interest groups were overrepresented in their parliamentary delegations. The growing influence of union functionaries in the SPD, where they constituted more than 37 percent of the Reichstag delegation in 1930, severely limited the party's freedom of movement in precisely those issues of social policy that were of decisive importance for the future of parliamentary democracy. The Center Party, by contrast, had to contend with strong internal tensions between its middle-class and working-class constituencies. But it was in the DVP and DNVP that the influence of special-interest groups

was most apparent. It was not without some justification that in 1929 Stresemann considered the public financing of political parties as a way of reducing
their susceptibility to interference by outside business interests.

The obvious dysfunctionality of the Weimar party system notwithstanding,
the deeper causes of the parliamentary crisis that descended on Germany in the
second half of the 1920s lay in the veto power that established economic interests—such as the Reichswehr, heavy industry, large-scale agriculture, and, in
the early phase of the Weimar Republic, organized labor—were able to exercise
in the name of transcendent national objectives. These elements found their
counterpoise at the upper echelons of the state bureaucracy and in the Bureau of the Reich President, whose officials almost invariably favored a system
of government that bypassed the parliament whenever possible in accordance
with Defense Minister Geßler's motto: "Governing with the Reichstag is impossible." Otto Braun repeatedly pointed out, though always in vain, that the
indiscriminate use of emergency powers could only undermine the parties'
sense of parliamentary responsibility even further. In this respect, it is particularly revealing that Braun was eventually excluded from meetings of the
national cabinet—meetings that he was entitled to attend in his capacity as
Prussian minister president—whenever the Reich president, who was normally
represented by state secretary Otto Meißner, chose to attend in person.

Illegal rearmament and attempts to circumvent obligations imposed by the
Versailles peace treaty had given rise to a parallel bureaucracy at a fairly early
stage in the history of the Weimar Republic. The role of the president as a surrogate legislator as well as the close relationship between the bureaucracy and
certain interest groups only intensified this tendency. But it was only against
the background of the deep-seated antipathy that a large part of the professional elites, the media, the judiciary, the academic establishment, and the
educated middle classes harbored toward the parliamentary system that made
it possible for the executive to assert its autonomy vis-à-vis the legislature in a
process that started in late 1923 and culminated in the presidential cabinets of
the late Weimar Republic. The widespread resentment of parliament received
added impetus from the fact that the experiences of the revolution and postwar inflation had done much to intensify antagonism toward social democracy,
which was held responsible for the leveling of social privileges as a result of
long-term social and economic factors.

The antagonism between middle-class interests and organized labor, however, was overshadowed by the asymmetry that characterized the respective
fields of foreign and domestic politics. The Luther government lived on the
expectation that the consequences, or *Rückwirkungen*, of the Dawes Plan that
Stresemann had promised would soon make themselves felt. These, however,
failed to materialize. Just how precarious the diplomatic situation was after the
London Conference can be seen in the fact that the German Foreign Office—

acting on advice from Ramsay MacDonald, who otherwise prophesied a "catastrophe for Germany and the world" — failed to issue the formal declaration on the war-guilt clause that Stresemann had promised to make in return for the DNVP's help in securing parliamentary acceptance of the Dawes Plan. At the same time, the discussions on the suspension of interallied military controls, which the Western powers were willing to undertake after a final general inspection, led to a major foreign policy confrontation. For the inspection of German military installations produced such negative results that the Allies were obliged to postpone the withdrawal of Allied occupation forces from the area around Cologne that had originally been scheduled for 10 January 1925.

The incumbent chancellor, Wilhelm Marx, was stunned by these developments and warned of a return to the policy of sanctions that had led to the occupation of the Ruhr in January 1923. By no means, however, was this the case. Aside from the fact that German violations of the disarmament clauses of the Versailles peace treaty were undeniable, the manner in which Seeckt was trying to limit and obstruct the armament controls could only have strengthened French mistrust of German military policy. But the most important reason for the great importance Herriot attached to the general inspection of German military installations is to be sought in his desire to persuade Great Britain to sign the Geneva Protocol for the creation of a European system of security that had been submitted by the League of Nations in October 1924. Although the matter of security had been assiduously avoided, French pressure kept it on the agenda of international politics. As long as France's security needs had not been adequately addressed, Paris clung tenaciously to its right to impose sanctions on Germany.

The German public, which accused France of an insatiable thirst for continental hegemony, had no sympathy whatsoever for the French obsession with security. Even the Anglo-Saxon powers regarded the tenacity with which France continued its occupation of the Ruhr and Rhineland as the consequence of a legalistic and, in the final analysis, backward-looking foreign policy. France's unfavorable demographic development, a sense of economic inferiority, and the traumatic experience of the First World War were the defining elements of a French foreign policy that had committed all of its resources to preventing the resurgence of Germany. Both the British and the French governments were well aware of the fact that Allied military controls could not be continued indefinitely. The refusal to evacuate the zone around Cologne, therefore, was little more than an expedient by which Herriot sought to involve Great Britain more directly in French security policy.

German foreign policy, on the other hand, sought to prevent implementation of that clause in the Geneva Protocol stipulating that disputes already decided by a unanimous vote in the Council of the League of Nations could not subsequently be submitted for revision to the League's arbitration board.

This was true not only of the recent decision on Upper Silesia but of the entire Versailles system, despite the revision clause in Article 19 of the League of Nations Covenant. In the opinion of Friedrich Gaus, the influential head of the legal division of the German Foreign Office, the Geneva Protocol "effectively closed the road to a peaceful revision of the Versailles treaty." Yet the German experts felt strongly that Germany's admission to the League of Nations would be meaningless unless it afforded Germany an opportunity to work for the revision of the peace treaty. The Foreign Office reacted with great concern to the efforts of the League of Nations to use the demilitarized zones that had been established in different parts of Europe as the point of departure for universal European disarmament.

Similar considerations informed German fears that Allied military controls might be transferred to the League of Nations and thus perpetuated indefinitely. Along with the French refusal to withdraw from the zone around Cologne, this fear played an important role in Stresemann's decision to revive the stalled negotiations for an end of military controls and the premature evacuation of the Rhineland by offering to sign a security pact with other European powers. The stimulus for Stresemann's initiative had come from Lord d'Abernon, who for his own part was concerned that Foreign Secretary Austen Chamberlain might give in to his pro-French feelings and agree to the conclusion of an Anglo-French security pact that for all intents and purposes would be directed against Germany. Even if this did not come to pass, Stresemann still had to anticipate that France might be able to extract from the new Conservative cabinet under Stanley Baldwin "physical guarantees" on the Rhineland that would preclude the evacuation of Allied occupation troops for the foreseeable future.

The offer of a security pact that Stresemann circulated first to the British in January 1925 and then to the French cabinet contained not only a purely defensive component designed to prevent Germany's diplomatic isolation but also an offensive component that Stresemann hoped would lead to the early evacuation of the Rhineland and perhaps to the return of the Saar as well. On 4 June 1925 Stresemann confided to the American ambassador Alanson Houghton that the peace Germany was offering France "might be compatible with ten more years of occupation in the Rhineland," though without specifying this in the wording of the proposed pact. The German draft also guaranteed that the demilitarization of the Rhine frontier would be respected, thereby implicitly abandoning German claims to Alsace-Lorraine without, on the other hand, saying anything about Eupen-Malmedy or about German guarantees for its eastern borders.

With Luther's approval, Stresemann submitted the German offer to the Allies without first informing the cabinet for fear that this would give the Nationalists an opportunity to talk it to death. Contrary to the assurances of

Lord d'Abernon, the German proposal elicited mixed reactions from Chamberlain and other members of the Conservative cabinet. While firmly denying British suspicions that this was simply a way to reopen the issue of Germany's eastern borders, the Wilhelmstraße nevertheless made it quite clear that Germany would eventually seek revision here as well. In response to the German offer, Chamberlain proposed that at a later date Germany should become part of the Franco-British alliance that he personally favored. The majority of the cabinet, however, vigorously opposed entering into any commitments on the continent as long as a limited revision of the Treaty of Versailles had not yet taken place. Such a revision, the Conservatives pointed out, could only be envisaged several years down the road and would have to make provisions supporting the Polish position in the questions of Danzig and the Polish Corridor. Even then, Chamberlain considered the Rhine Pact preferable to no pact at all, for his main concern was to prevent Europe from breaking up into antagonistic alliance systems and Germany from joining forces with Soviet Russia. By mediating between Germany and France, Chamberlain hoped that Great Britain would be able to avert the outbreak of armed conflict in Europe and thus eliminate the danger that Britain might be drawn into direct military involvement on the continent.

Because of a change in France's government that saw the Radical Socialist Aristide Briand ascend to the leadership of the Quai d'Orsay, it was not until the middle of June 1925 that the French reacted to the German offer. In light of the British attitude, outright rejection seemed unwise. Moreover, Briand shared Herriot's insight that it was necessary to abandon the crude strategy of threatening Germany with military sanctions and replace it with guarantees in international law that consolidated the territorial status quo. Along with the inclusion of Belgium and German recognition of Article 16 of the Covenant of the League of Nations, France made its participation in the proposed security pact contingent on a link between the security pact and French guarantees of the German-Polish and German-Czechoslovakian borders. Briand also wished to include a statement stipulating that the security pact would have no effect on German obligations under the Versailles peace treaty, a stipulation that preserved the possibility of imposing sanctions in the event that Germany failed to fulfill its military and economic obligations.

On top of all of this, France also demanded that the security pact be linked to Germany's entry into the League of Nations as a way of containing its rival within a system of collective security. Unfortunately, the attitude of the major powers toward the Geneva Protocol meant that such a system was not yet a reality. After considerable hesitation and against strong domestic opposition, Stresemann announced Germany's fundamental willingness to join the League in September 1924 but made such a step contingent upon a series of conditions that included a permanent seat for Germany on the League Council, assurances that Article 16 of the League Covenant would not be applied against Germany, and Germany's eventual participation in the system of League mandates. Moreover, Stresemann sought assurances that Germany would not be obligated to acknowledge its guilt for the outbreak of the war or any other comparable moral responsibility. Under no circumstances was Stresemann willing tc allow what little freedom of movement Germany enjoyed in foreign affairs to be further curtailed by membership in the League of Nations. While the major powers readily agreed to Germany's petition for a permanent seat on the League Council, the German request that in view of its military weakness it be exempted from participating in the enforcement of sanctions under Article 16 of the League Covenant proved particularly controversial since it did not conform to the anti-Soviet containment strategy pursued by the League of Nations.

French efforts to link the security pact to Germany's entry to the League of Nations created domestic political difficulties that prevented Stresemann from taking on the issue of the League of Nations immediately. Stresemann had hoped that the conclusion of a security pact guaranteeing the present Rhine border would make it possible for him to bring about an end to the occupation of the Ruhr and an early evacuation of the Rhineland. In a conversation with Soviet Commissioner for Foreign Affairs Maxim Litvinov, who expressed grave misgivings about a German accommodation with the League of Nations, Stresemann downplayed the obligations this would impose upon Germany. "Keep in mind," Stresemann continued, "that for the foreseeable future Germany's objective in the west is not the revision of the Versailles treaty but rather the containment of France within the limits established by the treaty, that is to say, to guarantee the security of the Rhineland." The conditions that the French had attached to their participation in the proposed security pact, however, had forced the German Foreign Office to address the question of Germany's entry into the League of Nations without being able to link this directly to the revision of the Versailles peace treaty. There was little that Germany could do but reiterate its opposition to making guarantees for its eastern borders. The fact that Britain was not willing to support the French position on eastern European borders was a factor that in this respect worked in Germany's favor.

Stresemann realized much more clearly than any of his domestic opponents that Germany was neither militarily nor economically in a position where it could choose between the Western powers and Soviet Russia. Indeed, the proposal for a security pact guaranteeing Germany's western borders was designed precisely to reestablish Germany's freedom of choice in foreign affairs within the limits to which this was still possible. The German foreign minister emphatically rejected the idea held by circles in the Reichswehr and DNVP that an alliance with Soviet Russia would make it possible to break out of the encirclement of the Little Entente, disrupt the cooperation among the Western powers, and force, if necessary by military means, a revision of the German-Polish border. None of this took cognizance of the fact, however, that the Soviet Union was preoccupied with severe domestic problems caused by the implementation of the New Economic Policy or that the Polish Republic was clearly in the process of stabilizing itself under the leadership of Marshal Józef Piłsudski. Aside from these facts, there was no chance whatsoever that Germany could militarily survive a limited conflict with Poland even if it were provoked by the Soviet Union. As long as France was still in the Rhineland and could use this as a base for the deployment of force on Germany's exposed flank, German intervention in Poland could only lead to a new defeat.

In this context the Allied disarmament note of 4 June 1925 should have had a sobering effect on German policy makers. On the contrary, it only encouraged Stresemann's political opponents both inside and outside of the cabinet to intensify their agitation against the proposed security pact. The extent to which Germany's political leadership was still hostage to the foreign policy illusions of the Wilhelmine era was apparent in the cabinet meeting of 24 June, where Stresemann was criticized not only by the ministers from the DNVP but also by spokesmen from the Center as well as by the defense minister and the chancellor for having "betrayed the nation" when he renounced Germany's claim to Alsace-Lorraine. Stresemann responded by pointing out that the return of Alsace-Lorraine could only be achieved by a war against France for which the necessary means were simply not available. By the end of the meeting the cabinet majority had compelled the foreign minister to limit himself to excluding the use of force in the matter of Alsace-Lorraine, a stipulation that Stresemann as an advocate of a national Realpolitik found absurd.

Forced onto the defensive by Stresemann's superior argumentation, General Hans von Seeckt stated the position of the Locarno opponents who categorically rejected any foreign policy concessions or modification of Germany's revisionist stance with the pithy formula: "We must get power, and as soon as we have power we will of course go after everything we have lost." The diplomatic team of the Foreign Office, headed by State Secretary Carl von Schubert, the successor of Ago von Maltzahn, could only respond to such a grotesque assessment of Germany's diplomatic situation with gestures of utter dismay. The Wilhelmstraße tried in vain to impress upon the Reichswehr command that the mere mention of military action or intensified secret rearmament would only strengthen French resistance to ending the occupation in Germany's western regions. A year and a half later, Schubert commented somewhat ironically on the margins of a war-games plan for a German-Polish conflict predicated upon Russian neutrality and French passivity: "The assumption seems to be that England had fallen victim to a seaquake, and that America has been devastated in part by tornados, in part by misguided speculation, whereas Czechoslovakia was fully preoccupied by its negotiations for a concordat."

It was only in connection with changes in the leadership of the German general staff, culminating in the replacement of Seeckt by General Wilhelm von Heye, that a more realistic attitude toward Germany's foreign policy prospects began to develop. A strategy memorandum written by Colonel Joachim von Stülpnagel in 1926 recognized that the long-term goals of regaining the Polish Corridor, achieving *Anschluß* with Austria, and ending the demilitarization of the Rhineland could be attained only through a long-term revision of the Versailles peace treaty based on the principle of universal disarmament. Operational war-game plans, the memorandum continued, had revealed just how limited German military power was, at best sufficient for defensive action in the event of a conflict with Poland. In spite of this, however, the secret rearmament agreements with Soviet Russia continued intact. In 1926 a tank training school near Kazan and a military airport at Lipezk that was to be shared by German and Soviet planes were placed in operation. Technical cooperation in the use and manufacture of poison gas was also initiated. But this aspect of the secret rearmament lost much of its significance, in part because German industry was not willing to finance major rearmament projects in Russia and in part because the problems associated with the Soviet Union's New Economic Policy severely limited the possibility of closer cooperation.

Under these circumstances, the Reichswehr command shifted its emphasis to the long-term preparedness of the German people, including the use of guerrilla tactics, for the eventuality of an armed conflict. While the military did not abandon its plans for illegal mobilization or the extensive buildup of border patrols and militias that had taken place during the Seeckt era, it was able to dissociate itself from Seeckt's wishful thinking that Germany would be able to deploy a substantial number of combat-ready divisions in the event of a general mobilization. Instead, Germany's military leadership began to concentrate its attention on the modernization of weaponry and on increased tactical mobility. The military had not abandoned the idea of an armed conflict with France but simply conceded that Germany would not be ready for such a conflict before 1935–40. In the meantime, the illegal financing of Germany's secret rearmament, which was monitored by a committee of high-ranking government officials and which appeared in the budget under a number of spurious headings, had led to a series of corruption scandals, the most spectacular of which was the bankruptcy of the Phöbus Film Company (Phöbus-Film Gesellschaft), which in 1927 resulted in the resignation of Defense Minister Otto Geßler.

Prior to the conclusion of the Treaty of Locarno, Stresemann encountered determined resistance from Seeckt, who was responding to criticism in the Allied disarmament note regarding the fact that the German chief of military operations was responsible to no one but the Reich president and that the German general staff continued to exist in open violation of the Versailles peace treaty. When Paul von Hindenburg, who considered Seeckt's sober and intellectual demeanor a sign of arrogance, assumed the Reich presidency in the spring of 1925, the position of the chief of military operations declined in significance relative to the Ministry of Defense. Nevertheless the Reichswehr command did not abandon its political ambitions. Instead of the critical distance it maintained toward the political arena during Ebert's tenure as Reich president, the Reichswehr now called for a "positive attitude toward the state," a stance most strongly advocated by the increasingly influential Colonel Kurt von Schleicher. This correction in the Reichswehr's political course, however, must not be seen as a change in the deep-seated antiparliamentary bias of the military. The authoritarian proposals for constitutional reform that Schleicher circulated in 1926 already indicated that the period of military self-restraint in domestic policies had come to an end.

The Reichswehr no longer saw itself as a "state within the state" but rather as an integral part of a statist-authoritarian potential at the disposal of the Reich president. The reorientation that had taken place at the upper echelons of the Reichswehr leadership was predicated on the strategic insight that in the future a total war could not be fought in opposition to the existing political system or without the consent of large segments of the population. The program of national military preparedness therefore implied intensified efforts to isolate and neutralize those political parties that were deemed "nationally unreliable," a term that applied primarily to the SPD. In the area of foreign policy, the military fully supported Stresemann's newly developed strategy of using the disarmament issue as a tool for securing military parity for Germany. Seeckt's resignation, which Geßler received in 1926 after the chief of military operations had permitted the eldest son of Crown Prince Wilhelm to participate in the autumn maneuvers in a uniform from the prestigious 9th Infantry Regiment, was no more than a reflection of the change that had taken place in the military's medium-range strategy and of the new relationship that had developed between Germany's military and civilian leadership.

The change that took place in the Reichswehr's concept of its role in Germany's political life must also be seen as a reaction to the setbacks that German diplomats had suffered at Locarno in their efforts to secure greater freedom of movement for the German military. In the summer of 1925 Stresemann was still hoping to achieve immediate success in issues related to disarmament and the evacuation of the occupied territory. Under pressure from the DNVP, which was determined to sabotage the security pact before the French response had even arrived, Stresemann included a demand for the evacuation of Allied troops from the Ruhr and Rhineland even though the diplomatic advantages of such a step were far from clear. Since Briand, who had considerable sympathy for the domestic political problems of his German colleague, was resolved to bring the negotiations to a successful conclusion, he did not address the

German reservations but reached an understanding with Chamberlain that the legal experts of the participating nations would draw up a draft treaty to be initialed at a conference of foreign ministers that would meet in Locarno on 15 September 1925. Chancellor Luther, whom Stresemann had kept on board only by threatening to resign earlier that summer, opposed the DNVP's motion that Stresemann be sent to Locarno by himself in order to emphasize the supposedly "nonbinding" character of the meeting. The actual intention of the DNVP motion, however, was to isolate the German foreign minister and to undercut his position in the cabinet. Once again, the foreign minister was obliged to take along the statement that he had refrained from issuing at an earlier stage of the negotiations on the war-guilt question, the evacuation of the zone around Cologne, and disarmament. Trotting out these perfectly well known positions at Locarno would be all the more unfriendly in view of Briand's apparent willingness to accommodate the Germans by completing the evacuation of the Ruhr as early as 31 July and of Duisburg and Düsseldorf by 15 August.

The central problem of reaching an understanding with Germany did not lie in peripheral issues such as these, for, as Briand well knew, they would be resolved as soon as the more complicated matter of security had been settled. The central problem was Germany's firm determination to avoid guarantees pertaining to its eastern borders and to keep the relationship it had established with the Soviet Union under the auspices of the Treaty of Rapallo from being jeopardized by closer ties to the West. The latter objective proved an unusually challenging diplomatic problem, for the USSR had bluntly informed the German government that it would consider Germany's entry into the League of Nations a breach of the principles laid down in the Treaty of Rapallo. The USSR had further indicated that even if Germany were exempted from compliance with Article 16 of the League of Nations Covenant and did not have to grant France to the right of transit across German territory, it would feel compelled to protect itself against the threat of Allied intervention through separate agreements with Poland as well as with France.

The neutrality pact that the Russians offered to sign with Germany and by which Germany would pledge not to participate in any economic, political, or military alliance directed against the USSR came as something of an embarrassment to Stresemann, if only because it conveyed the impression that Germany might be entertaining thoughts of revising its Polish border by military means. The foreign minister had every reason to avoid the appearance of bad faith and a repetition of the Rapallo coup that would have endangered the signing of the security pact. At the same time, Stresemann also had to contend with the pro-Russian influence of Count Brockdorff-Rantzau, Germany's ambassador in Moscow, and was worried that the Russians might leak some of the ambassador's earlier indiscretions about "pushing Poland back into its ethnographic frontiers" in an effort to sabotage his Locarno policy.

On the other hand, the overtures from Moscow helped Germany reach a compromise with respect to Article 16 of the League Covenant by which Germany would be obliged to participate in the League's punitive actions only to the extent that this was "compatible with its military posture and in accordance with its geographical position." The possibility of an alliance with Russia remained an important tool for pressuring the French into concessions on the important question of Germany's eastern borders. With respect to sanctions, Stresemann indicated that Germany would not participate in any action against Soviet Russia on the grounds that it ran the risk of becoming the battleground in a major war between east and west. At the same time he proposed that as a member of the Council of the League of Nations Germany would not use the veto to which it was entitled to block sanctions in the event of Soviet aggression. In this respect, Stresemann explicitly endorsed the principle of collective security without surrendering any specific German interests.

In addition, Stresemann could be sure that if it reached a point where sanctions were under consideration, the arbitration procedures this would set in motion would provide him with ample opportunity to safeguard German interests. Firmness on this particular point strengthened the German position with respect to the unusually persistent Soviet overtures that went beyond mutual guarantees of neutrality to consolidating the status quo in the East, something that Stresemann was determined to avoid. In the final analysis, the comprehensive consultations authorized by the Treaty of Berlin that Germany and the Soviet Union concluded at the latter's urging in April 1926 proved far more favorable to Germany's revisionist aspirations than a formal alliance. In any event, the Polish question could only be reopened indirectly, namely, by impeding Poland's economic consolidation and offering generous economic aid in exchange for a revision of Poland's western boundary.

At Locarno Stresemann succeeded in his goal of blocking French efforts to attach guarantees to the arbitration treaties Germany concluded with Poland and Czechoslovakia. In point of fact, these treaties were essentially nonbinding and signified a substantial weakening of the French treaty system insofar as Germany was able to avoid guarantees of its eastern borders. The unmistakable contrast between this situation and the renunciation of military force by Germany and France with respect to their common border in the west virtually challenged Germany to entertain the prospects of revising its borders with Poland and Czechoslovakia in the not-too-distant future. To this extent Stresemann was right in viewing the Treaty of Locarno as a defeat for Poland. This, however, was also true for France, which in the case of a conflict that was not provoked by Germany would have been obliged to provide military assistance. By the same token, the treaty undercut French efforts to persuade Great Britain to specify its obligations in the event that Germany failed to honor its promise regarding the demilitarization of the Rhineland. Direct sanctions without recourse to the cumbersome procedures demanded by the Covenant of the League of Nations had thus become practically impossible even if the relevant clauses of the Versailles peace treaty had not been formally rescinded.

When the heads of the governments of England, France, Germany, Italy, Belgium, Poland, and Czechoslovakia convened at Locarno in early October 1925, the essential elements of the security pact were already in place. The fact that Germany would henceforth be treated as a complete equal represented a prestige triumph for German diplomacy that cannot be overestimated. The "Spirit of Locarno" as a symbol for a new era of international understanding and commitment to avoid European military conflict, however, concealed a tenacious struggle over the interests of national states in which Stresemann, unlike Aristide Briand, showed no inclination whatsoever to make generous concessions. The memorable words of the French premier that Locarno marked "the beginning of an era of trust" never became reality despite the fervent hopes of the crowds that, summoned by the sound of church bells at the end of the conference, believed that the foundations of a new era of peace had been laid at the shores of Lago Maggiore.

Locarno represented hope—and so Chamberlain could say that from this point on there would no longer be victors or vanquished. In a similar vein, Stresemann stated on the occasion of the formal signing of the treaty in London on 1 December 1925 that there was "every reason to speak of the idea of Europe." But only the future would show whether Briand's will to maintain the status quo could be reconciled with the undiminished German desire for revision, a desire that was betrayed by Stresemann's statement that the task at hand was "to push back France trench by trench since a general attack is no longer possible." To be sure, this statement, as well Stresemann's remark in his controversial letter to the Prussian crown prince from September 1925 that before anything else Germany had to get the strangler off its back, can also be interpreted in a tactical sense. But the fact remains that Stresemann's foreign policy was informed by an ironclad nationalism and that for him the idea of Europe would assume validity only if and when Germany had regained full sovereignty as a nation-state and with it the power to conduct its own military affairs.

In Stresemann's verdict, Locarno represented no more than a first step on the road to the "gradual reacquisition of German sovereignty through a network of European treaties." The phrase "silver streak on the horizon" (*Silberstreif am Horizont*) that entered the popular vocabulary at this time betrays the extent to which German politicians felt that they were embarking on a long and rocky road at whose end the German Reich, enlarged by *Anschluß* with

Austria, would have regained its position as a power in the heart of Europe. Originally Stresemann had ascribed relatively little importance to the security pact. It was the Western rhetoric of peaceful cooperation that made the treaty appear as a fundamental turning point in international relations. But as far as the concrete issues of evacuation and disarmament that had been discussed in the early phase of the negotiations were concerned, disappointingly little had been accomplished from the German point of view. The chancellor Luther returned to Berlin deeply depressed and fearful of reprimands from his colleagues in the cabinet, and the German delegation had to be protected by cordons of police on its arrival in the German capital. Stresemann correctly emphasized that his diplomacy had achieved all that could achieved under the existing circumstances. Even in the final session and then again in the interval between the initialing and the formal signing of the treaty, Stresemann tried to pressure Briand and the Allied ambassadors' conference responsible for the disarmament issue to make some concession that might make the treaty more palatable at home. In the end he obtained Briand's promise that the evacuation of the Cologne area could occur as early as 1 December 1925. But hopes that the evacuation of the entire Rhineland might take place ahead of schedule remained unfulfilled. To be sure, Briand tried to accommodate Stresemann by agreeing to reduce the number of troops and to restrict the authority of the occupation administration. But this gesture of goodwill, which the French premier had to defend against his own domestic opponents, went unrecognized by the German public.

The ratification of the Locarno treaty by the Reichstag constituted a new test of strength for Luther's *Bürgerblock* cabinet. Luther still clung to the hope that he could persuade the DNVP to acquiesce in the ratification of the treaty in spite of the fact that the party had done everything in its power to thwart Stresemann's policy. That the nationalist and *völkisch* press sharply criticized the treaty and attacked the renunciation of Alsace-Lorraine and Germany's entry into the League of Nations could only have been a bad omen. On the other hand, there were good reasons why the DNVP might still go along and help the treaty clear the parliamentary hurdle. For failure to do so would almost certainly jeopardize the continued existence of a cabinet that had largely accommodated the interests of the DNVP in the area of agrarian, tax, and financial policy. But here the DNVP's lack of internal cohesion became increasingly apparent. With the active support of Alfred Hugenberg and his press empire, the party's local and regional organizations brought increasingly heavy pressure to bear upon the DNVP party leadership. Unable to withstand this pressure, the DNVP Reichstag delegation instructed its ministers in the Luther cabinet to oppose Locarno and eventually forced them to resign from the cabinet without calling for the formal dissolution of the governing coalition.

The DNVP's effort to remain in power through this blatantly transparent maneuver and yet vote against the ratification of the Locarno treaty in the firm expectation that it would still pass with the support of the Social Democrats was thwarted by the SPD's Otto Braun, who made his party's support of the treaty contingent upon the DNVP's formal exclusion from the governing coalition. Thus the Luther government was dissolved in late November 1925 after the treaty had been ratified with the votes of the moderate bourgeois parties and the SPD and against those of the DNVP, NSDAP, Business Party, and KPD. Under normal conditions, this constellation of forces that had rallied to the support of the treaty should have served as the basis of a new government based on the parties of the Great Coalition. Both the SPD and Center favored such a policy. But although the exigencies of foreign policy—namely, the fact that a rejection of the Locarno treaty would have represented a catastrophe with incalculable consequences—was able to generate a parliamentary majority that reached from the Left to the center, this alliance was not sufficiently strong to provide a consensus for the formation of a new cabinet.

Ernst Scholz, the chairman of the DVP Reichstag delegation, asserted that "for well-founded reasons related to the German economy" the implementation of a domestic and economic political policy in whose formulation the Social Democrats were involved was impossible. Scholz's position enjoyed the full support of the presidential office, which had urged the reestablishment of the *Bürgerblock* cabinet even before the vote on the Locarno treaty had taken place. The behind-the-door intrigues that State Secretary Otto Meißner initiated with the tacit approval of the DNVP party leadership were designed to bring about a collapse of the negotiations over the social-political demands of the Social Democrats. When the Reich president asked the DDP's chairman, Erich Koch-Weser, to form a government based on the parties of the Great Coalition but set a deadline that left him with little time in which to accomplish this task, Koch-Weser failed to see the way in which he was being used as a pawn in the political intrigues of Meißner and his associates. This was equally true of the Social Democrats, who, despite the urging of its ministers in the Prussian cabinet, entered only halfheartedly into the negotiations without first obtaining the DVP's commitment to a compromise solution.

When the SPD withdrew from the cabinet negotiations, Meißner had accomplished his goal of forming another bourgeois minority government under Luther's chancellorship. This government, however, could only function with Social Democratic toleration, for the DNVP, despite Hindenburg's personal intervention, refused to share responsibility for Germany's entry into the League of Nations as provided for in the Locarno treaty. Once again, foreign policy constraints made it impossible to dispense with the need for establishing parliamentary unity with the moderate Left and kept the focal point around which the national political agenda formed from gravitating to the antirepublican Right. Under these circumstances, the new cabinet remained dependent on the authority of the Reich president, who still sought to bring the DNVP into the coalition at the earliest possible suitable opportunity. It was only a few months, however, before Luther himself fell from power as a result of a controversy over the colors of the German flag, which he had brought to a head through his own initiative. The flag decree of 5 May 1926 was predicated upon the assumption that the right to make changes in the regulations concerning Germany's national banner lay with the Reich president and was beyond the legislative competence of the Reichstag. The new decree authorized the use of the old black-white-red commercial banner of the Second Empire at Germany's trade establishments abroad. Vigorous protests from the DDP and Center against this obvious concession to Germany's antirepublican parties drove Luther from office and revived the prospect of a transfer of power to the Great Coalition.

After the Center's Konrad Adenauer failed to form a government of the Great Coalition because the DVP still entertained hopes of forming a bourgeois cabinet in opposition to the Social Democrats once the issue of the League of Nations had been resolved, the only alternative was to form a new bourgeois minority cabinet with Marx and not Luther at its head. All of this highlights the precarious situation in which the republic found itself as a result of the intransigence of the DNVP and the dilemma of the SPD, whose support for Stresemann's foreign policy had not been rewarded with domestic political concessions. The situation would probably not have been substantially different even if the SPD had had a clear political line. Most of the SPD officials still believed that participation in government was a sacrifice they accepted more out of a sense of political responsibility than to exercise greater influence on governmental decisions. Time and time again the SPD executive committee was frustrated in its own tactical deliberations by the SPD Reichstag delegation, in which the representatives from the ADGB frequently exercised a veto. It was precisely when it came to the most important sociopolitical conflicts, such as the issue of working hours, that the party's freedom of maneuver was most seriously curtailed.

The tendency of the Social Democrats to concentrate more and more on their own internal affairs was in part a consequence of the repeated failures their party had experienced since 1919. To be sure, the SPD still regarded itself as the genuine "republican state party" (*republikanische Staatspartei*). In the Görlitz party program it had adopted in 1921 in a state of euphoric expectation of inevitable democratization, the SPD had endorsed without any reservations whatsoever Germany's new democratic republic as "the state system that had irrevocably evolved out of history." Since then, however, the realities of republican government stood in increasing contradiction to the vision of the future socialist society that bound the party together. Nowhere was the ambivalence the SPD felt toward the parliamentary system more eloquently expressed than in Gustav Radbruch's lament that the party considered democracy "a mere ladder to socialism" to be discarded when the goal was attained, while in truth democracy represented "at least half of its program, namely, the great half that had already been achieved and was capable of being achieved at any moment." It would still take many bitter lessons before the party as a whole realized that the republican form of government was in itself worthy of defense.

The SPD's retreat to the more traditional and introspective conception of itself was reflected in the program it adopted in 1925 at Heidelberg following its merger with what still remained of the Independent Socialists. In many respects reminiscent of the Erfurt tradition, the Heidelberg Program tended to recast the SPD in the oppositional role to which it had become accustomed in the prewar era. At the same time—and particularly under the pressure of competition from the KPD—the SPD's left and emphatically Marxist wing gained importance even though it was unable to articulate constructive political alternatives to the policies of the party leadership. The seriousness with which the socialist Left, whose most prominent theoreticians were Max Adler and Paul Levi, took the threat of dictatorship that the Austrian socialists had addressed in their Linz Program of 1927 reveals that it, no less than the reformist majority that controlled the party, had been forced onto the defensive and had abandoned the initiative to the bourgeoisie. Still, the party's notorious abstinence in matters of coalition politics must be attributed not so much to the continued use of an orthodox Marxist vocabulary in the socialist press and in official speeches at party congresses as to the shortsightedness of labor leaders unable to look beyond their own immediate interests. Even some of the leading representatives of the wing that had come over from the USPD, including Rudolf Hilferding and Rudolf Breitscheid, urged the party to become more actively involved in the affairs of the republic.

The fundamentally defensive character of Social Democratic party politics must be seen against the background of stagnating membership figures. This stemmed from the fact that after 1918 the number of industrial workers no longer grew in relation to the "new middle class" and that the party was not entirely able to compensate for the loss of elements on its left wing to the KPD by attracting new supporters from the German middle class and peasantry. In this respect, the agrarian strategy the party had adopted before the war proved to be a liability in terms of its ability to attract rural support, despite its efforts to articulate a more attractive farm program. Given the political climate of the Weimar years, the prospects of transforming the SPD from a party of the industrial working class into a peoples' party were indeed very poor. For all intents and purposes, the SPD remained a party of the industrial proletariat and saw itself cast back into the multilayered Social Democratic subculture that in these years was experiencing something of a renaissance. At the same time, the aging of the party's leadership and the lack of turnover in positions of responsibility undercut the party's appeal to young people, who remained decidedly underrepresented in its rank-and-file membership.

In 1921 the SPD's membership reached its nadir with 800,000, although this was partly mitigated by the return of some 200,000 Independent Socialists over the course of the next several years. This decline contributed in no small measure to the party's reluctance to take part in a coalition government after 1923, even though the outcome of the December 1924 elections temporarily rekindled hopes that it could recapture some of the terrain it had recently lost. For all that the party had accomplished in the interest of the general welfare since the revolution of 1918, a distinct gulf still separated it from the parties on Germany's bourgeois Left. A fear of contact on both sides that was rooted in continuing social prejudices was reinforced by an awareness of divergent social and economic interests. The relative isolation of organized labor became more apparent as pressure for accommodation with the Western powers abated. The notion that the SPD had to be "on board" in matters of foreign policy but that domestic policies were best left to the parties of the bourgeois Right had become a self-evident principle of German political life among those who served in the Marx and Luther cabinets. But it would have been virtually impossible for the Social Democrats, even had they entered the government, to neutralize the preponderant influence that industrial and agrarian interest organizations exercised in the formation of the national political agenda outside as well as inside the existing parliamentary framework. Any attempt to change this would only have strengthened the tendency to return to a government by emergency decree without effective control by the Reichstag.

The increasing independence of the national cabinet from the political forces that were at work in the country at large was encouraged by the exigencies of German foreign policy, which in light of Germany's dependence on the continued influx of American capital precluded any fundamental changes in Germany's constitutional system. At both extremes of the party spectrum, this situation gave rise to two contradictory expectations. For if some hoped that a purely right-wing government from which the Social Democrats were to be excluded would assume power after the uncertainties of the current international situation had been resolved, others expected that Germany would return to a government of the Great Coalition, which unlike that of 1923 would be more than a crisis government. The second of these alternatives, however, proved to be an illusion. Until the Reichstag elections of 1928, coalition politics was distinguished by the fact that the formation of a cabinet in which the Social Democrats were represented was routinely blocked by extraparliamentary influences and became acceptable only when Germany was confronted with a revision of the Dawes Plan for which the parties of the bourgeois Right did not want to assume political responsibility.

The leveling of the international playing field for which Stresemann had worked so hard at Locarno and that would have eliminated the need for the constant oscillation between opposing majorities on domestic and foreign issues never materialized. As a result, German revisionism was cast back upon a diplomacy of small steps that the nationalist Right immediately attacked in the sharpest possible terms as a sign of German weakness and insufficient national resolve. The obstacle that the unresolved claims by Poland, Brazil, and Spain to a permanent seat on the League Council posed to Germany's entry into the League of Nations was eventually overcome, and in September 1926 the German Reich was festively received into the League of Nations. Stresemann was determined to use the League as a forum for promoting German interests, particularly with respect to the German minorities in Poland and Czechoslovakia, which indirectly supported Germany's revisionist aspirations with secret funds from the Reich. Ultimately, Germany hoped to use Article 19 of the League Covenant as a lever for bringing about a fundamental revision of the Versailles peace treaty. This, in turn, accounted for the constant vacillation between the great powers and smaller nations that characterized German policy at the League of Nations.

The most important issues of German foreign policy were discussed outside the League of Nations, even though Stresemann used meetings of the League Council to cultivate informal contacts with the British and French prime ministers. Stresemann placed particularly great hopes in the exchange that took place between himself and Briand at Thoiry on 17 September 1926. Here they discussed, among other things, the possibility of an early withdrawal of the occupation troops from the Rhineland in exchange for German assistance in strengthening the ailing French franc. This project, which would have obliged the Germans to issue railway and industrial bonds ahead of schedule, collapsed not only because of internal opposition in France but also because American banks were reluctant to endorse the early issuance of the bonds. The diplomatic breakthrough for which Stresemann had been hoping, therefore, never materialized because Briand had overestimated his freedom to maneuver at home. The only thing that ever came of all that Stresemann and Briand discussed at Thoiry was the removal of military controls at the end of January 1927. Otherwise, the conversation was a disappointing failure.

In March 1929 Stresemann wrote to Lord d'Abernon that those who "had worked for the Locarno policy only see their hopes in ruins." With increasing bitterness Stresemann had to recognize that the so-called *Rückwirkungen* of Locarno had been extremely limited in scope and ultimately failed to materialize. The only major fruit of the "Locarno spirit," namely, the premature evacuation of the Rhineland in the summer of 1930, took place after Stresemann was no longer alive. It is remarkable that in the lavish celebrations of the "liberation" of the Rhineland the name of the late foreign minister was never mentioned. That he was not particularly well liked either in his own party or among his parliamentary rivals and opponents was something of which he had been well aware. For Stresemann there had been little, if any, relief from defamatory and libelous attacks, including from the crown prince whose return to Germany Stresemann had made possible. Stresemann thus suffered the fate of those who have the courage to assume responsibility for unpopular decisions in the face of limited political options. In the final analysis, his indispensability as German foreign minister in the six critical years from 1923 to 1929 stemmed in no small measure from the fact that, at least from the perspective of German revisionists, he never achieved a decisive success.

As far as the relationship between foreign policy and domestic politics was concerned, Stresemann never realized that his efforts to restore Germany's full sovereignty as a nation-state played into the hands of those political factions that viewed the republic as a temporary expedient that one had to endure until the power of the German state and its hegemony in foreign and domestic affairs had been restored. In this sense, Stresemann's failure to achieve the decisive breakthrough for which he had hoped at Thoiry contributed indirectly to the temporary stabilization of Weimar's constitutional system. Stresemann realized that Briand's reluctance to make concessions regarding the evacuation of the Rhineland was related to the militancy of the national defense associations in France and that the Western powers could not be expected to view the DNVP's participation in the national cabinet, where it had received several major portfolios, as a sign of Germany's peaceful intentions. In hindsight it is still difficult to understand why Stresemann did not call for the dissolution of the Reichstag after the Nationalists had rejected the Locarno treaty and work for the DNVP's defeat in the ensuing electoral campaign. Instead, Stresemann repeatedly—and not merely to placate his own party's right wing—supported the DNVP's inclusion in the national government. It is precisely because he agreed with the Nationalists in the essential elements of their foreign policy aspirations that he overestimated the possibilities of domesticating the extreme Right, which, as opponents on the Left ironically observed in 1927, had suddenly become as meek as lambs on foreign policy questions. In the final analysis, Stresemann failed to understand that the nationalist appetites of those like Hugenberg, Claß, Seldte, Hergt, and Hitler could never be satisfied by advances in foreign affairs, however convincing they might seem to others.

To the extent that Stresemann's own party failed to achieve its domestic political agenda and suffered the continual loss of its electoral support, he came more and more to believe in the "primacy of foreign policy." Until his death he consistently worked to integrate divergent interests and sought—even to the point of threatening to resign from the cabinet and the party he still led—to bring the recalcitrant wings of the various parties together and to force coalition partners to cooperate with each other in a more constructive and responsible manner. Out of a sense of profound national commitment,

Stresemann resisted the increasing polarization of German domestic politics and the declared intention of the nationalist Right to drive the Social Democrats into permanent political isolation. It is indeed remarkable that in this context Stresemann used to cite the SPD's patriotic record during the World War and pointed out that more men from its ranks had died on the battlefields than from all of the parties combined. In a similar vein, Stresemann justified his hundred days as chancellor with the argument that otherwise a "battle of one Germany against the other" would have ensued.

Stresemann's fundamentally bourgeois nature and his liberal political convictions hampered him in his search for a basis on which permanent political cooperation with the Social Democrats might be possible. There were material as well as personal factors that made it impossible for him to work for an opening to the Left and thus for a permanent stabilization of the republican system. Aside from considerations of economic policy that included the antipathy of Anglo-Saxon capitalism to socialist experiments, Stresemann's deep distrust of the SPD on issues related to national defense played a central role. In retrospect it is indeed difficult to explain why in the Locarno negotiations Stresemann ascribed such great importance to the evacuation of the Ruhr and Rhineland or why he pursued the termination of Allied armaments controls with a persistence that often offended his negotiating partners. He certainly could have helped allay French concerns about German rearmament—concerns that manifested themselves in 1925 in the French decision to build the Maginot line—by endorsing the proposal that a civilian control commission be appointed to supervise the demilitarization of the Rhineland under the terms of the Locarno treaty. The fact is, however, that he failed to do this just as he failed to oppose Germany's secret rearmament with the necessary forcefulness.

There is no evidence to suggest that the foreign minister ever envisaged going to war to realize Germany's revisionist aims, even though it is unlikely that he could have been ignorant of military plans that considered an armed conflict with France in the foreseeable future as a foregone conclusion. If Stresemann emphatically endorsed the Kellogg Pact proposed by Henry Stimson, he did so for more than purely tactical reasons. For Stresemann was very much aware of the dangers that another war in central Europe posed to the continued existence of the German Reich. The award of the Nobel Peace Prize to Stresemann and Briand in 1926 expressed the satisfaction of world public opinion that these two politicians had put an end to Franco-German enmity and had thereby created the preconditions for a lasting peace in Europe.

Stresemann was one of the most outstanding European statesmen of his time. But he never was a European at heart. Given the profoundly nationalistic character of the German political culture that was his spiritual home, this simply was not within his nature. His great merit as a statesman was that he sought direct understanding with France instead of pursuing the chimerical notion of his predecessors and his successors that France could be diplomatically isolated. On this point Stresemann broke with the basic fundamentals of Bismarckian foreign policy and, in so doing, set an example that Konrad Adenauer was to follow after 1945. To be sure, it is true that in September 1923 there was no alternative to direct negotiations with Paris. Stresemann succeeded in persuading the French that it would be impossible to keep Germany permanently tied down on the Rhine. At the same time, however, Stresemann was never able to embrace the politics of trust that Briand proposed to him. No doubt this was in part the result of the revisionist pressures to which he was constantly subjected. Tactical considerations that manifested themselves in the sharp contrast he drew between himself and his opponents in the DNVP were always present in his brilliantly formulated desire for reconciliation. It is no surprise that the French would feel so ruthlessly betrayed after the posthumous publication of his *Vermächtnis* in 1932–33.

In the final analysis, the German foreign minister was never able to escape his Prussian-German heritage, even if he did consider replacing military dominance with economic power. He could never conceive of national policy except on the basis of a strong military and used the League of Nations' desire for universal disarmament as a tactical means of achieving parity for Germany's military establishment. Within these limits, however, Stresemann did his best to achieve an understanding among the European powers. Had he been able to transfer his characteristic prudence and discretion from the diplomatic to the domestic political arena, then the course of Weimar's political development might very well have been different. Under the circumstances, however, Stresemann's success in foreign policy was to have precisely the opposite effect in domestic politics. The Dawes Plan and the Treaty of Locarno had done much to initiate a period of reconstruction that did not translate into the internal consolidation of Germany's parliamentary democracy but, on the contrary, prompted a general assault against the social achievements of the first years after the war. To be sure, attempts by the German Right to overthrow the Weimar system ceased almost entirely in the face of Germany's dependence on foreign powers. At the same time, however, authoritarian trends became more and more pronounced within the existing political system, which was now dominated by a coalition of the bourgeois center and Right. By contrast, the Social Democrats found themselves forced more and more onto the defensive, though in the short term their support was still essential for the reconstruction of German foreign policy. For the moment the direct and indirect integration of the republic into the Atlantic system of states, as well as its increasing dependence on credits from the United States, precluded overt constitutional experiments. Under the influence of the economic interest groups, the antirepublican Right found itself obliged to work out some form of accommodation with existing parliamentary institutions. The *völkisch* movement, including the temporarily banned NSDAP, had become hopelessly fragmented and was reduced to the role of splinter parties. Yet even then there was a clear disparity between the political stability that the republic seemed to have gained and the weakness of the political forces responsible for its continued existence. How long this precarious domestic balance could be maintained would depend primarily on the peculiar constellation of international politics.

CHAPTER SEVEN

The Extraparliamentary Offensive

A G A I N S T the background of the Ruhr crisis and the runaway inflation of the early 1920s, the middle phase of the Weimar Republic appears to be a period of remarkable political and economic consolidation. With the Treaty of Locarno and Germany's entry into the League of Nations, the German Reich had achieved a position of parity with other European powers. Although from the German point of view the reparations problem remained unresolved, the fact that it had been accorded the same status as the problem of interallied war debts meant that it had been effectively decoupled from the punitive and compensatory principles provided for in the Treaty of Versailles. Germany's reparations payments were now seen as the nation's contribution to rectifying the long-term financial damage resulting from the First World War. The postwar phase of economic warfare seemed to have come to an end.

On the basis of a steady stream of international loans that helped Germany compensate for its lack of indigenous capital, the German economy experienced a period of rapid growth after 1924. The Marx and Luther governments assigned the highest priority to preserving the stabilization of the currency and maintaining a balanced budget, if for no other reason than the fact that this constituted an indispensable precondition for the success of Germany's negotiations on reparations and international credits. This policy, however, took place at the expense of those sectors of society with low and middle-range incomes, while the ownership of capital benefited from an array of tax advantages and direct as well as indirect subsidies. Even after the reorganization of the national cabinet in January 1926, the interests of big business and large-scale agriculture, which in part were directly represented in the cabinet, continued to receive preferential treatment. To be sure, nominal wages rose rapidly as a result of the booming economy. But since the cost of living rose almost as quickly, the standard of living of most wage earners showed only marginal improvement.

This constellation characterized the social and political climate of the next several years. Economic recovery was achieved largely at the expense of consumers, while social policy definitively assumed a compensatory function. The fiscal reform that the Luther cabinet introduced in the summer of 1925 was perfectly consistent with the principle articulated by Johannes Popitz from the

Ministry of Finance that "the tax burden must be economically defensible." Clearly rejecting the way in which Erzberger had used tax reform as a way of redistributing income, the new reform reduced the 60 percent tax rate for those in the highest tax bracket by a good third, whereas the minimal tax rate of 10 percent remained intact. It was only with the fourth child that an increase in the tax exemption from 1 to 2 percent took effect and the amount of one's monthly income that was exempt from taxation was lowered to eighty marks. The latter provision encountered widespread dissatisfaction among entrepreneurs in spite of the fact that the rate remained lower than it had been in Prussia before the war.

The obvious tax advantages that property owners received from this arrangement ran into sharp criticism from the reparations agent, who recommended strengthening the domestic market through limited wage raises. The growth in revenues from income and sales taxes stood in sharp contrast to the stagnation of revenues raised from all other sources. As a complement to the tax reform, the Finance Ministry obliged industry even further with substantial tax deferments and subsidies. The latter, often paid without the authorization of the Reichstag, primarily benefited heavy industrial concerns such as Röchling, Stinnes, Krupp, Mannesmann, and Flick as well as the shipbuilding industry, where orders were scarce. That Friedrich Flick was the government expert appointed to evaluate the need for subsidies to the United Upper Silesian Foundries (Vereinigte Oberschlesische Hüttenwerke) just as they were about to pass into his own hands revealed the potential for corruption that existed in the increasingly close ties between industry and the ministerial bureaucracy. The use of governmental subsidies abated somewhat over the next several years before reappearing in full force during the world economic crisis of the early 1930s. Here the most celebrated case involved the spectacular purchase of more than 110 million shares of stock in the Gelsenkirchen Mining Company (Gelsenkirchener Bergwerks A.-G.) at vastly inflated prices by the Brüning cabinet shortly before its fall from power in the late spring of 1932. In the meantime, the improvement in the financial status of Flick took place at the insistence of the Reichswehr leadership and was directly related to highly secret efforts to protect German industrial assets in Upper Silesia from liquidation. In this respect Friedrich Flick functioned as something of a straw man for the German government, which was heavily involved in the area.

Support, particularly for heavy industry, was deemed necessary after Hjalmar Schacht, the new president of the Reichsbank, tightened credit and raised the discount rate after having detected what he saw as the first signs of an inflationary price trend. The effects of Schacht's restrictive credit and interest policy revealed that the German economy remained extremely vulnerable to disruption despite the extensive rationalization it had undergone during the recent inflation. When the banks of issue more or less erased the difference in interest rates between the United States and Germany, the influx of loans came to an almost immediate stop while private and institutional investments declined precipitously. This, in turn, led to severe economic disturbances. By the end of 1925, unemployment once again exceeded 2 million. The period of virtually full employment thus came to a definitive end. Still, Germany was able to soften the social effects of this crisis by countercyclical measures and public work programs that exhausted the government's fiscal reserves.

The stabilization crisis of 1925–26, which stemmed in no small measure from the defective manipulation of market forces and at that time had no counterpart in other industrialized countries, soon gave way to the rapid economic recovery of 1927, which ran out of steam in 1928 and fed into the worldwide recession in the late 1920s and early 1930s. None of this, however, had much bearing on the agrarian sector, which had been in a state of chronic recession since 1926 as a result of declining agricultural prices on the world market. The stabilization crisis only intensified existing socioeconomic tensions. On the one hand, the national government had to cope with the social consequences of structural mass unemployment once it recognized that permanent unemployment could no longer be blamed on those who were out of work or be attributed to their unwillingness to find a job. On the other hand, the principle of the *Sozialstaat* was about to undergo a severe test. State intervention in the economic process encountered intensified opposition from influential industrial interest groups that attributed Germany's economic difficulties to an ill-conceived financial and wage policy and once again chanted the old lament about the excessive tax burden on business. In a memorandum on "German Economic and Financial Policy" submitted to the Reich president in late December 1925, the National Federation of German Industry demanded the right to veto expenditure decisions by the finance minister and formally requested that the national government free itself from the haggling of party politicians.

It is no coincidence that renewed attempts to replace the parliamentary system with authoritarian forms of government under Article 48 surfaced at the precise moment that the collapse of the *Bürgerblock* cabinet over the Locarno legislation opened up the prospects for a coalition on the Left. Heavy industry, which looked upon the DVP as its parliamentary arm, was adamantly opposed to efforts by the Social Democrats and its affiliated labor unions to keep the possibility of a return to the eight-hour day open by persuading the government to sign the Washington Working Hours Agreement. In the Langnam Association, the most important pressure group for the Ruhr anthracite mining industry, and the "Ruhrlade," an informal association of the leading mining and steel magnates that had been meeting since 1927, as well as in the increasingly influential National Federation of German Industry, the industrial elite of Rhineland-Westphalia possessed a powerful and well-organized lobby that was not at all hesitant about promoting its social and political objectives by means of financial contributions to the various political parties or by exercising direct economic pressure in the form of threats to torpedo the Franco-German steel negotiations.

At a meeting of the membership of the National Federation of German Industry in Dresden in September 1926, Paul Silverberg from the soft-coal mining industry gave a remarkable speech in which he affirmed the entrepreneurs' loyalty to the existing political system and called for a policy of "responsible collaboration" with the Social Democrats. Silverberg's words came as something of a shock to his associates in the RDI and provoked a sharp protest from those pressure groups that were associated with German heavy industry. In the bitter and protracted controversy that followed, the representatives of the finished products and export sectors were unable to mobilize much support for their more moderate point of view, even though Silverberg had explicitly rejected the demands of radical trade unionists for codetermination and socialization and made the revival of the Zentralarbeitsgemeinschaft contingent on union acknowledgment of management's primacy. But the dominant elements within German heavy industry were less interested in a compromise than in a strategy for dealing with the crisis that had as its ultimate goal the permanent exclusion of the Social Democrats from government responsibility, the systematic destruction of the parliamentary system, and the installation of a government that would rule by means of the special emergency powers provided for in Article 48 of the Weimar Constitution.

The deeper cause for the massive pressure that Rhenish-Westphalian heavy industry sought to exert in the domestic political arena had less to do with the social paternalism of a relatively homogeneous group in terms of its social background and political ideology than with the increasingly severe problem of rising production costs. This problem had been concealed for some time by the trend toward vertical and horizontal concentration that the inflation of the early 1920s had set in motion only to be greatly accelerated in connection with the stabilization crisis of 1925–26. The most tangible expression of this trend was the founding of the United Steelworks (Vereinigte Stahlwerke), which took place in early 1926 and brought together 50 percent of Germany's iron and steel production. The national government did nothing to curtail the concentration of economic power on such a large scale. On the contrary, it favored the concentration of capital by waiving the merger taxes to which it would otherwise have been entitled, as it did in the case of the merger of Germany's leading chemical firms to form I.G. Farben (Interessengemeinschaft Farben A.-G.) in 1925. The government also ignored the unions' demand for the amendment of the antitrust legislation of 1923, which would have provided the means for an effective control of monopolistic price fixing.

In a parallel development, heavy industry was able to increase its productive capacities so that by 1925 iron and steel production had already returned to its prewar level in spite of the territory Germany had lost as a result of the Versailles peace treaty. This was accomplished by the continual construction of new facilities and by increased technological rationalization, which had its principal effect upon the technical coordination of individual production processes. By contrast, there was little improvement in working conditions or in the demands placed upon the industrial work force. In contrast, these demands seemed to increase with the development of more uniform methods of production. As a result, industry was able to effect a considerable increase in labor productivity. By 1925 it already stood at 14 percent above the prewar level and continued to rise throughout the second half of the decade. At the same time, the expanded capacities achieved by greater rationalization made it possible to reduce unit production costs as long as increased fixed costs could be met through the full exploitation of a plant's productive capacities. In 1925, however, steel plants were on the average producing at only 60 percent capacity; by the beginning of 1926 this had fallen to about 50 percent.

The need to fulfill Germany's reparations obligations had greatly encouraged the expansion of productive capacities in the hard-coal sector and had led management to believe that it would soon match and surpass the production levels of the prewar years. Once the economy had stabilized, however, it became clear that the market was no longer capable of absorbing the increased coal production. This stemmed, on the one hand, from the excess capacity of western Europe's mining industry as a result of Germany's efforts to expand and rationalize its own plants in order to offset the decline in steel production that had occurred with the loss of Lorraine and, on the other, from the stagnation of the world economy and the use of new energy sources such as petroleum. Just as the Rhenish-Westphalian Coal Syndicate (Rheinisch-Westfälische Kohlensyndikat) had tried to deal with this problem through a pricing strategy that saw it maintain high prices in those areas where there was no competition and dump surplus production on the international market in those areas in which it faced competition, the German steel industry also adopted a policy of price fixing. Established in November 1924, the Raw Steel Association (Rohstahlgemeinschaft) not only instituted fixed production quotas but also formed marketing syndicates, or *Verkaufsverbände*, for the various products of the metallurgical industries, thereby virtually eliminating all competition in the domestic market.

Through the price monopoly of the Steelworks Association (Stahlwerkverband), the steel industry was able to make certain that high prices in the domestic market would compensate for the low prices it had to charge its international customers. But then, under the terms of the so-called AVI Accord (AVI-Abkommen) that the members of the Association of Iron-Processing Industries (Arbeitsgemeinschaft der eisenverbrauchenden Industrien) concluded at the end of 1924, the processing industries received a refund for the steel used in the production of export commodities, a third of which went directly to the processing plants of the steel industry itself. In order to prevent the Lorraine steel industry from underselling German steel on the domestic market, the International Association of Raw Steel Producers concluded an agreement in 1926 by which the German partner was granted a higher export quota in return for concessions in the south German market. The purpose of this arrangement was to make it possible for German producers to work at increased capacity and thus lower their production costs. But this did not materialize, since the cartel failed in its efforts to achieve higher prices for steel products on the international market. At the same time, the German plants, unlike those in Lorraine, surpassed their quotas and had to make substantial compensation payments (*Ausgleichszahlungen*), with the result that they quickly terminated the agreement while the territorial monopolies remained intact. These were then extended in 1933 in the form of a general cartel of the export syndicates.

In the anthracite and steel-producing industries, which tended to separate marketing from production, cartelization and a pricing policy intent on achieving production at full capacity mitigated against a contraction of the heavy industrial sector that would have been beneficial to the national economy as a whole. Noneconomic motives were also involved, among them the conviction within Germany's ruling classes that a systematic expansion of the nation's economic potential would expedite a revision of the Versailles peace treaty. This, along with the effectiveness of heavy industrial interest organizations, explains why the manufacturers of consumer and finished goods were unable to assert themselves despite their prominence in the most important business associations. Even in the inflation it had become clear that the heavy industrial lobby was able to exercise a virtually invincible veto in Weimar's political system by virtue of its ability to undercut the price levels established by national economic policy. Moreover, the "gentlemen from the West," as the leaders of heavy industry in Rhineland-Westphalia were called with a mixture of respect and irony, could also take advantage of their close contacts in the Reich Finance Ministry, if not in the Bureau of the Reich President itself.

While the preferential treatment that the Marx and Luther cabinets granted to big business facilitated Germany's economic recovery after the Ruhr crisis, it also contributed to the fact that an economic reorientation in favor of the so-called new industries was slow in coming and never occurred with sufficient strength. By the same token, improvements in the infrastructure of the economy as a whole, such as the installation of a network of public utilities, were sacrificed to the special interests of heavy industry. Excessive coal and steel prices in the domestic market made investments in the processing industries more expensive and limited the export possibilities of enterprises that did not participate in the AVI Accord. The hard-coal sector, whose sales were boosted for a short period of time by the British miners' strike of 1926, was enduring a notorious crisis in the costs of production, or *Selbstkosten*, that was only partially mitigated by subsidies and special reductions in transportation costs. With the outbreak of the world economic crisis, the national government found itself obliged to assume a part of the coal industry's social welfare costs, among them the employers' share of the miners' insurance.

For their own part, the employers in heavy industry objected as vocally as possible to supposedly excessive government outlays for social welfare and the tax burden this entailed, but without mentioning the portion of the social welfare budget that was earmarked for the support of war victims and sur- vivor benefits or that the growth of public expenditures in relation to the gross national product was generally exaggerated. It was psychologically unfortu- nate that the immediate costs of the lost war had been taken care of by the inflation until the fall of 1923 and that normal fiscal conditions only came into existence at a time when tax increases, social welfare benefits, and losses in in- come were no longer seen in the context of the destruction of capital that had occurred during the war but as a consequence of reparations and conflicts over the allocation of the social product.

Simultaneously the employers' associations intensified their pressure not merely with respect to the controversy over the length of the workday but above all in the area of wage policy. As a result of the powerful position that heavy industry held in the employers' associations as well as in national politics, the system of tariff autonomy in the key industries had little practical significance. Since the stabilization of the currency at the end of 1923, there was no wage contract in the Ruhr mining industry that had not been concluded without state arbitration. After the stabilization of the currency, no wage contract was concluded in the mining enterprises of the Ruhr without the participation of a government arbitrator and, in most cases, binding arbitration. The situa- tion was not appreciably different in the iron and steel industry. The failure of collective bargaining, therefore, could not be blamed on the labor unions. After 1924 the socialist, Christian, and liberal unions as well as the Polish Pro- fessional Union (Polnische Berufsvereinigung) found themselves pushed more and more onto the defensive. They had virtually no chance whatsoever of sus- taining themselves vis-à-vis increasingly united employers' associations, which now began to resort to lockouts and, if necessary, closing down plants. In place of the open struggle between labor and management, there emerged a new war of experts' reports on the different weight that should be attributed to cost-effectiveness and labor productivity, while both negotiating partners were more than happy to let the state-appointed arbitrator deal with decisions related to wages and the length of the workday.

In spite of the bitterness that existed in the camp of the industrial working class, radical tendencies within the unions had been on the wane ever since the early 1920s. The change in trade-union strategy by the KPD, which dissolved the Union of Manual and Intellectual Workers (Union der Hand- und Kopfarbeiter) in 1923 and proclaimed the slogan "Into the unions" (*Hinein in die Gewerkschaften*), met with a cool response from the leaders of the more reformist unions, who systematically excluded Communists from their steering committees. The Revolutionary Trade-Union Opposition (Revolutionäre Gewerkschaftsopposition) Group that had surfaced in 1928 remained numerically insignificant. By the same token, efforts during the economic crisis to found independent Communist unions ended in failure. The KPD, which had no appreciable support among factory workers and recruited the great mass of its adherents from the ranks of the unemployed, had no direct influence over the practical politics of organized labor, although its continual attacks against the leaders of the trade-union movement severely crippled its capacity to make decisions. The external consolidation of the trade unions was accompanied by steady decline in their membership. What this suggests is that those who had streamed into the unions in such large number in the early 1920s had not been sufficiently integrated into their new organizational homes. As in the prewar period, skilled workers still constituted a clear majority of those who belonged to the organized labor movement, whereas trainees and unskilled workers tended to fall by the wayside. While this tended to strengthen the position of the more moderate factions within the union apparatus, it also undermined union willingness to engage in bitter and prolonged wage conflicts.

The National Rural League and heavy industry tried to take advantage of the changed economic situation to break organized labor's collective bargaining monopoly and to propagate the notion of factory unions, or *Werkgemeinschaften*, that would be under the effective control of management. This was also the aim of the German Institute for Technical Labor Training (Deutsches Institut für technische Arbeitsschulung or DINTA) that had been founded in 1925 by the heavy industrial employers' associations. Directed by Karl Arnhold, DINTA sought to win the "heart and soul" of the German working class and to create a new type of worker who would be loyal to his firm, willing to work long hours, and conscious of his national identity. At the same time, the institute pursued research in "human economy" that would increase labor productivity through the rationalization of work processes and improve the workers' psychological adaptation through on-the-job pedagogical counseling. In political terms, DINTA represented an attempt supported by a large part of Germany's entrepreneurial elite to introduce the concept of the *Volksgemeinschaft* into the industrial workplace. In this respect, DINTA anticipated the "Work Is Beautiful" Program of the German Labor Front (Deutsche Arbeitsfront) as well as more modern techniques for creating attachment to the workplace.

The turn toward the principle of the *Werkgemeinschaft* and the increasingly strong anti-union sentiment that had surfaced within the ranks of Germany's entrepreneurial elite came as a bitter disappointment to the nationalist and Christian unions that in 1920 had united to form the German Trade-Union Federation (Deutscher Gewerkschaftsbund or DGB). The Christian unions, including the right-wing German National Union of Commercial Employees (Deutschnationaler Handlungsgehilfen-Verband or DHV), were outraged since such attitudes seemed to make a revival of the Zentralarbeitsgemeinschaft impossible. On issues related to wages and the length of the workday, the Christian unions found themselves forced more and more into a common front with the socialist General German Trade-Union Federation (Allgemeiner Deutscher Gewerkschaftsbund or ADGB). In contrast to Adam Stegerwald, the national leader of the Christian labor movement, Heinrich Imbusch from the Union of Christian Mine Workers (Verband christlicher Bergarbeiter) openly advocated socialization of the Ruhr mining industry and employed language that was more radical than that of the Socialist Miners' Union (Der Alter Verband). At the same time, relations between the nonsocialist unions and the National Rural League and the right wing of the DNVP became increasingly strained in view of the latter's opposition to collective bargaining and the statutory regulation of working hours.

Such a shift in the balance of social forces had a particularly profound impact on the Center, the only nonsocialist party with an appreciable working-class constituency. To be sure, the disaffection of those who identified themselves with the Center's left wing—made manifest in Westphalia with the emergence of the Christian-Social People's Community (Christlich-Soziale Volksgemeinschaft) and the expansion of Vitus Heller's Christian-social movement party from Bavaria to other parts of the country—had been contained in the two 1924 Reichstag elections. But in 1925 Joseph Wirth's sensational resignation from the Center Reichstag delegation in protest against his party's move to the right and the increasing dissatisfaction of the party's working-class wing bore dramatic testimony to the existence of a severe crisis of confidence within the Center Party. In the referendum on the expropriation of the Hohenzollerns and other German ruling houses, a significant portion of the Catholic working class had voted for the bill being proposed by the parties of the German Left.

Labor Minister Heinrich Brauns, who for reasons of national policy had repeatedly advocated the formation of cabinets based on the so-called *Bürgerblock*, had gradually come to the conclusion that a continuation of an arbitration policy that favored management was no longer prudent in view of the increasing opposition of the Christian working class and the improvement in Germany's economic situation that was anticipated for 1927. With his Work Hours Emergency Law (Arbeitszeitnotgesetz) that provided a surcharge for overtime and his increasingly pro-union stance in arbitration awards, Brauns encountered increasingly severe criticism from the employers' associations, which were determined to maintain the three-shift system in the steel industry despite arbitration decisions to the contrary and to resist further wage increases. To fight what an internal memorandum of the Northwestern Group of the Association of German Iron and Steel Industrialists (Nordwestliche Gruppe des Vereins der Deutschen Eisen- und Stahlindustrieller) called the "wage dictatorship of the state" (*Lohndiktat des Staates*), the leaders of the Rhenish-Westphalian industrial establishment decided to create a war chest and make preparations for a comprehensive shutdown, which was to take effect if the labor minister persisted in his notions about a reform of working hours. Confronted with the united opposition of the Northwestern Group, the government beat a tactical retreat when it came to the actual application of the Work Hours Emergency Law. Although the wage conflict in the steel industry had ended with an arbitration award that favored the employers, the Northwestern Group began to make preparations for an open test of strength in the area of social policy, whereby its aim was to deprive the Labor Ministry of the power of compulsory arbitration and to break the back of the socialist as well as the Christian unions. This set the stage for the so-called Ruhr Iron Dispute in the fall of 1928.

If the compensatory social policy that Brauns had pursued with great persistence and discretion had little effect on the relative strength of the competing parties in the labor market, it had nevertheless materially improved the wage earners' chances for equality by expanding not only the scope of existing labor law but also social insurance coverage and health and safety protection in the workplace. Arguably Brauns's most important achievement was the Unemployment Insurance Act that was finally passed in July 1927 after having existed in draft form for the better part of two years and that established a comprehensive system of unemployment insurance as well as job counseling for those who had lost their jobs. As in the case of the Work Hours Emergency Law, Brauns was able to secure a parliamentary consensus on this bill by working through the National Economic Council (Reichswirtschaftsrat) in which the Christian trade unions occupied an important mediating position. The new law supplemented existing unemployment benefits and emergency aid by establishing the principle that the worker had a right to limited financial security in the event he had lost his job and that he could secure this right through a system of unemployment insurance to be administered by the collective bargaining parties. In many respects, this law represented the high point of the republic's development as a social welfare state even if it benefited only part of the labor force and was never adequate in dealing with the problem of long-term unemployment.

In spite of the high structural employment—between the end of 1925 and the beginning of 1927, for example, the rate of unemployment never fell below 15 percent—economic planners were confident that the economic rationalization would eventually make it possible for the economy to absorb the surplus workers. The premium of 3 percent that was to be raised from employer and employee contributions and a special emergency fund that was to be administered by the National Agency for Job Placement and Unemployment Insurance (Reichsanstalt für Arbeitsvermittlung und Arbeitslosenversicherung) made the support of 1.4 million unemployed workers possible. After workers' eligibility for this support had expired, they would then be eligible for government loans. But since unemployment benefits were limited to twenty-six months, those who had been without work for a longer period of time became the responsibility of public welfare agencies, whose sole criterion was acute need. By 1928 seasonal workers were declared ineligible for unemployment insurance, and in 1929 this was extended to part-time workers and married women. When the Unemployment Insurance Act was adopted by the Reichstag on 16 July 1927, its passage had been predicated on assumptions about the development of the German economy that failed to materialize.

The same kind of fiscal euphoria gave rise in the last two years of the republic's economic boom to a plethora of initiatives at the municipal level for long overdue improvements in the infrastructure, the construction of new transportation systems, and the incorporation of smaller communities into large metropolitan centers. This was accompanied by a construction boom that not only provided new housing but also served as the vehicle for projecting a cultural and political self-image. Extensive new housing developments, many of which survived the Second World War, and public parks testify to an uninterrupted tradition of municipal self-awareness and pride. In the cities there developed a mass culture that transcended class barriers as well as the beginnings of a consumer society. In many cases, popular resentment against the innovative features of modern urban life reinforced a justifiable concern over the frequently shaky financial condition of the municipalities, which relied on short-term credits to finance long-term projects.

Criticism of irresponsible financial behavior by public authorities came from various quarters, ranging from those like reparations agent Parker Gilbert, Reichsbank President Hjalmar Schacht, Gustav Stresemann, and Heinrich Brüning, who feared the effects of becoming excessively dependent upon foreign loans, to Germany's industrial leadership, which was adamantly opposed to any increase in the current level of public spending. Nevertheless, Reich Finance Minister Heinrich Köhler from the German Center Party took it upon himself to initiate increases in civil servant salaries of more than 20 percent. Köhler's reform of civil servant salary structure continued the leveling of salary scales in the public sector and was therefore met with a mixed response from the National League of Higher Civil Servants (Reichsbund der Höheren Beamten) under the leadership of Ernst Scholz, simultaneously chairman of the DVP Reichstag delegation. The new pay raises constituted a form of compensation for the introduction of unemployment insurance and increased civil servants' salaries to a level comparable with the highest wages of skilled workers. The reform was passed in a moment of fiscal euphoria in which comparatively low interest payments did not pose an immediate burden to public finances.

Made without first consulting the leadership of the Center Party, Köhler's unilateral promise of a reform of civil servant salaries ran into sharp criticism not only from Parker Gilbert, who pointed out that civil servants' salaries were low in other Western countries as well, but also from Heinrich Brüning and the Christian labor unions under the leadership of Adam Stegerwald. From the outset, it seemed that the only way the bill could be financed was by making certain that government subsidies to the unemployment insurance fund remained within limits. Even more important, however, was the fact that this action undercut efforts by the employers' associations to hold the line against wage hikes in the private sector. Using governmental labor contracts as the basis for comparison, the labor unions were able to bring real wages up to their prewar level and in some cases even exceed that standard. In any event, there were substantial shifts in Germany's wage structure. Miners, for example, found it impossible to maintain their position at the top of the wage scale. In addition, the wages of skilled industrial workers clearly exceeded the wage levels established by collective bargaining.

Heavy industry complained bitterly about the "wage dictates" of the Reich Ministry of Labor as well as about the excessive costs of the government's social welfare programs. In their argumentation, the leaders of German heavy industry tended to equate parliamentarism with social policy and to denounce the political system as a "union state" (Gewerkschaftsstaat). Yet the rise in real wages after 1925 can be ascribed neither to the system of governmental arbitration, which tended to depress wages during periods of economic uncertainty, nor to the influence of the labor unions, which had been severely weakened by the inflationary crisis of the early 1920s. Real wages, which had declined drastically during the inflation and had only just begun after 1924 to adjust to inflationary expectations, climbed much more slowly than labor productivity, so that it is altogether misleading to suggest that the wage increases exceeded the growth in industrial productivity. On the contrary, the net income of all those who were employed did exceed the growth of the national economy. What this reflected was an increase in the number of gainfully employed persons of 11.3 percent vis-à-vis the prewar era, whereby the proportion of white-collar employees and civil servants grew from 10.3 to 17.3 percent of the total labor force between 1907 and 1925, while that of blue-collar workers declined from 54.9 to 49.2 percent over the same period of time. The relatively high salaries of white-collar workers, public employees, and civil servants rather than high wages for industrial workers meant that there was indeed a limited disparity between increases in earned income and labor productivity.

The widespread argument in management circles that the German economy suffered from excessively high wages failed to recognize the underlying structural problem that plagued German industry in the postwar period. At the heart of this problem lay an unwillingness to innovate, the concentration of technological improvements in structurally weak sectors of the economy, and the monopolistic restriction or distortion of economic competition to the detriment of small and middle-sized enterprises. The price-fixing practices of heavy industry resulted in an indirect increase in the cost of living, which in turn had repercussions on wages and wage demands. But since the system of collective bargaining never functioned properly because of the weakness of the unions — particularly in the highly paid industrial sectors — the reduction of excess capacities in heavy industry from the corrective economic effect of higher wages failed to materialize. Not even a much lower wage level would have dramatically improved the long-run market position of German heavy industry. Moreover, investment activity in the industrial sector was severely hampered by the substantial subsidies to large-scale agriculture east of the Elbe.

Measured against prewar standards, Germany's industrial growth in the Weimar Republic lagged behind that of comparable industrial countries. It had become quite apparent at a fairly early stage in the world economic crisis that Germany, along with Great Britain, was among the losers in the industrial race. The lack of a national policy for planned economic growth and a tendency to subsidize unprofitable sectors contributed to the structural weakness of the German economy, as did a substantial increase in interest rates over prewar levels and insufficient internal capital formation. The latter was an indirect result of the hyperinflation, which had consumed the savings of the old middle class. But political factors, among them the Reichsbank's credit policy as well as national and international protective tariffs, also had a negative effect.

In the final analysis, the effects of state-subsidized capitalism were not as pronounced in the industrial as in the agrarian sector. To be sure, the hyperinflation had played a crucial role in making it possible for large-scale agriculture to liquidate its indebtedness. Still, the lack of capital for the rationalization of production combined with the collapse of agricultural prices on the world market to prevent the economic recovery of German agriculture. In addition to comprehensive credit initiatives in which the Prussian government played a major role — the SPD's Carl Severing spoke of the need to erect a "solid bulwark of reliable German peasants" to keep German agriculture from being flooded by foreign Slavic influences — the national government instituted a comprehensive program of agrarian subsidies, which, in conjunction with the Eastern Aid Program (Osthilfe) and support for East Prussia, exceeded several times over the amounts earmarked for industry, without, however, halting the growing indebtedness of agriculture or restoring its profitability.

New customs legislation that took effect after a prolonged parliamentary debate in August 1925 sought to restore tariffs in the agricultural sector to their prewar level. Fundamentally different from the protectionist commercial treaties that took effect at the same time, agricultural tariffs translated into an immediate and substantial increase in the cost of living. Government-mandated price controls were essentially window dressing and aroused strong opposition among the artisanry. The economic and fiscal policies of the *Bürgerblock* cabinets were therefore well on their way to redressing the social balance sheet to the disadvantage of the working masses and important sectors of the lower middle classes. This was also possible because the National Rural League was able to assert its influence as a powerful agricultural interest organization by virtue of its close ties to the DNVP and other nonsocialist parties. The triumph of agrarian protectionism, however, had an immediate effect upon those small and middle-sized farms in the western part of Germany that were dependent upon imported feed and was particularly harmful to the German export industry, which had to fear retaliatory measures by Germany's trading partners. In defending its economic interests, the agrarian lobby was able to avail itself of traditional nationalist shibboleths such as the much-evoked mystique of East Prussia and Germany's eastern frontiers. The pretext of national necessity was repeatedly invoked to defend the interests of a small caste of agrarian magnates. By the same token, the leaders of Ruhr heavy industry succeeded in portraying themselves as the decisive force in the struggle against French ambitions, although by no means did this prevent them from accepting payment for their patriotic merits in the form of the Ruhr donation.

The interpenetration of economic interest organizations and nationalist associations was a defining feature of Germany's political culture in the 1920s and early 1930s. Once the republic had achieved its external consolidation with the stabilization of the currency and the acceptance of the Dawes Plan, the functions of the extraparliamentary organizations on both the Right and Left underwent a profound change. For instead of seeking the overthrow of the existing constitutional order through a coup d'état, they now placed themselves in the service of efforts to revise that order in a more authoritarian direction. In this respect, they could take advantage of the fact that the authority of the Reichstag and the various government parties had been severely eroded by the strongly statist character of the *Bürgerblock* cabinets — the national government and the ministerial bureaucracy had made themselves increasingly independent of both parliament and the government parties — and by the increasing unpopularity of the government's currency, tax, and social policies. The extraparliamentary offensive against the parliamentary system of government despite the latter's economic and political stabilization revealed that Germany's republican parties had failed to integrate the social and economic interests they represented into a viable political consensus both within themselves and with each other in parliament.

The domestic consolidation of Germany's republican system in this phase of the *Bürgerblock* governments was accompanied by a decline in the con-spiratorial activities of the patriotic combat leagues and the gradual eclipse of hopes on the radical Right for a violent overthrow of the hated Weimar system. The adoption of a long-range strategy for Germany's secret rearmament and the Reichswehr's formal acceptance of the new republican order cut the ground completely out from under the military antics of the patriotic leagues. As a result the combat leagues sought to gain direct political influence. From a veterans' organization the Stahlhelm evolved into the most important of Germany's numerous national-conservative combat leagues. Its success stemmed in no small measure from the efforts of Franz Seldte, a reserve officer who was severely wounded in the First World War and who in 1919 played a major role in the consolidation of a number of local-front soldier organizations into a national association. Since the middle of the 1920s some of the formerly in-dependent combat leagues, including the Viking League (Wiking-Bund), the Olympia League (Bund Olympia), and Erich von Ludendorff's Tannenberg League (Tannenberg-Bund), joined the Stahlhelm, which at the same time entered into close relations with the United Patriotic Leagues (Vereinigte Vater-ländische Verbände). By 1924 the Stahlhelm together with the Young Stahlhelm (Jungstahlhelm) already accounted for more than 400,000 members.

The same path was taken by the Young German Order (Jungdeutscher Orden) under the leadership of Artur Mahraun. Mahraun had come out of the German youth movement and had participated with his followers in the fight-ing in Upper Silesia in 1921. Until 1923 the Young German Order had placed primary emphasis upon its paramilitary activity and was therefore banned for a short time by the Prussian government in 1923. After 1924, the Young Germans began to pursue broader political objectives without, however, sacrificing their nonpartisan character. The Order's seemingly antiquated organizational struc-ture, which drew its inspiration from the traditions of the Teutonic knights in the late Middle Ages and manifested a number of parallels to the neoconserva-tive Ring Movement (Ring-Bewegung), was perfectly consistent with the mis-sion it had set for itself in its charter, namely, to translate the principle of the *Bund* into political reality and thus make the existing party system super-fluous in the not-too-distant future. Mahraun, whose *Jungdeutsches Manifest* from 1927 revealed a close affinity to certain neoconservative ideas, sought to replace the parliamentary system and the existing party system with an organi-cally structured corporatist order in which the concept of the neighborhood (*Nachbarschaft*) would be merged with the leadership principle.

With almost 100,000 members, the Young German Order was the second strongest political combat league on the conservative scene. It recruited its support primarily from the milieu of the Protestant middle class. Many of its more active members came from the youth movement. Mahraun propagated the inner renewal of the German nation, which he sought to bring about not through military exercises as in the case of the Stahlhelm but through physical fitness, internal colonization, and labor on the German frontiers. In this respect, Mahraun was the first to propagate the idea of a voluntary work corps, and the Order was later to become deeply involved in the work camp movement. In foreign policy, the Young German Order supported Stresemann's efforts on behalf of an understanding with France, while in the east it advocated the elimination of the Polish Corridor and a far-reaching program of colonization.

Stresemann did not hesitate to mobilize the potential of the combat leagues in support of his Locarno policy. In an article written for the *Hamburger Fremdenblatt*, Stresemann stressed that "the great living forces of the nation" were "not represented by the parties alone." Nevertheless, the Stahlhelm fell more and more under the influence of Theodor Duesterberg, a former combat officer who had been promoted to the Stahlhelm's second-in-command in March 1924, and joined the ranks of those groups on the German Right that opposed the Treaty of Locarno. Whereas Franz Seldte continued to think in the categories of Wilhelmine nationalism, the Stahlhelm developed an outspoken national-revolutionary wing that included among its most prominent representatives a number of neoconservative writers like Ernst Jünger, Franz Schauwecker, and Werner Beumelburg, who used the Stahlhelm's official organ to propagate the notion of "soldierly nationalism." The radical rejection of parliamentary democracy merged with the call for a national dictatorship to produce the vague goal of creating a "state of front soldiers" (*Staat der Frontsoldaten*) modeled after the "community of the trenches" (*Schützengrabengemeinschaft*). As an alternative to representative democracy, the Stahlhelm offered a corporatist program developed primarily by Heinz Brauweiler, one of the Stahlhelm's most important ideologues. The manipulative use of the mythos of the "front experience" became increasingly apparent in 1926, when the Stahlhelm dropped combat experience as a prerequisite for membership and transformed itself from a veterans' organization into what its advocates called a "political nationalist freedom movement."

The sudden arrival of the paramilitary combat leagues, or *Bünde*, upon the German political scene in the second half of the 1920s only intensified the feeling of an impending generational change. It was, interestingly enough, not the generation that had served at the front but rather the generation that succeeded it that appropriated the ideology of the front soldier for its own purposes, that most eagerly embraced the neoconservative myth of a new national beginning based upon the *Volksgemeinschaft*, and that saw itself inadequately represented in the aging leadership cadres of the established political parties. Uniforms and military parades, which were used to spectacular effect by the Stahlhelm at its annual Front Soldier Rallies, as well as political demonstrations directed for the most part against Locarno and the League of Nations, became increasingly prominent features of a political culture in which extraparliamentary actions were becoming more and more common.

In response to the increasing politicization of right-wing combat leagues like the Stahlhelm and Young German Order, those forces that were loyal to the republic founded the Reichsbanner Black-Red-Gold (Reichsbanner Schwarz-Rot-Gold) as an umbrella organization serving all of Germany's republican parties in Magdeburg, the birthplace of the Stahlhelm, in 1924. In spite of the official participation of the Center Party and DDP out of largely tactical considerations, the Reichsbanner remained a mass organization sponsored primarily by the Social Democrats. Within a short time the Reichsbanner had more than a million members and far outstripped the numerical strength of the combat leagues on the Right. The Reichsbanner was founded as an organization for Germany's front soldiers and modeled itself in many essential respects after right-wing combat leagues. Like Hitler's SA, the Reichsbanner was responsible for protecting meeting places and keeping order at republican rallies. But the *bündisch* element and military rituals never overshadowed the Reichsbanner's outspoken prorepublican orientation.

In 1927 Karl Höltermann succeeded Otto Hörsing as leader of the Reichsbanner. Under Höltermann's leadership the Reichsbanner and its more militant nucleus, the Iron Front (Eiserne Front), approximated the political style of the nationalist Right, both in its cultivation of the leadership principle and in its self-conscious use of paramilitary forms. Under the motto "Struggle for the Second Republic" and with its emphasis upon the principle of nonpartisanship, the Reichsbanner found itself among those who were openly critical of the existing party system. It is therefore not surprising that the Reichsbanner — and not simply because of Hörsing's frequently headstrong leadership style — should have aroused strong distrust not only within the Center and DDP but also within the SPD executive committee. At the heart of this situation lay not only the difficulties the Center was experiencing as a result of its entry into Luther's *Bürgerblock* cabinet but also the stormy political temperament of the new generation that was just emerging on the political scene, a generation that rejected the routinized, symbolically empty, and directionless political praxis of the party functionaries and revealed little sympathy for a species of associational democracy (*Vereinsdemokratie*) they dismissed as obsolete.

In contrast to the Reichsbanner, which conceived of its mission in essentially defensive terms and eschewed violent confrontation with political adversaries whenever possible, the Red Front Soldiers' League (Roter Frontkämpferbund or RFB) and its auxiliary, the Red Youth Front (Rote Jugendfront), were intentionally founded as fighting combat leagues. Their behavior only intensified the anti-Marxist fears of the German bourgeoisie and provided right-wing combat leagues with an opportunity to present themselves as defenders of law and order. Despite its official proclamations of nonpartisanship, the Red Front Soldiers' League led by Ernst Thälmann functioned as an auxiliary organization of the KPD that appropriated the external trappings of the right-wing combat leagues and worked for the establishment of a united proletarian front from below.

After the adoption of the new leftist tactic at the Sixth World Congress of the Communist International in the fall of 1928, the outward behavior of the KPD became more and more radical. As a result, the party found itself involved in increasingly frequent brawls with the SA and Reichsbanner. Even then, however, responsibility for the bloody clashes that took place between Communist demonstrators and the Prussian police in Berlin in the first days of May 1929 and that resulted in death and injury to countless numbers of people must be attributed to the use of excessive force by the police. The decree banning demonstrations on 1 May provoked the KPD into calling for mass protests that had, contrary to the claims of Berlin police chief Karl Zörgiebel and Prussian Minister of the Interior Karl Severing, nothing do with Communist plans for a coup attempt. The fact that after "Berlin's Bloody May" — as these events were soon to be known in the Communist press — the Red Front Soldiers' League was banned in Prussia and a number of other German states did little to relieve existing political tensions. Communist propaganda, on the other hand, used the ban to justify its agitation against the Social Democrats in accordance with the newly proclaimed thesis of "social fascism." In point of fact, the Red Front Soldiers' League, which could claim about 80,000 members at the time it was banned, never constituted a serious threat to the existing political order. The same was true of its various illegal successor organizations. For the most serious threat to the survival of the Weimar Republic came not from the political Left but was being mounted by the paramilitary units of the political Right.

Of the unremitting efforts to unite the paramilitary combat leagues on the nationalist Right into an effective extraparliamentary block, none was more important than the initiative undertaken by Baron Wilhelm von Gayl on behalf of the presidential candidacy of General Hans von Seeckt at the end of 1924. Gayl's ultimate goal was to use Seeckt's election as the point of departure for a comprehensive revision of the Weimar Constitution in a more authoritarian direction. Gayl's plans, however, were undercut by the premature call for new presidential elections as a result of the unexpected death of Reich President Friedrich Ebert on 28 February 1925. Ebert's death was in no small measure the consequence of an unprecedented campaign of vilification that the German Right had unleashed against the Prussian government in the wake of the Barmat scandal. In itself there was nothing unusual about the bankruptcy of a company run by the Barmat brothers. Even the Stinnes empire had collapsed shortly after his death as a result of excessive speculation on the credit market and insufficient capital reserves. But the fact that the Barmats had received loans from the Prussian State Bank and the National Post Office combined with the fact that the two brothers were Jews who had immigrated from Poland after 1918 to produce a spate of unfounded allegations of corruption against the SPD that assumed distinctly anti-Semitic overtones. Even Ebert, who was falsely accused of having granted special favors to the Barmats, became a preferred target of inflammatory attacks from the right-wing DNVP. The campaign reached its high point with the accusation that Ebert had committed high treason when he joined the strike committee of the Berlin munitions workers in early 1918. While the Magdeburg court before which Ebert sued a newspaper editor for libel did condemn the defendant, it did not invalidate the accusation of high treason.

This was one of those notorious cases in which the judiciary allowed itself to be used as the lackey of a blind nationalism that discredited the parties of the Left and other republican institutions through a campaign of systematic vilification. The republic was now paying a price for its failure to take effective measures aimed at securing the loyalty of an overwhelmingly social-conservative judiciary to the new constitutional order, if necessary through a revision of the disciplinary code and the procedures for promotion. Expressions of support from public figures and members of the national cabinet, which otherwise did not find the courage to censure the decision in public, did little to compensate for the outrage that Ebert felt at not being able to take legal steps against the systematically inflated accusations of high treason until after the Magdeburg decision had been successfully appealed. The official cause of Ebert's death was a ruptured appendix for which the physically robust fifty-four-year-old received treatment too late.

The new presidential elections confronted the political parties with the difficult task of nominating candidates who could unite a majority of the people behind their candidacies. For the parties of the Weimar Coalition, the obvious solution would have been to agree upon a common candidate, who most likely would have been Otto Braun, the highly respected Prussian minister president who had declared himself willing to accept the nomination. This step never got off the ground, however, since the Center Party opposed the nomination of a Social Democrat. In Social Democratic circles, on the other hand, it was more or less a foregone conclusion that, in light of Ebert's party affiliation, the presidency would remain in their party's possession. When the moderate bourgeois parties broached the possibility of uniting behind the candidacy of Defense Minister Otto Geßler, they were sharply rebuffed by Stresemann with reference to the disastrous affects the election of the defense minister to the Reich presidency would have upon his foreign policy. Since the electoral law provided for a runoff election in the event that no candidate received an absolute majority in the first round of voting, each party proceeded to field its own candidate: Ernst Thälmann for the KPD, Otto Braun for the SPD, Wilhelm Marx for the Center, Heinrich Held for the BVP, Willy Hellpach for the DDP, Karl Jarres for the DVP and DNVP, and Erich Ludendorff for the National Socialist Freedom Party. None of these candidates obtained the absolute majority needed to win in the first round. Jarres received 10.7, Braun 7.8, and Marx 4 million votes.

The first round of voting revealed just how deep the cleavages between the various political parties were and how little support the existing party system enjoyed among the broad masses of the German people. Whereas the republican parties now took the step they should have taken earlier in the process by withdrawing the candidacies of Braun and Hellpach to unite behind the candidate of the so-called People's Bloc (Volksblock), the Center's Wilhelm Marx, the political Right, which attributed much greater importance to the gaining control of the Reich presidency than did the republican parties, revived a longstanding plan to form a joint nominating committee under the auspices of the ostensibly nonpartisan National Citizens' Council (Reichsbürgerrat) headed by Friedrich Wilhelm von Loebell, Prussian minister of the interior during the war. This committee then proceeded to nominate as its candidate the victor of the Battle of Tannenberg, Paul von Hindenburg und Beneckendorff.

Having already retired from active political life, the seventy-eight-year-old general accepted the candidacy only after emissaries of the DNVP, including former Grand Admiral Alfred von Tirpitz, appealed to his sense of patriotic duty and assured him of the undivided support of the parties on the German Right. The assurance was in itself somewhat rash, since there were profound misgivings that extended deep within the DNVP as to whether Hindenburg was equal to the task of carrying out the duties of the Reich presidency. Baron von Gayl rightly feared that the aging field marshal might not be willing to go along with open violations of the Weimar Constitution. Heavy industry, on the other hand, preferred the mayor of Duisburg, Karl Jarres, although he stood virtually no chance whatsoever of defeating Marx. For their part, Stresemann and the DVP were correct in pointing out that there were compelling foreign policy considerations that weighed against Hindenburg's candidacy and that his election to the Reich presidency would almost certainly be greeted with alarm and consternation in Paris and London. Even though the Loebell committee, having renamed itself the Reich Bloc (Reichsblock), mustered a majority for Hindenburg, his candidacy remained controversial on the political Right as a whole. Even immediately before the election, Chancellor Luther considered forcing Hindenburg's withdrawal. It was symptomatic for the evolution of German politics that Hindenburg's candidacy was launched by a group of right-wing politicians who felt little, if any, sympathy for the principles of parliamentary democracy and that they could comfortably ignore the opinions of the individual party leaders when it came to nominating a candidate.

The principal campaign theme of the bourgeois Right was that Marx, as leader of the Center Party, was the prisoner of the Social Democrats, who were bent on "selling out" the Republic. Hindenburg, on the other hand, was depicted as someone who stood above the parties, as the champion of the national interests of all "patriotic-minded" Germans. Implicit in this propaganda was a denigration of all political parties. As Fritz Schäffer from the Bavarian People's Party so aptly expressed it, Hindenburg's candidacy was born of the "misery of Germany's party politics." Hindenburg, who had his staff compile a collection of "patriotic maxims" that he could use in the campaign, had no experience whatsoever in parliamentary or electoral politics. He made almost no personal appearances during the course of the campaign, though much to the distress of the DNVP he did offer public assurances that he would uphold the constitution. Although the campaign exploited the myth of the victor of Tannenberg at every conceivable opportunity, his nomination represented neither an encouragement to monarchist circles nor a distinct advantage for the military. Even before accepting the candidacy, Hindenburg had secured the approval of the exiled Kaiser Wilhelm II, though he directed his staff to deny this. It was precisely because Hindenburg enjoyed the loyalty of circles close to the former Kaiser that his presidency constituted such an obstacle to plans for the eventual restoration of the monarchy.

The second round of voting took place on 26 April 1925 with no clear indication as to who might win. With 14,655,000 votes Hindenburg obtained a relative majority over Marx, who polled 13,751,000 votes. What was particularly significant about this outcome was that almost a third of the core electorate of the Bavarian People's Party ignored the instructions of the party leadership and voted for the Protestant Hindenburg. The KPD, which against the Comintern's advice had refused to withdraw its support for Thälmann's candidacy, failed to improve upon its position in the first election. This, in turn, bore dramatic testimony to the party discipline of Social Democratic voters, whose party strongly supported Marx's candidacy in return for the Center's willingness to go along with Otto Braun's election as Prussian minister president. The republican Reichsbanner also wholeheartedly supported the former chancellor and head of the Center Party, Wilhelm Marx. The common struggle against the Right no doubt helped strengthen the sense of solidarity among the republican parties.

In the final analysis, it turned out that not only the DDP, particularly in Saxony and Hamburg, but also the Center — last, but not least, in Westphalia and Silesia — had to absorb heavy losses at the polls. By no means, therefore, was Hindenburg's narrow majority to be attributed solely to the Bavarian People's Party, which refused to join forces with the Social Democrats under any circumstances whatsoever. Nor could the outcome of the election be attributed to the intransigence of the KPD. The election results made it clear that resentment against the Social Democrats had played a central role in the voting behavior of the bourgeois electorate and that in large segments of the German middle class this went hand in hand with the rejection of the parliamentary system. The decisive factor, however, was that of the 3.5 million voters who participated only in the second round of balloting, an estimated 3 million cast their votes for Hindenburg. The mobilization of anti-Marxist and nationalist sentiments thus afforded the political Right access to that dangerous arsenal of nonvoters the republican parties could not hope to reach.

Demonstrations by right-wing associations and the prominent display of the imperial black-white-red flag greeted Hindenburg as he traveled to Berlin for his inauguration. Wary of confrontations and misunderstandings, the Reichsbanner maintained a distinctly low profile. This, in itself, captured the symbolic essence of the change in political style that was to characterize the next five years of the republic. On the other hand, the concerns of those loyal to the republic that Hindenburg would depart from the constitution in the exercise of his office proved unfounded. To be sure, Stresemann had a great deal of difficulty convincing the new Reich president that the foreign policy constraints under which the Reich was laboring did not permit him to "pound his fist on the table" as the president wanted him to do. Nor was it a good omen that the Reich president was unwilling to affix his signature to Germany's application for membership in the League of Nations as the constitution required. Far more troubling still was the constant influence that representatives of the DNVP, large landowners, and the "imperial party"—as Otto Meißner, whom at the urging of the chancellor Hindenburg had retained as state secretary in the Bureau of the Reich President, called the old monarchist entourage, including the crown prince—were able to exercise over the thinking of the new president.

Even though Hindenburg was widely regarded as a figure of national integration, the outcome of the presidential election nevertheless represented a defeat for the republic. The political polarization that had expressed itself in the formation of the People's Bloc and Reich Bloc reached much deeper than one might guess from the ad hoc character of the alliances concluded before the second round of voting and revealed the progressive isolation of Germany's parliamentary forces. That Marx failed to obtain a majority stemmed, aside from the endorsements of the parties, first and foremost from the combination of anti–Social Democratic sentiments and the association of his name with the unpopular coalition politics pursued at the national level since November 1923. A similar constellation arose in 1926 in connection with the referendum and plebiscite on the expropriation of dynastic properties. During the course of this action, it became increasingly clear that significant sectors of the German electorate, irrespective of individual party affiliation, were opposed to a purely reactionary policy oriented toward a restoration of prewar conditions. To this extent, the chances for the survival of the republican system were still quite good in the middle of the 1920s.

Various issues such as the one-sidedness of the *Bürgerblock* in policies related to the distribution of the social product, the absence of concessions on the part of industry in the matter of working hours, and unemployment that reached a new peak at the beginning of 1926, as well as the cabinet's inflexibility in the revaluation conflict, had led to the buildup of resentments and frustrations that now exploded over an issue of purely secondary significance, the settlement of the fortunes of the German dynastic houses. The failure to deal with this matter at the time of the republic's founding—a failure not unrelated to fears of Allied intervention—finally caught up with the republic in late 1925 just as negotiations between the Hohenzollerns and the Prussian state seemed to be drawing to a close. Excessive claims for restitution that the German dynastic houses filed against the various state governments prompted the Social Democrats to press for a legal settlement to this problem at the national level in the hope that this would put an end to protracted litigation with the administrators of princely estates.

The psychological effects of the tremendous transfer of wealth that had taken place during the runaway inflation of the early 1920s soon transformed an issue of secondary significance into one of the most exhaustive and most bitterly contested political conflicts in Germany since the end of the war. The DDP took the first step toward a resolution of this conflict by introducing a motion that would have authorized the state governments to settle claims pertaining to dynastic properties outside the judicial system. The Democrats were no doubt hopeful that the SPD would cooperate in this effort, particularly since the DNVP had rejected the Treaty of Locarno. This initiative, however, was frustrated from two sides. On the one hand, the KPD—which had abandoned its earlier opposition to the SPD and the socialist labor unions to embrace the policy of a united front—became involved in the issue when it submitted to the Reichstag a bill that provided for the expropriation of dynastic properties without compensation to the princely houses. On the other hand, the DNVP mobilized German constitutional scholarship on its behalf and succeeded in having Carl Schmitt pronounce the DDP's relatively moderate proposal unconstitutional in a number of different respects. The DDP immediately tried to defuse this opinion by calling for the appointment of a special court by the national government that would determine the judicial merits of the case once and for all. This solution, which in itself was problematic because it failed to take into consideration the antirepublican bias of the German judiciary, became so distorted in the subsequent negotiations among the government parties that it was no longer appropriate as the basis of a consensus within the cabinet. The issue was further complicated—and in some respects disastrously so—by the fact that Reich President Hindenburg adopted the position of the minister of justice and proclaimed that a law determining the status of dynastic wealth would require an amendment to the Weimar Constitution despite the fact that Article 153, Paragraph 2, of the constitution provided for the expropriation of such properties if such action lay in the public interest. While Hindenburg's opinion was open to legal challenge, it blocked a parliamentary solution to the problem even though the SPD and bourgeois middle parties worked diligently in search of a viable legal compromise.

In January 1926 the German League for Human Rights (Deutsche Liga für Menschenrechte) submitted a petition with the approval of the KPD that called for a referendum on the fate of dynastic properties in accordance with the relevant clauses of the Weimar Constitution. The SPD and socialist labor unions immediately cosponsored the motion so that it would not appear as if the initiative had been left to the KPD. At the same time, the socialists rejected the KPD's offer of joint action under the auspices of an ad hoc *Aktionsgemeinschaft*. The Social Democrats, who sought to mobilize the free trade unions in order to give the action a nonpartisan character and to undercut the presence of the KPD, could hardly refuse to cooperate in the conduct of such a referendum, particularly since the increasing isolation of the bourgeois minority governments from the German public suggested that the recourse to plebiscitary measures such as this was appropriate. In point of fact, the demand for the expropriation of the royal houses possessed a popularity that extended far beyond the parties of the Left. For in addition to the strong antimonarchist sentiments that characterized German public opinion, the prospect that the government might restore dynastic properties to the ruling houses stood in direct contrast to the government's handling of the revaluation question. This, in turn, prompted middle-class voters who, on most other issues, stood on the right wing of Germany's political spectrum to support expropriation. Despite well-organized counterpropaganda from the German Right that employed anti-Semitic imagery, despite efforts to hamper circulation of the petition in East Elbia, despite the opposition of the BVP, the Center, the DVP, and elements of the DDP as well as from the leaders of both religious confessions, the petition for a referendum on the expropriation of dynastic properties still obtained the signatures of more than 12.5 million voters.

When the parliamentary delegations of the various German parties failed to reach a compromise in June 1926, the referendum became inevitable. It immediately triggered both a totally unanticipated mobilization of the German electorate and a process of extreme political polarization that exploded the existing confines of German party politics. Although there was virtually no prospect whatsoever that the issue could be decided by means of a referendum, it nevertheless expanded into a fundamental debate over social policy. Behind the slogan "Republic or monarchy" stood the conflict between those who sought to solidify the republic as a means of achieving greater social justice and those who hoped to return to a conservative-governmental regime committed to the defense of inherited social privileges. If on 13 June the Social Democratic *Vorwärts* editorialized that "the future of the German Republic was at stake," this was an understandable reaction to the propaganda of the German Right, which used every conceivable argument to brand the referendum as a fundamental violation of an individual's right to private property or—as Otto Dibelius, superintendent general of the Protestant churches of Kurmark, stated on behalf of his congregation—as "the beginning of Bolshevism in Germany."

Whereas the DVP and the DDP were more moderate in their argumentation and warned that the conflict might lead to a presidential crisis, the DNVP unleashed a wild propaganda campaign that conjured up the specter of Bolshevism and carried markedly anti-Semitic overtones. In this respect, the DNVP fell in line with the NSDAP, which had reconstituted itself after Hitler's premature release from prison and now added extra fuel to the campaign by calling for the expropriation of property belonging to east European Jews who had immigrated to Germany after 1 August 1914. Hitler, who characterized the expropriation of the princes' property as a "Jewish swindle," unfalteringly led his party into the camp of the German Right. At a hastily convened leadership conference in Bamberg in February 1926, Hitler prevailed over Gregor Straßer, who argued on behalf of the party's district leaders (*Gauleiter*) from the northern and western parts of the country that the NSDAP should support the referendum. Hitler's triumph marked the beginning of the NSDAP's expressed support for the continued existence of the capitalist economic system, a course that Hitler explicitly endorsed in a speech before a contingent of Ruhr industrialists in the summer of 1927.

The right-wing parties received support from monarchist circles, including the German Nobles' Society (Deutsche Adelsgenossenschaft), which denounced the referendum as an "inexpiable crime," as well as from representatives of the Protestant church. Even the Vatican was prevailed upon to do its part in defeating the referendum. Referendum opponents also received support from the National Rural League, the Stahlhelm, the Young German Order, the German National Union of Commercial Employees, and elements of the entrepreneurial elite. At the same time, Loebell tried to resuscitate the Reich Bloc and succeeded in persuading the Reich president to issue a public statement, in blatant disregard of his responsibility for exercising discretion, in which he denounced the referendum as a violation of the law that would set the nation on a "helter-skelter downward course" (*der auf abschüssiger Bahn haltlos bergab*). Although this was immediately dismissed as a purely private remark, it nevertheless appeared on billboards and leaflets throughout the country. Not only did this unleash a storm of protest in the Reichstag from the SPD and the other parties that supported the referendum, but was all the more damaging to Hindenburg's reputation because it coincided with the disclosure of plans for a right-wing dictatorship that must have had his tacit approval.

The opponents of the referendum enjoyed a tactical advantage in that all they needed to do to defeat the referendum was to persuade voters to abstain.

In spite of obstructionist tactics that in certain rural districts singled out those who took the time to vote for public ostracism, 14.5 million people voted for expropriation without compensation, to which Wilhelm II responded: "This means that there are 14 million sons-of-bitches [*Schweinehunde*] in Germany." Both churches lamented the outcome as a sign of the moral decadence of the times. The Catholic episcopacy identified this as the principal reason why so many Catholic workers as well as a fairly substantial percentage of the Center's own rank-and-file membership had disregarded their party's official position to vote for expropriation without compensation. In this respect, it is indeed remarkable that both the Windthorst Leagues (Windthorst-Bünde), the youth organization of the Center under the leadership of Heinrich Krone, and the National League of German Democratic Youth (Reichsbund der Deutschen Demokratischen Jugend) under the DDP's Ernst Lemmer spoke out against the "excessive claims of the princes." Under heavy pressure from its rank-and-file membership, the DDP decided to leave how one voted on the referendum up to his or her individual conscience, whereupon several members of the party, among them Hjalmar Schacht, resigned from the DDP in protest. The German Trade-Union Federation (Deutscher Gewerkschaftsbund or DGB), the umbrella organization of the nonsocialist unions, maintained a distinctly low profile, while the Christian labor unions spoke out in favor of expropriation. The Reichsbanner, whose members openly sympathized with the demand for expropriation, maintained the forms of complete neutrality, with the unfortunate result that agitation in the streets was left in the hands of the Red Front Soldiers' League and the Communist youth organization. When the KPD expanded its activities into the countryside—if only to counter the obstructionist tactics of the National Rural League and the abuse it heaped upon those who took part in the referendum—anticommunism of a particularly virulent nature spread throughout the rural population.

In itself, the struggle over the expropriation involving the princes was no more than an episode. Still, it revealed profound differences in the mentality of German society and uncovered a generational conflict that went beyond party lines. The outcome of the referendum indicated that a significant portion of the German population—possibly a majority—was still in the republican camp and was opposed to the reactionary allegiances of Germany's bourgeois elites, which had voted for the interests of the Hohenzollerns out of a concern for their own privileged status. The political polarization that had been triggered by the referendum campaign thus went significantly beyond the issue at stake. The mobilization of anti-Bolshevik and anti-Semitic sentiments by the German Right anticipated the constellation of political forces that would eventually lead to the destruction of what was still left of the parliamentary system after 1931. In 1926 the threat that this posed to Germany's republican system was so imminent that it prompted all republican forces to draw more closely together in the belief that even at this point they could still construct a lasting foundation for the parliamentary order. The summer vacation camps for workers' children, intentionally nicknamed "children's republics" or *Kinderrepubliken*, that had been established by the Socialist Workers' Youth (Sozialistische Arbeiterjugend) and the Red Falcons (Rote Falken) bore dramatic testimony to this era's abiding faith in the future of a social democracy.

Under these circumstances the Center Party decided to pay closer attention to the interests of its working-class and trade-union constituencies. This, in turn, provided Heinrich Brauns with the push he needed to have them more firmly anchored in the republic's social constitution. The SPD, forced by external circumstances into an unwelcome alliance with the KPD, blew its chance to place the DNVP in the wrong when it failed to approve the compromise legislation proposed by the government on the expropriation of the dynastic properties. Had the Social Democrats accepted the government's compromise bill, this would have established the preconditions for the long anticipated transition to the Great Coalition. As in the past, negotiations for an extension of the coalition to the Left foundered on the intransigence of the DVP.

The final break between the SPD and the bourgeois middle parties took place not as a result of the dispute with the DVP over the length of the workday but over the issue of domestic armament controls. During the course of protracted negotiations, the Prussian government and SPD had struggled to reach a compromise on the clearly antirepublican recruitment of officers for the Reichswehr, the use of illegal weapons depots, and the army's close relations with the paramilitary Right. The purpose of the SPD's intervention in this matter was not so much to repudiate the government's military policy as to bring it under tighter republican control. Kurt von Schleicher, who in his efforts to rearm the German people was opposed to any accommodation with the allegedly pacifist SPD, did his best to sabotage the compromise that Prussian Minister President Otto Braun offered in an attempt to resolve the deadlock. Scheidemann's spectacular but politically ill-advised speech in the Reichstag, in which he exposed the Reichswehr's illegal cooperation with the Red Army and the nationalist combat leagues at home, unleashed a storm of indignation within all of Germany's bourgeois parties. Although virtually all of these facts had already been reported in the foreign press, Stresemann denounced Scheidemann's revelations as "unforgivable." For his own part, Scheidemann demanded the resignation of Defense Minister Otto Geßler, whom the SPD held principally responsible for the folly committed by the Reichswehr. Schleicher immediately seized upon this purely perfunctory demand to strengthen the Reich president in his conviction that it was impossible to govern with the SPD.

Further isolated by its opposition to the proposed Trash and Filth Law (Schmutz- und Schundgesetz) that radical racists had introduced with an unmistakably antiliberal and anti-Semitic thrust in an attempt to discredit the DDP's Minister of Interior Wilhelm Külz, the Social Democrats forced the resignation of an already unstable minority cabinet that had remained in office with the support of the DNVP. Schleicher had thus succeeded in carrying out his two-pronged intrigue. For not only was he able to prevent the dismissal of Geßler — who shortly thereafter was obliged to step down as a result of his involvement in the Phoebus film scandal — but he had managed to drive the DDP and SPD into political isolation and to clear the way for the formation of a new *Bürgerblock* cabinet that included an unusually high number of ministers from the DNVP and was once again headed by the Center's Wilhelm Marx. Hindenburg, who claimed the right to appoint the defense minister as a prerogative of his office, exercised a decisive influence on the formation of the cabinet. With threats of a dissolution of the Reichstag and "other possible measures," Hindenburg and his advisors were able to pressure the various government parties into making the necessary concessions. The chain of events that culminated in the installation of the fourth Marx cabinet bore dramatic testimony to the fundamental disenfranchisement of the parties vis-à-vis the social interests that now focused their attention on the Bureau of the Reich President.

Even if it is true that at the beginning of his tenure as Reich president Hindenburg refrained from directly interfering in the government's business, his office soon became the venue of choice for the interests of big business and large-scale agriculture. These interests found well-disposed advocates in men like the DNVP party chairman Count Kuno von Westarp, the president's future neighbor and confidant Elard von Oldenburg-Januschau, and the president's son Oskar von Hindenburg, who served as a liaison between the Reich president and Kurt von Schleicher. The gift of the one-time family estate in Neudeck in East Prussia on the occasion of Hindenburg's eightieth birthday was financed by public subscription and registered in the name of Oskar von Hindenburg in order to avoid inheritance taxes. This proved to be a shrewd move not only on the part of Oldenburg-Januschau but also for the large landowners from east of the Elbe, even though the latter contributed less than 5 percent of what had been needed to purchase the estate. While Hindenburg continued to make a point of remaining politically neutral, he frequently evoked false hopes through indiscretions in talks with representatives from the DNVP. There is no way in which this can be construed as the nonpartisan exercise of the powers of the presidential office. It was more through Stresemann's consummate skills than through the energies of Chancellor Hans Luther, who had yielded to pressure from the Reich president and DNVP and was on the verge of jettisoning the Locarno policy, that the embarrassment of a presidential veto against its continuation was avoided.

The powers of the Reich president depended ultimately on the close and confidential relationship that Hindenburg established with Defense Minister

Wilhelm Groener and the latter's "cardinal in politics," General Kurt von Schleicher. The result of small and almost imperceptible changes in the constitution, the expansion of presidential authority was aided by the unabashedly conservative character of contemporary constitutional law, the judiciary, and the bureaucracy. At a conference of German constitutional lawyers in April 1924 Carl Schmitt and Erwin Jacobi had already argued that the emergency powers the existing constitution had conferred upon the Reich president gave him the sovereign power to violate that constitution without legal recourse. After Hindenburg's election the overwhelming majority of Germany's constitutional lawyers endorsed the expansion of presidential powers and found widespread support for its position in the bourgeois middle parties, including the DDP.

With his rear effectively covered, Hindenburg felt free to raise major objections to the proposed law governing the exercise of presidential emergency powers under Article 48 of the Weimar Constitution that was sent to him in November 1926 and to request that its implementation be postponed until after a "general constitutional reform" had taken place. Intent on expanding the powers of his office, Hindenburg rejected the law's proviso that presidential decisions were subject to review by the courts. He also felt that it was not necessary to secure the countersignature of the chancellor but only that of the minister whose portfolio was most directly affected by the exercise of emergency powers. For all practical purposes, Hindenburg would have arrogated to himself the right to appoint the ministers of the national cabinet—and in particular the minister of defense on the basis of the powers the constitution vested in his position as commander in chief of German armed forces. At the same time, Hindenburg did not shy away from becoming involved in current government business by refusing to approve bills he did not like and, if necessary, by threatening to resign. Given the prevailing sentiments of German public opinion, the latter threat inevitably raised the specter of a constitutional crisis.

On the surface, the *Bürgerblock* cabinet that assumed office in early February 1927 represented a return to government by parliamentary majority. Yet the very heterogeneity of the parties represented in the cabinet precluded effective government action. There was, for example, no agreement on social policy, which the Center, as the dominant coalition partner, clearly wanted to strengthen. Further conflicts arose over the school question, which Marx had included in the government program more or less on his own authority. While an understanding on the expansion of confessional schools was certainly possible among the Center, BVP, and DNVP, such an arrangement could never include the DVP, whose cultural policy embodied the legacy of classical liberalism and was very close to that of the SPD as well. In foreign policy, by contrast, an understanding between the DNVP and the other coalition parties was not likely, even though Stresemann had finally received assurances from

Westarp that his party would accept the constitutionality of the Locarno treaty. In point of fact, the DNVP's participation in the government was possible only because no major foreign policy decisions were pending at the time. To maintain its position within the government, the DNVP was even prepared to support an extension of the Law for the Protection of the Republic, albeit in a watered-down version. At the same time, a shift to the right was reflected in the personnel policies of the nationalist minister of the interior Walther von Keudell, who reorganized his ministry for the specific purpose of undercutting the position of those who were loyal to the republic. One of the principal casualties of this policy was State Secretary Arnold Brecht, who subsequently found a high-ranking position in the Prussian civil service.

The governing coalition was based on the temporary alliance of antagonistic interests. The Center Party used its position within the coalition to advance its social policy. As a counterploy, the right-wing DNVP succeeded in incorporating principles that were of vital importance to the National Rural League into a new trade bill. But the coalition eventually broke apart, as everyone had expected from the outset, over the Center's attempt to introduce school legislation that had been on the shelf ever since the school compromise of 1919 with the explicit goal of making confessional schools the accepted educational institution for the entire country. The new school bill that the minister of interior introduced in the early spring of 1927 encountered immediate resistance from the DVP, which vigorously opposed efforts to roll back the nondenominational common schools, or *Simultanschulen*, that had been established by the Weimar National Assembly as the norm for elementary and secondary education.

The dissolution of the government coalition over the school issue had a tactical component as well. With an eye to a new round of diplomatic negotiations that would take place in 1928, Stresemann believed that governmental stability at home was absolutely essential for the success of his foreign policy. By late 1927, when the school conflict came to a head, it was no longer possible to postpone new elections even if the current legislative period would not end until December 1928. To the Center Party, the break over an issue that involved confessional differences represented a favorable point of departure for new elections. The DNVP, by contrast, was anxious to avoid the unpopularity that responsibility for the revision of the Dawes Plan would almost certainly bring with it. The *Bürgerblock* was therefore already an empty shell when in the middle of February 1928 the end of the coalition was officially proclaimed and a month and half later the Reichstag was dissolved. In the long run, ad hoc alliances between different economic interests within the government could not compensate for the loss of authority the Reichstag and the government parties had suffered in the eyes of their diverse political constituencies. The challenge of the extraparliamentary forces had undermined the willingness of the parties and their parliamentary delegations to cooperate with each other. At the same time, ideological antagonisms had become increasingly pronounced.

Although both Hindenburg and Stresemann pleaded in vain for the continuation of the Marx cabinet, its resignation resulted from the internal exhaustion of the governing coalition and did not even require action by its parliamentary opposition. After it had passed an emergency program consisting of a supplemental budget for 1927 and the budget for 1928, the Reichstag was formally dissolved on 31 March 1928. In the election campaign that followed, the parties of the Left placed the proposed increase in military spending—and especially the proposed payment of the first installment for the construction of the "battle cruiser A"—at the heart of their campaign with slogans such as "Food for children, not battle cruisers" (*Kinderspeisung staat Panzerkreuzer*). The propaganda of the DNVP, NSDAP, and Business Party, by contrast, was directed primarily against Stresemann's policy of understanding and provided a mantel of self-righteous justification for the humiliating attacks that the foreign minister had to endure in Bavaria. In the meantime, the Center found itself under increasingly heavy pressure from its middle-class constituencies for a move to the Right, while its working-class wing still agitated for an opening to the Left.

For the opponents of the republic, the outcome of the Reichstag elections of 20 May 1928 was uniformly disappointing. Of the 103 seats the DNVP had held in the previous Reichstag, it now held only 73, although some of these losses could be ascribed to the success of the newly founded Christian-National Peasants and Farmers' Party (Christlich-nationale Bauern- und Landvolkpartei), which managed to win ten seats in the new parliament. The NSDAP, on the other hand, lost 100,000 votes and elected only twelve representatives to the Reichstag. A portion of these losses benefited special-interest parties that received approximately 14 percent of the total popular vote. At the same time, the erosion of the liberal middle parties continued with intensified vigor. This was particularly true of the DDP, which saw the size of its parliamentary delegation reduced to twenty-five deputies. But the DVP also suffered heavy losses in spite of Stresemann's indisputable foreign policy accomplishments and lost six of its fifty-one seats in the Reichstag. Moreover, the Center Party was forced to absorb heavy losses for the first time since 1920. All told, these results indicated the existence of a severe crisis within the bourgeois party spectrum. The clear winners of the election, on the other hand, were the SPD and, to a somewhat lesser extent, the KPD, which elected a total of fifty-four deputies. With 154 Reichstag mandates, the Social Democrats emerged from the election as by far the strongest party. The consistent policy of opposition the SPD had pursued since the end of 1923 seemed to have paid off.

In Prussia, where Landtag elections were held in conjunction with the national elections, the parties of the Weimar Coalition attained a secure parliamentary majority. This stemmed in part from the fact that the Prussian election law did not permit splinter parties that had failed to receive a direct mandate at the district level to pool its votes, or *Reststimmen*, toward the election of candidates on a statewide slate. Without waiting for coalition negotiations to begin at the national level, Otto Braun moved decisively in continuing the government of the Weimar Coalition despite vehement protests from the DVP, which had been excluded from a role in the Prussian government ever since 1925. Outside of Prussia, however, the triumph of the political Left had done little to strengthen Germany's republican forces. Whatever votes the Social Democrats managed to win were almost invariably offset by losses on the part of the DDP and Center as well as by the growth of an increasingly intransigent KPD. At the same time, the Center's closest ally, the Bavarian People's Party, had fallen — in large part through the interference of the Bavarian episcopate — under the domination of an emphatically antiparliamentary clique.

The outcome of the May 1928 Reichstag elections meant that the only conceivable way of forming a government that rested upon a parliamentary majority lay in a government of the Great Coalition. This path, however, was blocked by a number of formidable obstacles. Reluctant to entrust the chancellorship to a Social Democrat, Reich president Hindenburg considered appointing Ernst Scholz, chairman of the DVP Reichstag delegation, as chancellor until the DNVP's Westarp convinced him that it might be more advantageous to let the SPD exhaust itself in running the government on the assumption that the governing coalition would not last for more than a few months. In the end, Hindenburg assigned the task of forming a new government to Hermann Müller, the SPD's national party chairman. Well respected outside of his own party for his conciliatory attitude and his ability to negotiate compromises, Müller eventually developed a positive working relationship with Hindenburg, who later said that Müller was the best chancellor he had ever had even though he was a Social Democrat. By no means, however, was Hindenburg willing in 1928 to give Müller his unconditional support. For example, Hindenburg refused to accept Joseph Wirth as vice-chancellor, since he could not permit, he explained to the chancellor-designate, one party to dictate the composition of the cabinet. At the same time he threatened to resign if General Wilhelm Groener, who had replaced Geßler at the Ministry of Defense, was not retained in the cabinet.

Presidential interference also made it impossible for Müller to carry through with his initial decision to leave the Labor Ministry in the hands of Heinrich Brauns. As a result, the right wing of the Center was able to block the party's full participation in the new government and limit its representation in the cabinet government to one person, Transportation Minister Theodor von Guérard, who served as little more than a liaison and listening post. Brauns, whom the Center Reichstag delegation recalled very much against his will, was replaced by Rudolf Wissell from the SPD. These developments forced Müller to present his government as a "cabinet of personalities" that was free of formal commitments to the various government parties and would seek nothing more than parliamentary approval of the declaration that accompanied its installation in office. The second difficult hurdle that Müller had to clear was the delaying tactics of the DVP Reichstag delegation, which at the urging of its Prussian Landtag delegation made the DVP's participation in the new national government contingent upon a reorganization of the government in Prussia in which the DVP would receive two ministerial portfolios.

This complication might have been avoided if the SPD party leadership had nominated Otto Braun for the chancellorship in the place of its esteemed party chairman. The personal union between the offices of the Reich chancellor and the Prussian minister president would also have afforded the SPD an opportunity to influence the current discussion about a reform of Germany's federal structure in a way acceptable to the Social Democrats. Of the two, Braun was without a doubt the more energetic statesman, and he possessed a clear tactical and strategic concept of what he wanted to accomplish. But there was more to his reluctance to commit the full force of his personality to the fight for the dual appointment than concerns for his health. In part, his reluctance stemmed from the realization that the existing constellation of domestic political forces precluded, at least for the foreseeable future, a political offensive aimed at bringing about a merger of Prussia with the Reich with the simultaneous grant of autonomy to the south German states. Although in 1927 Braun had publicly advocated a reform of Germany's federal structure along unitarian lines, he assiduously avoided committing himself to any of the reform plans that were discussed at a special conference of representatives from the various German states at the beginning of 1928. Instead, he concentrated on strengthening Prussia's position within the existing federal structure by promoting administrative mergers with smaller and politically untenable entities. A personal union between Prussia and the Reich might possibly have averted the impending constitutional crisis of the Reich. But even if Braun had pursued this course of action, he would most likely have failed as a result of opposition from the Center and DDP, neither of which would have been comfortable with such a concentration of power in the hands of the Social Democrats. By the same token, Hindenburg and the presidential camarilla would almost certainly have resisted with all the means at their disposal the merger of Prussia with the Reich under the wrong—namely, Social Democratic—auspices.

As far as the SPD executive committee's choice of a candidate was concerned, strategic considerations—aside from a distrust of the willfulness of the "red czar" of Prussia and the rivalry between the party's parliamentary delegations in Prussia and the Reich—were far less important than the party's attachment to Müller as the ranking member of the party and its adherence to well-established patterns of mobility within the party organization. Thus Braun retreated, disappointed by the attitude of his own party, to his Prussian stronghold. With consummate skill he managed to fend off the DVP's repeated demands for an expansion of the governing coalition in Prussia, since in view of the impending negotiations with the Vatican on a concordat with the Prussian state he had found an ally in the Prussian Center that was not willing to abide by the directions of the Center's new party chairman, Monsignor Ludwig Kaas.

It was no secret that Otto Braun, his fundamentally conservative attitude notwithstanding, had earned the enmity of influential circles in the Reichs-wehr by virtue of his relentless attacks against the political abuse of military power. Schleicher, who worked behind the scenes through his close friend and associate Wilhelm Groener to exercise enormous influence over the for-mation and final shape of the government, would have done everything in his power to block Braun's appointment as chancellor. But a majority cabinet headed by Hermann Müller also met with strong resistance from the bourgeois parties and their social constituencies. It was only through the intervention of an ailing Stresemann that the Great Coalition finally came into existence. From his sanitarium in the Black Forest, Stresemann intervened directly in the cabinet negotiations by sending Müller a telegram—immediately dubbed "the shot from Bühlerhöhe"—and forced the DVP Reichstag delegation to go along with the formation of the new government by threatening to retire from active political life if it persisted in its obstructionist tactics. In spite of continual interference from Hindenburg and the presidential entourage, Stresemann's forceful assistance made it possible for Müller to present his "cabinet of per-sonalities" to the Reichstag on 5 July 1928. In the ensuing vote, not even the Social Democrats were able to provide Müller's government with unanimous support. It was only in April 1929, when Wirth and Stegerwald from the Ger-man Center Party joined the cabinet, that a normal coalition government came into existence. The Center had triggered the crisis that led to the reorganiza-tion of the cabinet by withdrawing Guérard from the government. Even though all the members of the new cabinet were competent and experienced parlia-mentarians, its effectiveness was limited from the very outset. This stemmed in the first place from the pressure exerted by the Bureau of the Reich President, which in a number of important matters simply presented the cabinet with one fait accompli after the next. Moreover, the fact that Germany stood before a new round of reparations negotiations as well as the still-unresolved question of how unemployment insurance was to be financed foreshadowed potentially divisive conflicts, to which must be added an anticipated industrial offensive against the entire system of binding arbitration and a deepening controversy over the construction of "battle cruiser A."

The issue of "battle cruiser A" was the first instance in which the intervention of the Reich president came close to precipitating a government crisis. The outgoing Marx government had included the first installment of the construction cost for the cruiser in its supplemental budget, but this item had met with firm opposition in the Reichsrat. Arguing that this body should not reject a national budget at a time when the Reichstag was already dissolved, Prussia had succeeded in persuading the other states to vote for a postponement in the construction of the proposed battle cruiser until the fall of 1928. Braun no doubt supported such a postponement on the assumption that the upcoming elections would so alter the composition of the Reichstag that a majority for the navy's new object of prestige could no longer be found. But in the middle of August, Groener submitted a request to the national cabinet that sought authorization for the payment of the first construction installment. In the course of doing this, he hinted that the rejection of this request would result in his resignation and, if necessary, in that of the Reich president as well. The willingness of the Social Democratic ministers in the Müller cabinet to give in on this matter left Braun deeply embittered and created a state of general malaise within the ranks of the SPD. As Carl von Ossietzky sarcastically remarked, on this occasion the Social Democrats had played the "fifth Marx government."

The program for the construction of four armed cruisers whose tonnage would not exceed the 10,000-ton limit imposed by the Versailles peace treaty but whose fighting power would be equal to that of modern fighting ships and whose radius of action was 2,000 nautical miles was purely a matter of national prestige. Groener's argument that the ships were needed to protect East Prussia in case of a Polish attack was farfetched and had been rejected even within the Reichswehr by Schleicher. Braun pointed out with a great deal of justification that these sums would be better spent on solving East Prussia's social problems. In point of fact, however, the controversy over the construction of the battle cruisers obscured the fact that Germany was now operating on the basis of a four-year armament budget—of which the naval construction program was only a part—that had been drafted with the approval of the cabinet but without parliamentary knowledge. Properly characterized as a marginal problem by Julius Leber, the conflict over "battle cruiser A" drew the public's attention away from the extensive rearmament programs and military contingency plans that had been hatched by the commanders of the Reichswehr and made it easier for them to shield the Reichswehr budget from parliamentary scrutiny. This, in turn, accounted for the equanimity with which the Social Democratic cabinet ministers prepared themselves for the impending budget debate in the Reichstag.

In this situation a fateful flaw in the chancellor's leadership ability became increasingly apparent. As long as he intended to avoid prior consultation with the SPD Reichstag delegation, he should have followed Braun's advice and postponed a discussion in the party caucus until public interest in the issue had subsided. Having taken a clear position against the construction of the proposed battle cruisers during the recent election campaign, the SPD feared with some justification that Communist propaganda would do its best to capitalize upon the SPD's sudden about-face. The cabinet decision to proceed with the construction of "battle cruiser A" had been reached by secret vote out of consideration for the embarrassing plight in which the Social Democratic members of the cabinet found themselves. Although it was clear that a cabinet vote to proceed with the program of naval construction would place the chancellor in an extremely difficult situation, the cabinet majority willingly took this risk. As expected, the SPD Reichstag delegation disavowed its hapless ministers and called for a clarification of the decision on the floor of the Reichstag. This embarrassing spectacle reached its climax when on 15 November 1928 the chancellor and other Social Democratic members of his cabinet were forced by the imposition of party discipline to leave the government bench and vote against their own government's bill. Fortunately, the bill found the necessary votes for parliamentary approval, thereby making continuation of the coalition possible.

While Schleicher was correct in his calculation that the right wing of the SPD could be persuaded to go along with an active rearmament program, his hopes that this issue would bring about a major split within the SPD failed to materialize. At the SPD's 1929 party congress in Magdeburg the moderate wing disregarded the intransigent stand of the pacifist Left and succeeded in softening the party's stance on the defense issue. But this did not lead to a qualitative improvement in relations between the SPD and the Reichswehr. After all, the Reichswehr's pursuit of illegal rearmament for the purpose of preparing the nation for war was fundamentally incompatible with the SPD's goal of making armed conflict impossible through universal disarmament. And even though Groener relaxed ties between the Reichswehr and the Stahlhelm and dissolved the western border patrols once Allied controls had been lifted, the Reichswehr's biased recruitment practices remained unchanged. Schleicher continued to wage a war of words against the Social Democratic government in Prussia and remarked to Groener in September 1928 that the "strong man of Prussia" would continue to do everything in his power "to make the chancellor's life as miserable as possible in all military questions."

Schleicher, whom Groener blindly trusted in all political questions and who, as head of the newly created ministerial office (*Ministeramt*) within the Ministry of Defense, held a key post in the leadership of the Reichswehr, had been working for a sweeping realignment of political forces in Germany for some time. As early as 1926–27 Schleicher had first broached the idea of a "Hindenburg cabinet." In this respect, he found himself in fundamental agreement with the Reich president that in the future it was essential to limit the role of parliament in the process of government formation. But while Schleicher did not believe that the Müller government would last all that long, he was concerned about the situation in Prussia and agonized over how the power of the Prussian government might be curtailed or circumvented. Yet the return to a right-wing government that would not oppose the Reichswehr's program of national rearmament presupposed the successful conclusion of the recently initiated negotiations in Paris on a new plan for the payment of reparations that would supersede the Dawes Plan. This also presupposed the creation of an effective and constructive German Right, and on this point both Schleicher and Hindenburg were in fundamental agreement that this could not be accomplished with Alfred Hugenberg.

Contrary to the expectations of the Reichswehr command and the Bureau of the Reich President, Hermann Müller's cabinet of the Great Coalition proved to be one of the most durable in the history of the Weimar Republic. This stemmed in no small measure from the fact that the negotiations over the Young Plan, for which the DNVP did not want to accept political responsibility, took longer than expected on account of differences among the Allies. But Schleicher had also failed to recognize the profound shifts that had taken place within the bourgeois party spectrum in the wake of the May 1928 Reichstag elections and that had resulted in a completely unforeseen strengthening of the faction around Hugenberg. The external impetus for this shift came from the pressure of middle-class interest groups, which in their frustration over being inadequately represented by the moderate and right-wing bourgeois parties pressured those parties into nominating candidates more attuned to their own needs or issued electoral programs of their own. The net effect of all this was to accelerate greatly the fragmentation of the existing party system.

The heavy losses the DNVP had suffered in May 1928 stemmed in no small measure from the defection of many of its traditional supporters to special-interest parties like the Reich Party of the German Middle Class (Reichspartei des deutschen Mittelstandes), the Christian-National Peasants and Farmers' Party, and the German Peasants' Party (Deutsche Bauernpartei). The DNVP's gamble in January 1927 to enter the national cabinet, in spite of its out-spoken antiparliamentary orientation, in hopes that this would enable it to hold together the divergent social and economic interests that constituted the party's material base had clearly not paid off. And with the failure of this gamble came Alfred Hugenberg's moment of opportunity. Hugenberg had stood in sharpest opposition to the DNVP party leadership ever since the beginning of 1927 and polemicized with all the means at his disposal against his party's participation in the coalition on the grounds that this represented an implicit recognition of the parliamentary system. Hugenberg's stance found widespread approval within the Pan-German League and the Stahlhelm. With the support of local chapters in the party organization that blindly obeyed his every command, Hugenberg was able to incorporate into a special reform program he presented to the party leadership in September 1927 a demand for the repeal of Article 54 of the Weimar Constitution and the principle that parliament was ultimately responsible for the formation of the national cabinet. Under the circumstances, the adoption of this program constituted nothing less than a vote of no confidence in the party leadership and a repudiation of the four Nationalist ministers who sat in the Marx cabinet.

The former director of the Krupp Steelworks had used funds from heavy industry during World War I to lay the foundation of a press concern, which he used to promote annexationist war aims and the political objectives and policies of the German Fatherland Party (Deutsche Vaterlandspartei). Even after he left Krupp, Hugenberg continued to maintain close relations with German heavy industry through his presidency of the Mining Association (Zechenverband) and the Mining Society (Bergbaulicher Verein). With the patronage of Hugo Stinnes and Albert Vögler, director of the German-Luxemburg Mining and Smelting Company (Deutsch-Luxemburgischen Bergwerks- und Hütten A.-G.), Hugenberg presided over extensive funds that were to be used in building up a comprehensive movement, or *Sammlungsbewegung*, of Germany's bourgeois Right. Hugenberg's efforts to isolate the Stresemann wing within the DVP and to effect a merger of that party with his own DNVP, however, encountered strong opposition from influential industrial circles that did not approve of the DNVP's obstructionist tactics. Stinnes soon turned away from Hugenberg to create his own press organ in the *Deutsche Allgemeine Zeitung*, which represented the perspective of the DVP's right wing. Nevertheless, the "man behind the scenes"—Hugenberg's sobriquet as late as 1926—was able to build up an extensive network of personal ties to all sorts of right-wing organizations. This network permeated the associational structure of the political Right from the Christian-social wing to *völkisch* extremists before converging in the so-called Hugenberg Concern that stood at its center. Although Hugenberg originally functioned as little more than an administrator of the funds he received from heavy industry, with the help of political friends from the old Prussian landowning elites he was able to use his press empire to further his own interests.

By no means did the ambitious Hugenberg limit himself to bringing the various organizations on the German Right, from the National Rural League to the nationalist trade-union associations, under his control. For at the same time Hugenberg was no less determined to subordinate the neoconservative Ring Movement to his influence. As cofounder of the Berlin chapter of National Club of 1919 (Nationaler Klub von 1919) and as the principal patron of Oswald Spengler and his somewhat esoteric intellectual entourage, Hugenberg had made himself indispensable to the leading advocates of the so-called New Right. His League for the Protection of Germandom on the Frontier and Abroad (Schutzbund für das Grenz- und Auslandsdeutschtum) that had originally been founded in connection with his plans for settlement in the East functioned as the organizational backbone for the intricate network of neoconservative *Gesinnungsgemeinschaften* that had constituted themselves as quasi-private "clubs" and "rings" in conscious rejection of the liberal principle of association. Hugenberg lavished particular interest on the June Club (Juni-Klub) that had been founded by Eduard Stadtler after his withdrawal from the Anti-Bolshevist League of 1919 (Anti-Bolshewisten Liga 1919) and that was dedicated to the struggle against the Versailles peace treaty at home and abroad.

With the founding of the Political College (Politischer Kollege) as a conservative alternative to the prorepublican German Institute for Politics (Deutsche Hochschule für Politik) that had been established by the followers of Friedrich Naumann, the June Club moved to the forefront of right-wing politics in the early Weimar Republic. The College, renamed the Institute for National Politics (Hochschule für nationale Politik) in 1922, was the creation of Heinrich von Gleichen, editor in chief of the club's leading organ, *Das Gewissen*, and its principal liaison to neoconservative publishing circles. Working closely with the Lutheran Seminary of Saint John (Johannesstift), the Political College originally served as a training school for the leaders of the nationalist labor unions. Hugenberg provided the funds that made it possible for the renowned Catholic historian Martin Spahn to take a leave of absence from his academic post at the University of Cologne so that he could teach at the Institute for National Politics after the Faculty of Arts and Science at Humboldt University — and not the Prussian Ministry of Culture — had rejected his appointment. Originally a Reichstag deputy for the German Center Party, Spahn had defected to the DNVP in 1921 and was considered its most important Catholic spokesman. In contrast to Gleichen's revolutionary conservatism, Spahn espoused a Wilhelmine imperialism that was close to Hugenberg's own ideological orientation. Although as an academic the nationalist historian wielded considerable intellectual influence, he devoted most of his energies at the Institute for National Politics to political pursuits, not the least of which was an articulation of the ideological assumptions that informed the Ring of German Universities (Deutscher Hochschulring), an umbrella organization for neoconservative student organizations that had sprung up at a number of different universities throughout the country.

In his efforts to attract representatives of the younger generation to his program of national concentration, Hugenberg promoted the political careers of men like Gottfried Treviranus, Hans-Erdmann von Lindeiner-Wildau, Paul Lejeune-Jung, and Hans Schlange-Schöningen, all of whom later belonged to the young-conservative opposition within the DNVP. At the same time, Hugenberg used his close ties to Germany's neoconservative intelligentsia — after the June Club dissolved itself in the wake of Moeller van den Bruck's death, Hugenberg shifted his support to the influential German Lords' Club (Deutscher Herrenklub) of Berlin, where Gleichen did his best to perpetuate the spirit of its predecessor—to free himself through literary endeavors of the stigma of being merely a businessman. From 1927 on, Hugenberg was engaged in a systematic campaign to wrest the DNVP party leadership from Westarp and Hergt and to transform the party from an organization of notables into a plebiscitarian mass movement.

In his bid for control of the DNVP, Hugenberg could put the powerful press apparatus he had built up since the last years of the First World War to good use. Not only did the Hugenberg concern publish a number of important newspapers and magazines with mass circulation, but it exercised considerable influence over the local and provincial press by controlling wire services and advertising agencies. In 1927, the Hugenberg concern acquired the Universal Film Corporation (Universum-Film Aktiengesellschaft or UFA), so that from then on the new medium of feature and documentary films was almost entirely under Hugenberg's control. Only the great liberal newspapers of Berlin, such as the *Berliner Tageblatt* and *Vossische Zeitung*, as well as the prestigious *Frankfurter Zeitung* and the *Deutsche Allgemeine Zeitung* were able to sustain themselves in the face of the increasingly effective control that the Hugenberg concern was able to exercise over the German press.

A particularly deft move in Hugenberg's bid for control of the DNVP was his decision—a decision that Westarp himself never saw through—to buy up the financially ailing party press service and combine it with his own news agency. This afforded Hugenberg an excellent opportunity to expound his own views in opposition to those of the party leadership. Within the party this strategy proved extremely effective. The preponderant position of the Hugenberg concern in the press of the Weimar Republic contributed in no small measure to the exacerbation of political tensions and to the polarization of the general political climate. Yet even so, the attempts to influence German public opinion in favor of the DNVP's own political ideas had relatively little effect on the steady stream of Germany's middle-class voters from large ideologically oriented parties like the DNVP to regional and special-interest parties and eventually to the NSDAP.

In the final analysis, it was not so much propaganda as the manipulation of party personnel through the use of funds that heavy industry had placed at his disposal that made it possible for Hugenberg to mobilize the DNVP regional organizations (*Landesverbände*) against the Reichstag delegation and the party executive committee and thus cause Westarp to step down from the party chairmanship in the summer of 1928. Westarp had failed to assure himself of the loyalty of the DNVP party apparatus. At a meeting of the DNVP Party Representation (DNVP-Parteivertretung) in October, Hugenberg was elected chairman, presumably by a margin so narrow it was never made public. Hugenberg's bid for the chairmanship had been helped by the fact that Westarp, whose base of power within the DNVP had always been the Central Association of Conservatives (Hauptverein der Konservativen), could no longer count on this faction's support because of its implacable opposition to the DNVP's recent entry into the national government. The old-line Prussian conservatives upon whom Westarp had traditionally depended were still captive to the spell of Wilhelmine ideology and emphatically demanded the restoration of the Hohenzollern monarchy. Hugenberg, on the other hand, took steps to assure himself of the support of the Stahlhelm, which under Duesterberg's leadership had just embarked upon a militantly antirepublican and extraparliamentary course.

The takeover of the DNVP by its nationalist right wing came at a heavy price. For Hugenberg's success was closely related to the collapse of the Lambach revolt within the DNVP. Walther Lambach, who functioned as a liaison between the DNVP and Germany's largest white-collar union, the German National Union of Commercial Employees (DHV), had intentionally triggered the crisis that led to Hugenberg's election by publicly questioning the DNVP's adherence to the monarchist principle. According to Lambach, the party's commitment to monarchism was directly responsible for its devastating defeat in the 1928 Reichstag election and played a major role in its inability to attract the support of the younger generation. Lambach implicitly criticized the resurgence of feudal tendencies within the DNVP, which in his opinion could only lead to the neglect of the party's social task and to a policy of empty phrases. Lambach's "self-criticism" was directed above all else against the Hugenberg wing of the party. Under Hugenberg's influence, the DNVP had turned its back on the nationalist unions to become an instrument of German heavy industry by virtue of its support for the "yellow," or *wirtschaftsfriedlich*, factory unions and their concept of the *Werkgemeinschaft*. Lambach's plea for a constructive national policy on the basis of the republican system of government found support among precisely those young conservatives who owed their political careers to Hugenberg's patronage. Committed to the principle of "Christian-social self-help," this faction—henceforth referred to as the People's Conservatives—advocated a revival of the Zentralarbeitsgemeinschaft and recognition of the trade-union principle. The People's Conservatives also endorsed a constitutional reform of the existing political system and opposed as utopian the idea propagated by Hugenberg and his entourage of a "completely new and radical reorganization of the present state system."

The protest by Lambach, who managed to remain in the party despite a concerted effort by Hugenberg and his associates to have him expelled, was only the first of a number of parallel initiatives by representatives of the younger generation within the bourgeois party spectrum that sought to bring about a fundamental reorientation of German political life in which a constructive politics based on the republican form of government would be possible. There was simply no room for such a concept in Hugenberg's DNVP. Under the motto "Bloc, not mush" (*Block, nicht Brei!*), the new party chairman sought to transform the DNVP from a loose association of notables that attracted a broader constituency only through its ties to right-wing interest groups and combat leagues into a plebiscitarian mass movement organized according to the "leadership principle." With its center of gravity in the extraparliamentary realm, the "unparliamentary party" in the country at large was to become "the conscience of the delegations working in today's parliaments." Over Westarp's determined opposition, Hugenberg proceeded to carry out a reorganization of the party that effectively subordinated the DNVP Reichstag delegation to the formal control of the party's reconstituted executive bodies.

For all his bureaucratic prowess, Hugenberg lacked political sensitivity and creativity in formulating his program. The Lambach conflict, for example, resulted in the isolation and finally the secession of the party's younger, more activist leadership cadre. An unreconstructed Wilhelmine reactionary, Hugenberg was incapable of harnessing the impulses of the conservative revolution for the purposes of the national opposition. The path along which he led the DNVP amounted to nothing more than a dogmatic frontal assault against the existing political system, including the person of Hindenburg. At no point, however, was Hugenberg able to define a vision of the "new" Germany that could have transformed the DNVP from a motley crew of right-wing outsiders into a fascist movement modeled after what Benito Mussolini, a figure much admired in DNVP circles, had created in Italy. And within two years Hugenberg was obliged to relinquish his claim to leadership of the radical opposition to the Weimar Republic to Adolf Hitler.

In the short term, the socially reactionary thrust of the DNVP's new political course under Hugenberg enjoyed the open sympathy of influential circles within the Rhenish-Westphalian industrial establishment, which under the impact of the Emergency Work Hours Law had embarked upon a policy of all-out confrontation with the socialist and Christian labor unions. The decisive role that heavy industrial interests had played in the establishment of the League for the Renewal of the Reich (Bund zur Erneuerung des Reichs) under the chairmanship of former chancellor Hans Luther made it abundantly clear that German industry believed that a general retrenchment in the area of social policy could be achieved only by means of a fundamental revision of the Weimar Constitution and the curtailment of parliamentary sovereignty. The new organization, which enjoyed close ties to the moderate wing of the DNVP and commissioned a series of studies on constitutional reform that culminated in the 1932 recommendation for a "strengthening of the leadership concept," represented only the most recent in a series of attempts to overcome the stasis of the existing party system through the nonpartisan association of an impressive number of prominent and politically influential notables. The Renewal League's plans for constitutional revision, which centered on the need to abolish the dualism between the Reich and Prussia and to dismantle the parliamentary system in the various German states, did not go far enough to satisfy Hugenberg. What the DNVP party chairman wanted was the literal implementation of the program that had been proclaimed in the Renewal League's founding appeal, namely, the "welding together [*Zusammenschweißen*] of the entire nation."

Hugenberg's rigid attitude, which led the DNVP into sterile opposition and open conflict with the Reich president, met with strong opposition in heavy industrial circles. For the most part, the leaders of Germany's industrial establishment favored the continuation of the *Bürgerblock* cabinets and hoped to use the trend toward concentration that manifested itself in the bourgeois party spectrum from 1930 on as a tool for the advancement of their own special interests. The Ruhrlade, which under the leadership of Paul Reusch coordinated the collection and allocation of political contributions from German heavy industry and which had earlier tried to support Westarp with substantial financial donations, regarded Hugenberg's election to the DNVP party chairmanship as an unmitigated defeat. Reusch rejected the Stahlhelm's proposal for a referendum on a revision of the Weimar Constitution as well as the subsequent campaign against the Young Plan as utterly hopeless and a dangerous experiment with populist methods. Unlike Hugenberg, the Ruhr industrial magnates threw their influence behind the creation of a comprehensive party alliance extending from the moderate wing of the DNVP to the DDP as a preliminary step toward the ultimate goal of strengthening the position of the Reich president.

Hugenberg's isolated initiative notwithstanding, the chances for a genuine renewal of the bourgeois party system as it existed at the end of the 1920s were extremely slim. Within the DVP, movement in this direction had been stimulated by the Reich Association of Young Populists (Reichsgemeinschaft junger Volksparteiler or RjV), an organization for representatives of the so-called younger generation that consisted primarily of white-collar employees. Working closely with Stresemann, the RjV criticized the DVP's increasingly close identification with the interests of big business on the ground that this prevented the party from developing a broad base of support within the German middle classes. But in the final analysis, the reform-minded elements within the DVP were no more successful than the People's Conservatives in the DNVP. After Stresemann's death, the party chairmanship fell to Ernst Scholz, who over the course of the preceding several years had become increasingly dependent on the DVP's industrial wing. The change in the leadership of the DVP put an end to the negotiations that the DDP national chairman Erich Koch-Weser had initiated with Stresemann shortly before the latter's death with a view toward the creation of a "bloc of national awareness" (*Block des Nationalbewußten*) and the eventual merger of the two liberal parties. But whereas the faction around Lambach seceded from the DNVP in late 1929 and helped accelerate the party's internal disintegration with the founding of the People's Conservative Association (Volkskonservative Vereinigung), Scholz was able to avoid an open split within the party. The negotiations for the creation of a parliamentary coalition among the DVP, the DDP, the People's Conservatives, and the Business Party came too late to prevent the collapse of the bourgeois center in the face of the Nazi threat.

If movements for the consolidation of the bourgeois Right ended in failure, this was no less true of parallel efforts on the bourgeois Left. These efforts received much of their impetus from the rise of a new leadership cadre throughout bourgeois associational life that sought to exercise more direct influence on the existing political system and to take a stand on behalf of Germany's beleaguered middle classes against the rising tide of industrial and agrarian interest politics. It was in the context of these developments that the Young German Order decided to shed its esoteric and elitist profile in order to gain more direct access to the parliamentary process. With the founding of the People's National Reich Association (Volksnationale Reichsvereinigung) in early 1930, the Young German Order entered into direct competition with the established bourgeois parties. When the People's National Reich Association subsequently merged with the German Democratic Party in July 1930 to found the German State Party (Deutsche Staatspartei), this represented an almost heroic attempt to rejuvenate the forces of bourgeois liberalism by infusing them with the spirit and idealism of the German youth movement. At the same time, the founding of the State Party was seen as the first step toward the concentration of the political center into a united front committed to the support of Germany's republican system.

Whatever hopes Erich Koch-Weser and Artur Mahraun may have had that this union of fundamentally disparate elements — the bündisch-corporatist ideas of the People's National Reich Association with the parliamentary and unitarian orientation of the DDP — would establish itself as the crystallization point around which not merely the People's Conservatives and the dissidents on the DVP's left wing but the rest of the DVP, the Business Party, and other bourgeois organizations would coalesce failed to materialize. On the contrary, the principal effect of the founding of the German State Party was the further weakening of the DDP, which officially merged its organization with that of the new party but whose left wing either defected to the Social Democrats or reconstituted itself as an independent political entity between the State Party and SPD. The People's National Reich Association, on the other hand, seceded from the State Party within months of its founding and retreated more and more into the bündisch milieu out of which it had emerged. In the meantime, efforts to counter the increasing fragmentation of the bourgeois middle had assumed a somewhat more modest form in the promulgation of the Hindenburg

Program as a rallying point for the DVP and the parties of the moderate Right in the campaign for the September 1930 Reichstag elections.

The realignment of the bourgeois party spectrum did not stop at the Center Party in spite of the remarkable stability of its own electorate. The referendum on the expropriation of the dynastic houses bore dramatic testimony to the increasing self-confidence and assertiveness of its working-class wing. Yet the position that this group had secured for itself in Catholic politics seemed threatened from two directions. On the one hand, the founding of the Catholic Action that Papal Nuncio Eugen Pacelli announced at the National Catholic Day (Reichs-Katholikentag) in September 1928 was designed not only to redefine the Center Party's role as the principal spokesman for Germany's Catholic population but also to terminate the independence of the People's Association for Catholic Germany (Volksverein für das Katholische Deutschland), which had long functioned as an auxiliary for the Center among Catholics throughout the country. On the other hand, the Christian labor unions now found themselves under increasingly heavy attack from the more conservative Catholic workers' associations (Arbeitervereine), which were strongly opposed to the idea of an interconfessional Christian people's party that Christian labor leader Adam Stegerwald had proposed in his famous "Essen Program" of November 1920. At the heart of all this lay both a distinct trend within the bourgeois camp away from parliamentary democracy to corporatist modes of social and political organization and — this was particularly characteristic of the final phase in the Weimar Republic's history — a return to the political confrontations that had existed at the time of the republic's founding. This was clear not only in the debate over the resurrection of the Zentralarbeitsgemeinschaft but also in Schleicher's reference to the corporatist components of the wartime economy.

At the Cologne party congress of the German Center Party in December 1928, the antipathy that the party's middle-class and civil servant constituencies felt toward the social and political ideas of Stegerwald, Joseph Joos, and Heinrich Imbusch exploded with emotional ferocity. This set the stage for a bitter defeat for Stegerwald, who was wrongly identified with the more outspoken elements on the party's left wing, and led to the election of prelate and canon law professor Ludwig Kaas to the chairmanship of the Center Party. Here, as in the DNVP, the tendency to separate leadership of the party as a whole from the chairmanship of the party's Reichstag delegation asserted itself when Kaas carefully avoided a break with the party's rebellious labor wing by choosing Stegerwald for the latter post. At the same time, Kaas moved to reassure the leaders of the Christian labor movement by dissociating himself from the one-sided confessional orientation of those who supported the Catholic Action.

As in the DNVP and DVP, the change in the chairmanship of the Center

Party signaled a clear-cut shift to the right. Kaas had repeatedly made disparaging comments about Stresemann's foreign policy, which he now considered "finished" (*erledigt*). Kaas was not merely an agent for the confessionalization of the Center but favored a resolute nationalist and authoritarian course that would break with the democratic and social traditions of German political Catholicism and foster the trend toward a revision of the Weimar Constitution in a more authoritarian direction. At the National Catholic Day at Dortmund in October 1929, Kaas declared his belief in "leadership on a grand scale" and stressed the need to make the party impregnable to the "unpredictable coincidences of changes in the parliamentary weather." The reservations that the new party chairman felt about participating in a government of the Great Coalition was reflected in the fact that his party was slow to respond to Müller's offer of a cabinet reorganization. In fact, it was not until April 1929 that the Center finally joined the national government.

When Heinrich Brüning succeeded Stegerwald as chairman of the Center Reichstag delegation, he made certain that the swing to the right extended to the party's parliamentary activities as well. From this point on, the Christian labor unions found themselves more and more isolated. The bitterness that many Catholic workers felt over the social halfheartedness of their party manifested itself in an increasing number of defections to the KPD. Nevertheless, the Center emerged from the leadership crisis of 1928 ideologically strengthened. Not only had Kaas's election identified the Center more closely with the Catholic Church, but Catholic associational life had been significantly strengthened in relationship to the party. Moreover, the Vatican had displayed an increasing tendency to abandon its role as a patron of confessional parties in favor of direct negotiations with the state governments, as, for example, in the case of the concordats that were currently under discussion with Prussia and Bavaria. All of this foreshadowed the semiparliamentary course of action that Heinrich Brüning was to follow—perhaps against his original intentions—on his appointment as chancellor in the spring of 1930.

Nowhere in the bourgeois party spectrum had the reform-minded representatives of the younger generation succeeded in gaining the upper hand. As a reaction to the increasingly heavy pressure of organized economic interests, the parties became increasingly fixed in their ideological positions and demonstrated less and less flexibility in cabinet negotiations. The long overdue rejuvenation of party leadership cadres never materialized. The various efforts at bourgeois concentration, whether in the form of an extraparliamentary bloc as envisaged by Hugenberg or by a renewal of the bourgeois center, failed to check the increasing fragmentation of the German party system. After 1930 all the parties that had at one time existed between the Center and DNVP found themselves in a state of virtually total dissolution.

The cabinet of the Great Coalition was not immediately affected by the transformations that were taking place in the bourgeois party spectrum and that represented the first step toward government by presidential decree. The frontal assault that Hugenberg had planned to institute against the existing constitutional system in the form of a referendum from the Stahlhelm remained little more than a momentary distraction. A far more serious threat to the government's position was the attack that the iron and steel industry launched against the system of compulsory state arbitration on 1 November 1928 by closing all of its plants in the Ruhr. The most serious wage conflict of the Weimar Republic did not take place unexpectedly. Management had already prepared itself for such an eventuality by establishing a special fund to which the participating firms contributed the equivalent of 2 percent of their total payroll. The showdown would have taken place in late 1927 had not a downturn in Germany's economic situation forced management to postpone the planned action until a more propitious moment.

The formation of a new coalition government under Social Democratic leadership in the summer of 1928 had the immediate consequence that heavy industry no longer felt obliged to exercise the restraint it had shown during the period of the *Bürgerblock* cabinets. Even before the current conflict erupted with the expiration of the existing wage agreement on 1 November 1928, industry had initiated negotiations with Labor Minister Rudolf Wissell on the legality of compulsory state arbitration. Even the representatives of the socialist unions were prepared to concede that the responsibility of the negotiating parties should be increased. At its Hamburg convention in 1928, the General German Trade-Union Federation (ADGB) had stressed that existing collective bargaining arrangements were not viable without movement in the direction of "economic democracy" and the full-scale involvement of organized labor in the economic decision-making process. The program that Fritz Naphtali and other trade-union theoreticians presented at Hamburg demanded that union representatives be given far-reaching control over entrepreneurial and economic decisions without, however, ever envisaging the assumption of direct responsibility for the country's economic policy.

The concept of "economic democracy" was predicated upon the assumption of uninterrupted economic growth. Drawing on Hilferding's theory of "organized capitalism," this concept represented a departure from the orthodox Marxist thesis that capitalism would inevitably collapse on account of its own internal contradictions and postulated a gradual reorganization of the private enterprise system in the direction of socialism. This would take place through an increase in the number of factories under state and union ownership, through greater state involvement in economic planning, and through the creation of institutions for economic self-administration (*wirtschaftliche Selbstverwaltung*) that would simultaneously function as instruments for the systematic transfer of the means of production from private to social control.

To be sure, Naphtali stressed the importance of improved education for the workers if economic democratization was to succeed. Still, he showed surprisingly little interest in expanding the worker's right to participate in the decision-making process within the plant itself and assigned the factory councils a clearly subordinate role relative to that of the unions in his proposals for cooperative economic planning on an industry-wide or national level. All of this Naphtali based on Article 165 of the Weimar Constitution and its provisions for a national economic council with subordinate representative entities.

Aside from the fact that there was no indication of how the program was to be implemented in the absence of a parliamentary majority willing to support it, the fundamental weakness of "economic democracy" lay in its comparatively mechanistic understanding of economic processes. It was assumed that these processes operated more or less autonomously according to their own inherent laws and that they should be subordinated to extensive union control, which at the same time would prevent the large-scale concentration of economic power. The role of the market as a controlling mechanism was generally underestimated and the possibilities of state intervention in the economic process overestimated. Its call for democratization notwithstanding, Naphtali's program contained statist and bureaucratic features and amounted to an indirect rejection of a purely parliamentary system, which was to be supplemented by corporatist structures analogous to Wichard von Moellendorf's concept of a planned economy, or *Gemeinwirtschaft*. In some respects, the program constituted a form of social and psychological compensation for the weakness the unions had displayed in the most recent wage conflicts, which they had managed to survive only with the help of state arbitration.

It was not just the ambivalence of the trade-union program but the very notion of an expanded role for the unions in the economic decision-making process that led Germany's employer associations to view it as a dangerous challenge requiring a vigorous propaganda response. For industry it was a matter of rolling back the influence of the unions, softening up the system of collective bargaining, and limiting the conduct of wage negotiations to the plant level. Only then would it be possible to resuscitate the factory unions (*Werkgemeinschaften*) that industry had abandoned in 1918 and in which it had paid a relatively high share of the social benefits. Only then would industry be able to force the employees of a given plant to accept wage cuts by threatening that plant's economic survival. In principle, industry was struggling for the "restoration of its freedom of contract [*Vertragsfreiheit*]," which it equated with an end to state intervention in the collective bargaining process and the abolition of the existing system of compulsory arbitration.

From the Reich labor minister management demanded the elimination of the legally binding character of all arbitration awards as well as the "depoliticization of arbitration," by which it meant the exclusion of the Labor Ministry from arbitration deliberations. Compulsory state arbitration was to be reserved for cases in which there was a direct threat to the "livelihood of the population as a whole" and not for the mere settlement of labor disputes. For his own part, Wissell rejected these demands on the grounds that a change in existing arbitration procedures could take place only through a parliamentary vote, although he did agree to devote particular attention to the concerns of the west German steel industry about cost-effectiveness and profitability in the next round of arbitration negotiations.

In spite of all this, the Northwestern Group of the Association of German Iron and Steel Industrialists proceeded to circumvent the arbitration decision that was scheduled for publication in the second half of October 1928 by notifying its workers that their employment was to be terminated as of 1 November. Although the Ministry of Labor declared that its decision was legally binding and in spite of the fact that the unions felt compelled to accept it even though the wage increases it awarded were minimal, the Northwestern Group considered it illegal and immediately instituted a massive lockout. In light of the extremely modest supplemental costs the decision imposed on industry, this action could only be interpreted as an act of intentional noncompliance with government arbitration procedures and as an attack against the labor unions, which immediately took legal recourse. The fact that various labor courts that dealt with the matter offered differing and sometimes conflicting opinions constituted a defeat for the Ministry of Labor insofar as the original arbitration award it had confirmed had been nullified on procedural grounds.

Aside from the complicated legal issues in which management had achieved at best a Phyrric victory, the political dimensions of the conflict worked almost entirely to the disadvantage of the entrepreneurs. The lockout of 260,000 workers, 160,000 of whom received no maintenance payments from a union, even before court decisions on the legality of the arbitration award had been rendered was considered highly unfair by large segments of the population. In addition, the strategy of the Northwestern Group represented a clear slap in the face to the labor minister, particularly after he had indicated his willingness to make allowances for the marketing difficulties that faced the steel industry. Wage costs, to be sure, were only a small part of these problems, which had more to do with the fact that the industry was now selling a greater share of its product in international markets where prices were still low. Since the workers who had been kept from working were ineligible for benefits from the National Agency for Job Placement and Unemployment Insurance—by law the agency had to remain neutral in all wage conflicts—the Social Democrats and Center Party submitted a bill to the Reichstag for a change in the law that would have authorized retroactive payments to those who had not been covered. The bourgeois middle parties were able to forestall the introduction of this bill on the floor of the Reichstag only by promising to make funds for unemployment relief available to local communities to be administered without going through normal bureaucratic channels.

With the approval of a majority in the Prussian Landtag that included the DVP, Prussian Welfare Minister Heinrich Hirtsiefer instituted immediate relief for the workers who had been locked out without requiring repayment or proof of need and without deducting the support payments they had received from their unions. The social hardships that had been caused by the prolonged lockout had also had a negative effect upon small business. In the final analysis, the near unanimity of German public opinion forced the parties to ignore the objections of the employers' associations, which argued rather unconvincingly that the sum total of the support payments the unemployed workers had received from different sources exceeded what they would have normally earned. Even the National Federation of German Industry, which had not been consulted by the Northwestern Group before it initiated the lockout, was reluctant to take a public stand against the support payments. As a result, heavy industry suddenly found itself politically isolated.

Even though the immediate cause of the conflict was clearly related to the ongoing struggle over wage policies, there could be no doubt that the leaders of German industry in the west had hoped that the lockout would accomplish the twofold aim of rolling back the existing system of compulsory state arbitration and weakening the socialist and Christian labor unions, whose ties to the various bourgeois parties were a source of suspicion to both the Northwestern Group and the Mining Association. The same goal also lay at the heart of industry's plans for a new wage offensive in the Ruhr mines, which had been postponed in 1929 so that the mineowners could take advantage of favorable market conditions that had been created by the British miners' general strike of 1926. That the Northwestern Group finally agreed under increasingly heavy pressure from German public opinion to arbitration by the Reich minister of the interior, Carl Severing, meant that it had lost its bid for a definitive victory over the concept of the social state. As a representative of the Ruhrlade, Paul Reusch had strongly opposed any concessions to the unions. But the instigators of the lockout could no longer count on the support of the leading employer associations and backed down at the urging of the DVP cabinet officers — whom Albert Vögler had won over to a political solution to the conflict — because the potential risks and the danger of eventual state intervention were simply too great. The employers had, however, succeeded in circumventing the arbitration of the one person who was legally authorized to act in this function, namely Labor Minister Wissell.

The conflict that soon came to be known as the "Ruhr Iron Conflict" had far-reaching political consequences. Since management had failed to force the unions to accept "free" wage settlements, the industrial leadership of the Rhine-Ruhr basin intensified its fight for a "free economy" by extraparliamentary means. The fact that even the DVP could ignore the pressure of its right wing and vote in favor of support for workers who had lost their jobs as a result of the lockout only increased the fundamental doubts of German heavy industry in the possibility of a satisfactory parliamentary response to its demands that business be freed from excessive social costs and the fetters of collective bargaining. From this perspective, it appeared obvious that this issue should be addressed in the next round of reparations negotiations and that Germany's approval of the new commitments that this would certainly entail should be made contingent upon the adoption of a "domestic Young Plan" and the exclusive use of any financial savings that might result for the relief of German industry.

For the time being, the challenge that the Ruhr Iron Dispute posed to the national government produced a consolidation of the governing coalition, since the Center Party had been forced to the side of the SPD. On the other hand, it was only a matter of time until the profound differences that separated the DVP and SPD on the tax and fiscal reform that would have to be enacted in order to deal with the growing deficit in the national budget and the inadequately funded state unemployment insurance system led to a rupture in the governing coalition. For the moment, however, Germany's industrial elite was interested in postponing a major overhaul of the national government until after the conclusion of the negotiations on a revision of the Dawes Plan so that, as Ludwig Kastl, the general secretary of the National Federation of German Industry, expressed it, the Social Democrats "would not be allowed to avoid responsibility for the Young Plan and the reform program" that would bring industry the relief it so desperately needed.

The Great Coalition's period of grace would unceremoniously end as soon as the ratification of the Young Plan had deprived it of its raison d'être in foreign affairs. In the meantime, the republic had succeeded in defending itself against the assault of the extraparliamentary forces since the early summer of 1928. The Stahlhelm's petition for a referendum on the revision of the existing constitutional system as well as the NSDAP's monotonous tirades against the parliamentary system were essentially neutralized by the restraints rooted in the connection between financial reform and a revision of Germany's reparations burden. In the fall of 1929 it remained an open question as to whether there was still sufficient time for a regeneration of the bourgeois party spectrum. It soon became clear, however, that most of the moderate bourgeois parties, including the Center, had fallen under the control of those forces that were most strongly opposed to collaboration with the SPD and organized labor and sought, insofar as they had not already inscribed the call for a *völkisch* dictatorship on their political banner, to transform the parliamentary system into a presidential regime. Encouraged by the Reichswehr command, the Stahl-helm, and the newly formed "Green Front," pressure on the Reich president to hand governmental responsibility over to the representatives of the "national Germany" continued to mount.

CHAPTER EIGHT

Dissolution of the Parliamentary System

GERMANY had already taken the first fateful steps toward a rejection of parliamentary government before the disastrous effects of the world economic crisis were first felt. The deterioration of Germany's domestic economy could be seen as early as the spring of 1929 in the contraction of foreign credit from abroad and a decline in tax revenues at home. Although the New York stock market crash of October 1929 did not come as a complete surprise, no one expected that it would trigger a major economic recession. Industry and the banks, however, were quick to take advantage of this development by intensifying pressure on the cabinet to lower taxes as a way of alleviating the acute domestic capital shortage. The prospect of lower reparations payments only intensified this pressure further.

Originally the German government had wanted to postpone negotiations on a new reparations agreement so that it might concentrate instead on negotiating an early evacuation of the Rhineland. This option was based on the assumption that no change in the U.S. attitude on the repayment of interallied debts, to which the reparations question was closely tied both objectively and subjectively, was likely before the 1928 presidential elections. At the same time, the German government also believed that if negotiations took place at a later point in time, Germany's economic situation would not appear as strong as it currently was in light of the continued decline in the influx of foreign capital, which had totaled approximately 20 billion marks since 1924. On the other hand, the anticipated budget deficit for 1928 spoke in favor of revising the Dawes Plan as soon as possible since a reduction in the amount of Germany's annual reparations payments would improve the Reich's financial situation.

The impulse for reopening the reparations question came initially from Park Gilbert and only secondarily from Reichsbank President Hjalmar Schacht. The two men pursued fundamentally different aims in spite of a common thrust their efforts seemed to share on the surface. Gilbert had become increasingly concerned over the fact that 54 percent of the foreign loans Germany currently received were being used for expenditures in the public sector and that this tended to encourage government wastefulness, particularly at the municipal and state level, where unproductive investments were frequently being financed with foreign loans. Gilbert feared that this endangered Germany's ability to raise the sums of money necessary to meet its annual reparations obligations under the terms of the Dawes Plan as well as the modalities of their transfer. In view of the Reich's chronically negative trade balance, Gilbert had been obliged to cover the transfer payments out of the Reichsbank's substantial foreign currency reserves even though export revenues remained negligible. That this "artificial transfer" could not be continued indefinitely was something of which both he and the American banks, which were anxious to secure their investments, were fully aware. The only alternative, which the Reichsbank president temporarily sought to implement, lay in an immediate halt to all transfer payments. This, however, would have given rise to widespread doubts about Germany's ability to meet its fiscal obligations, which, in turn, would not only have made it difficult for Germany to secure new loans on the international capital market but would also have led to the withdrawal of short-term foreign credits.

Gilbert explicitly warned against the idea that Schacht had thrown into the discussion of trying to accelerate the pace of developments by deliberately creating a transfer crisis. The cabinet ministers involved in this problem also realized that an end to the influx of foreign loans would cause severe economic dislocation and dramatically reduce the German standard of living. The Reichsbank president's argument that by not acting now the crisis would only be postponed for two years and would eventually erupt under much less favorable circumstances was rejected by Hilferding as irresponsible *Katastrophenpolitik*. For Schacht this argument was primarily a tactical ploy by which he hoped to induce Gilbert into reducing the amounts of Germany's transfer payments. Privately the Reichsbank president admitted that the normal annual payments provided for under the terms of the Dawes Plan could be made "without further ceremony" (*ohne weiteres*). At the same time, he conceded to Stresemann, who agreed with him, that the real issue that Germany had to address in the next round of international negotiations was not so much the reduction of its reparations payments as the "reacquisition of Germany's freedom of movement in international affairs."

Acting on the assumption that increased indebtedness to foreign investors limited the Reich's ability to act in foreign affairs, Schacht had been trying for some time to slow down the influx of foreign loans by manipulating the discount rate and simultaneously imposing restrictions on the use of credit. This initiative failed in part because of the resistance of the American banks but also because the Reichsbank continued to permit the influx of short-term loans at the same time that it took measures to limit the influx of long-term loans. To be sure, the enormous inflow of foreign capital reflected the confidence of American investors in the German economy. But the main cause was the difference in interest levels between the United States and Germany, which, aside from the German deficit in productive balances, stemmed last but not least from the fact that part of the liquidity resulting from the international loans was immediately consumed in the transfer of reparations payments. The discrepancy between the demand for credit and domestic credit formation, which was generally cited as proof of Germany's acute capital shortage, increased even further after 1928 when the United States adopted a policy of high interest rates, whereas at the same time the Reichsbank maintained its inflated discount rates to prevent the flight of foreign capital and permitted domestic investments to decline even further. With long-term foreign indebtedness at 5.5 billion marks and short-term debts in the amount of 7.6 billion marks, the German economy found itself in an extremely precarious situation at the end of the economic upswing of 1927–28.

Under these circumstances, the proposal by the reparations agent that Germany's reparations obligations be determined once and for all and that the transfer protection clause of the Dawes Plan be dropped met with the approval of France, which was interested in the immediate conversion of German reparations payments into commercial obligations so that it could use them to finance the repayment of its debts to the United States under the terms of the Mellon-Berenger Agreement of 1926. Given the state of French public opinion, there was no way any responsible French politician could have committed France to obligations with respect to the United States and England that exceeded German reparations payments to France. At the same time, however, France was obliged to ratify the treaty and make substantial supplemental payments to Washington by the end of 1929. Poincaré was willing to consider concessions on the withdrawal of Allied troops from the Rhineland in order to obtain a German guarantee for payments in the amount of the French war debt. Stresemann was quick to exploit this link by bringing up the reparations question at the September session of the League of Nations. The six powers agreed to start immediate negotiations on the situation in the Rhineland and a final settlement of the reparations problem.

In assembling a German delegation for the meeting of experts that was to take place in Paris in February 1929, Stresemann spoke of the need for the various German parties to unite in a "community of responsibility" (*Verantwortungsgemeinschaft*) and paid particular attention to the forces of the so-called national opposition. This accounted for the fact that in addition to Schacht, who was an ex-officio member of the German delegation by virtue of his presidency of the Reichsbank, Stresemann also appointed Albert Vögler, by now chairman of the board of directors of the United Steelworks (Vereinigte Stahlwerke A.-G.), as one of the delegation's special experts, with Ludwig Kastl of the National Federation of German Industry and the Hamburg banker Carl Melchior as deputies. When Paul Silverberg protested against the choice of Melchior, Stresemann replied that "against what will no doubt be the strong opposition of Hugenberg, we must erect a bulwark of personalities that can withstand the assault of Hugenberg's press." As far as Schacht and Vögler were concerned, this expectation was not fulfilled.

Stresemann, who was already seriously ill at the time, and Chancellor Müller overestimated the loyalty of the president of the Reichsbank. In order not to jeopardize the delegation's formal status as a commission of experts, they were reluctant to limit its initiative with precise instructions. Schacht harbored the misconception that in exchange for the protection that Germany had received under the transfer clause of the Dawes Plan and for converting a part of the annual reparations payments into commercial obligations he would be able to secure far-reaching political concessions in the direction of a revision of important points of the Versailles treaty. Under the pretext of securing the productive capacity of the German economy, Schacht demanded not only a "guaranteed source of raw materials from overseas"—in short, a demand for the return of the German colonies and "the reconstruction of German agriculture through the return of the [Polish] corridor"—but also a guaranteed market for German exports. Although the government warned Schacht and Vögler against pushing these "secondary points" into the foreground, Schacht tied them to the offer of annual German payments in the amount of 1,650 million marks, of which only 450 million would be unprotected by a transfer clause similar to that in the Dawes Plan while the remaining amount would be protected in one way or another.

Schacht seems to have believed that this proposal would receive American support. But the American negotiators were by no means prepared to overload the financial transactions with political demands of this nature and proved remarkably conciliatory in an effort to prevent an open confrontation with Schacht. Even the wide gap that separated the German and Allied positions on the issue of annual reparations payments threatened to scuttle the conference. That, however, had little effect on the German delegation. The Reichsbank president, supported in this respect by Vögler, was obviously determined to see the proposed agreement fall on its face and return to the terms of the Dawes Plan. When Schacht suggested the possibility of a halt to all transfers, the French immediately interpreted this as a deliberate attempt to sabotage the negotiations. In Paris the French finance minister, Emile Moreau, remarked that Schacht's position was undermining German credit. A few days later, there was a massive flight of foreign currency from Germany. This was precisely what the Reichsbank president had tried in vain to prevent with his restrictive credit policy. These withdrawals, however, were not prompted by the intervention of the Banque de France, as the German press claimed, but rather by a reversal in the interest rate differential between Berlin and New York. Once again, it became abundantly clear that Germany's financial dependence upon the international capital market did not permit unilateral initiatives in the area of reparations policy.

At this point the German government felt compelled to intervene. Until then it had not become involved in the activities of the German delegation at Paris in spite of mounting criticism at home and abroad of Schacht's conduct. Schacht, who now asked for instructions after having earlier insisted on his independence as an expert, was told to sign the compromise prepared by Owen Young. At the urging of the National Federation of German Industry, Vögler promptly resigned from the delegation, whereas Kastl withstood the enormous pressure to which he was being subject and eventually agreed to sign the document. In sharp contrast to the claims he would later make, Schacht argued at a convention of the German Chamber of Industry and Commerce (Deutscher Industrie- und Handelstag) at the end of June 1929 that, in view of the incalculable financial damage that might otherwise ensue, Germany had no choice but to accept the "New Plan."

The payment plan that now bore the name of the American delegate Owen Young was generally denounced in Germany as unsatisfactory, although Hilferding had predicted obligations of a similar magnitude. The deadline for a settlement of the reparations problem stood firm from the very outset, since for psychological reasons it was impossible to exceed the time frame that currently existed for the repayment of interallied debts to the United States. At the same time, it was in Germany's interest to reduce the size of its annual payments by amortizing them over a longer period of time. The plan stipulated that for thirty-seven years the German Reich was to make payments averaging 2.05 billion marks, including the liquidation of the Dawes loan with interest. For an additional twenty-two years—that is, until 1987–88—annual payments of almost 2 billion Reichsmark were to be made. Transfer protection, on the other hand, was by and large eliminated. In the event of a severe economic depression, however, Germany could apply for a two-year delay in payments. In return, Germany could point to the abolition of the institution of the reparations agent, the restoration of national management of the railroad, and the suspension of international administrative oversight of the Reichsbank, which had never been particularly successful in the first place. Germany thus regained complete sovereignty over its national finances. Moreover, the initial annual payments of 1.7 billion marks were to be increased gradually before reaching the final level stipulated in the Young Plan. For the moment, this afforded, in comparison to the Dawes Plan, substantial relief—though by no means to the degree for which most Germans had hoped—for the ailing national budget.

The adoption of the Young Plan by the experts' commission, however, did not put an end to bitter fights both at home and abroad over the reparations question. At the First Hague Conference in August 1929 Stresemann, who was making his last appearance in an international forum, did his best to secure a promise for the early evacuation of the Rhineland from Aristide Briand, who finally agreed to a deadline of 30 July 1930. It was not this issue, however, but rather the rivalries between Great Britain and France over the formula for the distribution of reparations payments and each country's share of those payments no longer protected by the transfer clause that threatened to bring the conference to an end. Once again Stresemann was able, albeit by means of relatively minor financial concessions, to forge a compromise between the two Allied powers. All in all, the negotiations of The Hague represented a major success for Germany. The evacuation of the third occupation zone in the Rhineland thus began five years earlier than provided for in the Versailles peace treaty. All restrictions on German sovereignty had been eliminated.

Nevertheless Schacht took immediate advantage of the relatively minor concessions that Stresemann had to make to the Allies in order to prevent the conference from falling apart as the pretext for publicly dissociating himself from the Young Plan and for resigning from the German delegation in what amounted to a major political sensation. In the background of these developments stood the initiative of Hugenberg, who together with Hitler and the Stahlhelm's Theodor Duesterberg had begun to make preparations for a national referendum against the Young Plan. Schacht's memorandum from December 1929 stated that the Reichsbank would not participate in the proposed Bank for International Balance of Payments (Bank für Internationalen Zahlungsausgleich) if Germany's terms of payment under the new plan became less favorable. International opinion interpreted this as a last-moment attempt to sabotage the agreement that had been reached by the Hague Conference. In point of fact, Schacht was primarily interested in avoiding any personal responsibility for the new reparations plan. On 23 January 1930 the German government accepted the final protocol of the Second Hague Conference. For budgetary considerations alone, Germany was no longer in a position to dissociate itself from the results of the conference. Not only was Schacht politically isolated after his interference in the budgetary process that made the tax cuts for which everyone had hoped impossible, but this left Hindenburg with no alternative but to accept his resignation from the Reichsbank in March 1930, a move that was supposed to bring about the collapse of the Müller cabinet and initiate a reorganization of the national government. The president of the Reichsbank was obviously counting on a severe transfer and financial crisis for which he did not want to be held publicly accountable.

Whereas the nationalist Right bitterly attacked the Young Plan as proof of Germany's continued economic enslavement, in reality the plan had virtually united the European powers into a debtors' front against the United States, whose rigid insistence on the repayment of the interallied war debt had contributed in no small measure to the psychologically acceptable connection between reparations and the liquidation of the interallied war debt. This, in turn, helped foster the impression that the reduction, if not the cancellation, of Germany's reparations obligations was only a matter of time. The participating financial experts all assumed that once the United States had canceled the interallied war debt a reduction of Germany's reparations payments would soon follow. With the adoption of the Young Plan the connection between reparations and the Versailles peace treaty had been definitively severed. A return to the demands of the London Ultimatum of 1921 was therefore out of the question.

To be sure, abandoning the protection of the transfer clause of the Dawes Plan represented a major concession. In point of fact, it was precisely Schacht's tactics that led the Allies to deprive Germany of the principal instrument with which it could impede the commercialization of its reparations obligations and thus bring the delicate mechanism of international debt-management out of balance. It was also detrimental from the German point of view that the new payment plan fixed the gold parity of the Reichsmark. In the context of declining prices as a result of the world economic crisis, this translated into an increase in the real value of the reparations payments. For all of that, however, the plan, which in 1929 encumbered 3.5 percent of the German national income for the payment of reparations, represented a major step forward. It is difficult to see why Schacht could say Germany would "sink in the next thirty to fifty years to the level of an American labor province [Arbeitsprovinz]" if the reparations burden remained intact.

Whoever hoped that the conclusion of the reparations negotiations would bring with it a relaxation of domestic political tensions could only have been sorely disappointed. As it became increasingly evident that the Young Plan legislation could no longer be blocked for fear of the severe economic repercussions this would almost certainly have, interest groups with close ties to the German People's Party moved quickly to exchange their support of the Young Plan for some fundamental commitments in the area of social and fiscal policy. In doing so, they made use of the somewhat spurious argument that a comprehensive budgetary reform was necessary to correct the political weakness that had forced the Reich to make concessions at The Hague. It was only through the adoption of an "internal" Young Plan that Germany could overcome the "external" Young Plan that had been imposed upon the Reich. Therein lay a certain analogy to the myth that the external defeat of November 1918 could somehow be rectified by a new upsurge in national feeling. Behind this sort of nationalist cant stood concrete material interests intent upon dismantling the social and political compromises on which the founding of the Weimar Republic had been based. The fact is that the end to transfer protection exposed the German currency to new instabilities should it prove impossible for Germany to cover the annual payments and interest obligations that were due under the terms of the Young Plan out of genuine tax surpluses.

The Great Coalition cabinet of Hermann Müller, beleaguered as it was by all sorts of internal conflicts, proved unequal to the task of producing a balanced budget. For all intents and purposes, its internal cohesiveness was thoroughly exhausted after the first Hague Conference. The budget proposal for the 1929 fiscal year that Social Democratic Finance Minister Rudolf Hilferding submitted after laborious negotiations with the individual parties fell apart in the cross fire of special-interest groups even though it came close to meeting the expectations of the DVP and its industrial backers. It was only through Stresemann's personal intervention that a provisional compromise on the budget was finally reached. This compromise, which delayed action aimed at balancing the budget, was accepted only because the fall of the government during the current round of reparations negotiations had to be avoided at all costs.

Hilferding was unusually well versed in matters of financial policy, but he lacked the ability to accomplish his political objectives, particularly when it came to dealing with the left wing of his own party. The central controversy focused on the use of the surplus revenue that was anticipated from the temporary reduction in Germany's annual reparations payments. The National Federation of German Industry moved quickly to draft a detailed memorandum on German financial and economic policy entitled *Aufstieg oder Niedergang*, in which it demanded immediate relief for the German business community and protested vehemently against plans to use the savings from the Young Plan to cover the existing budget deficit. Under increasingly heavy pressure from its own industrial wing, the DVP balked against going along with an otherwise perfectly acceptable compromise by Labor Minister Rudolf Wissell on government subsidies to the national unemployment insurance fund. Stresemann spent the last hours of his life locked in conflict with the DVP's right wing to make certain that his party would not bolt the existing governmental coalition. His death on 3 October 1929 marked not only the end of an era in foreign politics but also the definitive defeat of those forces within the DVP that were disposed to accommodation instead of confrontation.

Declining tax revenues left Hilferding with no other choice but to maintain the liquidity of the government finances through short- and medium-term borrowing. This expedient, however, encountered strong opposition from the president of the Reichsbank, who frustrated all attempts to arrange international loans. In this respect, Schacht received ill-advised support from Parker Gilbert, who refused to approve the Kroeger loan that the finance minister had negotiated on his own initiative or similar credit arrangements with the Dillon and Reed banking house. Not only did Gilbert fail to appreciate the increasingly desperate state of the German budget but he felt that these loans would jeopardize financing for a new reparations loan. Schacht knew perfectly well that unless the government borrowed money, it would not be able to pay the civil servants' salaries. He used the independence of the Reichsbank to force the cabinet and the Reichstag to pass a law for the retirement of the public debt that had the practical effect of mandating the use of all future savings in reparations for the liquidation of Germany's national debt.

His recent conduct at the Hague Conference notwithstanding, Schacht continued to stand as a symbol of Germany's creditworthiness. This image, as well as his influence in Germany's largest banks and the leading industrial interest organizations, enabled him to exert a persistent influence on the financial policies of the national cabinet. In the German public there were rumors that someone was about to establish a financial dictatorship over which the parliament would have no control. Not even the DVP shied away from the suggestion that the reparations agent, who did little to discourage speculation of this sort, be replaced by an independent command for financial affairs, which, among other things, would have usurped the parliament's control over the budget. This was simply a new variant of the demand for an economic dictator that had been raised with regularity since the middle of the 1920s.

Under this sort of pressure, the financial program submitted by Hilferding and his state secretary Johannes Popitz in early December 1929 was rejected in spite of the fact that it actually went quite far in accommodating the DVP with the promise of an early tax reform that featured not only relief for property taxes and a reduction in income taxes but a heavier tax burden for the broad masses of the German people. As in the past, all that one could get through the Reichstag was an interim financial program that authorized numerous budget cuts, particularly in the area of social insurance. Frustrated by the fate of their program, Hilferding and Popitz promptly resigned. It would not be long before Paul Moldenhauer, who now assumed the helm at the Ministry of Finance, would find himself confronted with a similar constellation of forces. For the moment, however, the survival of the cabinet had been secured.

The attempt to force the cabinet into undertaking a fundamental reorientation of German financial policy prior to the enactment of the Young Plan laws had failed for the time being. In large part, the contradictory strategies of the bourgeois Right had contributed to this outcome. When Hugenberg led the DNVP down the path of uncompromising obstructionism, he cut across the pressure tactics of Schacht, whose primary goal was to reduce the Reich's financial dependence upon the Western powers, whereas the DNVP leader thought in terms of nothing less than the complete overthrow of the existing parliamentary system. Under these circumstances, the political Right now availed itself of a tactic that had previously been reserved for the use of the German Left, namely, the enactment of legislation through popular plebiscite. When in early 1929 the leaders of the Stahlhelm debated initiating a petition for a referendum on the "prerogatives of the Reich president," this was an attempt to repeal Article 54 of the Weimar Constitution and with it the principle of parliamentary responsibility for the formation of the cabinet. This proposal, which would have enabled Hindenburg to appoint a cabinet of his own liking, seemed somewhat adventurous even though Hindenburg's state secretary in the Bureau of the Reich President, Otto Meißner, let it be known that the Reich president was fundamentally in favor of it. Formulated by the Stahlhelm ideologue Heinz Brauweiler and approved by the DNVP party chairman Alfred Hugenberg, the plan was symptomatic of the distance that had come to separate the conduct of parliamentary business from the actual needs and longings of large segments of the German population. Stresemann, who remained firmly committed to the principle of parliamentary government, refused to let the DVP take part in the efforts at constitutional revision through popular plebiscite. But even within the DNVP and the National Rural League, the Stahlhelm's proposed referendum evoked little enthusiasm in spite of the fact that it would have given the Reich president the right to veto the parliament's approval of the Young Plan. Hitler, on the other hand, simply ridiculed the whole project as overly academic.

Duesterberg, however, remained firmly committed to the "creation of a great national front" (*Schaffung der großen nationalen Front*) through a popular referendum in the hope that this would pave the way for the formation of a new government of the German Right. While revision of the constitution may not have been an altogether appropriate goal of such a referendum, the struggle against the Young Plan could not have been better suited for this sort of action. Moreover, the leaders of the Stahlhelm believed that Hindenburg could be persuaded to repeal the Young Plan legislation either on his own initiative or on the grounds that the plan had been rejected first by a third of the deputies in the Reichstag and then in a subsequent referendum. But the Reich president, for all his sympathy with the efforts of those who sought to strengthen his constitutional position, was unwilling to run a risk of this magnitude. Under these circumstances, it was not difficult for Hugenberg to give the Stahlhelm initiative a somewhat different thrust and to fashion not only a referendum against the Young Plan but also a law that would be enacted by popular referendum against the hated "war-guilt lie." The decisive strategic difference between this and the Stahlhelm's action was that Hugenberg showed no reluctance whatsoever in attacking the president himself. There was also a constructive dimension to the Stahlhelm initiative in that it would have culminated in the formation of a new Hindenburg cabinet invested with the mantle of plebiscitary legitimacy. Hugenberg's action, on the other hand, aimed at the complete destruction of the existing constitutional system, although his own concept of the "national dictatorship" that was supposed to replace it, aside from the fact that he himself was supposed to lead it, remained characteristically vague.

The National Committee for the German Referendum (Reichsausschuß für das Deutsche Volksbegehren) that Hugenberg established on 9 July 1929 aimed at the creation of a national counterparliament. In terms of its basic form, the National Referendum Committee was a nonpartisan institution sponsored by the Stahlhelm, the Pan-German League, the National Rural League, and the United Patriotic Leagues. In point of fact, however, the initiative rested on a tactical alliance among the DNVP, the Christian-National Peasants and Farmers' Party, and the NSDAP. The last of these decided only after considerable hesitation to use this as an opportunity to gain a wider audience for its propaganda but stipulated from the very outset that its participation in the project would be limited to the time frame of the referendum itself. Such a stipulation undercut the broader purposes of the National Referendum Committee, which was to create a movement of national concentration that embraced all of the parties and organizations on the German Right. Over the misgivings of his more moderate conservative partners, Hugenberg proceeded to commit the movement to a radical obstructionist course from which he could no longer deviate on account of pressure from the NSDAP, which was admittedly pursuing its own objectives. The demagogic character of the crusade against the Young Plan, however, went back to Hugenberg's initiative.

The draft of the Law against the Enslavement of the German People that Hugenberg circulated among his closest supporters in the late summer of 1929 and finally published in September called on the national government to renounce without delay the "war-guilt clause" of the Versailles peace treaty, to demand the end of the occupation of German territory, and to reject any new burdens or obligations, but in particular those connected with the Young Plan. Moreover, Article 4 of the so-called Freedom Law threatened those cabinet members or their authorized deputies who did not comply with these demands with imprisonment for high treason. In its original version, the Reich president was explicitly included among those who were subject to such a threat, no doubt on the assumption that this would force him to repeal the Young Plan laws that were expected to work their way through the Reichstag in September and thereby give the proposed plebiscite a chance of success. The vilification of Hindenburg as a potential traitor, however, encountered strong opposition from the National Rural League, the Stahlhelm, and the Westarp wing of the DNVP. As a result, Hugenberg found himself obliged to moderate the language of the already published draft by exempting the Reich president from the clause providing for sanctions against those responsible for the ratification and implementation of the Young Plan. This, however, did little to alter the fact that Hindenburg, outraged by Hugenberg's intransigence, viewed the campaign against the Young Plan as an attack on his personal integrity. Although he was ambivalent about the Young Plan itself and avoided coming out in support of the national cabinet, Hindenburg regarded the action of the extreme Right as a dereliction of patriotic duty and felt that his closest ideological allies had suddenly deserted him.

The threat of sanctions against those government officials who were held responsible for the enactment of the Young Plan was taken from the propaganda arsenal of the Pan-German League and equated the German foreign policy throughout the entire history of the republic with high treason. This encountered opposition on all sides, prompted the Young German Order into speaking out against the referendum, moved heavy industry to withdraw its financial support from the project, and provoked strong protest even among the leaders of the nationalist Free Corps. But the NSDAP was quite forceful in making the retention of this clause a condition of its own participation in the referendum campaign. Hugenberg was therefore compelled to leave Article 4 in the text of the proposed freedom law, albeit in a somewhat attenuated form. This, however, only intensified the criticism of Hugenberg's obstructionist tactics both within his own DNVP and from other right-wing organizations. To be sure, the People's Conservatives decided once again to postpone their planned secession from the DNVP, while Count Westarp was doing his best to keep the deepening party crisis within acceptable limits. At no time, however, could one discern the slightest sign that a comprehensive national *Sammlungsbewegung* was about to take shape. In the parliamentary debate on the Freedom Law, which ended with its rejection by an overwhelming majority, Hugenberg suffered a severe defeat. In the voting on the controversial Article 4 the unity of the DNVP Reichstag delegation fell completely apart. Count Westarp promptly resigned as the delegation's chairman after having heretofore resisted Hugenberg's efforts to encroach upon the prerogatives of his office. Twelve Nationalist deputies, including G. R. Treviranus and Walther Lambach, left the party.

Only for tactical considerations did the leaders of the National Rural League remain in the National Referendum Committee. After the negative outcome of the referendum they, like the NSDAP, discretely dissociated themselves from the organization. Under these circumstances, Hugenberg's dream of a wave of plebiscitary actions that would eventually transform itself into an all-embracing movement of national mobilization was no longer plausible. At the same time, the normally more than adequate financial resources of the right-wing opposition began to dry up as well. Nevertheless, Hugenberg poured all the resources at his disposal into the campaign against the "Paris Tribute Plan," flooding the public with pamphlets and brochures that reviled the existing political system with biting sarcasm and painted a totally distorted picture of the Young Plan negotiations. Once again he took aim at the person of Hindenburg, who bitterly repudiated all allegations. At the same time, the NSDAP tested for the first time its new propaganda apparatus and pulled out all the stops in the struggle for the Freedom Law, which it portrayed, much to Hugenberg's dismay, as a purely National Socialist action.

Contrary to the expectations of most observers, 10.02 percent of Germany's eligible voters attached their signatures to the referendum petition, thereby meeting the quorum mandated by the Weimar Constitution but only by the scantiest of margins. Yet in the referendum that took place on 22 December 1929 only 5.8 million voters — a figure considerably smaller than what the right-wing parties had received in the last Reichstag elections — voted for the proposed Freedom Law, which required 21 million votes to take effect. The indirect support of Hjalmar Schacht, who now publicly denounced the Young Plan on the farfetched grounds that its "intents and conditions" were being disregarded by the government, could do nothing to change the outcome. The national government decided not to take legal action against the referendum and plebiscite in spite of the fact that the Freedom Law would have interfered with the administration of public finances in violation of their constitutional exemption from plebiscitary legislation. In bringing such action the cabinet ran the risk of being rebuffed in the courts and was wary of the pressures that might be brought to bear upon the person of the Reich president. On the other hand, the government now had the means at its disposal to wage an effective countercampaign under the direction of Reich Interior Minister Carl Severing. Both the national and Prussian governments forbade their public employees to support the referendum on the grounds that Article 4 was incompatible with the loyalty required of civil servants. In point of fact, only the Prussian government made a consistent effort to take action against the numerous high-ranking civil servants who disregarded this injunction. National Socialist infiltration of the civil service as well as the increasingly obvious failure to enforce discipline within the civil service only underscored the slow but sure erosion of the republic's authority.

The campaign of the national opposition against the Young Plan ended in a political fiasco. The 5.8 million votes that had been cast for the Freedom Law made it clear that a plebiscitary surprise attack against the existing political system stood no chance of success. The principal beneficiary of the campaign was the NSDAP, which had succeeded with the help of the right-wing bourgeois press in casting itself as the major driving force of nationalist politics. Nevertheless Hugenberg was able to contain the secession of the party's moderate wing — which proceeded to reconstitute itself either under Treviranus's leadership as the People's Conservative Association (Volkskonservative Vereinigung) or as the Christian-Social People's Service (Christlich-Sozialer Volksdienst) — through his control of the DNVP party apparatus. In this respect, Hugenberg was no doubt helped by the posture of Count Westarp, who despite truly irreconcilable differences with Hugenberg remained loyal to the DNVP. In the eyes of most bourgeois conservatives Hugenberg was seen as a political eccentric. Of the national unity that Hugenberg had promised, little, if anything, could be seen.

Paradoxically, the defeat of the campaign against the Young Plan did not translate into the stabilization of the existing parliamentary system. To be sure, the right-wing opposition had failed in its most recent attempt to prevent the

Reich president from signing the Young Plan laws after they had been passed by the Reichstag. Still, the enactment of these laws on 12 March 1930 marked the end of the Great Coalition and, with it, the demise of the last government that rested upon a parliamentary majority. Candid voices in the presidential entourage let it be known that it was time to form a cabinet of the bourgeois Right now that domestic political problems had moved to center stage. And the Social Democrats had become expendable after they had done their part in helping to bring about temporary relief on the reparations front. Under these circumstances, it was no longer possible for the Reich president to withstand pressure for a reform of German finances that would create the fiscal prerequisites for a new political offensive on reparations and a revision of the Versailles peace treaty. The fact that the end of interallied controls would supposedly usher in a new phase in the struggle against Versailles was a consideration of enormous importance in the political calculations of the German Right.

As early as the spring of 1929, General von Schleicher had been pressing for the replacement of the existing governmental coalition by a cabinet of the bourgeois Right under the leadership of either Ernst Scholz, Hans Luther, or, above all, Heinrich Brüning. The fact that Brüning was a former combat officer who had been decorated with the Iron Cross recommended him for the chancellorship in the eyes of both Schleicher and Hindenburg, although the latter was still somewhat reluctant to entrust the chancellorship to a Catholic. In a personal meeting between Brüning and Schleicher the two found themselves in essential agreement on the Reichswehr's demands for increased defense appropriations. Brüning, however, felt that a change of governments should be delayed until after the evacuation of the Rhineland. At the same time, he let it be known that he would not turn his back upon an appeal from the Reich president to assume the leadership of a government that enjoyed Hindenburg's confidence. For the time being, however, it never went beyond tentative overtures of this nature. For as long as the Young Plan had not yet been implemented, the existing cabinet would have to remain in office. In December 1929, when the coalition threatened to fall apart because of the DVP's opposition to the way in which the cabinet planned to balance the budget, Hindenburg extracted a promise from the DVP ministers that they would remain in the cabinet even if this meant expulsion from their party. This constituted a reaction against Hugenberg, whom Hindenburg still accused of "deserting the colors." In early 1930 Hindenburg tried without success to persuade the DNVP party leader to pursue a policy of constructive collaboration with the moderate Right.

The radicalization of the DNVP under Hugenberg dealt a severe blow to the strategy that Schleicher had planned with such consummate care. There was no way in which the Hindenburg cabinet he envisaged could be expanded to accommodate the Hugenberg movement. Under these circumstances, the Bureau of the Reich President with support on its flanks from heavy industry did everything in its power to strengthen the anti-Hugenberg opposition within the DNVP in the unrealistic hope that it might still be possible to have him replaced. As it was, Hugenberg enjoyed particularly spirited support from the influential Pan-German League as well as unexpectedly strong backing from the DNVP's district and regional organizations. At the center of conservative hopes for a sweeping realignment on the Right, the key figure was Gottfried Treviranus, who had founded the People's Conservative Association in late January 1930. But those who had hoped that the People's Conservatives would form the nucleus of a DNVP that had returned to its political senses were sorely disappointed. Nor was Count Westarp able to assert himself against Hugenberg's intransigent political course. For the time being, there was no alternative but to write off the possibility of concentrating the various factions on the German Right into a united political front. In the light of these developments Schleicher now began to focus his attention on a new version of the *Bürgerblock* that would depend upon the confidence of the Reich president and that would help lay the foundation for a government of those elements on the Right that were prepared to work within the existing political system to bring about its fundamental overhaul and regeneration.

Hindenburg was essentially open to the ideas that Schleicher outlined for a reorganization of the national government. In the middle of January 1930 Hindenburg assured Count Westarp that after the implementation of the Young Plan he would return to a conservative government of the "middle." State Secretary Otto Meißner elaborated upon what the Reich president had in mind by stating that the proposed presidential cabinet would be "antiparliamentary" and "anti-Marxist" in terms of its basic orientation and that its appointment would be accompanied by a reorganization of the Prussian government. The fact that his support for the ratification of the Young Plan had provoked such strong public criticism only heightened Hindenburg's interest in such a government. Hindenburg was all too easily swayed by the blandishments of the Right, which claimed that the imposition of this most recent "dictate" by the victorious Allies—as Brüning referred to the Young Plan—was the result of parliamentary malfeasance for which the SPD was held directly culpable. It was perfectly consistent with this position that Hindenburg should prove so receptive to the arguments of Schacht and Brüning that only a fundamental reform of public finances along the lines that industry had been demanding for some time would make it possible for the Reich to stand up to the foreign powers in future negotiations on the revision of the Versailles peace treaty.

The implementation of the Young Plan gave new impulse to the efforts of the oppositional forces on the German Right. This became most apparent in the ratification of the German-Polish liquidation agreement, which was closely related to the Young Plan but for tactical reasons was being handled separately. In point of fact, it involved a settlement of the endless disputes that had arisen between the two countries over the Polish government's expropriation of property that had belonged to the Prussian government and of real-estate holdings of Germans who had opted to remain in the areas acquired by Poland under the terms of the Versailles peace treaty. The Polish government had used the unresolved status of this question to justify large-scale interference in the material existence of the German minority that had remained in Poland, whereas the German government had endeavored to transfer property that had previously belonged to the state to independent agencies as a way of exempting it from the claims that Poland was entitled to make under the terms of the Versailles peace treaty. By requiring both parties to waive any claims to compensation, the liquidation agreement effectively guaranteed the material status of the German minority as of 1929. In return Germany was abandoning its claim to compensation for losses that for all intents and purposes were irrevocable.

The liquidation agreement appeared to contradict what had become a fundamental maxim of German foreign policy, namely, that any treaty commitments with Poland that might be interpreted as a de facto recognition of the postwar boundaries must be avoided. In point of fact, however, Germany's acceptance of the agreement effectively undercut Poland's intention of having its reparations claims spelled out in the Young Plan and did much to defuse Józef Piłsudski's incessant clamor for an eastern Locarno. At the same time, Germany's efforts to secure protection from the League of Nations for the German minority in Poland gained credibility from the conclusion of this agreement. From this perspective, Stresemann had expressly applauded the efforts of Ulrich Rauscher, the German envoy to Poland, on behalf of a normalization of German-Polish relations, in spite of the fact that this encountered strong opposition from large-scale agriculture. In exchange for German concessions pertaining to financial and commercial ties, the agreement greatly increased the German government's freedom of action in the foreign policy arena. Even though Polish public opinion was sharply critical of the agreement, it was immediately attacked by the nationalist Right in Germany—but above all by the NSDAP—as an abandonment of German demands for a revision of Versailles. Although this was by no means the case, the liquidation agreement nevertheless represented tacit acknowledgment of the fact that Germany's efforts to bring Poland to its knees through the exercise of economic pressure had been counterproductive.

The agreement that Stresemann had endorsed shortly before his death was concluded by Julius Curtius, his successor at the German Foreign Office. This represented a preliminary step toward the conclusion of a German-Polish commercial treaty that the German export industry desperately sought but whose implementation Brüning delayed so that it did not take effect until after the Nazi conquest of power. The successors to the cabinet of the Great Coalition thus missed their opportunity to expand commercial ties with Poland and to establish the foundations of a lasting political equilibrium that might very well have defused the problem of the Polish Corridor. Instead, mutual distrust, as in the case of German plans to construct a battle cruiser, grew so strong that Marshal Piłsudski was prompted to consider the strategy of a preventive war against Germany. This, in turn, unleashed vastly exaggerated reactions on the German side and had a negative impact upon German domestic politics in the critical year of 1932.

In typical fashion Hindenburg used the ratification of the German-Polish liquidation agreement—which provoked a storm of protest from the East Elbian landowners and whose constitutional validity the nervous Reich president had to have examined—as the pretext for demanding that the Müller cabinet draft a comprehensive program of financial assistance for "the East in its desperate struggle for survival" (*den verzweifelten um seine Existenz ringenden Osten*). Hindenburg further demanded, in what amounted to a clear repudiation of Prussia's policies in the east, that "the agricultural representatives and spokesmen from the eastern provinces"—in a word, the agricultural chambers (*Landwirtschaftskammer*) that were already in the firm control of the large landowners and the National Rural League—should be given a major role in the deliberations. Even before the fall of the Müller cabinet, Hindenburg had not only promised the Ministry of Agriculture to the president of the National Rural League, Martin Schiele, but indicated his willingness to provide the east with the necessary funds, if necessary by presidential emergency decree. Meißner remarked upon handing Schleicher the text of the appeal the Reich president had prepared for publication on 18 March: "This is the first step and the bridge to your solution. It is the starting point to the best of what we can possibly have, to the leadership of Hindenburg [*zum Führertum 'Hindenburg'*]." Most observers were surprised by the decisiveness with which Hindenburg shed his customary reserve and began to ply the cabinet with instructions that frequently went into the most minute details. By the same token, his initiative on behalf of financial aid to the east was a well-calculated stab in the back of the existing governmental coalition, which was struggling in vain to balance the budget. In fact, Hindenburg's own entourage was not particularly concerned over the fact that the opposition of the Social Democrats would almost certainly make it impossible to secure parliamentary approval of the aid package for East Elbian agriculture.

The increased pressure of organized agricultural interests was a direct response to the deepening agrarian crisis, which had first become apparent in 1926 before assuming truly alarming proportions in 1928–29. This crisis, which stemmed in part from international factors beyond the control of any German government, could not be blamed upon the shortcomings of the Great Coalition. The Social Democrats, whose Kiel agrarian program called for the support of domestic agricultural prices through the introduction of a grain monopoly, were well aware of the need to provide assistance to the agrarian sector, but most of all to the predominantly agricultural areas east of the Elbe River. But the cabinet found its ability to deal with the problem hampered by the fact that it could not directly defy the directive from the League of Nations for the gradual elimination of all trade barriers, particularly since the limited protective tariff that Germany had adopted in 1925 as a way of maintaining the price structure for basic agricultural commodities had gradually transformed itself into a comprehensive system of agrarian protectionism.

At the insistence of Reich Agricultural Minister Hermann Dietrich, the Müller government adopted a middle-of-the-road policy, which instead of intensifying the existing system of agrarian protectionism by increasing the tariffs for agricultural products relied on government subsidies aimed at maintaining domestic rye prices as well as a series of structural reforms in East Prussian agriculture. But various initiatives—and particularly those undertaken by the Prussian government under its East Prussian Assistance Program (Ostpreußen-Hilfe)—to improve agricultural productivity remained virtually ineffective despite vigorous efforts on the part of the Braun government. The Prussian government had every reason to seek greater financial involvement by the Reich. At the same time, it also sought to correct the one-sided emphasis that the East Prussian Assistance Program had always placed on agriculture and to initiate changes in the structure of the East Prussian economy by expanding the existing transport system as well as by providing incentives for commerce and the establishment of industrial settlements. These measures, as well as the efforts of the Prussian government to convert long-term agricultural indebtedness through the division and resettlement of those estates that could no longer be saved from bankruptcy, provoked vigorous protests from precisely the same organized agricultural interests that had earlier called for a government-sponsored settlement policy aimed at slowing down the slide in the price of agricultural real estate. Hindenburg identified himself with these interests when he let it be known that he wanted the Eastern Aid Program (Osthilfe), which was no longer to be limited solely to Prussia but should include all of the eastern provinces, to be used exclusively for the restoration of agriculture's economic viability "in all of its forms, whether it be large estates or small peasant holdings."

Under these circumstances, it seemed only logical for the government to use the funds that would become available through the implementation of the Young Plan for what one memorandum from East Elbian farmers called the "salvation of the German East." Hindenburg's suggestion to this effect referred back to an agrarian program that Paul Silverberg had presented to the National Federation of German Industry (Reichsverband der Deutschen Industrie or RDI) in 1929 and that sought to limit Germany's dependence on foreign imports and to achieve relative self-sufficiency in meeting the nation's nutritional needs. The RDI was by no means as altruistic as it might have initially appeared. On the one hand, the reduction of agricultural tariffs was a necessary precondition for the increase in industrial tariffs being sought by sectors of the German business community. On the other hand, this represented an attempt to wrest the leadership of the economic rehabilitation of the German east from Prussia. Whatever the RDI's motives might have been, the accord between industry and agriculture was quickly destroyed by the excessive demands of agricultural interest organizations, which used Hindenburg's initiative as the pretext for requesting tax reimbursements over several years' time and subsidies in the amount of a billion marks.

Within the Müller cabinet there was complete agreement that in the face of declining national revenues there was no way an agrarian program of this magnitude could be financed at this point in time. The chancellor was reluctant to jeopardize the budget compromise that had been hammered out in painstaking negotiations among the government parties and was in complete agreement with Finance Minister Paul Moldenhauer on this particular issue. Despite repeated attempts to influence him to the contrary, Hindenburg was still operating on the assumption that he could maintain the existing cabinet even if the DVP were to leave it and was prepared to give Müller full authority to dissolve the Reichstag and use presidential emergency powers. Schleicher tried to counter such a proposal with the dire warnings that this would not only produce an alarming "surge of power" for the SPD but would further alienate the national opposition from the Reich president. It was only when the cabinet responded somewhat diffidently to the Reich president's ultimatum on the Eastern Aid Program that he decided to dispense with it. The cabinet had been kept in office so that it could oversee the ratification and implementation of the Young Plan. Now that this had been accomplished, there was no reason why it should remain in office. The full extent of Hindenburg's identification with the interests of the East Elbian landowners did not become fully apparent until after the collapse of the Great Coalition. The final blow to the Brüning government two years later came in the form of allegations from Germany's landowning elites that the chancellor and his cabinet had played into the hands of "agrarian Bolshevists."

The resignation of the Social Democratic majority cabinet on 27 March 1930 was brought about by irreconcilable differences among the coalition partners. These differences came into sharp focus when the government was notified that Hindenburg would not grant the chancellor the special emergency powers that were provided for in Article 48 of the Weimar Constitution. In point of fact, the collapse of the Müller cabinet had been carefully scripted. In February 1930 Ernst Scholz, Stresemann's successor as chairman of the DVP, had been informed of Schleicher's plans for a cabinet that would constitute itself and govern independently of the various parties in the Reichstag. The cabinet was to be headed by Brüning after both Scholz and Hans Luther, who opted instead for the presidency of the Reichsbank, withdrew their names from consideration. Schleicher's initiative was undertaken in close consultation with G. R. Treviranus, who functioned as a liaison to the forces on Germany's moderate Right, and was consistent with the decision that the right wing of the DVP had reached in December 1929 to bring about the collapse of the existing governmental coalition as soon as the Young Plan had been adopted. In this respect, Scholz enjoyed the full support of the Federation of German Employer Associations (Vereinigung der Deutschen Arbeitgeberverbände), whose chairman Ernst von Borsig had warned Finance Minister Paul Moldenhauer in March 1930 that any further increase in employer contributions to the unemployment insurance fund would almost certainly result in the withdrawal of his organization from the National Agency for Job Placement and Unemployment Insurance (Reichsanstalt für Arbeitsvermittlung und Arbeitslosenversicherung). But, as always, the DVP Reichstag delegation was reluctant to be saddled with responsibility for bringing down the government. At the DVP's Mannheim party congress in the third week of March, the party leaders manifested an unusual willingness to compromise, though without committing themselves to any of the financial measures that would become necessary with the ratification of the Young Plan.

Under these circumstances, the decisive role fell to the German Center Party. Brüning, who during this time met repeatedly with Hindenburg and maintained informal contact with General von Schleicher, was still reluctant to take the final steps that were necessary to bring down the Müller cabinet. In this respect, he had no doubt whatsoever that a dramatic reduction in the current level of public spending and in particular drastic cutbacks in the benefits of the unemployment insurance program were absolutely necessary. In the fall of 1929 Brüning had committed the Center Reichstag delegation to a reform of unemployment insurance before the implementation of the Young Plan and regarded this, along with a program for cutting taxes that went back to Hilferding's tenure as Reich finance minister, as the most critical point of the budget deliberations. In late January 1930 Brüning made this a condition for his party's consent to the Young Plan.

In setting this condition, Brüning had been guided by the tactical consideration that the Social Democrats should not be spared the onus of far-reaching cuts in the budget for social welfare, particularly since the rapid increase in unemployment would most likely trigger movements of social protest throughout the working population. At the same time, Brüning sought to frustrate the DVP in its efforts to postpone fundamental decisions in the area of fiscal policy until the need for solidarity in matters of German foreign policy made it possible for the party to state its demands as forcefully as possible. For their own part, the Social Democrats, who had already made substantial concessions on the question of eligibility for unemployment compensation, were particularly concerned that a delay in a reform of unemployment insurance would bring a new reduction in benefits. In the final analysis, however, Brüning's efforts to link the reform of public finances to acceptance of the Young Plan did not have the effect he desired. For instead of strengthening the cabinet's internal cohesiveness, it forced the members of the cabinet to complete the budget under incredible time pressure.

The bill that Finance Minister Paul Moldenhauer submitted in an attempt to eliminate the chronic deficit of the National Agency for Job Placement and Unemployment Insurance did not seek to do this by increasing employer contributions or government subsidies but by merging its budget with those of other social agencies, including the public housing authorities, and covering any deficits that might result through savings—practically speaking, through a reduction in benefits—in the agency's budget. This represented a further retreat from the principle of insurance that had been at the heart of the system ever since its inception and limited the reform to the collective liability of those who were already insured so that social expenditures remained at the same level. The Social Democrats and their trade-union affiliates responded with a counterproposal that provided for an emergency levy of 3 percent on the wages of all full-time wage earners. Such a proposal seemed logical since civil servants and employees in the public sector had been hardly, if at all, affected by the widespread unemployment and simultaneous losses in income.

Although Moldenhauer eventually warmed to the idea of an emergency levy, his party remained adamantly opposed to it. The reason for this lay not so much in the fact that Scholz, as president of the National Association of High Civil Servants, was looking out for the interests of the state civil service but rather in the determination of the DVP's industrial wing to force a reduction in unemployment insurance benefits in spite of the fact that the various business groups that supported the party also agreed that the salaries of the civil servants were entirely too high. Renewed efforts to reform the existing system of unemployment insurance were effectively blocked several weeks later by the obstructionism of the DVP and the self-restraint of the Center. At this point, the ministerial agencies that were involved with the program hammered out a compromise under which the insurance carriers would continue to do their part, but with the understanding that any future shortfall in revenues would be covered through the creation of an emergency fund at the National Agency for Job Placement and Unemployment Insurance and through an increase in the employers' contributions from 3 to 4 percent.

It was against the background of these developments that the DVP jeopardized the extremely fragile compromise that seemed to be taking shape on the budget by demanding that tax reductions for the 1931 fiscal year be passed into law in connection with the budget for the current year. The sweeping reduction in personal taxes—and especially for those at the upper-income levels—that had been wrested from Hilferding in 1929 in anticipation of lower reparations payments proved a fateful and self-inflicted handicap. For it soon became apparent that tax increases were unavoidable in view not only of the relatively minor savings accruing from the Young Plan—most of which were earmarked for mandatory debt retirement—but also as a result of a rapid decline in tax revenues and the increasing deficit in the government's unemployment insurance program. Yet the DVP blocked any increase in property taxes. The Reich Emergency Levy (Reichsnotopfer) represented an attempt to get around the DVP's intransigence. Whereas the SPD criticized the fact that the budget deficit was to be covered primarily by indirect taxes that weighed most heavily upon the lower classes, the DVP demanded, in addition to what it had already asked for, a reduction of real taxes and greater flexibility in municipal taxes, which was intended as a device to bring psychological pressure to bear upon the municipalities to reduce their expenditures for unemployment compensation. With its litany of demands for more and more tax cuts, the DVP Reichstag delegation had effectively stabbed their own ministers in the back. What the delegation wanted was not a compromise on the budget but the collapse of the existing governmental coalition.

For his own part, the chancellor insisted on introducing his government's original budget proposal and eventually forced Brüning to go along with this decision. Yet the leader of the Center Reichstag delegation met with the Reich president immediately before the vote on the Young Plan was scheduled to take place in the Reichstag and reassured himself of Hindenburg's willingness to enact the budget reform by the use of Article 48 should this prove necessary. "You can count on it," Hindenburg told him, "we will have a finance reform. If the parties don't go along, I'll do it without them." By promising to make use of all constitutional means to introduce new taxes for the purpose of deficit reduction in the fiscal year that was to begin on 1 April 1930, Hindenburg had given Brüning what amounted to a blank check to do whatever he deemed necessary in the area of fiscal reform. Unwilling to use it just then, Brüning preferred to achieve his objectives through a compromise on unemployment insurance. But when the DVP learned that the Müller government had received neither an order for the dissolution of the Reichstag nor presidential emergency powers, the time frame for an agreement was extremely narrow.

Brüning's compromise proposal accommodated the DVP to the extent that while it provided for premiums in the amount of 3.5 percent, it postponed a more general solution until some point in the future. In the light of subsequent developments, the compromise appears relatively acceptable even though it avoided answering the question of whether unemployment insurance should be financed by higher premiums or tax increases. By now, however, the Social Democratic Reichstag delegation was no longer willing to go along with the compromise, whereas the DVP accepted it for purely tactical reasons. For Reich Labor Minister Rudolf Wissell, who had already balked at an earlier compromise within the cabinet, the compromise represented the first step toward a blatant reduction of benefits that the unions could not possibly accept. Spokesmen for the unions in the SPD Reichstag delegation correctly pointed out that, given the unequivocal attitude of the DVP and the Center Party, the Brüning proposal would lead to further cuts in unemployment insurance, and they expressed a preference for the government's original proposal. The chancellor, alluding to the danger of a general state crisis, pleaded in favor of the Brüning compromise but was unable to persuade even his own party.

From a tactical perspective, the decision of the SPD's Reichstag delegation to make no concessions beyond those that were already contained in the compromise that had been hammered out in the cabinet proved to be a virtually irreparable mistake. In the deliberations on financial reform the SPD found itself pushed to the very limits of its ability to compromise. The Socialists could very well have yielded once again to the DVP, but once they had refused to become an instrument of the DVP's deliberate drive for a reduction of social benefits, they felt compelled to reject Brüning's compromise proposal. Had they on this one occasion managed to set aside their fundamental misgivings, they would have come under similar pressure from the DVP in the debates over the other pending tax bills. The fact is that Brüning's compromise proposal was designed to precipitate a break not from the side of the DVP but from that of the Social Democrats. The DVP then used the SPD's rejection of the Brüning proposal as a pretext for blocking both the discussion of proposals for deficit reduction in the tax committee and a debate on the government's proposals in a plenary session of the Reichstag. Hermann Müller's chances of securing the passage of his fiscal program in what Carl Severing called "open battle" had been effectively dashed. A last-minute reversal of the SPD's position might have frustrated Moldenhauer's tactical maneuver. But it is unlikely that the government would have survived the subsequent battles over deficit reduction, particularly since Müller, in deteriorating health, no longer had the strength to fight.

On the evening of 27 March 1930 the chancellor submitted the resignation of his cabinet. Only hours later, Hindenburg entrusted Brüning with the task of forming a new government. The next day Brüning, after consultation with the Center Party's Reichstag delegation, requested the president to form "a cabinet that was not bound to the parties" (*ein nicht an die Parteien gebundenes Kabinett*) by invoking the emergency powers that Article 48 of the Weimar Constitution had invested in his office. Much relieved, Hindenburg consented. He had finally found the man who he believed would be able to govern without out the Social Democrats, would lead the parties of the national opposition back to the principle of "political" (*staatspolitische*) responsibility, and would free the Reich president from the image of serving the interests of the political Left. For the SPD this decision meant its deliverance from a situation that had become intolerable. Even Rudolf Breitscheid, who at the SPD Magdeburg party congress in 1929 had opposed any link between his party's participation in the national government and guarantees regarding the future of unemployment insurance and had warned explicitly against a cabinet of civil servants as nothing more than a "thinly veiled dictatorship," approved of the decision by the SPD Reichstag delegation. In the cabinet the Social Democrats had found themselves constantly on the defensive with respect to their bourgeois coalition partners and had never been in a position to act in accordance with their political ideals. Going into opposition seemed a more honest and—in view of the widely anticipated dissolution of the Reichstag—tactically appropriate response.

The force of circumstances obliged Brüning to complete the transition to a government independent of constantly changing majorities in the Reichstag more rapidly than he had expected. By early 1930, if not earlier, Brüning had already made up his mind to use the change of government to initiate a comprehensive reorientation of German foreign and domestic politics, of which the reform of German finances would only be the first step. At the heart of his domestic program stood the liquidation of the reparations problem, in whose service fiscal policy and fiscal reform were to be placed. From the very beginning Brüning had felt that reparations represented an intolerable burden on the German people and a fundamental constraint upon the Reich's freedom of action in domestic and foreign policy. To the Center Party he assigned the "historic mission" of guaranteeing—in the face of changing coalitions and, if need be, by setting aside the principle of parliamentary responsibility—the continuity of Germany's foreign policy, including the reduction of reparations and a "fiscal policy necessary for success" in this endeavor. A solution to the reparations problem, Brüning believed, was possible only on the basis of a thoroughgoing financial reform. For only a "solid financial economy of the Reich" could maintain foreign creditors' confidence in its creditworthiness, which in turn constituted a necessary precondition for the success of any policy aimed at a revision of the Young Plan.

In his capacity as the Center Party's financial and tax expert, Brüning had severely criticized the changes that had taken place in the 1925 tax reform under the impact of recession. In doing so, he pointed out that measures to create new jobs and the extension of credit to industry had created a budgetary deficit that continued to grow and grow. In point of fact, the national government had accumulated a growing debt through unsecured loan guarantees that, as late as 1929, had severely limited its freedom of action in the negotiations at The Hague. Brüning did not need Schacht's exhortations or the bitter memories of the withdrawal of French loans in the spring of 1929 to reach the conclusion that in the absence of a responsible fiscal policy it would be impossible to avoid future capitulations to the Western powers in the reparations question. Not only was Brüning concerned about the possible restoration of international financial controls such as those Parker Gilbert had instituted in 1929, but he also believed that the only way in which the reparations issue would be resolved in Germany's favor would be by playing off the interests of private investors against those of the reparations creditors.

When Brüning assumed the chancellorship, he was convinced that Germany was not in a position to raise the annual payments it owed under the terms of the Young Plan. As early as the fall of 1929 Brüning, together with Center party chairman Ludwig Kaas, had begun to envisage a revision of Germany's reparations burden once the evacuation of the Rhineland had been completed on 30 June 1930. For Brüning, therefore, the link between financial reform and the adoption of the Young Plan was far more than a simple tactical maneuver. For it was precisely after the adoption of the Young Plan laws, Brüning insisted, that the need was greatest for a fiscal policy that would establish "certain guarantees for the future" and make it impossible for Germany's international creditors to blame difficulties in transferring the annual reparations payments on a policy of calculated default by the German government. An economic crisis, Brüning warned, should not be allowed to create, as it had in 1926, a phantom financial economy (*Schattenfinanzwirtschaft*) that in critical situations left Germany dependent on international loans.

Brüning did not think of the various symptoms of the crisis that had hastened the demise of the Great Coalition as an independent factor but rather as a consequence of the reparations problem. Until the late fall of 1930 Brüning, like many influential representatives of the German business and industrial communities, continued to attribute the crisis, which manifested itself primarily in a dramatic increase in unemployment, to largely endogenous causes. In this respect, Brüning agreed with Hjalmar Schacht that irresponsible financial mismanagement had occurred at all levels of government and that the principle of Prussian frugality had been violated in the most egregious manner. Unlike Schacht, however, Brüning did not think that the principal goal of state economic policy should be the formation of domestic capital, a goal that had been used by various special-interest groups to demand tax reductions and to justify Schacht's restrictionist credit policy. As far as Brüning was concerned, the fight against the recession was always secondary to the goal of revising the Young Plan. The deflationary policy that Brüning pursued from the very outset of his chancellorship was driven to a far greater extent by the primacy of reparations policy than by the lingering trauma of the hyperinflation. Nor was Brüning influenced by the argument to be found in contemporary economic theory that a balanced budget constituted the only way in which an economic crisis could be overcome. Brüning's own view of Germany's fiscal and economic development since 1926 had transformed him into an outspoken opponent of government programs for the creation of credit and of public works projects aimed at combating unemployment. In his opinion, the countercyclical policy that Germany had employed to get out of the stabilization crisis of 1926 was to be rejected primarily on account of its implications for Germany's reparations policy.

These views, to which Brüning clung with quasi-doctrinaire rigidity, coincided with a profoundly nationalist temperament, unconcealed monarchist sympathies, and a deeply conservative philosophy of the state shaped by traditional Prussian virtues and prejudices. Just as Brüning considered the revolution of 1918–19 a misfortune that could have been avoided, so he saw the Weimar Constitution as a political form that had been forced upon Germany from abroad and that was incompatible with the traditions of the German state. Along with many opponents of the republic, he harbored a deep-seated antipathy toward the alleged arrogance of the German party system. In his view, a sound and functional administration was more important than viable parliamentary institutions. Even though he had begun his political career as an associate of Adam Stegerwald and as secretary general of the German Trade-Union Federation (Deutscher Gewerkschaftsbund or DGB), Brüning had never developed particularly close relations with the working class in his capacity as a financial expert.

The outwardly reserved, ascetic intellectual who had made himself indispensable to his colleagues by virtue of his unusual efficiency, his wide-ranging circle of contacts, and his imposing command of facts was inconspicuous in his personal demeanor and studiously avoided any hint of emotionality. He was not a forceful speaker and lacked the confidence-inspiring charisma of a populist politician. Those who had to deal with him were often irritated or offended by his behavior. He always kept his feelings close to himself, and not even his closest associates were privy to his fundamental political intentions. His tendency to make political decisions while talking to informal advisors, to inform the cabinet and parliamentary committees only after the fact, and to go deliberately over the heads of the responsible cabinet ministers became more and more pronounced during his tenure as chancellor. "Nobody knows what Brüning really wants"—this heartfelt sigh uttered by Bernhard von Bülow, a state secretary in the German Foreign Office—paints a telling picture of the private character of the chancellor's governing style.

The sobriety of Brüning's public manner, interpreted by many as coldness and diffidence, was a mask behind which there existed a deeply sensitive and complex personality that had been shaped by the highly romanticized front experience of the younger generation, of which he considered himself a part, and by an uncritical admiration for the Prussian military tradition that lay at the heart of his relationship with Hindenburg. A trained political economist, Brüning understood politics primarily as the action of individuals. Although he had reached the chancellor's office through intrigues and personal contacts, he failed to understand that his eventual fall from power was not the work of malicious rivals but the result of political conditions that he himself had helped create. On the other hand, this life-long bachelor was possessed of a natural optimism that made him believe that dogged perseverance would eventually pay off, even in political situations that had little to do with the strict adherence to principles. Without a doubt Brüning distinguished himself as a politician of incomparable tactical skills that made it possible for him to pursue the long-range goals that he had set for himself by means of discretely and carefully selected alternatives to the point where both contemporaries and later observers felt that tactics were all there ever was to his style of leadership. The secret of Brüning's success was his tenacious and sometimes doctrinaire adherence to the options on which he had decided. On the other hand, his inability to adapt to radically altered political constellations was a major factor in his political demise.

In late March 1930 Brüning was still convinced that his goal of an "absolutely clear and reliable financial policy" could be attained in the near, if not immediate, future. Aside from the absence of the Social Democrats, the only significant difference between the previous cabinet and the one he had assembled with surprising speed was the inclusion of Martin Schiele as minister of agriculture, Gottfried Treviranus as minister for the occupied territories, and Victor Bredt from the Business Party as minister of justice. Although Schiele remained a member of the opposition DNVP, he resigned his seat in the Reichstag. Even though the Bavarian People's Party and the Business Party were indirectly tied to the government, the cabinet was not based on a formal coalition and lacked the support of a majority in the Reichstag. In presenting his government, Brüning stressed the fact that it enjoyed the backing of the president and characterized its formation as the "last attempt" to carry out the crucial tasks that faced the Reich on the basis of the existing Reichstag. Despite this thinly veiled threat, Brüning hoped to avoid a dissolution of the Reichstag for the time being. By the same token, he hoped to reserve use of presidential emergency powers for the sweeping administrative and financial reforms he was planning to introduce.

Aside from the fact that the Social Democrats were now in opposition and responded to the presentation of the new cabinet with an immediate motion of no confidence, the parliamentary constellation that greeted Brüning upon his appointment to the chancellorship was remarkably similar to what Hermann Müller had faced when he first became chancellor. Brüning's first decision was to submit Moldenhauer's bill for covering the deficit as part of a package that included emergency aid for East Elbian agriculture in the hope that the DNVP could be persuaded to vote for it in the Reichstag. This strategy worked remarkably well in that Hugenberg decided not to support the Social Democratic motion of no confidence. The proposals for covering the deficit were accepted by the majority of the DNVP Reichstag delegation, though not without massive pressure on the recalcitrant Hugenberg by the leaders of the National Rural League. It soon became clear, however, that this had produced only a temporary improvement in Brüning's political position. For in the meantime the world economic crisis had descended upon Germany in all of its fury, with the result that revenues fell far below budget projections. In order to balance the budget, it would be necessary to submit a supplementary budget in connection with the deliberations for the 1931 budget. At this point, Brüning ran into opposition from precisely the same groups that had brought about Hermann Müller's fall from power.

In an effort to cover the mounting budgetary deficit, Moldenhauer not only resorted to tax increases but also proposed the resurrection of the Reich Emergency Levy in a new form known as the Reichshilfe der Festbesoldeten, with provisions for a levy on fully employed wage earners in the amount of 2.5 percent of their salary. Stegerwald, the new minister of labor, had made it clear before accepting his appointment that under no circumstances would he agree to unilateral reductions in unemployment insurance that were not matched by sacrifices in other areas. Brüning, who in principle favored salary cuts for the civil service, although he would like to have postponed them until the fall, now faced the passive resistance of the DVP. In late June, following a formal ultimatum, the DVP withdrew Moldenhauer from the cabinet. The controversial bill, however, received immediate support from Treviranus, who shared Brüning's dislike of the civil service salary reform of 1927. The Business Party, on the other hand, made its support of the deficit reduction package contingent on a reduction in the sales tax that weighed so heavily on its predominantly middle-class constituents. Brüning's efforts to secure Hugenberg's cooperation, however, foundered on the DNVP party leader's insistence on a reorganization of the Prussian government — which both the Prussian Center Party and the Reich chancellor considered inadvisable — and his party's inclusion in the cabinet without any conditions whatsoever. By now Hugenberg had consolidated his position within the DNVP. Despite the protests of the Westarp group, the DNVP executive committee had given Hugenberg and the new chairman of the DNVP Reichstag delegation, Ernst Oberfohren, a unanimous vote of confidence and had reiterated the party's commitment to a policy of unconditional opposition to the existing system of government.

Brüning believed that he could overcome the resistance of the Bavarian People's Party and the right-wing interest parties by seducing them with concessions. Still, he did not abandon the idea of an emergency levy on full-time earners, which Hermann Dietrich, Moldenhauer's successor as finance minister, tried to make somewhat more palatable to the average citizen by extending its provisions to higher-income groups and by taxing the royalties (*Tantieme*) received by the board members of large businesses. For the chancellor, this not only was a way to meet the demands of his own party that the burden of balancing the budget should not fall exclusively upon the shoulders of lower-income groups and the unemployed but also represented a response to a bill from the Social Democrats that provided for an emergency levy of 10 percent on monthly salaries exceeding 8,000 marks. After a second reading of the bill in the Reichstag, Brüning made one last effort to gain the DVP's support by amending it to include a head tax (*Bürgersteuer*), which was extremely unpopular in the public at large—it was frequently stigmatized as a "nigger tax"—because it failed to differentiate among income levels.

The chancellor had wanted to avoid a break with the SPD because he needed its agreement for a special expenditure law (*Ausgabensicherungsgesetz*) that would have limited the legislative competence of the Reichstag and therefore required a two-thirds majority for passage. The SPD was willing to consider voting for the bill after its press had launched into agitated and excessive attacks against the new chancellor. The SPD let the first part of the budgetary package that Brüning submitted through the Reichstag but made it clear in the course of subsequent negotiations that it could not go along with the head tax. As far as revenues were concerned, whatever this tax might raise was insignificant. But Brüning, mindful of Hindenburg's determination to exclude the SPD from a meaningful role in the governmental process, could not and would not drop it. He therefore abruptly broke off negotiations that Breitscheid had conducted with exemplary fairness, without, however, having assured himself of the DVP's support for his budget legislation.

Brüning's defeat in the decisive vote was caused by the rigidity of the DVP and the intransigence of Hugenberg, who joined forces with the SPD, KPD, and NSDAP in opposing the government budget bill. It would be difficult to take exception with the attitude of the SPD, for it could not have possibly drawn a clearer line between accepting a share of responsibility for the nation's political course and becoming co-opted into a reactionary social policy than it did in the case of the ill-conceived head tax. Only later would the socially regressive character of this tax be mitigated slightly through the indexing of incomes. Brüning was already trying to juggle a whole array of tactical expedients and could not for a moment claim that he was following a clear line unaffected by special economic interests. In the final analysis, it was not the conflict over a half-percent increase in the premiums for the state unemployment insurance program but the failure to index a municipal tax whose revenues were of no significance whatsoever that brought about the formal collapse of Germany's parliamentary system.

Bereft of political alternatives but true to his promise, Brüning resorted to the expedient of a presidential emergency decree to enact his tax program and dissolved the Reichstag on 18 July 1930 after it had voted to rescind his authorization to act in such a manner. Speaking for the SPD Reichstag delegation, Otto Landsberg explained that his party had rejected the emergency decree because the intent of Article 48 was not to make it possible for the government to enact a bill that had been previously defeated in the Reichstag but to maintain security and order in the event of parliamentary paralysis. While Landsberg's position was objectively correct and ethically motivated, it soon became superfluous in the course of subsequent events and was not even shared by the leading Social Democrats. When the Reich president proceeded to enact the emergency decree that had been rejected by the Reichstag in a slightly modified form, his action found the unanimous approval of judiciary and constitutional experts. The majority of the parties did what they could to reconcile themselves to the new situation.

Even after Brüning had crossed the Rubicon of government by presidential decree, he still believed that he could persuade the newly elected Reichstag to cooperate in the implementation of his program. He failed, however, to understand that he had allowed himself to become the instrument of those interests which were determined to use the depression to dismantle the existing system of social benefits and to initiate sweeping wage cuts. His close ties with the Reich president precluded the possibility of a reconciliation with the Social Democrats who, with one eye on their stronghold in Prussia and the other on the rising threat of the NSDAP, did not want to burn all their bridges behind them. Instead, Brüning cast his lot with the faction around Treviranus and Westarp, which officially broke with Hugenberg just before the decisive no-confidence vote in the Reichstag and on 23 July 1930 — much too late for it to play a significant role in the upcoming election campaign — and reconstituted itself as the Conservative People's Party (Konservative Volkspartei). Its appeal for the concentration of all conservative forces behind Hindenburg, however, did little to prevent many former Nationalist deputies from joining the Christian-National Peasants and Farmers' Party (Christlich-nationale Bauern- und Landvolkpartei) and the Christian-Social People's Service (Christlich-sozialer Volksdienst) that had been founded in late 1929. In spite of alliances with conservative splinter groups, the moderate Right won no more than forty seats, while the DNVP emerged from its inner-party debacle with forty-one deputies.

The only visible success of the Brüning cabinet was the evacuation of the last French troops from the Rhineland on 30 June 1930. The government celebrated the achievement of this long-desired political goal with a ceremony at Ehrenbreitstein castle, where the traditional banners of the Reichswehr were flown instead of the black-red-gold of the Weimar Republic. It was as if one had suddenly returned to the days of Wilhelm II. Yet the ceremony was not without its note of political discord. For in spite of a petition from the Prussian government, the public statements by the Reich president and the national cabinet assiduously avoided mentioning the name of Gustav Stresemann. Moreover, the Reich president threatened to cancel his participation in the official cere- mony because the Prussian interior minister, Albert Grzesinski, refused to lift the ban on the west German Stahlhelm that he had imposed six months earlier. Although the status of the case was perfectly clear—by holding formal military maneuvers in Langenberg in 1929 the Stahlhelm had violated a number of dis- armament clauses—the Reich president, who was still an honorary member of the Stahlhelm in spite of its role in organizing the recent referendum against the Young Plan, insisted that the Prussian government repeal its prohibition of the Stahlhelm. The true irony of the situation lay in the fact that restora- tion of German sovereignty over the Rhineland was actually a consequence of the very Young Plan that the Stahlhelm continued to revile. On this particular point neither the Reich president nor the chancellor nor the right-wing press had anything to say.

The liberation of the Rhineland did not bring the Brüning cabinet the politi- cal breathing space it so desperately needed. On the contrary, it definitively and unambiguously broke the foreign policy vise that had hitherto held the parties from the SPD to the DNVP together. Partly in response to the growing challenge of the NSDAP, the right-wing parties abandoned all restraint in their nationalist propaganda. Within a few weeks, 14,000 members of the Stahlhelm held a rally at the Deutsches Eck on the Rhine to demand the return of Alsace- Lorraine and Eupen-Malmedy under the slogan "No statute of limitation for injustice!" (*Unrecht verjährt nie!*). At a demonstration of the Eastern Associa- tions of Loyalty to the *Heimat* (Heimattreue Ostverbände) marking the tenth anniversary of the East and West Prussian referendum, Gottfried Treviranus, the Reich minister for the occupied territories, pleaded for an active revisionist policy in the east and spoke of the "still lost German lands that must be re- gained some day. . . . The stagnation of German blood in the east [*Ostdeutsche Blutstockung*]," he continued, "is a concern and a danger for Europe." Such a statement by a ranking cabinet member was hardly designed to strengthen the confidence of creditors from the West in the political stability of the Reich. The withdrawal of foreign loans—but also the flight of German investment capital that had begun with the referendum against the Young Plan—had aggravated the Reich's financial difficulties well before the outcome of the September 1930 Reichstag elections sowed further confusion over Germany's ability to survive the deepening economic crisis.

Whereas Brüning advocated savings in the public sector that were to be complemented by simultaneous, comprehensive cuts in wages and prices, the full fury of the world economic crisis descended upon Germany. This, in turn, greatly intensified existing social tensions and evoked within the middle-class circles upon which the presidential cabinet was dependent a sense of grow- ing bitterness. By the spring of 1930, industrial production had declined by

one-third in comparison with the previous year. At the same time, mass unemployment continued to rise and had already reached the 3 million mark by
the beginning of 1930. Hardest hit of all were the urban industrial workers. The
number of union members who were either out of work or were employed on
a part-time basis rose from 17 to 45 percent in the space of a single year. In the
textile industry that figure exceeded 50 percent by the fall of 1930. Unskilled
and semiskilled workers were more directly affected by the increasing unemployment than other sectors of the industrial work force. With the cuts that
had taken place in unemployment insurance benefits over the course of the
previous year, more and more of those who were out of work had to depend
on emergency assistance or municipal relief programs.

Unemployment also affected Germany's white-collar population on a much
larger scale than ever before. This came in the wake of widespread dismissals
that had taken place, particularly among older employees, as a result of the
increasing rationalization of German economic life in the preceding period. By
the same token, many previously independent small entrepreneurs and artisans
had to close their businesses. The incidence of bankruptcy rose at an alarming rate. The so-called old middle class that had already been severely hurt
by the inflation and revaluation had to endure the continued deterioration of
its economic situation. The retail sector, which had only temporarily recovered from the losses suffered during the years of inflation and revaluation, now
faced intensified competition from department stores and discount chains.
High interest rates and a chronic capital shortage endangered the existence of
middle-class artisanal and manufacturing enterprises. Many of those who had
at one time been economically independent before seeking work in the employ
of someone else as a result of the trend toward concentration once again saw
their livelihood in jeopardy.

There was also a perceptible decline of salaries in the white-collar sector.
This was particularly true of women employees, who were frequently forced
as a condition of their employment to accept salaries that were considerably
below those which had been established for their male counterparts by collective bargaining. The fashionable polemic against "double earners" was aimed
specifically at working women. While many older employees — and particularly
female employees — were thus being eliminated from the work force, there was
also an alarming rise in unemployment among those who had been born in
the years just before the outbreak of World War I when the birthrate had been
particularly high. Many juveniles could not find an apprenticeship and had
to eke out a living with odd jobs and part-time employment. Moreover, they
were not entitled to unemployment insurance or emergency relief aid. Pensioners and welfare recipients, as well as disabled war veterans and the widows
and orphans of those who had been killed during the war, also had to accept
drastically reduced benefits.

Cuts in wages, pensions, and welfare benefits in the public sector along with a general reduction of retirement incomes struck hard at a stratum of society that had already suffered a great deal as a result of the personnel cutbacks in 1924 and the partial revaluation of those paper mark assets that had been destroyed by the inflation. The infringement upon the civil servant's "well-earned rights" (wohlerworbene Rechte) that had taken place with the Reichshilfe der Festbesoldeten evoked a strong protest from civil servant unions, which contested the legitimacy of the pension and salary cuts with arguments that sounded plausible. Considerations of status, however, prevented not only the "old" but also the "new" middle class from working together with organized labor. All of these circles looked on the Social Democrats as the true cause of the crisis. The anti-Marxist agitation of Germany's right-wing parties thus found an increasingly warm reception among diverse middle-class elements that seemed to be driven more than anything by their own social frustrations.

Within the German middle class economic distress was most apparent among the owners of small and middle-sized farms, who derived little, if any, benefit from the subsidies that large agricultural enterprises had been receiving. The excessive price of rye—the domestic price was twice that on the world market—threatened the economic viability of meat and milk producers in the northern and western parts of Germany who depended on cheap feed grains imported from abroad. The combination of rising production costs as a result of high import duties with falling prices on the domestic market forced many small farmers to the brink of economic collapse, in part because they had been obliged to contract short-term loans at high interest in order to pay for seed, machinery, and other necessities of life. The decline in agricultural prices had made it impossible for enterprises that were still economically viable to make the necessary investments. In the period between 1928 and 1930 the number of agricultural enterprises that went out of business doubled.

Signs that the political system had begun to break down could be seen most prominently in those agrarian regions in which small and middle-sized farms specializing in cattle production were predominant. Since 1928 the bitterness of the peasantry had expressed itself in public demonstrations that sowed anxiety and terror within the propertied bourgeoisie. Spontaneous resistance against tax collections, foreclosures, and the garnishment of property escalated into a protest movement that spread throughout northern Germany. The geographical center of the Rural People's Movement, or Landvolkbewegung, under the leadership of "peasant king" Claus Heim was Schleswig-Holstein, where the effects of the agrarian crisis had been particularly severe. The movement's more militant elements used all means at their disposal—ranging from the nonpayment of taxes, consumer strikes, and boycotts to terrorism and bombs—in their struggle against the police and local authorities to prevent the destruction of the time-honored structures of ownership in peasant society. Archaic forms of peasant resistance thus merged with *völkisch* and racist slogans to produce a species of anticapitalism with strong anti-Semitic overtones. The Artaman League (Bund der Artamanen), which preached the renewal of the nation through a return to "blood and soil," provided the movement with a steady stream of new ideas. Nationalist revolutionaries of all nuances, including the Salomon brothers, Friedrich Wilhelm Heinz, Friedrich Hielscher, and Otto Straßer, became the principal ideologues of this increasingly anarchistic movement, which had its counterpart on the extreme Left in various Communist actions.

The Rural People's Movement was a particularly conspicuous symptom of the general loss of political orientation that increasingly large segments of the German middle class began to experience in the last years of the Weimar Republic. This phenomenon was rooted in status anxieties that were greatly intensified by the economic uncertainties of the late 1920s and that resulted in a weakening, if not dissolution, of existing political ties. In the agriculturally less productive areas of Schleswig-Holstein, for example, the migration of voters to the extreme Right had manifested itself ever since 1920 in support for a series of extremist protest parties, the most notable example of which was the NSDAP. As the emergence of the Christian-National Peasants and Farmers' Party clearly revealed, the radicalization of Germany's rural population threatened the previously unchallenged leadership of the National Rural League and DNVP. The close identification of the National Rural League and the so-called Green Front that it had helped launch in the spring of 1929 with the interests of East Elbian landowners who had already received preferential treatment in the administration of the Eastern Aid program combined with a general lack of confidence in Hugenberg, who was widely perceived as a representative of German heavy industry, to produce a radical agrarian opposition that relied on direct action and the mobilization of the peasant masses instead of working through the parliament and the various political parties. Efforts by the National Rural League to bring the increasing radicalization of its followers under control were unsuccessful in preventing its own regional affiliates, among them the Pomeranian Rural League (Pommerscher Landbund), from falling under the influence of the Landvolkbewegung. These developments marked the beginning of the dissolution of the DNVP's core constituency and of National Socialist infiltration of agricultural interest organizations.

The erosion of authority that all of Germany's nonsocialist parties with the exception of the Center had experienced and that had led to a series of singularly unsuccessful efforts to unite the German bourgeoisie manifested itself from 1930 on within Germany's middle-class and agricultural interest organizations as well. These organizations were forced to defend themselves against the charge that they had failed to provide the needs of their constituents with sufficient protection. The obvious failure of the capitalist economic system had fueled a particularly zealous form of anticapitalism that was driven by nationalist and anti-Semitic ressentiment and that endowed the slogan of the *Volksgemeinschaft* as propagated by the German Right with incomparable appeal. What became increasingly clear was the dissolution of the parliamentary system from within. The fact that Brüning systematically forced the parliament to the margins of the decision-making process only accelerated the collapse of the bourgeois party spectrum. As a result, even those forces that were loyal to the republican form of government began to put some distance between themselves and the existing constitutional system. Left-liberal constitutional scholars as well as Social Democratic theorists began to consider ways of limiting the sovereignty of parliament and strengthening the authority of the Reich president. The criticism of "party squabbling" (*Parteigezänk*) and the charge that the Reichstag had become a clearinghouse for special economic interests met with a positive response even among certain elements of the Social Democratic working class. The feeling that Germany was on the verge of a radical and comprehensive intellectual and social change pervaded the atmosphere. This was the hour of those intellectuals who had embraced the "conservative revolution." Having fallen out of fashion during the period of Weimar's political and economic stabilization, the champions of the "conservative revolution" now assumed center stage in the fateful discussion over the direction in which the nation was presumably headed.

Under the impact of the deepening economic crisis, the cultural pessimism that had gripped Germany's educated elite in the last years before the outbreak of World War I gained new ground. The deep-seated ressentiment against modern industrial society that now was accused of having contributed to the dissolution of the "natural" and religious bonds between the individual and his society and of having placed politics in the service of the raw, unbridled "passions of the masses" reinforced existing bourgeois prejudices against the "cultural Bolshevism" of the large cities, against movies, commercial advertisements, jazz, and showgirls—in short against the various manifestations of modern life as such. Berlin's rise as a cultural metropolis was, on the one hand, a source of pride and satisfaction and, on the other, a sign of cultural and moral decay. The widespread status anxieties of the German bourgeoisie exploded in vitriolic attacks against the "asphalt press," the earliest manifestations of "mass culture," the rapid growth of a consumer society, and the reign of an unrestrained "materialism."

Such attitudes almost invariably went hand in hand with a subliminal anti-Semitism, which under the prevailing conditions was expressed more and more openly. By contrast, organized anti-Semitism was not particularly widespread. Following the ban of the German Racist Defense and Defiance League (Deutschvölkischer Schutz- und Trutzbund), it was most evident in the NSDAP, without, however, having been the primary factor on the part of its sympathizers in their decision to join the party. Anti-Semitic excesses like the assaults that had taken place in Berlin's Scheunen neighborhood in November 1923 remained isolated incidents. On the other hand, anti-Semitic feelings, particularly toward nonassimilated Jewish groups, began to pervade German public life as a whole. As a result, incidents of anti-Semitic behavior were rarely prosecuted under the law, particularly since anti-Semitism was rampant in the judiciary, where it had been stimulated by professional competition against Jewish colleagues. Nor was the right-wing press shy about mobilizing anti-Semitic prejudice in its campaign against the SPD. This was particularly true in the case of the bribery scandals involving the Barmat and Sklarek families. These techniques were also used in connection with the referendum on the expropriation involving Germany's dynastic families. As its systematic defamation of the black occupation troops in the Ruhr clearly revealed, not even the DNVP was above using racist polemics in its propaganda when it could be made to serve its own purposes.

The Central Association of German Citizens of the Jewish Faith (Centralverein deutscher Staatsbürger jüdischen Glaubens) tried to combat the anti-Semitism that had become so widespread throughout German society primarily by means of the written word but had met with meager success. In the meantime, anti-Semitism in the German universities assumed alarming proportions through the influence of the Germanic University Ring (Hochschulring deutscher Art). Under these circumstances, attempts by the ministries of education in several German states and by concerned faculty members to have a ban imposed on student anti-Semitic activities stood little chance of success. Symptomatic of this situation was the constitutional dispute that pitted the Prussian student associations against the Prussian minister of education, Heinrich Becker. As early as 1927, Becker had taken exception to the way in which the charter of the parent organization of student associations throughout Germany and Austria had excluded Jewish students from membership. Those prorepublican student groups that expressed solidarity with Becker represented a tiny minority in comparison with the prevailing nationalism of German student life. The political extremism of Germany's university students, however, was only partly motivated by their economic difficulties and the poor employment prospects for university graduates. More than anything else, it was a manifestation of the increasing disintegration of Germany's educated bourgeoisie, or *Bildungsbürgertum*, and the status anxieties this produced throughout the German bourgeoisie as a whole. This, in turn, explains why the National Socialist German Students' Association (Nationalsozialistischer Deutscher Studentenbund) often set the tone for an entire university community. Its demand that the admission of Jewish students be subject to a quota — supposedly as a way of relieving overcrowding at the universities but in point of fact a thinly veiled pretext for excluding Jewish students altogether — frequently found the support of a majority within the student body of a particular institution.

The spread of anti-Semitic sentiments was a clear indicator of the increasingly antiliberal character of German political and intellectual life. Of the various species of antiliberalism that surfaced during the last years of the Weimar Republic, none had a broader appeal or a greater impact upon German political life than neoconservatism, which received organizational support from the Ring Movement (Ring-Bewegung) and called upon the services of influential publishers such as the Hanseatic Publishing Institute (Hanseatische Verlagsanstalt) and the Eugen Diederichs Publishing House (Eugen Diederichs-Verlag). The neoconservative ideology had grown out of the nationalist idealization of the so-called front experience, in which class antagonisms and the certainties of bourgeois life had dissolved in a new type of warrior who found his way back to a new, more meaningful life through his willingness to sacrifice himself for the sake of the community as a whole. *Der Kampf als inneres Erlebnis*, as the title of Ernst Jünger's 1920 war novel so aptly put it, alluded to the tendency so typical of the political irrationalism of the times to replace content with mere form and to depict struggle as an end in itself without reference to the aims it purportedly served. The reduction of all time-honored values to empty forms to the point where they became devoid of any meaning whatsoever was characteristic of this unrealistic and voluntarist mode of thinking. For all of its revolutionary posturing, "soldierly nationalism," as this trend has been called, was merely a more recent version of the "philosophy of life" and tragic nihilism of Friedrich Nietzsche and, from this perspective, represented a reaction to the cultural crisis of the late nineteenth century. At the same time, it blocked any honest attempt to come to terms with the meaning of the great war and stood in sharp contrast to Erich Maria Remarque's classic *All Quiet on the Western Front* and a host of similar war novels published by other authors. The fact that the NSDAP could provoke an incident at the premiere of the film based on Remarque's novel and bring about a ban on its public performance suggests that the glorification of war in the writings of Ernst Jünger, Ernst von Salomon, Franz Schauwecker, Werner Beumelburg, and Edwin Erich Dwinger had taken a firm hold on the public mind. This was possible precisely because it was the generation that had risen to political maturity since the end of the great war that identified itself most closely with the mythos of the front soldier.

What distinguished Germany's neoconservative intelligentsia from more traditional conservatives was its unabashed activism, which received its consummate expression in the concept of the "conservative revolution" that Hugo von Hofmannsthal had coined in 1927. The common denominator of this extremely complex and many-faceted trend was the postulate that liberal capitalism had outlived its usefulness and must be replaced by a new species of national socialism that would translate the "ideas of 1914," with their emphasis on the inner solidarity of the nation, into practice and establish a new form of society that was opposed to the Western constitutional state yet commensurate with Germany's indigenous political traditions. The most important source of these ideas was Oswald Spengler, whose widely read book *Preußentum und Sozialismus* linked the notion of a wartime command economy to a romanticized and highly stylized interpretation of Frederick the Great's concept of rule. As the myth of the front soldier and the related idea of a community of warriors sworn to a common cause make clear, it was a socialism of sentiment rather than one rooted in a particular economic theory. It was not simply a matter of abolishing the contradiction between capital and labor through a fundamental reform of the existing economic system and a stronger commitment to the principle of social justice. What distinguished Germany's neoconservative authors was rather their cynical contempt for the "masses," their unabashed elitism, and their outspoken hostility toward the principle of equality. Just how society was to be organized remained unclear in the writings of all of these authors, who borrowed heavily from the corporatist theories on which the Viennese social thinker Othmar Spann had based his concept of the organic state. In the final analysis, however, Germany's neoconservative intelligentsia was less interested in institutions as such than in personal bonding and charismatic leadership. The leadership principle and the need for a nationalist dictatorship were propagated and popularized by a broad spectrum of neoconservative publicists. The leader for which they all longed assumed the aura of a providential messianic "savior."

Like the much-celebrated "ideas of 1914," the idea of a German "socialism" as an alternative to Marxism's materialism and emphasis upon class conflict had a markedly anti-Western thrust. The notion of a specifically German form of socialism proceeded from the idea of a corrupt and degenerate capitalist West that stood in direct contrast to the untapped energies of the "young nations" (*junge Völker*) to the east. All of these ideas could be traced back to a propaganda pamphlet that Moeller van den Bruck had written in the summer of 1918 for the Supreme Military Command. Inventing the slogans that the Nazi movement would subsequently use with such devastating effect, the brochure conjured up the idea of a "national revolution" and a future "Third Reich" that would conquer for a "new German race" its rightful place in the domination of the world. Although it clearly contributed to the development and spread of Weimar irrationalism, Oswald Spengler's more pessimistic view of the world paled in comparison to the visionary activism of those who embraced the "new nationalism." At the same time, the diffuse nature of these ideas mitigated against their absorption into the existing party spectrum. By no means was this unintentional. National revolutionaries like Ernst Niekisch combined their nationalist vision with outspoken sympathies for the Soviet Union, while Karl Radek's tactical maneuvers were designed to secure the support of "the leftists on the Right" (*linke Leute von rechts*). The central thrust of these ideas, despite their different nuances, was directed against Bolshevism and Social Democracy. The rejection of liberalism and the Enlightenment, on the other hand, was common to all positions and frequently went hand in hand with a tendency to idealize Russia, which was supposed to have preserved its original culture and an unbroken continuity of its religious traditions. At the heart of all this lay the categorical rejection of Western industrial civilization and the atomization of society that had been its universal legacy.

The uncritical way in which Germany's neoconservative intelligentsia glorified the life of the simple peasant almost always went hand in hand with a deeply resentful polemic against the forms of urban life and its alleged "cultural Bolshevism," a term that immediately evoked a wide range of anti-Semitic associations. This, in turn, was complemented by a reassessment of nature and the rediscovery of one's special relationship to natural life. Initially an affectation of the educated middle classes in the last years before the outbreak of World War I, the idea of communion with nature became a fascinating experience for increasingly large segments of German society in the postwar period, extending even to the proletarian youth in the tents of the Communist "Red Falcons." This attitude could easily be harmonized with the ecological impulses of the times, which manifested themselves in the resettlement movement, the idea of garden cities, and the plea for less concentrated housing and for bright and airy apartments as an alternative to the tenements that had been inherited from the previous century. Informed by the spirit of the Bauhaus and the "New Objectivity," the urban architecture of the 1920s represented a constructive response to the social problems of modern industrial society.

The positive attitude toward technological progress that could be seen in the architecture and literature of the 1920s and that frequently merged with the vision of a new society was not free from a measure of ambivalence. For on the one hand it represented an opening to the West, the acceptance of a consumer society, and a positive response to the emerging mass culture. On the other hand, it concealed strategies of social control that ran counter to basic values of the liberal tradition. By the end of the 1920s the tendency to open society up to impulses from the outside had reversed itself and was in the process of being transformed into a mood of national introspection that fused the idea of a fundamental reform of society with notions of community that had been appropriated from the *völkisch* tradition to combat the rise of the masses and the atomization of modern society. The remarkable enthusiasm for modern technology that manifested itself in an uncritical admiration of Fordism and Taylorism, a surprisingly strong interest in the industrial development of the United States, and an astounding eagerness to adopt American techniques of production and marketing stood in sharp contrast to the widespread reemergence of preindustrial values and modes of thought. Even politicians like

Hermann Dietrich, Adam Stegerwald, and Heinrich Brüning—all of whom were trained political economists—were convinced that Germany's industrial capacity had developed far beyond the nation's economic needs and harbored the illusion that the best way to get the unemployed masses off the streets was by accelerating the pace of agricultural resettlement.

The contrast between the vision of a "national breakthrough" (*nationaler Aufbruch*) and the longing for a return to the social and economic circumstances of the imperial era was reflected not only in the fascinating cultural life of the "Golden Twenties," a period that was characterized by the tension between extreme modernity in a few cultural centers and the relative backwardness of life in the provinces. This tension carried over, albeit in a somewhat different form, into the political system itself. The established political elites, whether they stood on the right or left wing of the Weimar party spectrum, were all focused on the positive and the negative aspects of the imperial experience. They looked back to the Second Empire either to reestablish contact with prewar conditions or to use them as a standard for judging the present. To the younger generation, which had been politically socialized in the first years after the end of the war, this attitude lacked passion and perspective. What it offered by way of contrast in differing political variants was the vision that Germany's military defeat constituted the point of departure for a fundamental inner renewal of the nation. Although the *Burgfrieden* had been exposed as a farce, right-wing intellectuals still evoked the war experience, though without referring to the civil war that followed in its wake, as proof of the nation's unity of purpose.

The undisguised class conflict that had resulted in the paralysis of Weimar's parliamentary system was complemented by a marked contrast in political mentalities that reflected pronounced intergenerational tensions. The antibourgeois affectations of a significant portion of Germany's front and postwar generations expressed itself in an emotionally charged rejection of interest politics. In his autobiography Ernst von Salomon captured the mood of this rebellious generation when he wrote: "What we thought to be political was a matter of fate. Outside of our world, politics was simply a matter of interests." It was the same sort of political irrationalism that prompted Ernst Jünger to issue his famous dictum that instinct was superior to intelligence. In both authors an extreme subjectivism clearly prevailed. Yet both were representative of their own cohort group—and not merely among the neoconservatives—in the sense that they called for a politics based on ethical values and dismissed its unheroic everyday conduct as "political horse trading."

From the outset, the Weimar political system was handicapped by its inability to attract the support of the younger generation and by its failure to mobilize those more activist elements that stood under the influence of the German youth movement. Without a doubt, the hardships of everyday life in the crisis-ridden early years of the Weimar Republic had forced the various youth groups that were just beginning to reconstitute themselves after the end of the war and that had expected the collapse of the Second Empire to produce a fundamental renewal of German society to the periphery of everyday political life. Whereas the front experience had led German youth to embrace the vision of a new society that transcended existing class differences and abolished established social hierarchies, social reality was characterized by a state of virtual civil war, intensified conflicts over the distribution of the social product, and uninterrupted bureaucratic authoritarianism. Under these circumstances, the more activist elements of the younger generation tended toward either radical protest or political abstinence. This factor accounted not only for the early growth of the Communist Youth Leagues (Kommunistische Jugendverbände), which were only gradually subordinated to Leninist principles of party discipline, but also for the persistence of the apolitical *Wandervogel* tradition. The great majority of the *bündisch* youth thus organized itself outside of the existing political parties, which it denounced in unequivocal terms and to which it opposed its own vision of an integral and organic society that was free from internal conflict.

Even those republican youth organizations that were prepared to take part in the political life of the newly founded German Republic found themselves excluded from any sort of meaningful political role. Neither the Hanover Circle (Hannoveraner Kreis) that was influenced by the Marxist ideas of Max Adler nor the reformist-minded Hofgeismar Circle (Hofgeismar-Kreis) of Young Socialists found a home within the SPD. Indeed, the independent status of the Young Socialists remained a constant source of friction with Social Democratic functionaries who expected their docile subservience to the party organization. At the same time, the Socialist Workers' Youth (Sozialistische Arbeiterjugend) and the various youth organizations attached to the socialist labor unions had to accept the fact that fewer and fewer youths were willing to join. Aside from changes in the structure of the German economy that benefited the white-collar sector, the principal cause of this phenomenon lay not so much in the undeniably greater appeal of the Reichsbanner as in the failure of the SPD and socialist labor unions to take cognizance of the fact that the experiences of the war had increased the self-confidence of their younger members to the point where they were no longer willing to serve indefinitely as simple lackeys for an increasingly decrepit apparatus of functionaries. As a result, a considerable age differential began within both the SPD and its affiliated unions between their leadership cadre and their rank-and-file membership. The average age of the membership was 42.5 years, whereas the group of those who were younger than 25 years of age was grossly underrepresented in comparison with its percentage of the total population.

The KPD, many of whose functionaries had come from the socialist youth movement, was in comparison to the SPD a much younger organization with a more favorable age structure. Its politics of radical opposition found greater sympathy among the young, even if the imposition of Stalinist party discipline had had a negative effect upon the attractiveness of the Communist Youth League. For in the larger working-class parties, the more activist elements among their younger factions voiced increasingly sharp criticism of the bureaucratic ossification of the party organizations. The various factions that broke away from the two parties—whether it was the Socialist Workers' Party of Germany (Sozialistische Arbeiterpartei Deutschlands or SAPD), the Class Conflict Group (Klassenkampf-Gruppe), the International Socialist Combat League (Internationaler Sozialistischer Kampfbund or ISK), the Opposition Communist Party of Germany (Kommunistische Partei Deutschlands [Opposition]), or even the right wing of the opposition that had crystallized within the SPD around the faction associated with the *Neue Blätter für den Sozialismus*—were all motivated by the same concerns, namely, to overcome the all too obvious immobility of the organized workers' movement and to develop more effective and up-to-date modes of resistance and agitation.

The bourgeois parties were threatened to an even greater extent than the SPD by the aging of their leadership cadre in spite of the fact that they had all made a concerted effort to encourage the development of their own party youth organizations since the middle of the 1920s. But the conflict over the expropriation of German princes had done much to expose the deeply rooted psychological cleavages that separated the different generations. To be sure, the problem of generational conflict had already been a major topic of public debate for some time. The judicial and social policies of the Weimar Republic, after all, had displayed an exemplary degree of sensitivity to the needs of German youth and had gone to great lengths to give it the necessary space for self-development in the areas of pedagogy, criminal justice, and rights to social benefits. Yet the "young generation," as one generally referred to those who had reached maturity either during the war or in the immediate postwar period, found its opportunities for advancement to positions of leadership and responsibility within the existing political system extremely limited. From this perspective, the scathing criticism that Theodor Haubach of the circle around the Neue Blätter für den Sozialismus directed against the "chained barrier [*Absperrungskette*] that has been drawn between the institutions of German public life and the German youth" was very much on target.

The increasing age of the republic's leadership cadre provided a convenient target for its enemies on the Right, which portrayed themselves as champions of German youth and denounced the Weimar parliamentary system as the "final bankruptcy of the older generation." The NSDAP's Joseph Goebbels spoke contemptuously of the "republic of senile old men" (*Republik der Greise*), while Gregor Straßer attacked its leadership cadre by saying that "these characters are the same ones who were around before the war and revolution, before upheaval and the new breakthrough." This was a common refrain that harkened back to a motif that Max Hildebert Boehm, a leading figure in the Berlin June Club, had expressed as early as 1919 in his tract *Der Ruf der Jungen*: "For us the war means the collapse of the old generation and its world and the breakthrough [*Aufbruch*] for the young." Nowhere was the neoconservative appropriation of the cult of youth expressed more powerfully than in these words.

The generational conflict of the Weimar Republic stemmed in no small measure from the fact that demographic factors made the cohort groups that entered the labor market in the 1920s and early 1930s unusually large whereas the economic system, on the other hand, remained relatively stagnant. Conflicts over the distribution of the social product were therefore resolved at the expense of the younger generation, which had also borne the brunt of structural unemployment during the period of Germany's political and economic stabilization. Yet the psychological differences that separated the older and younger generations arose not so much out of socioeconomic factors as out of the radically different ways in which each generation had responded to the shattering experience of World War I. Complaints from war veterans that they belonged to a "lost generation" that had been excluded from meaningful participation in the political life of their country were only partly justified. In any event, the chronic crisis of Germany's parliamentary development during the Weimar Republic tended to insulate the bourgeois parties and the SPD from the full effect of the generational change that began to transform German society in the period after 1928. The failure of Walther Lambach's attempt to advance the cause of the younger generation within the DNVP against the monarchist elements that controlled the party was only symptomatic of this situation.

The literature and journalism of the 1920s were imbued with a youth mythos that proceeded from the fiction that the younger generation had been chosen as the driving force of a fundamental social and cultural change. Hans Zehrer applied this concept to the political crisis of the Weimar Republic and predicted that those age cohorts which had been relegated to the periphery of German political life would bring forth new forms of political action and dissolve the factionalism and interest politics that had become the order of the day under the republican system of government in a "Third Front." Similar expectations could be found in the area of pedagogical reform. Once education had been freed from the dead ballast of the previous century, a new generation no longer corrupted by moral relativism and Western materialism would finally be in a position to restore the lost unity of spirit and power, of nature and art, of society and state.

Hans Zehrer, who helped give these ideas their classic form, had welcomed

Brüning's appointment as chancellor. Still, he did not think the time had come for the young generation in whose name he spoke to realize the full promise of the failed "national revolution" of 1918. "Attention, young front: Stay out!" (*Achtung, junge Front: Draußen bleiben!*) was his slogan from the fall of 1930. The parties had not yet completely ruined themselves, and so the young generation must not exhaust its energies by assuming responsibility for Germany's political destiny before the proper moment had arrived. The dangers inherent in the myth of a breakthrough in which one generation was called upon to atone for the failures of its predecessor could be seen in Zehrer's own misreading of the NSDAP as the first step toward Germany's self-liberation in the spirit of the young generation. As late as 1932 Zehrer spoke of the NSDAP and KPD as the end results of a dying liberalism "that were destined to soak up and gather together the masses that had once been part of the liberal spiritual world." The future, Zehrer believed, belonged not to the party but to the *Bund*, and it was essential that the *bündisch* nucleus of the NSDAP find its way back to the principle of the *Bund*.

The National Socialist movement made effective use of the way in which Germany's educated elites had deluded themselves into believing that the idealism of the younger generation constituted an antidote to the plague of interest politics and did not hesitate to manipulate this for its own partisan ends. At the beginning of the 1930s there had been resistance in certain intellectual circles to the idealization of youth. In the final analysis, the youth cult was the symptom of profound social uneasiness and constituted an attempt to mask the status anxieties that were related to this situation as the consequence of intergenerational change. The close relationship that developed between neoconservatism and the youth cult helped create the illusion of a viable future political and social alternative to the beleaguered parliamentary republic. At the other end of the political spectrum, authors in the style of Kurt Tucholsky articulated a radical critique of the bourgeois-liberal tradition that likewise laid special claim to the idealism of the young generation, though from a perspective that was much more deeply committed to the Enlightenment and Marxism than to the cultural pessimism of the Wilhelmine era.

The dilemma of the young German appeal for the regeneration of the Reich stemmed last but not least from the complete absence of a concrete political strategy and of concepts that one could translate into political reality. This defect stood in sharp contrast to the self-confidence with which men like Edgar Jung and Heinrich von Gleichen attacked the parliamentary system. The cultural and social-economic change the young conservatives hoped to bring about was perceived more as an act of spiritual transformation than as one of political organization and mobilization. Here lay the fundamental difference that separated the idealism of the young conservatives from the political pragmatism of the NSDAP, notwithstanding the fact that the two continued to manifest significant ideological affinities and, in the case of the Straßer brothers, direct personal ties. The intellectual structure that neoconservatives and their Catholic counterparts—first and foremost, the adherents to the notion of a Christian Reich—as well as the "decisionist" school of German constitutional thought had all helped popularize could be easily manipulated by the NSDAP for its own partisan purposes. Despite their far-reaching social and political connections, the young conservatives were kept by the esoteric nature of their political program from exercising direct influence on the course of events in the late Weimar Republic with the possible exception of the short-lived Schleicher chancellorship.

In retrospect, it is remarkable that when the long-dormant potential for antirepublican protest was finally mobilized by the emergence of the presidential system in the middle of 1930, it found its greatest resonance at the German universities. This stemmed in part from the fact that, despite the strenuous efforts of Prussian Education Minister Heinrich Becker, a university education remained a privilege reserved for the children of the upper classes. Although some of the universities had remained loyal to their liberal traditions, the majority were clearly hostile to the republican system of government, while those prorepublican academics who had organized in the Weimar Circle of University Professors Loyal to the Constitution (Weimarer Kreis verfassungstreuen Hochschullehrer) constituted a distinct minority within the profession as a whole. At the same time, the social influence of anti-Semitic fraternities went unchallenged. A significant portion of the university professorate sympathized with the DNVP and felt threatened by the progressive erosion of its social and professional status. This contributed in no small measure to their readiness to embrace the flight into political irrationalism and to justify it with presumably professional arguments. The increasingly partisan character of German university life prompted progressive scholars to abandon hopes of an academic career, particularly since the conflicts involving Günther Dehn, Julius Gumbel, Hans Nawiasky, and Theodor Lessing had shown that the prospects for advancement in their chosen fields of study were virtually nonexistent. The incomparably rich intellectual and artistic life of the Weimar Republic thus took place largely outside the confines of public universities and academies. By the same token, its influence on the course of political events was negligible.

As long as the basic interests of German society were at least partially mediated by the Weimar party system, the republic had little difficulty surviving the intellectual protest movement that drew its energy from the cultural and social crisis of the late 1920s. The vitriolic attacks that neoconservative pundits from Arthur Moeller van den Bruck to Ernst Jünger and Edgar Jung launched against parliamentary democracy had little impact on the decision-making process except in the areas of jurisprudence and cultural policy. It was only when powerful economic interest groups—but particularly sectors of heavy

industry and large-scale agriculture—began to use the neoconservative movement as a battering ram for the destruction of the political system that this
began to change. Beginning in 1929 the ideas of the neoconservative movement
were used to legitimate a policy whose primary objective was the exclusion
of organized labor from a meaningful role in determining Germany's political
destiny and to eliminate what still remained of Germany's badly decimated
parliamentary system.

The dissolution of the Reichstag in July 1930 provided the definitive impetus for the realignment of Germany's conservative Right. The outcome of the
Reichstag elections that had been set for 14 September would in the final analysis depend on whether it would be possible to isolate Hugenberg politically and
win over a majority of the Nationalist electorate for the newly founded Conservative People's Party. The defections from the DNVP Reichstag delegation
that had begun in 1929 continued unabated. Of the seventy-eight deputies the
party had sent to the Reichstag in 1928, only thirty-five were still with the party
two years later. As a result of Count Westarp's indecision—he had avoided
a break with the party in April 1930 when the DNVP's agrarian wing voted
solidly against Hugenberg—efforts to gain control of a substantial part of the
DNVP party apparatus had ended in failure. By the same token, the normally
agile Treviranus failed in his efforts to establish the People's Conservative Association as an attractive magnet around which those elements on the moderate
Right that supported Hindenburg could coalesce. That Hindenburg did not so
much as lift a finger to help the People's Conservatives in their campaign for
the September 1930 Reichstag, even though they had strongly supported proposals for strengthening the powers of the presidential office, contributed to
their poor performance at the polls and to the fact that they emerged from the
elections with only four mandates.

In the final analysis, the efforts to reorganize and realign the parties of the
bourgeois Right were overwhelmed by the breakthrough of the NSDAP as a
mass political movement. In this respect, the NSDAP had succeeded in mobilizing much of the protest potential that had accumulated over the course
of time for its own purposes, particularly since it had managed to persuade
the German electorate that, in contrast to the DNVP, the Stahlhelm, and the
conservative Right, it sought a radical break with the existing constitutional
system and would never become a party to negotiations or partial compromises as the Hugenberg movement had done. Despite large areas of ideological
agreement between the bourgeois Right and National Socialism, Germany's
antirepublican voters regarded the NSDAP as the more consistent alternative
to the existing system inasmuch as Nazi propaganda had assiduously avoided
embracing any of the established political options or committing the party to a
specific economic philosophy. Nazi polemics focused instead on condemning
the increasingly powerful role that organized economic interests had come to

play in German public life and the progressive atomization of society that this had left in its wake. To this latter ill, Nazi propagandists opposed the fiction of a "national community" that transcended all social and economic antagonisms.

As the votes were being counted on the night of 14 September 1930, the Brüning government discovered much to its dismay that it had suffered a disastrous defeat at the polls. To be sure, the Center Party was able to improve on its position in the Reichstag by increasing the number of its parliamentary mandates from sixty-two to sixty-nine. But the parties of the middle and moderate Right were forced to absorb heavy losses. In spite of its merger with the People's National Reich Association (Volksnationale Reichsvereinigung or VNR), the newly founded German State Party won only twenty mandates, six of which immediately vanished with the VNR's secession in early October. With 4.9 percent of the popular vote, the DVP, saw its strength in the Reichstag cut by a third, while the DNVP received scarcely 7 percent of the popular vote. Regional and special-interest parties, on the other hand, received more than 14 percent of the popular vote and remained remarkably strong. The Social Democrats, receiving 143 seats in parliament and 24.5 percent of the popular vote, still suffered appreciable losses, most of which benefited the KPD, which emerged from the elections with 13.1 percent of all votes cast and entered the new Reichstag with seventy-seven mandates. The uncontested winner of the election, however, was the NSDAP, which, contrary to State Secretary Hans Schäffer's prediction that it would receive thirty to forty seats at most, won 18.3 percent of the popular vote and emerged with 107 seats as the second strongest delegation in the Reichstag.

The outcome of the September 1930 Reichstag elections meant that the more moderate bourgeois parties, including the special-interest parties, would not possess a parliamentary majority even if they managed to form a coalition with the DNVP. Given Hugenberg's intransigence, this was never a realistic possibility in the first place. The only way in which a government that enjoyed the support of a parliamentary majority might assume office seemed to lie in a return to the Great Coalition, the very thing that the dissolution of the Reichstag had been designed to prevent. Since neither Hindenburg nor Brüning was prepared so much as to consider inviting the SPD to join the government, it is pointless to speculate from the perspective of numbers alone whether a return to government by parliamentary majority might have been possible. Not even with the inclusion of the NSDAP could this have been accomplished. The goal of the election had been to free the government from its dependence on Social Democratic toleration. It now appeared, however, that the continuation of the presidential cabinet itself was possible only on the basis of an understanding with the SPD. But when Brüning, under the force of circumstances, had the temerity to propose such a course, both the DVP and the Business Party, which eventually instructed Justice Minister Victor Bredt to resign from the cabinet, adamantly refused to go along. In the meantime, the presidential entourage looked upon the composition of the new Reichstag as further confirmation for its argument that it was no longer possible to govern with parliament, just as Brüning, who feared that the Reichstag might rescind his previous emergency decrees, had no choice but "to go to Canossa" and beg for the toleration of the SPD.

The possibility of a Nazi landslide in the September 1930 Reichstag elections had loomed increasingly large since the spring of 1929. Whereas in 1928 the NSDAP had been relegated to the position of a splinter party with a mere 2.6 percent of the popular vote, the party had consistently increased its percentage of the popular vote in a series of municipal elections beginning in the spring of 1929. The party's emergence on the national level began in the municipalities, where the NSDAP had frequently entered into coalitions with the bourgeois parties against the German Left. The upward trend then continued in state and regional elections throughout the country. In June 1930, shortly before the dissolution of the Reichstag, the Nazi percentage of the popular vote in Saxony reached 15 percent after having jumped the previous fall to 7 and 8 percent in Baden and Lübeck respectively. In December 1929 the NSDAP tripled its vote in the Thuringian Landtag elections and emerged with 11.3 percent of the popular vote. This prompted Hitler to intervene on behalf of Wilhelm Frick's appointment as the Thuringian minister of the interior and cultural affairs in return for his party's participation in a right-wing coalition government.

In the summer of 1930 the rise of the NSDAP was as predictable as the collapse of the bourgeois center. The regional elections that had taken place over the course of the previous year revealed that both the SPD and the KPD would maintain their position, with some slippage from the former to the latter, in spite of the fact that the bourgeois parties as well as the NSDAP had concentrated their efforts against the two working-class parties. The outcome of the September 1930 elections reflected a radical polarization of the electorate and indicated that a qualitative change in the political climate had taken place. The Bürgerblock coalitions at the local and state levels had prepared the way for the rejection of the Weimar compromise by the bourgeois political establishment. The dissolution of special-interest and regional splinter parties in favor of the NSDAP and the erosion of the bourgeois center signaled the end to an era of bourgeois Honoratiorenpolitik that was accompanied by the triumphant protest of the provinces against large urban centers.

Brüning failed to comprehend the full significance of the outcome of the September 1930 elections. From the outset he was focused on the task of reconstructing the parliamentary system in an authoritarian direction. He regarded the Reichstag as little more than a disruptive force and was determined to use the Reich president's emergency powers as the rule rather than as the exception in order to lay the foundation for a fundamental revision of the existing constitutional system at the first opportune moment. In doing this, however, he failed to realize that in the long run he would be operating in a vacuum. For the radical opponents of the existing political system in the DNVP and NSDAP were united with the remnants of the more moderate bourgeois parties in their determination to eliminate the SPD as the republic's only ally of consequence. Out of foreign policy considerations Brüning decided for the time being to rely on Social Democratic toleration. In this respect, he left his Social Democratic partners in the dark about his plans for a revision of the constitution. But even had Brüning wanted to keep open the option of a return to parliamentary government after the newly elected Reichstag had convened on 13 October 1930, this would have been impossible given the attitude of the Reichswehr and the various interest groups exerting influence on the Reich president. The parliamentary constitution thus became an empty shell whose only function was to conceal the gradual transition to authoritarian government.

CHAPTER NINE

The Nazi Breakthrough

THE breakthrough of the NSDAP as a mass movement was the decisive event in the last phase of the Weimar Republic. At times the NSDAP was able to mobilize more than a third of the electorate at the expense of the moderate bourgeois parties. Its inroads among these voters revealed that large sectors of the moderate bourgeoisie were unwilling and unable to accept the social and political conditions of postwar Germany. Now that a stagnating economy and the consequences of the war had led to intensified conflict over the allocation of resources, the social restructuring that had been under way since the imperialist epoch made itself more keenly felt than before. This, in turn, produced an unprecedented rise in protest voting that benefited first and foremost the NSDAP, a party that was extremely adept at exploiting the social resentments of the German middle classes.

As late as 1928, no one would have imagined that the NSDAP could possibly break out of its marginal position. In the Reichstag elections of May 1928, the NSDAP had received no more than 2.6 percent of the votes, which was even less than its share in the elections of December 1924, even though it had made every conceivable effort to achieve a breakthrough into the national political arena. Disciplinary measures against the NSDAP no longer seemed necessary. The Prussian Ministry of the Interior, for example, saw no reason to continue banning Hitler from speaking in public after the original prohibition of the party as a whole had been lifted in 1925. Nevertheless, its severe defeat of 1928 bore the seeds of the NSDAP's future rise.

In 1928 the NSDAP had organized its campaign around the goal of winning the support of the working masses. The most important of those groups the National Socialists targeted, however, remained largely impervious to the party's propaganda. The election results in the large urban centers were an unmitigated disaster for the party. In greater Berlin, for example, the NSDAP polled only 1.4 percent of the popular vote, with similar results in other major west German cities. Only in Munich and Augsburg, and in some middle-class towns like Coburg and Weimar, was it able to register as much as 4 to 6 percent of the popular vote. The party's poor showing in urban areas, however, was offset by some unexpected gains. In several rural regions the NSDAP did disproportionately well, particularly in Dithmarschen and other parts of Schleswig-Holstein and in southern Lower Saxony, Upper Hesse, Franconia, and Baden.

In addressing the party's leadership conference that took place in Weimar in the early fall, Gregor Straßer, who in January 1928 had moved over from the post of propaganda chief to assume leadership of the party organization, interpreted these seemingly disappointing election results in a surprisingly good light as a relative success for the party's work over the past four years. From the perspective of the NSDAP leadership, the party's growth since the fiasco of 9 November 1923 was quite encouraging. At that time, after all, the movement was on the brink of dissolution. The Bavarian government had joined Prussia in proscribing it, and the *Völkischer Beobachter* had been closed down. Many functionaries escaped prosecution by fleeing abroad, while others left the movement. And Hitler had been condemned to five years' imprisonment by the Munich People's Tribunal.

At the same time, the Nazi movement split into a number of rival factions. Hitler had rather casually appointed Alfred Rosenberg as his deputy, even though Rosenberg was completely lacking in the practical political and organizational skills necessary to hold the party together. Moreover, Hitler chose not to provide Rosenberg with any clear directives from prison even though the unusually lenient conditions of his confinement afforded him sufficient contacts and possibilities to exercise influence. With the cooperation of Hermann Esser and Julius Streicher, Rosenberg founded a successor party called the Greater German People's Community (Großdeutsche Volksgemeinschaft). This organization, however, was unable to compete against the Racist Bloc (Völkischer Block) in Bavaria, which had established itself as an independent regional branch of the German Racist Freedom Party (Deutschvölkische Freiheitspartei or DVFP), and the German Workers' Party (Deutsche Arbeiterpartei or DAP) in Franconia. In addition to the leadership rivalries that tore it apart in Bavaria, the party organization in north Germany remained loyal to Hitler but not to the Bavarian clique and moved to assert its independence from the rest of the NSDAP.

The German Racist Freedom Party was a splinter group of the German National People's Party, which had established itself in 1922 under the leadership of two Reichstag deputies, Albrecht von Graefe and Count Ernst zu Reventlov. Largely unaffected by Prussian suppression of right-wing activities, the DVFP took advantage of the confusion that existed on the extreme Right and assumed leadership over the Völkisch–National Socialist movement. One of its main assets was General Ludendorff, whom the Munich tribunal had left alone and who, after Hitler's ignominious flight on 9 November 1923, saw himself as the providential leader of the national liberation movement. Ernst Röhm, who had illegally reorganized the outlawed SA as an athletic association and had brought it together with the remnants of the German Combat League (Deutscher Kampfbund) in the so-called Frontbann, recognized Ludendorff's authority, although he was careful to avoid a break with Hitler, whose fame had spread beyond the party faithful as a result of his stunning performance before the Munich People's Tribunal. As late as March 1925, Röhm made the officers of the Frontbann take an oath of loyalty to Hitler as the "leader and moving force of the National Socialist movement" and to Hindenburg as its patron and protector.

Gregor Straßer, an activist in the Bavarian Free Corps since 1919, had established contact with Ludendorff and Hitler as early as 1921. Elected to the Bavarian Landtag as a candidate of the Racial Bloc after the Munich fiasco, Straßer occupied a key position in the *völkisch* movement and was subsequently elected to the Reichstag in the December 1924 elections. Sincerely believing that he had Hitler's approval, Straßer agreed to the formation of a leadership consortium consisting of Ludendorff, von Graefe, and himself as Hitler's representative. At the unification congress held in Weimar in August 1924, the DVFP and National Socialists merged to form a united delegation calling itself the National Socialist Freedom Movement (Nationalsozialistische Freiheitsbewegung).

Hitler, however, had deliberately sought to prevent the party from participating in the May 1924 elections and had the support of the north German NSDAP, which had formed a leadership consortium of its own. Informed of Straßer's initiative that had given the NSDAP a disproportionately high number of mandates — in Bavaria alone the Racial Bloc had received twenty-five seats — Hitler demonstratively resigned his chairmanship of the party for the duration of his imprisonment after he had delayed in responding to the request from the north German leadership consortium that he assume its chairmanship. Hitler's reaction puzzled many of his supporters. For the party leader did nothing to help resolve the internal conflicts that had developed over the movement's future course but had simply let it be known that no one was allowed to speak in his name on any subject whatsoever. Hitler's goal was fairly clear. He wanted to postpone a regeneration of the movement until he was in a position to take action himself so that he would not once again be forced into accepting compromises with other patriotic and racist groups. In particular, Hitler was anxious to neutralize Ludendorff as his chief rival. In this respect, Hitler used Ludendorff's outspoken anti-Catholicism, which was further strengthened by the sectarian circle that had crystallized around his wife Mathilde, to turn certain members of the Bavarian government against him. Moreover, Hitler fanned the distrust against the upper-bourgeois character of the German Racist Freedom Party that still smoldered in important sectors of the original NSDAP membership. Such social elitism seemed indeed incompatible with the fundamental goal of a social revolution that was being pursued in particular by the north German National Socialists.

Under these circumstances, the Völkisch–National Socialist alliance, a stop-gap solution in the first place, fell apart even before the December 1924 Reichstag elections, although Ludendorff did not officially terminate his role in the triumvirate until early February 1925. Many National Socialist groups had declined to field candidates and called upon the party to refrain from taking part in the elections. When the National Socialist Freedom Movement emerged from the elections with a mere fourteen seats—of which four went to true National Socialists—Ludendorff's claim to national leadership lost much of its credibility. At this point, the DVFP tried to revive its esoteric Ludendorff cult in an effort to defend the prominent position that he had assumed in the racist camp following the ban against the NSDAP. The elections for Reich president were just what Hitler needed to rid himself of his troublesome competitor. In a sudden about-face, Hitler strongly urged his followers to participate in the elections and enjoined them to vote for Ludendorff as the candidate of the "national opposition" in spite of the fact that Hitler's hard-core supporters in Munich had been particularly vicious in their attacks on the general. The DVFP, on the other hand, had endorsed the candidate of the Right, Karl Jarres, in order to spare Ludendorff the embarrassment of a completely hopeless first-round candidacy. Hitler, however, persuaded Ludendorff to run. But when Ludendorff received only 1.06 percent of the votes in the first round of elections, he was politically dead. At this point the DVFP abandoned its leadership cult since it could find no other symbolic figure to take Ludendorff's place. The road to Hitler's second takeover of the National Socialist movement had thus been cleared.

The low profile that Hitler maintained during the period of his confinement at Landsberg made it possible for him to devote himself to a voluminous programmatic manuscript, which he dictated to his fellow inmate Rudolf Hess. A revised version of this manuscript was published in 1925 by Franz-Eher-Verlag as the first part of Hitler's book *Mein Kampf*. That Hitler write such a book had been suggested by Gregor Straßer, who had the ulterior motive of sparing Hitler's fellow prisoners the strain of listening to the party leader's interminable political and pseudophilosophical tirades. But before he could conclude this project, Hitler was paroled after having served just six months of his sentence. Hitler owed his early release to the fundamentally unbroken nationalist and restorationist attitudes of the Bavarian government. He had many patrons in these circles, not least of whom was the chief of the Munich police force, Ernst Pöhner, who died a few weeks later in an accident. Hitler's release was originally scheduled for 1 October 1924, but was postponed until 20 December as the result of a protest from the public prosecutor's office, which was alarmed by Röhm's activities in the Frontbann. The next reasonable step would have been to deport Hitler to Austria. But overtures to the Christian-Social cabinet under Chancellor Ignaz Seipel came to nothing, since the Austrian government felt that Hitler's presence in Austria would be a serious threat to its domestic and foreign affairs. In Munich one regarded high treason from the Right as a gentlemanly indiscretion. Moreover, the Bavarian Right had been so deeply implicated in the putsch that it would have given the government a guilty conscience had it denied Hitler the parole promised him by the People's Tribunal or expelled him from the country.

Hitler soon discovered, however, that his political maneuverability was severely limited. To be sure, the Bavarian minister president Heinrich Held, whom Hitler had visited on Pöhner's advice, agreed to lift the ban on the NSDAP and the *Völkischer Beobachter* in return for a promise by the Nazi party leader that he would respect the authority of the state and confine himself to the pursuit of power by legal means. But in late February 1925, when in his tried and true manner Hitler announced the refounding of the NSDAP at a meeting in Munich's historic Bürgerbräukeller and asserted his claim to its sole leadership, the Bavarian government wasted little time in issuing an injunction that barred him from appearing as a speaker in public meetings. The majority of the other German states quickly followed suit. As a result, Hitler was deprived of his most effective weapon in internal party affairs, namely, his ability to speak in public. Over the next several years he tried to compensate for this disability by systematic visits to local NSDAP branches, but his propaganda efforts were limited to speaking at internal meetings, writing editorials for the *Völkischer Beobachter*, and completing the second part of *Mein Kampf*.

Hitler had carefully prepared his return to the public political arena. Having left the party membership in the dark as to his intentions for two months after his release from prison, Hitler announced the refounding of the NSDAP under his leadership without so much as mentioning Ludendorff. The DVFP had earlier rejected Hitler's claim to leadership; all it was prepared to grant him was the role of the "drummer" marching by the side of the inspired military commander. Now it was Hitler who called for unity in the *völkisch* camp, whereas the German Racist Freedom Party was fostering discord. The choice between Hitler and Ludendorff provided a clear definition of the fronts that existed within the National Socialist movement and did much to obscure its real internal conflicts. When Hitler promoted the presidential candidacy of Ludendorff and thus isolated him from the DVFP, many of that party's followers found their way to the NSDAP, while their former party became an insignificant splinter party before folding altogether in 1929.

At the same time, Hitler secured his claim to the unconditional leadership of the National Socialist movement by anchoring it in the organization and the bylaws of the party. Formal responsibility for deciding questions of party membership and maintaining the party organization rested with the general membership caucus, or *Generalmitgliederversammlung*, in Munich. This body was identical with the Munich chapter of the NSDAP party organization and was controlled by Hitler's closest associates. Party bylaws stipulated that the acceptance of new members was the sole responsibility of the NSDAP's Munich headquarters and that it had a right to all initiation fees, which were also to be paid by former party members, as well as to a certain percentage of all membership dues. Only individuals could apply for membership, a requirement that was designed to prevent racist splinter groups from joining en bloc. Members were also barred from belonging to other political organizations — though this practice continued for some time to come — so as to make certain that mergers encouraged by other racist groups could not be used to obtain concessions in matters of program or personnel.

This organizational structure meant that the new party was effectively an affiliate, or *Dépendance*, of its Munich local chapter. This also meant that Hitler retained his dominant place within the movement even though its main strength after 1924 had shifted to northern and western Germany. The party's new bylaws were based on the so-called *Führerprinzip*, although for the time being a rudimentary party board continued to exist. Subsequent general membership meetings further dismantled whatever might have remained of democratic organizational principles. The crucial rule was that motions submitted to the general membership or to the party convention required the prior approval of the party leader. Moreover, the leader was for all practical purposes not subject to control of any kind from within the party, nor was he bound to abide by the decisions of any party committee. Personnel decisions lay exclusively in his hands. According to the bylaws, those who held offices in the party organization exercised administrative functions only. By the same token, party conventions or delegates' meetings were not to have decision-making powers.

This organizational structure was built entirely around the person of Adolf Hitler. Its full significance, however, was not immediately apparent, for it took several years before the autonomy of the local and regional organizations outside of Bavaria could be eliminated. Yet the main principle that the leader's power must override any and all decision making within the party organization itself existed from the outset. The fact that the NSDAP had no collective leadership group of any kind made it a unique political phenomenon, even if one compares it with the Fascist Party in Italy. It also made its internal structure fundamentally different from the that of the Communist parties, which always — even in the aberrant Stalinist era — retained the principle of collective leadership. The leadership conference, which for a time continued to handle matters of political coordination and the reconciliation of conflicting interests, had no authority to undertake action on its own initiative but could only submit suggestions to the leader.

In the beginning, however, Hitler saw no need to act in accordance with the leadership concept as spelled out in the party's statutes. Both the ban on public speaking and Hitler's growing taste for a Bohemian life-style, which led him to rent the "Haus Wachenfeld" on the Obersalzburg and then to move into the highly prestigious Prinzregentenplatz in 1929, had the consequence that the task of rebuilding the party organization fell more and more on the shoulders of a group of subordinates including, among others, Gregor Straßer and later his brother Otto, Joseph Goebbels, Franz Pfeffer von Salomon, and Karl Kaufmann. Their rise to responsible positions within the party organization not only stemmed from the fact that outside of Bavaria Hitler needed their help but was also a consequence of the NSDAP's break with the DVFP and of a changed political climate that required a new type of party functionary who no longer strutted about with the affectations of the Free Corps.

Hitler sought to counteract the persistent centrifugal tendencies within the National Socialist movement by granting far-reaching authority to act in his name to a number of party leaders on whose personal loyalty he could count. As soon as the Prussian ban against the NSDAP was lifted, he entrusted the task of building up the party organization in northern Germany to Gregor Straßer, who had severed all ties with the DVFP. But unlike Bavaria and Franconia, where the refounding of the National Socialist Party did not require the creation of a leadership body and where each local unit was subordinated to the authority of the Munich party leadership, Hitler had to work within existing party structures in western and northern Germany and, in contrast to the constantly traveling Straßer, was unable to exert direct personal influence.

At Straßer's insistence, Hitler agreed to grant district leaders, operating under the formal title of *Gauleiter*, far-reaching decision-making powers. This move represented a clear departure from the command structure that had been adopted with the reorganization of the NSDAP in 1925 and effectively transferred the leadership principle from the national to an intermediary level. It may have been a sign of weakness, but Hitler realized that only in Bavaria and Franconia could he count on the unequivocal support of the party faithful—and even here their ranks had been thinned by his turn against Ludendorff following his release from prison. The fact is that although the refounding of the NSDAP in late February 1925 had provided a welcome and clear-cut break with the DVFP and other racist groups, this had entailed a painful loss of membership. If at the end of 1923 the movement still counted some 55,000 members, by the beginning of 1925 its active support consisted at best of 25,000 followers.

In the following years the NSDAP presented the checkered image of a disparate, if not somewhat haphazard, collection of ideological and political groupings. Individual districts varied greatly in size and organization, and rivalry and high-handedness were rampant among district leaders, something about which the party's national leadership could do relatively little. Even though the party's charter required the appointment of the *Gauleiter* by the central office, Munich was frequently not consulted but only informed after the fact. The far-reaching decentralization of the party's personnel and propaganda policies was not merely a concession to the pressure of regional peculiarities, but it was also consistent with Hitler's tendency to think of the party more as a company of followers personally loyal to him than as a bureaucratic apparatus. At Hitler's insistence, the election of local unit leaders, or *Ortsgruppenleiter*, was to be continued on the assumption that this would yield more effective leaders through a selection process that conformed to his social Darwinist view of politics. Even then, the district leaders retained the right to veto the election of anyone of whom they did not approve. In the administration of party finances, the Munich central was able to assert its primacy only gradually, even though Philipp Bouhler made certain with his typical bureaucratic stubbornness that it received its rightful share of the membership dues.

The contradiction between bureaucratic forms of organization and Hitler's preference for personal ties to lower-level party functionaries was bound to exacerbate rivalries within the party. It is doubtful whether the party could have been held together without the tenacious organizational work of the leadership cadre around Straßer, which by and large operated independently of the directives issued by Munich. This, however, meant that Hitler's intention of basing the NSDAP exclusively on the principle of personal loyalty to the leader while at the same time giving the party's local chapters sufficient freedom of action was for the most part frustrated. Styling himself the sole guardian of the "National Socialist idea," Hitler intended to make blind obedience to the leader's will the guiding principle of the movement. Its strength, he explained, lay by no means "in cultivating the greatest possible spiritual independence of individual members, but in maximizing the discipline with which its members followed the intellectual [*geistige*] direction of the leader." From this perspective, Hitler regarded discussions within the party about the direction in which it should be headed as superfluous. Party conventions, he declared in 1926 at the first muster of his troops in Weimar, were "not the place where half-baked and uncertain ideas can possibly be clarified." Hitler's conviction that the work of the party should be concerned exclusively with the recruitment of new members and followers and that it should take on the character of a pure campaign organization was only realized in steps.

During his political apprenticeship in Munich, Hitler had begun to strike the pose of a politician who tackles a crisis, mobilizes political resentments for his cause, and pursues the vision of a mass movement inspired by fanatical will to fight without worrying about any of the intermediary steps. By contrast, Straßer and the north German district leaders faced the necessity of creating a solid party apparatus that could compete with the DVFP. Unlike Munich, where the movement could always operate within a broad current of *völkisch*-restorationist sentiment, the cities of the Ruhr basin and northern Germany, as well as greater Berlin, where the party competed with the tightly knit organizations of the SPD and KPD, offered little opportunity for the rowdy anti-Semitism of Bavarian vintage to take root and grow. Finding itself in the diaspora, as it were, the party needed a platform that addressed concrete issues, not least of which was the social question.

Clearly visible after 1924, the rift between the west and north German wings of the movement and the Bavarian-Franconian party also stemmed from a different pattern of social recruitment for those younger leadership cadres upon whom the Prussian local chapters were based. In the Bavarian and Franconian organizations, small-town and middle-class elements imbued with the *völkisch* ressentiment of the early twenties held the upper hand, whereas the new recruits, who soon outnumbered the older constituency, were both socially less homogeneous and more urban and antibourgeois than their older counterparts. This gave rise to considerable tension that could not be resolved in either programmatic or practical terms. Since the structure of the NSDAP precluded the collective formulation of objectives, conflicts over the direction in which the movement should be headed invariably took the form of personal rivalries. Straßer, who successfully portrayed himself as Hitler's loyal follower, managed to isolate the NSDAP party leader from the full effect of these rivalries, although the north German faction continually criticized the increasing popularity of a Byzantine personality cult for which they held Hermann Esser primarily responsible.

Joseph Goebbels, who had worked as editor in chief of a *völkisch* newspaper in Elberfeld, joined the NSDAP in 1925. He shared Straßer's dislike of the "messy pigsty" that existed at the party's national headquarters in Munich. When he remarked that Hitler was surrounded by the wrong people, he only said aloud what the party's district leaders from the northwest believed in their hearts. In 1926 Gregor Straßer still believed that he could bring Hitler under his influence but failed to realize the man's stubbornness in holding on to the goals he had set for himself. Straßer felt that Hitler's vision could be transformed into a practical political strategy only if it were possible to create an effective counterweight to the privileged position the Munich clique held within the party organization without at the same time openly challenging Hitler's leadership monopoly. In the fall of 1925 Straßer united the district organizations he had established under the aegis of an organization that called itself the Working Group of the North and West German District Leaders of the NSDAP (Arbeitsgemeinschaft der nord- und westdeutschen Gauleiter der NSDAP). From the outset, this organization embraced divergent tendencies and was characterized by strong internal contradictions. Joseph Goebbels and Gregor Straßer's younger brother Otto, who was deeply influenced by the national revolutionary Ernst Niekisch, represented an outspoken socialist position within the organization. "First salvation of socialism [*sozialistische Erlösung*], then national liberation will sweep in like a storm," wrote Goebbels, who called for a full-scale attack on the "bosses in Munich" and perceived the conflict primarily as one of generations. For all his tactical shifts, the National Socialist agitator abandoned the militant anticapitalism that characterized his early thinking. Goebbels's antipathy toward the capitalist economic system was not rooted in a commitment to the social emancipation of the proletariat but in an intractable and irrepressible hatred of the upper bourgeoisie that was driven by the neurotic ambition of a socially declassé academic failure.

The Northwestern Working Group founded its own organ, the *National-sozialistische Briefe* edited by Straßer and Goebbels, the latter himself a member of the NSDAP leadership group. This was the first step toward the establishment of the Kampf-Verlag, which, under the direction of Otto Straßer, soon brought out the biweekly *Der National Sozialist* and eventually came to control seven of the seventeen party organs. In this respect, the Kampf-Verlag represented an important counterweight to the Munich-based Franz-Eher-Verlag under the direction of Max Amann. In the meantime, the organizational consolidation of the northwestern districts had aroused the suspicions of the autocratic party clique in Munich, which was by no means unaware of the mounting opposition to its high-handed leadership style and its posture of infallibility. Straßer and his closest associates, among them Karl Kaufmann and Joseph Goebbels, sought to isolate Hitler from the camarilla and to win him over to a course of political action that would concentrate the party's efforts on fighting the DVFP, National Rural League, and Stahlhelm, and on dissociating itself as unequivocally as possible from the capitalist economic system in order to gain the support of organized labor.

Gregor Straßer failed to realize that Hitler was, at all costs, determined to avoid clear political positions and sought instead to commit the party to a messianic faith in his own leadership abilities. Otto Straßer, by contrast, became more and more convinced that in the final analysis Hitler's actions were driven by sheer intuition, that in reality he was a "sleep walker," or perhaps a "medium like those that arise in the most confused eras of human history," and that he had no capacity for constructive political action. His somewhat more naive brother Gregor labored under the illusion that he was acting in agreement with Hitler when in the summer of 1925 he circulated, without consulting the Nazi party leader, the draft of a program that was designed to resolve the contradictions contained in the Twenty-Five-Point Program from February 1920. This initiative represented a direct challenge to Hitler's claim that the party program was immutable and violated the first premise of his leadership style, namely, that he should not allow his hands to become tied in programmatic matters. The party dictator immediately recognized that he must avoid taking a position that could be interpreted as hostile either to the socialist idea as he understood it or to the national concept. As a practical visionary, he had come to the conclusion that a majority could only be achieved, as he explained in an address to the Hamburg National Club (Hamburger Nationalklub) in

1926, through the dissolution of the two mutually antagonistic political blocs, one international-socialist and the other nationalist in character, that currently dominated German public life.

In Hitler's mind, his own claim to absolute leadership and the ideological unity of the movement were simply two sides of the same coin. As he countered Straßer's efforts by summoning the leaders of the party to a conference in Bamberg in February 1926, he was acting out of this twofold motive. The external occasion for his intervention was the decision of the party's leaders in the north to side with the Left and against national conservatives in supporting a referendum for the expropriation of the German ruling houses. Hitler's appeal to the principle of law to block this initiative was no more convincing than the anti-Semitic campaign he launched shortly thereafter. Straßer felt abandoned by his partisans, above all by Goebbels, who experienced his "conversion on the road to Damascus" in Bamberg and defected to Hitler; obliged to withdraw his draft program, Straßer gave in on one point after another in order to avoid an open break with Hitler.

The Bamberg leadership conference, which represented a formal concession to the internally divided group of northwestern district leaders, revealed Hitler's characteristic way of resolving conflicts. By calling for unity, eschewing personal attacks, and showering his opponents with signs of his personal trust while at the same time demanding their unconditional loyalty, Hitler was able to disarm the emerging opposition and enhance his own personal prestige by restoring the outward unity of the movement. It was equally characteristic of Hitler's leadership style that he refrained from taking a position on the merits of the conflict itself, invested the controversial Gottfried Feder with responsibility for the party program, and appointed Gregor Straßer to the central committee, where he was given the task of coordinating the party's propaganda effort. Shortly after the conference Hitler also appointed Franz Pfeffer von Salomon chief of the SA and Goebbels, by now an unabashed Hitler zealot, district leader in Berlin.

The conflict that had been papered over in Bamberg was not so much a matter of substance as one of differing strategies. In their commitment to reduce the existing system of government to its very foundations as well as in their indecision as to whether or not this was to be accomplished through parliamentary methods, the differences between Hitler and the younger party leaders who had met at Bamberg were little more than differences of degree. In northern Germany participation in parliamentary elections was even seen as a violation of the National Socialist ideal. The party's break with the DVFP had emphasized this point. As the 1924 election campaign began, Hitler maintained a low profile, so much so, in fact, that contemporaries spoke of his incomprehensible mania for neutrality. The temporary alliance between the NSDAP's successor organization and the DVFP spared Hitler from having to make a decision. Tactical calculations and inner uncertainty prompted him, as late as 1926 and 1927, to have the question of participation in parliamentary elections placed on the agenda of the leadership conferences held in conjunction with the party congresses. It was, therefore, not just because Hitler was ineligible to run for office that he declined to have his name placed at the top of the NSDAP's national slate of candidates, or *Reichliste*, in any Reichstag election.

During his confinement in the Landsberg fortress, Hitler had come to the conclusion that, unlike in 1923, he would have to pursue his conquest of undivided political power without resorting to the kind of armed uprising that had brought him into conflict with the Reichswehr. Even then Hitler was not comfortable with the putsch plans of the German Combat Alliance. Dissociating himself from paramilitary methods was closely related to his hopes of an early parole. His call for the refounding of the NSDAP expressly stated that in the new version of the SA military considerations were to be excluded. After Ernst Röhm was released from prison, he had merged the remnants of the Combat League and various nationalist defense militia to form the Frontbann, which, conceiving of itself as an armed combat group, placed itself under Ludendorff's military leadership. When Hitler handed command of the SA over to Röhm, the latter sought to create an organization that was independent from the NSDAP and that would represent the military arm of the national opposition. Hitler, however, refused to deviate from his hopes of building up the SA as a civilian political entity within the framework of the NSDAP. In April 1925 it came to a open break between the two men. Röhm resigned his command of both the Frontbann and the SA and went off to Bolivia.

Even later in his career, Hitler strongly opposed the militarist tendencies of the SA. In May 1926 Hitler permitted the merger of the SA units that since the party's refounding in 1925 had existed only at the local level into a centrally run organization headed by Pfeffer von Salomon. In doing so, Hitler effectively rescinded Röhm's refusal to subordinate the SA to the party. Hitler now enjoined the SA and SS (Schutz-Staffel der NSDAP)—the latter founded in November 1925 as a special elite corps—to bear witness to the unshakable will and fighting resolve of the National Socialist movement through their own unity and discipline. The SA was thus supposed to project the ideal image of the party. In every respect, it was to function, at times through the use of terror, as an instrument of National Socialist propaganda.

By no means did this decision—a decision that had the full support of the group around Gregor Straßer—mean that the NSDAP was now resolved to gain power by parliamentary methods. At the general membership conference in May 1926, Hitler made it perfectly clear that the acquisition of mandates in the Reichstag and state parliaments served one purpose and one purpose only, namely, to expand the scope and effectiveness of the party's propaganda. It was, Hitler continued, understood that National Socialist deputies would stay away from the elected bodies and that their work on behalf of the party would be remunerated only with the customary perks such as per diems, parliamentary immunity, or free railroad passes. In February 1931, when the NSDAP delegation joined the DNVP in boycotting the Reichstag, party leaders stressed that one of the goals behind the action was to use all the means at their disposal for the ongoing campaign of popular mobilization. Furthermore, the NSDAP leadership did not want to become involved in elections where its prospects of victory were slim for fear that defeat would result in a loss of party prestige. It was, therefore, not until the late fall of 1926 that the NSDAP participated in the Saxon and Thuringian Landtag elections; in later years it fielded candidates in municipal and regional elections only on an ad hoc basis.

At this juncture, Gregor Straßer and his followers did not expect that by "poking its nose into the Reichstag," as Hitler put it, the party would be able to achieve much in the way of a political revolution. By concentrating their energies on building up a powerful party organization, they sought to transform the NSDAP into "a community dedicated to a single world view, or what Hitler called "eine verschworene Weltanschauungsgemeinschaft." At the same time, however, they needed an effective leadership apparatus that, like those of the Left, could make tactical adjustments as circumstances demanded. As for the conquest of power, National Socialist activists remained haunted by the memory of November 1918. This explained in large part their lack of interest in working within parliament or in increasing their electoral strength. Their primary goal was to build up a strong National Socialist organization in Germany's large urban centers.

The group of district leaders who were most intimately involved in the everyday work of the party realized full well that Hitler was indispensable as a symbol of the party's unity and as a purveyor of ideas. Privately the Straßer brothers, Kaufmann, Pfeffer von Salomon, and initially Goebbels as well harbored misgivings about Hitler's leadership style and his tactical acumen. They criticized his poor understanding of human nature, his excessively ambitious plans, and his tendency to avoid conflicts and decisions. Even though Gregor Straßer went along with the cult of the leader, which was reflected in the introduction of the obligatory "Heil Hitler" greeting in 1926, he felt a strong sense of personal distance from the party leader at the same time that he recognized his undisputed powers of intuition and his visionary gifts. Straßer viewed Hitler more as an artist than as a practitioner of Realpolitik and felt that as such he was incapable of "well thought-out, systematic work" and did not have "both feet on the ground." Such people, he said, can "sometimes achieve unprecedented effects, if they can do it at a single stroke and if others are ready to draw the necessary conclusions before a reaction has had time to materialize." Straßer was fully aware that Hitler's propensity for autosuggestion, and his belief, fostered by partial successes, in his "personal infallibility" made it impossible to counter his intuitions with logical arguments. Though deeply impressed by Hitler's dilettantish pronunciamentos about the nature of the world, Pfeffer von Salomon was concerned that the Führer would lose all sense of proportion. It was therefore important, as he confided to Otto Wagener, the deputy commander of the SA and one of the party's future specialists on economic affairs, "that those around him keep a clear perspective regarding the true measure of things" (*das Maß der Dinge nicht aus den Augen verlieren*). Straßer shared this view and conducted his policy accordingly.

The draft of Straßer's program that Hitler had dismissed so cavalierly contained the strategic elements of what has come to be known as the NSDAP's "urban plan." This strategy was based on the premise that the only way in which the NSDAP could hope to tap the socialist parties' electoral reserve was to stress the socialist elements of its own program and to formulate a program of constructive social policies. At the same time, the draft represented an attempt to commit Hitler to some kind of program. Aside from the fact that the Straßer draft replaced Gottfried Feder's appeal for an end to the bondage of interest slavery with a more realistic assessment of the existing economic system, differences between it and the Twenty-Five-Point Program were slight. A number of counterdrafts were submitted, among them a much more radical proposal by Goebbels that has not survived as well as an exposé by Pfeffer von Salomon, whose racially determined social Darwinism anticipated the future policy of racial extermination. The ideas contained in Straßer's proposal can be traced back to his brother Otto, who in most respects was his intellectual superior.

Gregor Straßer's proposal had been prompted not so much by any single issue as by the need to advance a reasonably binding program to help the NSDAP in its confrontation with the political Left. In this respect, Straßer realized that racially anti-Semitic fantasies in themselves did not add up to a program that could effectively counteract Communist agitation. As a result, his draft program addressed the future economic order in considerable detail. Calling for a "far-reaching transfer of the means of production to public ownership," he also wanted to preserve the "private management of individual firms." That his special proposals as to how this was to be accomplished were rather vague suggests that his program, which opposed big industry and the large-scale concentration of capital, harkened back to preindustrial modes of production and in many respects represented a relapse into the utopian socialism that was so popular in certain artisan circles.

By the same token, the Straßer draft called for breaking up large agrarian estates in an attempt to create new peasant holdings. These ideas were poorly suited to bridge the gap between the proletarian Left and the bourgeois nationalist Right that had become such a prominent feature of German society. From a tactical perspective, proposals like this placed the NSDAP squarely between the existing party fronts without addressing the needs of the industrial working class even if profit sharing and the co-ownership of stock represented sensible demands. Within the framework of an extreme anti-Semitism that reduced capitalist exploitation to the alleged Jewish takeover of German economic life as a whole, these ideas amounted to no more than rhetoric.

The portion of Straßer's draft that was devoted to constitutional questions was remarkable for its moderation. His call for the establishment of a "national dictatorship" by extending the authority of the Reich president coincided with the goals of the conservative Right. This was also true in large measure of his sketch for a corporatist state structure that would take the place of the existing parliamentary system and the political parties. There was no mention of the fascist model of the party as the embodiment of the state despite the more general influence of the Italian example. The points of contact with neoconservative themes such as Oswald Spengler's "Prussian Socialism" and Othmar Spann's theory of the corporatist state were unmistakable. Straßer's program differed from kindred neoconservative projects only by virtue of its greater emphasis on a pseudosocialist element that was directed against large-scale capitalism and large-scale agriculture. The constitutional ideas of Edgar Jung were already anticipated in much of what Straßer proposed.

What the draft had to say in the area of foreign policy reflected the influence of Otto Straßer's associates in the national-revolutionary movement and was rooted in the juxtaposition, common to the entire Right, of the "long-standing ossification of the capitalist West" to the "continuous flow of the East" (noch im Fluß befindlicher Osten). Straßer's call for an alliance with Bolshevist Russia, however, was rejected out of hand by Hitler, who had just committed himself to a strategy of creating the conditions for Germany's expansion through an understanding with England and the cultivation of closer ties with Italy. In spite of the sharp opposition he encountered on account of his willingness to abandon South Tyrol, Hitler succeeded in having this adopted as the official party line and was subsequently always concerned that the party maintain a unified position on foreign policy questions.

By comparison with Hitler's boundless dreams of hegemony, Straßer's eclectic draft program must have appeared quite moderate. Although it envisaged Anschluß with Austria and, as its ultimate goal, the restoration of Germany's 1914 borders, Straßer's foreign policy program lacked the customary thrust in favor of imperialist expansion into eastern Europe. It also provided for the creation of "United States of Europe" through a gradual trade and tariff union that in the first phase would embrace Germany, Switzerland, Hungary, Denmark, Luxemburg, and Holland and in the second France and the other west European countries. The stridently nationalist tone that characterized Hitler's and Goebbels's utterances on foreign policy was absent from Straßer's draft.

This alone would have made it impossible for Straßer's program to find the necessary support within the NSDAP party organization.

After the debacle at Bamberg Straßer abandoned his efforts to formulate a binding program for the NSDAP. This, however, did little to weaken his determination to fight the watering down of National Socialist principles by the Munich clique and to secure the party's "socialist" commitment. Against Alfred Rosenberg, who favored the "national" over the "socialist" moment in the party's political orientation, Straßer emphasized the latter, but in such a way that it amounted to little more than a declaration of ethical principles. Like most neoconservative pundits, Straßer rejected the French Revolution's postulate of equality and felt that it should be replaced by an assessment of each individual's contribution to the welfare of the community and that this criterion should determine the rank order of society. At the same time, Straßer favored corporatist ideas that were incompatible with contemporary industrial society. Straßer's notion of socialism was conceptually imprecise and failed to recognize the economic pressures of the modern capitalist system. The neo-conservative character of Straßer's socialism was reflected not only in his claim that the Marxist parties were materialistic but also in his concept of labor as the fulfillment of the individual's duty to the community. In short, Straßer cannot be seen as the representative of a Nazi left wing, even though he did conceive of himself as a leader of the working class and rejected Hitler's cynical comments about the proletarian masses. In contrast to his brother, Otto Straßer tended toward a stronger socialist position. Under his influence, the publications of the Kampf-Verlag functioned as a forum for the party's left wing, which in Saxony and western Germany enjoyed widespread sympathy.

The outcome of the May 1928 Reichstag elections dealt a serious, if not fatal, blow to the party's previous strategy of winning the support of Germany's urban population at the expense of the countryside. The organs of the Kampf-Verlag attributed the NSDAP's lack of appeal among industrial workers to its ambiguous attitude with respect to the capitalist economic system. By intensifying their socialistic rhetoric, the leaders of the party's left wing only found themselves forced more and more to the periphery of the movement. The party's rank-and-file membership, however, continued to look upon the NSDAP as a workers' party and felt that its task was to free the laboring masses from the influence of Marxist internationalism and to convert them to a genuine "German Socialism." Hitler represented this point of view *expressis verbis*. One of the NSDAP's most important organizational and propaganda goals, he insisted, was "to bring the workers into the national community as a unified sector of society that feels and wants to be part of the nation."

The NSDAP's call for the "nationalization of the working class" had nothing to do with real social responsibility or with a deeper insight into the

problems of the working population. Hitler and his closest associates were incapable of developing even the slightest comprehension of the modern industrial world and the social condition of the factory workers. The party's leader
made extremely disparaging comments time and time again about the masses
of manual workers. Yet there were two reasons why the NSDAP could not dispense with the industrial work force in its entirety. The first was that without
the potential mass support of the industrial proletariat the party remained
essentially dependent on the bourgeois forces whom Hitler considered — and
this was the extent of his socialism — utterly incapable of shaping a political
movement. The second was that the NSDAP could command the respect of
the ruling elites, especially in the Reichswehr and in big industry, only as long
as it was able to live up to its claim that it would free the German working
class from the influence of "Marxism" and neutralize it as a factor in the political class struggle. It was precisely this expectation that not only accounted for
Hitler's toleration after 1923 but also led to the alliance with the conservatives
that culminated in his appointment as chancellor.

Communist and Social Democratic charges that Hitler was nothing more
than the lackey of high finance and big business held true only for the idealized
image of the NSDAP that Hugenberg and right-wing industrialists had created.
Only by means of an elaborate propaganda effort and considerable deception
on its part was the NSDAP able to keep this image alive. In this respect, there
can be no doubt that Hitler knew how to create such expectations and how to
use them without scruple for his own political purposes. For all the energy he
spent on trying to win the favor of big business, Hitler retained the pseudosocialist vocabulary he had used since the earliest days of the movement. In
internal party deliberations, however, Hitler assiduously avoided any remark
that would reveal the respective weight he gave to the words "National Socialism" in charting the party's political course. In public statements he would
avoid having to commit himself by stressing that he was neither a bourgeois
nor a Marxist politician.

On the level of practical politics, Hitler supported the strategic reorientation the party undertook in the early summer of 1928, which entailed the
abandonment of the NSDAP's urban plan and the concentration of its efforts
on winning the support of previously neglected sectors of the electorate, the
most important of which was the farmers. Before 1928 such a strategic reorientation would have been virtually impossible. The NSDAP originally was a
movement with a predominantly urban profile, something that changed only
very gradually, if at all. Farmers were always underrepresented in the party
leadership as well as in its membership. Its invocations of "Blood and Soil" —
a formulation taken from the arsenal of *völkisch* slogans — and its evocation of
a healthy peasantry as the fount of the nation's life notwithstanding, the party
paid insufficient attention to agricultural interests. At the beginning, in fact,

the NSDAP was positively hostile to large-scale agriculture. By the same token, its pseudosocialist agitation alienated Germany's peasant population, particularly since the party showed no interest in supporting the farmers' demands for fiscal relief at the same time that it catered to the victims of the currency revaluation. In the final analysis, the movement could offer farmers no more than the tired propaganda cliché that their plight was caused by the baneful influence of the Socialists' allies, the "usurious Jewish capitalists."

In spite of its essentially negative attitude toward agriculture, there was increasing evidence from 1927 on that significant gains were within the NSDAP's grasp, particularly in those crisis-stricken areas where the Rural People's Movement, or Landvolkbewegung, had begun to undermine the rural population's traditional allegiance to the National Rural League and the DNVP. Even before the elections of 1928, the party leadership tried to adapt its propaganda apparatus to the new situation. Still, the main target of the election campaign was the urban middle class. The fact that the NSDAP won votes in several rural regions where it had no more than a rudimentary party apparatus testified to its appeal as a radical protest movement. Recognizing rural Germany as a potential source of support, Hitler decided in April 1928 — quite against his custom — to offer an authoritative interpretation of Point 17 in the NSDAP party program whereby the call for expropriation was limited to the "Jewish real-estate speculation societies" and did not affect the institution of private property.

The NSDAP leadership was quick to grasp the lessons of its unexpectedly poor performance in the 1928 Reichstag elections. Henceforth the party's election campaigns were to be coordinated from its national propaganda office in Munich, now under the direction of Heinrich Himmler, and would be designed to tap the electoral potential of protest voters eager to vent their rage against the existing political system. The preconditions for this change of direction had been established back in 1926, when Straßer was head of the party propaganda office and Himmler his deputy. By making the relevant officials in the local or regional party organization directly answerable to the central propaganda office, they had created a vertically integrated apparatus that ensured a uniform use of language everywhere. In 1930, when Goebbels replaced Himmler as head of the national propaganda office so that the latter could devote his full attention to building up the SS, the foundations for this unique and unprecedented propaganda apparatus were already in place.

The transition to a relentlessly intensifying propaganda campaign that in the fall of 1928 grew out of the party's defeat at the polls the previous May would have been inconceivable had not party leaders simultaneously succeeded in transforming a movement held together by little more than the Führer mythos and the camaraderie of those who belonged to the party's second tier of leaders into an unusually effective and disciplined machine. Hitler's notion of a movement sworn to his person and defined by its fanatical ideology provided Gregor

Straßer and the young functionaries he had brought into the party leadership
the shell they could fill through the construction of a hierarchically structured
organization. Straßer's motives as well as his methods stood in sharp contrast
to Hitler's vision of a party structure that was unbureaucratic and based on the
principle of direct subordination and personal allegiance. For without the tight
organization of its individual parts, a mass organization like the NSDAP could
not survive for long.

Straßer consciously understood his role in the party leadership as a corrective to Hitler's excessive ambitions and his arbitrary interference in the work of
the party. In this respect, Straßer was realistic enough to realize that any new
attempt to specify the content of the party program was bound to fail because
of Hitler's resistance. Yet in his eyes the fact that the NSDAP had "only an
ideological but not a constructive program" would be a weakness in the event
that the party ever entered the government. "We are fighting for power without
actually knowing what to do with it once we have gotten it." Straßer therefore
adopted a twofold approach when he became head of the party organization in
early 1928. On the one hand, he sought to establish more comprehensive control over the entire party apparatus. At the same time, however, he decided to
create a planning mechanism that would be in a position to issue clear political
directives after the party seized political power.

It was only to be expected that the organizational changes Straßer pursued
with inexhaustible energy would encounter strong opposition from within the
party. Nevertheless, he succeeded in establishing a uniform structure at the
district level of the party's national organization. Before doing this, however,
it had required all of Straßer's powers of persuasion to convince Hitler that
he should divide up his personal fiefdom, the district of Upper Bavaria, and
divest it of its character as an entity that stood directly under the authority of
the Führer. Moreover, Straßer sought to curtail the power of his erstwhile partisan Goebbels, who since his change of heart in 1926 had become his keenest
rival. Through the expansion of the propaganda and organizational leadership of the party, the erstwhile apothecary from Landshut was able to push
older party leaders — and, in particular, the party secretary Philipp Bouhler —
to the periphery of party affairs. Only the party treasurer, Franz Xaver Schwarz,
was unaffected by these changes, whereas the Investigatory and Arbitration
Committee (Untersuchungs- und Schlichtungsausschuß) headed since 1926 by
Walter Buch, Otto Dietrich's Press Office, and large parts of the propaganda
office stood under Straßer's indirect control. To be sure, Hitler denied Straßer
the position of secretary general of the party. This, however, did little to change
the fact that, next to the Führer, Straßer was the most influential person in
the NSDAP.

Straßer also sought to replace the overlapping competencies that had
plagued the party for some time with a clearly delineated vertical organization

that one could supervise with a minimum of effort. In this respect, Straßer tried to curb indirectly Hitler's spontaneous interventions by directing subordinate party authorities to go through proper channels when dealing with the central office. A major innovation in this regard was the installation of regional and national inspectors as the key ingredients of a vertical control system that would make it possible for Straßer to influence party appointments at the district level as well as the increasingly important task of selecting candidates for election to the state legislatures and the Reichstag. These measures met with ferocious opposition from the party's district leaders, who appealed directly to Hitler in an attempt to protect the far-reaching autonomy to which they had become accustomed. Hitler, who was loath to dismantle the system of district leaders who were directly subordinate to him, responded by introducing a dualistic element into the structure of the party. The system of Reich inspectors was thus the first institution of centralized control that Hitler abolished at the end of 1932.

A particularly telling sign of Straßer's own political agenda was the creation in 1929 of the Organizational Division II (Organisationsabteilung II) under the leadership of Konstantin Hierl, who was not only a close personal friend but the future commander of the National Work Corps (Reichsarbeitsdienst). The purpose of the agency was to act as a general staff that would make the necessary preparations for a future takeover of power without regard for the exigencies of everyday politics. This planning organization was patterned after the departmental structure of the national government. Straßer sought to staff it with qualified experts who did not necessarily come from the more established leadership cadres of the NSDAP. This only strengthened the technocratic character of the Organizational Division II, which for reasons of personnel was reunited with Division I in June 1932. By then, the demands of constant campaigning were so great that as many staff members as possible were pulled out of the planning organization. Hitler himself was deeply hostile to bureaucratic planning, which he considered incompatible with the ideological character of the National Socialist movement. At the end of 1932 he also dismantled this element of Straßer's organizational legacy.

Straßer was unable to come up with an adequate solution to the problem of how the upper echelons of the party leadership should be organized. For example, the SA, which was growing rapidly under Pfeffer von Salomon, remained an alien body that had not been sufficiently integrated into the party as a whole. Not only changes in the chain of command, but also complaints about lack of funding for the SA sparked repeated internal conflicts within the party, to which Walter Stennes, the deputy commander of the eastern branch of the SA, responded with such defiance that Pfeffer was obliged to resign as SA chief in August 1930. Hitler's reaction to these developments was to place both the SA and the SS directly under his own command. It soon became clear, however, that this would not be sufficient to put an end to the increasing friction that stemmed both from the greater self-confidence of the SA and its claim to meaningful participation in the party's affairs.

In 1927 Straßer had vigorously opposed a proposal from Artur Dinter, a spokesman of the *völkisch* ideology and district leader of the NSDAP in Thuringia who was subsequently expelled from the party, that the NSDAP create a party senate. For his own part, Straßer had hoped that the bureaucratic apparatus he had created would hold Hitler's interventions in check. In the place of the party congresses, which had been held at Nuremberg since 1927 and which no longer served as an appropriate forum for serious political discussion, Straßer advocated regular meetings of the party's district leaders and special conferences as a way of achieving the necessary degree of political coordination. But since these meetings had no decision-making power — with the result that Hitler could accept or reject their suggestions as he saw fit — they had no institutional standing. At the level of the party's national leadership, there was no formal communication among the various party agencies, which were acting completely independently of each other. By the same token, the leaders of the party organization were unable to keep a hold on the special agencies and professional committees that proliferated with great rapidity in the period of the party's expansion. But as long as the party concentrated its efforts on electoral agitation and avoided making political decisions, the dualism between the amazingly efficient bureaucratic planning and supervisory apparatus that Straßer had designed and Hitler's predilection for free-floating decisions did not become fully apparent. Hitler's disinterest in routine decisions meant that there was a tacit division of labor that required his attention only when negotiations with the bourgeois Right were on the agenda.

By virtue of his relentless organizational energy and his performance in parliament, Gregor Straßer earned increasing respect both inside and outside the party. Admiration for Straßer was in fact so great that he ran the risk of coming into competition with the Hitler cult. Straßer's personal charisma as a speaker at public rallies had been an important asset during the period of the NSDAP's breakthrough. Only in the hectic 1932 election campaigns was it surpassed by the speeches that Hitler tailored specifically to the psychotic public mood that had been created by the deepening crisis. Right-wing associations and parties interested in collaborating with the NSDAP after its strategic reorientation in September 1928 generally regarded Straßer as their most important negotiating partner. No doubt these organizations hoped that Straßer's fundamental willingness to redirect his party toward a more constructive course of action would weaken the NSDAP's more radical factions and prompt Hitler to cooperate with the presidential cabinets that seemed to be just around the corner.

The NSDAP's frenetic campaigning from 1928 on was orchestrated by a national propaganda office that operated on the premise that propaganda actions must be so concentrated in time and space that public opinion will be totally saturated. In this respect, the party did not limit its activities to the election campaigns themselves but staged continual publicity offensives with regional emphases. Neither the bourgeois nor the socialist parties were able to offer anything remotely comparable with the highly centralized campaign of the NSDAP, which, unlike the other parties, poured all of its energies into political propaganda. All members of the NSDAP contributed to this propaganda effort, if only by wearing the party's lapel pin. The logistics of every campaign were carefully worked out beforehand; for major events all the available resources in a given district were mobilized. No one was more innovative in the use of unconventional campaign methods than Joseph Goebbels. Under his direction, the election campaign of 1930 became a classic example of fascist mobilization strategies. The number of rallies the NSDAP held exceeded those of any other party by fourfold. In the last four weeks of the campaign alone, the NSDAP planned to hold no fewer than 34,000 public demonstrations. In order to ensure uniform procedures and to convey the impression of political unity, local party units were instructed to conduct their propaganda in strict conformity with directives issued by the central propaganda office in Munich, which prescribed virtually every detail of the techniques that were to be used. In addition to the customary public rallies, there were information booths, band concerts, SA parades, church attendance, mailing campaigns, and the constant distribution of leaflets. The central office supplied the local party agencies with a constant flood of materials, including postcards, stickers, lapel pins, brochures, leaflets, and posters. There was nothing that escaped the ingenuity of Nazi propagandists. A case in point was the use of film. Under Goebbels's influence the party had begun to exploit the potential of the political propaganda film to an unprecedented extent as early as 1930. Such films were shown mostly in places where Hitler and other prominent party leaders were not able to appear as speakers. For the manufacture of outdoor sound film, the NSDAP turned to an American company, Twentieth-Century Fox. The NSDAP's most spectacular use of modern technology could be seen in Hitler's airplane trip through Germany in the July 1932 election campaign.

In addition, the national propaganda office in Munich also decreed that the same publicity techniques should be employed simultaneously throughout the country. Since it proved difficult to print and distribute the campaign materials from a central location, the text and pictures to be used in the campaigns were sent to local propaganda offices for duplication. This procedure insured that the content of the propaganda, which would be coordinated with releases in the party press, would be uniform throughout all of Germany. To enhance its effectiveness, Nazi propaganda concentrated on a limited number of themes such as the fight against the Young Plan or the corrupting influence of special interests in public life. Through the uniformity of propaganda the party was able to create an impression of unity and fighting resolve. These techniques proved unusually effective in other respects as well. Insofar as the local propaganda offices were required to file regular reports on the success of the propaganda techniques they had used as well as on the mood of the local electorate and were encouraged to submit proposals for new propaganda initiatives, the party's central leadership could rely upon an effective network of communications that anticipated the use of modern polling techniques.

Feedback from the local areas made it possible for the national propaganda office in Munich to focus its propaganda on specific groups and, if necessary, to make adjustments in the course of the campaign itself. In later campaigns, however, the party abandoned the technique of uniform propaganda and modified its message to fit the specific social structure of the election district, especially in areas where it had not yet tapped the seemingly inexhaustible potential of new voters. At the same time, the party addressed the needs of particular occupational groups in separate election rallies that were held specifically for those groups. Taking into account the increasing fragmentation of voter interests, this technique allowed the party the luxury of making a different set of promises at each of these meetings. Moreover, campaign messages and ideological themes were carefully tailored to address the concerns of the various target groups. For example, the party realized at a fairly early point in its development that a radical emphasis on racial anti-Semitism would be repugnant to the very bourgeois voters who constituted its most important reservoir of potential support. As a result, it limited its polemics against Jews to attacks against the alleged Jewish takeover of German economic life. Even Hitler conformed more or less to this mode of discourse, so that in the decisive campaigns between 1930 and 1932 anti-Semitic themes figured less prominently in Nazi propaganda than in that of the DNVP and other right-wing parties.

The mobilization of voters as an end in itself was advantageous only as long as the NSDAP did not participate in government at the state level, where it would have been forced to make good on the hodgepodge of mostly contradictory promises it had made during the campaign. On the other hand, this system afforded the party greater flexibility in adapting its message to the constant stream of protest voters and in winning over those who had previously remained aloof from all forms of party politics. Taking the results of the 1928 Reichstag elections to heart, the NSDAP intensified its propaganda in the open countryside and in small and middle-sized towns. The NSDAP thus made its first inroads into the existing party landscape in places where the more traditional bourgeois parties had failed to develop strong local and regional organizations. Occupying the position in municipal politics that had been previously held by independent voter blocs, the National Socialists laid claim to the legacy of Germany's special-interest parties in the period after 1930.

An indispensable prerequisite for the success of the NSDAP's propaganda offensive was the institution of the speakers' bureau. The founding of a National Socialist school of oratory can be traced back to Fritz Reinhardt, the district leader in Upper Bavaria-Swabia and later a state secretary in the Reich Ministry of Finance. Reinhardt, whose expertise was in the area of correspondence courses, established a private training program for party speakers, which by 1933 had been attended by more than 6,000 persons. A graduated scale of speakers' fees ensured that the speakers' bureau was financially self-supporting and attractive to its participants. Since the NSDAP charged admission for its meetings, the party's local chapters were interested in organizing events that fell outside the period of election campaigns. This, in turn, provided a regular income for party speakers. The commercialization of the Nazi propaganda effort constituted an amazingly simple device, which, however, could work only within the context of a steadily increasing party membership.

The rapid influx of new party members after 1929 greatly improved the NSDAP's financial situation even though the rising salary costs for full-time party functionaries threatened to outstrip revenues. The party's national leadership, therefore, became interested in increasing the number of NSDAP deputies at both the state and national level, where they would be supported by expense accounts from which the party would receive a portion. By the same token, they could spare the party the high costs of travel that propaganda work inevitably entailed by traveling at public expense. As for himself, Hitler refused to be supported from party coffers and financed his increasingly expensive lifestyle with income from *Mein Kampf*, the articles he wrote for the *Völkischer Beobachter*, and his speaker's fees. Even then, Hitler did not decline gifts from the Munich notables who had befriended him, such as the Bruckmann family. Nor was he modest in setting his own speaker's honoraria that were collected by his private secretary, Rudolf Hess.

Unlike the moderate and right-wing bourgeois parties, the NSDAP was not dependent on contributions from large firms or economic interest organizations. Its main sources of income were membership dues, revenues from party rallies and other events, and supplemental fund drives among the membership. In spite of the deepening economic crisis, the party's local branches were able to raise considerable sums of money, the better part of which was sent to the NSDAP's district and central offices. The income the NSDAP generated from this source was many times larger than the dues raised by the SPD. The SA, on the other hand, financed itself by acting as a sales organization for the cigarette industry and similar enterprises. It also collected regular payments from sympathizers who were not yet ready to join the party. Moreover, some of the party's publications made a considerable profit by selling advertising space.

Until the National Socialist assumption of power on 30 January 1933, financial contributions from big industry remained comparatively modest. Indeed, the business community as a whole was distinctly reserved when it came to giving to the NSDAP in spite of Hitler's appeals in appearances before the Düsseldorf Industrial Club (Düsseldorfer Industrie Club), the Hamburg National Club, and in private meetings with industrial leaders. One major exception was Emil Kirdorf, who was introduced to the party through Elsa Bruckmann and temporarily joined it in 1927. A former board member of the Gelsenkirchen Mining Company (Gelsenkirchener Bergwerks A.-G.), Kirdorf met with little success in his efforts to help Hitler establish contact with German heavy industry. In 1928 Kirdorf returned to the DNVP, where he advocated an alliance with the NSDAP in spite of misgivings about its social and economic program. The large advances that the NSDAP received for its participation in the referendum against the Young Plan were used to reduce the party's long-term indebtedness. The credit that Fritz Thyssen extended to the party was used primarily for the purchase of the former Barlog Palace, now dubbed the "Brown House," in Munich. For this expenditure, the party's rank-and-file membership was charged a one-time supplemental assessment of two marks.

Further financial contributions came to the NSDAP from the ranks of middle-sized entrepreneurs and manufacturers, sometimes in exchange for protection from physical aggression or public polemics. This was even true in the case of I.G. Farben, a giant chemical cartel that sought tariff protection for its newly developed synthetic fuel. Rumors about foreign — and particularly French — financial contributions notwithstanding, the NSDAP financed itself essentially through its own efforts until the summer of 1932, when the July Reichstag elections sapped its financial strength. From this point on, the party became increasingly dependent on subsidies and loan guarantees from industry. The business world now began to make regular payments to certain high-ranking officials of the NSDAP. A case in point was Emil Georg von Stauß, director of the Deutsche Bank und Diskonto Gesellschaft, who established a close relationship with Hermann Göring in an attempt to influence the NSDAP's economic policy in favor of industry. This, in turn, made it possible for Göring to enjoy a luxurious life-style before the party ever came to power, one that exceeded Hitler's own efforts in this direction.

More important were the contacts that Gregor Straßer was able to establish with August Heinrichsbauer, the Berlin liaison for Rhenish-Westphalian heavy industry, and Walther Funk, the economics editor of the *Berliner Börsenzeitung* who joined the NSDAP in 1931 and became a member of its economic policy staff. Through these contacts Straßer received regular donations from Ruhr industry. By the same token, funds from heavy industry were made available for the founding of a new newspaper, the *Essener Nationalzeitung* through the mediation of Funk in conjunction with Ludwig Grauert, executive director of the Northwestern Group of the Association of German Iron and Steel Industrialists (Nordwestliche Gruppe des Vereins der Deutschen Eisen- und Stahlindustrieller) and later state secretary in the Prussian Ministry of the Interior. Whatever money the NSDAP received from these sources, however, did not come close to meeting its operating expenses through the summer of 1932. And its electoral victories occurred before any such subsidies might have been available. All of this underscored the willingness of the NSDAP's followers and sympathizers to make material sacrifices in spite of the worsening economic situation. This, in turn, was the decisive prerequisite for the development of the National Socialist propaganda machine, which in an increasingly tense political climate began to pull much of the electorate with it.

The NSDAP supplemented its agitation among the masses with a concerted effort to expand its popular base by infiltrating the middle-class interest groups affiliated with the parties of the bourgeois Right and by gaining influence within ostensibly nonpolitical associations. The NSDAP was particularly successful at the municipal level in politicizing not only the network of bourgeois clubs but also artisan associations and other local organizations and in using them as vehicles for the transmission of its propaganda message. By 1930 artisan organizations were already largely under the control of the NSDAP. Characteristic of the Nazi strategy was the way in which it exploited the 1932 elections to the church council of the Old Prussian Union, where it was able to wrest no less than a third of the seats on the church council away from the conservative notables who had traditionally run its affairs. This, in turn, gave the German Christian movement that was closely associated with the NSDAP a measure of respectability within church circles at large. Nazi infiltration of middle-class associations and social institutions proved a particularly effective technique in smaller communities and towns for expanding the party's base of support beyond the lower middle classes into the ranks of the local elites.

Of even greater significance were the NSDAP's efforts to gain leverage within national interest organizations by bringing pressure to bear from the local level. In 1932, for example, a Nazi front organization known as the Combat League for the Commercial Middle Class (Kampfbund für den gewerblichen Mittelstand) under the leadership of Theodor Adrian von Renteln succeeded in taking over the Central Association of German Retailers (Hauptverband des deutschen Einzelhandels). The party's greatest success in this regard could be seen in the case of the National Rural League (Reichs-Landbund). The idea of a Nazi agricultural association had originated with the Landvolkbewegung and the Artaman Association in the late 1920s. It was subsequently taken up in 1930 by R. Walter Darré, a völkisch-oriented agricultural expert who already enjoyed a considerable following in these circles and whom Straßer approached with the suggestion that he establish a bureau for agrarian policy in the NSDAP's central office. Darré proceeded from the assumption that the Nazi conquest of power in the large urban centers presupposed effective control of the agrarian sector, either to avert a food boycott such as that of 1918–19 or to use such a boycott as a political weapon.

Relying on the services of volunteer experts at the district level, the Agrarian Political Apparatus (Agrarpolitischer Apparat) was able to develop an extensive network of confidants, or *Vertrauensmänner*, in a remarkably short period of time. Aside from its original function of gathering information, this apparatus was soon given the assignment of bringing local agricultural organizations and associations under the control of the party. This took place through the special training of agricultural specialists, or *Fachberater*, to use their expertise under ostensibly nonpartisan auspices to gain influence within the peasant associations and the National Rural League. The Rural League, which had just entered into an alliance with the NSDAP against the rival Christian-National Peasants and Farmers' Party, was particularly vulnerable to National Socialist infiltration, which Darré encouraged with the slogan "Hinein in den Landbund!" When the elections to the Prussian chambers of agriculture took place in late 1931, the Agrarian Political Apparatus had established the NSDAP as the controlling force in a large number of the local agricultural associations. Under these circumstances, the executive committee of the National Rural League felt obliged to create a special seat on the RLB presidium for one of Darré's closest associates, Werner Willikens. In March 1932 the National Rural League broke with Hindenburg and publicly endorsed Hitler's candidacy for the Reich presidency. Nothing could have more clearly demonstrated the fundamental vulnerability of the DNVP and the interest groups that stood behind it to the skillfully disguised threat of Nazi subversion from below.

The organizational opportunism that characterized the NSDAP's quest for power necessarily led it to seek a rapprochement with the bourgeois Right. Unlike the Center and the parties on the socialist Left, the bourgeois Right proved particularly susceptible to National Socialist propaganda. This was reflected, among other things, in the elaborate network of National Socialist occupational associations and other special organizations that the NSDAP had developed since 1929. In addition to artisan associations, a number of professional organizations were founded, including the National Socialist Teachers' League (Nationalsozialistischer Lehrerbund) under Hans Schemm, the Combat League of German Architects and Engineers (Kampfbund Deutscher Architekten und Ingeniere), the National Socialist League of Physicians (Nationalsozialistischer Ärztebund), the National League of National Socialist Lawyers (Reichsbund nationalsozialistischer Juristen), the National Socialist League of University Lecturers (Nationalsozialistischer Dozentenbund), and the National Socialist German Students' League (Nationalsozialistischer Deutscher Studentenbund) as well as the National Socialist civil servant societies that the Prussian government tried to get around by banning state civil servants from belonging to the NSDAP. What seems most remarkable in this context was the vulnerability of the educated bourgeoisie to National Socialist propaganda. Alfred Rosenberg's Combat League for German Culture (Kampfbund für deutsche Kultur) mobilized the resentment that the more conservative elements of the German bourgeoisie felt toward modern art and literature—the closing of the Bauhaus in 1932 was a prime example of this attitude—without, however, committing the party to a unified cultural policy.

Even though the NSDAP proved increasingly attractive to members of the German middle class, its position within the general milieu of bourgeois associational life was not particularly strong. The membership of the Combat League for the Commercial Middle Class, which attracted attention with the virulence of its anti-Semitic agitation, consisted almost exclusively of small merchants and petty entrepreneurs who attributed their own economic misery to the influence of Jewish capital. The NSDAP, however, was not successful in drawing the German National Union of Commercial Employees (Deutschnationaler Handlungsgehilfen-Verband or DHV) into its political orbit in spite of the fact that a high percentage of its members sympathized with its goals. Under Hans Bechly and Max Habermann the DHV leadership was not yet ready to follow Hitler into a frontal confrontation with the Brüning government. Indeed, DHV leaders could not set aside their suspicions that the NSDAP—a "DNVP in youthful makeup" (*jugendliche geschminkte DNVP*)—was using the interests of organized labor only as a cover for its own purposes. Despite the DHV's markedly anti-Semitic and distinctly nationalist attitude, it refused to become part of the NSDAP's organizational network.

It was not so much on the level of national associations as on that of local bourgeois clubs and interest groups that the NSDAP was able to secure its breakthrough into the bourgeois party spectrum. Except in Catholic regions, the systematic infiltration of bourgeois organizations proved highly effective. Contacts with ostensibly nonpartisan middle-class interest groups often afforded the party an opportunity to win over local notables and through them to address increasingly large sectors of Germany's bourgeois electorate. Particularly susceptible in this regard were those segments of the middle class that feared and resented large enterprises and business conglomerates. These elements, for the most part artisans and small entrepreneurs, felt that the DVP and DNVP were not sufficiently sensitive to their vital interests.

In sharp contrast to its success with specific sectors of the German middle class, the NSDAP had a hard time gaining a foothold within the camp of organized labor. Since 1928 there had been considerable interest on the party's left wing in the establishment of a National Socialist trade-union movement. This, however, encountered strenuous opposition from Hitler, who feared—not without reason—that such organizations would be in a hopeless minority vis-à-vis the socialist and Christian unions and that this situation could not but have a negative effect on his propaganda campaign. More important, it would have been tactically unwise for him to alienate the business leaders whose support he was seeking by becoming involved in labor initiatives. These reservations notwithstanding, Hitler eventually permitted the creation of the National Socialist Factory Cell Organization (Nationalsozialistische Betriebs-zellenorganisation or NSBO). First limited to Greater Berlin, this organization was established throughout Germany in 1931. Headed by Walter Schumann and Reinhard Muchow, it copied the system of in-plant organization that had been developed by the KPD. The NSBO was particularly popular in small and middle-sized firms and in public enterprises like the German Railway Corporation (Deutsche Reichsbahn) and only occasionally successful in large enterprises such as the Siemens Electrical Works. Still, in the 1931 factory-council elections (*Betriebsratwahlen*) the NSBO managed to win 12 percent of the blue-collar vote. Its appeal among white-collar employees, however, was even greater, as shown by the fact that it received 25 percent of the votes. The NSBO's original task was to disseminate National Socialist propaganda among those who were affiliated with the existing labor unions, which were generally successful in warding off its attempts at infiltration. Still, this did not preclude the NSBO from representing its membership at the plant level or from taking part in strikes and other work-related job actions. In comparison with the ADGB, which had an estimated 5.8 million members, the NSBO was relatively insignificant, with at most 300,000 members. Still, it would continue to make considerable organizational progress as long as it preserved its labor-union orientation.

Despite persistent internal conflicts, the NSBO's efforts to establish a foot-hold within the industrial working class received strong support from the National Socialist press, which tried to create the impression that it was un-equivocally on the side of the workers. This was particularly true in the case of Berlin, where the anticapitalist tenor of Goebbels's *Der Angriff* was not sub-stantially different from that of Otto Straßer's rival *Berliner Arbeiter-Zeitung* and other publications of the Kampf-Verlag. The party was consistently sup-portive of labor actions and defended the Berlin metalworkers' strike of 1930. In the Reichstag the NSDAP lent its support to generous financial aid for the unemployed and voted with the SPD and KPD against further reductions in unemployment insurance benefits. Goebbels's demands for profit sharing and co-ownership by the workers came straight out of Straßer's program of 1926.

Despite Hitler's overtures to big business, the NSDAP preserved the anti-capitalist rhetoric of its earliest days, which carried a distinctly anti-Semitic flavor with its polemics against big capital and stock market speculation. As late as the fall of 1931, the NSDAP Reichstag delegation resurrected the pseudo-socialistic ideas of Gottfried Feder and demanded, among other things, nation-alization of the major banks, a ban on trading on the stock market, a 5 percent limit on interest (including a 1 percent liquidation fee), and the confiscation of profits derived from war, inflation, and unjustifiable stock market trans-actions. Industrial circles were extremely alarmed by the NSDAP's periodic fits of state-socialistic weakness, which in their eyes moved the party dangerously close to Communist views. This formed the background of subsequent efforts by Hjalmar Schacht and other representatives of heavy industry to exercise a constructive influence on Nazi economic programs.

Organized labor was not taken in by the NSDAP's anticapitalist rhetoric. This was particularly true since it almost invariably went hand in hand with the uncompromising rejection of the SPD and KPD, which the NSDAP regarded as its principal opponents. But Joseph Goebbels's systematic efforts as district leader of Berlin to break the domination of the "Communards," as they were known in National Socialist parlance, were also designed to impress bourgeois sympathizers and mobilize the anti-Communist sentiments of the middle classes. By staging highly visible SA parades in working-class neighborhoods, Goebbels hoped to discredit the KPD in the eyes of the masses and to provoke it to violent confrontation. Despite the intervention of the Prussian police force and repeated bans against the NSDAP organization in Berlin, fights with the Red Front Soldiers' League (Roter Frontkämpferbund) and occasionally with units of the Reichsbanner broke out in meeting halls and in the streets with great regularity. Deaths or severe injuries frequently ensued. The cynicism with which Goebbels encouraged the escalating violence in the streets of Berlin reached a climax with the glorification of Horst Wessel, an SA platoon leader and author of the song that bears his name. Even though Wessel had received his fatal wound in a brawl with pimps in a seedy Berlin neighborhood, Goebbels made certain that the disgruntled student was transformed in the Nazi press into a martyr for the movement.

Goebbels's ambition to make a name for himself in the struggle for Berlin and the unscrupulous methods by which he pursued this end formed the background to his conflict with the Straßer group. It was a conflict that soon became a struggle over the future direction of the party. The rivalry that went back to the Bamberg meeting was turned into irreconcilable enmity by an article that Erich Koch, later district leader of East Prussia, published at the instigation of Otto Straßer. Koch, who had just become an editor at Straßer's Kampf-Verlag, struck a most sensitive nerve with a quasi-anti-Semitic allusion to Goebbels's crippled foot. Without the active help of Goebbels, the smoldering conflict between Straßer's publishing house and the Munich party leadership surely would not have exploded as violently as it did in the early summer of 1930. The editors of the Kampf-Verlag did not conceal their disapproval of Hitler's decision to join Hugenberg and Seldte in the referendum against the Young Plan. In their eyes, this amounted to nothing less than a relapse into political horse trading and an option in favor of big capital.

Fundamental differences of opinion had surfaced before in connection with the NSDAP's participation in the governments of Saxony and Thuringia. In both states the NSDAP held the balance of power in its hands. The Saxon

NSDAP, led by the former lieutenant commander Helmut von Mücke, had offered to join a coalition government with the SPD and KPD. Though informed of this step, Hitler forced Mücke to withdraw the offer, whereupon he resigned from the NSDAP. While the Kampf-Verlag sympathized with the Left and defied the NSDAP's national leadership by supporting the Saxon metalworkers' strike, Hitler advocated an alliance with the bourgeois parties. Although negotiations toward this end in Saxony had ended in failure, Hitler decided in January 1930 to bring the NSDAP into the Thuringian state government. With Wilhelm Frick as minister of the interior and public education, Thuringia became a testing ground for the strategies the NSDAP was to adopt in its bid for national power.

The group around Otto Straßer, which since 1929 had found increasingly strong support among the younger social activists within the NSDAP, regarded this as an unforgivable betrayal of the party's principles. Hitler could easily have ignored the internal conflict this issue threatened to precipitate, but tactical considerations dictated otherwise. Now that the NSDAP had withdrawn from the National Committee for the German Referendum (Reichsausschuß für das deutsche Volksbegehren), the time had come for cautious overtures to the Brüning cabinet in an attempt to isolate the Hugenberg wing of the DNVP. Otto Straßer categorically rejected Hitler's tactical vacillation. A two-day meeting with the party leader in late May 1930 failed to reconcile their differences of opinion. Whereas Straßer demanded an unequivocal commitment to the NSDAP's socialist program, Hitler spoke cynically about the workers, who wanted nothing more than "bread and circus" and "had no understanding of ideals whatsoever." Max Amann and Rudolf Hess were also present at the meeting, which deeply upset Hitler. Although he was incensed by Straßer's counterarguments, he hesitated to draw the obvious conclusions until Straßer openly provoked him by publishing a pamphlet entitled *Ministersessel oder Revolution?* At that point Hitler authorized Goebbels to purge the party of its "destructive elements," lest it become a "debating society for uprooted literati and chaotic parlor-Bolshevists."

Even before Otto Straßer published his appeal on 4 July 1930 proclaiming the socialist secession from the NSDAP, Goebbels had forced Straßer's supporters onto the defensive through a massive deployment of the SA. Gregor Straßer now left the Kampf-Verlag and publicly attacked his brother. Otto Straßer's more prominent associates, among them Count Ernst zu Reventlov and Erich Koch, renounced their allegiance to him. No more than a few hundred of his followers joined his new organization, the Action Group of Revolutionary National Socialists (Kampfgemeinschaft revolutionärer Nationalsozialisten), which later transformed itself into the "Black Front." The final result would not have been much different had Gregor Straßer gone along with the opposition. As it was, he had been estranged from his brother for some time and at this point was still hoping to become the Saxon minister of the interior. From a tactical point of view, Otto Straßer's open break with Hitler was a major blunder, for it made it possible for Hitler to portray himself as the advocate of moderation and legality. This image served Hitler well in the upcoming Reichstag elections as well as in his efforts to win the favor of German big business.

The conflict with Straßer and the pretext for Goebbels's disciplinary action that forced Otto Straßer's followers to leave the party can only be understood against the background of the close ties that had developed between this faction and a group of social-revolutionary National Socialists in Thuringia. With support from the so-called leftists on the Right (*linke Leute von rechts*) and incorporating elements of the *bündisch* ideology, this faction set for itself the goal of creating an "anticapitalist youth front stretching from the Right to the Left" and of replacing the NSDAP with a comprehensive *Sammlungsbewegung* that united social-revolutionary groups of all shades into what was to be a left-wing variant of Hans Zehrer's vision of a "Third Front." The myth that "youth will break the power of the parties" and that revolutionary renewal will come about by the sheer force of conviction had long been preached by Ernst Niekisch, who was soon to denounce Hitler as a "German calamity" (*deutsches Verhängnis*) and a "political imposter" (*politischer Kreditschwindler*). But the mythos of youth was no match for the well-established power of the National Socialist mass organization and the fanatical Hitler worship that had become a decisive sociopsychological factor outside the NSDAP itself.

The "Fourteen Theses of the German Revolution" that Otto Straßer had published in August 1929 had several points in common with the strategies pursued by Ernst Niekisch and the National Bolshevists. It was characteristic of Hitler's tendency to delay taking sides as long as possible that the open conflict with Otto Straßer became irreversible—though only with a strong push from Goebbels—only in the summer of 1930. Straßer's followers did not realize that, in sharp contrast to their own hopes, Hitler had always sought to take an unambiguous stand against the bourgeois Right. From this perspective, they could only have regarded his willingness to participate in coalition governments with bourgeois parties as a surrender of the NSDAP's antiparliamentary orientation. The contacts with the DNVP, from which Hitler began to dissociate himself after the formation of the Harzburg front in the fall of 1931, was seen as a betrayal of their own principles. It was in this connection that Konrad Heiden observed that the history of true National Socialism had come to an end with the elections of 14 September 1930. But the gradual expansion of the NSDAP's power base, which up until this time had rested solely upon the plebiscitary mandate of the leader, utilized government participation as simply one tool among many for gaining power and did not signal the end of the "national revolution" as propagated in party propaganda.

Even after Otto Straßer and his modest circle of followers had left the party, the ambivalence between a procapitalist and a prosocialist line was not resolved until some time after the Nazi assumption of power on 30 January 1933. Nevertheless a gradual shift in the social character of the movement had undeniably occurred since the early years of its existence. This was particularly apparent in the style and demeanor of the party's youth group. Under the leadership of its founder Kurt Gruber, the Hitler Youth (Hitlerjugend or HJ) had assumed a distinctly proletarian character and had addressed itself primarily to working-class youth. In 1931 Gruber was replaced as leader of the Hitler Youth by the *völkisch* writer Baldur von Schirach, just after he had succeeded in purging one of Straßer's supporters, Wilhelm Tempel, from the leadership of the National Socialist Student League. Under Schirach the Hitler Youth began to imitate the cultured and bourgeois style of the *bündisch* youth movement. The National Socialist League of High School Students (Nationalsozialistischer Schulerbund) also accommodated itself to the prevailing trend toward bourgeois respectability. Despite these corrections in its political course, the National Socialist youth organization never came close to matching the size or strength of the Catholic or socialist youth groups. By the same token, the *bündisch* movement, which had come out of the *Wandervogel* tradition, was repelled by the militarist tendencies of the Hitler Youth.

Paradoxically, the influx of new members and the growing success in the elections that the NSDAP had experienced since the spring of 1929 did not result so much from a clearer programmatic focus as from its opportunistic exploitation of the potential for protest. The NSDAP's national propaganda office consciously concentrated its election propaganda on winning the support of voters who had changed parties, were young, or who had not voted in previous elections. Such people were rarely found in the ranks of the industrial work force, which by and large remained immune to the NSDAP. Hitler's public appearances followed the same pattern in that he always sought to adapt his speeches to his audience and its prejudices. A major factor in the NSDAP's success in the decisive years after 1929 was its ability to mobilize the social resentments of the German electorate and to transform irreconcilable hopes into campaign promises without regard to their practical feasibility.

At the same time, the NSDAP profited from the increasingly negative attitude toward the activity of political parties that had been consciously nurtured by conservatives with phrases like "party appointees in the civil service" (*Parteibuchbeamten*) or "party strife" (*Parteienhader*). In emphasizing its categorical rejection of Weimar's political system, the NSDAP sought to present itself as fundamentally different from the existing "system parties" (*Systemparteien*). While it disparaged the different parties as the puppets of influential special interest groups, the NSDAP portrayed itself as a popular movement totally devoted to the welfare of the community as a whole and determined to restore the nation's "unity of will." As long as the NSDAP did not have to deliver on its promises by taking part in the work of parliament, this campaign strategy proved quite successful.

By comparison with the bourgeois parties and even the SPD, the NSDAP had the distinct advantage of being a party of the young and did not hesitate to mobilize the widespread cult of youth for its own purposes or to appropriate the mythos of "national awakening" (*nationaler Aufbruch*) and Moeller van den Bruck's "right of the young nations" (*Recht der jungen Völker*). In this way, it was able to take advantage of the generational tensions that had become such a prominent feature of Weimar political life by the late 1920s. Despite its backward-looking ideology, the NSDAP exercised great appeal on the younger generation by virtue of its openness to new technologies, its rejection of bourgeois notions of order, and its essential dynamism. Much of the NSDAP's appeal stemmed from the fact that it compensated its followers for their failure to move up in society by creating honorary positions at all levels of the party organization.

The leadership cadre of the NSDAP had been recruited for the most part from the ranks of active officers or combat soldiers of the First World War, almost all of whom were between the ages of thirty-five and forty. The average age of those party members and functionaries who had joined the party after 1925 was even lower. The average age of the membership declined after 1925, but rose again after 1927; by 1932 it stood at thirty-one years. In relation to the population as a whole, men between the ages of eighteen and twenty were clearly overrepresented in the NSDAP, although this must be seen against the background of the demographic preponderance of the younger age cohort in the 1920s. The average age of female members, who represented 7.8 percent of the membership — and this was even lower than in the other parties — was appreciably higher. The NSDAP exercised a strong appeal on young people who were at the beginning of their working careers. The largest occupational group among the younger party members comprised workers, many of whom had never found work as a result of Germany's structural unemployment and therefore had not come into contact with the labor unions. As the upper middle class began to join the party in increasingly large numbers after 1930, the average age of the membership rose slightly. The youthfulness of the NSDAP, particularly in the SA, conveyed an image of vigor and militancy that contrasted starkly with the preponderance of the elderly in the other Weimar parties, and particularly in their parliamentary elite. The Nazi electorate came from all age groups. The party even recorded considerable success among pensioners and housewives living alone, who voted for the NSDAP as a protest against the social hardship they had suffered from the inflation, economic crisis, and resultant cuts in their social security benefits.

Another peculiarity of the NSDAP was the unusually high fluctuation in its membership, a phenomenon with no parallel in German politics except for the KPD. This peculiarity could be traced back not just to the party's unique organizational development since 1929 but also to certain structural features of German political life. Insisting that, unlike the other Weimar parties, it did not represent any particular set of special interests, the NSDAP mobilized different social groups at different points in its development as a political party. Indeed, its success in small and middle-sized towns brought about a radical change in the profile of its voters. In the autumn of 1928 the NSDAP had no more than 97,000 members; by January 1933 this number had risen to 746,000. These figures, however, hide a much higher turnover. In the period before it came to power, the NSDAP lost more than a half of those who had joined the party before 1930 and a good third of those who had joined after 1930. The rapid pace of the party's absolute growth until the fall of 1932 concealed a simultaneous loss of members. In short, the NSDAP was a rather unstable organization that could keep alive only by snowballing growth. The hard core of NSDAP members consisted of hardly more than 300,000 persons. It was only by gaining power in 1933 that it could absorb and permanently integrate the flood of new members that joined it after 1931.

What was true for the NSDAP's membership applied even more to its voters. While it did experience exceptional growth in the number of votes obtained — increasing its share from 18.3 to 37.3 percent between September 1930 and July 1932 — it was unable to hold on permanently to its voters before 1933. Despite the short intervals between elections, the NSDAP lost up to a third of its voters from the previous election, but was able to offset these losses with gains from the DNVP, DVP, bourgeois interest parties, and regional parties. The spectacular setback the NSDAP suffered in the November 1932 Reichstag elections stemmed in part from to the loss of many peasant voters who had supported it in 1930 but now returned to the DNVP. Another factor was the disproportionately heavy losses the NSDAP incurred through diminished voter participation. Most detrimental of all, however, was the extreme heterogeneity of its followers. All of this makes it clear that the NSDAP was successful only as long as its incessant campaigning and the creation of a general mood of crisis kept the voters in a state of frenzied excitement.

The rise of the NSDAP since 1929 had taken place primarily at the expense of the moderate bourgeois parties, but also affected the DNVP and the bourgeois interest and regional parties that attracted the bulk of their support from former Nationalist voters. The main reason for the breakdown of the bourgeois center was the economic weakening of the "old middle class," which since the end of the war, if not earlier, had lost much of its former standing and had been affected more than other groups by the hyperinflation and devaluation of the currency. This category included artisans, small and middle-sized retailers, businessmen, and small entrepreneurs. Many of these, but particularly the independent operators, were Nazi sympathizers. As the agrarian crisis worsened, they were joined by family farmers who no longer felt adequately represented by the DNVP. As a result, the NSDAP fared considerably better in small towns and rural communities than in the big cities. Fifty percent of its votes came from communities and towns with fewer than 5,000 inhabitants, whereas in cities and metropolitan areas it received no more than 40 percent, which was less than its national average. Nonetheless, in comparison with rival parties, the NSDAP was largely successful in its efforts to bridge the urban-rural dichotomy.

The disparity between the party's performance in urban electoral districts, on the one hand, and in middle-sized and small towns as well as rural districts, on the other, was compounded by unmistakable confessional cleavages. In Protestant regions the NSDAP generally enjoyed better electoral prospects, no doubt as a result of the strong nationalist orientation of the local Protestant consistories. Moreover, the party was able to mobilize the movement for a national church, the "German Christians," for its own purposes. In Catholic regions, by contrast, the party's performance lagged considerably behind its national profile. The internal cohesiveness of the Center Party and the Bavarian People's Party (Bayerische Volkspartei or BVP), along with the initially well publicized misgivings of the clergy concerning the anti-Christian slant of the National Socialist Weltanschauung contributed to the reserve with which the Catholic population viewed National Socialism. In Catholic regions, as opposed to their Protestant counterparts, the NSDAP was only rarely able to penetrate the network of middle-class clubs and associations that had played such an important role in its expansion in northern Germany.

For all its efforts, the NSDAP made no appreciable inroads into the ranks of the political Left. The combined share of the votes cast for the parties of the German Left remained constant after 1930 in spite of the fact that the total number of voters was increasing. The KPD in particular remained almost totally immune to the National Socialist propaganda. The frequently assumed migration from the KPD to the NSDAP was actually limited to a handful of intellectuals. Unlike the KPD, the SPD lost a few of its marginal voters to the NSDAP; about a tenth of the floating voters who made their way to the NSDAP came from the ranks of the SPD. The NSDAP's constantly reiterated claim that it was also a workers' party was only very partially borne out. The percentage of party members from working-class backgrounds declined from 45.9 percent in 1927 to 35.9 percent for 1930–32 and lagged considerably behind the percentage of wage earners in the population as a whole. Among voters and their families, the percentage of those who supported the NSDAP was lower still and stemmed overwhelmingly from those sectors of the working population that manifested a strong middle-class profile. The NSDAP did relatively well among workers employed in artisanal and small-scale enterprises, municipal employees, and agricultural laborers. To the extent that it was able to win over industrial workers, its success was limited almost exclusively to permanently unemployed younger workers who found a field of activity in the SA.

Despite the varying degrees of sympathy the NSDAP could muster in the different occupational groups and the religious confessions, it succeeded in playing down contrasts of class and religious affiliation. This "omnibus effect" enabled it to make major gains in all social groups after the spring of 1932. By infiltrating the interest structure of the bourgeois parties, the NSDAP was able to gain entry into the ranks of bourgeois notables and to counteract the social prejudices that these circles had harbored against National Socialist functionaries because of their predominantly petit bourgeois background. Many members of the ruling elites decided to support the NSDAP, not because they sympathized with it, but because they were captivated by Hitler's personal charisma and expected him to do away with parties altogether. As a means of gaining the sympathies of the upper classes, the *Führer-Kult* proved unusually effective. Similar to women voters whose share of the vote in November 1932 — a time when the party was already registering a marked decline in the support of those who had earlier voted for it — exceeded that of male voters, the NSDAP's upper-class sympathizers were slow to honor the party with their vote.

The NSDAP's efforts to attract the support of civil servants by appeasing that group's social resentments with promises to reinstate a purely professional civil service and to provide guarantees for its rightfully acquired status were particularly successful. Despite a ban by Prussia that prevented civil servants from belonging to the NSDAP and disciplinary action against those who defied this ban, civil servants were overrepresented in the party well before 1933. By comparison, the other groups of the "new middle class" proved much less responsive to National Socialist propaganda. This only confirms the observation that by and large those social groups that sympathized with the NSDAP were those that were subjectively and objectively threatened with the loss of social status, a factor that was certainly the case with civil servants. In this respect, it is striking that the majority of the National Socialist functionaries, including members of the highest leadership group — Heinrich Himmler, Joseph Goebbels, Hermann Göring, and Reinhard Heydrich are good examples — had abandoned middle-class careers or were insecure in their own social status. This was no less true of the SA leadership, which was permeated with the social ressentiment that represented the driving force behind the rise of the National Socialist movement. Some early defectors from the highest stratum of German society also joined. The most prominent of these was August Wilhelm, Prince of Prussia, who became a member of the NSDAP in 1930 and soon rose to a high position in the SA.

The NSDAP was more successful than any of its rivals in overcoming social cleavages and in presenting itself as a movement that transcended class divisions. In spite of the fact that they represented highly divergent social and economic interests, National Socialist voters were united in protest against the intolerable social and political conditions that existed throughout the country. If in terms of its social composition the NSDAP came close to the ideal image of a people's party, it earned this character only in a negative sense. For at no point in its history was the NSDAP able to commit its followers to a positive program. Nor could it ever hope to attain an absolute majority in free elections. At the time of the July 1932 Reichstag elections, it was already clear that the NSDAP recorded only marginal gains in its traditional strongholds and that it could offset its losses among the rural and urban lower middle classes — its major constituency — only by making inroads into the ranks of the upper middle class and by mounting concerted efforts in parts of the country it had previously ignored. The myth of the movement's irresistible growth as emphatically propagated by Hitler had, as Gregor Straßer himself knew, no basis in reality. Only the extreme voter mobilization in the first half of 1932 and the cumulative effect of the National Socialist electoral victories during this period made it possible for the party to temporarily attract the support of more than a third of the voting population.

The spurious — that is to say, specifically fascist — character of the National Socialist movement would almost certainly be revealed once growth ceased to be an end in itself and the permanent mobilization of the party's followers had run out of steam. It was precisely this situation that arose in late 1932 and that led to a severe crisis within the party. Gregor Straßer decided to embark on what he considered a course of constructive cooperation with the bourgeois Right. Hitler, on the other hand, held steadfastly to his previously successful strategy of not siding with any of the established political factions so that he could present himself as an uncompromising adversary of the existing political system. That his gambit proved eventually successful had little to do with a change in voter attitude, although the outcome of the Lippe state elections on 13 January 1933 was interpreted in this sense. Hitler could not afford to risk new elections any more than could Franz von Papen, unless he first found a way to break out of his increasingly dangerous political isolation and present his followers with a visible success by taking over control of the government. Hitler sensed that, in the final analysis, he and his opponents were engaged in a war of nerves. And indeed, his opponents did not have the nerve to challenge the NSDAP in an open election in which, as things stood, it would have gone down to a devastating defeat.

The central significance of the electoral politics of these years lay in the use of the Führer cult to neutralize the social reservations of the ruling elites against the NSDAP. Without the votes of the middle classes, especially in the upper levels of the civil service, the cumulative effect that provided the NSDAP with its victory in the July 1932 Reichstag elections — even though it fell short of the absolute majority for which party leaders had hoped—would not have taken effect. Germany's conservative elites were willing to give their votes to the NSDAP—and this occurred frequently before the referendum against the Young Plan—because of their prejudices against the KPD and SPD. This was an important factor in making the NSDAP, in spite of the contradictory nature of its program, respectable in the eyes of high-ranking military officers and the architects of the presidential system, many of whom now looked on it as a constructive political force. The leaders of big industry and their busy liaisons with the national government believed that Hitler's outward adaptation to the forms of bourgeois sociality represented the first sign of tangible success in their efforts to bring about the political taming of the NSDAP.

CHAPTER TEN

Government in Crisis

W H I L E the outcome of the September 1930 Reichstag elections left Heinrich Brüning's advisors somewhat bewildered, the chancellor himself remained remarkably cool. Brüning regarded the outcome of the election, which had put an end to any prospect of parliamentary support for his cabinet, as further proof that it was simply not possible to govern with the Reichstag and the parties that constituted it. Nevertheless, contemporary political pundits expected him to form a new cabinet based on the parties of the Great Coalition with the Prussian prime minister Otto Braun as his vice-chancellor. Among the leaders of the Reichswehr and in influential industrial circles, there was strong support for a cabinet that rested on as broad a political base as possible and that would conceivably include the SPD as well. For the combined strength of the KPD, the NSDAP, and the DNVP precluded the use of an enabling law that would have made the government independent of the approval of the Reichstag.

To be sure, a return to the Great Coalition would have done much to stabilize the domestic political situation. But this step was not a practical reality, since a parliamentary majority required the votes of the Business Party, which was siding more and more openly with the NSDAP. Yet the formation of a broadly based crisis government in the Reich and Prussia was doomed from the outset not only by Brüning's apparent coolness to the idea but also by the veto of Hindenburg, who had not forgiven Braun for his role in his government's conflict with the Prussian Stahlhelm. A right-wing coalition that would include the NSDAP was also out of the question, for it not only encountered the adamant opposition of the Center Party, but was also considered unnecessary by Brüning and the leaders of the Reichswehr. Despite mounting pressure from the political Right, the Reich president therefore refrained from reshuffling the cabinet.

Still, Brüning was confronted with the problem of persuading the Reichstag majority to go along with his long-standing plan for an emergency decree that would make it possible for him to carry a reform of German finances. Whereas negotiations with the remnants of the moderate parties made only slow progress, Brüning was surprised by the flexibility of the SPD and the ADGB, although this did not keep him from threatening to bring about the collapse of the Prussian government if the SPD failed to go along with his conditions for solving the fiscal crisis. Under the influence of Otto Braun, the Social Democratic Reichstag delegation voted to tolerate the Brüning cabinet, whose dismissal it had demanded during the election campaign, as the lesser evil. In justifying this step, the SPD national executive committee declared that the alternatives were either an authoritarian-conservative dictatorship of the German Right or a "Hitler government" with Hugenberg serving as chancellor. Voting against the emergency decree would, the party argued, result in the collapse of public finances, in which case unemployment insurance would be the first casualty.

With these assurances in hand, Brüning decided to enter into negotiations with the NSDAP. Earlier efforts to obtain Hugenberg's toleration of his government had collapsed when the DNVP party chairman announced that he would not consider such a step unless the government dissolved the Prussian coalition and immediately halted all reparations payments. In a wide-ranging conversation with Hitler, Frick, and Straßer on 6 October 1930 — just before he submitted the package of emergency decrees to the Reichstag — Brüning outlined virtually every aspect of his long-term domestic and foreign programs. In vain he tried to convince Hitler that with respect to the reparations question he could do little but pursue a delaying tactic until the completion of his proposed fiscal reform. The Nazi leader did, however, take great interest in Brüning's offer to encourage coalitions between the Center Party and NSDAP in the individual states and to reopen the Prussian question at some point in the future. The chancellor indicated not only that he fully appreciated Hitler's need to remain in the opposition for at least the time being but also that he welcomed such a role for the NSDAP from the perspective of his foreign policy.

Although in the following months Brüning had frequent and highly secret contacts with leading representatives of the NSDAP, he never received a pledge of the party's support or toleration. At the same time, the Brüning cabinet softened its position on the controversial matter of subsidies to the Thuringian police department, which it had suspended when members of the NSDAP were appointed to high positions. To be sure, Minister of the Interior Joseph Wirth backed down in this matter because he was unsure whether the supreme constitutional court would regard the NSDAP as an "anticonstitutional party." Brüning's conciliatory attitude indirectly benefited the Thuringian National Socialists, whose high-handed personnel policies had become so irritating to their bourgeois coalition partners that Frick was forced to resign in April 1931. The chancellor was careful to maintain a low profile throughout this controversy. While in public statements Brüning repeatedly stressed the contradictions of National Socialist propaganda, he clearly avoided burning all of his bridges to the NSDAP.

Brüning's accommodating attitude toward the NSDAP stood in sharp contrast to his deep-seated distrust of the SPD. In this respect, there was little that separated him from the bourgeois Right, which now held the fate of the republic in its hands. In conservative-nationalist circles it was generally assumed that with a little time and patience it would be possible to bring the NSDAP around to a constructive attitude toward the state and integrate it into the process of national regeneration. Speaking for the DNVP, Hans-Erdmann von Lindeiner-Wildau felt moved to warn the government against falling into the same error "that earlier generations had committed when socialism came into being." He strongly urged that "a way be found to enlist the positive energies contained in National Socialism for rebuilding the nation." Similar notions prevailed among the leaders of the Reichswehr, who anticipated the reinstatement of conscription and did not want to lose the "national human material" of the SA. All of this was part of the widespread illusion that Hitler would be easier to deal with than the opinionated and intractable Hugenberg.

Only the flexibility of the SPD enabled the Brüning cabinet to survive the motion of no confidence that the DNVP, NSDAP, and KPD brought against it when the new Reichstag convened in October 1930. This also made it unnecessary for the cabinet to rescind the emergency decrees of 26 July and 6 October. At the same time, the chancellor succeeded by means of massive pressure on the moderate parties and in the face of fierce polemics from the opposition in adjourning the Reichstag until 3 December 1930 and, after a brief session, once again until February 1931. It was not so much the climate of the Reichstag debates as the chancellor's deliberate strategy of introducing emergency legislation only when the Reichstag was not in session that forced parliament to choose between the Scylla of having to bring down the government and the Charybdis of going along with its intermittent exclusion from a meaningful role in German political life. The latter was precisely what Brüning had in mind. After the December vote, Hermann Pünder, one of his closest associates in the Reich Chancery, noted that it made no difference with whose help the government stayed in power since the chancellor had no intention of working with a "nonfunctional Reichstag" and only asked that the Reichstag refrain from interfering.

By no means did those who were closest to the chancellor regard the increasing independence of governmental authority from all legislative control as a temporary expedient. To the contrary, the government looked upon this development as a preliminary step toward a more radical reform of Germany's federal structure. As a consequence, Brüning was quick to use the not altogether unprovoked obstructionist tactics of the right-wing parties and KPD to curtail dramatically the powers of the legislative branch of government. In February 1931 he forced the parliamentary majority that tolerated his government to accept a procedural change stipulating that bills requiring expenditures could be introduced only if they included proposals for how they might be financed. While this did put a stop to the numerous bills introduced by the opposition for purely demagogic purposes, it also severely limited parliament's legislative initiative.

The DNVP, the NSDAP, and the KPD—the last named, however, only temporarily—responded to this change in the Reichstag's manner of operation by walking out of parliament in a demonstration that was also joined by the Christian-National Peasants and Farmers' Party (Christlich-Nationale Bauern- und Landvolkpartei). While the absence of the opposition parties might have made it easier for the Reichstag to conduct its business, it was also a matter of concern for Brüning in that the SPD and KPD now possessed the ability to pass social legislation to which he might be opposed. It was thus an illusion to assume that the temporary absence of the Right would help stabilize the political situation. This development simply meant that from now on the pressure on the government came from sources outside parliament. A case in point was the resumption of the referendum the Stahlhelm had initiated in December 1929 in an attempt to force the dissolution of the Prussian Landtag, a project that revived the political constellation of the 1929 fight against the Young Plan. By means of a referendum that took place in February 1931, the "national opposition" compelled the Prussian government to conduct a plebiscite, or *Volksentscheid*, on 9 August 1931. At this time, the nationalist Right, together with the KPD, was able to mobilize 37 percent of the popular vote in favor of the dissolution of the Prussian Landtag.

The parties of the German Right believed that they could turn the Reich president against Brüning and persuade him to dissolve the Reichstag. The unrestrained agitation of the opposition, which depicted the chancellor as a stooge of the SPD's Otto Braun, contained an element of truth in the sense that only the SPD's toleration of the Brüning government provided the chancellor with the parliamentary majority he needed to remain in office. Still, the national cabinet was afraid of arousing Hindenburg's distrust by taking Braun's side and flatly refused to support Severing and the Prussian government in their struggle with the "national opposition." When Severing issued an emergency decree that forced the press in Prussia to print a semiofficial government statement in which the demagogic character of the referendum was exposed, the national cabinet disavowed his action. Even though the referendum eventually failed, this did little to strengthen the position of the Prussian government since the "national opposition" only intensified its efforts with the Reich president to put an end to Brüning's informal cooperation with the SPD.

In the summer of 1930 the chancellor was not particularly concerned about losing Hindenburg's support. By curtailing the power of the Reichstag and thereby neutralizing the influence of the political parties, Brüning had taken the first steps toward a fundamental reform of national finances and the elimination of reparations that, in turn, would make it possible for him to enlist the support of the German Right for an authoritarian revision of the Weimar

Constitution, which, among other things, might include the restoration of the Hohenzollern monarchy. For the time being, the chancellor did not want to touch the institution of the Reichstag itself, even if he was already in the process of relegating it to the role of a rubber-stamp legislature. The relationship between emergency decree and normal legislation was reversed insofar as the government began to implement all important measures by means of emergency legislation, which, though contained in only a few sweeping decrees, was more voluminous than legislation enacted by normal parliamentary procedures. The loss of the Reichstag's importance was reflected in the number of times it met during the Brüning chancellorship. Whereas it had met forty-one times in 1931, there were only thirteen plenary sessions in 1932.

Brüning also had no qualms about mobilizing the Federal Council, or Reichsrat, against unwelcome initiatives of the Reichstag and frequently relied upon the help of Otto Braun to have troublesome resolutions revoked by the veto of the upper house. Even then, Brüning did not rely for long upon the support of the Federal Council, for as he grew tired of having to cater to the diverse interests of the individual German states he began to undercut the Federal Council's earlier position as a sort of emergency legislature by narrowing the scope of legislation that required its ratification. In this respect, Brüning no longer informed the Federal Council of pending legislation and usually presented it as a fait accompli. Yet through all of this, the state governments remained supportive of the national government in spite of the way in which it had curtailed the rights of the federal states and in spite of the divergent interests that came to the fore in the discussion of important national issues. Under the pressure of the deepening economic and political crisis, they, like the national government, had to contend with an increasingly aggressive parliamentary opposition.

The declining influence of popularly elected institutions and of the political parties was further reflected in the fact that consultations between the chancellor and party leaders became increasingly infrequent. By the same token, the power of the administrative apparatus was greatly increased. The ministerial bureaucracy came to assume a key position in the legislative process, particularly since Brüning had his emergency decrees formulated in a deliberately abstract judicial terminology that made it all the more difficult for his critics to mobilize public opposition against them. Without the help of administrative jurists, it was no longer possible to decipher the increasingly sweeping emergency degrees. In this situation certain state secretaries, notably Hermann Pünder and Hans Schäffer, came to wield considerably more political influence than any cabinet minister. State Secretary Curt Joël, who after the departure of Minister of Justice Victor Bredt became head of that department, also played a major decision-making role in helping to determine the areas in which emergency legislation was applicable.

The internal consolidation of the presidential system was further reflected in the increased willingness to use emergency decrees in areas hitherto considered exempt from emergency legislation, such as civil servant pay scales. In this respect, the use of emergency decrees violated the sovereignty of the states and preempted the administrative autonomy of municipalities. Whereas emergency decrees were originally limited to a specific period of time, this restriction was discarded along with the principle that the budgetary powers of the Reichstag were inviolable. Leading constitutional scholars such as Gerhard Anschütz and Walter Jellinek—moderates who were in no way whatsoever identified with the conservative Right—endorsed expanding the areas in which emergency legislation could be used even if this required a change, if not a breach, of the constitution. The fact that the dictatorial authority of the Reich president was now seen as an independent legislative right encountered little resistance. This policy, however, proved as disastrous as it was shortsighted. The Bavarian minister president Heinrich Held was quite correct when he warned the chancellor in early 1932 that it would be impossible to prevent "a dissident government of one kind or another" from invoking earlier precedents to justify misuse of Article 48.

While constitutional scholars and the Constitutional Court generally went along with Brüning's efforts to expand the scope of his emergency legislation and deviated from his position only in isolated cases, such as the question of civil servant salary scales, the opposition parties protested more and more vehemently against the unconstitutional character of presidential government. The NSDAP's threat to charge Hindenburg before the German Supreme Court with violating his oath to uphold the constitution was not without effect. By the end of 1931 Otto Meißner, the state secretary in the Bureau of the Reich President and an early supporter of efforts to expand the president's emergency powers, had begun to express increasingly strong reservations as to whether the government's proposed measures were consistent with the constitutional use of Article 48 and even went so far as to threaten a presidential veto if this were in fact the case. The greater the distance that Brüning put between himself and the parties in the Reichstag, the more dependent he became upon the Reich president and the political forces that stood behind him, that is, not just the Reichswehr leadership but also conservative special-interest organizations that had become accustomed to working through the ministerial bureaucracies without allowing the Reichstag and the parties that belonged to it to perform their indispensable integrative function.

In the late fall of 1930, Brüning hoped to use his increased freedom of maneuver in domestic politics to undertake a comprehensive reform of German finances that would bring him closer to his ultimate goal of putting an end to reparations. The emergency decree of 6 October 1930 represented an initial step in this direction and implemented painful reductions in social services and the salaries of public employees as well as substantial cutbacks in public investments. State Secretary Hans Schäffer, Brüning's closest advisor in budgetary matters, was hoping that these measures, together with a $125 million loan from the banking house of Lee, Higginson & Company, would carry him through the budget year that ended in April 1931. A foreign loan of this magnitude had become necessary because the contraction of the German economy since the middle of the previous year meant that revenues had fallen significantly behind expenditures. The cost of emergency social services, for example, exceeded earlier estimates.

In point of fact, this loan ran counter to Brüning's general political strategy. Lee, Higginson & Company had extended the loan on the twofold condition that Germany abide by the Young Plan and that a debt liquidation law be enacted by parliamentary means. For his own part, the chancellor was determined to reduce Germany's foreign indebtedness and to consolidate its short-term debts in the public sector. He therefore sought to impose strict limits on government borrowing. But it was no longer possible to cover the deepening budget deficits with foreign loans, particularly since these were accompanied by political conditions that obliged Germany to defer negotiations with the French for a revision of Germany's reparations burden. This only strengthened Brüning in his resolve to do without foreign financial help insofar as this was possible. The chancellor rejected the idea of economic self-sufficiency for the Reich as propagated not only by large-scale agriculture but also by the NSDAP and former Reichsbank president Hjalmar Schacht and agreed with the National Federation of German Industry that a major expansion of exports was the only means by which Germany could regain its former position of power. If Brüning still endeavored to decrease his country's dependence on foreign loans, this was to avoid the situation of 1929, when in his opinion the government had had no choice but to accept Allied conditions.

Brüning, however, went a step further. In this respect, the chancellor sought to turn the foreign debt into a tactical weapon for achieving the cancellation of Germany's reparations obligations and for "preparing all the nations for a general settlement," namely the revision of the Versailles treaty. A debt-free and crisis-proof national budget coupled with a deeply indebted but functional economy would create a situation in which Germany would be unable to raise enough money to cover reparations, debt retirement payments, and the interest on foreign loans. The idea of playing private debts against Germany's reparations obligation was directed mainly against France, which held only a small share of private commercial investment in Germany but was the principal reparations beneficiary. Germany's private creditors could have no interest whatsoever in seeing the credits raised abroad used for the payment of reparations, as had been the case since 1924. Yet if such loans were not forthcoming, the transfer of reparations payments could only be ensured by expanding German exports to the point of dumping, an alternative that was equally unappealing to Germany's foreign creditors.

The chancellor sought to reduce the internal indebtedness of Germany's public budgets through a broadly based deflationary policy. In this respect, he believed that austerity in public expenditures—an unquestionable duty of the state to begin with—would lay to rest Allied objections that Germany was deliberately sabotaging the financing of reparations. At the same time, reducing the tax burden was the only way in which the international competitiveness of German industry could be restored. Moreover, Brüning hoped to use the economic crisis to bring about a reduction of wages and prices that, once the reparations had ended and the low point of the economic crisis had passed, would be complemented by a devaluation of the mark. This, in turn, would create the preconditions for a major German export offensive. As the first country to accept unpopular sacrifices on the home front, Germany would, as the chancellor explained to Hitler in early October 1930, "move into first place" (an die Spitze kommen).

Even under normal conditions, the risks of such a strategy would have been enormous. The effects of the global economic slump on Germany compounded these hazards beyond all measure. Nevertheless, Brüning was initially successful in overcoming the reservations of his cabinet and the German industrial establishment. This was due in part to the devastating collapse of the domestic economy, which caused unemployment figures to rise precipitously, brought all private investment to a virtual standstill, and left the leaders of industry, labor, and the civil servant unions totally overwhelmed. Their disorientation stood in sharp contrast to the chancellor's outward and initially sincere determination to do everything in his power to overcome the crisis. But there was not much he could do. To be sure, he accepted the prevalent doctrine of political economy that deflationary measures offered the only way in which the crisis could be effectively combated. He was also convinced that such measures would cause the recession to "bottom out" sooner and would lead to a healthy contraction of the economy. But Brüning was not a consistent deflationist, for the main objective of his fiscal and economic policy was not to combat the recession but to eliminate reparations—a factor that he, to be sure, considered a contributing factor to the world economic crisis.

At the outset, the German business community tended to attribute the collapse of the economy, which had become fully apparent only in the second half of 1930, to endogenous causes, such as excessive tax burdens and social expenditures. They failed to recognize that a recession had been clearly foreshadowed as early as 1929, when the economy was outwardly prosperous, by a decline in investment and an increase in savings deposits. By the same token, prices began to decline even before Brüning instituted measures to reduce prices and wages. These measures, however, affected cartelized products only after a certain delay and had no initial effect on agricultural products, which were subsidized by the government. Big industry attributed the recession mainly to a misguided social policy and was determined to use it to cut production costs. Industry was slow to realize that the crisis, which progressed by fits and starts, could trigger a contraction of the economy for which lower wages and reduced taxes were no remedy and that it posed an immediate threat to the continued existence of many business enterprises. By 1932-33, industrial production had declined by 43 percent from its high point in 1927-28; steel production alone had declined by 65 percent. Due to unusually high interest rates on loans that resulted from the currency policy of the Reichsbank and its dependency on the American capital market, investment activity came to a virtual halt, while withdrawals of capital exceeded new investments by a substantial margin.

Even though the international character of the crisis soon became obvious, Brüning, at first in agreement with the leading industrial associations, felt that he should stick to his fiscal and economic policies and that, for the time being, he could turn his back on offers of international cooperation. The recession was indeed conducive to the lowering of production costs that he wished to bring about. Industry—and the labor unions as well—approved of his consistent deflationary policy as the only way to combat the crisis. If the pressure of organized economic interests on the cabinet temporarily abated, this was not true in the case of agricultural subsidies. Still, decreasing tax revenues and the rapidly growing expenditures for the support of the long-term unemployed more than offset these political advantages. Despite reductions in public expenditures and investments at the national, state, and municipal levels, the actual decrease in public spending did not amount to more than 17 percent, whereas the proportion of unproductive to productive expenditures grew rapidly. Instead of lowering taxes as it had sought to do, the national government found itself obliged to increase the tax burden even on industry. Since interest rates were also kept high to protect the currency, tax increases served to constrict economic growth.

The average decline in national income, nominally amounting to 41 percent per person between 1929 and 1932, would surely have been less precipitous had not special political consideration for the powerful East Elbian agricultural interests provided this group with economically unjustifiable subsidies. This, in turn, saddled the working class and the commercial middle class with the main burden of the crisis. Incomes derived from agriculture and capital, by contrast, decreased on the average only by a third, a fact that can only be attributed to the protection of agriculture and tax privileges for big industry. The crisis, then, brought about a major redistribution of income that fell heaviest on workers and the lower middle classes, including recipients of pensions and public welfare, whereas a different economic policy could have mitigated the extent of their deprivation.

To knowledgeable political observers, the redistributive effects of Brüning's crisis policy were predictable as early as the fall of 1930, for it corresponded to the wishes of the industrial and agricultural interest groups. Yet this restructuring process, though perfectly visible in the social statistics, was not the result of long-range economic and financial planning. To the national government, the totally unexpected scope of the crisis was mainly a disruptive factor that prevented Brüning from going ahead with the implementation of his reparations and fiscal policies. In the light of the steady decline in tax revenues, every effort to fund public budgets turned into an increasingly futile race for time. Brüning and Reichsbank President Hans Luther refused to heed the warnings of the experts. Wilhelm Lautenberg of the Ministry of Economics, for instance, pointed out that the continuous decline in public investments, combined with the decline of prices below production costs, was bound to accelerate the downward spiral of the economy. Brüning and Luther did not realize that the only remedy for the deepening economic crisis was for the state to "prime the pump."

The national cabinet looked upon the struggle against mass unemployment in primarily fiscal terms. Direct and indirect measures to create a limited number of jobs, such as those proposed by an ad hoc committee under the chairmanship of former Minister of Labor Heinrich Brauns, had no independent political standing but were used exclusively as supplementary measures in balancing the budget. They also conflicted with the cabinet's goal of lowering prices and wages, a goal that Brüning, who underestimated the effects of international protective tariffs, expected to stimulate exports. This strategy would also have been beneficial from the point of view of reparations, but was incompatible with the subsidies to agriculture, whose continuation was politically unavoidable. Compounded by the banking crisis of June 1931, these factors effectively shattered the original framework within which the cabinet had expected to accomplish its domestic and foreign policy goals.

Since the political survival of the Brüning cabinet depended on its ability to achieve at least a partial solution of the problems that faced it, it tended to usurp regulatory functions previously reserved to other agencies. The cabinet thus assumed responsibility for establishing wage policies, supervising the banks, aiding the eastern provinces, and conducting foreign trade. There is no doubt that the constant expansion of the government's responsibilities greatly overtaxed its resources, particularly since Brüning was unwilling to give the acute crisis priority over his long-range goals of settling the reparations problem and revising the constitution. As a result, the conduct of government business soon became mired in a welter of tactical expedients, in which even long-range foreign policy plans were pressed into the service of short-term domestic calculations. As long as the chancellor's predictions of an improvement in Germany's foreign and domestic situation failed to materialize, he reacted to the pent-up resentment of the interest groups by trying out a muddle of tactical measures. None of these reassured the public of the government's ability or its will to deal with the problems of mass poverty and economic decline.

The mass unemployment unleashed by the depression passed the 4 million mark in early 1931 and reached 6.1 million in February 1932. Actual unemployment was considerably higher, since many workers who had no claim to unemployment compensation or who had given up looking for work did not appear in the official statistics. The temporary rise in the number of self-employed workers also suggests that many of the long-term unemployed took up peddling in an attempt to eke out some kind of a marginal living. At the same time, unemployment benefits were subject to systematic cutbacks; after June 1931 they were paid for only twenty weeks — sixteen weeks for seasonal workers — with the result that increasingly large numbers of workers, particularly the young and many women, were removed from the rolls altogether. A curious consequence of this was that, at the height of the unemployment crisis, the unemployment insurance fund registered a growing surplus while expenditures for emergency support and local welfare agencies rose steeply. Given the rapid increase of long-term unemployment, the temporary emergency support provided by the national government to cushion this effect had only a minor effect.

The situation of the permanently unemployed in a society that still considered idleness a social stigma for which the victim was to blame defies adequate description. The hardship in the large cities, where unemployment was most prevalent, was unimaginable, while in the countryside, where wages had fallen to extremely low levels, the suffering was held within limits. Desperate people roamed the streets carrying signs reading "Seeking Work at Any Price" and were forced to rent a cheap place where they could sleep for a few hours because they could not afford to stay in an emergency shelter. Some spent all their time in municipal warming places because they had no money for heating materials and accepted the most menial jobs simply to survive. Unable to afford a single cigarette or a single beer, they stared with envy at those who drank alcohol in proletarian bars and went through the garbage cans of the rich in search of food. Hardest hit were young workers and women, since they were the first to be fired. They were also most likely to have their public support benefits reduced or eliminated on the basis of humiliating means tests.

Unemployment among the young was compounded by the presence of a disproportionately large cohort that stood on the threshold entering the labor force. Under these circumstances, a considerable part of the younger generation was unable to earn a respectable living. This, in turn, contributed to the rapid rise of social militancy, especially in the extremist parties, the KPD and NSDAP. After the proscription of the Red Front Soldiers' League (Roter Frontkämpferbund), the KPD resorted more and more to terrorist violence, much of which was provoked by violent acts by the SA. The SA became a refuge for the youthful unemployed, given a meager livelihood in SA homes and through public fund drives that anticipated the future *Winterhilfe* of the Third Reich. Unemployed young people who had never found work and therefore had no contacts with labor unions, occupational associations, or workers' clubs were recruited into the rapidly growing armies that the Left and especially the Right were forming in preparation for civil war. Independently of these developments, long-term unemployment, which eventually affected well over a third of all salaried workers, also weakened the sense of solidarity and activism of the salaried work force. The demoralization that spread throughout society in the wake of mass unemployment was further reflected in an increase in protest voting that often benefited the KPD. Public pressure to do something about mass poverty even affected Hindenburg, who for his own part urged the government to create "work and bread."

The extent of unemployment was totally unexpected and quickly led to a crisis of the social welfare system. In a concerted effort to reduce its expenditures in the area of social welfare, the national government had taken a number of critical steps that included the curtailment of unemployment insurance benefits through the reduction of the categories of recipients and the amounts paid, repeated cuts in supplemental support, reduced social and health care benefits, lower welfare and pension payments, and the removal of unemployment insurance from the national budget. Yet in spite of all of this, the costs of social welfare represented a disproportionately high percentage of the decreasing public expenditures. Moreover, these costs were being shifted from the national government and public insurance agencies to the municipalities. From this perspective, the dispute over the contributions by employers and employees to unemployment insurance premiums, which in the meantime had reached 6.5 percent, seemed of minor importance. Nevertheless, it was the Social Democratic decision to tolerate the Brüning cabinet that accounted for its willingness to continue the unemployment insurance program and, for the moment at least, to fund its share of the increased costs of emergency assistance, albeit with strict time limitations. Even then Carl Goerdeler, the newly appointed Reich commissar for price supervision (Reichskommissar für Preisüberwachung), contended that the system of unemployment insurance had been a complete failure and demanded that need criteria be applied to insurance benefits and that in the meantime the entire system of unemployment insurance be placed in the hands of the labor unions, which were to be transformed into public associations with compulsory membership. But Labor Minister Adam Stegerwald refused to change the existing system of unemployment insurance, even though it provided meager support to fewer and fewer of the unemployed.

In view of growing mass unemployment, it seemed sensible to establish public works projects that would create additional jobs and momentarily mitigate the effects of the recession. Plans to this effect had been discussed by the Provisional National Economic Council (Vorläufige Reichswirtschaftsrat) at the beginning of the crisis, and the so-called productive unemployment relief, practiced since 1926, pursued the same objective. Finance Minister Hermann Dietrich was the chief proponent of using government contracts to offset seasonal and economic fluctuations in employment. Efforts to this effect had been initiated in the early summer of 1930 but were limited to projects undertaken by the national railway system and the post office and involved sums of money that were far too small to stimulate the economy. Moreover, the financing of government contracts was made contingent on the reduction of prices. Of particular significance was the collapse of the construction industry as a result of the cutbacks in public spending. Instead of a highway construction project as proposed by a private planning group, the cabinet opted for a comprehensive program of street construction that was to be financed by foreign loans and therefore ran into a veto from the president of the National Bank. In the final analysis, public construction projects never went beyond a financially limited program for building small private homes.

Under these conditions, the government's economic policy confined itself to helping certain sectors of the German industrial community to bring down their production costs by authorizing reductions in wages and prices in the hope that this would stimulate a revival of trade on both the domestic and international markets. But this proved to be a dangerous experiment. For by using emergency decrees to bring prices and wages in line with the sagging domestic economy, the government ruined all chances for a recovery of the economy. Faced with declining prices, entrepreneurs could not be expected to show much interest in new investments. Nor was the government able to reduce the prices of major brand-name products to the same extent that it did with the prices of articles marketed by independent producers. Moreover, efforts to force a reduction in prices encountered fierce opposition not only from the most severely affected group—that is, the artisanry and small business sector—but also from large-scale industry, which complained that prices still did not cover production costs in spite of major wage reductions. At the same time, the government's efforts to bring about a reduction of prices offset the benefits of the higher income tax, which was now expanded to include the crisis-ridden agricultural sector. The collapse of prices, which eventually embraced the artificially protected agrarian sector as well, not only stifled the entrepreneurs' willingness to invest but did little to stimulate exports since the government had begun to resort to protective tariffs.

The British government's decision in September 1931 to devalue the pound dealt a further blow to the international competitiveness of German industry, which now urged its government to follow the example of other European countries and devalue its currency. Brüning, however, steadfastly refused to go along with these demands for fear of the consequences this might hold for his reparations policy. To justify his rigid attitude on the devaluation question, the chancellor invoked clauses of the Young Plan that obliged Germany to tie its currency to the value of gold. After other countries had begun to abandon the gold standard, a devaluation of the mark in the wake of the British devaluation would have been diplomatically feasible, even over French opposition. For his own part, Brüning envisaged a devaluation of the German mark by 20 percent but wanted to make certain that this took place in conjunction with his projected export offensive. The decline of German exports led to a further contraction of the domestic economy, which in the case of heavy industry led to a dramatic underutilization of existing capacities.

Under these circumstances, it made little sense to institute additional austerity measures in the public domain, since this would almost certainly lead to a further contraction of economic activity. In the meantime, the number of those who advocated a comprehensive government credit program as a way of reducing unemployment continued to grow. While Reichsbank President Hans Luther and other members of the cabinet questioned the wisdom of continuing Brüning's deflationary policy—and not even Brüning was so sure—the chancellor finally brushed aside all misgivings with the argument that measures to stimulate the economy must not be taken until the recession had bottomed out. Any earlier attempts, he felt, would have little more than a purely psychological effect. He therefore opposed demands from the labor unions and SPD for reduced working hours and a public works program that would create new jobs. At the same time, he rejected the proposal that Ernst Wagemann had made internally before going public in a lecture before the Study Group on Monetary and Credit Reform (Studiengesellschaft für Geld- und Kreditreform) in early 1932. Anticipating a program that was to resurface in a slightly modified form within the General German Trade-Union Federation and the free trade unions, Wagemann called on the government to increase the money supply by making credit available for purposes of economic reconstruction. Brüning condemned Wagemann's independent initiative in the sharpest of terms, claiming that by suggesting that there were means other than deflation for "improving our situation" he was sabotaging the government's reparations program. Surely the French would accuse the Germans of duplicity, Brüning contended, if it appeared that measures to revive the economy had been delayed until after the Basel commission had certified Germany's inability to pay. To this, Luther added that Wagemann's initiative endangered efforts to reform the civil administration and to reduce social benefits, thereby giving his personal stamp of approval to the cabinet's political priorities.

The recommendations of the Brauns commission for mitigating the social and economic effects of unemployment, therefore, never went beyond a few thin palliatives such as proposals to form a voluntary labor service and to create emergency jobs, the number of which remained woefully inadequate. Even proposals for the construction of public housing on a very limited scale were effectively quashed by industrial interest organizations, which maintained that the time had come to liquidate rent controls and to abandon the construction of housing with public funds in favor of private housing construction. That industry opposed all measures to create new jobs unless they, as in the case of the railroad and post office, did not affect the private sector went without saying. The official explanation for this position was that such measures would inhibit efforts to lower production costs. In the same manner, the Federation of German Employer Associations (Vereinigung der Deutschen Arbeitgeberverbände or VDA) rejected Dietrich's proposal to create an incentive for additional hiring through payroll subsidies that would be paid by the government on the grounds that this would disturb competitive balance. Under these circumstances, it is not surprising that Brüning saw little reason to set aside his fundamental reservations about proposals for the creation of new jobs.

Throughout all of this, the Social Democrats and labor unions were pressing for legislation to establish a forty-hour workweek as the norm for German industry. Emphatically supported by the Prussian government as well as by Brüning's minister of labor, Adam Stegerwald, this proposal had much to offer. Small and middle-sized entrepreneurs in particular saw it as a way to keep the nucleus of their work force gainfully employed. The Harburg Oil Company (Harburger Ölwerke), for example, had had good experience with a four-shift system and a thirty-six-hour workweek. Other companies had also tried to reduce their actual working hours by canceling shifts to avoid firing more and more of their workers. Even I.G. Farben, the giant chemical cartel, gave serious consideration to shortening the length of the workday. Carl Bosch, chairman of I.G. Farben's board of directors and a presidial member of the National Federation of German Industry, came to view this as an absolute necessity. "In light of the continuing overproduction of goods, the worldwide surplus of labor, and the long-run impracticability of excluding parts of our population from production," the only realistic solution, he concluded, was "reducing the working hours." Under heavy pressure from the public, the cabinet decided to include authorization for reducing the workweek to forty hours in the emergency decree it sent to the Reichstag in December 1931. In practice, however, the cabinet only recommended that companies reduce working hours instead of laying off workers. An outright ban on layoffs, as proposed by Prussia, was not approved.

It is not surprising that Bosch's proposal for reducing the working hours by law encountered the massive opposition of German heavy industry, even though Bosch—in agreement with the labor unions—did not call for wage equalization, or *Lohnausgleich*. Publicly, heavy industry argued that shorter working hours would lead to an unacceptable increase in production costs.

Internally, however, its leaders were concerned that since the workers had already absorbed a 17 percent decrease in real wages, further reductions were not feasible because they would depress workers' incomes below the poverty line. Under these circumstances, shorter working hours would not appreciably lower labor costs. Ludwig Grauert, executive secretary of the Northwestern Group of the Association of German Iron and Steel Industrialists (Nordwestliche Gruppe des Vereins der Deutschen Eisen- und Stahlindustrieller), therefore circulated the proposal that industrial employers be permitted to pay less than the minimum wage in the event of overtime. Otherwise, he claimed, it would not be possible to achieve a reduction of production costs in the area of wages. Even Gustav Krupp urged the government to authorize such a step, which would have meant the end of collective bargaining and was thus rejected by Stegerwald out of respect for the SPD and organized labor.

Even then, the government was not able to commit itself to energetic measures for increasing the number of jobs. To be sure, the chancellor did authorize some steps in this direction, but with the proviso that such programs be kept as small as possible so that funds for programs that might become necessary in the future would be available. In this respect, he fully agreed with Ernst von Borsig, chairman of the Federation of German Employer Associations, and Eduard Hamm, secretary of the German Chamber of Industry and Commerce (Deutscher Industrie- und Handelstag), that job creation programs must not be allowed to jeopardize future efforts to stimulate the economy. One should not, argued the chancellor, deprive future generations of work. His dogmatic faith in the power of the economy to heal itself, however, was not the only and certainly not the dominant element in the chancellor's attitude. His obsession with reparations precluded supplementary appropriations even in cases where the budget could have made funds available. Only when such expenses could be hidden in separate budgets, as in the case of the state-owned railroad, did he authorize government projects that produced new jobs.

A policy of employment creation by means of government loans would have sabotaged efforts by leading industrial associations to use the crisis to force a thorough reform of German social policy and undercut their plans for lower wages. At the same time, industry hoped to put an end to the government's involvement in collective bargaining and to reduce social welfare benefits. Nor did the leading industrial associations hesitate to advance deflationary arguments to counter the demands of organized labor and the white-collar and civil servant unions for measures that would increase the purchasing power of the public and combat the depression, which in the eyes of many resulted from insufficient consumption, by stimulating demand. The adherence of the employer' associations to a deflationary strategy was not, however, primarily a matter of dogmatic belief and even less a reflection of the trauma of hyperinflation that continued to haunt the middle class. Much more important was the argument that a deflationary economic policy was the only way to achieve a comprehensive reduction of wages along with an end to the existing systems of compulsory state arbitration and collective bargaining. On questions of foreign trade, however, the National Federation of German Industry departed from the deflationary principle and successfully pressured the cabinet to finance sales to the Soviet Union with comprehensive credit guarantees that amounted to the creation of artificial credit.

The Brüning cabinet underestimated the danger inherent in the determination of western Germany's heavy industry to rescind the social compromises upon which the Weimar Republic had been founded. Heavy industry would cooperate with the government's economic policy only if it was allowed to reform the existing system of collective bargaining. As early as April 1930 an influential employers' organization known as the Northwestern Group of the Association of German Iron and Steel Industrialists anticipated future challenges to the sanctity of collective bargaining agreements when it encouraged the Becker Steelworks to avoid shutting down operations by imposing a 10 to 15 percent wage reduction upon its work force. At the same time Arbeit Nordwest made the price reduction that the government sought contingent upon prior wage reductions. Labor Minister Stegerwald had decided to give in to the employers on the question of wage levels, but not in the matter of the inviolability of wage contracts. The arbitration decision in the wage conflict with the northwestern iron and steel industry that was handed down at Bad Oeynhausen and immediately endorsed by the government on 6 June 1931 was adopted over the opposition of the labor unions. Authorizing average wage reductions of 7.5 percent, it also canceled the piecework clause that had been agreed upon in the settlement of the Ruhr Iron Conflict. In the light of these concessions, the government's concurrent demand for lower iron prices was disproportionately modest. The arbitration decision was a clear signal to industry that it did not have to limit itself to the reduction of real wages through the curtailment of overtime and the widespread practice of short-term hiring. The government thus assumed primary responsibility for a far-reaching decline in industrial wages. By agreeing to a link between price cuts and wage cuts, it gave additional impetus to the employers' demand for undermining the system of collective bargaining.

Even before the promulgation of the emergency decree of 6 October 1930, the government found itself under massive pressure from employer and industrial associations to permit changes in existing wage contacts and to implement across-the-board wage reductions as high as 15 percent. An earlier arbitration decision had deferred settlement of the wage conflict in the Ruhr mining industry until after the September 1930 elections, but in late December the government was forced to show its true sociopolitical colors. Before the negotiations had even begun, the government had promised to compensate the Mining Association (Zechenverband) for a reduction of coal prices with a wage reduction of 8 percent along the lines of the precedent that had been established in the arbitration decision in the Berlin metal industry. Yet the government soon realized that in the Ruhr this could be done only at the risk of severe strikes and social unrest. The Mining Association, however, did not wait for the arbitration efforts of the labor minister and announced massive layoffs for 15 January 1931 in an attempt to coerce the workers to accept wage cuts in violation of their contract.

To be sure, it was possible in this instance to avert an open conflict by means of a special emergency decree that eliminated voluntary participation of the negotiating partners in the arbitration procedure and placed responsibility for setting wage levels in the hands of the cabinet. But this makeshift solution, which saddled the government with full responsibility for industrial wage policies, was bound to intensify pressure from the entrepreneurs, who were determined to do away with wage contracts and the existing system of binding arbitration. To Paul Silverberg, after all, arbitration was the "ultimate source of all our social and much of our economic misery." Although Brüning advocated a more flexible wage structure and indicated his willingness to make concessions to industry, it was quite clear that yielding to the demands of the Northwestern Group of the Association of German Iron and Steel Industrialists and the Mining Association was bound to radicalize the workers, including the Christian unions, and thus make it impossible for labor to continue its toleration of his government.

Shortly thereafter, the United Steelworks (Vereinigte Stahlwerke A.-G.) attempted to force the employees at its Ruhrort-Meiderich plant to accept a 20 percent cut in wages and salaries in order to avert closing of the plant. This underscored the determination of heavy industry to break the sanctity of existing wage contracts at the level of the individual plant should this prove necessary. In the Meiderich case, this attempt failed because of resistance from the workers, who rejected the wage cuts despite the prospect of unemployment, so that in the final analysis management was prepared to hire unemployed steelworkers in order to close the plant down. The reopening of the plant in May 1933 must be seen against the background of these events. It represented a spectacular propaganda coup for the NSDAP.

To be sure, those heavy industry leaders who were fiercely determined to remain "masters in their own house" did not command a majority in the National Federation of German Industry. When Paul Silverberg and Hans von Raumer attempted to reach an agreement with the labor unions in the fall of 1930, they did so without the backing of the leaders of heavy industry, who were intent on dismantling the existing system of social welfare. Their efforts to unite the unions and employers in support of the projected austerity measures, however, were not entirely hopeless. For while a revival of the Zentralarbeitsgemeinschaft as envisaged by von Raumer was out of the question, the unions did demonstrate a willingness to enter into serious negotiations with the employers and were prepared to make major concessions in the area of wages in order to save the beleaguered system of collective bargaining and state-sponsored arbitration. For the most part, the SPD and labor unions were convinced that the deflationary path taken by the Brüning government was unavoidable. What they bitterly opposed was the tendency of employer organizations to place the burden of the crisis on the working and commercial middle classes. They thus demanded the coordination of price and wage cuts and a program of public investments that would benefit the economy as a whole.

Efforts to encourage cooperation between management and labor reached a climax in early June 1930, but encountered the increasingly adamant resistance of west German industry and the Federation of German Employer Associations. Speaking for the VDA, Ernst von Borsig expressed the conviction that time was on the entrepreneurs' side so that there was no reason to make concessions to the unions. Silverberg's initiative, though endorsed by the board of the National Federation of German Industry, eventually foundered on the open obstruction of entrepreneurs who belonged to the Ruhrlade. The Ruhrlade was an informal body of twelve Ruhr industrialists under the chairmanship of the Gutehoffnungshütte's Paul Reusch that coordinated the representation of heavy industrial interests. In the late summer of 1931, this body began to intensify its pressure on the cabinet to break with the SPD and reorganize the cabinet in a clearly authoritarian sense.

Ruhr heavy industry had already dissociated itself publicly from the Brüning cabinet at a convention of the Langnamverein on 3 June 1931. Through the mediation of Albert Vögler, the various protest resolutions adopted at the convention were softened to avoid a personal affront to the chancellor. In this respect, Brüning was able to enlist the cooperation of not only Vögler, but also Fritz Springorum, whom the chancellor warned about the dire consequences that would result from the collapse of his government. But even in its more moderate version, the resolution was little more than a quasi ultimatum that called for "the end of tribute," the removal of party representatives from the cabinet, and the noninterference of the state in wage policy and amounted to an open declaration of war against Stegerwald's conciliatory attitude toward the unions. To be sure, said Ernst Poensgen in a declaration that expressed the prevailing mood of western industry, his group did not want a dictatorship but rather "economic and fiscal leadership that will save the German economy from imminent collapse."

The hard line taken by German heavy industry was shaped in large measure by the economic difficulties of the iron and steel industry and the dramatic decline in the sale of coal in the wake of the British pound's devaluation. By the spring of 1931, more and more industrial entrepreneurs had become skeptical about Brüning's ability to act forcefully and were disappointed by his continued dependence on the SPD. The declaration that Germany's leading business associations published on 29 September 1931, in which they came out in strong support for the principle of "individual wage structuring" (*individuelle Lohngestaltung*), signaled the end of further cooperation with the government. Aside from the fact that Stegerwald enjoyed close ties to the Christian labor unions and had declared in the cabinet that he was neither willing nor able to treat the wage earners as "outlaws," the preservation of collective bargaining and the state-sponsored system of binding arbitration represented the very minimum necessary to keep the ADGB and SPD from abandoning their toleration of the Brüning cabinet.

Although the leading industrial associations agreed in principle with Brüning's deflationary policy, important areas of disagreement existed from the outset. The first indication of this could be seen in the preliminary deliberations on the emergency decree of 3 December 1930, which mandated comprehensive cuts in the areas of civil servant salaries, unemployment and social insurance programs, and public housing. In the end, however, the more moderate elements of the German industrial establishment were persuaded by the argument that a change of governments would accelerate the flight of foreign credits and thus indicated their willingness to continue working with the chancellor. The same group also exerted pressure on the DVP, which advocated the NSDAP's participation in the national government and demanded budget cuts of 300 million marks in the 1931–32 budget, to drop its call for the convocation of the Reichstag, a sword of Damocles that threatened the presidential cabinet.

While the national government could be reasonably confident of the support of the National Federation of German Industry in spite of the vociferous opposition of heavy industry, it found itself in irreconcilable conflict with agrarian interest organizations. Brüning did his best to accommodate the agrarian interests in the area of foreign trade. He had, for example, prevented the German-Polish trade agreement from taking effect and declared Germany's earlier ratification of the International Customs Agreement (Zollfriedensabkommen) null and void when Great Britain failed to ratify it. He also worked for the removal of the most-favored-nation clause and for the expansion of the government's authorization to impose duties on processed agricultural products. Agricultural Minister Martin Schiele, on the other hand, went far beyond these steps and demanded a complete overhaul of the system of trade agreements and the imposition of still higher import duties on processed agricultural products. Since these changes would result in a long-term weakening of German exports to northern Europe and the Benelux countries, Carl Duisberg protested vigorously on behalf of the National Federation of German Industry. This conflict, which outlasted the Brüning cabinet, shifted to the question of import quotas for all agricultural products and Schiele's demand that the export of agricultural products be subsidized in an arrangement similar to the AVI Accord for the iron processing industry. Government concessions of this nature, however, did little to inhibit the increasing radicalization of the farm electorate in Prussia's eastern provinces, Schleswig-Holstein, and Lower Saxony.

A similar conflict arose with respect to the Eastern Aid Program known as the Osthilfe. The National Federation of German Industry had advocated that the industrial assessments originally slated for the payment of reparations be shifted to agriculture following the declaration of a moratorium on all reparations payments by Herbert Hoover. At the initiative of Baron Tilo von Wilmowsky, deputy chairman of the board of directors of Friedrich Krupp A.-G., heavy industry and the National Rural League began to exchange ideas under the auspices of the Esplanade Circle (Esplanade-Kreis). The extraordinary financial demands by the RLB's Schiele, along with his plans for the administrative handling of loan guarantees and debt conversion, encountered strong opposition from industrial circles, which agreed with Schiele that the Prussian government should be excluded from the administration of the Osthilfe but not that the program should be delivered into the hands of organized agricultural interests. Brüning too was hesitant to put Schiele in sole charge of the Osthilfe, particularly since, for financial reasons, he did not want to lose the participation of the Prussian government, which refused to work with Schiele but was willing to accept Transportation Minister G. R. Treviranus as commissar for the Osthilfe.

Brüning, who had a strong personal commitment to the Osthilfe program and who knew that the Reich president was pressing for comprehensive aid measures, remained skeptical as to whether a sweeping rehabilitation of eastern agriculture could be achieved within the foreseeable future. Although he shared the misgivings of banking and industrial circles who felt that solutions that involved extensive state regulation were bound to undermine the free play of capitalist market forces, he nevertheless approved Schiele's request for a comprehensive moratorium on agricultural credits in the east. Since Finance Minister Hermann Dietrich persistently refused to use revenues from the industrial surcharge tax to write off agricultural debts, the amounts earmarked for this purpose in the emergency decree of 26 July 1930 were relatively small, with the result that debtors were not always able to meet the conditions for protection against foreclosure.

Under pressure from the DNVP, the National Rural League, and the Christian-National Peasants and Farmers' Party, the Brüning government presented the Reichstag with a comprehensive Eastern Aid Program in February 1931. This program represented a response to a plan proposed by the DNVP's Alfred Hugenberg, whose extreme demands were ironically dismissed by the Social Democrats as "the socialization of the capital lost by east German agriculture" and regarded as entirely out of the question by industrial circles.

Despite the unusually generous guarantees contained in the bill, it too was essentially a failure. This stemmed in no small measure from the fact that the banking crisis had severely affected capital liquidity, made Prussia financially insolvent, and led to excessively high interest rates that stood in the way of any major program of debt conversion. Moreover, the measures that had already been enacted for a restructuring of German agriculture had been blocked by administrative institutions under the domination of agricultural interest organizations. Revelations that in a number of cases the allocation of funds had been accompanied by gross mismanagement and that large landowners had used these credits to finance their lavish life-style only helped discredit the program in the eyes of the public.

Brüning's hopes that a broad expansion of the Eastern Aid Program would lead to a relaxation of domestic political tensions were never realized, largely because the demands of organized agriculture greatly exceeded what was possible within a capitalistic economic system. Instead of accepting bankruptcy protection based on the individual's ability to achieve recovery, agricultural interest organizations demanded the cancellation of all debt payments, lower interest rates, and increased subsidization of agricultural prices. After the reshuffling of the Brüning cabinet in late 1931, Brüning gave in to pressure from organized agriculture once again and undertook a further expansion of the Eastern Aid Program, which was now headed by Hans Schlange-Schöningen. Contained in the Fourth Emergency Decree for Protecting the Economy and Finances, these measures entailed, among other things, a general reduction of interest rates as well as the appropriation of funds from the industrial levy and the use of supplemental credits for the purposes of agricultural recovery.

Enacted on 20 November 1931, the new version of the Eastern Aid Program did not preclude the use of coercive measures to refinance the indebtedness of large agricultural estates, particularly since those that were beyond help were to be divided up into new farms for resettlement. Schlange-Schöningen placed the National Settlement Society (Reichssiedlungsgesellschaft) that had been created for this purpose in the service of internal colonization, which he and other nationalists regarded as a national mission insofar as they sought to stem the exodus of Germany's rural population from the east and thus prevent the German east from becoming little more than a steppe. A landowner himself, Schlange-Schöningen was nonetheless not ready to adopt the line of his peers but pursued instead a recovery program that was based on the principle of profitability and aimed to convert hopelessly indebted estates into plots for new settlers. In this respect, however, Schlange greatly overestimated the prospects of rapid administrative action. The euphoria that the idea of renewed colonization of the East aroused in these years—for it was combined with corporatist ideas and the hope that it would provide an inexpensive means of taking care of the unemployed masses—stood in sharp contrast to the numerically modest success of resettlement itself. The Fifth Emergency Decree, which stemmed from Schlange-Schöningen's initiative but was never promulgated, came under heavy fire before it was ever published from organized agricultural interests, which did not hesitate to go to the Reich president with the charge that the chancellor was selling out agriculture in the East.

The Eastern Aid Program instituted in late 1931 did nothing to calm the noisy opposition of the right-wing parties, which on 11 October 1931 formally launched their campaign against the Brüning cabinet by forming the Harzburg Front. In economic terms, the Eastern Aid Program and the protectionist measures that complemented it stood in diametric opposition to the chancellor's deflationary strategy. Measures to lower prices had little impact as long as they did not include foodstuffs. There were even temporary increases in the price of bread, which Stegerwald sharply criticized on the grounds that this made further reductions in wages impossible. Artificial price supports, on the other hand, had little long-term impact in light of the general decline in consumer purchasing power.

In point of fact, the Eastern Aid Program represented a policy that provided large-scale agriculture with unjustified and economically as well as politically damaging privileges. Approximately 3 million small agricultural enterprises were excluded from the program's subsidies, while only 2 percent of an estimated 2 million middle-sized enterprises benefited from it. By contrast, 5 percent of the 13,000 large-scale enterprises had their debts converted, while 81 percent were given tax exemptions, bankruptcy protection, and lower interest rates. Moreover, the way in which Germany's tariff regulations were biased in favor of grain producers discriminated against the consumer to the extent of 2 billion marks in additional imports. The money that was squandered in this way could have been used to finance the creation of a considerable number of new jobs.

The effects of this were not fully apparent until late 1930, when Brüning was about to implement his long-awaited comprehensive reform program. In spite of the increasing skepticism of industrial interest organizations and the heightened polemics of agricultural interests, Brüning withstood the critical situation created by the promulgation of the First Emergency Decree for Economic and Financial Security in October 1930 and its subsequent tightening in December in remarkably good shape. With characteristic rigidity, Brüning proceeded with his budgetary reform according to plan in spite of unexpected difficulties on all sides, not the least of which was the fact that the countercyclical effects of the emergency decrees had led to a far more severe decline in tax revenues than any budget projections had anticipated.

At the same time, the Finance Ministry found it increasingly difficult to procure the necessary loans from the German banks, particularly since the Reichsbank had experienced a serious depletion of its own gold reserves and was therefore unable to help the government with its cash-flow problems. The outcome of the September elections had thoroughly shaken the confidence of many foreign creditors in the internal stability of the Weimar Republic and had triggered a widespread flight of capital from Germany. The immediate cancellation of short-term foreign loans resulted in a considerable reduction of the Reichsbank's foreign currency reserves. Reichsbank President Hans Luther, who felt that maintaining the stability of the currency was his paramount task, responded to this situation by raising the discount rate, thereby making credit even more scarce. By early 1931 the cabinet had decided that drastic new cuts in public spending represented the only way that the budgetary expenditures could be covered.

At the same time, the government had to contend with increasing pressure from organized economic interests to suspend the payment of reparations. In this respect, the declarations of the civil servants' associations, the labor unions, the German Urban Conference (Deutscher Städtetag), and the most important industrial associations differed only in tone from the attacks against the government's alleged "lack of backbone" that had gone out from Hugenberg, the Stahlhelm, the National Rural League, and, last but not least, the Christian-National Peasants and Farmers' Party and that had been exceeded only by the shrillness of National Socialist agitation. In the cabinet virtually everyone agreed that halting reparations payments—a step that would have lessened but by no means eliminated the budget deficit—would be interpreted by foreign powers as a declaration of bankruptcy and would almost certainly lead to the widespread recall of credits. This concern was not unfounded. Not only the international banking experts whom the government consulted, but also the British ambassador, Sir Horace Rumbold, had expressly cautioned the Germans against requesting a moratorium on the payment of reparations, even though the Young Plan permitted them to do so for a portion of their annuities. Moreover, the formal appeal that Germany would have to make to the Bank for the International Balance of Payments (Bank für Internationalen Zahlungsausgleich) would have led to a time-consuming investigation of Germany's ability to pay without providing immediate relief. In fact, it would have involved indirect control measures to which Brüning was opposed in principle and that would have unleashed a new storm of indignation from the "national opposition."

Brüning had long planned to postpone reopening the reparations question until at least the late autumn of 1932, since any solution of the closely related interallied war debts question would have to await the outcome of the presidential elections in the United States. Yet in early 1931 Brüning began to have serious doubts whether the "fulfillment offensive" demanded by Reichsbank President Luther could be delayed much longer in the face of the mounting budget deficit and a declining economy. Like Brüning, Dietrich and Luther were fully committed to a strategy of proving Germany's reliability through the scrupulously exact fulfillment of its reparations obligations. At the same time, however, they planned to use Germany's revived competitive strength in world markets to pressure its creditors into canceling its reparations obligations. But it was difficult to gain domestic political support for this strategy, particularly since the government was no longer in a position to prepare the campaign for revision quietly behind the scenes.

Brüning believed that he could create a situation in which the proposal for canceling reparations would come from one of the creditor nations. From his point of view, this was necessary if the recall of foreign credits was to be kept within limits. But in late January 1931 when Foreign Minister Julius Curtius suggested to Aristide Briand that France should "let the air out of the Young Plan," the chancellor was not pleased, since a French initiative was precisely what he wanted to avoid. His foreign policy, which had the wholehearted support in the Foreign Office of State Secretary Bernhard von Bülow, was in fact aimed at isolating France, the main reparations creditor, and subjecting it to English and American pressure. In the summer of 1931, when he found himself obliged to visit Paris in preparation for the London Conference, Brüning deliberately avoided taking along Hans Schäffer, who advocated more open relations with France. A few months later Schäffer resigned his position as state secretary in the Ministry of Finance, for he considered the policy of fictitious budgetary reform to which Brüning had resorted an exercise in futility.

The chancellor had set his sights on a global solution to the reparations question. He was intent on avoiding premature negotiations and did not want to obtain French loans at the price of political concessions. One of his main arguments against the NSDAP's participation in the national government was that Hitler might be willing to meet France halfway, a concern for which there were indeed concrete indications. Similar reasons also led Brüning to reject the idea of requesting a moratorium on reparations payments. Such a request would have meant that negotiations on a definitive solution of the reparations problem would have to take place at a time when Germany had presumably overcome the current economic crisis or at least would be in a better position to pay. But things did not work out this way. In the summer of 1931, President Hoover proposed, on his own initiative, a one-year moratorium on the payment of reparations and other interallied debts related to World War I. For the sake of its credibility, the German government was obliged to react to this step with enthusiasm in spite of the fact that it had undercut its own reparations strategy.

As long as the reparations were not canceled, the German Reich had to avoid foreign policy conflicts in order to protect its credit worthiness. Nevertheless Brüning, who maintained a low profile in this matter, gave Foreign Minister Curtius the authorization to proceed with the implementation of a German-

Austrian customs union. Under consideration since Stresemann's days but in the planning stage only since the fall of 1931, this initiative carried the risk of damaging Germany's formally correct relations with France. But the chancellor did not expect the French to accommodate Germany on the central issues of ending the reparations, revising the eastern frontiers, and establishing parity of armaments. In short, he had adopted an aggressive foreign policy line that had taken hold in the Foreign Office after the death of Stresemann and that was expressed in personnel decisions such as the appointment of Bernhard von Bülow as state secretary for foreign affairs. Von Bülow was well known as a strong advocate of an active revisionist policy. His ultimate aim was to circumvent the principle of collective security by means of bilateral agreements and intensified disarmament negotiations to establish military parity for Germany.

Nothing revealed the new course of German foreign policy under Brüning more clearly than the manner in which German diplomacy reacted to the memorandum on the formation of a Federated European Union that Aristide Briand submitted to the League of Nations in May 1931. For all his attachment to the idea of a powerful national state, Stresemann had never allowed the discussions with Paris to be broken off. His successors, however, believed that they could isolate France and confront it openly on the international level. Briand's European plan was rejected out of hand by the German Foreign Office and national cabinet. Instead of submitting it to a serious evaluation, the German government was interested only in exploiting whatever advantage a negative German response might give it in the domestic political arena. Curtius remarked that the German note would help to provide Briand's initiative with a "first-class funeral."

To be sure, Briand's carefully worked-out memorandum, which was also rejected by Italy and Great Britain, was not immediately realizable in practical political terms and was never meant to be. Its underlying assumption was that the lasting peace and the economic future of Europe depended on its political federalization, a goal that could only be achieved in the long term. In contrast to simultaneous negotiations of the League of Nations for a dismantling of customs barriers, Briand's proposal emphasized the importance of a political accord as a prerequisite for a European common market. Neither State Secretary von Bülow nor Foreign Minister Curtius was willing to give any credence whatsoever to the potential for the future of this program and claimed that Briand's only aim was to "place new shackles on Germany." Brüning, on the other hand, nonchalantly told the British ambassador Sir Horace Rumbold that Briand meant to force Germany to abandon its demands for the revision of its eastern frontiers once and for all, even though Briand had issued a clear statement to the effect that this was not the case. In the cabinet the chancellor observed that the German Reich could not exist "without sufficient natural living space," to which Curtius added that the Briand program was exclusively designed to uphold French hegemony.

The plan to use a customs union to circumvent the ban on a German-Austrian *Anschluß* that was contained in the Treaty of Saint-Germain was the work of Bernhard von Bülow. The legal department of the German Foreign Office had drafted a treaty whose wording did not violate the terms of the existing treaties, particularly the Geneva Protocol that Austria had signed in 1922. At that time the Austrian Republic, in return for major financial aid provided by the League of Nations that came primarily from the French, had had to promise that it would not make any commitments that would directly or indirectly curtail its independence, including the granting of special economic privileges. In point of fact, von Bülow's draft treaty did not affect Austrian sovereignty and did not imply special status for Germany since it also contained a clause that explicitly permitted third parties to join. He could therefore hope to weather the storm of public indignation that was expected in France by sheer stubbornness.

The initiative for the conclusion of a customs union agreement came from the Austrian vice-chancellor and foreign minister Johann Schober. Schober anticipated that this agreement would prompt Germany to provide the help the Austrian Republic so urgently needed in view of its increasingly desperate economic situation. At the same time, he hoped that it would give a boost to the Greater German People's Party (Großdeutsche Volkspartei), which in the past had been relegated to a minor political role compared to that of the Christian-Social and Socialist camps and which recently had had to contend with increased competition from the Austrian NSDAP. Schober did not have to fear any serious opposition from the Social Democratic Party, for its leading representatives, among them Otto Bauer and Karl Renner, had always been emphatically in favor of an *Anschluß*. By contrast, the Christian-Socialist Party—whose leader, Monsignor Ignaz Seipel, had signed the Geneva Protocol in 1922—increasingly dissociated itself from the idea of an *Anschluß*. The press leak that forced the German and Austrian governments to announce the plans for a customs union prematurely on 17 March 1931 was not at all unwelcome to Berlin, since it forced Vienna to commit itself publicly to the foreign policy line that the two governments had agreed upon.

The customs union concluded under the Austrian chancellor Otto Ender marked the beginning of a reorientation in Austrian foreign policy, the primary goal of which was to break the republic's political dependence on the Western powers. In fact, this dependence had been a decisive factor in sustaining the viability of the Austrian parliamentary system in spite of increasingly intense domestic political conflicts that reached a climax in 1927, when a spontaneous popular uprising and the burning of the Ministry of Justice created a state of

virtual civil war that abated only with the adoption of the constitutional compromise of 1929. The fall of Ignaz Seipel in 1929 and the increased activity of the
Heimwehr, which favored close contacts with fascist Italy, created a political
stalemate that made it possible for Foreign Minister Schober to pursue plans
for an Austrian-German customs union without parliamentary consultation
and in the face of opposition from certain sectors of Austrian industry. This,
then, was Austria's first step in the direction of an *Anschluß* and must be seen as
an attempt to bring its own government in line with the German presidential
system.

Although German foreign policy tried to depict the proposed customs
union as a way of furthering the League of Nations' announced goal of doing
away with customs barriers throughout Europe, it had much broader aims from
the outset. Brüning spoke of it as a first step that would "permit economic solutions on a large scale [*im großen Stil*] in central Europe." What this statement
conveniently omitted was that Germany planned to supplement its accord with
Austria with preferential trade agreements with Rumania, Bulgaria, Hungary,
and Yugoslavia, which would lay the foundation for a broad trade offensive in
southeastern Europe. Efforts in this direction had been under way for several
years, promoted in particular by the Central European Economic Conference
(Mitteleuropäischer Wirtschaftstag), a planning group sponsored by German
industry. But these efforts took on a new accent when German diplomacy,
strongly influenced by von Bülow, initiated a trade offensive in southeastern
Europe designed to break up the Little Entente, which was closely allied to
France. The thrust toward the southeast, which had the full support of the German ambassador in Belgrade, Ulrich von Hassell, also sought to cut off Poland
from its normal trade partners. The hope was that in the foreseeable future
an active central European policy would isolate Poland and eventually make it
amenable to a revision of its western borders.

Paris and London were only vaguely aware of the implications of the proposed German-Austrian customs union, the details of which Curtius had negotiated with Schober during an official visit to Vienna in March 1931. Yet the
German initiative, which had not received the endorsement of the staff of the
German Foreign Office, came as a major affront to Aristide Briand, who had
lost that year's French presidential election to the emphatically nationalist candidate Paul Doumer. The departure of Briand, who a few weeks earlier had laid
a wreath at Stresemann's grave in a gesture that drew very little attention by
the German press, marked the end of a diplomatic era in which the hope that
the former enemies of the First World War might come to an understanding
had not been altogether illusory. Germany's unilateral initiation of the customs
union, however, revived the methods of the prewar era and was reminiscent
of the "panther leap" (*Panzersprung*) to Agadir devised in 1911 by Alfred von

Kiderlen-Wächter. Von Bülow was von Kiderlen's pupil and shared with him the illusion that Germany's foreign policy partners could be duped.

For his own part, Curtius succumbed to the illusion that he could brush aside French protests since the British government was generally sympathetic to closer cooperation between Germany and Austria. But he lost the goodwill of the British when he failed to heed their advice to avoid unilateral proceedings and to act only in consultation with the British cabinet. It soon became clear that it was a serious mistake to believe that France could be diplomatically out-maneuvered, particularly since German diplomacy had already done its best to embarrass the forces of reconciliation represented by Briand. Even though Curtius repeatedly admonished his Austrian partners to remain firm and "keep the faith of the Nibelungen," Vienna was not in a position to withstand the diplomatic pressure mobilized by the French. While the German Foreign Office denied that the League of Nations had any jurisdiction in the matter, Austrian Vice-Chancellor Schober was compelled to permit that body or the International Court in The Hague to decide whether the German-Austrian customs union was compatible with the provisions of the Geneva Protocol.

On 5 September 1931 the International Court agreed, albeit by a surprisingly narrow margin, with the League of Nations that the German-Austrian customs union project was a violation of existing treaty obligations. By this time, how-ever, the customs union was already politically dead for the simple reason that Austria's growing economic instability ruled out a sudden change of direction in the conduct of its foreign policy. In reality, the collapse of the Austrian Credit Institute (Österreichische Creditanstalt), the country's most important private bank and one that commanded great international respect because of its close connection with the House of Rothschild, was not directly related to the fiasco of the planned customs union. This sensational event was caused primarily by the fact that the Austrian Credit Institute had lost almost all of its own capi-tal reserves in the purchase of the nearly bankrupt Real-Estate Credit Institute (Boden-Kreditanstalt) and, unable to recall its own loans and faced with the collapse of its own securities, experienced a severe liquidity crisis. Since this bank either directly or indirectly controlled more than two-thirds of Austrian industry, its insolvency triggered a severe crisis throughout the entire banking system and economy. Foreign creditors responded by immediately recalling their loans. France, in turn, took advantage of this crisis to pressure the Aus-trian government, which collapsed as a result of this crisis, into abandoning the proposed customs union with Germany.

Although the German government attempted to mount a program of finan-cial support for Austria, it was the Bank of England that provided the Austrian Credit Institute with the loan of 150 million Austrian schillings it needed to contain the international repercussions of a collapse of the Austrian banking system. This undercut French policy, which sought to attach political conditions to financial aid to Austria. Vienna was reluctant to fulfill these conditions, feeling that in doing so it would lose what face it had left in Berlin. The Banque de France retaliated by selling all of its pound reserves, an action that placed severe pressure on the British pound and indeed set the stage for the devaluation of the British currency in September 1931. For the moment, however, France's position in international finances was quite solid, partly as a result of the excessive devaluation of the French franc in the wake of the Ruhr crisis. By comparison, Germany's financial position was too weak for it to be of effective help to Austria.

It is quite certain that a German-Austrian customs union would have done little, if anything, to relieve Germany's increasingly desperate economic situation. That German foreign policy took up the customs union project in the first place stemmed in large part from the government's desire to have at least one success to its credit in revising the order that had been created by the Versailles peace treaty to help counter massive right-wing agitation against reparations. Moreover, the German initiative might have aggravated latent friction between Great Britain and France, a prospect that was by no means unwelcome to Brüning. The failure of the German initiative, however, severely damaged the prestige of Curtius, who was also attacked by the Right for his willingness to negotiate with Poland. Only the fact that in the heated matter of rights for German minorities the League of Nations had decided in favor of the German position saved Curtius from having to resign at this time, although Brüning assiduously avoided showing support for his beleaguered foreign minister.

The effects of the Austrian credit crisis, which had been aggravated by the conflict over the customs union project, on the German economy were disastrous. For the withdrawal of foreign loans, which began in Austria with the insolvency of the Austrian Credit Institute, spread to Germany within a matter of days as the financial difficulties of the Karstadt department store chain became known and as the North Star Insurance Company (Versicherungskonzern Nordstern) had to admit serious financial losses in May 1931. The banking crisis that now broke out in Germany was directly related to Brüning's decision to consolidate political support for his proposed fiscal reforms by issuing a public statement on the reparations question. Whereas Brüning usually paid little attention to public opinion, he now declared in the cabinet that the German people could not be asked to make further financial sacrifices without "determined steps" in the reparations question. But the furor over the German-Austrian customs union project had prompted the British to ask that the visit the chancellor had planned to make to Chequers, the country estate of the British prime minister, in May 1931 be postponed until the following month.

Not without some justification, Brüning feared that the Third Emergency Decree for the Reform of the Economy and Finances, which had been prepared behind closed doors and was published on 5 June 1931 immediately after the Social Democratic party congress, would produce a storm of public protest. In order to avoid coming under pressure from economic interest organizations, Brüning had ordered a news blackout during the preparatory work on the emergency decree. Since some details nevertheless leaked out, the public was even more critical of the severe measures the decree contained than it would have been had it received prudent advance warning. The *Berliner Tageblatt* described the public's reaction to the decree as "general horror." Cuts in the salaries and wages of public employees, reductions in social services, increases in sales taxes, expanded emergency taxes, cuts in national subsidies to states and municipalities, and the elimination of exemptions on the wage and salary tax affected not just selected social groups but the entire population with the exception of those belonging to the highest income groups in the private sector. All of this, it seemed, justified combining the emergency decree with an appeal to the Allied powers stating that the economic condition of the Reich "makes relieving Germany of the unbearable reparations payments an imperative necessity."

The so-called Tribute Appeal was issued on 6 June 1931 and contained the phrase that the "limit of what we can impose on our people" had been reached. In this respect, however, Brüning fell victim to the disastrous miscalculation that he could keep the reparations question in abeyance on the diplomatic front while creating the impression at home that he had actually embarked on a revisionist course of action. From the point of view of social psychology, it was also a mistake to appeal to the population to make sacrifices without explaining their exact purpose. Brüning's conviction that reparations negotiations could only be conducted from a position of financial strength was difficult to convey to the public at large, which as a matter of course assumed that in this desperate situation all payments would have to stop. Similarly, Brüning should have known that foreign governments were bound to conclude from the Tribute Appeal that Germany would soon be unable to fulfill its reparations obligations and that the appeal was an indication of its complete insolvency.

If foreign creditors felt prompted to withdraw their short-term loans from Germany, it was not so much because they saw cracks in the country's financial system as because they felt that the Tribute Appeal signaled the end of Germany's willingness to pay. Under these circumstances, they no longer trusted Germany to fulfill the financial obligations it had assumed. Subsequent developments were to prove them correct, for they lost much of the capital they had left in Germany and thus helped "finance" the German crisis. The flight from the German currency, which had already begun, now reached totally unexpected proportions. The Reichsbank found itself confronted with an outflow of foreign currency that it had never before experienced in this form. Only with the help of short-term discount credits from the Bank of England was it possible for the Reichsbank to avoid falling below the 40 percent currency reserves required by the Young Plan.

The impending collapse of the German capital market confirmed the worst fears of those who condemned the excessive use of short-term foreign credits as a dangerous threat to Germany's economic health. The withdrawal of loans compounded certain structural weaknesses in the German banking system. In comparison with the prewar period, credit institutions operated with very little capital of their own and with much smaller liquid reserves. The high proportion of short-term foreign credits was not a particular problem as long as it was possible to compensate for their withdrawal by contracting new short-term loans. The outcome of the elections of September 1930, however, had brought about a major change in this practice, for it seriously inhibited the influx of new loans, whether short- or long-term. At the same time, the banks found themselves faced with the problem that the time limits the majority of the creditors had placed on their loans made it impossible to make these credits liquid. In many instances, declining prices and falling values in the stock market deprived credit institutions of sufficient investment opportunities, so that they were increasingly forced to include their own stock in their portfolios. In the event of a cash-flow crisis, these assets were of practically no value whatsoever. Even the securities of other companies were adversely affected by the decline of the stock market, with the result that Germany's larger banks were often forced to absorb extensive losses.

The banking crisis had disastrous effects on bank clearinghouses and savings institutions, which had long suffered from the government's deflationary policy. To be sure, savings banks, which had become more important than the banks as institutions for financing municipal projects, could claim increased savings deposits, but they shared the financial plight of the municipalities insofar as the mounting costs of services for the unemployed made it impossible for them to repay short-term loans. This revealed a fundamental flaw in Weimar's fiscal structure. During the period of stabilization, municipal governments had gone into excessive debt and frequently financed long-term investments with short-term loans. In this respect, it is important to remember that they bore the principal burden of the profound changes that had begun to take place in the structure of German society before the war and of improving an economic infrastructure that in Germany had not kept pace with those of other developing industrial nations. Under the conditions of the crisis, the municipalities experienced a further increase in their social responsibilities and had to deal directly with the problems of mass poverty at the same time that their own finances were adversely affected by cuts in the social budget and the elimination of government subsidies for the construction of public housing.

The widespread criticism of the municipal fiscal policy failed to appreciate the fact that the social-political accomplishments of the municipalities were among the lasting successes of the Weimar Republic. Large towns in particular, many of which had grown even larger through the incorporation of outlying areas, did much to shape the highly innovative social and cultural climate of the Weimar Republic through new social and educational initiatives, new communications and housing policies, and new municipal businesses that were promptly attacked by entrepreneurial circles as instances of "socialism through the back door" (*kalte Sozialisierung*). At the level of municipal administration, there was a remarkable degree of interparty cooperation despite efforts in the late 1920s to isolate the parties of the Left through the formation of local bourgeois blocs. Such cooperation stood in sharp contrast to the dismal situation in the Reichstag.

The insolvency of the municipal banking system produced by excessive demands on the fiscal resources of local government severely compromised the credibility of public finances. This, however, was little more than a side effect of the more general credit crisis that materialized in early June 1931. This crisis, intensified by opposition to the Emergency Decree of 5 June 1931, temporarily threatened to bring down the cabinet. Only by threatening to dissolve the coalition government in Prussia was Brüning able to dissuade the SPD from convening the budget committee of the Reichstag, while the DVP, on the other hand, was moved to self-restraint by the intervention of influential industrialists and the Reich president. While concern about the negative effects of a cabinet crisis on Germany's credit rating abroad might have helped insure the continued existence of the presidential government, reassuring the world on this point could not avert the collapse of Germany's capital market.

On 17 June 1931 the collapse of the North German Wool Carding Company (Norddeutsche Wollkämmerei) in Bremen set in motion a series of fateful events in the area of credit policy. Largely caused by irresponsible speculative ventures, the bankruptcy of Northern Wool affected its principal creditor, the Darmstadt and National Bank (Darmstädter und Nationalbank), which under Jakob Goldschmidt had become one of Germany's most important industrial banks. However, the bank's insolvency and the impending failure of Karstadt, at the time the largest of Germany's department store chains, did not become known for a few days. The bankruptcy of the North German Wool Carding Company alone triggered a wave of capital withdrawals from the Reichsbank. Having already lost most of its reserves of gold and foreign currency, the Reichsbank now found itself in the unfortunate position of being unable to guarantee the minimum currency reserves mandated by law.

In order to stem the flight of capital, the Reichsbank began to make the refinancing of loans difficult for private banks and to curtail the volume of loans in spite of the fact that this policy was bound to lead to further business failures and to an increase in unemployment. For the moment, however, there was no alternative unless the government was willing to risk the currency and its reparations policy by circulating unsecured banknotes, a course that was firmly rejected by Reichsbank President Luther. Luther's efforts to secure rediscounted credits from the Bank of England had run into strong opposition from Montagu Norman, who only indirectly alluded to the impending weakening of the British pound. French credits might have been available — and indeed the British recommended applying for them — but the German government did not wish to accept them because of the political conditions the French would almost certainly attach.

The debacle of the Reich's financial policy was primarily the result of Brüning's precipitous action in the reparations question. Luther, who feared for the security of the currency, had protested in vain against Brüning's course of action. At the time of his visit to Chequers in early June 1931, it became clear to the chancellor that his Tribute Appeal had had a most unfortunate psychological effect in American financial circles, whose willingness to come to the aid of the German government with large-scale credits had all but evaporated. Under these circumstances, a German initiative in the reparations policy was out of the question. The creditor nations thus agreed among themselves to react with complete silence to Brüning's announcement that by November 1931 Germany would no longer be in a position to make reparations payments.

Contrary to Brüning's optimistic reports, the participants in the meeting at Chequers had parted with a feeling of helplessness. In the meantime, the run of foreign creditors on the major German banks continued unabated. When President Hoover decided to take matters in his own hands and proposed a one-year moratorium on the payment of international political debts, it was as if he had cast the Germans a life preserver, which Brüning, in spite of fundamental reservations, did not hesitate to seize. Yet the American president's message did not bring immediate relief, for after a brief respite the flight of capital resumed on an alarming scale in early July. This stemmed in part from the opposition of the French government, which as the largest reparations creditor felt hurt by the moratorium and did not yield to United States pressure until 7 July. In this respect, it was psychologically damaging that Luther entered into originally secret negotiations for a rediscount loan of 100 million dollars that was to be funded jointly by the national banks of the United States, France, and England and the Bank for the International Balance of Payments. The coincidence of Germany's search for credit with the moratorium was bound to create the impression that Germany had reached the end of its solvency, since the rediscount loan would be by no means sufficient and since the gold and foreign currency reserves necessary to secure Reichsbank notes had already fallen below the minimum prescribed by law. It was thus only a matter of time before German currency reserves were exhausted and foreign accounts in Germany would be frozen.

The run of German and foreign creditors on the major German banks threatened to bring about the total collapse of the German credit system. The government was still trying to rescue the North German Wool Carding Company, and the Reichsbank struggled in the face of resistance from the banking industry to create a guarantee consortium of major banking institutions in an attempt to meet the claims of the creditors. It was in the midst of these developments that the Darmstadt and National Bank, Germany's fourth-largest credit institution, depleted its liquid assets and ceased cash transfers. At the same time, the State Bank for the Rhine Province (Landesbank der Rheinprovinz), a public credit institution that provided cash to the savings banks of the Rhineland, declared its insolvency. Then, just as the Reichsbank, the government, and the banking industry were engaged in feverish consultations on how to bring the crisis under control, news that the Dresdener Bank, Germany's second largest credit institution, had also become insolvent suddenly broke.

Although the national government publicly pledged to "guarantee all deposits," the closing of the Darmstadt and National Bank's windows on 13 July 1931 led many German customers to withdraw their deposits. The cabinet briefly considered alleviating the crisis by issuing emergency currency but finally decided against it. Despite immediate efforts to restore the liquidity of the banking system by appropriating public funds, the cabinet found itself obliged to declare banking holidays on 14 and 15 July, using this respite to work around the clock on an emergency decree for the protection of the credit system. The resulting emergency decree provided for the creation of an acceptance and guarantee bank, the very kind of shared-liability consortium that the banks had previously rejected. The decree provided for tighter government oversight of the credit system by giving the national government far-reaching control over private credit transactions and making it the majority shareholder in the Deutsche and Dresdener Banks. The reprivatization of the banking system did not take place until 1933. In the meantime, the principal victims of the credit restrictions contained in this decree were the municipalities. Savings banks and bank clearinghouses were instructed to exercise the utmost restraint in granting loans to municipal institutions.

The government's efforts to deal with the banking crisis through extensive regulations did little to enhance its prestige in the eyes of the public. The fact that the Emergency Decree for the Protection of Credit had been modified at the last moment—after it had been signed by the Reich president but without Brüning's visible involvement—created a general impression of helplessness. Nevertheless Brüning was able to persuade the DVP to go along with the promulgation of the emergency decree by pointing out that a change of government in the middle of the credit crisis could have incalculable consequences. The price the chancellor had to pay for the DVP's support, however, took the form of sweeping promises to put an end to the binding character of state arbitration in wage disputes and to introduce a more flexible system of collective bargaining as well as to give the Right more influence in the government. While the move to increased governmental regulation irritated the leading industrial interest organizations, Paul Silverberg still shied away from an open break with the cabinet.

At the very least, responsibility for the extent of the credit crisis can be traced to the failure of the government and the Reichsbank, whose actions were characterized by conflicting objectives and thus contributed in no small way to the fact that the crisis spilled over into the monetary sector. Brüning's fixation on the primacy of the reparations question prevented him from initiating domestic measures to combat the crisis. Luther's main preoccupation, by contrast, was maintaining the stability of the currency. For these reasons the two politicians were unable to conduct an orderly retreat from the gold standard and the principle of maintaining a minimum of convertible reserves. Concern about an increase in the circulation of banknotes led Luther to pursue a restrictive credit policy that eventually brought about the collapse of the banking system itself and a sharp increase in the number of bankruptcies and plant closings, all of which severely complicated Germany's budgetary difficulties. A further problem was an increase in the discount rate to 17 percent.

In the final analysis, Luther—whom the banking community would like to have replaced with Schacht—believed that the flight of capital would eventually abate on its own. The passivity for which foreign observers criticized Luther stemmed in part from his desire not to give the reparations creditors a reason to interfere in Germany's fiscal affairs, something that would have certainly happened had he instituted controls on foreign currency transactions. Yet the international banks were not prepared to help the Reich by extending credit as long as the German government did not take effective measures to halt the flight of capital. As Montagu Norman correctly pointed out, most of the withdrawals were made by German investors. As a result, Luther had no alternative but to institute controls on foreign currency transactions that he himself had earlier rejected. The government's Emergency Decree against Capital Flight and Tax Evasion was, however, unduly harsh and even provided for severe prison sentences in certain cases of hiding or illegally exporting foreign currency. The National Socialist regime later used this legislation to prevent Jews from transferring capital out of the country. In point of fact, controls on foreign currency, the abandonment of minimum reserve requirements for the Reichsbank, and the Hoover moratorium placed the Reich in a position where it could relax its rigid deflationary domestic policies.

A further cause for the German credit crisis was the fact that Brüning sought to avoid negotiations with France, even though the British, realizing that they were dependent on France in the area of fiscal policy, were very much interested in the development of direct Franco-German contacts. The German side, however, chose to ignore Montagu Norman's subtle hints in this direction. Discussions that Brüning and Curtius conducted reluctantly with the French prior to the Chequers meeting produced, as expected, negative results. The chancellor, after all, was not willing to make the political concessions that France demanded in exchange for a major loan, namely, the promise to forgo revision of the Young Plan for a period of ten years, the formal abandonment of the German-Austrian customs union project, and the cancellation of the program for the construction of a naval cruiser. Brüning was not altogether unjustified in stating that no German government would be able to comply with the French conditions. Germany's foreign policy was now paying the penalty for its earlier betrayal of Aristide Briand and the moderate elements in France.

There is of course no definitive answer to the question of whether a consistent policy of allowing the waves of distrust and nationalism between France and Germany to die down naturally and establishing genuine economic cooperation between the two countries could have confined the effects of the world economic crisis to central Europe. Brüning was convinced that the French were intent on systematically undermining Germany's position as a major power. Just how strongly the chancellor's strong bias against France impaired the rationality of his domestic economic decisions was revealed by his perplexing conduct in the Gelsenberg affair, which was irreconcilable with his own principle that state intervention in the economy should be reduced. In March 1932 Brüning and Dietrich decided at the urging of Friedrich Flick that the government should acquire Flick's shares of Gelsenberg stock at what amounted to a highly inflated price. Concluded in May, this transaction— which did not become public until after the chancellor's fall from power— was not so much a matter of helping the ailing United Steelworks (Vereinigte Stahlwerke), in which Flick owned a considerable amount of stock, as one of bailing out the run-down Flick concern. The motive for Brüning's unusual procedure—only the chairman of the board of the Steel Association (Stahlverein) was informed in the strictest confidence—was to prevent any of the Gelsenberg stock shares from falling into French hands, a development that would have had far-reaching repercussions on Germany's secret economic rearmament. This instance is only one more illustration of the way in which Brüning's obsession with foreign policy affected his decisions in the field of economic policy.

In the early summer of 1931 it became increasingly clear that Brüning's hopes of isolating France were quite illusory. By the same token, Germany was unable to have the reparations question placed on the agenda of the London Conference in late July 1931 since the Anglo-Saxon powers were reluctant to undertake any action in the matter without French involvement. Instead, American Secretary of State Henry Lewis Stimson facilitated negotiations on private moratorium agreements between the creditor nations and Germany, which had to commit itself to maintain state controls over foreign exchange transactions. At the same time, however, there was no willingness to provide Germany with the international loan it so desperately needed. As far as the reparations question was concerned, all that Brüning achieved was that the Bank for the International Balance of Payments established a special committee to examine the financial viability of the Reich. The Wiggins Committee that was charged with this task submitted a report on Germany's financial and economic situation in mid-August 1931. Written by the British financial expert Lord Walter Layton, this report pointed out that because Germany continued to contract short-term foreign loans, it was unable to pay more than a fraction of its obligations and that the payment of reparations between 1924 and 1930 had been financed exclusively with foreign loans. Although none of this was new to the experts, official confirmation of these facts represented a certain success for Germany's efforts in its struggle to have the reparations canceled once and for all. The Layton Report, however, did not address the question of how the extensive capital losses that Germany had suffered since the early 1920s were to be replaced.

Measured by the expectations that had been raised by the Tribute Appeal of 6 June, the results of the London negotiations could only be described as disappointing. An official moratorium would have been tantamount to an acknowledgment of Germany's inability to pay and would have completely destroyed the Reich's creditworthiness. As it was, the moratorium agreements with Germany's international creditors and the German commitment to maintain state controls over foreign currency transactions removed the pressure that the threat of loan withdrawals had posed to the conduct of German affairs since 1929. To Brüning, the new situation meant that "the endless threats and extortions by France were no longer possible."

On account of Germany's continued inability to pay, the moratorium agreements were extended several times. Since the German Reich did not permit free transfers of capital until after the Second World War, the London agreements meant that the destruction of German capital was borne in large part by foreign financial interests. To be sure, this could not have been foreseen in the summer of 1931. Still, there were signs that the Allied powers might accommodate Germany in the reparations question by accepting lower annual payments or possibly a one-time final payment. Yet Brüning insisted on the complete cancellation of reparations. He did not expect this to occur before the summer of 1932, for he realized that the conference of experts that was scheduled to take place in Basel in early 1932 would only partly accede to Germany's demands. Brüning did not feel that an extension of the Hoover moratorium — which was successfully opposed by the American financial establishment — was a viable solution to Germany's problems. On the contrary, he wanted to limit the moratorium to six months or a year so that its expiration would not coincide with the end of the German economic crisis.

Against the background of these developments, the chancellor pleaded with the members of his cabinet to continue the policy of balancing the budget at all costs and not to initiate any measures that might give the Allies the impression that Germany still had some freedom of action in the financial arena. A few months earlier Brüning had emphasized that the government must not admit to the world that domestic political considerations had forced it to "pull the emergency cord of the reparations." If it ever leaked out that the budget was not covered, he warned, Germany's foreign policy options would evaporate. Even in the face of mounting resistance at home, Germany must, he insisted, stay its deflationary course until the summer of 1932. Under no circumstances must Germany admit its financial collapse, for this would leave it defenseless against the demands of the Allies. But the obsessive pursuit of a deflationary policy that began to face increasing criticism within the cabinet itself no longer made much sense following the imposition of government controls over foreign currency transactions and the moratorium agreements that Germany reached with its international creditors. Brüning's decision to take advantage of protections afforded by the Young Plan and to apply to the Bank for the International Balance of Payments on the basis of the Layton Report amounted to a tacit admission that his previous strategy had failed. Nevertheless he continued to stake the very existence of his cabinet on a global solution to the reparations question.

As the contraction of the German economy began to affect healthy enterprises and their investment activity, Brüning's deflationary credo lost much of its persuasive power in spite of the fear of inflation that the cabinet had conjured up and that had struck a responsive chord even within Social Democratic circles. Not even Brüning was convinced that continuing the deflationary policy was appropriate. There was a point, he told State Secretary Schäffer, where deflation turned into inflation. This was true in the sense that as production continued to decline, fixed costs could be covered only with borrowed money. Reichsbank President Luther also began to waver in his commitment to deflation and wondered whether the relaxation of domestic credit might not be a more appropriate response to the deepening recession. Nevertheless, the government and the Reichsbank remained firmly opposed to the demands of heavy industry that the devaluation of the pound and other major currencies be followed by a devaluation of the mark. To compensate for the devaluation of the pound, industrial circles planned for a systematic reduction of wages and prices under the unpopular motto "In keeping with the national emergency."

The system of piecemeal solutions by which the cabinet had tried to stabilize the national budget since the late summer of 1931 had the effect of leveling the entire structure of prices and wages, including the reduction of interest rates, social benefits, and administrative costs. The government's decision to lower interest and discount rates by emergency decree triggered a bitter conflict with Reichsbank President Luther, who at the urging of the economic interest organizations vehemently opposed the flight into government economic regulations. Among the cumulative austerity measures the government announced was the proposal that the existing system of unemployment insurance should be replaced by a general program of support for the unemployed. In some areas, however, growing political resistance succeeded in limiting further cuts in public expenditures that had been made necessary by the disappearance of foreign loans. Reductions in agricultural subsidies and in the defense budget, for example, were out of the question. As State Secretary Schäffer so pithily expressed it: "From the budgetary point of view, we are already living in a military dictatorship."

The high point of the austerity program that Brüning pursued with unflinching consistency was the Dietramzell Emergency Decree of 24 August 1931, which was followed by two equally stringent emergency decrees on 6 October and 8 December. The cuts mandated in all areas with the exception of agriculture were particularly drastic with respect to salaries and wages in the public sector. Not including the elimination of benefits, these cuts amounted to a 20 percent reduction of salaries in the public sector. In a sense, this made Stegerwald's call for rescinding the civil servant salary reform of 1927 unnecessary. A whole raft of related measures authorized reductions in pensions and retirement benefits, benefits for wounded war veterans and invalids, subsidies for children and public housing, and travel assistance. At the same time, they also penalized "double earners," namely, married women. Against the warnings of his closest advisors, Brüning continued the fiscally convenient practice of progressive salary reductions. Yet by June 1931 he found himself obliged to introduce an emergency income tax for self-employed persons and employees in the private sector that largely neutralized the economic benefits of lowered prices.

The salary reductions in the public sector provoked vigorous protest on the part of the affected interest organizations, which argued that salaries in the civil service were protected by the constitution. On this issue they had the support of the president's office, which warned that Article 48 must not be used to reduce public pensions, since this would constitute a violation of the civil servants' "duly acquired rights" (*wohlerworbene Rechte*). And indeed, the decision to raise the length of service at which legal salary guidelines became applicable had transformed a one-time emergency levy into a permanent salary reduction. Although the government, with the help of Carl Schmitt, had for the most part succeeded in deflecting the opposition of the Supreme Court, resistance to further salary reductions was clearly mounting. It is a telling point in this respect that certain groups of civil servants, among them the Reichswehr, the police, and the judges of the superior courts, had to be exempted from the salary reductions.

In the Dietramzell Decree, Brüning began to interfere with public institutions in ways he had originally wanted to delay until the end of the reparations. Among other things, Brüning had wanted to empower state governments to implement salary reductions and other austerity measures by administrative decree without securing the approval of their parliaments or elected municipal councils. This measure, which was defended with reference to the acute short-age of public funds, strengthened authoritarian tendencies at the state level and went hand in hand with dramatic reductions in the general level of national funding for the states. Since states and municipalities were virtually prohib-ited from contracting new loans, the result was an austerity psychosis that only further increased unemployment. Austerity measures were particularly harsh in the personnel-intensive educational area, where they affected adult education, public libraries, the public school system, and, last but not least, the universities. Unemployment among university teachers and graduates cre-ated great hardships, which the Emergency Organization for German Scholars (Notgemeinschaft für die deutsche Wissenschaft) was unable to relieve in any significant way. The abolition of emeritus status, which yielded very little in the way of financial savings, only alienated the comparatively small group of university teachers who had manifested a distant, yet loyal attitude toward the Weimar Republic.

In the meantime, Brüning was determined to use the increasingly severe fis-cal crisis at the state level to advance his proposal for a reform of Germany's federal structure. For the time being, the chancellor did not go along with the creation of administrative consortia that some of the smaller states had pro-posed. Anticipating that state parliaments would be incapable of carrying out the austerity measures that had been forced upon them, Brüning believed that he could overcome the opposition of some of the north German state govern-ments to an abolition of the parliamentary system. In the case of Prussia, he wanted to wait for the full effects of the fiscal crisis to make themselves felt so that he could accomplish Prussia's merger with the Reich and the abolition of its Landtag in one fell swoop. This plan had the support of Luther, who made a reform of Prussia's finances contingent upon its merger with the Reich. For these reasons, Brüning was not pleased with the temporary success of the austerity measures adopted by Prussian Finance Minister Hermann Höpker-Aschoff and his successor Otto Klepper. In this respect, Brüning criticized Klepper for unnecessarily upsetting the Prussian electorate by introducing a tax on butchered meat before the Landtag elections of April 1932.

Over and above this, Brüning and Luther insisted on streamlining the ad-ministration. But it was impossible to go beyond the merger of a few local courts and administrative districts. The only savings that could be achieved involved not filling vacancies and reducing supplies to administrative offices. While the cumulative effect of these measures was to reduce the cost of govern-ment to a considerable extent, the expenditures for crisis support and social services were exploding all bounds. As a result, the total expenditures of the central government, the states, and the municipalities were reduced by only 1,736 million marks in the 1932–33 budget year from the level of 1929–30. The moratorium on reparations accounted for 1,474 million of this sum, so that the actual reduction of expenses came to no more than 262 million marks. The political cost of these savings was by no means commensurate with their deflationary effect on the budget.

Brüning's deflationary policy had severely reduced his room for political maneuver. By the fall of 1931, industrial circles were thinking about having him replaced by ex-chancellor Wilhelm Cuno. At the same time, the Reich president, under the increasing influence of Major General Kurt von Schleicher, was becoming impatient to see the long-awaited extension of the government to the Right. Once again, however, Brüning was able to dispel the president's misgivings, particularly since on this occasion he brought up the subject of Hindenburg's reelection by parliament, though only after having first discussed the matter with the Reichswehr leadership. In the meantime, Brüning was hoping to achieve a decisive breakthrough at the Lausanne meeting on international debts that had been scheduled for April 1932 and to use the prestige that this would bring him on the home front to undertake a revision of the constitution, perhaps in the direction of a constitutional monarchy. At the same time, Brüning believed that he could keep the NSDAP politically isolated. The collapse of its negotiations with the Hessian Center Party had convinced the chancellor that Hitler's party was not suitable as a coalition partner and that its success was only a "fever symptom" of the current economic crisis. The immediate task, therefore, was for Brüning to consolidate his own position by ensuring the reelection of Reich President von Hindenburg. "In domestic politics I had reached the point," Brüning wrote in hindsight, "where I could envisage spending the summer working for the legal restoration of the monarchy." The chancellor, however, failed to realize that in the eyes of his conservative partners he had become superfluous once a final solution of the reparations problem was achieved and only constituted an obstacle to the long-awaited government of the nationalist Right.

CHAPTER ELEVEN

The Road to Presidential Dictatorship

THE Brüning cabinet had not emerged from the severe stress that was associated with the banking crisis and the devaluation of the pound in the summer of 1931 entirely unscathed. These developments, however, had less of an effect on cooperation within the cabinet than on the chancellor's relationship with the Reich president, who from Brüning's perspective had fallen increasingly under the influence of his own circle of advisors and seemed less and less willing to accept the views of the chancellor. The petition campaign that the nationalist Right had mounted against Brüning prior to the Harzburg rally in early October 1931 and that deluged the Reich president with baskets full of letters demanding Brüning's dismissal, however, proved far less effective than the steady stream of complaints that Hindenburg received from spokesmen for the patriotic associations and other notables who enjoyed his respect. The intrigues in the presidential entourage proved increasingly worrisome to the chancellor and can only be regarded as a symptom of his increasing isolation.

Hindenburg, who demanded from Brüning that he initiate an opening to the Right, had little sympathy for the chancellor's argument that a break with the majority in the Reichstag would eventually lead to an open constitutional conflict. In contrast to the unsolicited advice he received from General Kurt von Schleicher, Brüning was under no illusion that either Hugenberg or Hitler would ever go along with his leadership of the cabinet. The Reich president, on the other hand, was reluctant to accept this fact and demanded that Brüning realign his government with the Right when the chancellor submitted his cabinet's resignation on 7 October 1931 in an attempt to produce a clarification of the existing political situation.

In addition to the long-sought resignation of Foreign Minister Julius Curtius, Hindenburg also demanded that Brüning dismiss Joseph Wirth, whom he distrusted on account of his close ties to the SPD, and Theodor von Guérard, so that aside from Brüning the only representative from the Center to remain in the cabinet was Minister of Labor Adam Stegerwald. Although Baron Konstantin von Neurath had been suggested as Curtius's successor at the German Foreign Office, Brüning decided to assume this responsibility himself. For the Ministry of the Interior Brüning favored Otto Geßler despite the fact that the Social Democrats were almost certain to be offended by his appointment. Geßler, however, agreed to join the cabinet only on the condition that it implement a comprehensive package of reforms that would have abrogated important provisions of the Weimar Constitution, a course of action for which Hindenburg was not yet prepared. In the end Brüning followed Schleicher's suggestion that he appoint Wilhelm Groener to the Ministry of the Interior in a move that would unify the two portfolios in the person of the current defense minister. This was a clear indication that the Reich president and his advisors, above all General von Schleicher, viewed the cabinet as a temporary solution that would be replaced by a new government once the upcoming reparations negotiations in Lausanne had been concluded.

Brüning's attempt to placate his critics in big business by appointing several of its more highly respected representatives to posts in his cabinet ended in complete failure. Paul Silverberg, to whom Brüning offered the Ministry of Transportation after he had overcome his own fears that this might fuel a "mounting anti-Semitism," declined on the grounds that he did not enjoy the confidence of a majority of the industrial leaders in the west, while Albert Vögler's close ties to the DNVP ruled out any possibility that he might cooperate with the chancellor. Eventually Brüning was able to persuade Hermann Warmbold from I.G. Farben to accept the Ministry of Economics. Still, he had failed to line up the necessary support of Germany's most important business associations, which in late September 1931 had issued a joint declaration that amounted to an open declaration of war against the social and economic policies of the Brüning cabinet. Moreover, it soon emerged, to the utter dismay of Reichsbank President Hans Luther, that the new economics minister was a strong adherent of the plans for the expansion of credit that had been aired by financial expert Ernst Wagemann as a way out of the deepening economic crisis. By the same token, Brüning's appointment of Hans Schlange-Schöningen as the Reich commissar for eastern development failed to provide an effective counterweight to the vigorous representation that large-scale agriculture had received within the cabinet from Martin Schiele in his capacity as the Reich minister of agriculture.

On top of all of this, Brüning found himself obliged to establish a national economic council, or *Reichswirtschaftsrat*, along the lines of a proposal submitted by the former chancellor Wilhelm Cuno. This was conceived as a sort of crown council to the Reich president and was to consist of fifteen representatives from the German business community recruited primarily from heavy industry in the Rhine-Ruhr basin as well as from newer industries such as chemicals and electronics, banking, and agriculture. It was typical of the increasingly prevalent antiparliamentary mood that had become manifest throughout German society that the chancellor was urged to establish a "Supreme Economic Command" (*oberste Wirtschaftsleitung*). The demand for greater expertise in the formulation and implementation of national economic policy coincided with authoritarian efforts to place the responsibility for economic decision making in the hands of the Reich president without going through parliament. Needless to say, Brüning experienced considerable difficulty in maintaining a measure of parity in the appointment of those who were to serve on this constitutionally questionable body, with the result that the National Rural League and the Christian-National Peasants and Farmers' Party left the council under protest before the three-week-long negotiations on Germany's future economic program had reached a conclusion. The situation within the council was complicated by massive pressure from heavy industry in the west. The leaders of German heavy industry presented the cabinet with a virtual ultimatum demanding that it make a definitive break with the Social Democrats and socialist labor unions. This was hardly a promising start for the second Brüning cabinet, which differed from its predecessor not so much by virtue of its stronger orientation to the right as by the complete absence of parliamentarians. The external impression was nevertheless one of considerable continuity. The fact, however, that Hindenburg had exerted direct influence on the personal composition of the cabinet and was resolved to determine the course of future German policy without regard for the sentiments of the parliamentary majority indicated a clear shift of power in the direction of the Reich president.

In the view of the offensive it faced from organized economic interests, the reorganized Brüning cabinet owed its survival to the fact that Hugenberg's intransigence temporarily ruled out the formation of a government of the nationalist Right. Under the circumstances it seemed far more expedient not to "change horses," as Schleicher put it, until there had been a final settlement of the reparations question. This was also the view of the moderate Right. *Die Tat* spoke of Brüning as "the folding-screen [*Wandschirm*] behind which new forces could take shape." In a similar fashion, Count Westarp commented in the middle of October, after Brüning had just secured a small majority that made it possible for him to remain in office: "Only after an agreement has been reached with our creditors and a revision of our reparations burden has been achieved will it be possible, indeed necessary, to attempt the formation of a new government under National Socialist leadership. The DNVP party leadership unfortunately no longer comes into question for such a task." In short, Brüning's days as chancellor were numbered.

With the reorganization of his cabinet the chancellor found himself totally dependent upon the Reich president. In the meantime, the Reichstag had been left with nothing to do but to defeat the no-confidence motions that the Right and the Left introduced with each new package of emergency decrees. At no point did anyone try to mobilize the parliamentary forces that stood behind the cabinet. Even the public became accustomed to looking at the cabinet as a mere tool in the hands of the Reich president that he could use without regard for the majority in the Reichstag. The chancellor, who continued to hope that a breakthrough in the reparations question would produce a dramatic change in the domestic political landscape, failed to realize that he himself was in danger of becoming a pawn of the special interests that bypassed the ministerial bureaucracies in going directly to the president. At the same time, he believed he could dismiss the reorientation of his government to the right as a consequence of the political games he had been obliged to play in order to remain in office. The unpleasantness that Brüning experienced in this respect only strengthened his resolve to stay the political course upon which he had embarked, even if the price he had to pay for such a decision was his temporary political isolation. As a result, Brüning secluded himself from his cabinet colleagues more than necessary and maintained close ties to only those members of the Center Reichstag delegation whose loyalty was never in doubt, among them Joseph Joos and Hans Bell. When traveling by train, Brüning pulled the blinds of his compartment tightly shut so that he would not be recognized in public. To critics he reacted with a fit of doctrinaire self-righteousness.

At the outset Brüning's disdain for what he sarcastically called the "general assault of the Pan German–Hugenberg clique" seemed to have been fully justified. The display of force by the national opposition in the small resort town of Bad Harzburg on 12 October 1931 only underscored the disunity of his right-wing opponents. The presence of a number of prominent personalities, including the Hohenzollern princes Eitel Friedrich and August Wilhelm, former generals such as Walther von Lüttwitz and the retired chief of army command Hans von Seeckt, high-ranking members of the Prussian aristocracy, and the leaders of the DNVP, the Business Party, the Pan-German League, the Stahlhelm, the United Patriotic Leagues, and, last but not least, the NSDAP assured the rally of a substantial public resonance. The leadership of the National Rural League under Count Eberhard von Kalckreuth was represented in its entirety. Of the business leaders who had been invited to attend, however, most excused themselves on one pretext or another. Aside from Karl Brandi from the Mining Association (Zechenverband), heavy industry and big business were represented only by intermediate-level executives. The rally's principal organizers, DNVP Reichstag Deputy Otto Schmidt-Hannover and Herbert von Bose, had sought to transform what had been originally conceived as a closed meeting of the leaders of the national opposition into a demonstration involving the entire spectrum of bourgeois forces. In this respect they were hardly successful.

There were several reasons for the absence of prominent industrial entrepreneurs. In the first place, most of them were extremely critical of Hugenberg's politics without, however, going so far as to support Brüning. Moreover, Brüning had threatened reprisals against the large firms that were dependent on the largess of the Reich if they took part in a demonstration directed against his government's retention in office. Even the leaders of heavy industry in the west sought to avoid an open confrontation. This was not true, however, of Hjalmar Schacht, who used the Harzburg rally to deliver an unscheduled speech that created something of a sensation when the former Reichsbank president publicly attacked the policies of his successor Hans Luther and denounced the Reichsbank's current gold reserves as insufficient. For the most part, however, the attacks against the government did not go beyond the already time-worn arguments of the so-called national opposition. As Hans Zehrer aptly expressed it, the "mass rally [*Massenauftrieb*] of all the old leaders" was more reminiscent of 1921 than of 1931.

Hugenberg's plan to use the Harzburg rally as the forum for creating a shadow cabinet of the "national Germany" under his leadership and for uniting the Right behind a single candidate for the upcoming presidential elections never materialized. From the very outset Hitler had done his best to deflect Hugenberg's overtures in his direction. On the eve of the rally itself Hitler had failed to attend a meeting with the other leaders of the "national opposition" on the contrived pretext that he had to return to Berlin in order to take care of indigent SA men whom the police had evicted from their quarters. On the next day he demonstratively left the reviewing stand as soon as the SA units had marched by and indicated just what he thought of the Stahlhelm and the paramilitary units of the bourgeois Right. Hitler was thus able to disguise his own social insecurity as tactically intended personal affronts that attracted far more attention than the common goals Hugenberg highlighted in his appeals for the solidarity of the Harzburg Front.

Hitler was determined to avoid all political commitments and to stress at every conceivable opportunity the independence of the National Socialist movement. From the very outset Hitler viewed the meeting at Harzburg with considerable skepticism and formally apologized to his subordinates for having to attend as a result of certain tactical necessities. At the same time, the Harzburg rally reinforced Hitler's resolve to organize a mass demonstration in Brunswick, where the NSDAP had just entered a coalition with the DNVP, in lieu of the party congress that was now long overdue. Only eight days after the Harzburg rally more than 70,000 SA men descended on Brunswick to demonstrate the strength of their movement. Although the SPD and Reichsbanner exercised remarkable self-restraint, bloody clashes nevertheless occurred when units from the SA marched through working-class neighborhoods. Even then, the Reichswehr's official observer issued a positive report on the discipline of the National Socialist units.

Prior to the meeting in Harzburg, Hitler had met privately with Kurt von Schleicher and had been officially received by the Reich president. Although these meetings had produced little in the way of concrete results, they had nevertheless done much to elevate Hitler's self-esteem. The meetings, however, had been arranged by Brüning, who sought to take the wind out of Hugenberg's sails and to isolate the DNVP. In his first visit with the Reich president,

Hitler was accompanied by Wilhelm Frick and Hermann Göring. Hitler explained the general goals of his movement and complained that the excesses of which his party had been accused stemmed from the need to defend itself. The meeting only strengthened Hindenburg's antipathy toward the Nazi party leader, who scarcely let him utter a word. From the Hindenburg house surfaced the rumor that after his meeting with Hitler the Reich president had supposedly said that the "Bohemian corporal" might be acceptable at best as postal minister. At the same time, the Reich president had admonished Hitler to tolerate the reorganized Brüning cabinet. Hitler was no more willing to do this than he was to ally his party with those elements around Hugenberg whom he held in such deep contempt. Even in the unlikely event that the "national opposition" should, with the help of the KPD, succeed in defeating the most recent emergency decree and in finding a majority for a no-confidence motion against the Brüning government, a significant improvement in the NSDAP's strategic position was not to be expected.

In contrast to the other members of the Harzburg Front, Hitler had no intention of joining a Hindenburg cabinet. On the contrary, he wanted to bring about new national elections at the earliest conceivable opportunity in order to provide tangible proof of his movement's rapidly growing strength. A convenient opportunity to do precisely this presented itself in connection with the upcoming presidential elections. When Brüning initiated negotiations with Hitler on the possibility of extending Hindenburg's term of office by means of a Reichstag resolution that would require an amendment to the Weimar Constitution, the Nazi party leader at first reacted negatively but then wrote a long letter in which he outlined his constitutional reservations against a parliamentary extension of the president's term of office. At the same time, Hitler hinted that if new elections were to be held without delay in the Reich and Prussia, he would regard the newly formed Reichstag as competent to extend the president's term of office for an additional two years.

Hitler's tactical line was fundamentally different from that of Hugenberg, who made his support for extending the president's term of office contingent upon Brüning's immediate resignation and the dissolution of the Prussian coalition in hopes that this would make it possible for him to control the new right-wing government that would subsequently assume power. In order to keep from being outflanked by the DNVP, Hitler eventually went along with Hugenberg's maximal program. It was certainly not in Hitler's best interests to see the Brüning cabinet replaced by a new right-wing coalition as long as the relative strengths of the different parties in the Reichstag had not changed in favor of the NSDAP. Normal presidential elections could be used to help accomplish this goal even if Hitler shied away from a direct confrontation with the Reich president.

Brüning had pursued the idea of extending Hindenburg's term of office ever since the late summer of 1931 and felt certain that he could count on Schleicher's full support. Brüning acted in the belief that respect for the person of the venerable field marshal was the lowest common denominator upon which the antagonistic interests of the dominant political elites could be reconciled. The procedure that had been adopted in 1923 of extending the president's term of office through a parliamentary resolution requiring a two-thirds majority in the Reichstag recommended itself almost immediately in the situation that existed in 1932. Not only the moderate bourgeois parties but the SPD as well signaled their agreement, if for no other reason than the fact that it seemed a good idea to avoid a presidential election in the midst of a severe social and economic crisis.

For Brüning these pragmatic, if not opportunistic, concerns went hand in hand with his determination to use the Reich president as an instrument for the realization of his plans for the reconstruction of state and society. This goal outweighed whatever reservations Brüning might have had about the fragile health of the eighty-four-year-old Hindenburg. Just how much of his plans for the restoration of the Hohenzollern monarchy Brüning revealed to Hindenburg is unclear, particularly since the question of which of the Prussian princes would assume the throne had not been decided. In the meantime, Hindenburg recoiled at the idea of serving as a temporary replacement for the monarch, for he could conceive of a restoration only in terms of the reinstatement of the Kaiser in his full hereditary rights. From the monarchist perspective, the rigidity with which the exiled and largely isolated monarch had dealt with the question of the succession had exacted its own revenge. As head of the House of Hohenzollern, Wilhelm II vetoed the succession of Crown Prince Wilhelm just as he had earlier rejected the idea in early April 1932 of allowing the crown prince to stand as a candidate for the office of Reich president in the second round of voting in the presidential elections.

It was symptomatic of the agony in which the republican system found itself that no effort was made on the part of the more moderate political parties to nominate a candidate with a clearly identifiable party profile. For a while the SPD's Carl Severing considered nominating Hugo Eckener, who was widely known as captain of the airship *Graf Zeppelin* and was known to be a moderate liberal, but he changed his mind when the Hindenburg solution presented itself. The idea that the Reich president must not be a party politician was tacitly accepted by a majority of Germany's political parties. This, in turn, reflected the pervasive antiparliamentary sentiments that now embraced even the parties of the bourgeois Left. The SPD maintained a low profile throughout the nominating process in recognition of the fact that any candidate it might present — the name of Otto Braun was mentioned — would always be politically isolated. Exploratory talks with the Communists had established that the KPD would make its cooperation contingent upon an end to the SPD's toleration of the Brüning cabinet and the formation of a "united front from below." None of this was acceptable to the SPD.

Despite Hindenburg's reticence in the matter of restoring the monarchy, Brüning exerted strong psychological pressure in persuading the Reich president to remain in office. In doing so, he availed himself of the very arguments that the Reich president had always used and appealed to his sense of patriotic duty. If the president refused to stand for election, Brüning argued, there existed the danger of civil war. Faced with arguments like these, Hindenburg finally agreed to the parliamentary extension of his term of office for life. At the same time, Hindenburg recognized the wisdom of Otto Braun's argument that reelection by popular vote would be preferable since the outcome would not depend on negotiations among the various political parties. When Brüning had to abandon his plans in the face of resistance from Hitler and Hugenberg, the Reich president insisted that he would stand for election only if the nonpartisan character of his candidacy could be guaranteed.

Brüning's carefully cultivated fiction that the presidential regime was nonpartisan effectively precluded the Reichstag and the individual political parties from taking an active role in the choice of the Reich president. The moderate parties therefore raised no objections to Hindenburg's nomination by a nonpartisan entity. The Bureau of the Reich President conducted preliminary negotiations with a number of patriotic associations, including the Kyffhäuser League (Kyffhäuser-Bund), to determine if they might be willing to sponsor Hindenburg's nomination. Not only would this help minimize the consequences of Hugenberg's defection from the ranks of Hindenburg's supporters, but it would have also helped create the impression that the patriotic Right was fully committed to the reelection of the Reich president. By now, however, it was becoming increasingly clear that the Stahlhelm was having reservations of its own about a Hindenburg candidacy. Whereas Rüdiger von der Goltz from the United Patriotic Leagues dissociated himself as unequivocally as possible from Hindenburg, Max von Horn, the chairman of the Kyffhäuser League, agreed in spite of considerable resistance from the rank and file of his own organization to come out in support of the Reich president's reelection. In the meantime, Hindenburg had responded to the Stahlhelm's rejection of his candidacy by making his willingness to accept the nomination contingent upon the support of at least a part of the patriotic Right.

Parallel to the efforts of the presidential office, the lord major of Berlin Heinrich Sahm had begun to lay the foundation for Hindenburg's nomination on a purely nonpartisan basis by forming special Hindenburg committees throughout the country and by collecting signatures in support of Hindenburg's reelection. As a result of the ambivalence of the patriotic organizations toward a Hindenburg candidacy, the task of persuading the still hesitant Hindenburg to accept the nomination fell to Sahm. Impressed by the more than

3 million signatures that had been collected in support of his candidacy, the Reich president allowed himself to be hailed as a symbol of the "conquest over party factionalism" (*Überwindung des Parteigeistes*) when Sahm officially announced his candidacy on 16 February 1932.

The Hindenburg committees brought together first of all politically unaffiliated representatives of the German Right, although the DVP and the State Party also took part in this initiative. On several occasions, members of the cabinet such as Hermann Dietrich were prevented from speaking at local rallies on Hindenburg's behalf because they allegedly stood too far to the left. The Hindenburg committees, like the Loebell committee of 1925, were not to be confused with elements loyal to the republic, and they stood in an ambivalent relationship to Brüning's policies as Reich chancellor. The Center, Bavarian People's Party, Social Democrats, and Reichsbanner as well as the State Party and DVP all held their own campaign rallies on Hindenburg's behalf. The discipline exhibited by the rank-and-file membership of the SPD was truly astonishing, as the overwhelming majority of the Social Democratic voters cast their ballots for an unpopular president whose election represented the only chance of averting a Hitler dictatorship.

Hindenburg refrained from taking any role whatsoever in the campaign. The government's electoral propaganda depicted the Reich president as a model of selfless devotion to duty who had sacrificed himself for the sake of the fatherland in its hour of need and who had been Germany's savior during and after World War I. The fact that neither political parties nor the Reichstag was ever mentioned in the official propaganda for Hindenburg's reelection amounted to an implicit abdication of responsibility by Germany's republican system. On the contrary, it was the venerable field marshal's role as the guarantor of national unity and the need to overcome the factionalism of political parties that received primary emphasis. Adapted to the tenor of National Socialist and DNVP propaganda, the campaign for Hindenburg called for an end to "party rule" in what represented the swan song of parliamentary liberalism.

One of the more disingenuous features of Hindenburg's bid for reelection was that his campaign went to great lengths to conceal the fact that the president's support came from precisely those parties that had opposed his election in 1925. When Otto Braun called upon the president to assure him of his loyalty, no news of this ever made its way to the public. Hindenburg reacted vigorously to the allegation that he was a candidate of the Left whose campaign was directed against the "national Germany." If the Social Democrats did not have a candidate of their own, it was not his fault, he argued, that they supported his candidacy. But Hindenburg went far beyond apologetic statements such as this in trying to defend his candidacy to his former supporters on the German Right. The very way in which the NSDAP and DNVP portrayed him as an exponent of the "system parties" compelled the Reich president to commit himself well in advance of the election to the establishment of a right-wing government. "Despite all the blows that he had taken to the back of his neck," he would not abandon his efforts to bring about "a healthy swing to the Right" and promised to work for the formation of a government of national concentration after the Prussian Landtag elections.

There can be no doubt that Hindenburg violated his pledge of nonpartisanship and made a determined effort to win the support of the very groups that opposed his reelection. Hindenburg was particularly embittered that the Stahlhelm was not willing to repay the favors he had bestowed upon it time and time again with its unconditional support. Under Hugenberg's influence, the leaders of the Stahlhelm had hoped to barter their support of Hindenburg's candidacy for major political concessions pertaining to the reorganization of the Brüning cabinet. As a result, the Stahlhelm fell between all stools and, in the final analysis, was obliged to nominate its second-in-command Theodor Duesterberg for the first round of voting in the hope that Hugenberg would be able to come forward with the long-awaited unity candidate of the Harzburg Front when the runoff elections took place four weeks later.

The major reason why the dream of a single candidate for the Harzburg Front never even came close to being realized lay in the attitude of the NSDAP, which was willing to cooperate in the specially constituted Steering Committee of the National Opposition (Arbeitsausschuß der nationalen Opposition) but steadfastly refused to commit itself in the question of a candidate. Efforts by Hugenberg, who had no intention of running himself, to make the nomination of Albert Vögler or one of the Hohenzollern princes palatable to the Nazi party leader only confirmed the former's lack of tactical acumen and had to be abandoned in the face of Nazi criticism that the "national front" was pursuing a socially reactionary course of action. Hitler, who had instructed Göring and Frick to play for time in their negotiations with the Stahlhelm and the DNVP, sowed further confusion when in the course of a discussion over the proposed government of national concentration he demanded not only the chancellorship but also the Ministries of the Interior and of Defense. This prompted immediate criticism from the leaders of the Stahlhelm and effectively stalled the negotiations. Hitler temporarily considered nominating either Göring or Ritter von Epp as a candidate in the first round of voting. He himself was reluctant to run, although efforts to provide him with German citizenship were already under way. His hesitancy stemmed from the combination of his chronic antipathy toward institutional ties of any sort and a subliminal fear of not being able to win against Hindenburg.

To the extent that the Hindenburg candidacy began to take shape, the NSDAP found itself under increasingly heavy pressure to go beyond simply nominating someone to run in the first round of voting and to respond to Brüning's challenge by presenting, as the regional party press had already been suggesting, Hitler as its official candidate. According to the NSDAP's inflated campaign rhetoric, large numbers of the party faithful would have found Hitler's refusal to accept the challenge of running against Hindenburg incomprehensible. On 22 February 1932 Goebbels, who had been urging Hitler to run for weeks, proclaimed Hitler's candidacy at a mass rally in the Berlin Sport Palace. His carefully orchestrated announcement triggered a storm of applause from those in attendance and effectively shattered whatever hopes the "national opposition" still had of uniting behind a single candidate for the upcoming presidential elections. Embittered by this turn of events, the DNVP and the Stahlhelm proceeded to nominate Theodor Duesterberg as the candidate of the Harzburg Front. The KPD, on the other hand, chose to support Ernst Thälmann as it had done in 1925. The Social Democrats, who had prematurely announced their support for Hindenburg's candidacy, waited until 27 February before coming forward with their own campaign slogan: "Defeat Hitler! Therefore vote for Hindenburg" (*Schlagt Hitler! Darum wählt Hindenburg*).

For Hitler the lack of German citizenship did not prove to be a major obstacle. After the collapse of Frick's efforts to have Hitler appointed police commissar in Thuringia and after the refusal of the Technical University in Brunswick to grant Hitler an adjunct professorship to teach a special course on the "Foundations of National Politics," the Nazi party leader was appointed to the post of councillor, or *Regierungsrat*, in Brunswick's Department of Cultural Affairs and Measurements and was given responsibility for representing the interests of the state in Berlin. Although this maneuver was hardly convincing, an attempt by the DNVP to deny Hitler the award of citizenship that went with this appointment would have done little to change the existing political constellation. Insofar as Hitler was preparing to run as a representative of the "new Germany" against the aged field marshal as the symbol of an inwardly moribund system, he demanded an end to the presidential regime in favor of his own party dictatorship. This placed Germany's republican forces completely on the defensive. It became increasingly clear that, under these circumstances, a Hindenburg victory would do nothing to halt the republic's slow drift to the right. The only chance of salvaging anything from the existing situation was to preserve as much as possible of the republic's formal structure in the hope that this could be carried over into a new stage of development when improved economic conditions had reversed the radicalization of increasingly large sectors of the German population.

In the first round of voting on 13 March 1932 Hindenburg barely missed the absolute majority he required for election with 49.6 percent of the popular vote, while Hitler, on the other hand, fell far below the necessary majority with 30.1 percent of all votes cast. Since Duesterberg withdrew his candidacy in favor of Hindenburg in the second round of voting that was scheduled to take place on 10 April, Hindenburg's election was assured. Hindenburg, however, was able to increase his share of the popular vote to no more than 53 percent. In contrast, Hitler achieved, with 36.8 percent of the popular vote, the NSDAP's best result thus far. Both adversaries were bitterly disappointed by the outcome of the election. Hindenburg had suffered his most severe setbacks in precisely those parts of the country where his personal following was strongest. In the electoral districts of Pomerania, Merseburg, Thuringia, Chemnitz-Zwickau, and Schleswig-Holstein he placed behind Hitler, while in the west the wide margin he enjoyed over Hitler stemmed in no small measure from the votes of the Center and SPD. The heterogeneity of the Hindenburg electorate became increasingly apparent in those regions where state and municipal elections coincided with the second round of voting in the presidential campaign. Many of those who had voted for Hindenburg in the presidential campaign supported the extreme Right on the regional level. Hindenburg's victory, therefore, signaled anything but a stabilization of Germany's domestic political situation and was at best a brief respite for Germany's increasingly beleaguered republican forces in their struggle against the rising tide of nationalist extremism.

The relative insignificance of the results of elections at the state and local level for the actual conduct of governmental affairs stood in sharp contrast to the vehemence with which these elections were contested. Almost without exception the campaigns seemed to degenerate into opportunities for demonstrating the potential power of the party armies on the Left and Right. That was no less true of the presidential campaign, which according to the terms of a special "Easter truce" imposed by the government had been compressed into a few short weeks. This provided Joseph Goebbels with a perfect opportunity to personalize the campaign. To be sure, there was nothing original in this stratagem, particularly since the republicans had done everything in their power to place Hindenburg's personality and character at the forefront of the campaign and to deemphasize the less attractive features of Hindenburg's political profile almost to the point of directly falsifying what the Reich president actually stood for. This was precisely why Goebbels, who assumed control of the entire Nazi propaganda apparatus for the campaign effort, was determined to portray Hitler as the alternative of the future, as "our last best hope." The Hitler mythos, which was decisive for the cohesion of the party and its inner circle of followers, was pounded into the public consciousness with every propaganda trick at Goebbels's disposal. In this respect, he even took advantage of the contrast between Hitler and the highly respected hero of World War I to elevate the simple front soldier of humble origins into a symbol of national renewal. The NSDAP conducted its campaign with considerable energy and all its customary professionalism. In addition to pamphlets, posters, and countless rallies with either Hitler or Goebbels as the principal speaker, the party surprised the nation in the campaign for the second round of voting with Hitler's plane flight across Germany. As a result, Hitler was able to appear in more than twenty large cities in the first week of the campaign alone. By staking everything on the election, the party leadership was reassuring its voters that the new Reich president would be none other than Adolf Hitler.

Prior to the first round of voting on 13 March 1932, circles within the NSDAP and SA had convinced themselves that the takeover of power was imminent. Hitler's subsequent defeat triggered a sense of deep depression throughout the party organization and obliged Goebbels to use all the resources at his disposal to counter the mounting defeatism that expressed itself in talk of "the movement's Kunersdorf," an explicit reference to the site of Frederick the Great's most crushing defeat. Contrary to Hugenberg's hopes of fielding a single candidate for the entire German Right in the second round of voting, Hitler decided to continue his bid for the presidency, even at the risk of a new defeat, with every means at his party's disposal. The national campaign committee of the NSDAP intensified its quasi-religious glorification of Hitler as the guarantor of Germany's "national resurrection." The leadership cult proved indispensable in holding the party together at this particularly critical juncture in its internal development. Particularly sharp criticism was directed against the public demeanor of the SA, which many party functionaries held responsible for Hitler's disappointing performance in the preliminary campaign. The activists within the SA, on the other hand, failed to see the point of further electioneering and called for a violent uprising.

Goebbels succeeded in mobilizing the party's disappointment over Hitler's failure in the presidential elections for an intensified effort in the campaign for the state and local elections that were scheduled to take place throughout much of the country on 24 April 1932. The landslide victories the NSDAP recorded in Prussia and most other German states came as no surprise to German public opinion. With the exception of Bavaria, the NSDAP emerged from the elections as the strongest party. In the "republican bastion" of Prussia, the NSDAP increased the size of its parliamentary delegation from nine to 162 seats and could, with the KPD's 57 votes, prevent the passage of any legislative bill. Along with the moderate bourgeois parties, the main losers in Prussia were the SPD, which saw its parliamentary strength reduced from 137 to 94 mandates, and the DNVP, which lost 40 of its 71 seats in the Prussian Landtag. The parties of the governing Weimar Coalition, which salvaged only 163 seats of the 230 it had previously held, found themselves in a hopeless situation. The NSDAP, however, failed to translate its victory at the polls into political power. Other than in small states like Thuringia, Brunswick, Oldenburg, and the two Mecklenburgs, where it was already a member of the governing coalition, or in Anhalt, where it subsequently joined a coalition government, the NSDAP found itself excluded from a role in the new state governments. This was particularly obvious in large and politically influential states like Bavaria and Württemberg. On the other hand, the elections had severely weakened the more moderate bourgeois parties and had intensified the process of political polarization to such a degree that many states—with the notable exception of Baden, where state elections were not scheduled to take place until November 1932—were reduced to the expedient of appointing permanent caretaker governments. Public respect for Germany's parliamentary institutions was severely damaged by this state of affairs.

In Prussia the governing coalition had anticipated its defeat at the polls by taking precautions against the possibility that the parties of the radical Right might try to assume power unilaterally. Over the strenuous objections of the opposition parties, the Prussian government had adopted a change in parliamentary procedure immediately before the elections whereby the minister president was to be elected by an absolute majority of the Prussian Landtag. Otto Braun remained skeptical about this stratagem, which was designed to prevent the NSDAP from gaining control of the Prussian minister presidency. It made sense only if the Center Party's delegation to the Prussian Landtag could work out an arrangement with Brüning's government that guaranteed the viability of the caretaker cabinet in Prussia. In the months that followed, there were repeated attempts to keep the Social Democratic members of the cabinet in the background or to replace them with members of other parties so that possible opposition in the presidential palace to the government's tacit understanding with Brüning could be minimized. This expedient, however, was soon overwhelmed by the pace of events.

To be sure, the purely formal continuation of the current Prussian cabinet was not exactly what the minister president had in mind. On 24 May Braun thus announced the resignation of his cabinet before the hastily convened Prussian Landtag. Braun felt that he was at the end of his energies and no longer saw any possibility of successfully defending the democratic republic from the minority position in which the SPD and its allies on the bourgeois Left found themselves. Although the current government remained in office as a result of the peculiar constellation of forces that existed in the Prussian Landtag, Braun delegated his responsibilities as Prussian minister president to Heinrich Hirtsiefer and retired for the time being from the day-to-day affairs of state. Illness, political resignation, and the realization that he was powerless to protect the sovereignty of the Prussian state against the machinations of the Brüning government all played a role in causing Braun to take a step that at times was criticized within his own party as desertion under fire.

In the preceding months the Prussian government had gone to great lengths to prevent a political constellation in which it would no longer be possible to govern. On the domestic front Braun had absolutely no room to maneuver as a result of the strict austerity measures that Brüning had forced upon him and the central government's virtually total refusal to provide him with the credit assistance he had requested. Time and time again the Prussian government found itself embarrassed by the antics of the Right, as in the case of the Stahl-helm's referendum for the dissolution of the Prussian Landtag in the summer of 1931. In spite of all this, Braun did not waver in his determination to ini-tiate a reform of Germany's federal structure by bringing about the personal union of important posts in the Reich and Prussian cabinets. In this respect, Braun was able to utilize the draft of a bill that Arnold Brecht had submit-ted to the *Länderkonferenz* in August 1931 and that aimed to solidify Brüning's parliamentary support by having several Prussian ministers join the national cabinet. Brüning had already endorsed the idea of merging the Prussian and Reich Finance Ministries. But he hesitated to take the decisive political step that Braun had challenged him to take—in November 1931, for example, Braun went so far as to offer Brüning his own post as Prussian minister president— for fear of the protest this might evoke from Hindenburg and his entourage.

As in a number of other instances, Brüning's penchant for tactics clearly exceeded the limits of what was politically possible. Brüning had been deter-mined for some time to bring about absorption of Prussia into the Reich. In this respect, however, Brüning was more inclined to unify a number of key Prussian cabinet posts with their counterparts in the Reich than to appoint a special Reich commissar for Prussia. The financial savings that would result from such a step played an important, though by no means decisive, role in Brüning's calculations. For Brüning believed that Prussia, like the other Ger-man states, would eventually become financially dependent upon the Reich and would have no choice but to acquiesce in the transfer of important admin-istrative responsibilities to the Reich. The reserve that Brüning exhibited in his financial policies toward Prussia, a state with national responsibilities particu-larly in the area of the police, was thus part of a deliberate strategy that Prussia managed to counter through severe emergency decrees of its own.

The draconian austerity measures that first Brüning and then Franz von Papen imposed on Prussia had a much more devastating impact at the state than at the national level, for they resulted in severe cuts in the administrative bureaucracy, in the cultural and educational sector, and in municipal finances. Most of the government's austerity measures were based on emergency de-crees that had been authorized by the Dietramzell enabling act and took effect without the collaboration of the Landtag. The net result of this practice was the effective abolition of the autonomy of the individual German states. Under these circumstances, the Prussian Social Democrats began to wonder whether there was any point in continuing the fight for the authority of the state gov-ernment. Through all of this, Severing was determined to retain control over the Prussian police force until the next Reichstag elections.

Brüning dismissed the pledges of loyalty he received from the caretaker Prussian government with an air of almost casual indifference. For his own part, he was far more inclined to see whether it might be possible to induce the NSDAP into joining his cabinet on the national level by first incorporating it into a coalition with the Center and DNVP in Prussia. In this respect, he planned to have Carl Goerdeler, who was currently acting as the Reich price commissar, assume the office of the Prussian minister president at the same time that he was appointed vice-chancellor in Brüning's own cabinet. In the event that the cabinet negotiations in Prussia escaped his control, Brüning had prepared an emergency decree that would have placed the Prussian Ministries of the Interior and of Justice under the sovereignty of the Reich. Despite fears in the entourage around Schleicher that such an eventuality might come to pass, it does not appear that Brüning ever gave serious consideration to the possibility of an alliance with Braun.

It soon became clear that Brüning no longer held the threads of government together, that he allowed himself to be bypassed in important matters, and that he was no longer able to control the activities of the presidential entourage. Indeed, the chancellor turned out to be the major loser in the presidential and Landtag elections of the spring of 1932. To be sure, Hindenburg had declined to accept Brüning's offer to resign before the elections because this struck him as a form of political extortion. By no means, however, did this prevent Schleicher in his negotiations with Hugenberg and the leaders of the Stahlhelm from promising a reorganization of the national cabinet in return for their support in the presidential election. Hermann von Lüninck and Hugenberg were slated to become chancellor and vice-chancellor, respectively, while Brüning would either remain on as foreign minister or be replaced by Baron von Neurath. But given the intransigence with which Hugenberg issued his totally unrealistic demands for an immediate solution to Germany's political and economic problems, all of this was mere speculation. In the meantime, the highly offensive attacks that the Hugenberg press had directed against the Reich president had left permanent scars. Hindenburg could hardly have been expected to authorize an extension of the governmental coalition to the DNVP as long as Hugenberg remained at its helm, which is precisely why Paul Reusch called in vain for his removal as DNVP party chairman. At the same time, Hindenburg had not forgotten the pledge he had made to his peers in the aristocracy that he would initiate a change of course no later than the Prussian Landtag elections, from which time he would govern not with, but against, the Social Democrats. For his own part, Brüning was criticized behind his back for having forced the Reich president into an impossible situation.

At no point did the chancellor appreciate how dangerous the intrigues in the presidential entourage were to the continued existence of his cabinet. Schleicher used his personal ties to Hindenburg's son Oskar—they had both served in the same Prussian regiment—to turn the Reich president against Brüning. In the meantime, the influence of the East Prussian aristocrats—and especially that of Elard von Oldenburg-Januschau, whose comment that a lieutenant and six men would be sufficient to send the Reichstag packing was widely quoted — only compounded the insecurities that the Reich president already felt regarding his ability to fulfill the duties of his post. For all of this, however, the aged field marshal remained remarkably impervious to the intrigues of his camarilla and to the increasingly widespread rumors of Brüning's supposedly compromising relations with the German Left. The situation was complicated even further by the fact that Hindenburg's increasing inclination to withdraw to his estate at Neudeck made it difficult for Brüning to see him, particularly since Otto Meißner, the state secretary in the Bureau of the Reich President, used occasions like these to insulate the aged field marshal from undesirable influences.

It was no coincidence that fundamental decisions about the direction of German policy were being shaped to an increasingly large extent by purely personal idiosyncrasies and antipathies. Brüning himself had contributed in no small measure to this state of affairs with the establishment of the presidential system and through his own style of leadership. Under these circumstances, the institutional foundations of political decision making as well as its parliamentary oversight had been severely undermined. The personalization of the decision-making process was typical of German political life in the last years of the Weimar Republic and stemmed in no small measure from Brüning's tendency to attach inordinate significance to the purely tactical aspects of his policies. The inscrutability of Brüning's political intentions necessarily led to greater reliance on personal contacts and intrigues and helped create that murky atmosphere in which men like General von Schleicher who were accustomed to operating in the dark could exercise considerable influence behind the scenes. Not only Brüning but also Groener and later Franz von Papen and Baron Wilhelm von Gayl lived in an almost obsessive fear of spying and leaks.

The ambiguous nature of political life in this crucial phase of the late Weimar Republic reflected the fundamental dishonesty of a political strategy that deliberately exploited the loyalties of the Social Democrats, the German State Party, and the left wing of the Center to bring about a shift to the right. As a political pragmatist who assiduously avoided an open break with legality, Brüning was obliged to walk a tightrope in order to avoid having to make a choice between fundamental political options. At no point was this ambivalence more apparent than during the presidential elections, which afforded the chancellor one last opportunity to postpone the decision between a more moderate policy based on the political center and a definitive turn to the Right. Only the fact that the presidential cabinet was forced on the eve of the Prussian Landtag elections to defy the German Right in the matter of the SA brought this situation to an unexpected end. This action irrevocably undermined the very existence of the

Brüning cabinet. To the outside observer, however, this turn of events seemed to be have been brought about by the fateful conjunction of malicious intrigues and personal incompetence.

The appearance of nonpartisanship that the second Brüning cabinet had carefully cultivated by seeking authoritarian rather than parliamentary sanction for its political program was hopelessly compromised at the very moment that it decided to intervene in the escalating civil war between Communist and National Socialist paramilitary units. Although the right-wing press preferred to ignore it, the increasingly violent confrontations between the Combat League against Fascism (Kampfbund gegen den Faschismus) and the illegal Red Front Soldiers' League (Roter Frontkämpferbund) on the one hand and the SA and its affiliated National Socialist terrorist units on the other were almost invariably initiated by the latter. State governments throughout the country had grown increasingly concerned about the growing political influence of the SA since the summer of 1931. The SA, with an estimated 100,000 members in January 1930, had grown to approximately 291,000 members a year later and to 445,000 by August 1932. The Nazi party leadership exercised little control over the increasing aggressiveness of the SA and did little, if anything, to curb it. For the party it had become a dangerous instrument of political power that could no longer be held in check by the police alone.

Intelligence analysts within the Reich Ministry of the Interior had been working with the Prussian police force ever since the late summer of 1930 to compile a comprehensive dossier on the SA and its activities, which, in the opinion of those who conducted the investigation, provided ample evidence of the subversive and traitorous character of the SA. The discovery of the so-called Boxheim documents in September 1931 only tended to confirm this impression. Hidden on a farm in the Hessian village of Lampertheim and brought to light through the indiscretion of a former NSDAP functionary, these documents cast a strong light on what circles within the SA were planning to do in the event of a revolutionary upheaval and contained relatively detailed plans that would presumably take effect in response to a Communist coup attempt. Prepared primarily by the future SS lawyer Werner Best, these plans confined themselves largely to what the SA had to do in order to secure its own power during a situation of revolutionary turmoil. To be sure, the plans made it clear that the SA planned to move against potential enemies with considerable force and to enforce martial law in the sharpest possible manner but contained no directive pertaining to the declaration of a state of emergency.

The Boxheim documents indicated — and this was later confirmed by leaks to the Prussian state police — that the NSDAP regarded an uprising by the Communist working class as well as parts of the SPD and socialist labor unions as highly probable. Should this happen, the SA would withdraw from the cities to take control of the countryside, where it would proceed to starve out the putative "proletarian" revolution by preventing food supplies from reaching the large urban centers. Considerations of this nature had already prompted R. Walter Darré to establish the Agrarian Political Apparatus of the NSDAP (Agrarpolitischer Apparat der NSDAP), an agency that was to be instrumental in organizing the Nazi infiltration of the National Rural League and other influential agricultural interest organizations. Memories of the November Revolution played a large part in shaping the plans of the SA. In this respect, the Prussian police force was wrong when it tried to prove the existence of a Nazi conspiracy to overthrow the existing political order.

In spite of the fact that all sorts of plans for a violent overthrow of the republican system were in the air, the leaders of the NSDAP and the SA had no concrete idea of how they should go about gaining power. This, however, did not mean that they had committed themselves to attain power by means of a parliamentary majority. The SA in particular continued to attach considerable significance to the extraparliamentary struggle. For his own part, Hitler avoided taking a stand in the matter. To be sure, he characterized the contingency plans that Best had drafted as a statement of personal preference that did not commit the party in one way or another, and he emphatically warned the party against being provoked into a confrontation with police and military authorities. At the same time, however, Hitler assiduously avoided endorsing the parliamentary road to power in his response to the criticism that disclosure of the Boxheim documents had evoked. His visionary concept of the political process was reflected in this rhetorical flourish: "Of its own accord and with the certainty of natural law destiny will deliver power into our hands."

Actively supported by Carlo Mierendorff, a future member of the German resistance, the efforts of Wilhelm Leuschner, the Social Democratic minister of the interior in Hesse, to use the Boxheim documents as the basis for bringing a charge of high treason in the German Supreme Court failed because of the disinterest of the bourgeois middle parties, which did not want to preclude the possibility of an understanding with the NSDAP. Similarly unsuccessful were the raids the Prussian police conducted against SA installations after the formation of special SA commando units following the first round of voting in the presidential elections, which had given rise to concern that the NSDAP would try to seize power by force in the event of an electoral victory. The danger of an SA strike in the event of a Nazi victory at the polls was first broached within the Reich Ministry of the Interior. In spite of this, Groener disavowed his Prussian colleague Carl Severing when the latter took action against the SA. Severing suffered a further defeat when the German Supreme Court ruled in favor of the NSDAP that the Prussian police force must return all the material it had confiscated from the SA. Groener, who still believed that the SA could be disciplined, was soon to learn better.

By now the SA had long ceased to be merely a self-defense organization responsible for keeping order at Nazi party rallies. Its main purpose now seemed to be the provocation of political adversaries. The use of violence had received Hitler's express approval, for it had a propaganda function that was all the more palpable because significant sectors of the German bourgeoisie looked upon the deployment of violence against the political Left with considerable sympathy. The various institutions that the SA had erected to shelter and house mostly unemployed SA men became a breeding ground for violence and functioned as bases from which more or less spontaneous operations against those with differing political opinions were frequently launched. This sort of activity was designed to intimidate political opponents and to foster a sense of insecurity within the population at large. The SA, however, was careful to avoid direct confrontations with the police and, to a lesser extent, with its Communist rivals. Over time the militancy of the self-defense organizations on the Right and Left continued to escalate to the point where injuries and soon deaths became more and more frequent.

The state governments, which were responsible for the maintenance of public safety and which had become increasingly alarmed by the growing brutality of political confrontations, found the passivity of the national government in the face of the threat this posed to public order incomprehensible. In point of fact, Brüning was inclined to ignore the role of the SA since he still hoped to defuse the NSDAP's radicalism by involving it in "positive government work" through its integration into a series of governmental coalitions at the state level. The chancellor therefore hesitated to use specific civil service regulations to stem the National Socialist infiltration of the civil service in spite of the fact that a number of ministries had begun to complain about the irregularities this had produced in their subordinate agencies. At the same time, the increasingly cozy relationship that had developed between the NSDAP and the Reichswehr tended to, as the Prussian minister of the interior sarcastically put it, dim the "shooting light" (*Büchsenlicht*) the police needed in order to take effective action against the increasing number of SA terrorist actions.

The leaders of the Reichswehr viewed the problem of the paramilitary organizations from the perspective that they made it unnecessary for the army to become involved in domestic political conflicts. This corresponded to the rigid stance that Groener had adopted, to the annoyance of many officers with outspoken nationalist sentiments, regarding the nonpartisan role of the Reichswehr. The medium-term goal of the Defense Ministry was to depoliticize the paramilitary organizations by first withdrawing them (in the form of a military sports club) from the influence of the political parties and then transforming them into a national militia as soon as this could be reconciled with the course of negotiations at the Geneva Disarmament Conference. As early as January 1932 Schleicher began to lobby for the creation of the Reich Curatorium for Youth Fitness (Reichskuratorium für Jugendertüchtigung) that was eventually founded under the leadership of retired General Edwin von Stülpnagel. With a view toward the specific interests of the Reichswehr, Schleicher pleaded for a close bond between the SA and the state. By the same token, Defense Minister Groener felt that he could avoid a political choice with the motto "We want to win over [einfangen] the Nazis, but without forcing the Sozis into opposition." His unabashed optimism concerning the government's ability to defuse the radicalism of the Nazi movement was further reflected in his remark after the April Landtag elections that steps would have to be taken "to prepare the Nazis for government participation since a movement that is certain to keep on growing can no longer be suppressed."

Groener's equanimity was thoroughly shaken when he attended a conference of state ministers of the interior in early April 1932. All of them demanded immediate intervention against the SA and indicated that if it were not forthcoming, the state governments would have no recourse but to act on their own. Groener, who was deeply wounded by charges from the south German states that he had been derelict in the performance of his duties, conceded that a "prophylactic strike" against the SA was justified in light of the widespread rumors that it was planning to take power by force following the second round of the presidential elections. In this respect, Groener was unable to refute the argument from his fellow ministers at the state level that the existence of an "independent party army" undermined the long-term authority of the state and that speedy action was therefore necessary. With the observation that the "elimination of the SA" was a foregone conclusion, Groener expressed his fundamental support for the petitions of the state ministers of the interior, though with the qualification that the "good elements" within the SA would have to be recruited for service to the state. In an effort to gain time, Groener finally persuaded the states to agree to a postponement of their demand for an immediate ban against the SA until 13 April so that the outcome of the presidential elections would not be affected by the action. Groener felt bound by the promise he made to the state representatives and therefore went ahead with the ban against the SA despite the fact that this was not necessarily in his best interests as Reich defense minister.

Groener was not fully aware of the explosion that might be ignited by the dissolution of the SA and other quasi-military formations of the NSDAP. Otherwise he would hardly have spoken of solving the problem of the combat leagues through the creation of "a large universal military sport club" in the official text with which he promulgated the Emergency Decree for the Protection of the Authority of the State. Hitler had nothing but sarcasm for this idea, even though he outwardly complied with the ban against the SA and expressly forbade resistance to its implementation as advocated by SA Chief of Staff Ernst Röhm. Groener failed to appreciate the social energies that had come together in the SA during its emergence as a mass organization or that these energies could possibly be deflected through the creation of a nonpartisan association for premilitary training. At the same time, Brüning also failed to appreciate the enormous importance of this decision. By no means was it taken at the behest of the Prussian government alone. Both Bavaria and Württemberg, neither of which could be accused of prosocialist sympathies, had expressly advocated the ban. Yet, aside from the papers loyal to the Center, the bourgeois press depicted the ban against the SA as a deliberate attempt to boost the electoral prospects of the Social Democrats.

Brüning and Groener underestimated the emotional resistance the ban against the SA encountered at the upper echelons of the Reichswehr command and in the presidential entourage. To be sure, Schleicher initially placed himself squarely behind his defense minister and backed up his position with the argument that the proper "psychological moment" for drastic measures against the SA had arrived and that its prohibition was absolutely necessary to protect the authority of the state. At the heart of these statements, however, lay the illusion that the NSDAP could be held to the path of legality by disciplining the SA. Schleicher therefore rejected proposals from several army commanders that the scope of the ban be expanded to include the Reichsbanner, particularly since this would have meant an end to the SPD's toleration of the Brüning government.

Within the Defense Ministry, however, the mood underwent a dramatic and abrupt change. The military was highly sensitive to the storm of protest that had engulfed the entire German Right and that drew its energy from the antisocialist resentment of broad sectors of the German bourgeoisie. Crown Prince Wilhelm made himself the spokesman for such sentiments when in a letter to Groener he lamented the smashing of the "wonderful human material" in the SA and depicted its prohibition as "a danger to domestic peace." Under the influence of arch-conservatives, Hindenburg began to have misgivings of his own. The Reich president was concerned that the ban on the SA might be construed as a belated reward to the SPD for its support of his reelection. In this respect, his son Oskar played a particularly pernicious role. He wanted to protect the Reich president from once again having to take responsibility for an unpopular emergency decree and was irritated over rumors from the members of the Harzburg Front that he had functioned as liaison between the president's entourage and the SPD.

After a sleepless night Schleicher reversed his position and proposed that the ban against the SA be temporarily postponed and that Hitler be given a formal ultimatum instead. This, of course, was nothing more than a ploy to gain time. Groener refused to go along with it, for it was clear to him that the cabinet would suffer a severe loss of face if he backed down in this matter. At the same time, he refused to be swayed by the diversionary suggestion from the

Bureau of the Reich President, which with the help of the army's chief of staff, General Kurt von Hammerstein, and presumably with Schleicher's knowledge as well, had hastily compiled a detailed dossier of incriminating materials on the Reichsbanner that would have justified including it in the ban against the SA. Groener saw through the spurious character of the dossier, which concerned events that had occurred some time ago and had entered the public domain through an indiscretion in the press. Groener tried to undercut the initiative of the Bureau of the Reich President by persuading Karl Holtermann to voluntarily dissolve the paramilitary defense units the Iron Front (Eiserne Front) had formed to protect itself against the SA. At the same time, Groener promulgated a ban of dubious constitutionality against Communist freethinkers' and atheist organizations in an attempt to offset Hindenburg's perception of favoritism toward the Left. By demonstrating that the allegations against the Reichsbanner did not withstand close scrutiny, Groener eventually prevailed over the vacillating and seemingly helpless Reich president.

The personal estrangement that these matters produced in the relationship between Hindenburg and Groener was very much a part of the general campaign against the defense minister in which Schleicher, whose own relations to Groener had deteriorated for largely personal reasons, played a critical role. The resentment that the rank-and-file soldier had felt against Groener as a result of his role in the Leipzig trial of three junior officers for high treason were revived almost overnight. Another element of the general's loss of prestige was his remarriage and the premature birth of a son in apparent violation of the moral standards of the social class to which he belonged. The fact that this man was unceremoniously sacked despite his highly valuable services to the army was symptomatic not only of the extremely tense atmosphere that existed on the German domestic scene but also of the almost pathological distrust the German Right harbored against those whose opinions did not conform exactly with their own counterrevolutionary view of the world.

As head of the Defense Ministry, Groener should have taken disciplinary action, including dismissal, against Schleicher's insubordination as well as against those military commanders who openly criticized him. Groener, however, felt that in view of the Reich president's attitude he no longer possessed the backing he needed for such a step. Groener now had to pay a heavy price for the fact that for some time the defense minister had been nothing more than the figurehead of a technically and politically independent military apparatus. The connections that Schleicher enjoyed to the Reich president, not only through the person of his son Oskar but also through his state secretary Otto Meißner, provided him with unparalleled influence and led to the formation of the presidential camarilla that to an increasing degree shaped the decisions at the helm of the Reich. The bitter polemics that were directed against Groener by circles within the government as well as by the bourgeois press were fueled by a combination of accumulated political ressentiment and the defense of vested interests.

Since the first years of the Weimar Republic the leaders of the Reichswehr had cultivated a wide range of contacts with the Free Corps, the patriotic associations, and especially the Stahlhelm, whose leadership cadre stood in close social contact with the middle and upper echelons of the German officer corps. The Reichswehr's support of the paramilitary combat leagues had originally served the purpose of helping the military circumvent the government's efforts to fulfill the armament provisions of the Versailles peace treaty. The border patrol units that the Reichswehr had built up primarily in the eastern provinces depended above all upon the informal cooperation of the Stahlhelm and other bourgeois combat leagues. Since the end of the 1920s, however, the expansion of the border defense units had changed this situation. From this point on, border patrol units were integrated into plans for a general mobilization of German armed forces. This, in turn, presupposed close cooperation with the civilian administration. For, as the demands placed on the German military apparatus continued to grow, it could no longer function simply on the basis of an informal understanding with East Elbian landowners, Stahlhelm functionaries, and local dignitaries. The fact that the Prussian minister of the interior, Social Democrat Carl Severing, eventually decided to tolerate these more or less illegal military arrangements despite the fact that they helped consolidate the bases of conservative power at the local level was typical of the power relations that existed in the last years of the Weimar Republic.

The rapid growth of the SA, particularly in the eastern provinces, had an important effect upon the work of the border patrol units. Initially, directives from the Reichswehr command prohibiting SA members from participating in border patrol activities were scrupulously obeyed. Even Hitler had repeatedly opposed SA participation in these operations. Still, there was a wide range of contacts with the SA at the local level, even though the primary base of support for the border patrol units was still the Stahlhelm. Since Röhm had returned from his Bolivian exile to assume command as SA chief of staff, the SA's relations with the Reichswehr had undergone a qualitative change insofar as he sought to strengthen its military character and model it after the German army. By March 1931 Röhm had reached an understanding with the leaders of the Reichswehr, whereby the existing ban against both the use of Nazi party members in any Reichswehr operation and the SA's participation in the border patrol units was lifted. In certain parts of the country, the SA soon became indispensable for the work of the border patrol units. This was particularly true in East Prussia, where membership of the SA greatly exceeded that of the Stahlhelm. Relations between the SA and the German officer corps, however, remained severely strained by pronounced social prejudices on both sides of the equation.

In spite of continual friction arising out of the arrogant behavior of the SA, the leaders of the Reichswehr regarded the SA as an important source of potential recruitment for the militia that the Geneva Disarmament Conference was expected to approve. The idea of a militia was attractive as a temporary expedient, for it seemed to offer the only realistic chance of raising the full complement of troops in the event of a general mobilization of Germany's armed forces. The twelve-year period of military service that had been adopted with the creation of the 100,000-man army meant that the number of reservists who were fit for service continued to decline at the same time that the segment of the population that had received military training became older and older. In the short term, the Reichswehr could remedy this situation only by relying on the paramilitary combat leagues. From this perspective, however, the SA was much more valuable than the Stahlhelm, since its membership was relatively young, whereas the Stahlhelm, except for the Young Stahlhelm (Jung-Stahlhelm), enrolled a high percentage of veterans.

The expanded activities of the border and regional self-defense organizations did much to exacerbate conflicts between the Prussian government and the paramilitary aspirations of the Stahlhelm. These conflicts stemmed from the fact that the abolition of Allied military controls and the diminished risk of Allied sanctions following the adoption of the Young Plan, as well as the anticipated outcome of the Geneva disarmament negotiations, made it possible for Germany to accelerate the pace of its rearmament program. This, in turn, was accompanied by the adoption of a more aggressive foreign policy stance under the state secretary in the German Foreign Office, Bernhard von Bülow, after Stresemann's death in the fall of 1929. In the meantime, the increasing involvement of the Reichswehr in German domestic politics and its close ties with right-wing paramilitary combat leagues did not augur well for the military's standing policy of nonpartisanship in German party politics. The use of the SA for border patrol activities in particular created a real danger that the army might become involved in latent civil war situations. For the German Left had not remained passive in face of the SA's turn to terrorism. The Reichsbanner responded to this turn of events by founding the Iron Front and by forming special self-defense units known as *Hammerschaften* that had a military character of their own and that were partly trained by retired Prussian police officers.

Since its origin, the Reichswehr had always combined the principle of strict nonpartisanship in domestic political affairs with the cultivation of an essentially homogeneous conservative and nationalist point of view in its officer corps. Nevertheless, in the late 1920s the German military experienced growing internal tensions that were directly related to the phenomenon of generational change. For whereas most of the older officers remained wedded to the basic values and aspirations of the imperial tradition, the more recent generation of officers tended to have a more positive attitude toward technology and was more receptive to racist and National Socialist intellectual currents. The leaders of the Reichswehr, however, were unable to convince the younger officers of the credibility of its political agenda. The "itch in the ranks of the young lieutenants," as one of Schleicher's confidants expressed it, revealed the existence of widespread dissatisfaction with the political course of Germany's military leadership and pointed to a deepening crisis of confidence within the German officer corps. All of this seemed to place the homogeneity of the Reichswehr in serious question.

At no time did this become more apparent than in the Leipzig trial of three young Reichswehr officers that opened several days after the September 1930 Reichstag elections. The defendants were three lieutenants from Ulm—Hans Friedrich Wendt, Richard Scheringer, and Hanns Ludin—who had supposedly advocated the formation of National Socialist cells within the Reichswehr. The accused officers had established contact with the Nazi party leadership in an effort to reach an agreement with the new armed power in the event that the NSDAP's prophecies of a "national revolution" actually came true. General Ludwig Beck, the defendants' superior officer, testified that sympathies with the NSDAP and support for its political objectives were widespread among the younger members of the officer corps. Groener's excessive reaction to the alleged attempt to sow subversion within the ranks of the Reichswehr thus met with universal dismay. Most army leaders felt that the three defendants were guilty of at most an infraction of regulations that was already covered by appropriate disciplinary measures and failed to see why an incident that had taken place more than a year earlier had given rise to charges of high treason in the Leipzig High Court.

Groener had intentionally played up the disciplinary issues in the Leipzig case out of fear that the inner cohesion and discipline of the army had been seriously compromised. A number of his public statements, including a controversial promise to give a watch to those who informed on such behavior in the future, served a similar purpose. Groener's disciplinary measures, however, did little to stop the criticism that had surfaced within the officer corps in connection with the Leipzig trial and that reflected outspoken *völkisch* and antiparliamentary attitudes. When Groener proceeded to state at a conference of Germany's military commanders that the army, as the strongest element of the state, had to be kept free of all political influences and had to stand above all political parties and that these objectives could be achieved only through the proper instruction of the officer corps and its unconditional obedience to established authority, he failed to appreciate the deeper reasons for the criticism. For this criticism stemmed in large part from the ambivalence the Reichswehr leadership felt toward the new nationalism and the program of "national rebirth" as represented by the NSDAP. The appeal to the tradition of the Reichswehr's nonpartisanship and its relationship to an abstract concept, however, was no longer sufficient to retain the confidence of the troops.

In the final analysis, the course of the Leipzig trial did little to clarify the question of the Reichswehr's relationship to the NSDAP. For whereas the Ulm officers were sentenced to several years in prison, they became celebrated heroes in the right-wing press, with the exception of Scheringer, who changed camps while in prison and declared his allegiance to the KPD. Ludin's attorney, the National Socialist Hans Frank, had not expected that the court would overrule the objections of the Prussian prosecutors and permit Hitler to take the witness stand on behalf of the defendants. This afforded the Nazi party leader a unique opportunity to assert under oath and with the widest possible publicity that the NSDAP remained entirely within the bounds of legality and that it had no intention whatsoever of interfering with the independent role of the armed forces. In committing himself and his party to the path of legality, Hitler was acting in perfect conformity with the purely formal concept of constitutionality that was to be found in contemporary legal scholarship. Yet in the same breath Hitler announced to the great satisfaction of most of those in attendance that after a National Socialist takeover "heads would roll" and that those responsible for twelve years of bad government would be made to suffer the consequences. In this context, legality meant little more than a promise to respect the Reichswehr's monopoly on the possession and use of armed force. Hitler's refusal to become involved in open conflict with the legally constituted armed forces was a consequence of the lessons the Nazi party leader had learned from the events of November 1923.

For the Reichswehr leadership Hitler's commitment to the principle of legality came as something of a surprise and was immediately interpreted as a conciliatory gesture. To be sure, the leaders of the Reichswehr had not forgotten the sarcastic propaganda campaign that the NSDAP had directed at Germany's military institutions and leading representatives of the German military establishment. But Hitler's effort to overcome the fundamental misgivings of the Reichswehr command to the NSDAP's participation in various military operations was intentionally continued by Ernst Röhm. In dissociating himself in a meeting with Schleicher from the former deputy commander of the eastern division of the SA, Walter Stennes, and his rebellion against the Nazi party leadership, Röhm assured the military that in the future "revolutionary action" by the SA was out of the question. Hostage to the illusion that the SA might be tamed, the leaders of the Reichswehr chose to believe the assurances of Hitler and Röhm. At the end of 1931 the Reichswehr command established with a great sense of relief that no new "cases of subversion" — or attempts by the

NSDAP to gain influence within the Reichswehr—had been confirmed. Such a conclusion, however, completely ignored the fact that the SA's principal goal was to establish good relations with the rank-and-file soldier and, if necessary, to enlist his support for the domestic political struggle. At the same time, the SA was in a position to reap the benefits of military training.

Otto Braun did his best to shake the Reichswehr's naive faith in the SA by detailing cases of alleged military treason and by making the most of Hitler's Lauenburg speech of April 1932, in which the Nazi party leader stated that co-operation with the border patrols was contingent upon the overthrow of the existing political system. As early as 1929, the Prussian minister president had vigorously objected to the general's Program for the Military Preparedness of the German People and had realized that the full implementation of these plans was incompatible with the survival of Germany's democratic institutions. The Reich president, by contrast, fully approved of the almost imperceptible change in the German constitution that had made it possible for the Reichswehr to assume an increasingly independent position in the political system. By 1930 Groener could state with evident satisfaction that on the German political scene not a single stone could be moved "unless the full weight of the Reichswehr's word was thrown into the balance."

The Reichswehr continued to harbor the hope that within the foreseeable future it would be able to free itself from the fetters of the demilitarization clauses of the Versailles peace treaty. In this respect, it took the position in disarmament negotiations that Section V of the Versailles treaty should be rendered ineffective through international agreements. This represented a clear change from Stresemann's cautious behavior in the armament question. The tough and persistent manner in which the German delegation now pressed for concrete results could only intensify the security concerns of the French. In anticipation of the gains it expected to make during the Geneva Disarmament Conference in February 1932, Germany's military leadership had already begun long-term armament planning. Plans for an army with the strength of twenty-one divisions in the event of a general mobilization had been in various stages of development since 1929. The border patrol assumed an important place in these plans. After 1931 this program was replaced by the "second rearmament program," which was to be implemented between 1 April 1931 and 31 March 1938 and whose goal was to place no less than thirty-four divisions in the field. This program included a comprehensive economic plan for the manufacture of weapons and provided for the possible mobilization of the civilian sector as well. In a parallel endeavor, the Reichswehr embarked on a systematic re-organization of existing paramilitary organizations, particularly with respect to their weaponry and technical ordnance. As a corollary of this planning, the German military establishment was determined that the most recent disarma-ment negotiations should eliminate Allied oversight of Germany's military budget and give Germany the right to shorten the term of service from the current twelve years so that more men could be trained for military service.

When the Reichswehr submitted its far-reaching financial demands, including the so-called billion mark program for military rearmament, the Brüning government proved to be as accommodating as possible, even though it could only cover part of what had been requested. The first attempts to remove military expenditures from the budgetary control of the Reichstag had been initiated during the Müller cabinet. Since rearmament planning was always conducted in the strictest possible secrecy, public debate on this subject was necessarily limited. To all of those who were involved, however, it was clear that such planning and the far-reaching mobilization of Germany's economic resources it entailed could be implemented only over the opposition of the SPD. The Defense Ministry therefore placed the Brüning cabinet under increasingly heavy pressure to dissolve the existing government coalition in Prussia and to end its dependence on the toleration of the Social Democrats. A significant aspect of Germany's rearmament program was the expansion of the regional and border patrols, which was to be continued as long as the Versailles peace treaty prevented Germany from rearming openly. This, in turn, necessarily affected the Reichswehr's relationship to right-wing paramilitary organizations. Given the scope of the Reichswehr's efforts to build up a large civilian militia that would compensate for its own personnel shortages, the ban against the SA was regarded within the Reichswehr as a most unfortunate development, particularly since it was in this organization that Germany's military planners hoped to find the manpower necessary to bring troop levels up to the desired strength. Within the Reichsbanner and Iron Front, on the other hand, the military saw only those elements of society that were unwilling to serve.

Apparently Brüning, who at the time was deeply involved in the disarmament negotiations, did not attach much significance to the ban against the SA, particularly since the NSDAP offered no resistance to the actions of the police aside from a vigorous propaganda campaign in the official party press. The fact that the ban against the SA offered psychological encouragement to Hitler's adversaries, however, also prompted the bourgeois Right to come to the support of the NSDAP. Nevertheless, the government's intervention interrupted the escalating cycle of violence long enough so that the elections on 24 April 1932 could be held in relative peace. But the outcome of these elections did not bring about a dramatic change in Germany's political course. The national cabinet lacked the necessary resolve not only to dissociate itself as unequivocally as possible from the NSDAP but also to take advantage of the window of opportunity that had temporarily opened for cooperation with the Prussian government. For his own part, Brüning did not want to destroy his chances of future cooperation with the NSDAP at the state and provincial level. The relatively optimistic mood that prevailed within the more moderate parties despite signs of an imminent crisis suddenly changed to one of disorientation and resignation in the aftermath of the disastrous defeat they suffered in the elections of 24 April. At the same time, the German Right intensified its pressure against the supposedly one-sided ban against the SA.

By this time, Groener's dismissal was only a matter of time. It was only a question of finding the proper pretext for forcing his removal from office. This was to be provided by a meeting of the Reichstag on 10 May 1932. When the defense minister defended the measures the government had taken against the SA with clear and rational arguments, his words could hardly be heard over the cacophony of abuse that came from the ranks of the NSDAP and DNVP. At this point, Groener knew that he was politically dead. As a result, the defense minister was completely defenseless against the scandalous attacks of the National Socialists. In the very same meeting of the Reichstag, a young deputy by the name of Kurt Schumacher earned the respect of his colleagues by objecting to Goebbels's charge that the Reich president had been elected by the "party of deserters," that is, the Social Democrats. In the right-wing press Groener was roundly criticized for having made a fool of himself in the Reichstag, as if proper parliamentary behavior was suddenly something that actually mattered. Even Count Westarp succumbed to the psychosis that had been unleashed by the attacks on Groener when he told the Reich president that the defense minister was no longer "fit to serve." On top of all this, Schleicher threatened the resignation en bloc of all the generals in the ministerial office if Groener refused to step down.

Groener had been anticipating that Hindenburg would ask for his resignation for several weeks. He thus preempted Schleicher's initiative by asking to be relieved of his responsibilities as defense minister. At the same time, he wished to continue in his post at the Ministry of the Interior in order not to jeopardize the status of the Brüning cabinet. But this did encounter strong resistance from the Reich president, who refused to sign the documents that were necessary to implement this arrangement. Throughout all of this, Brüning remained loyal and did his best to prevent Groener from leaving the government. As a result, the request for Groener's dismissal was never formally submitted. Nevertheless, Groener's voluntary resignation as minister of defense resulted in the dismissal of the entire cabinet. Hindenburg was not ready to appoint a new defense minister, with the result that Schleicher withdrew the demand that he be appointed to this post on the flimsy pretext that he did not want to add to Groener's embarrassment. Carl Goerdeler was briefly mentioned as a possible successor for Warmbold, who resigned as minister of economics. In the meantime, Schleicher was already busy at work providing the Reich president with alternatives to the Brüning cabinet and urging him to make a complete break with the chancellor.

When reminded by the Reich president of his promise to form a right-wing cabinet immediately after the Prussian elections, Brüning asked that he be given until the completion of the Lausanne negotiations scheduled for early June. Hindenburg, however, regarded this as a breach of Brüning's word. The chancellor, who protested vigorously against efforts to influence the Reich president behind his back by referring to the gravity of Germany's diplomatic situation, secured nothing but a promise to postpone negotiations with the leaders of the various parties until after the convocation of the recently elected Prussian Landtag. At all costs Brüning wanted to avoid the impression that a change of governments was imminent. In this respect, however, he was undercut by the machinations of Schleicher, who with the full support of Oskar von Hindenburg and State Secretary Meißner had established contact with Hitler. In two meetings with the Nazi party leader on 22 April and 8 May—that is, before the parliamentary controversy over the person and performance of Groener had drawn to a climax—Schleicher had sought Hitler's toleration for a future right-wing cabinet. These conversations, which were never recorded in writing, produced a less than convincing commitment from the Nazi party leader to support the new cabinet until the next Reichstag elections on the threefold condition that the Reichstag be dissolved, the ban against the SA be rescinded, and its "full freedom of action" be restored.

When Brüning learned of the agreements that had been reached behind his back, he immediately warned against not including the NSDAP in the proposed right-wing cabinet as well as against new elections that would greatly intensify the process of political polarization and accelerate the dissolution of the bourgeois center. In a conversation with Count Westarp, who had been mentioned as his possible successor, Brüning pointed out that it would be an almost catastrophic mistake to permit Hitler the luxury of a new election campaign without having first tied his hands by including his party in the governing coalition. Yet the NSDAP's only chance lay in maintaining a stance of uncompromising opposition to all of Germany's bourgeois parties. The NSDAP had therefore rejected Brüning's repeated invitations to join his cabinet as a junior partner that would have to subordinate its policies to those of other political parties. Against his better judgment, Schleicher criticized Brüning for having failed to win the NSDAP over to a policy of constructive cooperation with the state. In point of fact, the chancellor had made repeated efforts to reach an understanding with the NSDAP at the state level. Even Groener—and on this point he was in complete agreement with Schleicher—was adamantly opposed to giving Hitler power at the national level.

Most political observers failed to comprehend just what had prompted the leaders of the Reichswehr to stake their future on an alliance with Hitler. There is no doubt that Schleicher greatly overestimated his own political acumen and failed to recognize the risks of a tactical accommodation with the NSDAP. The Reichswehr's lack of critical distance toward the NSDAP and its inability to arrive at a purely objective assessment of National Socialism and the personality of Adolf Hitler stemmed in no small measure from the extent to which its revisionist demands and antiparliamentary sentiments coincided with those of the NSDAP. After a conversation with Hitler in September 1931, Kurt von Hammerstein concluded, somewhat ironically but nonetheless seriously, that they both wanted "the same thing" down to the question of timing itself. The efforts of the Reichswehr leadership were therefore directed to dissuade Hitler from his "false methods" and "revolutionary ideas." Groener had spoken of an "educational process over a long period of time" that would only succeed if one could attract the well-meaning National Socialists to the service of the state, whereas the "troublemakers" would have to be systematically excluded from the movement. A struggle against the movement as a whole was therefore inappropriate. Only "excesses" were to be repressed with all due severity. At the heart of these considerations lay the increasingly widespread conviction that one must not reject the National Socialists as the socialists in their own time and place had been rejected. This, in turn, was typical of the way in which the thinking of the military was still shaped by the clichés of the November Revolution and how Germany's military leadership might in the same breadth accuse the SPD of high treason and equate it with the KPD.

The wishful thinking of the military caused it to believe that Hitler's demagogic tirades were primarily designed to keep the more "radical" National Socialists who were working for the revolutionary overthrow of the existing political system under control. The unusually positive assessment of Hitler's personality shared by Schleicher, Groener, and Hammerstein stemmed in part from the fact that the Nazi party leader maintained a deliberately low profile and did his best to appear conciliatory in private conversations with Germany's military leadership. The way in which many Nazis ingratiated themselves with the generals produced a state of virtual euphoria on the part of the latter. This was particularly true of Hermann Göring, who in these months emerged as Hitler's most important liaison to the national government and the right-wing parties.

For all of this, the military continued to harbor a certain distrust toward the NSDAP that was rooted in inherited social prejudices. The benign condescension with which they treated Hitler led them to commit incredibly grotesque errors of judgment. Through intelligent and accommodating handling Hitler could be persuaded to dissociate himself from the more radical elements within his own movement. It was therefore essential—in Schleicher's casual way of speaking—to tie Hitler two and three times to the "pillar of legality." This sort of self-deception was directly related to the way in which the National Socialist movement had chosen to present itself not as a party in the traditional sense of the word but as the catalyst for the formation of a "genuine national community." Nationalistic emotions only fueled the illusion that the extremism of the Nazi movement was brought on only by the discriminatory treatment it had suffered at the hands of the Weimar political establishment and that fair treatment would provide new impetus for the "healthy" national forces that were to be found in the NSDAP.

The illusion that Hitler was prepared to cooperate also influenced the decisions of Hindenburg, who had withdrawn to his Neudeck estate. Brüning's last parliamentary triumph on 11 May 1932 came too late to stem the tide of events. In spite of the Groener debacle, the chancellor had once again managed to enlist the support of a wavering Business Party, which sympathized with the NSDAP, in defeating motions of no confidence from the Right and Left with majorities of 286 and 259 votes, respectively, and in securing authorization for a number of loans that had once again become necessary. In his final speech as chancellor, Brüning called on the nation to stay the current course. From the reparations and disarmament negotiations that were to take place in Lausanne in early June, Brüning hoped for a decisive breakthrough. For all the hardships that had been visited upon the German people through the lack of Allied sympathy, Brüning contended, the course on which he had embarked some two years earlier had been right. He was not about to lose his nerves "a hundred meters before the finish line."

The fact that the Reichstag had readily approved the loans for which Brüning had asked gave the chancellor renewed hope that it still might be possible — in the short run, at least — for him to stabilize his cabinet. The demonstrative resignation of Economics Minister Hermann Warmbold on 6 May over the length of the workday, however, signaled the defection of industry, which for reasons of foreign policy had generally supported Brüning despite all of the misgivings its leaders might have had about his domestic policies. To be sure, the leadership of the National Federation of German Industry had once again assured the chancellor of the backing of the "sensible men of the German business community" as recently as 17 May. Heavy industry and large-scale agriculture, on the other hand, were determined to support the reorganization of the cabinet that Schleicher had initiated and were strongly opposed to Goerdeler's appointment as the new economics minister.

In the second half of May 1932 Brüning devoted all of his energy to the preparation of a new package of emergency decrees that included even more drastic austerities in the area of social services. The increasingly urgent problem of mass unemployment, the cabinet believed, could only partially be solved by an improvement in the existing economic situation. The extreme economic pessimism that was reflected in this observation and the legitimate need to cushion further reductions in social services by compensatory measures explain why the question of agricultural resettlement suddenly moved to the foreground of political deliberations. From this perspective, therefore, the notion of agricultural resettlement assumed the function of a social safety valve. It was symptomatic of Weimar's political crisis that it was this issue that brought about the collapse of the Brüning cabinet. The crisis over agricultural resettlement was preceded by a prolonged conflict over jurisdiction within the cabinet between Hans Schlange-Schöningen and Adam Stegerwald. This conflict, in turn, must be seen against the background of the increasingly desperate situation of the German working class and Stegerwald's desire not to be seen as a man favoring social cutbacks. These tensions, which also reflected the extreme nervous strain under which the cabinet was obliged to operate during its last days in office, contributed to the fact that news of the proposed resettlement program reached the public and in particular the large landowners before the fifth emergency decree had received its final stamp of approval from the national cabinet.

The comprehensive resettlement program that Dietrich and other members of the cabinet were pushing in the hope that the creation of small agricultural holdings would alleviate the problem of mass unemployment rested upon the expectation that it would be possible to accelerate the pace by which irremediably indebted estates were to be made available for subdivision and resettlement. The plan—or as much of it as existed—had not yet been thoroughly thought out, and Schlange-Schöningen's faith in the ability of his own dynamism to achieve immediate and tangible results in the area of agricultural resettlement was unrealistic. Moreover, his hasty reaction to the emergence of opposition from organized economic interests—for example, he tendered his resignation to the Reich president without first consulting the chancellor—was to prove extremely damaging to the success of his mission.

Nevertheless, it would be misleading to assume that the ineptitude of those who were involved in the planning of this project was the sole reason why the East Elbian landowners openly lobbied Hindenburg on behalf of Brüning's dismissal. It did not require the written protests of Baron Wilhelm von Gayl, the representative of the East Prussian provincial estates in the Reichsrat, and Magnus von Braun, the spokesman for large-scale agriculture, to arouse Hindenburg's deep-seated distrust of Brüning now that the chancellor could no longer count on the unconditional backing of big business. The very fact that the Reich president once again found himself in the position of having to sign a controversial emergency decree was sufficient to arouse his anger, particularly in the light of threats from the DNVP and NSDAP to bring suit against him in the German Constitutional Court for having authorized enactment of the legislation. After Hindenburg refused to receive Brüning at Neudeck, Meißner presented him with the text of the decrees for his signature. He protested against a new round of cuts in the pensions of war victims and criticized the resettlement program because it expedited the foreclosure and compulsory auction of hopelessly indebted estates. But the real bone of contention was that Hindenburg refused to confirm Groener as minister of the interior and that he demanded a fundamental reorientation of the cabinet to the Right. Brüning was no longer in a position to comply with the latter demand.

With Hindenburg's permission Schleicher summoned Franz von Papen to Berlin as Brüning's presumptive successor as early as 26 May 1932. Brüning, on the other hand, was prevented from seeing the Reich president until after his return from Neudeck. When the chancellor requested with specific reference to the upcoming negotiations in Lausanne an extension of his authority to issue emergency decrees, Hindenburg brushed him aside and withdrew his support from the cabinet. Brüning suddenly realized that he stood alone. On 30 May the cabinet unanimously decided to submit its resignation. To be sure, Brüning kept hoping until the last moment that he could change the president's mind. But this was no longer possible, if only because the schedule for the parade of the naval guards commemorating the Battle of Skagerrak left too little time for the discussion of substantive issues at the reception.

Despite the snubs from the Reich president, Brüning had loyally tried to do what he could to resolve the crisis, even if he did decline Hindenburg's offer that he remain on as German foreign minister in the new cabinet on the grounds that he would not have the authority he needed to bring the negotiations at Lausanne to a successful conclusion. Nevertheless Brüning indicated that he was fully prepared to support his successor with his wide-ranging experience and unquestioned international prestige. Brüning hoped that he might be able to recommend either Carl Goerdeler or Count Westarp for the chancellorship. With greater determination on Brüning's part, efforts on their behalf might have been successful, for by no means was Hindenburg committed to the outside candidate that Schleicher was pushing in the person of Franz von Papen.

Brüning attributed his fall from power to Schleicher's intrigues. These intrigues, however, only reflected the long-standing determination of the forces behind the presidential regime to decouple the exercise of executive authority from the control of parliament and to neutralize not only the KPD but the SPD and socialist unions as well. To be sure, the hard-won fruits of Brüning's tenacity on the reparations question were to be reaped by his successor. But in domestic politics this no longer mattered for the simple reason that it had brought with it relief from Germany's fiscal burden. By the same token, the chancellor's deflationary policies no longer enjoyed the approval of organized economic interests or broad social forces. In the final analysis, the decisive fact was that not only had Brüning cleared the way for the exclusive rule of the German Right but also that he had helped lay the legal or pseudolegal foundations for its rise to power.

As Brüning's successor Schleicher presented the Reich president with Franz von Papen, who had just arrived in Berlin. In many respects the appointment of the gentleman horseman and Center Party politician from Westphalia was a most congenial solution to Hindenburg. As a former officer in the Uhlan cavalry and as a one-time military attaché in Mexico and Washington, Papen came to the chancellorship with the proper pedigree. To be sure, his Catholicism might have been a minor flaw, but it was more than compensated for by the deeply conservative views and staunchly monarchist loyalties that Papen shared with the local nobility of the area around Münster. Only a few weeks earlier, Papen had confidently asserted that he would be able to form a presidential cabinet totally independent of all party ties. It is possible that a remark to this effect in a letter to Schleicher had prompted the latter to suggest the aristocrat from Westphalia for the chancellorship. Schleicher had met Papen, who through his wife was closely related to the Saar industrial elite, at the German Lords' Club (Deutscher Herrenklub) in Berlin. It was particularly telling for the character of the newly emergent presidential dictatorship that once the political parties seemed to have abdicated all responsibility the network of conservative and neoconservative organizations known as the Ring Movement should become an increasingly important source of political patronage.

As far as Schleicher was concerned, the fact that his candidate for the chancellorship was a former member of the Center's delegation to the Prussian Landtag who had consistently advocated an end to his party's coalition with the Social Democrats was an added virtue. Along with one other renegade Centrist deputy, Papen had also voted against the controversial change in the Prussian order of business that had blocked the National Socialists from laying immediate claim to the office of the Prussian minister president. Within the Center Party, Papen had remained something of an outsider, even though as a majority shareholder in the party newspaper *Germania* he had done his best to pressure its editors into adopting a more conservative line. Like his aristocratic peers from east of the Elbe River, Papen was an outspoken nationalist, though without embracing the more doctrinaire species of German nationalism espoused by Hugenberg. The strongly ideological but unclear political ideas that Papen espoused reflected the conservative-reactionary clichés regarding the collapse of 1918, a vague Christian corporatism with an extreme authoritarian component, and a conservatism that was directed against the accomplishments of the postrevolutionary era and that bore outspoken elitist and reactionary features. It is no surprise that he strongly opposed the ban against the SA from the very outset.

Papen's previous political experience made it appear as if he were ideally suited to fulfill Hindenburg's desire for the formation of a cabinet "of national unity." But if Schleicher had felt that the nomination of Papen would make it easier for the Center to accept Brüning's dismissal and to reconcile it to the new presidential cabinet, he could not have been more thoroughly mistaken. The replacement of Brüning by the apostate Papen sent severe shock waves throughout the Center Party. This stemmed in part from the fact that shortly before his appointment as chancellor Papen had reassured the Center party chairman, Monsignor Ludwig Kaas, who had pleaded with him not to accept Hindenburg's offer, that he would abide by party discipline. But when Hindenburg appealed to his "patriotic sense of duty" and "obedience," Papen apparently forgot about his promise to Kaas and accepted the task of leading a governmental team that for the most part had already been chosen. In defending his decision, the newly minted chancellor informed Kaas, who felt a deep sense of betrayal after he had gone to great lengths to praise Papen's party loyalty at a meeting of the Center Reichstag delegation, that he had acted as a German and not as a party man. Such a statement could only have fueled the party's outrage at such an obvious breach of trust.

In the organization of the cabinet, which Schleicher pursued with all of his customary vigor while Papen assumed a much more passive role, a number of prominent political figures who enjoyed close ties to Brüning were first contacted. Count Westarp, who felt a strong sense of solidarity with Brüning, did not think the proposed government, which would govern against the will of the more moderate bourgeois parties and without the participation of the DNVP and NSDAP, could possibly succeed. Carl Goerdeler, who was being considered for the Ministry of Economics, submitted to the Reich president a detailed memorandum for a reform of the existing system of government that would, among other things, have placed responsibility for the Ministries of Economics and of Labor in the hands of a single person. Hindenburg's apparent refusal to consider this proposal led to the collapse of the negotiations with Goerdeler. Since politicians with a high parliamentary profile were either out of the question or unavailable, Schleicher had a hard time finding appropriate candidates for the various cabinet posts, with the result that the completion of the cabinet proceeded very slowly. In the final analysis, the Bureau of the Reich President ended up relying upon personalities who belonged to the extreme Right without being affiliated with a specific political party. The phrase "cabinet of barons" that was frequently used to describe the new cabinet was only partly correct.

What finally emerged from the efforts of the Bureau of the Reich President to bring about a "shift to the right" stood in no relationship whatsoever to the evolutionary revision of the constitution in a more authoritarian direction that Brüning had hoped to bring about. By no means did the composition of the new cabinet reflect the actual constellation of political power that existed in the Reich. The parties that had worked so hard for the reelection of the president only two months earlier were no longer represented in the cabinet. The new minister of the interior was the same Baron Wilhelm von Gayl who had successfully lobbied Hindenburg against Brüning's supposedly "Bolshevist" plans for rural resettlement. As the provincial representative of East

Prussia in the Reichsrat, Gayl had looked after the special interests of the large landowners and had become an implacable foe of the Prussian government under Otto Braun.

The political color of the remaining members of the cabinet only strengthened the impression that the wheel of history had been reversed. Baron Magnus von Braun, who as director general of the Raiffeisen Cooperative was closely tied to large-scale agriculture from east of the Elbe, was put at the helm of the Ministry of Agriculture. Because of his involvement in the Kapp Putsch, the Prussian government had dismissed him from his post as *Regierungspräsident*. The Foreign Office was entrusted to a career diplomat with close ties to the monarchist camp, Baron Konstantin von Neurath, who was currently serving as the German ambassador to London. He had temporarily resigned from the diplomatic corps as a gesture of protest against the Weimar Republic. The new finance minister was Count Lutz Schwerin von Krosigk, a former budget director in the Ministry of Finance who had not been previously active in politics. Neurath and Schwerin von Krosigk could only be persuaded to join the cabinet by personal appeals from Hindenburg. They were joined by Paul Baron Eltz von Rübenach as the minister of transportation and postal services and by Franz Gürtner at the Ministry of Justice. In 1923 Gürtner, an outspoken German nationalist who was serving at the helm of the Bavarian Ministry of Justice, had supported Hitler. Although his appointment was intended as a friendly gesture toward the south German states, the Bavarian cabinet immediately dissociated itself from its former member. The Economics Ministry finally went to the rather bland Hermann Warmbold, whose only real merit seemed to be the fact that he had resigned from the Brüning cabinet just in time. Appointed to the Labor Ministry was the previously unknown president of the National Insurance Office (Reichsversicherungsamt), Hugo Schäffer. In all of this, perhaps the most significant change was that Hermann Pünder, state secretary in the chancellor's office, was replaced by one of Schleicher's closest confidants, Erwin Planck.

Aside from the nucleus of the "cabinet of gentlemen," as Papen described it in a conversation with Magnus von Braun, its composition was far more heavily slanted to the Right than Hindenburg had originally desired, regardless of how warmly he welcomed the social and political homogeneity of the cabinet members. Schleicher, who assumed control of the Ministry of Defense, had overestimated his ability to retain control over the frequently spontaneous and always opportunistic decisions of the new chancellor. Baron von Gayl, on the other hand, was to pursue the antiparliamentary course on which the new government had embarked with much greater consistency than Schleicher would have liked in light of the commitments he had made to Hitler prior to the fall of the Brüning cabinet. For his own part, Schleicher regarded new elections as a thoroughly unnecessary distraction that would only delay the revision of the constitution in a semiabsolutist direction.

The general public looked on the formation of the new government without any regard for the respective strengths of the different parliamentary blocs in the Reichstag as a clear challenge and provocation. At the same time, it was astonished by the rarefied social composition of the cabinet, for which the sobriquet "cabinet of barons" seemed quite justified. In order to live up to the government's claim of being a cabinet free from ties to the various political parties, the ministers publicly resigned from their respective parties insofar as they had such ties in the first place. Papen, for example, resigned from the Center Party before it had a chance to expel him, a gesture that did nothing to alter the fact that remaining cabinet officers continued to cultivate close ties to the bourgeois Right, if only under the auspices of organizations like the German Lords' Club. In the final analysis, the cabinet represented the political world view held by those segments of Germany's conservative elites that regarded themselves as the backbone of the state. Of a "government of national unity," as it officially called itself, nothing could be seen.

The reaction of the various political parties and their affiliated labor unions to the surprising appointment of Franz von Papen as chancellor was universally negative and ran the gamut from sharp polemics on the Left and unequivocal rejection by the Center and the bourgeois middle parties to indirect rejection by the DNVP, which immediately announced that it had not made any commitments to the new cabinet. The NSDAP, on the other hand, refrained from attacking the new chancellor directly because it did not want to jeopardize the dissolution of the Reichstag or the suspension of the ban against the SA. At the same time, however, it failed to comply with Schleicher's request for a written promise of toleration for the period after the elections. Nor did the cabinet appear to have much support from the various economic interest organizations, with the exception of those that represented different sectors of the German business community. Sustained by the power of the Reichswehr and the authority of the Reich president, the new cabinet was consistent with the political fantasies of those segments of Germany's conservative elite that had either succumbed to the myth of a "new front" as propagated by Hans Zehrer, Walther Schotte, and other neoconservative pundits or still adhered to an authoritarian conception of the state whose political premises had long since vanished. Since toleration by parliament was no longer to be expected, the new cabinet could function only as a presidential dictatorship in an open breach of the Weimar Constitution.

CHAPTER TWELVE

Government by the Threat of Coup d'État

O N 2 June 1932, the very day that Franz Papen took the oath of office, his cabinet decided to dissolve the Reichstag on the grounds that its composition no longer reflected the "will of the [German] people" as revealed in the most recent state elections. The new government thus fulfilled Schleicher's promise to Hitler, who had made his toleration of the cabinet contingent on new national elections and the suspension of the ban against the SA. It was consistent with the new cabinet's antiparliamentary attitude that Papen did not wait for the Reichstag to meet but published his government's own program on 4 June. The program stated that despite the Reich's precarious financial situation the chancellor would stay the course of the Brüning cabinet. At the same time, however, the program represented far more than the statement of a "transitional cabinet" insofar as it disparaged the work of all of its predecessors since the founding of the republic and made vague promises about the creation of a "New Germany." To Count Harry Keßler, the document represented a "poorly concocted extract of political reaction at its worst [*finstere Reaktion*], in comparison with which the government declarations of the imperial era are like rays of enlightenment." The declaration's tirades against Brüning, the spread of "Cultural Bolshevism," and the "moral deprivation [*Entsittlichung*] of the German people" under the influence of the "state socialism" of all the postwar cabinets and its invocation of the "immutable principles of the Christian world view" constituted an intolerable concoction of cultural ressentiment and socially reactionary interests.

The comprehensive emergency decree published ten days later made no secret of the government's pronounced antisocial bias or its favoritism toward the interests of large-scale agriculture and big business. Whereas the controversial agricultural resettlement program had been dropped following Hindenburg's veto, the emergency decree made far-reaching cuts in the area of social insurance and unemployment compensation. Particularly callous was the introduction of means testing for those applying for the dramatically sharply reduced unemployment insurance benefits. For all of the government's high-sounding declarations of adherence to the basic principles of Bismarck's social policy, this decree amounted to the end of social insurance as it had existed since the end of the nineteenth century. The program for job creation that was proclaimed at the same time was neither sufficiently comprehensive nor appropriate to compensate for the drastic reductions that had taken place in the social budget.

The government's program came under sharp attack from every conceivable direction. The Center Party stressed that the emergency decree lacked "any generous constructive element," an obvious allusion to Papen's cancellation of the program for the resettlement of small farmers upon which Stegerwald had placed such high hopes for combating urban unemployment. In point of fact, however, the decree only implemented budget cuts that the Brüning cabinet had already prepared, although these cuts went much deeper since in the meantime the budget deficit had grown considerably larger. The decree authorized further cuts in social benefits at the same time that it reduced the burden on large capitalist interests. It therefore triggered bitter protests within the socialist, Christian, and liberal labor movements. Particularly caustic was the comment of the Social Democratic organ *Vorwärts* that Papen and his cabinet apparently no longer felt the need "to take the overwhelming mass of the German people into consideration."

The cabinet's willingness to make the "down payment" that Schleicher had promised the NSDAP by lifting the ban against the SA signaled a clear break with Brüning's political course. This action provoked strong protests in several of the German states, and even the Reich minister of the interior expressed misgivings. But on 14 June 1932 the government promulgated a Decree to Combat Political Excesses in which it revoked the ban against the SA as well as the decree of 8 December 1931 that had prohibited the public display of uniforms and insignia. The state governments protested to little avail against these new regulations and proceeded to enact their own bans against uniforms, whereupon the Papen government issued a second decree that deprived them of the right to pass any regulations that exceeded the defense of the public order in individual cases. Heinrich Held, the Bavarian minister president, protested in vain against the arbitrary infringement upon the sovereignty of the individual German states. On the dubious grounds that the "important upcoming electoral decisions" made it necessary to restore "political freedoms" that had been curtailed by emergency decrees, the Papen government yielded to pressure from the NSDAP.

The retreat of government authority in the face of the Nazi challenge had immediate consequences. Along with the SA, all the other political self-defense organizations mobilized their forces for the upcoming election campaign. The wave of violence that accompanied the campaign surpassed anything that Germany had previously witnessed. Just in the final ten days before the election, 24 persons were killed and another 284 injured in Prussia alone as a consequence of political violence. The catalyst for the escalation in political violence was no doubt the SA. The mixture of hatred and impotence that the Communists and Social Democrats felt at this turn of events made them increasingly eager to strike back. The Reichsbanner, which normally maintained a nonmilitant posture, now became regularly involved in brawls and confrontations that were provoked either by the Communists or National Socialists. Even some of the bourgeois parties began to organize defense leagues of their own. The Bavarian People's Party, for example, founded the Bavarian Watch (Bayernwacht) to defend itself against increasingly frequent attacks by the SA. Uniforms and military rituals pervaded the political landscape and conveyed an impression of order that in point of fact no longer existed. The desperation that gripped unemployed youths found an outlet in militant civil war. When the KPD leadership attempted to curb the senseless and costly clashes with political enemies, it encountered strong resistance from activists at the grass roots of the party organization. By the same token, the use of violence had become an end in itself for the SA.

The escalation of violence usually began with an attempt to break up or disrupt campaign rallies of political rivals. In large cities, SA parades through working-class neighborhoods were often designed to provoke the Left to open battles in the streets. Organized workers defended their turf but usually avoided going on the offensive against the SA. The SA, by contrast, did not hesitate to operate from motor vehicles and to attack Social Democratic or Communist newspaper offices, party headquarters, union halls, workers' shelters, and even socialist youth camps. In small towns and the countryside where local police forces were weak, the SA conducted an uninhibited reign of terror that severely hampered the freedom of movement of its opponents on the Left. This was particularly true in the provinces of eastern Prussia. The National Socialist press celebrated the party's strike against the Communist movement and conveyed to its already biased readers the impression that these incidents had been provoked exclusively by its adversaries on the German Left. The NSDAP thus portrayed itself as the only reliable force that could maintain public order in the face of Communist terrorism and sought to substantiate this claim through the disciplined public behavior of the SA.

The increasingly violent confrontations between the self-defense leagues on the Left and Right provided the outlet for the release of potential social aggression that could no longer be contained within the existing political system. Starting with the Landvolk movement in the second half of the 1920s, the use of violence spread like wildfire to the Communist and National Socialist movements. Following the Prussian Landtag elections in the spring of 1932, the NSDAP exploited the militancy of the SA for the strategic purpose of making the position of the caretaker Prussian government untenable. After 16 June the party organized a series of militant demonstrations that began in the large urban areas of the Ruhr and spread from there to engulf the rest of the Prussian state. These, in turn, provoked counteractions by the KPD. It was not long before these incidents overwhelmed the capacities of the Prussian police. At the same time, National Socialist propaganda criticized Severing's police force for its insufficient energy in dealing with the Communist threat and held it responsible for "the descent into Marxist civil war." Unless the national government immediately declared a state of emergency in Prussia and outlawed the KPD, the NSDAP warned, it would be forced to resort to "decisive measures" of its own.

Accusations by the NSDAP and DNVP that the Prussian police force was working in collusion with the KPD only reinforced the antisocialist biases throughout the bourgeois camp. Even though the Reich minister of the interior and other cabinet members had access to classified information to the contrary, most of them continued to believe that an effective fight against the Communists was impossible as long as Braun and Severing remained in office. Having decided some time ago that the Prussian government must be destroyed, they now used the escalation of street violence as a pretext for achieving that goal and were all the more sensitive to charges in the Nazi press of timidity in dealing with the Prussian Social Democrats. In early July, Goebbels's newspaper *Der Angriff* began to call for the appointment of a Reich commissar "for the rebellious red Prussia." While the NSDAP had no hopes that one of its own functionaries might be chosen for this post, it nevertheless expected that military intervention against the sitting Prussian government would be extremely helpful to its own electoral prospects. The clashes between the NSDAP and KPD reached an initial climax on 17 July 1932, the so-called Bloody Sunday in the Hamburg suburb of Altona. The police had reluctantly granted permission for a march of at least 7,000 Nazi supporters. The demonstration, however, ran into armed resistance when the marchers reached the Communist working-class neighborhood of Altona. In an exchange of gunfire between the police and the Communists, eighteen persons were killed, most of whom were either local residents or innocent bystanders. In addition, there was a large number of people wounded or injured in the clash. In retrospect, there can be little doubt that the local police force failed to request reinforcements from Hamburg at the appropriate moment or that it failed to reroute the march into less volatile areas once the incidents had begun. The Antifascist Action (Antifaschistische Aktion) had demanded that the chief of police ban the demonstration and had threatened "self-help" (*Selbsthilfe*) in the event that its petition was denied. Out of the fear of being accused of favoritism, the police failed to respond to Communist pressure and thus contributed to the outbreak of violence.

While the Communist *Rote Fahne* accused the Prussian police of collusion with the "Hitler fascists," the *Völkischer Beobachter* portrayed the failure of the police in the most flagrant of terms and threatened indirect reprisals of its own. "Give us one week, and fifty thousand armed SS men will clean out Germany's headquarters for murder [*Deutschlands Mordzentrale*] without armored vehicles or a police bureaucracy. That will be the end of the civil war." With these words the NSDAP offered its services as a force for the maintenance of public order to the Papen cabinet. The NSDAP's unrelenting attacks against the Prussian government eventually had their effect. For although the Prussian government made virtually every effort possible to guarantee public security, it was powerless in the face of the systematic provocations by the NSDAP and desperate counterattacks by the KPD. As an added handicap, the Prussian police could no longer count upon the support of the courts. Police action against an SA unit that had provoked a disturbance at Dortmund's Schwanenwall in April 1932, for example, had led to dismissals and heavy fines for several police officers, although the SA men who had instigated the incident went scot-free.

On the day after the Bloody Sunday of Altona, the national cabinet promulgated an emergency decree prohibiting all outdoor rallies and marches. This did little, however, to curb political violence. Terrorist incidents continued unabated even after the Reichstag elections on 31 July. At this point, the national government had no choice but to reverse its position on political violence from the Right and to take stronger measures against it. An emergency decree to combat political terrorism promulgated on 9 August provided for the immediate establishment of special tribunals responsible for prosecuting political crimes and with the power to impose sentences that could not be appealed. The government also prohibited all public political rallies for the month of August. In doing so, it belatedly admitted that the actions the states had requested in June had been necessary. In the meantime, however, the wave of terror had served its purpose, namely, to provide a pretext for the removal of the Prussian government.

A murder case in the Upper Silesian village of Potempa that represented the climax of a systematic terrorist campaign by the SA throughout eastern Germany bore dramatic testimony to the decay of Germany's political culture. During the night of 9–10 August a group of five SA men attacked two Polish agricultural laborers who sympathized with the KPD. Both men were pulled out of their beds, and one of them was brutally murdered in the presence of his mother. When the special tribunal of the Beuthen law court condemned the murderers to death under the provisions of the emergency decree of 9 August, Goebbels unleashed a storm of protest in the National Socialist press in which publications from the right-wing DNVP joined. Hitler expressed his solidarity with the perpetrators in a telegram and did not hesitate to speak of a "monstrous miscarriage of justice." Despite widespread public outrage over the crime, the interim Prussian government commuted the death sentence to life in prison. As a pretext for its action, the government contended that the decree imposing more severe penalties for political crimes had taken effect only an hour and a half before the commission of the deed and that the defendants could therefore not be expected to be aware of it. The weakness of the national government in this matter was closely related to the review it had just conducted of its military preparedness in the event of an attempted coup by the NSDAP.

The Potempa affair was possible only against the background of the virtually neurotic anticommunism that had begun to spread rampantly throughout large sectors of the bourgeois public. The NSDAP both used and fueled this hysteria with its demand that the streets be opened for the fight against the Commune. Prominent Nazi politicians, including Hermann Göring, requested that the party be granted a temporary "right of self-defense" that would permit it to settle its score with the Left. In doing so, they intimated that in case of a KPD uprising they would be ready to fight side by side with the Reichswehr and whatever forces of order that might be left. The NSDAP's efforts to prepare the SA for this eventuality and to obtain access to the secret weapon deposits of the border patrols arose out of its expectation that after the Reichstag elections the NSDAP would settle its score with the Left once and for all. To the NSDAP activists, this meant nothing less than the takeover of political power.

In late July, Schleicher's chief of staff at the Ministry of Defense, Colonel Ferdinand von Bredow, called Hermann Göring and Ernst Röhm to his office and asked for an explanation of their efforts to secure weapons for the SA. Göring replied somewhat evasively that a violent coup mounted by Severing and the Iron Front was to be expected for the postelection period. In his opinion, the resources of the police were insufficient for suppressing such an uprising, whereas the deployment of the Reichswehr was no longer possible. The SA therefore had no choice but to prepare itself for armed conflict. Although this reasoning was largely spurious, Göring's candid statement shed light on the role in which many National Socialists saw themselves. Göring once again pleaded for a "right of self-defense" against the parties of the Left and suggested that the SA be given a few days to take its revenge. This was a veiled allusion to a possible Saint Bartholomew's Day massacre against the Left, an idea that Hitler too entertained.

Göring cynically remarked that Marxism had to be "wiped out completely," and that the SA had been "training" for some time to do precisely that. Comments like this were tantamount to an admission that the NSDAP would never be able to win the support of the socialist working class until it had ruthlessly destroyed its organizations and physically eliminated its leadership. Göring's conversation partners were aghast when he added: "However hard a time they might give us, and even if they try to starve us, we will not allow anybody to deny us right of revenge." The elemental need for the violent destruction of the political Left as the enemy with which the National Socialists had become obsessed was in part an irrational reaction to their frustration over the unshaken party loyalty of the socialist rank and file.

Despite unmistakable signs that the NSDAP was preparing to seize absolute power, Papen and Schleicher believed that they could persuade the National Socialists to cooperate with their government even after the elections had taken place. Baron von Gayl succinctly expressed the cabinet's tactical attitude toward the NSDAP when he said that "Adolf Hitler's young and constantly spreading movement" must be "freed of the fetters with which it has been shackled under Brüning and Severing and given support for its successful fight against international Communism." He could not have been more explicit about the cabinet's intention of using the NSDAP to silence the troublesome opposition of the extreme Left. The underlying assumption that appeared time and time again in Nazi propaganda was that once "Marxism" had been eliminated, the NSDAP would be willing to abide by the rules of the state.

When the Prussian Landtag convened on 24 May, the NSDAP and DNVP were unable to keep the caretaker government from exercising its functions. They did not, however, fail for the lack of effort. Shouting matches between the NSDAP and KPD erupted in the Landtag, and the Social Democrats were barely able to prevent a two-thirds majority necessary to secure passage of a Nazi and Communist motion demanding the dismissal of Berlin police chief Albert Grzesinski and other ranking police officers. The KPD had no qualms about resorting to obstruction against the SPD and concluding what amounted to a virtual alliance with the extreme Right. The pressure of the budget deficit had done much to exhaust the spirit of cooperation among the republican coalition partners. At this point, the increasingly antagonistic forces within the Prussian cabinet were held together only by the threat they faced of a Communist, Nazi, and DNVP majority. The Center Party's gradual turn to the right was already reflected in the compromises that had led to the election of the NSDAP's Hans Kerrl as president of the Prussian Landtag and the exclusion of the Social Democrats from the Landtag's presidium. With the death of Joseph Hess earlier that spring, the Prussian Center Party had lost its strongest advocate of an alliance with the Left. Only the Center's conflict with Papen — a conflict that Konrad Adenauer regarded as an utter dead end — afforded a measure of solidarity within the caretaker Braun government.

From the very outset, the triumvirate of Schleicher, Papen, and Gayl was determined to bring about the removal of the socialist-led government in Prussia. It continued Brüning's tactic of forcing the Prussian government into a public declaration of bankruptcy. It was symptomatic of the Reich's hostility toward the Prussian state that the Reich finance minister refused to authorize the transfer of 100 million marks that the national government owed to Prussia. Prussia, however, had a capable finance minister in Otto Klepper, who through a comprehensive administrative reform at the end of 1931 and the austerity decree of 8 June 1932 was able to thwart the national government's attempt to "cut off Prussia's water" (*Preußen aufs Trockene zu setzen*), as the former state secretary Hermann Pünder observed with a touch of malicious pleasure. There was something surreal about Prussia's efforts to resist the encroachment of the national government, because there was no longer an effective power behind the Prussian cabinet. Otto Braun was fully aware of this and refused to go on exercising the functions of the Prussian minister president, since he did not believe there was any way the Prussian government could prevent its dismissal by the national government.

The possibility of federal intervention in Prussia had been under discussion ever since the beginning of June 1932. Goebbels noted that the only alternative that still existed was between a National Socialist minister president and a Reich commissar. In the weeks that followed he revealed himself to be particularly well informed about the intentions of the Reich government. On 13 June he commented on a conversation that Hitler had had with Papen about the Prussian question: "Make up your mind. For us it's power or opposition." But since the Center Party refused to go along with Hitler's far-reaching demands, a reorganization of the Prussian government had to be postponed until after the next Reichstag elections. In the meantime, the right-wing press was united in its demands for the removal of the caretaker government and the appointment of a Reich commissar. This had been an essential component of the DNVP party program for some time and had been reaffirmed by Baron von Gayl at the annual meeting of the Society for the Eastern Marches (Ostmarkverein) in November 1931.

It was a troublesome sign of the erosion of the authority of the Prussian cabinet that the reliability of the civil service had become problematic and that Hirtsiefer and Severing could no longer count on the loyalty of high-ranking officials in the ministerial bureaucracies. Severing's earlier decisiveness and energy gave way to deep resignation. Like all his colleagues in the cabinet, he would have liked to see an end to the state of uncertainty in which the caretaker Prussian government found itself. Yet as the minister of the interior he was careful not to provide Papen with a pretext for intervening. Tough measures that Severing took against the illegal possession of weapons as a way of curbing the violence of the SA and the Antifascist Action and a decree permitting local authorities to ban demonstrations if their security forces were insufficient forced the national government to temporarily abandon its plans to accuse the Prussian government of passivity in dealing with the latent civil war that gripped Germany.

In intervening against the private armies of the Left and the Right, Severing was careful to treat both sides equally. The self-restraint that the police force was supposed to exhibit in its treatment of the SA and NSDAP found no sympathy whatsoever from the Berlin police chief Albert Grzesinski, whose Socialist party colleagues succeeded in dissuading him from openly attacking Severing's policies in the official party press only with the greatest of difficulty.

At the same time, Severing denied the Reichsbanner's request for authorization to deploy the defense units of the Iron Front as auxiliary police similar to the way in which those states with National Socialist governments were using the SA. By the same token, Severing maintained a surprisingly low profile at conferences of the state governments whenever the ban against the public display of party uniforms and insignia came up for discussion.

Severing had been expecting the takeover of Prussian police authority by the Reich for some time, even though the conditions that might justify this step according to the constitution did not, as *Vorwärts* carefully pointed out, yet exist. Severing was well aware of the fact that plans to this effect had already been drawn up by the Defense Ministry. As early as June 1932 he had addressed the possibility of a Reich commissar for Prussia in a conversation with the Reich minister of the interior, but Gayl refused to commit himself in response to Severing's comment that one should not wait too long before appointing a Reich commissar. Such a measure would no doubt help ease political tensions by shifting responsibility for the fight against political terrorism to the national government, which had previously obstructed the efforts of the Prussian government in this regard. Moreover, transferring control of the Prussian police to the national government would keep it from falling into the hands of the National Socialists. At the same time, federal intervention in Prussia would simplify the SPD's inevitable transformation into an opposition party once the upcoming Reichstag elections had taken place. Considerations of this sort help account for the equanimity with which the SPD faced the threat of federal intervention, which by now had become the object of a vigorous press controversy and countless public rumors.

Severing had originally thought that Papen would wait until after the upcoming Reichstag elections to move against the Prussian government. By early July, however, "every Tom, Dick, and Harry knew," as Grzesinski remarked, that the takeover was imminent. The Prussian government did not anticipate its formal dismissal but expected that it would be required to surrender certain police and judicial functions. Even then, enough about the details of Gayl's plans were beginning to trickle out to justify more serious fears. In light of the changed situation, Severing met with the SPD executive committee on 16 July and informed it that federal intervention could be expected to take place in the very near future and that Papen might very well go beyond the legal constraints of Article 48 and end the autonomy of the Prussian government. Pointing out that the police, though for the most part loyal to the republican government, could not hope to match the Reichswehr in either numbers or fighting ability, Severing made it clear that any attempt to resist would amount to little more than a brief demonstration. In point of fact, however, so few Reichswehr units were available for such an undertaking that the Prussian security forces quartered in barracks would have initially outnumbered the Reichswehr. On the other hand, there was no guarantee that those police chiefs who sympathized with the NSDAP would remain loyal to the Prussian government. Friedrich Stampfer, editor in chief of *Vorwärts*, rejected the idea of armed resistance with the argument that Severing did not have the right to be "brave" at the expense of his police officials. The SPD executive committee finally agreed to forgo any attempt at resistance and pledged that, "come what may, it would not abandon the principle of constitutionality." When two days later Severing considered having the completely isolated Social Democratic ministers resign from the cabinet, Otto Wels demurred with the argument that the party must not prematurely surrender any position of power. Prominent warnings in *Vorwärts* that the appointment of a Reich commissar would be unconstitutional, however, were not accompanied by the mobilization of the Berlin Social Democrats, in particular the Iron Front, in defense of the caretaker Prussian government. Such a step would no doubt have made a deep impression on the public mind and would have greatly increased the political risks that Papen would have had to face in intervening in Prussia.

For his own part, however, Papen was convinced before the fateful action on 20 July 1932 that the Social Democrats would not offer serious resistance. Nevertheless, the plans to depose the Prussian government presented the national government with the task of finding an appropriate constitutional pretext for taking such a step, particularly since the Prussian government had been careful not to do anything that might have been used to justify federal intervention. This, in turn, contributed to the fact that the final decision to intervene in Prussia was not taken until after the chancellor had returned from the reparations and disarmament negotiations in Lausanne. Whereas Papen was still vacillating, Gayl urged that action on the Prussian question could no longer be postponed. Petitions from the chairman of the DNVP Prussian Landtag delegation, Friedrich von Winterfeldt, and the president of the United Patriotic Associations, Rüdiger von der Goltz, were decisive in helping Gayl to prevail. On 11 July the Reich minister of the interior submitted plans for the proposed takeover of Prussia to the cabinet, which at first reacted with considerable reticence. State Secretary Meißner doubted that it would be possible to convict the Prussian government of the kind of dereliction of duty that would justify the assumption of dictatorial powers by the national government under Article 48 of the Weimar Constitution. Anticipating that Prussia might very well take legal action against the takeover before the Constitutional Court, Meißner suggested that the Prussian government be presented with an ultimatum on account of its lack of initiative with respect to the KPD, a suggestion that Schleicher dismissed as counterproductive. All participants were nevertheless in fundamental agreement that the removal of the Prussian government was absolutely essential. The differences in the cabinet pertained only to the question of how this was to be achieved in a way consistent with established legal norms.

The national government was inadvertently helped by a fatal blunder on the part of Wilhelm Abegg, the state secretary in the Prussian Ministry of the Interior and a member of the German State Party. In a conversation with two Communist members of the Reichstag, Ernst Torgler and Wilhelm Kasper, Abegg had urged them to help bring their party's terrorist campaign to an end so that it might join forces with the SPD in its struggle against National Socialism. Without Severing's knowledge, these overtures took place in the presence of senior government councillor (*Oberregierungsrat*) Rudolf Diels, who broke his vow of secrecy and informed representatives of the Ministry of the Interior of the conversation with the twist that it constituted an attempt on Abegg's part to win the support of the Communist deputies for a "merger of the SPD with the KPD." Gayl used this piece of deliberate misinformation to persuade the Reich president to sign a decree for the restoration of governmental authority in Prussia as well as a supplementary decree authorizing the declaration of a military state of emergency. In neither case, however, did the decree specify the date on which it was to take effect.

When Gayl called on Hindenburg at Neudeck, the date of the Reich's intervention in Prussia had not yet been decided. The action had been originally set for 18 July, but since no external pretext for intervention had materialized and since it was not yet clear who was to be appointed to the post of the Reich commissar of the interior, this target had to be dropped. Under these circumstances, it is indeed remarkable that Goebbels found out as early as 19 July that Franz Bracht, the lord mayor of Essen, had been chosen for this position. In the meantime, the events in Altona finally provided the national government with the pretext it needed to intervene in Prussia. Not only did the Prussian government's favorable treatment of the Communists — the "proof" of this allegation was the Abegg interview — in Altona constitute dereliction of its constitutional duty, but it was no longer in a position to guarantee public order and safety. In addition, the government cited a letter it had received on 19 July in which Landtag President Hans Kerrl reported a constitutional "emergency" in Prussia and requested that the national government temporarily assume the powers of the Prussian police force.

As part of Gayl's careful preparation, he had provided the commander of the Second Military District, General Gerd von Rundstedt, with orders to assume executive power in Berlin and Brandenburg on 19 July. In the meantime, Papen took steps to inform the south German governments of the action that was set to take place on the following day. The Prussian ministers Hirtsiefer, Severing, and Klepper were then invited to a meeting at the Reich Chancery for the morning of 20 July. At the same time, Gayl scheduled a meeting with a group of bankers for noon on 20 July in an attempt to avoid negative repercussions on the stock market by issuing reassuring statements from the government.

When the Prussian ministers arrived at the Reich Chancery on the morning of 20 July, Papen received them in the presence of the minister of the interior. The Prussians immediately realized that this was not the routine meeting they had been led to expect. The chancellor tersely read to them the text of the Presidential Decree for the Restoration of Public Order in the State of Prussia and informed them of the dismissal of Otto Braun from his post as Prussian minister president and Carl Severing from that of the Prussian Ministry of the Interior. He then informed them that Severing's responsibilities would be assumed by Reich Commissar Franz Bracht, while the chancellor would take over the minister presidency of Prussia as a specially appointed Reich commissar.

Hirtsiefer launched a formal protest against the measures of the national government, while Severing denounced them as a violation of the constitution and made it clear that he had no intention of abiding voluntarily by the orders of the Reich commissar. But Severing failed to follow up his statement that he would only yield to force with anything more dramatic than the gesture of leaving his office and retiring to his adjacent living quarters. The chancellor used Severing's pro forma act of resistance as the pretext for declaring a state of military emergency in Berlin and Brandenburg and for transferring executive power to Rundstedt. The significance of this step lay in the fact that it placed the Prussian security forces under military command and thus made it impossible for Grzesinski and his circle to undertake armed resistance. Early that afternoon Grzesinski, his lieutenant Bernhard Weiß, and the commander of the security police, Colonel Magnus Heimannsberg, were arrested, only to be released later that evening after they had resigned their posts. There was virtually no resistance from any side whatsoever. Still, the fact that after the putsch the security police received authorization to use armed force indicated that Rundstedt was well prepared for the possibility of protest actions from the Left. In the event of a general strike the national government would have immediately placed the entire Reich under martial law.

The Prussian ministers reacted to the events in the Reich Chancery by declaring the intervention of the national government unconstitutional and therefore null and void. They also pointed out that Papen did not have the right to invite them to a "meeting of the state government" that had been scheduled for that afternoon, since such a session must be presided over by a Prussian minister. The chancellor immediately used their legalistic protest to dismiss the entire Prussian cabinet on the grounds that it refused to cooperate with the Reich commissar. The responsibilities of the Prussian cabinet officers were thus transferred to the respective state secretaries, who registered no protest against this procedure. The fact that Gayl and Papen were perfectly content to leave the day-to-day administration of Prussian affairs in the hands of the state secretaries suggests that their primary objective was to gain control of the police and administrative apparatus. With the dismissal of the police chiefs as well as of four additional Social Democratic and left-liberal *Oberpräsidenten*, Bracht's systematic purge of the Prussian administration had begun. Within a few weeks, the painstaking efforts that Prussia had taken over the course of the previous decade and a half to "republicanize" its civil service were wiped out in favor of "a civil service appointed simply on the basis of its party affilia- tion [*Parteibuchbeamtentum*]" under the pretext of streamlining the adminis- tration. The purge was so thorough that Goebbels remarked virtually nothing had been left for the NSDAP to do.

In a radio address on the evening of 20 July, Papen sought to justify the action of the national government by citing the Prussian government's lack of inner resolve to take action against the "Communist terrorist groups" whom he held responsible for "the vast majority of the serious disturbances." With- out a doubt this positively grotesque reproach only showed just how far the triumvirate was prepared to go in order to conceal the illegality of its action in Prussia. Otto Braun, who had initially considered letting himself be arrested in his office only to realize how pathetic such a gesture would appear and stayed at home instead, indignantly rejected the chancellor's slanderous accusations in an open letter.

What rankled the Prussian prime minister most of all was the implication that he had been insufficiently loyal to the Reich. After all, Braun had fought for many years, often against his own party comrades, for close cooperation be- tween Prussia and the Reich, however great their differences might have been. With respect to the allegations of partisanship in the conduct of state affairs, Braun pointed out that "the incessant threats to 'make heads roll' and to inflict sundry other forms of death upon political opponents that prominent National Socialists, whom the Reich government now views as respectable negotiating partners, had been making with impunity for years have poisoned political life at least as much as the infamous Communist brutalities and murders." To be sure, Braun was right, but his response bore clearly defensive overtones. Braun no longer saw any possibility of fighting back and only hoped to free the Prussian government from the odium of illegal conduct.

Otto Braun and the Social Democratic ministers never contemplated violent resistance for as much as a single moment. This same was true of the SPD and ADGB, whose leaders decided on the same day that federal intervention oc- curred to concentrate their efforts on the current election campaign. The idea of responding to Papen's coup d'état with a general strike and actions by the Reichsbanner and Iron Front was quickly shunted aside. To be sure, some units of the Iron Front were eager to resist, while in Berlin the Academic Legion of the Reichsbanner (Akademischer Legion des Reichsbanners) and the plant workers of the Berlin Municipal Works (Berliner Stadtwerke) were prepared to strike back. But none of this revealed any systematic planning for actual resistance. At the same time, it suddenly became clear that defensive actions against the NSDAP could no longer be undertaken in conjunction with the Prussian police force or with the help of police weaponry.

Aside from the defensive and legalistic frame of mind in which the leading Social Democrats responded to the crisis in Prussia, party and trade-union leaders also realized that purely negative aims would not be sufficient to execute a general strike under the extremely difficult circumstances of mass unemployment. Nearly 44 percent of all union members were out of work, while another 24 percent had part-time work. More important still were the psychological factors that had led to a perceptible weakening of the ADGB and SPD executive committees. Otto Wels, for example, felt that he could act only in response to spontaneous mass protests, while the more activist elements within the party and labor unions waited in vain for a signal from above. Even the Reichsbanner leadership agreed with the official party line that the most important task was to ensure victory in the upcoming national elections. The idea of mobilizing the workers for the reinstatement of a caretaker government that stood not the slightest chance of regaining a democratic majority was, aside from preempting action by the Communists, quite illusory. Moreover, the Social Democrats lacked any revolutionary concept whatsoever. The commitment of the rank and file to the accepted line of defending the constitutional order, behind which the party and union leadership took refuge with the slogan "Save the elections," was equally unsatisfactory, particularly insofar as their opponents possessed the advantage of being able to parade their formal legality.

The tactical constellation that arose after the putsch in Prussia confirmed that the forces of democratic socialism had been outmaneuvered for some time. Organized resistance would have evoked precisely the response for which the Nazi party leadership had been hoping by making it possible for the NSDAP to exploit the confrontation between the state and the Left and to portray itself, as the NSDAP and SA tried to do time and time again over the course of the next several weeks, as Germany's salvation from Bolshevism. In Goebbels's comment of 21 July that "the Reds had missed their great opportunity" could be seen an undertone of regret that the NSDAP had not been directly involved in bringing about the fall of the Social Democrats and that the Papen cabinet had been temporarily strengthened by its role in resolving the crisis. Furthermore, the Social Democrats could not hope that active resistance against federal intervention would find much support from the south German states. To be sure, these states emphatically protested the form in which federal intervention in Prussia had taken place and denounced it as a precedent that threatened the principle of federalism. By no means, however, did this mean that they were prepared for an open break with the central government in favor of the Prussian republicans.

On the other hand, the hopes of the ousted Prussian cabinet officers that at least some of Papen's measures might be annulled by the State Constitutional Court (Staatsgerichtshof) were not altogether unrealistic, even if the court was unwilling to issue a temporary injunction against the central government. For his own part, Otto Braun viewed the court action, which from the Prussian side was prepared with extreme skill and expertise by Arnold Brecht, with great skepticism. The court issued its judgment 25 October 1932, that is, much too late for practical political purposes. Nevertheless, it exonerated the Prussian ministers, who had been treated with insulting condescension by the Reich commissar, of the charges of disloyalty to the Reich. It also upheld the federalist principle by denying Papen the right to have Prussia represented in the Reichsrat by members of the Reich commissariat. The decision, however, rested upon the fiction that a reasonable degree of cooperation between the caretaker Prussian government and the Reich commissariat was possible. This, of course, was out of the question. Papen rejected the compromise that Braun proposed on behalf of the formally reinstated cabinet with insulting nastiness and immediately expanded the scope of the federal intervention by abolishing the Prussian Ministry of Public Welfare and by implementing a presidential decree that curtailed the competence of the Prussian cabinet as of 11 November 1932. The Braun government was thus condemned to a "sham political existence," which ended only with its voluntary resignation in March 1933.

The decision of the Constitutional Court nevertheless represented a definite setback for Papen and Gayl in their efforts to reorganize the basic institutions of the German state. By upholding the principle that Germany was a federation of states, the decision prevented the formal absorption of Prussia into the Reich and unequivocally established that the implementation of reform of Germany's federal structure by means of Article 48 was unconstitutional. The fact that the Constitutional Court had examined the legality of the measures the Reich president had taken on the basis of his constitutional emergency powers only strengthened Hindenburg in his resolve to act within the bounds of the constitution itself. In the final analysis, therefore, the decision blocked the presidential cabinet's road to an open coup d'état and prevented it from using the Reichsrat as a constitutional surrogate for the Reichstag. In stormy negotiations with representatives of the south German states, the chancellor and the minister of the interior denied that they had intended to use federal intervention in Prussia as a model for implementing federal reform throughout the Reich. Gayl clearly sounded on the defensive when he referred to the "temporary need to concentrate the powers of the Reich and Prussia in a single entity." In point of fact, however, the real reason behind the Reich's intervention in Prussia was the long-standing desire on the part of the political Right to exclude the political Left from any role whatsoever in the conduct of state affairs.

To be sure, the national government did its best to avoid such an impression. The Reich commissar for the interior stated that before the elections the government would not undertake any action against the KPD in order not to violate its parliamentary rights. The occupation of Karl Liebknecht House, which had provoked furious protests from the KPD, was rescinded on 26 July in the course of lifting the state of emergency. On the other hand, the Communist threat was held up time and time again to justify the conduct of a government that had played so obviously into the hands of the NSDAP and that had deprived the SPD of its last measure of political security. Papen proudly declared, though from his perspective somewhat prematurely, that order had been restored in Germany and that the threat of communism had been banished. He emphatically objected to equating the extremism of the Left with that of the Right. Communism and National Socialism, he declared, had nothing in common. The former was "a threat to our national and social life," whereas the latter "seeks to bring about a national regeneration."

In reality, the intervention of the national government in Prussia was an example of class conflict from above conducted by administrative means and rested upon the indirect but extremely effective cooperation between, on the one hand, the deeply conservative presidential entourage and Reichswehr and, on the other, the NSDAP, SA, and SS. The driving forces behind the presidential dictatorship harbored the illusion that the elimination of the Left would placate the NSDAP without having to pay a heavy price for its cooperation. During the phase of authoritarian right-wing government, Schleicher declared, the NSDAP would either fall apart or "be brought to reason through the assumption of governmental responsibility." Yet by revoking the ban against the SA and by liquidating the republican Prussian police apparatus, the triumvirate of Schleicher, Papen, and Gayl had created a situation in which the only force in a position to bloc the NSDAP in its quest for power was the army.

Schleicher addressed the nation by radio to quell rumors of an impending military dictatorship. Such a government, he argued, would float in a vacuum and have no staying power. For his own part, Schleicher claimed to be favoring a government that rested on broad popular support. Given the current state of affairs, that could only mean the inclusion of the NSDAP in the governing coalition. The SPD, on the other hand, was simply ignored. In the course of his remarks, however, the defense minister conveniently failed to address the dilemma that, on account of its supposed nonpartisanship, the government was not in a position to issue unequivocal campaign endorsements. In their election appeal, the Reich president and cabinet had expressed the expectation that every German would do his or her duty to vote so that the Reichstag would be in a position "to work hand in hand with a strong government in fulfilling its constitutional obligations." In "the crisis of the times" there could be no alternative to a "government that truly stood above the parties" and that now occupied the place previously commanded by cabinets that were bound by commitments to the different political parties.

The claim to nonpartisanship was designed to gloss over the fact that except for the DNVP the government had no parliamentary support whatsoever. All the other bourgeois parties vigorously attacked Papen, with only the DVP exercising any restraint at all. At the same time, the south German states criticized the national government in unusually strong terms. In a campaign speech in Cologne, Bavarian Minister President Heinrich Held stressed the reactionary and markedly antifederalist orientation of the cabinet. Papen's reassurances to the non-Prussian states that the measures taken against Prussia had been temporary and exceptional were insufficient to quell their fear that federal infringement on Prussian sovereignty might be permanent. Their fears were reinforced by the fact that the Reich commissar for Prussia used the pretext of austerity to justify a comprehensive administrative reform replete with drastic personnel changes.

Papen had hoped that he would be able to bring spectacular results home from Lausanne. As it turned out, however, Papen had given in to pressure from France in the reparations question and agreed to a final payment of 3 billion gold marks. While this was certainly defensible on the merits of the case itself, to German public opinion, which had been whipped up for years by nationalist propaganda, Papen's rather inept diplomatic style appeared to have resulted in an outright defeat, particularly since the German delegation had been obliged to drop its demands in the armaments question and for the elimination of the war-guilt clause. Moreover, the Lausanne Agreement signed on 9 July would become effective only upon its ratification by the parties to the treaty. In a protocol that was originally kept secret, the Western powers made their ratification contingent upon the approval of the United States and, should this fail to materialize, entertained the possibility of returning to the provisions of the Young Plan. Yet in spite of all of these setbacks, the Lausanne Conference did bring about the long-awaited final settlement of the reparations question. But, as Papen himself admitted rather sheepishly to his cabinet, it had not brought about the relaxation of domestic political tensions.

For all of this, the chancellor faced the upcoming Reichstag elections of 31 July with astonishing equanimity. In this respect, Papen and his advisors seem to have become too deeply mesmerized by Carl Schmitt's argument that the popularly elected Reich president had the right to govern independently of the political composition of the Reichstag and that the parties in the Reichstag had no alternative but to accept this fact. With almost incredible naiveté, Papen entertained the illusion that he could achieve a political accommodation with Hitler, with whom he did not seem to have any objective differences. In the meantime, the fiction that the NSDAP was not a party but a movement that embraced the entire nation nurtured in Papen the illusion that Hindenburg and Hitler could work together as "ruler" and "leader" respectively. Walther Schotte, the ideologue of the "New State," seized upon these abstruse ideas of the chancellor and linked them to the bizarre idea that National Socialism "could only degenerate into a political party through the unnatural constraints of our electoral system within the framework of a party-run parliamentary democracy." Similar ideas were to be found in the writings of Hans Zehrer. The notion that the NSDAP would voluntarily dissolve itself after it had achieved the "national revolution" was not easily dispelled. As late as the spring of 1933, members of Hermann Göring's circle felt that the NSDAP was no longer necessary and that it should be transformed into a secular order for training the next generation of leaders.

The NSDAP did its best to escape the chancellor's embrace and responded with a torrent of demagogic attacks against the "obsolete Weimar System," in which Papen, his strenuous protests notwithstanding, was deliberately included. In the few short weeks of the election campaign, the NSDAP effectively dominated the presentation and substance of the debate. In this respect, it completely overshadowed its former partners in the Harzburg Front. Like the NSDAP, the DNVP promised a complete break with the mismanagement of the republic, for which it held the "Marxist parties" responsible. To the republican colors—the "symbols of a dying system"—it opposed the "liberation colors black-white-red." This, along with the call for a "national breakthrough" and the repudiation of the "dictated peace" of Versailles or the appeal to *völkisch* ressentiment, was no more than a pale imitation of National Socialist propaganda. The DNVP's efforts to distinguish itself from the NSDAP, on the other hand, were by and large unconvincing. Portraying itself as the only genuine conservative movement and as a necessary counterweight to the NSDAP with slogans such as "Only nationalism can save us, socialism deflects us from the goal," the DNVP tried to depict the NSDAP as a party that was deeply infected by socialist ideas. Claiming that it had a monopoly on political expertise, the DNVP insisted that it was indispensable, particularly in the area of economic policy. Even the DNVP's Pan-German wing, to the extent that it had not already defected to the NSDAP, nurtured the illusion that a government under National Socialist leadership could not possibly succeed without the economic acumen of the DNVP.

In the meantime, the rapidly collapsing bourgeois middle parties—the DVP, German State Party, Conservative People's Party, Business Party, People's National Reich Association, and Christian-Social People's Service—found it impossible to agree on a common agenda for the upcoming campaign. Despite the efforts of Paul Reusch and other representatives of west German heavy industry, the movement for bourgeois unity had definitively foundered, particularly since under the influence of DVP party chairman Eduard Dingeldey the People's Party had drifted to the right and had entered into an electoral alliance with the DNVP. The bourgeois-liberal camp was now reduced to the German State Party, which waged an uncompromising campaign against Papen and the NSDAP. However, the State Party's qualified defense of parliamentary democracy had lost much of its appeal, as its catastrophic defeat in the recent Prussian Landtag elections clearly revealed. As a result, only the SPD and KPD on the one hand and the Center and Bavarian People's Party on the other were left to face the imminent onslaught of the NSDAP. Even then, there was no possibility of cooperation between the SPD and KPD, since under the leadership of Ernst Thälmann and as a result of the shortsighted policy of the Comintern the latter had failed to anticipate the consequences of a National Socialist takeover and continued to view the "social fascism" of the SPD as the greatest danger.

The Center Party, which clearly dissociated itself from the SPD, conducted its campaign against the "apostate" Papen under the slogan "Back to Brüning." Rejecting all dictatorial schemes, the Center called for a "reformed democracy" and invoked the aura of the leadership cult for Heinrich Brüning, whose "triumphant march" through Germany proved a highly effective campaign strategy. For the first time, the Center Party made a major effort to appeal to Protestant as well as to Catholic Christians. Yet Brüning failed to draw a clear line separating his party from the NSDAP, however vigorously the Center might have protested the terrorist campaign methods of the Nazi Party. Nor did Brüning find it in himself to reveal the extent to which Hindenburg had capitulated to the antiparliamentary Right in the spring of 1932. This, in turn, only helped sustain the widespread illusion within bourgeois circles that the field marshal still possessed the will and stamina to hold the brown flood in check.

In the final weeks of the campaign, National Socialist propaganda achieved an unprecedented degree of technical perfection. Hitler's "freedom flight" over Germany, the holding of numerous mass rallies, the use of propaganda films and records—all orchestrated to great perfection by Joseph Goebbels, the Nazi propaganda director—eclipsed by far the campaign efforts of the other political parties. With remarkable skill, Goebbels sought to camouflage the weak point of the National Socialist strategy, namely, the fact that the NSDAP had refused to participate in the "government of national concentration" that had been responsible for lifting the ban against the SA and with whose opposition to Marxism and the restoration of parliamentary democracy it fully agreed. Hitler's repeated declarations that he was not fighting for "Reichstag mandates and ministerial portfolios" but for "the internal reorganization of our national life" were in fact a defensive ploy. For many right-wing voters failed to understand why he had challenged Papen in the first place.

In the new campaign format, party platforms were much less important than bold and simple polemics. The republican parties sought to imitate the methods of National Socialist propaganda. Demonstrations, marches, uniformed paramilitary units, and flags and symbols were the mainstays of the campaign. Continuing economic hardship translated into increased political mobilization that now began to embrace elements of the population that had previously remained aloof from partisan political activity. By the same token, the appeals the parties used during the campaign reflected a fundamental change in thrust and technique, no doubt as a result of the influence of newly developed techniques in advertising. Documentary films and radio advertisements became increasingly important. Traditional campaign meetings, at which a party sought to commit members and sympathizers to its goals in a rented hall, gave way to public open-air rallies, parades, and mass demonstrations. Military rituals added an aesthetic touch to the performances of parties and associations. The liberal emphasis on the role of rational discussion in the conduct of political affairs was swept away by the exchange of propaganda volleys and polemical stereotypes. The SPD, which had long adhered to the goal of educating rather than simply indoctrinating its members, reluctantly adapted to the new political style. This was particularly true in the case of the Iron Front, whose logo showing three arrows was a striking symbol of socialist assertiveness that gave the major demonstrations of the SPD a more distinctly combative character. The rallies of the Iron Front attracted as many adherents as the NSDAP's mass demonstrations. Yet there was something defensive in all of these attempts to counter the fascist propaganda of the NSDAP with methods that were essentially similar. Socialist propaganda, for instance, focused too much on the need for unity in the face of the Nazi challenge and failed to convey a vision of the social and political order for which the socialists were fighting. The emphasis in the campaigns of the republican parties on self-preservation found a counterpart in the rhetoric of the bourgeois middle parties, which focused exclusively on the need for order and clearly failed to distinguish themselves from other nationalist factions.

When the polling stations closed on the evening of 31 July 1932, one of the most vicious election campaigns of the Weimar years had come to an end. Earlier elections on the state level had already foreshadowed the changes that were to take place in the relative strength of the different parties. The clear loser was the liberal-conservative center, which received no more than a combined total of twenty-one seats and 4.8 percent of the popular vote. The Conservative People's Party vanished from the political landscape altogether. The Christian-Social People's Service saw its parliamentary strength reduced from fourteen to three seats in the Reichstag, the Christian-National Peasants and Farmers' Party from nineteen to three, the German People's Party from thirty to seven, the Business Party from twenty-three to two. The German State Party was reduced to four seats. The erosion of the bourgeois parties had reached devastating proportions. The DNVP, on the other hand, lost only four seats and returned to the Reichstag with a complement of thirty-seven deputies. Hugenberg, who in Bad Harzburg had posed as the true representative of the "national Germany," could at best aspire to the position of Hitler's junior partner. The Center Party and Bavarian People's Party were able to increase their share of the popular vote to 15.7 percent and sent a combined total of ninety-seven deputies to the Reichstag, no doubt as a result of their resolute opposition to Papen's political course.

For the Left, the election was a severe disappointment. The SPD's hopes that it might be able to profit from Papen's unpopularity went unfulfilled. It received only 21.6 percent of the popular vote and lost ten seats in the Reichstag. The party's extreme political isolation cost it whatever middle-class sympathizers it still had, while there was a sharp increase in the number of proletarian protest voters who cast their ballots for the KPD. The KPD won twelve new seats in the Reichstag and could improve upon its parliamentary position with 14.3 percent of the popular vote. The combined share of the popular vote for KPD and SPD, however, fell from 37.6 percent in 1930 to 36.2 percent in 1932. Although the parties of the Left remained relatively immune to National Socialist propaganda, it became increasingly apparent that their appeal to young voters was limited, and they attracted few voters outside the milieu of the industrial working class. Given the fact that the SPD had sustained a severe blow when it was forced to surrender Prussia without a fight, the loss of votes it suffered in the July 1932 Reichstag elections was actually quite modest.

Without a doubt the uncontested winner of the July 1932 Reichstag elections was the NSDAP. With 230 Reichstag mandates and 37.3 of all votes cast, the NSDAP achieved its best election result of all time and emerged as the strongest party in the Reichstag. The party's outward triumph, however, concealed an element of disappointment. For despite its unusually favorable starting position, the NSDAP was unable to achieve a significant increase in its share of votes vis-à-vis the second presidential election. Even more important, it was still far from the coveted absolute majority. A closer analysis of the election results indicated that it had been able to attract more votes from the upper middle classes and that it significantly strengthened its position in areas where it had been relatively weak. Yet in Nazi strongholds the defection of certain voter blocs and their replacement by new voters from different social backgrounds could be observed. Although the NSDAP's undeniable success at the polls concealed the relative instability of its potential voter pool, this fact did not escape the self-critical attention of Gregor Straßer and his associates in the party leadership. Goebbels too was aware that votes had been lost in the capital.

The depression in the inner circles of the NSDAP, which had operated during the campaign under immense pressure to succeed, stemmed from the fact that contrary to all expectations the party had not succeeded in attracting an appreciable number of voters from the SPD and Center. For in the final analysis, the Catholic and socialist camps remained remarkably stable. While the Center actually managed to improve on its performance in the 1930 Reichstag elections, the Social Democrats lost votes primarily to the KPD. In his campaign appeal of 22 June Hitler had proclaimed that a "decisive battle" was about to take place and that the power of the black and red parties would be broken once and for all. In his proclamation on the election results, by contrast, Hitler was somewhat more subdued and spoke of the need to "resume and continue the struggle with renewed vigor." Hitler's immediate entourage, on the other hand, attributed the NSDAP's failure to improve on Hitler's performance in the second round of the presidential elections to the government's decision to postpone the elections until the last possible moment. In point of fact, however, this had no bearing on the NSDAP's inability to score a substantial breakthrough into either the Catholic or proletarian milieu. Under these circumstances, it became clear that the party had to abandon its dream of somehow destroying the existing political system through a surprise attack at the polls. Within the party, those who regarded participation in the electoral process a betrayal of the NSDAP's revolutionary principle were gaining strength. On the day after the election, Goebbels noted that the time for opposition was at an end and that the NSDAP would have to come to power "in one way or another."

Although the outcome of the Reichstag elections was nothing less than catastrophic for Papen, by no means did it prompt him to step down as chancellor. On the contrary, Papen concluded that it was still necessary to continue the nonpartisan presidential cabinet, without, however, precluding the possibility that members of the NSDAP might participate in his government. Papen's thick-skinned behavior was extremely irritating to the Nazi party leadership, which tried to put the government under pressure by indirectly encouraging the SA to undertake terrorist attacks against its political adversaries. In the period after the elections the National Socialist wave of terror assumed frightening proportions. By such a campaign the NSDAP wanted to make clear that the only way in which law and order could be restored was through Hitler's appointment as chancellor.

At the same time the NSDAP quietly established contacts with the Defense Ministry. In the course of these contacts, the spokesmen for the NSDAP informed Schleicher, who had been spared the full brunt of Nazi polemics and who still enjoyed the confidence of the Nazi party leadership by virtue of his role in the discussions of the previous May, of Hitler's intention to take over the chancellorship. In the same context, Schleicher's Nazi informant also let it be known that Göring and Straßer were doing their best to dissuade Hitler from seeking the chancellorship. In any event, Schleicher responded to this overture and agreed to meet Hitler as early as 5 August without first consulting Papen.

Hitler came to the meeting with far-reaching demands. Aside from the fact that he sought the chancellorship for himself, the Nazi party leader also demanded the Ministry of the Interior in the Reich and Prussia for Wilhelm Frick, the Reich Labor Ministry for Straßer, the Aviation Ministry for Göring, and the Ministry of Public Education for Goebbels. Schleicher first tried to convince Hitler that his appointment as chancellor was not likely, then let himself be impressed by the novel argument that the NSDAP's leadership principle permitted practical work in the cabinet only under his stewardship. Schleicher realized that Hitler was not prepared to back down from his demand for the chancellorship. With a deep sigh Schleicher commented to one of his confidants: "So now I have to get the old man to go along with a Hitler chancellorship." With the Reich president, who in this matter concurred with Papen, Schleicher encountered clear rejection. With good reason Hindenburg declared that a Hitler chancellorship was incompatible with the principle of the presidential cabinet to which he was determined to adhere.

It is impossible to determine whether Schleicher had simply made a premature overture to the Nazi party leader or whether, what is more likely, Hitler happened to overhear the general's indiscretion. In any event, Hitler harbored completely unrealistic expectations that bore little relation to the situation in which he actually found himself. On 7 August Goebbels jotted down the complete list of all cabinet appointees, including the bourgeois ministers. He fancied the NSDAP to be standing "at the gates of power." Under the influence of the unbelievable expectations that existed at the upper echelons of the Nazi party leadership, Goebbels began to rave about his party's "historical mission" and asked the party's second tier of leaders, whom Hitler had invited to the Obersalzburg and then summoned to Prien, to prepare comprehensive plans for future personnel appointments. The NSDAP's district leaders were assigned the task of identifying qualified candidates in the party apparatus for positions in the civil bureaucracy. These persons would retain their posts in the party organization in order to demonstrate the "fundamental identity of party and state." At the same time, Goebbels also instructed the SA to make preparations for the assumption of power.

The maximal program that Hitler outlined at this point in time provided not only for Nazi control of the chancellorship in the Reich and the minister presidency in Prussia but also for the passage of an enabling act that would be forced through the Reichstag by the threat of dissolution. This, however, presupposed the transfer of presidential emergency powers to Hitler. While

Goebbels did his best to encourage these ideas, not only Gregor Straßer but also Göring, Frick, and the majority of the Reichstag deputies, whom Hitler had formally sworn to loyalty to his person, were generally skeptical about these goals and the way in which Hitler proposed to achieve them. For the most part, they tended to support the tactic recommended by Straßer, who felt that the party should first be satisfied with participating in a coalition government before attempting a frontal conquest of power. But to accept Schleicher's offer of the vice-chancellorship in addition to several other ministries would have been tantamount to abandoning Hitler's entry into the cabinet. Straßer, who anticipated the negative consequences of another dissolution of the Reichstag, felt that under these conditions negotiations with Papen stood no chance of success.

In point of fact, the attempt to isolate Papen politically and to make him totally dependent upon the support of the Defense Ministry proved a total failure. This strategy led directly to the debacle of 13 August, which occurred primarily because Hitler had been misled by his contacts with Schleicher to underestimate the importance of the close ties that existed between Hindenburg and Papen. Typically, Hitler entertained the illusion that the mobilization of massive pressure, including pressure from the street, would undermine the position of the current chancellor. Nevertheless, the Nazi party leader did succeed in moving Schleicher to explore the possibility of a Hitler chancellorship in spite of the Reich president's negative attitude to such a development. In a meeting of the cabinet on 10 August, Schleicher had predicted that there would be a crisis as soon as the Reichstag convened, since with the exception of the DNVP all of the parties opposed the government. To be sure, he pointed out that the Reichswehr and police were firmly committed to the government. But if a coalition between the NSDAP and Center were to come about and if Hitler were to claim the chancellorship on the basis of this coalition, it would be impossible to avoid a presidential crisis. Schleicher was under no illusion that Hitler could be satisfied with the vice-chancellorship and therefore advocated that he be summoned to assume leadership of the cabinet itself. By the same token, Schleicher felt that Papen's proposal to placate the NSDAP by inviting a number of National Socialists to join his government was hopeless.

Schleicher sought to buttress his position with the argument that after having come to power the National Socialists would presumably "take care of their SA and SS units themselves." Underlying this statement was the assumption that the militancy of the National Socialists should be understood as a simple reaction to Communist terrorism and that once "Marxism" had been eliminated the units would become superfluous. With calculations like this, the general had become hostage to the widespread psychosis that regarded the destruction of the parties on the German Left as an indispensable necessity. On the one hand, Schleicher believed that a Hitler chancellorship had the advantage of bringing a movement out of its "unproductive opposition" and putting it to work. On the other hand, the defense minister feared that the failure to include Hitler in the government would further radicalize his followers and deprive the government of the "good elements" of this fundamentally "valuable movement."

In the cabinet Schleicher failed to secure approval for his ideas. Although Franz Gürtner sided with Schleicher and characterized his plan to include the National Socialists in the government without offering them the chancellorship as an ideal solution to the current political crisis, Papen brushed aside all misgivings with the statement that he would try to find a "middle road" between the continuation of the presidential cabinet and a Hitler chancellorship. Schleicher, however, remained convinced that in the long run a mutually agreeable arrangement with Hitler was the only way out of the current political impasse. He thus remained open to informal contacts with the NSDAP, whereas Papen blindly placed his faith in the Reich president. The two men, each in his own way, decided to await future developments.

By contrast, Gayl in his capacity as minister of the interior called for an unequivocal decision and resolute action. He remained opposed to the NSDAP's participation in the national cabinet on the grounds that this would destroy the principle of nonpartisanship that lay at the heart of the presidential regime. At the same time, Gayl emphatically warned against overestimating the NSDAP and pointed out that in terms of numbers alone it was no stronger than the organized workers' movement. In view of the fact that the government expected to suffer a defeat when the Reichstag was reconvened, Gayl made a strong appeal for a "militant cabinet" and a "revolution from above" that would nullify the existing constitution. In this respect, Gayl proposed that, following the dissolution of the newly elected Reichstag, the Reich president should declare a national state of emergency. Furthermore, the next round of elections scheduled to take place according to the provisions of the Weimar Constitution would be postponed, the Prussian police force would be placed under the authority of the Reich minister of the interior, and the SA, SS, and other paramilitary combat leagues would be disbanded. The plans for such a coup d'état began to take definitive shape as early as August 1932. The long-range constitutional goals that lay behind these plans were outlined in a speech that Gayl delivered on Constitution Day on 11 August 1932.

An open break with the constitution as proposed by the Reich minister of the interior was not consistent with either Papen's character or Schleicher's preference for dilatory solutions in spite of the fact that this was the only way in which the presidential regime could be permanently secured. For their own part, both Papen and Schleicher hoped to avert a presidential crisis by direct negotiations with Hitler. After his meeting with Schleicher, Hitler had asked in vain that the date for his meeting with the chancellor be moved ahead. It was typical of Hitler's inflated sense of himself that he arrived in Berlin a day after his meeting with Papen was supposed to have taken place. Moreover, Hitler fully expected to achieve all of his goals in these negotiations. Goebbels had strongly encouraged him in this attitude despite Straßer's warning not to pursue an "all or nothing" strategy.

Hitler was well aware of the fact that he was staking everything on a single card. As a result, he became increasingly nervous and unfocused. He tried to disguise his inner uneasiness by turning to propagandistic visions. In demanding that all of his subordinates demonstrate unconditional loyalty to his leadership of the party, he was committing himself to a single course of action. As always, he staked everything on one card and refused to consider possible alternatives. In view of Schleicher's encouragement, Hitler felt that the threat of a coalition with the Center — and all the attendant dangers this posed to his own party — was no longer necessary as an alternative to the political course upon which he had decided to embark. On 12 August the *Völkischer Beobachter* prematurely rejected the overtures of the Center Party to begin negotiations with the NSDAP on the possibility of a coalition in both the Reich and Prussia. The editorial characterized the Center's offer as an example of "horse trading" and a "last-ditch effort" to save its own political hide. By now, Hitler wanted all the power to himself.

The negotiations that Hitler, in the company of Göring and Röhm, conducted with Schleicher and especially with Papen on 13 August 1932 proved a profoundly sobering experience. Hitler rejected the chancellor's offer of the vice-chancellorship and several additional cabinet posts as unacceptable and proceeded to outline his own demands for achieving power. He subsequently criticized himself for having agreed to Papen's suggestion that the final decision should be made in an interview with the Reich president. When he was received by Hindenburg a few hours later, he realized that the president was unwilling to go beyond what Papen had already offered. At this point, Hitler still believed that he was in a position of strength and could set his own conditions. With reference to his preliminary discussion with the chancellor, Hitler rejected the invitation to join the government and invoked the greatness of his movement to demand "full control of the state" for himself. Hindenburg replied that "before God, his own conscience, and the fatherland" he could not justify entrusting the entire power of the government to a single party. Scarcely twenty minutes later Hitler found himself dismissed with the injunction to act as the loyal opposition and a warning that any acts of terror on the part of the SA would be severely punished. Speaking to Papen, Hitler vented his outrage over the way in which he had been treated by the Reich president by intimating that the further course of events would "inexorably lead to the solution proposed by himself or to the fall of the Reich president." The break between the Nazi party leader and the Reich president had thus become inevitable even before the Bureau of the Reich President issued a sharply worded statement that stressed Hitler's demand for total power and maintained that this power would be used "in a one-sided fashion" to promote the goals of his own party. The entire episode constituted an embarrassing loss of face for Hitler.

The National Socialist movement looked upon the outcome of Hitler's negotiations with Papen, Schleicher, and Hindenburg as an unmitigated setback. Goebbels noted that "a sense of hopelessness prevails among the party comrades" and that the SA "is in a state of despair." More than any other element of the party, the SA had been psychologically prepared for the National Socialists to assume power, and they became increasingly insistent that the conquest of power by parliamentary means had to be abandoned in favor of direct action. Many of the SA leaders pleaded for an immediate strike against what still remained of the existing political order. In an attempt to contain the unrest within the ranks of the SA, the organization was placed on furlough until the end of the month. At the same time, the party leadership experienced considerable difficulty in explaining to its rank-and-file membership just why it had rejected Papen's offer of participation in his cabinet out of hand. Hitler, whose own reaction to this turn of events was extremely harsh, seized upon the verdict in the Potempa murder case on 22 August to launch into a series of scurrilous attacks against the Papen cabinet. These were immediately misinterpreted as signs of an impending insurrection and prompted the government to intensify its plans for declaring a national state of emergency.

Hitler was deeply committed to the view that the inexorable growth of his movement would simply overwhelm all countervailing forces and that this required no more than remaining steadfast to the principles that had already proved themselves as correct. This became abundantly clear in his defiant interview with the *Rheinisch-Westfälische Zeitung* on 16 August. On this occasion he stressed that "a movement must, without regard for the momentary ups and downs of its leaders, steadfastly and unwaveringly pursue the goal it has set for itself," in this case, the conquest of total and unconditional power. Indirectly Hitler contradicted the recently released démenti denying the existence of dissension within the ranks of the party. For after 30 August there were increasing doubts within the party that Hitler's strategy would lead to success.

Gregor Straßer, who was only slightly less popular than Hitler, was convinced even at this relatively early juncture that Hitler's determination to avoid a coalition and to achieve power through the continual mobilization of the party rank and file was not compatible with the conditions that actually existed. This had become increasingly clear after the debacle of 13 August, for now there was little likelihood that the Reich president would ever agree to a Hitler chancellorship. Papen had successfully conveyed the impression that Hitler's personal ambitions made it impossible for him to subordinate his own interests to the great common cause and to cooperate with other political groups in the national cabinet under the mantle of Hindenburg's leadership. Hitler could hardly reveal the deeper motives for his reluctance to do so, namely, his conviction that the movement had to avoid assuming partial responsibility lest it forfeit its claim to being the only viable alternative to the existing political system.

The more pragmatic Nazi party leaders realized that despite its spectacular success in the most recent Reichstag elections the NSDAP's chances of gaining power were still quite slim. A critical analysis of the election results showed that the party had exhausted its voter potential and that the lack of visible achievements had led to an erosion of its support. The profound disillusionment that existed among the party's rank and file could be seen in a growing number of resignations from the party, reduced financial contributions, and mounting internal criticism of Hitler's political course. Under these circumstances, the party leadership concluded that the NSDAP must make every effort to prevent the dissolution of the Reichstag and subsequent new elections, since these would almost certainly result in a major defeat. At the same time, it seemed more important than ever for the party to move beyond purely destructive opposition and demonstrate its credibility by constructive political work.

The first reaction of the Nazi party leadership to the shock of 13 August was to repair its broken ties to General Schleicher. The NSDAP's chief economic advisor, Otto Wagener, suggested to Schleicher's chief of staff, Ferdinand von Bredow, that he set up a meeting between Papen, Schleicher, and Hitler. Hitler insisted that the initiative for such a meeting must come from the government. Schleicher, however, was not interested in such a meeting for the simple reason that he did not feel that renewed conversations would lead to a relaxation of political tensions. Still, the contacts with the defense minister were not completely broken off. Straßer used his connections to Max Habermann and Hans Bechly from the German National Union of Commercial Employees (Deutschnationaler Handlungsgehilfen-Verband or DHV) to reassure Schleicher of his willingness to cooperate. At the same time, Straßer intensified his contacts with Günter Gereke, president of the German Conference of Rural Municipalities (Deutscher Landgemeindetag). Gereke, who had left the DNVP in protest against Hugenberg's leadership of the party and had joined the Christian-National Peasants and Farmers' Party, had attracted considerable attention with his proposals for the creation of new jobs and was now engaged in organizing the various employee groups throughout the country into a united front in support of his ideas. Cooperation with the labor unions, including the white-collar and working-class wing of the NSDAP, seemed to offer a chance to overcome the gridlock of domestic politics and to find a constructive way out of the current crisis. The Defense Ministry followed these developments with rapt attention, while Straßer felt that the emergence of such a *Querfront* constituted an excellent point of departure for recasting society in the National Socialist mold.

With these initially secret initiatives, the long-smoldering conflict between Gregor Straßer and Adolf Hitler finally erupted into the open. Straßer was adamantly opposed to the terrorist activities of the SA that Hitler both tolerated and encouraged for the simple reason that they had begun to hurt the movement. In a speech before the Reichstag on 10 May 1932 Straßer had brought forth his own program for job creation, and in a radio address on "The National Socialist Idea of the State" on the eve of the July Reichstag elections as well as in subsequent public statements he had repudiated the party's purely destructive tactics and affirmed the NSDAP's willingness to cooperate with like-minded groups, particularly within the ranks of organized labor. It was Straßer's firm conviction that only by participating in a coalition government could the NSDAP escape the political isolation that in the long run would certainly destroy it. What had served the party so well in the campaigns between 1929 and 1932 now threatened not only to deprive it of any influence over the conduct of the nation's affairs but also to trigger the defection of elements of its own electoral base.

With ideas like these, the Reich organization leader of the NSDAP incurred not only the displeasure of Hitler but also the fierce criticism of Goebbels and his entourage. Accusations of disloyalty that were frequently leveled against Straßer were, however, completely unfounded. Straßer identified himself much too strongly with the National Socialist movement to abandon hope of being able to convince Hitler of the political necessity of participating in a coalition government and of consolidating the party's position by coming forward with sociopolitical initiatives of its own. Behind this divergence of views lay a fundamentally different understanding of politics. For whereas Straßer planned to use the party's newly won parliamentary strength for constructive purposes, Hitler and Goebbels continued to think of propagandistic mobilization as an end in itself and were totally focused on the idea of achieving unlimited power.

Another way out of the isolation in which the party currently found itself would have been to resume the negotiations with the Center Party that had been broken off before 13 August. The possibility of a coalition with the Center Party remained a controversial issue within the Nazi party leadership. Hitler, who in this respect was strongly supported by Goebbels, was at no point prepared to consider such a coalition seriously, although this did not prevent him from initiating negotiations in which he occasionally participated in person. By contrast, Gregor Straßer, Hermann Göring, and a considerable number of NSDAP district leaders (*Gauleiter*), as well as the majority of the NSDAP Prussian Landtag delegation, felt that an alliance with the Center would afford their party a serious chance of gaining major influence both in Prussia and the Reich. Within the Center and Bavarian People's Party, on the other hand, there was substantial resistance to the idea of a Hitler chancellorship. Once again, the exclusive claims that Hitler made regarding the leadership of the national cabinet had negative consequences for his party.

The Prussian Center Party decided to resume the negotiations for a coalition with the NSDAP that had been broken off in June and continued this effort until the late fall of 1932. The decision to do this was motivated by more than the understandable desire to seek revenge for the fall of Brüning. When Papen's ill-advised course of action seemed to exclude the Center Party from the promised movement of national consolidation, the trauma of the Bismarck era repeated itself. It was compounded by the fact that the severe personnel cuts that Franz Bracht, the Reich commissar in Prussia, had begun to make in the Prussian civil administration were bound to have an adverse effect on civil servants affiliated with the Center. The main concern of the Center Party's leadership, however, was the cabinet's efforts to abolish the parliamentary system altogether and to erect in its place a "total state" that, despite its affinity with certain elements of Catholic social doctrine and particularly with the corporatist idea, threatened to restore the dominance of Germany's Protestant elites, with at best a sprinkling of Catholics. A further concern was the clearly antifederalist character of Papen's domestic policy.

All segments of the Center Party were in essential agreement that Gayl's "power hungry total state" must be blocked by an "authoritative state" grounded in obedience to the law. In October 1932 the Center Party's national chairman Ludwig Kaas stated that the "contempt for the elected representatives of the people" exhibited by the government, which refused to appear before the various Reichstag committees in the aftermath of the no-confidence vote of 12 September, was "intolerable." The Center and BVP feared that a fate similar to that of the Popolari under Mussolini lay in store for them. In the face of the latent threat of a coup d'état from above, Brüning also stressed the Center's character as a *Verfassungspartei* committed to the preservation of the existing constitutional order. By this, however, Brüning did not envisage a return to the parliamentary system, even though a coalition between the Center, the BVP, and the NSDAP would have yielded clear parliamentary majorities in both the Reichstag and Prussian Landtag. Instead Brüning advocated the creation of an "authoritarian democracy," which was reminiscent of his earlier plans for constitutional reform and in many respects coincided with Gayl's own ideas. Under no circumstances, however, was the Center prepared to tolerate an open violation of the constitution. Brüning also felt that the cabinet's tendency to pressure the Reich president into declaring a state of constitutional emergency constituted an extremely dangerous precedent, particularly since the Center had had to threaten to bring a suit against the Reich president in the State Constitutional Court. Paradoxically this brought the Center Party into an alliance of sorts with the NSDAP, which after the debacle of 13 August relentlessly depicted itself as the defender of Prussia's republican constitution and demanded that the commissariat restore full sovereignty to the Prussian Landtag.

For tactical reasons as well, the Center struggled to find a way out of the political isolation into which Papen had forced it and that stood in stark contrast to its record of participation in every national government since the imperial era. It was an unfortunate misjudgment by the Center party leadership that it tried to counter this threat by exploring the possibilities of an alliance with the NSDAP. Yet even Brüning, his deep misgivings about such a step notwithstanding, eventually decided in favor of it, though not without demanding "certain safeguards" for the interests of the Center Party. During this period the former chancellor overcame the resignation into which his removal from office had plunged him. He now sought to compensate for the passivity with which the Center party chairman, Monsignor Ludwig Kaas, had reacted to the hectic pace of recent political developments. Although Kaas continued as chairman, Brüning was now regarded as the actual leader of the Center. A Hitler-Brüning combination, which in terms of numbers alone might have produced a viable governmental coalition, stood virtually no chance of realization, under the assumption, of course, that Brüning would have been party to such a solution in the first place. Even the Reich president resisted the idea of a coalition between the Center and NSDAP for the simple reason that it would have eliminated the need for a presidential cabinet. Papen too considered the proposed coalition — and not without a certain measure of justification — as an "unnatural and unstable alliance." There can be little doubt that as soon as it had gained power the NSDAP would have tried to push its coalition partners aside, particularly after the enabling legislation upon which it was working had been passed.

There was no shortage of voices within the Center warning against cooperation with the NSDAP, particularly since Hitler's reaction to the Potempa verdict had caused widespread dismay in Catholic circles. Fritz Gerlich and Ingbert Naab, the editors of the Der gerade Weg, criticized the confusion of the Catholic parties, which seemed determined to "drive out the devil with Beelzebub" and failed to take Hitler's "absolute will to evil" seriously. Kaas himself could be invoked as a witness against such an alliance. In January 1931 he had vetoed a transfer of governmental responsibility to the NSDAP with the remark that while this would bring to light that party's "abysmal ignorance," nothing would be left to salvage afterward. To be sure, Kaas's attitude had changed in many respects under the impact of Papen's threat of a coup d'état. He had, for example, come to believe that the only way to avert the collapse of the entire state system was to force the NSDAP into assuming a share of responsibility, if only to prevent the Center Party from being forced into permanent opposition and torn apart by internal dissension. The BVP's Fritz Schäffer also regarded Hitler's appointment as chancellor as a lesser evil, as did the normally farsighted Konrad Adenauer.

When the Reichstag convened on 30 August 1932, preliminary negotiations between the Center and NSDAP had ensured the smooth election of the Reichstag's executive committee. With the help of votes from the Center, Hermann Göring was elected. The total exclusion of the Social Democrats from positions of influence within the Reichstag could be seen in the fact that although they had the second-largest parliamentary delegation, they were not represented in either the executive committee or secretariat. The Center and NSDAP had also agreed beforehand to adjourn both the Reichstag and Prussian Landtag immediately after the opening session. On behalf of the Center, Thomas Esser joined Hermann Göring in urging the Reich president to receive the leaders of the major parties before making the final decision, since in the opinion of the majority the Reichstag was "functional."

Another alternative was a presidential cabinet headed by Schleicher and supported by the NSDAP, Center, and BVP that would be closely tied to Prussia through the personal union of key ministerial posts. Gregor Straßer, who enjoyed Brüning's high personal esteem, sympathized with such a combination since it offered the possibility of drawing the NSDAP out of its purely negative opposition and of blocking Papen's constant threat of a coup d'état from above. The initiative for such a government was to come from all segments of the labor movement. Preliminary negotiations for the formation of a Schleicher cabinet backed by a parliamentary majority continued throughout the short interval between 30 August and the presentation of the government's program on 12 September. On 10 September, however, Schleicher, who had been kept abreast of the negotiations among the parties by Straßer, broke his silence and let it be known that he was "unwilling to lend a hand in the adulteration [Verfälschung] of an independent presidential government by assuming the leadership of a cabinet formed in effect by the parties." On the previous day, Hindenburg had received the executive committee of the Reichstag, whereupon he indicated to the utter dismay of the Nazi party leadership that he had no intention of dismissing the Papen cabinet even in the event of a parliamentary vote of no confidence. Consultation with the party leaders had clearly served no useful purpose whatsoever.

Nevertheless, Göring tried to arrange a meeting of the Reich president with the party leaders immediately following the debate on the government program but before the vote on various motions of no confidence. The parties' hectic efforts to avoid the dissolution of the Reichstag were motivated by their desire not to be dismissed as soon as they had assembled, since they wished to use the Reichstag to showcase their political involvement. In the case of the NSDAP, an added factor—at least in the opinion of Straßer and Göring—was the need to avoid new elections at any cost. Hitler and Goebbels, to be sure, were of the opposite opinion. As early as 8 September, they had reactivated their mobilization campaign with an eye toward the prospect of a new election. The NSDAP Reichstag delegation, however, was inclined to reach an understanding with the Center out of concern that Papen might succeed in his determination to submit the government program to a full debate in parliament. Furthermore, it was common knowledge that unless the Reichstag went along with its immediate adjournment, Papen planned to dissolve it before it had had a chance to vote on the various no-confidence motions that had already been announced.

The Reichstag that Göring called into session on 12 September fully expected that the discussion of the government program would last for several days. There was considerable speculation that during this time Hindenburg might change his position. At the very beginning of the session, the Communist delegate Ernst Torgler unexpectedly submitted a motion to place the debate on the KPD's motion of no confidence in Papen and its motion for the repeal of the emergency decree that it had just promulgated at the top of the legislative agenda. The plenary assembly reacted to this unusual occurrence with confusion and indecisiveness, particularly since the veto that the DNVP had been expected to make in the Reichstag's Council of Elders (Ältestenrat) and that would have rendered the Communist motion superfluous failed to materialize. Completely surprised by the changed parliamentary constellation, the NSDAP delegation asked for a brief suspension of the proceedings so that it might reach an understanding with the Center. This provided the chancellor with an opportunity to send for the presidential order dissolving the Reichstag that he had planned to use on the following day. At this point, Hitler intervened personally and instructed the NSDAP delegation, against the original commitment to the Center Party, to vote for the Communist motion of no confidence. When the session resumed, Göring immediately proceeded to the vote on the Communist motion and repeatedly prevented Papen from speaking on the grounds that the vote was already under way. As a result, the chancellor was finally obliged to place the red folder containing the presidential order dissolving the Reichstag on Göring's desk.

Göring's sleight of hand was a concrete demonstration of just how the National Socialists planned to deal with existing institutions once they had come to power. For it was clear to everyone that the no-confidence vote was constitutionally invalid for the simple reason that the chancellor had been denied the right to speak. Yet the legal and political postmortems in the Reichstag's Supervisory Committee (Überwachungsausschuß) had to admit that Papen had made a fatal mistake in not attending the constituent session of 30 August, so that he had missed the opportunity of making it clear that the government was determined to prevent a vote on a no-confidence motion. The chancellor's cynical disregard for the representatives of the people was perfectly consistent with his view of the constitution. Perhaps the most interesting aspect of this episode was that Papen had been meeting with Hindenburg at

Neudeck at the precise moment that Göring called the Reichstag into session and that the chancellor had been challenged by a parliament that sought to force his resignation without giving him an opportunity to present his government's program. Both of these facts bore dramatic testimony to the extremely low level to which the parliamentary system had sunk, and not merely because of the obstructionist tactics of the parties on the extreme Left and Right.

Politically, the fact that it received the support of only 42 votes, most of which came from the DNVP, against 513 that opposed it amounted to a severe and irreparable loss of prestige for the Papen cabinet. A defeat of this magnitude was virtually unprecedented in German parliamentary history. On the other hand, the dissolution of the Reichstag afforded the government an opportunity to implement at least the initial stages of its political agenda. Economic and social policy was at the heart of this agenda. The number of unemployed continued to hover around 5.5 million, and widespread poverty contributed to political radicalization. If it was to survive politically, the government had to improve its performance in the area of economics. The preconditions for doing so were not all that unfavorable. For in the summer of 1932 there were signs of a weak economic recovery, among them a rise in the price of raw materials and an upward trend in the stock market. Moreover, the end of reparations had eliminated many of the psychological inhibitions that had prevented Brüning from implementing large-scale programs to stimulate the economy. And finally, the climate for political initiatives in the field of economic policy had greatly improved. The devastating effects of the deepening economic crisis had prompted both economists and entrepreneurs, who up to this time had adhered to deflationary theories, to be somewhat more open-minded about experiments to stimulate the economy and create jobs.

The Twelve-Month Program for Economic and Social Policy (Zwölf-Monats Programm zur Wirtschafts- und Sozialpolitik) that Papen announced at a meeting of the Westphalian Peasants' Union (Westfälischer Bauernverein) in Münster on 28 August 1932 was designed to fuel economic recovery over the course of the next twelve months through the creation of jobs and the introduction of tax incentives for private businesses. An emergency decree to facilitate economic recovery that was promulgated on 4 September was the first concrete indication that a new economic course had been adopted. This decree provided for tax credits to businesses in proportion to the taxes they had paid and allowed them to use these credits to pay taxes they would owe after 1934. In effect, this amounted to the creation of artificial credit, which, because of its piecemeal nature and certain technical modifications in the tax system, was of primary benefit to large enterprises. The original idea that tax credits should be linked to employment of new workers fell by the wayside in subsequent cabinet deliberations.

In a parallel action, the government submitted a relatively comprehensive package of measures designed to stimulate the creation of new jobs. Reservations about such programs went back to the Brüning era but were expressed in the present context by Reichsbank President Hans Luther until he was effectively shunted aside by the chancellor, who suggested that he submit his resignation. Nevertheless, the effect of all this was to make the cabinet initially reluctant to approve schemes for the creation of jobs. Consequently, a mere 135 million marks was appropriated for government contracts, with the stipulation that contracts be awarded primarily to small and middle-sized enterprises. At the same time, the government moved to set up a comprehensive program of road construction, agricultural improvements, and the construction and rehabilitation of public housing. Much of this was to be carried out by the Voluntary Labor Service (Freiwilliger Arbeitsdienst), which had undergone considerable expansion in June 1932 under Reich Commissar Friedrich Syrup. To finance the creation of new jobs, the cabinet did not, as originally assumed, propose a compulsory loan but decided to introduce special job-creation vouchers (*Arbeitsbeschaffungswechsel*) that were to be issued under the auspices of the German Society for Public Works (Deutsche Gesellschaft für öffentliche Arbeiten A.-G.). In addition, the government's program also provided for small-scale suburban and rural housing developments.

A novel but highly controversial feature of the plan was the attempt to create new jobs indirectly by giving bonuses for the employment of new workers that were to be paid in the form of tax credits. Subsidies for the creation of new jobs, however, tended to discriminate against those firms that employed primarily highly paid skilled workers and that did not resort to mass layoffs when orders became scarce. On the other hand, this program tended to favor those enterprises that had laid off large numbers of workers in response to the deepening economic crisis. As a result, the use of bonuses to stimulate the creation of new jobs upset the competitive balance to the disadvantage of artisan enterprises. Nevertheless, the fact that the system of job-creation bonuses was based upon the norm of the forty-hour workweek had a positive effect on hiring practices that was partially offset by a reduction in the workers' take-home pay.

Although the actual number of jobs created was relatively small, the program represented a step forward in the sense that it broke with the principle of governmental nonintervention in the German labor market. To be sure, publicly funded measures to stimulate economic recovery came too late to do much for the economy in 1932. Nevertheless, the government placed great hopes in this program, which would have had the full support of the German labor unions had it not been coupled with far-reaching efforts to undermine the system of collective bargaining. The government expected that the system of bonuses for new jobs by itself would yield 1.75 million jobs for the unemployed. This, however, would not occur before the end of 1933, since the legislation would need some time to yield the desired results. Steps to create jobs directly would have a more rapid effect.

Finance Minister Schwerin von Krosigk regarded the link between subsidies to business and the creation of new jobs an indispensable social dimension to the otherwise austere and highly controversial Papen program. Papen was wedded to the conviction that a stimulation of the economy was possible only in conjunction with rigorous cutbacks in social spending. The second part of the Emergency Decree of 4 September 1932 stated that "social institutions must be simplified and rendered cost-effective in order to provide relief for business and financial institutions." What this amounted to was an enabling act in the area of labor and social law that would have permitted the government to intervene in existing statutory relations by means of special legislative decrees. The Decree for the Increase and Preservation of Employment of 5 September violated existing wage agreements by giving employers who increased their work force the right to cut wages by 5 to 25 percent for the thirty-first to the fortieth hour of the workweek. Enterprises threatened with collapse were permitted to establish pay levels that were as much as 20 percent below those that had been established through collective bargaining.

As early as 1 July unemployment insurance benefits had been reduced by 23 percent, and major cuts were made in emergency assistance and welfare payments as a consequence of the emergency decree that had taken effect the previous month. At the same time, the government introduced a universal levy for aid to the unemployed on the incomes of all employed persons and recipients of retirement benefits. The resulting savings realized by the National Agency for Job Placement and Unemployment Insurance (Reichsanstalt für Arbeitsvermittlung and Arbeitslosenversicherung) could then be applied to funding public works projects and the voluntary work corps. As a result of these regulations, "invisible unemployment" — that is, the number of unemployed who no longer applied to public agencies for work or assistance — showed a dramatic increase over and above the estimated 2 million workers who had been placed in this category before the new regulations took effect.

The net effect of the Papen program was to make the workers bear the entire cost of unemployment. It therefore elicited strong opposition from the socialist and Christian labor unions as well as from the various white-collar employee unions. Proposed changes in the workers' right of collective bargaining in particular were viewed with considerable misgiving, even by some employers, insofar as the revised system would have favored those enterprises unconcerned about the social welfare of their work force. Under the Papen program employers who hired new workers had the right to lower the wages of all employees in direct proportion to their total wage expenditures. With this proviso the cabinet had met the demand of the National Federation of German Industry for greater elasticity in the collective bargaining progress and adopted suggestions of heavy industry that had been rejected as recently as the Brüning cabinet. Wages had already fallen to such low levels that in many enterprises the workers reacted to attempts to implement the authorized wage cuts with frequently spontaneous strikes. To be sure, Papen intended to bring this situation under control by issuing a general ban on strikes in November. In practice, however, employers rarely availed themselves of the authorization to break their wage contracts by hiring new workers because at the time the demand for manufactured goods was weak.

The National Federation of German Industry had exercised considerable reserve in the first days of the Papen cabinet in apparent fear that "exorbitant plans" for the creation of new jobs were imminent. Yet by early August, the RDI had reversed itself and was calling for the allocation of funds for the immediate creation of new jobs in a move that placed it on the same track with the Reich economics minister. The RDI was enthusiastic about the Papen plan, even though the creation of artificial credit through the introduction of tax coupons went far beyond what industry had previously considered acceptable. Industry's positive reaction stemmed in part from the fact that Papen had involved leading members of the RDI, including Gustav Krupp von Bohlen und Halbach, Carl Friedrich von Siemens, and Robert Bosch, in the formulation of his program. The attitude of these industrial leaders was the first sign of a reorientation in government economic policy that did not automatically preclude the possibility of more active state intervention in the economic process.

Friction arose, however, over Magnus von Braun's intention to impose quotas on the import of food, which, as the National Federation of German Industry pointed out to Hindenburg and Papen, would only increase the deficit in Germany's trade balance even further. In light of the pressure he felt from the German industrial establishment, Papen tended to treat agricultural interests, aside from the general area of bankruptcy protection, somewhat cavalierly. The reduction of mortgage rates and related measures that Braun had promised had all been derailed by opposition from the business sector. This proved to be a serious political liability for the Papen government, particularly since the National Rural League, which had supported Hitler in the presidential campaign, had drawn closer to the NSDAP. For the moment, however, the conflict implicit in Papen's policy between industry and agriculture over the "return" to economic autarchy was still in its initial stages.

Even those in the heavy industrial faction, who, like Paul Reusch, had manifested clear sympathies for the NSDAP as late as the spring of 1932 — Reusch had supported Hitler against Hindenburg in the presidential elections — revealed a feeling of growing solidarity with the Papen cabinet. Particularly among the leaders of the Rhenish-Westphalian industrial establishment was it possible to discern far-reaching agreement with Papen's political agenda. The formation of a cabinet in which political parties no longer played any part had long been a desideratum of the industrialists who belonged to the Ruhrlade. In August 1932, for example, Reusch declared that Germany would move forward only if "in the future the parties were eliminated from the formation of governments. The reform project before us is so enormous that for the foreseeable future we cannot consider letting the parties get their hands on the government in Prussia or the Reich." It was particularly revealing of the attitude of heavy industrialists from the west that the Langnam Association invited Minister of the Interior Gayl and Reich Commissar Bracht to speak at its annual convention on 23 November 1932. When these two were unable to attend, the association asked Carl Schmitt to report on the outlines of their proposed administrative and constitutional reform. The increasingly close ties that were developing between German industry and Papen, who had also been invited to the Langnam Association's convention, constituted a major setback for Hitler and his efforts to win the support of German big business.

Papen's program of economic reform was designed in large measure to justify the cabinet's attempt to bring about a fundamental change in the existing constitutional order. To be sure, the Reich president's unwavering adherence to the presidential regime that possessed no backing whatsoever in the newly elected Reichstag was defended on the grounds that the measures that were necessary to revitalize the economy must not be watered down by party compromises and political horse trading. Insiders, however, knew perfectly well that what was at stake was the permanent dismantling of the existing parliamentary system. Even then, the strong words with which the chancellor sought to fend off the Damocles sword of a Nazi-Center coalition concealed an element of uncertainty about the future strategy of the cabinet. Of the various cabinet officers, the minister of the interior had strongly advocated the immediate proclamation of a state of constitutional emergency even before Hindenburg's fateful meeting with Hitler on 13 August. In conjunction with the Bendlerstraße, technical and legislative steps for the takeover of the Prussian police force and the proscription of the NSDAP and the paramilitary combat leagues on the Left and the Right had already been taken. In the crucial meeting of the national cabinet on 30 August Gayl emphatically called for the preemptive dissolution of the Reichstag on the grounds that further procrastination would deprive the cabinet of whatever initiative it might still enjoy. But Papen lacked the decisiveness to carry out his minister's plan of action, with the result that he failed to take sufficient advantage of favorable opportunities that came his way, as in the case, for example, of Hitler's outburst on 13 August or his threat of a public uprising on the occasion of the Potempa verdict.

In agreement with Schleicher, Papen continued to hope that it might be possible to avoid a formal coup d'état by keeping his adversaries on the defensive and dismantling the constitution in installments. At the very least the chancellor wanted to wait until the Reichstag had convened. In this way the *ultima ratio* of a coup d'état was replaced by the constant presence of the threat of a coup, by which the chancellor sought to keep the oppositional forces within the German party system in line. Gayl went along with this policy with considerable reluctance and continued to plead for a reform of the constitution, which in his opinion could be achieved gradually through a reform of the electoral law. An increase in the voting age to twenty-four would have inflicted considerable damage on the NSDAP but was not politically feasible.

None of the cabinet members doubted the necessity of dissolving the Reichstag unless the Reichstag made such an expedient unnecessary by voluntarily adjourning and refraining from a vote of no confidence. The cabinet also rejected Gayl's more far-reaching suggestion that the dissolution of the Reichstag be followed by the declaration of a state of national emergency. At this point the cabinet could still count on the promise it had extracted from the Reich president three weeks earlier of support for a postponement of new elections beyond the period provided for in the constitution. The undated order dissolving the Reichstag was issued on the constitutionally dubious grounds that there was a danger that the Reichstag would repeal the emergency decree of 4 September (as if it did not already have the constitutional right to do so). A compromise between Papen and any conceivable Reichstag majority, therefore, was out of the question from the very outset.

As Gayl had foreseen, the chances of a speedy and comprehensive reorganization of the German state quickly deteriorated as the cabinet lost what little respect it still possessed in the general public in the wake of the catastrophic vote in the Reichstag on 12 September and its capitulation to the radical Right in the Potempa matter. Although it clearly met with Hindenburg's approval, Papen's decision to grant clemency to the condemned murderers was widely interpreted as a sign of weakness in the face of Hitler's threat to ignite a civil war. Hindenburg's audience with Göring, the new president of the Reichstag, and his subsequent interview with the NSDAP's Hans Kerrl had by and large erased the negative impression created by Hitler's recantation of the promise he had made in October 1930 to pursue the conquest of power by exclusively legal means. The dissolution of the Reichstag thus diverted political energies into the election campaign and forced the impending conflict between the NSDAP and the presidential cabinet temporarily into the background. The Reich president refused to deviate from the constitution under any circumstances other than clear and present danger to public order. As a result, no break with the existing constitution ever occurred. That Papen postponed new elections until the last possible date, 6 November 1932, was another sign that the presidential government had been severely weakened.

Papen had missed his opportunity to act. As a result of the no-confidence vote of 12 September and his own refusal to cooperate with the Reichstag, he found himself forced more and more on to the defensive. The Nazi-Center majority in the Prussian Landtag kept him under continual pressure to revoke the changes in the Landtag's rules of procedure that he himself had called unconstitutional at the time and to restore the legislative prerogatives of the Prussian Landtag. Like a chameleon, the Prussian NSDAP transformed itself into a defender of the democratic-parliamentary constitution and was supported by the Center, which reproached the chancellor for the carelessness with which he had discarded the principles of the rule of law. Under these circumstances, any constitutional initiative by the Papen cabinet was construed by the public as confirmation of the charges that had been leveled against the Reich president. A further consideration in the cabinet's decision to temporarily postpone its plans for a revision of the constitution was the suit that Prussia had introduced in the State Constitutional Court.

In spite of all this, the government continued to elaborate on its plans for constitutional reform in its official government declaration and public statements by various members of the cabinet. This was tantamount to a latent threat of a coup d'état without it ever being clear just what form this might take. For a time Gayl even considered a popular referendum to legitimate a constitutional reform that had been decreed by the government from above. There was also talk of convening a new national assembly. Schleicher, on the other hand, temporarily entertained the possibility of founding a presidential party, but quickly changed his mind. Efforts to unite the more moderate elements of the German bourgeoisie received new impetus in September 1932 with the founding of the German National Association (Deutscher Nationalverein) in a conscious attempt to evoke the memory of the bourgeois role in Germany's struggle for national unity. Although the new organization tried to support Schleicher's policies as chancellor in December 1932 with an appeal to "combat the collectivist-Bolshevist tide from both the Right and Left," these efforts developed independently of Schleicher's political calculations.

The government officially continued to adhere to the program of the "New State" that Walther Schotte, the former editor of the *Preußischer Jahrbücher* and a contributor to *Der Ring* published under the auspices of the German Lords' Club, popularized in a brochure that appeared during the campaign for the November 1932 Reichstag elections. The official government line propagated in this brochure that "in the eyes of the German nation the system of formal democracy is bankrupt" corresponded in large part to the sentiments of an increasingly large number of contemporary observers. Schotte held the emergence of a multiparty system responsible for the disastrous course of Germany's domestic political development and claimed that such a system had falsified the meaning of the constitution and had substituted the conflict of petty party interests for the formation of large ideological fronts. It seems paradoxical that the ideologues of the "New State" bestowed so much praise on precisely those

Weltanschauungsparteien whose behavior had contributed so decisively to the functional weakness of the Weimar parliamentary system.

In contrast to Papen's confused and poorly developed ideas, Gayl had formulated relatively concrete views as to how the constitution should be changed. He made reference to the increasing splintering of the various political parties to cast doubt upon the viability of the party system itself. Criticism of the plethora of parties was a popular contemporary argument that Hitler never failed to invoke in his own campaign speeches. In point of fact, the number of parties in the Reichstag that failed to elect the fifteen deputies that were necessary to qualify as an official delegation (*Fraktion*) never surpassed that of the 1912 Reichstag. Aside from the bourgeois parties whose parliamentary strength had fallen to fewer than twelve mandates, splinter parties held at most thirty seats. The high number of parties that submitted lists of candidates—in July 1932 forty-two parties contested the election—was of little significance for the formation of parliamentary majorities. It was not the multiplicity of parties as such but the polarization of the entire party spectrum that contributed to the functional collapse of Weimar parliamentarism. The introduction of a new electoral system based on single-member constituencies rather than proportional representation would have done little to change this state of affairs.

The reorganization of German political life as propagated by the ideologues of the "New State" was designed to make political parties as such superfluous without being altogether clear as to what sort of institutions might take their place. Gayl was primarily interested in bringing about a fundamental change in the electoral law and envisaged the creation of single-member constituencies that would restore close contact between the voters and their elected representatives and eliminate the mediating function of party bureaucracies, particularly if this were combined with a system of indirect elections. Gayl would also have liked to raise the voting age by five years and was supported in this respect by Papen, who thought this would help calm the situation at the German universities. Lastly, Gayl advocated that the heads of families and war veterans should be entitled to vote more than once without having examined the demographic implications of such a change. The central point of Gayl's new order, however, was the elevated position of the Reich president, who would appoint the chancellor along with the other members of the cabinet. The government would therefore no longer be responsible to the Reichstag, whose competencies would be limited to the budget and the oversight of executive authority.

The program of the "New State" went far beyond a return to the constitutional system. By reorganizing the Reichsrat as an upper house, the powers of the popularly elected lower house would be severely curtailed. For the upper house was to be composed of dignitaries whom the Reich president had appointed for life. Moreover, it was to have an absolute veto over the legislative decisions of the lower house. New laws would therefore require the approval of both houses. It was typical of the naiveté of this unabashedly reactionary concept of the constitution that in the event of a conflict between the president and the government the latter would have no right of appeal. In the area of social policy, the program's reactionary nature could be seen in the fact that, in sharp contrast to its dramatic growth since the period before the war, the state's share of the gross national product was to be radically cut by reducing the scope of the republic's social welfare system.

Several details of this vague and, in many respects, contradictory proposal for constitutional reform went back to proposals that the DNVP Reichstag deputy Baron Axel von Freytagh-Loringhoven had circulated in the 1920s. The flirtation with the idea of an upper house possibly organized along corporatist lines did not pay sufficient attention to the federalist structure of the German Reich. An upper house, as a skeptical Carl Schmitt argued in his speech before the Langnam Association, was hardly a panacea for dealing with the current constitutional crisis. Such an institution could come into existence only after the creation of a "strong state" and not vice versa. The creation of an upper house was also seen as a means to keep alive the possibility of a restoration of the monarchy, even though the advocates of the "New State" admitted that at the moment this was not on their agenda. Particularly striking in this respect was the undisguised social elitism of the reform program, which was focused entirely on securing the rule of a privileged upper class. Nevertheless, when Papen presented his government program on radio, he claimed that the ideas of the "New State" marked the "spiritual turning point of the liberal century" and was shaped by "experiences of history and the uniqueness of our homeland."

Surprisingly the restorational character of the cabinet's constitutional plans found the support of large segments of the German upper class. Several pre-eminent constitutional scholars, including Carl Schmitt, defended the government's proposals for a revision of the existing constitution as a legitimate way out of the crisis in which the state currently found itself. Schmitt's willingness to sacrifice the first section of the Weimar Constitution in order to establish the sovereignty of the Reich president worked in a similar direction. The chancellor, in the meantime, had deluded himself into believing that he possessed sufficient political clout to translate his proposed revision of the Weimar Constitution into practice. Privately he remarked that under no circumstances should one wait until economic recovery was visible, since at this point the willingness to accept a radical change in the existing constitutional structure would begin to recede. Within the various bourgeois parties, including even the State Party, a reorientation had taken place in favor of constitutional and corporatist forms. This, however, did not meant that Gayl's semiabsolutist constitutional program could have obtained the support of broad segments of the population.

At the outset, the constitutional plans of Papen and his cabinet had no practical significance except in connection with the medium-term solution to the Prussian problem. Gayl, however, regarded federal intervention in Prussia as an important component of the impending reform of Germany's federal structure. In his mind, the crucial element of his efforts to reorganize the German state lay in the personal union of the Prussian and national governments. In this respect, he was prepared to do away with a central parliament in addition to the Reichstag and replace it with a state council composed of representatives who were to be appointed by either the provinces or the Reich president. In light of strong concerns expressed by the other German states, Papen was repeatedly obliged to qualify his support for these plans either by asserting that he had no intention of encroaching upon the sovereignty of the Prussian state or by admitting that no more than two Prussian ministries would ever be united with their equivalents in the national cabinet, to which an additional four Prussian ministers would belong. In defending these arrangements, Papen insisted that the dualism between the Reich and Prussia must never again become a prominent feature of Germany's political structure. In this respect, however, the decision of the State Constitutional Court effectively blocked the absorption of Prussia into the Reich. Still, the presidential cabinet was not willing to permit a return to the basic forms of parliamentary government in Prussia, regardless of how the different majorities in the Landtag might have appeared.

A more flexible posture on the part of the Papen cabinet might have prevented it from becoming completely isolated at the start of the new election campaign in September 1932. With a courage born of desperation, Papen now began to attack the NSDAP without restraint. In this respect, he skillfully exploited the tactical dilemma in which the National Socialists found themselves by portraying them as opponents of the "national" government and as the defenders of socialist principles. He also denounced Hitler's reaction to the verdict in the Potempa case as a deliberate rejection of the rule of law and as a stab in the back to a government engaged in a desperate struggle to restore the nation's military sovereignty and its equal rights in the international community. For his part, Hitler called Papen a "chancellor without a people," ironically referred to his cabinet as one that existed "by the grace of God," and characterized the government's economic stimulus package as "the most botched and incompetent job" imaginable. The NSDAP's relentless attacks against the supposed representatives of the hated Weimar "system" were not, however, a sign of unimpaired self-confidence. On the contrary, the trauma of 13 August was reflected in the defensive tone that Hitler struck in the vast majority of his campaign speeches. Presenting himself as the representative of "young Germany," Hitler challenged the "elderly excellencies of 1914," not even sparing Hindenburg, "who like every old peasant would some day have to pass on his farm."

A peculiar feature of the tragedy of these months was the fact that Hitler had no serious rival who possessed the personal charisma that was absolutely necessary during a period of extreme political disorientation to galvanize protest voters on the Left and Right in support of constructive efforts to overcome the crisis in which the German nation found itself. For all intents and purposes, the election campaign was a contest between Hitler and Papen over the choice between a fascist and an authoritarian dictatorship. The DNVP, DVP, Center, and Bavarian People's Party were able to do little more than maintain their current position, while those who were genuinely committed to the defense of the republic were relegated to the role of bystanders. Tactically the NSDAP found itself at something of a disadvantage. The propaganda slogans on which it had previously relied—the struggle against Versailles and the "November criminals"—had lost much of their effectiveness as the forces of the bourgeois Right had consolidated their position over and against the increasingly powerless parties of the German Left. The NSDAP conducted its campaign primarily against the socially reactionary "cabinet of the barons," that is to say, against a government that in its foreign and military policy, its rejection of party politics and parliamentary government, and in its pursuit of a strong national state found itself in essential agreement with National Socialism and had, in fact, adopted many of its formulations.

The Nazi campaign stressed the latent hostility toward the German working class that informed the social policies of the Papen cabinet. In this way, the NSDAP sought to outstrip the agitation of the working-class parties, seeing them—and not the bourgeois camp—as its true adversary. Moreover, the only prospect the NSDAP had of increasing its share of the popular vote lay in capturing large numbers of Social Democratic and Communist voters. As a result, Nazi propaganda relied, albeit with marked regional differences, on quasi-socialist slogans of its own, although Hitler was careful to avoid frontal attacks against the capitalist economic system itself. At Hitler's request, Rudolf Heß issued a directive that the party's propaganda efforts should refrain from excessive emphasis on the shortcomings of the "cabinet of the barons" for fear that this might alienate potential bourgeois supporters.

The ambivalence that the NSDAP had always manifested in the area of economic policy and that had always been a source of such great concern to heavy industrial circles was only underscored by the spectacular entry of the National Socialist Factory Cell Organization (Nationalsozialistische Betriebzellensorganization or NSBO) in the strike committee that the KPD and Revolutionary Trade-Union Opposition (Revolutionäre Gewerkschaftsopposition or RGO) had formed in connection with the Berlin transit workers' strike. Despite the limited success of efforts by the socialist unions to mediate between the different parties, the situation deteriorated on 3 November into a mutiny that had been organized by the RGO to protest the most recent wage cuts and that virtually paralyzed Berlin's transportation system for several days. The strike had been called by the RGO in conjunction with the NSBO, in other words, by a minority of the organized workers but with the consent of 66 percent of the affected transportation workers. It was a typical weakness of the KPD's trade-union policy that it immediately tried to put a political twist on a strike that had been solely motivated by economic grievances and thus presented an image of revolutionary preparedness that simply did not exist.

Joseph Goebbels, the Nazi district leader in Berlin who had actively supported the NSBO since 1931 with his operation "Into the Factories" (*Hinein in die Betriebe*), knew full well that an alliance between the KPD and NSDAP in the Berlin transit workers' strike carried considerable risks. But the initiative of the socialist public service unions had forced the NSBO to clarify its stance after having come under attack for its cavalier betrayal of the German working class. In Berlin's working-class neighborhoods, the NSDAP's support for the striking workers protected it against a heavy loss of votes, although in upper- and middle-class circles the NSBO's role in the strike only fueled suspicions that radical socialist trends were beginning to gain the upper hand within the Nazi party. These fears gave the otherwise colorless campaign slogans of the DNVP much greater potency. At the same time, the entire episode clearly demonstrated the ultimately insoluble dilemma the NSDAP faced in trying to find a common political denominator upon which the different protest groups out of which the party recruited the bulk of its membership and electorate could agree.

Gregor Straßer had hoped to avoid the dissolution of the Reichstag because from his perspective the NSDAP was neither psychologically nor materially prepared for another election campaign. On the basis of recent local and regional elections, the Nazi party leadership anticipated that it would suffer heavy losses in new national elections. As a result, the official party press was prohibited from publishing polling data. In contrast to the situation that had existed the previous summer when the NSDAP had benefited from the aura of irresistible growth, a sense of disillusionment had begun to set in among the party's potential voters and sympathizers. The mood within the party was extremely somber, so that even Goebbels was hard put to exhibit his usual confidence in victory. Reports of resignations by disappointed party members poured in from all sides, and new recruits could no longer compensate for the declining membership trend. At the same time, both contributions and revenues from membership fees lagged significantly behind what the party had received in recent years. As a result, the deeply indebted party had trouble finding the funds to cover the printing costs of posters and leaflets, and there was no money for the highly successful mass rallies of the past. Under these circumstances, word-of-mouth propaganda had to replace the use of campaign leaflets. An immediate effect of the widespread campaign weariness was that the enthusiasm of the party membership for participating in the campaign effort was severely diminished. Many local chapters found out much to their dismay that they were no longer able to fill the meeting halls they had rented for the campaign.

The failure of 13 August also affected the inner cohesion of the Nazi Party. Rivalries within the party leadership assumed grotesque proportions. Within the SA in particular there was growing opposition to the party leadership's continued commitment to the pursuit of power by parliamentary means. Many SA units, which in the past had always shouldered the main burden of the campaign, now balked at maintaining order in the meeting halls and at participating in election rallies. On the other hand, more moderate NSDAP functionaries complained that the militant behavior of the SA and the revelations about Röhm's homosexual tendencies had inflicted profound damage upon the reputation and image of the party. Within the SA, which saw itself as the target of financial and other forms of discrimination vis-à-vis the party's political organization, disciplinary problems continued to mount and occasionally degenerated into outright violence. Straßer moved to contain the dissatisfaction of the party's more militant elements by tightening the NSDAP's party organization. Hitler, on the other hand, looked for a remedy in the total concentration of the party's energies on the propaganda campaign, which must, he said, be waged as if it were "a matter of life or death" from which the NSDAP would "emerge victorious." With an incredible capacity for autosuggestion, Hitler simply pushed Straßer's objections aside.

On 6 November 1932, the electorate's weariness with the unending series of elections was reflected in an abnormally low rate of voter participation. No doubt the perception that election results had little impact on the course of events also played a role in the low election turnout. For the NSDAP, however, this meant that it could no longer count on permanently attracting the large number of protest voters whose support it had won in the past. What had already been foreshadowed in recent regional elections now became a reality. The NSDAP went down to a devastating defeat. Aside from the low rate of voter participation, the major reasons for the NSDAP's poor performance at the polls was the return of sizable electoral blocs to the DNVP and, to a lesser extent, to the DVP. Rural votes in particular returned to the parties of the bourgeois Right, while the NSDAP hardly won any new voters at all from the ranks of the industrial working class. In losing 14.6 percent of the votes it had received in July 1932, the NSDAP saw its share of the popular vote fall from 37.3 to 33.1 percent. Its heaviest losses came in the predominantly Protestant agrarian regions of eastern Germany and in electoral districts with a particularly high degree of industrial development. These losses were offset in part by gains in areas where the NSDAP had not done well the previous July. For the DNVP, on the other hand, the decision to focus its strategy on the NSDAP had paid off. By the same token, the frequently undisciplined and rowdy public behavior of the SA had scared away many a sympathizer.

The second largest loser in the November election was the SPD, which saw its share of the popular vote fall from 21.6 to 20.4 percent and whose losses, especially in its industrial strongholds, benefited the KPD. The Communists, by contrast, increased their share of the popular vote by 2.6 percent and now sent 100 deputies to the Reichstag. Moreover, the KPD did remarkably well in primarily rural regions where previously it had virtually no support at all. These results only underscored the fact that the proletarian camp had remained relatively stable in spite of all the voter shifts between the SPD and the KPD. The Center Party, on the other hand, barely managed to hold its own. Together with the Bavarian People's Party, it now commanded seventy seats in the Reichstag. The election results also revealed a dramatic recovery on the part of the DNVP, which received fifty-one parliamentary mandates, and the DVP, which increased its parliamentary strength to eleven seats. The combined total of the bourgeois-conservative voting bloc, however, still did not amount to more than 74 out of 584 seats. By comparison, the KPD and NSDAP could muster a majority of 296 parliamentary votes that would be sufficient to block any legislation to which the two parties were opposed. A parliamentary majority was not possible either on the basis of the great coalition or in the form of an alliance between the NSDAP, Center Party, and Bavarian People's Party. The only possible majority that could have been formed would have required the participation of the NSDAP, DNVP, Center Party, and BVP, but Hugenberg and Papen refused to have anything to do with such a configuration.

Strangely enough, Papen interpreted the outcome of the election as an endorsement of the nonpartisan presidential cabinet and of his proposed constitutional reform. The measures he instituted in Prussia, where Bracht had used the verdict of the State Constitutional Court to implement a comprehensive reorganization of the civil administration, made it clear that the pursuit of the "New State" had by no means come to an end. Schleicher, who had had major reservations about the plans for declaring a state of national emergency from the very outset, was on the verge of jumping ship. He was extremely concerned about the south German states' outspoken criticism of Papen's plans for the absorption of Prussia into the Reich and pleaded in vain with the cabinet to "deemphasize the matter of constitutional reform in view of the highly tense political situation." After all, the government still faced a firm phalanx of opposition parties and could only count on the support of the DNVP and a handful of small, right-wing splinter groups. The Center Party, on the other hand, continued to make it unequivocally clear that a presidential cabinet led by Papen stood no chance whatsoever of obtaining the toleration of a majority in the Reichstag. Hitler, who labeled the outcome of the elections a defensive victory, rejected "any compromise with the reactionary Hugenberg-Papen cabal" out of hand and issued a directive before the polls had closed calling upon the party to proceed "immediately with the preparations for a new propaganda campaign" and to put aside all internal organizational tasks.

At this point, the chancellor approached Hitler with a written request for a meeting to discuss the formation of a cabinet of "national consolidation." Hindenburg, on the advice of Schleicher, had promised Papen that he would be retained as chancellor on the condition that he initiate negotiations with the leaders of the various parties in order to secure a broader base of support for his cabinet. In a lengthy document, Hitler tersely ruled out his participation in the cabinet. At the same time, he let it be known that he did not intend to let himself be treated as he had been treated on 13 August. Moreover, he could not possibly approve of Papen's foreign and domestic policies and dismissed Papen's talk of a "new possibility of bringing together all the national forces" as a fiction, since not even Hugenberg was prepared to go along with it.

Since the bourgeois middle parties remained opposed to the Papen government, the prospects of a potential majority in the Reichstag remained unchanged. In a ploy to gain time, Schleicher raised the possibility of a change in the chancellorship and persuaded Papen to follow the proper parliamentary procedure by submitting his cabinet's resignation to the Reich president. Hindenburg, who was determined to retain Papen and the presidential system and to prevent a relapse into parliamentary government, formally accepted Papen's resignation with every intention of reinstalling him in office. Schleicher was thus free to initiate negotiations between Hindenburg and the leaders of the various German parties. But at the same time that the Reich president was receiving the various party leaders, Schleicher resumed his contacts with the General German Trade-Union Federation (Allgemeiner Deutscher Gewerkschaftsbund or ADGB), Günter Gereke's German Conference of Rural Municipalities, Gregor Straßer, and the Christian labor movement in quest for the *Querfront* of white-collar and working-class organizations that he had first envisaged earlier that summer.

Hindenburg first approached Hitler, whose refusal to enter into oral negotiations prompted a lengthy exchange of letters. The Nazi party leader persisted in his rigid attitude and again insisted on the chancellorship, including presidential powers. He also provided some indication of how he thought the current political crisis could be resolved. The Reichstag would have to pass an enabling law limited to a specific period of time, a step that could be achieved only by threatening to dissolve the Reichstag. Hindenburg, however, was not prepared to go beyond asking Hitler to form a cabinet that rested on a parliamentary majority and whose composition would be subject to his own approval. In particular, the Reich president reserved for himself the right to appoint both the minister of defense and the foreign minister. He also made it clear that a return to the dualism between Prussia and the Reich and a change in the purview of Article 48 of the Reich Constitution were nonnegotiable. In response, Hitler did not miss the opportunity to point out that from the point of view of common law the prerogatives the Reich president had claimed for himself were indeed unconstitutional. In point of fact, no reconciliation between the two was possible. Hitler stressed that it would be impossible to fulfill the mandate that Hindenburg had asked him to accept "because of its own internal contradiction" and proposed in response that he submit his own government program to the Reich president, upon the approval of which he would submit a list of ministers including Schleicher at the Defense Ministry and Neurath at the Foreign Office so that "the constitutional presuppositions for the work of the cabinet" would stem from the authority of the Reich president. Unimpressed by this ruse, Hindenburg instructed Meißner to inform Hitler that he could not justify "handing presidential powers over to the leader of a party that has never renounced its claim to absolute power" and that he feared that "a presidential cabinet headed by you would necessarily develop into a party dictatorship with all the consequences this implies."

The Reich president could not have been more succinct in stating the fact that Hitler sought to gain absolute power with no intention of ever relinquishing it. Yet the leaders of the bourgeois parties with whom he met either supported a Hitler chancellorship—this was the case with Ludwig Kaas from the Center Party and the BVP's Fritz Schäffer—or, like the DVP's Eduard Dingeldey, did not want to see the movement for national consolidation fall apart on this particular question. Only Hugenberg forcefully opposed Hitler's chancellorship. Hindenburg then asked Kaas, who had earlier advocated the formation of a "an emergency cabinet" (*Not- und Auffangskabinett*) by three or four courageous party leaders, to determine whether any alternative to Hitler's appointment might be found. Kaas's efforts, however, foundered on the intransigence of Hitler and Hugenberg, although Kaas blamed this on the indiscretions of government circles that would never have accepted the coalition he had in mind. The Reich president reacted indignantly to these charges by threatening to resign. Once it became clear that the negotiations with the party leaders had failed—the SPD, by the way, had never been consulted because Papen categorically refused to deal with it—Hindenburg called on his favorite chancellor to head a cabinet whose personnel was essentially the same as that of its predecessor.

Schleicher expressed severe reservations about the decision on 1 December 1932 to reinstate Papen as chancellor. Not only did he have doubts about Papen's own qualifications for the post, but he felt that Papen, like his predecessor, had been the victim of bad luck. By no means did Schleicher stand alone in the cabinet. Despite this opposition, Papen still planned to dissolve the Reichstag before it convened and to postpone new elections for six months. This could not be done under Article 48 of the Reich Constitution and could only be justified by an alleged state of national emergency. At this point, Papen decided to shore up his support in the Stahlhelm by appointing Franz Seldte Reich commissar for the Voluntary Labor Service. He had begun to court the Stahlhelm by having the government take part in the highly publicized Front Soldiers' Day, which took place at the Tempelhof airfield on 4 September, with more than 200,000 members of the Stahlhelm in attendance. In preparation for the conflict with the Reichstag that was certain to come, Papen had assured himself of presidential powers.

In the meantime, the cabinet also discussed the possibility of a Schleicher chancellorship, even though Schleicher's initial contacts with Gereke and Straßer had yielded no tangible results. Despite the completely negative outcome of his discussion with Hitler on 23 November, Schleicher still expected Straßer to "come to his rescue" should it prove impossible to persuade Hitler to join the government. He attempted to arrange another meeting with Hitler for 30 November, but failed. The Nazi party leader preferred to run off to campaign in Thuringia rather than travel to Berlin, where he never felt comfortable. The fact that Schleicher sent one of his closest associates, Colonel Eugen Ott, to inform Hitler of his renewed offer did nothing to change the Nazi party leader's intransigence. Nevertheless, the general remained determined to include the NSDAP.

The decisive factor in determining the fate of Papen's chancellorship was Schleicher's fear that the creation of a *Kampfkabinett* under Papen would quickly lead to a situation in which the Reichswehr would find itself at war with "nine-tenths of the population." At the decisive meeting of the cabinet on the evening of 2 December, first Neurath and then Schwerin von Krosigk firmly sided with the general, thereby starting what amounted to a palace revolution against the chancellor. It soon became clear that with one exception the entire cabinet was unwilling to go along with Papen's reappointment as chancellor. Transferring the office to Schleicher was the only way out of the predicament. In the meantime, Papen had approached retired General Joachim von Stülpnagel to see whether he might be willing to take Schleicher's place in a *Kampfkabinett* that might, under some circumstances, be obliged to use military force. Papen's attempt to minimize the "danger of strikes and domestic unrest" provided Schleicher with an opportunity to summon the well-prepared Ott, Schleicher's chief of military operations in the Defense Ministry, to report on the results of a war-game exercise that the military had recently conducted to deal with the threat of domestic upheaval.

Designed in close cooperation with military and civilian authorities on the occasion of the Berlin transport workers' strike, the exercise was predicated on the assumption that the Revolutionary Trade-Union Opposition and the socialist unions would call a general strike that was accompanied by violent clashes between the KPD and police. The exercise revealed just how perfect the planning for a military state of emergency, including the necessary emergency decrees, had been. The scenario postulated a secondary problem in the form of a simultaneous military threat from Polish insurgents in the eastern areas. The study assumed that the NSDAP would adopt a wait-and-see, though primarily hostile, attitude and that it would sympathize with the strikers on the local level. This corresponded exactly to the strategy that the NSDAP had previously pursued. The study also stressed the indispensable role of the NSDAP in strengthening the border patrols in East Prussia and made it clear that the forces committed to the maintenance of order would be overwhelmed by a general strike, particularly if the NSDAP should withhold its cooperation in the Technical Emergency Service (Technische Nothilfe), which for all practical purposes had been transformed into an antistrike organization. Ott indirectly alluded to the exclusive social character of the Papen cabinet by pointing out that it was important to avoid the impression that armed force was being deployed "to defend the interests of an upper class against the people as a whole."

Ott's presentation confirmed the wisdom of the defense minister's opposition to constitutional experiments. What was not immediately apparent, however, was the existence of a fundamental conflict over differing political goals. Schleicher was still intent upon taming the NSDAP and, should this prove impossible, upon attracting its more positive-minded elements to the service of the state; for Papen, on the other hand, the authoritarian program had become an end in itself. Within the cabinet, however, the decision had already fallen in favor of Schleicher even before it had had an opportunity to hear the report on the results of the war-game exercise. Later that evening the unexpectedly deserted chancellor reluctantly bowed to the decision of the cabinet majority and informed the Reich president that he would not stand in the way of a "Schleicher solution." Hindenburg reacted with his characteristic military terseness and told the deeply hurt and embittered Papen that he was too old to take on the responsibility for a civil war. "So then we must in God's name let Herr Schleicher see what he can do."

Papen's resignation marked the end of a period of conservative illusions that had been articulated by one of the leading contributors to *Der Ring*, the official organ of the arch-conservative German Lords' Club. The unexamined social and political resentments of a relatively small upper class that felt its traditional social and economic privileges threatened by the advance of the welfare state and that equated its private interests with those of the state were the underpinnings of a transitional regime that could only stay in power by continuous threats of a coup d'état. It was characteristic that this regime could easily crush the political Left through federal intervention in Prussia but was powerless to prevent populist mobilization from the Right in the form of the Nazi movement.

This deeply conservative regime was never able to summon up the energy for establishing a military dictatorship, the only means by which it could have preserved its domestic power and implemented the reactionary constitutional reforms of the "New State" against the will of an overwhelming majority of the German people. In the final analysis, the armed forces, which had promoted and sustained the political power of an exclusive social elite in the person of the aristocratic horseman Franz von Papen, refused to allow its strength to be consumed by the task of keeping a socially reactionary regime in power for fear that this would jeopardize its long-range goal of reestablishing German hegemony throughout central Europe. In the meantime, the Papen cabinet had contributed greatly to the paralysis of those forces that alone were capable of resisting the rising tide of National Socialism.

CHAPTER THIRTEEN

From Authoritarian to Fascist Dictatorship

WHILE the appointment of Kurt von Schleicher as chancellor on 2 December 1932 may have put an end to the speculation about the reorganization of the cabinet that was expected to take place after the November elections, the travails of the presidential system continued. In the preceding years Schleicher had always remained in the background. That he now felt obliged to abandon his customary place behind the scenes and assume responsibility for the everyday affairs of government was a sign of the internal fragility of the presidential system that he himself had helped to create in an attempt to give the Reichswehr a greater voice in the disarmament negotiations. The exclusion of the SPD and other pacifist groups from any meaningful role in shaping Germany's political course had cleared the way to a determined rearmament policy that the Reichswehr leadership managed to pursue in spite of the obvious effects of the domestic economic crisis. The primacy of military policy, however, had been seriously jeopardized by the impetuous behavior of Franz von Papen, who had come dangerously close to involving Germany's armed forces in domestic confrontations that threatened to erupt into open civil war. From the perspective of the Reichswehr, a conflict with the NSDAP was incompatible with the need for a comprehensive program of preparing the German nation for war.

In a situation such as this, Schleicher found himself left with no alternative but to try his own hand at bringing the foundering ship of state back on course. Schleicher flattered himself into thinking that he possessed the political expertise necessary to unite a badly splintered national opposition in a cabinet that enjoyed Hindenburg's support. The presuppositions for achieving this, however, were anything but favorable. On 29 November Hitler had backed out of negotiations that Frick and Straßer had urged him to attend. His decision was influenced in part by Göring, who was disappointed at being denied the minister presidency of Prussia, and by the agitation of Goebbels. Colonel Ott, whom Schleicher had sent to Weimar to meet with Hitler on the following day, was subjected to endless tirades explaining why the Nazi party leader could not under any circumstances accept the offer of government participation. As a result, the newly appointed chancellor came to the conclusion that he could treat Hitler as a political has-been and that he could bring Gregor Straßer, who had promised him to "come to his rescue," into the cabinet as vice-chancellor and

Prussian minister president. Therein, however, lay a fatal misreading of both Hitler's basic psychology and Straßer's freedom of maneuver and determination to act. The rarefied atmosphere of the presidential system had nurtured the illusion that the course of national policy was determined by the behavior and ideas of individuals. In point of fact, however, it was the irreparable break with the Social Democrats on 20 July 1932 that restricted the cabinet's freedom of movement and made its very survival conditional upon the goodwill of the NSDAP.

Schleicher's political course exhausted itself in tactical maneuvering and amounted to little more than an attempt to gloss over the break with the moderate Left in the coup d'état against Prussia by presenting a government program that had distinctly populist overtones and by portraying himself as a "social general." Schleicher was thus hoping to persuade the Social Democrats to adopt a wait-and-see attitude and at the same time mend his political fences with the socialist labor movement. The persistent economic crisis and mass unemployment were used to offer the Social Democrats a truce that did nothing to resolve the fundamental differences that divided the government and SPD in the area of military policy. It was therefore no coincidence that the *Tägliche Rundschau*, a daily newspaper with close ties to the chancellor, introduced the concept of a *Burgfrieden* into the public discussion. This coincided perfectly with Schleicher's own ideas. For Schleicher continued to use the command economy of World War I as a model on which his own thinking about the current economic situation was based. From this perspective, the only way in which the current economic crisis could be overcome was by enlisting the cooperation of the labor unions ranging from the left wing of the NSDAP to the General German Trade-Union Federation (Allgemeiner Deutscher Gewerkschaftsbund or ADGB) without regard for party affiliation. Since the late summer of 1932 Schleicher had gone behind Papen's back to establish contacts that made sense only if a break with the probusiness course of the Papen cabinet was forthcoming.

Burgfriede and *Querachse*, the two words that summed up Schleicher's strategy for dealing with the political and economic crisis, exercised a certain appeal only because the political parties were no longer as important as a result of the Reichstag's diminished authority and the increasing reliance upon emergency legislation at both the state and national levels. A general uneasiness over the activities of the political parties nurtured particularly in bourgeois circles the notion that one could simply dispense with them as the unloved children of the representative system. This in itself was a response to the increasing dissolution of the bourgeois middle parties. Count Kuno von Westarp, the former DNVP stalwart who had recently gone over to the People's Conservatives, spoke publicly of a "Twilight of the Parties" (*Parteidämmerung*) and demanded that the parties cease their efforts to participate directly in the conduct of government affairs. On the other hand, Westarp warned against the illusion that the parties could be entirely excluded from a role in government. Yet this was precisely what Hans Zehrer and his colleagues in the editorial offices of *Die Tat* had in mind. For it was their hope that the obsolete parties and their rigid bureaucracies would be supplanted by the front of the young generation, which had found its specific form of organization in the *bündisch* movement. Even then, it was not yet clear just how a politically effective force could be created out of a simple community of conviction, or *Gesinnungsgemeinschaft.*

Hitler exploited the general antipathy toward the existing party system for his own partisan purposes and promised that all political parties would be dissolved in the *Volksgemeinschaft* by which the Nazis pledged to subsume all social, confessional, and regional antagonisms under the unity of the national will. By the same token, the DNVP and Center tried to recast themselves as movements and went so far as to establish their own leadership cults. While this was an indirect triumph for Nazi propaganda, Hitler found himself confronted with the charge that his party was in the process of losing its character as a movement and was beginning to behave as simply another political party among the many that already existed. Criticism of this sort also came from the circle around Zehrer and reflected the widespread disappointment of influential bourgeois circles over Hitler's refusal to take his place in the Papen cabinet and to subordinate the interests of his movement to the general welfare. Complaints to this effect had in fact been passed on to Gregor Straßer in September 1932 by August Heinrichsbauer, whose admonitions almost certainly bore the imprimatur of Ruhr heavy industry.

The extent to which Schleicher shared in this sort of wishful thinking is difficult to assess. At any rate, Schleicher emphatically dissociated himself from the concept of a radical break with the existing constitutional system in favor of the "new order" that had been propagated by Papen and Gayl. He made no effort whatsoever to implement their plans for constitutional change or to anchor the presidential system in law. Nor did he take up the proposals for federal reform that had been drafted by the Bavarian government and initiate concrete steps in the Prussian question. Although he enjoyed the support of the so-called Tat Circle (Tat-Kreis), he clearly did not share Zehrer's belief in an epochal restructuring of the existing political order. For Schleicher's primary concern was always to avoid the constitutional conflict that weighed so heavily on Hindenburg's mind and to restore the effectiveness of the presidential regime under his leadership. In this respect, Schleicher was counting on a rapid economic upswing and was simply playing for time until that had materialized. Continuing to subscribe to the primacy of military policy, Schleicher sought to neutralize the opposition of the Left through a comprehensive program of job creation and, at the same time, win the support of the NSDAP, which appeared to have passed the high point of its development. In all of this, however, Schleicher greatly overestimated the Reichswehr's potential for influencing the course of Germany's domestic political development.

In the official statement of his government's objectives that Schleicher read over radio on 15 December 1932 in order not to become the target of repetitious no-confidence motions in the Reichstag, the chancellor gave every indication that he was prepared to reach a compromise with his critics. He stressed in particular that the cabinet he had formed was not a *Kampfkabinett* but a *Verständigungskabinett* that was willing to cooperate with all of those of genuine goodwill. In sharp contrast to Papen's style of governing, the new chancellor made sure that government spokesmen testified before the various Reichstag committees. By the same token, Schleicher had no intention of inhibiting efforts by the delegations of the major political parties in the Reichstag to demonstrate parliament's ability to act in a deliberate and responsible manner. Consequently he allowed the Center, SPD, and NSDAP to take the initiative in revoking the controversial changes that the Papen government had made in the existing system of collective bargaining and did not oppose a Reichstag resolution of 9 December 1932 repealing those sections of the September emergency decree that dealt with social policy. On the contrary, the Schleicher cabinet hurried to rescind these decrees and to move their expiration date up as much as possible.

To the uninitiated, the first actions of the new cabinet might very well be interpreted as a sign that it was about to reinstate the parliamentary system. The Reichstag, for example, decided with a majority that stretched from the extreme Left to the extreme Right to grant an amnesty for all political offenses except murder in a move that obviously did little to bridge the gap between potential adversaries in the event of an actual civil war. To be sure, the amnesty produced the release of highly visible political prisoners such as Carl von Ossietzky, the editor of *Die Weltbühne* who had been condemned to a lengthy prison term after his conviction for high treason in connection with revelations about the secret construction of a German air force that dated back to 1929. At the same time, however, the law represented a passport to freedom for right-wing political criminals insofar as they had ever been prosecuted in the first place. A bill the NSDAP introduced that would have transferred the right to represent the Reich president as his official deputy from the chancellor to the president of the German Supreme Court proved an unwelcome reminder of the negotiations the chancellor had conducted with Hitler after the November Reichstag elections. The presidential entourage, on the other hand, proposed an amendment to the constitution that would have barred Hitler, should he succeed in his bid for the chancellorship, from assuming the powers of the presidential office as long as the Reich president was still alive. The passage of these bills with the votes of the Social Democrats constituted a twofold affront to the new chancellor.

The truce between the parliament and the government could also be seen in the willingness of the Reichstag's Council of Elders to postpone the convocation of the Reichstag on several different occasions in order to avert an open conflict with the government. For the moment the NSDAP was not inclined to risk new elections, which under the current circumstances could have only resulted in another defeat. By the same token, the Center Party was fully prepared to go along with the chancellor's wish for the temporary continuation of the Reich commissariat in Prussia and to set aside any thoughts of inviting the NSDAP to join the government. The principal danger to the existence of the Schleicher cabinet, however, came not so much from the parliament as from the frustrated ambitions of his predecessor, whom Schleicher tried in vain to placate by offering him the ambassadorship in Paris. Hindenburg, however, regarded Papen's counsel as indispensable and wished to have him as near as possible. In retrospect, it is not at all surprising that Papen was never asked to move out of the official residence he had occupied as chancellor.

For the overall political situation it was significant that both the SPD and KPD assumed a purely passive role in the general constellation of political forces. To be sure, the KPD protested vehemently against the Schleicher cabinet as the "next highest stage in the development of fascism" and was always ready to introduce a motion of no confidence in the Reichstag. In real terms, however, the KPD lacked a concrete plan of action and remained on the periphery of events. Since the spring of 1932 the KPD had adhered to the official party line of "a united front from below" and clung rigidly to the dogma of the Antifascist Action (Antifaschistische Aktion) that the central thrust of its efforts should be directed against the SPD as a particularly pernicious form of "social fascism." Continued on instructions from the Comintern even after the putsch of 20 July 1932, this ultraleftist tactic went hand in hand with the consolidation of Ernst Thälmann's position as Communist party leader. With the help of the executive committee of the Comintern, Thälmann had succeeded in ridding himself of those critics who urged an intensified struggle against the NSDAP. Above all, Thälmann was able to neutralize his most formidable rival, Heinz Neumann.

Thälmann shared the illusion held by the leadership of the Comintern that the position of the KPD had grown steadily stronger and the circumstances in Germany were bound to produce a revolutionary crisis in the not too distant future. In this respect, the KPD misread the outcome of the November elections, in which it had increased its share of the popular vote from 14.3 to 16.9 percent as a result of substantial defections from the Social Democrats. The Berlin transit workers' strike, which Thälmann hailed as the Communist movement's "most important positive revolutionary achievement to date," was interpreted as the point of departure for the next wave of increasingly large mass actions in spite of the fact that it, like the few others that had been initiated by the KPD, had causes that were exclusively economic in nature. With approximately 350,000 members—the overwhelming majority of whom were unemployed—and plagued by the constant fluctuation of its membership, the KPD still lagged far behind the SPD and ADGB in purely quantitative terms, particularly since it had practically no support in large industrial plants. The Revolutionary Trade-Union Opposition and the Communist trade-union federations it had founded in 1931 received less than half the votes in the factory council elections that the Christian labor unions did and were hardly in a position to call a major strike without the participation of the socialist unions. With an estimated 40,000 members, the outlawed Red Front Soldiers' League (Roter Frontkämpferbund) projected a combat potential that simply did not exist, while the Communist Youth League (Kommunistischer Jugendverband), with about 55,000 members, remained disappointingly weak. The Red Front Soldiers' League and the military-political apparatus that Hans Kippenberger had built up were designed primarily to provide self-protection for a party that fully expected to be driven underground in the near future. The very existence of these organizations, however, only encouraged unchallenged reports in the right-wing press of Communist preparations for a general insurrection.

The KPD's claim to leadership in the united antifascist front for which it had appealed rested on shaky foundations, particularly since several of its more militant auxiliary organizations, such as the Communist Youth League, found it difficult to commit themselves to the contradictory policy line of the KPD central executive committee and preferred to make their mark by practicing acts of "individual terror." To be sure, the constant threat that the provocative behavior of the SA and SS posed to the socialist working class had led to isolated incidents of cooperation with Social Democratic organizations at the local level. Even then, however, the Communist Party failed to achieve a significant breakthrough into the ranks of the traditionally Social Democratic working class. The unrestrained polemics of the KPD, which continued to brand the SPD and the ADGB as "a pacesetter and driving force in the march of German fascism" and denounced their leaders as "social fascists," greatly compromised the credibility of Communist propaganda for the creation of a united antifascist front in which the Socialist Workers' Party of Germany (Sozialistische Arbeiterpartei Deutschlands or SAPD) and the Opposition Communist Party of Germany (Kommunistische Partei Deutschlands [Opposition]) were also represented. More than a simple nonaggression pact as proposed by Friedrich Stampfer after the formation of the Papen cabinet was never a realistic possibility.

Schleicher came to the chancellorship at a time when the SPD executive committee was engaged in a major effort to insulate itself against the agitation of the KPD. This, in turn, made it highly unlikely that the SPD would consider abandoning the oppositional role that had been forced upon it. For while Rudolf Breitscheid may have conceded that the new chancellor represented a definitive improvement over his predecessor by virtue of his "greater sense of reality and flexibility," the party remained unwavering in its opposition to the presidential regime. That the SPD leadership should refuse after Otto Braun's ouster in Prussia—an incident for which Schleicher was held primarily responsible—to cooperate with the new general out of concern for the effect this might have on the loyalty of the party's rank-and-file membership was fully justified. Only a few isolated voices within the party even went so far as to suggest toleration of the Schleicher cabinet in view of its sharp break with Papen's social policy.

By no means was the front against Schleicher as solid within the SPD as the party's semiofficial statements tended to suggest. It required the emphatic veto of the SPD executive committee to dissuade Karl Höltermann and the leadership of the Reichsbanner from cooperating with the Reich Curatorium for Youth Fitness (Reichskuratorium für Jugendertüchtigung), one of the new chancellor's pet projects. By the same token, the government's efforts to expand the Voluntary Labor Service (Freiwilliger Arbeitsdienst or FAD) met with a favorable response from within the ranks of the SPD despite reservations that party functionaries might have had about the paramilitary training that constituted such a prominent feature of life in the labor camps. The SPD's stance on the question of constitutional reform was also less unanimous than it seemed on the surface. A number of the party's more farsighted intellectuals, among them Carlo Mierendorff, Hermann Heller, Ernst Fraenkel, and Otto Kirchheimer, had become disillusioned with the paralysis of Weimar parliamentarism and were looking for ways to strengthen the government's authority through remedies such as the creation of a second chamber, the introduction of corporatist elements, or the limitation of parliamentary prerogatives. While these proposals all reflected the growing skepticism within Social Democratic ranks about the future of the liberal-parliamentary system, by no means did they signify a willingness to go along with Schleicher's policy. This was particularly true of the SPD party leadership, which was prepared to remain in the opposition for an extended period of time and was committed in the meantime to doing everything it could to defend the Weimar Constitution.

The defensive character of the SPD's strategy had become even more pronounced after the party's Leipzig party congress in October 1931. The policy of toleration had proved a failure, particularly since it had prevented neither the fall of Brüning nor the takeover of Prussia. Yet despite the defection of the SAPD, the solidarity of the party had to all outward appearances remained intact and had indeed been strengthened by its struggle against the NSDAP. Nevertheless, the Social Democrats continued to lose the confidence of the next generation. Many of the party's young members had either gone over to the SAPD or joined forces with the party's internal opposition under the auspices of the Socialist Workers' Youth (Sozialistische Arbeiterjugend or SAJ). Disappointment was also rampant among the representatives of the party's right wing, who either banded together in the group around the *Neue Blätter für den Sozialismus* or participated actively in the Reichsbanner and the Iron Front. Criticism of the increasing inflexibility of the SPD's policies, of the predominance of the party bureaucracy, and of an obsolete democratic style that no longer appealed to the masses was widespread among the party's younger members regardless of whether they belonged to the left or the right wing of the party. On the surface the party appeared to adapt itself to the changing political circumstances and in many respects went so far as to imitate the methods of recruitment and mobilization employed by the fascist movements. Still, it had become abundantly clear that despite the propaganda offensive of the Iron Front the Social Democrats were becoming less and less capable of acting on their own initiative.

Schleicher, therefore, had no more reason to fear the opposition of the Social Democrats than he could count on their cooperation. Still, it was vitally important for the success of *Querfront* strategy to enlist the support of the ADGB in addition to that of the Christian trade unions, on whose sympathies he could already count. In this respect, Schleicher took advantage of the increasingly pervasive trend toward the dissolution of ties between the German labor unions and the political parties with which they had been traditionally affiliated. The ADGB leadership, which in contrast to the SPD executive committee included outspoken advocates for the ideas of the Gereke circle, had reacted to the change of cabinets in December 1932 with much greater candor than the leaders of the SPD. The ADGB looked upon the new cabinet's repudiation of its predecessor's social policy as a major victory for organized labor. In this respect, however, the ADGB tended to overlook the fact that the protest strikes against governmental authority to break wage contracts had not been initiated by the labor unions and that management itself refused to make use of the authorization to deviate from existing collective bargaining law. Whether the chancellor would eventually succeed in integrating the labor unions into the existing presidential cabinet would ultimately depend on his ability to come up with a comprehensive job creation program in the public sector.

At an emergency congress in April 1932, the ADGB had unveiled a comprehensive program of job creation in the form of the Woytinski-Tarnow-Baade Plan (WTB Plan). The plan had been drafted on the initiative of the head of the ADGB's Office of Statistical Analysis, Wladimir Woytinski, with the assistance of Fritz Tarnow, chairman of the Woodworkers' Union, and the Social Democratic agrarian politician Fritz Baade. Submitted in late 1931, the plan that came to be known by its authors' initials provided for active state intervention in the business cycle through the large-scale creation of credit and sought to create a million new jobs in the public sector. By comparison with the job creation programs later implemented by Schacht and Hitler, the scope of the plan was modest indeed. A novel aspect of the WTB Plan, however, was its underlying assumption that the crisis could be overcome by stimulating consumption. Inflationary side effects were not to be feared since production could be quickly restored to full capacity to meet the increased demand that would result from greater consumer purchasing power.

With the WTB Plan the ADGB turned its back upon the purely reactive economic policies that had left the capitalist system free to function according to its own laws and that had only sought to control the mechanisms of economic distribution. The WTB Plan was the first step toward direct state intervention in the economic process. This, in turn, implied not only that the unions should assume responsibility for the economy as a whole but also that they would no longer subscribe to the purely mechanistic understanding of the economic process that had informed the program of economic democracy that the ADGB had unveiled in the late 1920s. The unions reluctant acceptance of the WTB Plan had been preceded by a bitter conflict with the SPD, during which Rudolf Hilferding, the party's leading expert on fiscal policy, had warned against its inflationary consequences in spite of Woytinski's observation that deflation had already overshot itself and was likely to lead to an arbitrary erosion of consumer purchasing power.

The skepticism with which the SPD party leadership responded to the WTB Plan was motivated not only by its commitment to an orthodox Marxist theory of economic crisis but also by the bitter experiences of its tactical alliance with Brüning, whose reluctance to implement a program of job creation had been shared by a majority of Social Democratic economic experts. Still, the party could hardly afford to repudiate the unions. The demands for job creation the SPD party leadership submitted in the final days of the Brüning cabinet and at the beginning of the Papen's term of office were therefore presented in muted tones and buried in a package of measures for "the reorganization of the economy." The far-reaching plans for the nationalization of the economy that appeared under this formula represented a retreat from the WTB Plan quite aside from the fact that the party's "Demands for the Economy of the Future" failed to address the specific economic problems of the day or the existing power relationships and thus amounted to a tacit admission of the SPD's political isolation.

In the spring of 1932 the ADGB received both support and competition from an unexpected quarter on the question of job creation. In a much cited speech to the Reichstag on 10 May 1932 the NSDAP's Gregor Straßer demanded an even more comprehensive program of job creation and alluded specifically to the "deep-seated anticapitalist longing" (antikapitalistischer Sehnsucht) that currently gripped 95 percent of the German people. Several days later the text of Straßer's speech was widely circulated under the title *Wirtschaftliches Sofortprogramm der NSDAP*. With his advocacy of a generous public works program, Straßer had succeeded in articulating what increasingly large sectors of the German population had come to feel. Moreover, his speech implied that the NSDAP would not categorically rule out the possibility of cooperation with the labor unions on this matter. But since Straßer's main tactical goal was the formation of a broad front in support of job creation, he failed to devote specific attention to the program's financial aspects, which were in the process of being finalized by Adrian von Renteln. Public opinion, however, was not aware of the fact that Straßer's turn toward a constructive social policy did not have the approval of Hitler, who, in response to vehement protests from business and economic interest organizations, ordered the withdrawal of the *Wirtschaftliches Sofortprogramm* in October 1932.

Straßer had been encouraged to undertake an initiative on the question of job creation by the Tat Circle, with which he maintained loose and mainly indirect relations. The *Wirtschaftliches Sofortprogramm* differed from union proposals for job creation, however, in that it sought to finance the creation of public credits by abandoning the gold standard and by adopting an economic policy committed to the far-reaching goal of economic self-sufficiency. Straßer's ideas on this subject found the support of a group of respected political economists who had come together in the Study Group for the Monetary and Credit System (Studiengesellschaft für Geld- und Kreditwesen). Among them were Ernst Wagemann, the principal critic of Brüning's deflation policy, and the Lübeck industrialist Heinrich Dräger, who had published a study entitled *Arbeitsbeschaffung durch produktive Kreditschöpfung* in the summer of 1932. Although Straßer and his supporters had no direct contact with the reform-minded union leaders around Woytinski, cooperation between the two groups seemed perfectly logical. Moreover, Gereke had been working since the fall of 1931 to formulate a platform on which individuals of different party backgrounds could unite. Through Hermann Cordemann, the head of the Berlin bureau of the economics division of the NSDAP national organization, Straßer maintained contact with the Gereke circle, which, in turn, enjoyed ties to Schleicher and was not only represented in the NSDAP, Christian-National Peasants and Farmers' Party, and Stahlhelm but also included representatives from the Reichsbanner and ADGB.

Schleicher was hoping to use the alliance of interests that had begun to coalesce on the issue of job creation to overcome the extreme isolation of the presidential cabinet and to persuade the various parties in the Reichstag to withhold their fire at least for the time being. To be sure, the chances of doing this were decidedly better in August 1932 than they were after the presidential regime had been thoroughly discredited by the dilettantism of Papen's solo venture. Still, the prospective allies of the chancellor remained suspicious as to whether his initiative in the question of job creation was merely a tactical expedient that lacked any real commitment on his part. In point of fact, he lacked the intrinsic credibility that would have made it possible for him to enlist the active support of such heterogeneous groups as the ADGB leadership, the Straßer wing of the NSDAP, the Christian labor unions, and perhaps even the Young German Order and the German National Union of Commercial Employees. In the final analysis, everything depended on Schleicher's ability to win over Gregor Straßer, who, next to Hitler, was the most influential man in the NSDAP, for the position of the vice-chancellorship. This, in turn, depended on the willingness of the NSDAP, as well as that of the Center Party and SPD, to forego direct interference in the conduct of government and to grant the Schleicher cabinet an implicit vote of confidence in the matter of job creation despite the fact that parliamentary approval was not required.

During the reorganization of the cabinet in December 1932 little could be seen of the impulse for job creation. While Schleicher insisted over the objections of the economics and finance ministers upon Gereke's appointment as Reich commissar for job creation, he was unable to transfer responsibility for these matters from the existing ministries. As a result, a comprehensive reform in the area of job creation was effectively blocked. Moreover, proposals to finance the emergency program that Gereke submitted to the cabinet encountered determined resistance from the other ministries. The only cabinet officer of any rank to support the proposal was Prussian Finance Minister Johannes Popitz, who argued that a comprehensive program of job creation was the only way in which the dismal financial situation of the municipalities might be remedied. Popitz's proposal to link such a program with a reorganization of the existing system of unemployment insurance, however, would have been unacceptable to precisely those labor unions whose support Gereke was soliciting. In this respect, therefore, Gereke found himself largely isolated even though he did not admit this in public and could still count on the journalistic support of the group around Hans Zehrer. Nor was the cabinet's attractiveness to organized labor enhanced by its continued adherence to orthodox fiscal theory.

Under the influence of Reichsbank President Hans Luther, who still regarded the threat of inflation as the most serious danger to the German economy, the amount of money the cabinet could allocate for the creation of new jobs was limited to the 500 million marks that had originally been set aside by the Papen government for premiums designed to encourage employers to hire additional workers but that had, for lack of applicants, remained largely unspent. In addition to this, there were several related measures to stimulate the construction industry and housing developments. In the final analysis, Gereke's emergency program fell far short of the expectations that Schleicher had aroused in his government declaration of 13 December. Big business, which continued to exert its influence in the cabinet and urged the chancellor in the strongest possible terms to maintain Papen's economic course, reacted with obvious relief. Yet the measures initiated by Gereke were very much on target, for by the end of February 1933 the municipal governments had already exhausted the funds that had been made available to them at the beginning of the year. What this shows is that job creation was a matter of great psychological importance even though the economic crisis was beginning to show signs of abating.

German public opinion tended to be favorably impressed by Schleicher's more conciliatory political style, which stood in sharp contrast to the aristocratic pretense of Papen. The civil servant union, for instance, noted that its concerns were no longer dismissed out of hand. Schleicher's popularity was growing not only among certain elements of the German working class but in large segments of the middle classes as well. It remained to be seen whether the chancellor would succeed in using this reservoir of goodwill to achieve the stabilization of his government. The major advantage that he possessed at the outset, namely, the fact that he was less firmly committed to a specific political course than Papen, became a handicap, however, as it became increasingly clear that his negotiations with different parties and associations were designed to do little more than buy time. Time and time again, Schleicher postponed a thorough reorganization of his cabinet. Aside from Papen, only Gayl and Hugo Schäffer had been dropped from the previous cabinet, the latter because he had lost credibility as labor minister. It remained unclear whether the chancellor's desire to broaden the cabinet's base was merely a formality designed to ensure toleration from various political forces or was intended to achieve a partial reactivation of the parliamentary system.

For all practical purposes, the chancellor could only count on the active support of the Christian and socialist labor unions and on the toleration of the Center. Out of respect for the Center, Schleicher was not in a position to comply with the exaggerated demands of Hugenberg and the DNVP. But by far the most important question was whether Gregor Straßer could be persuaded to join the cabinet as the indispensable cornerstone of the centerpiece of the labor-union axis upon which Schleicher sought to base his cabinet. Without Straßer it no longer made sense to seek the support of organized labor. Given the lack of real alternatives, it becomes somewhat easier to understand why Schleicher continued to believe, even after the break between Straßer and Hitler on 8 December, that this option remained open through the first part of January 1933. In point of fact, Schleicher had already lost the initiative several weeks earlier, so that by this time he was reduced to mere tactical diversions.

Without being informed in detail of Papen's intentions, Otto Braun recognized the desperate plight in which the chancellor and indeed the entire presidential regime found themselves. Unlike the SPD's national leadership, which in Braun's eyes had "allowed Communist demagogy to dictate its every action" and "let itself be maneuvered into a position of sterile opposition," he felt that the only chance of surviving the current political crisis lay in an alliance with General von Schleicher. On 6 January 1933, therefore, Braun offered to go along with the dissolution of the Reichstag and Prussian Landtag, as well as with the postponement of new elections until spring, in exchange for the end of the Reich commissariat in Prussia. Schleicher categorically rejected Braun's proposals. To be sure, it was extremely doubtful that the SPD executive committee would have approved Braun's obviously unconstitutional initiative. The decisive fact, however, was that Schleicher was neither psychologically nor politically capable of carrying out such a reversal of course. In earlier controversies such as the ban against the SA, the discussion of Gayl's plans for a state of national emergency, and Papen's decision to use military force against the NSDAP, Schleicher had consistently objected to a change of political course since this ran counter to the underlying objectives of his commitment to the presidential regime. Furthermore, such an arrangement would never have received the approval of the Reich president, who had not forgotten his conflicts with Braun.

The SPD'S distrust of Schleicher was fully justified. To be sure, Otto Wels's contention that as the person ultimately responsible for Papen's appointment he should also be held responsible for Papen's disastrous economic policy was little more than a purely tactical argument. But the general's intransigence in the Prussian question proved that he was neither willing nor able to pursue a genuine accommodation with the Social Democrats. Moreover, the appointment of Franz Bracht as Gayl's successor at the Reich Ministry of the Interior was certain to anger the SPD. After all, Bracht had been chiefly responsible for the purge of prorepublican personnel from the Prussian civil service. Schleicher's calculations were therefore predicated on the eventuality—for which there were indeed indications—that the socialist unions would break away from the SPD. As early as October 1932, in a much cited address to the labor-union school in Bernau, ADGB chairman Theodor Leipart had hinted at the willingness of organized labor to cooperate within the framework of the presidential regime provided that the government abandon Papen's outspoken anti-labor policy. Following the change of governments, Leipart had assumed an unusually positive attitude toward Schleicher in an interview with the Parisian newspaper *Excelsior*, although the SPD subsequently put pressure on him to retract some of his statements. The close ties between certain representatives of the ADGB and the Gereke circle also pointed in the same direction.

Within the socialist labor movement there were influential voices in favor of a rapprochement with the government, even, if necessary, at the expense of close relations with the SPD. In the *Gewerkschaftszeitung* of 24 December 1932, Clemens Nörpel spoke of the "unalterable duty" of the unions to "obtain the best possible salary and working conditions under every government and every constitutional system." A group of younger, national-minded union leaders, foremost among them Lothar Erdmann, seriously considered an understanding with the presidential regime based on the unions' integration into the state by means of some form of corporatist participation. Communist allegations, based in part on actual forgeries, that negotiations with the chancellor over the "nationalization" (*Verstaatlichung*) of the unions had taken place were factually untrue, although they did reflect a prevailing tendency within the socialist labor movement.

Despite original misgivings, the leadership of the socialist unions abandoned its opposition to the Voluntary Labor Service, even though suspicion at the local level that this was merely a way of undercutting the collective bargaining process remained fairly widespread. In terms of number alone, the Voluntary Labor Service (Freiwilliger Arbeitsdienst or FAD) had not met Schleicher's expectations. Led by Friedrich Syrup, the former head of the National Agency for Job Placement and Unemployment Insurance (Reichsanstalt für Arbeitsvermittlung und Arbeitslosenversicherung) and now Reich minister of labor, the Labor Service lacked the means to employ more than 243,000 young workers in public projects or in privately run work camps. In view of the persistent problem of juvenile unemployment, this was woefully inadequate. The Volunteer Labor Service had originally been founded with the intention of getting unemployed youth off the streets, in the obvious hope that this would prevent their political radicalization by the Right and Left. Schleicher also saw it as an important step toward the creation of a popular militia, which in turn would prepare the nation for compulsory military service.

It was symptomatic of the general psychological situation that existed in Germany during the last years of the Weimar Republic that the work-camp movement achieved widespread popularity that even extended to the socialist unions, which had to admit to themselves that they lacked the organizational capability to deal with permanent unemployment. The Reichsbanner was also interested in participating in the Voluntary Labor Service and in taking advantage of the special leadership training it had to offer. Conversely, Straßer's associate Konstantin Hierl, who had built up an independent National Socialist labor service corps, found it necessary to reach an arrangement with the FAD in order to protect his own recruitment pool. Right-wing organizations, but particularly the Stahlhelm, looked upon the subsidized work camps as an opportunity to obtain paramilitary training. Syrup, however, was able to prevent the work-camp movement from being entirely taken over by the bourgeois Right so that in the final analysis it remained a reservoir of heterogeneous political and social currents that, for the most part, had grown out of the German youth movement.

In a parallel effort, Schleicher advocated the creation of a "comprehensive emergency organization for German youth" that would foster self-help for the unemployed. This was seen as a substitute for the Reich Curatorium for Youth Fitness, whose work he considered inadequate. Given the shortage of funds, however, its effectiveness was equally limited. It was Schleicher's hope that all of these initiatives would help young people to overcome "the spirit of partisanship." In his mind, they represented the first step toward universal military service and participation in the militia. His offer to Höltermann to merge the Reichsbanner and Stahlhelm into a National Soldiers' League, or *Reichskriegerverband*, reflected the prevailing opinion within the Defense Ministry that the program of military preparedness for the German people could be used as an instrument of domestic political consolidation. In the manipulation of the military principle for domestic political objectives lay the specific weakness of Schleicher's political strategy insofar as his policies were based on a clear-cut concept to begin with. Even then, these ideas held some appeal for the socialist unions, while the reaction of the Reichsbanner revealed that they had also struck a resonant chord in the younger generation.

The neoconservative variant of the presidential regime that had emerged under Schleicher in the summer of 1932 possessed a certain appeal and integrative potential all its own. But after the failure of the Papen experiment—something for which his successor had to bear a good measure of responsibility—the preconditions for a political stabilization under authoritarian auspices no longer existed. For even though industry's extreme distrust of the cabinet seems to have abated when the scope of Gereke's job creation program was drastically curtailed and while both the National Federation German Industry and the German Chamber of Industry and Commerce (Deutscher Industrie- und Handelstag) appreciated the government's endeavors to rescind a trade policy that had discriminated against the interests of the export industry, fundamental differences persisted. At the same time, the cabinet faced increasing criticism from organized agricultural interests. Schleicher had so often changed his fundamental attitude in the past that his assurances of goodwill toward the SPD and the socialist labor unions now failed to earn him their toleration. Even if the desired alliance with Gregor Straßer had materialized, it still would have been difficult for a chancellor so enmeshed in constant political maneuvering to dispel the distrust that had built up against his commitment to the primacy of military policy.

On 3 December 1932, the day after he had assumed the office of chancellor, Schleicher offered the second most influential man in the NSDAP not only the vice-chancellorship but also the office of Prussian prime minister. At this point, Straßer was still hoping that the Nazi leadership cadre could be won over to a course of political compromise. The disastrous outcome of the municipal and district elections that took place on the following day in Thuringia, in which the NSDAP lost more than 40 percent of the votes it had obtained in the November Reichstag elections, only confirmed his contention that the party could not continue the purely destructive tactics it had previously pursued if it did not want to lose all credibility whatsoever. Before the elections he had been in a distinct minority with his proposal to enter a national cabinet under Schleicher's leadership. But now, after the Thuringian elections, a change in the thinking of the Nazi leadership cadre began to materialize as a large number of NSDAP Reichstag deputies came to realize that the dissolution of the Reichstag would bring heavy electoral losses with it.

On 7 December the situation drew to a head. Hitler, who had not even known of Schleicher's formal offer two days earlier, rejected Straßer's arguments for government participation out of hand. Straßer pleaded with the Nazi party leader to postpone a final decision until he had visited the party's most important district and state headquarters and had had an opportunity to assess the party's internal situation for himself. But Hitler did not respond to this suggestion any more positively than he had responded to earlier reproaches. The very sharpness of the exchange made a break between the two inevitable. Straßer had been contemplating his resignation ever since 30 November, when he found himself completely isolated in the Nazi leadership conference. Since a general secession from the NSDAP was for him out of the question, he accepted the personal consequences of what had become an untenable situation and announced his decision to resign all leadership functions in the party without, however, also renouncing his party membership.

Straßer was disappointed that none of the other leading figures within the party had supported him despite previous indications that many of them agreed with his analysis of the situation. Immediately after his meeting with Hitler, Straßer wrote the Nazi party leader a long letter in which he outlined the reasons for his resignation and assured him that he had no intention whatsoever of starting an opposition movement of any kind. At a hastily called meeting of the party's state inspectors in the Reichstag, Straßer explained both the political and personal reasons for his decision. Straßer's action could be interpreted as a last warning to Hitler to rid himself of the advisors to whose pernicious influence the increasing disarray of the party was to be attributed. For it was clear to him that Hitler's incomparable political talents had to be kept on track by a practical politician who kept the realities of everyday life in sight while the "Leader" pursued his visions. While Straßer accepted the charismatic function that Hitler exercised as party leader, this did not prevent him from maintaining an open mind and a sense of personal distance from the Hitler cult. At the same time, a sense of personal loyalty made it impossible for him to attack Hitler directly as many of his friends expected him to do. Later they would reproach him for his "paladin mentality."

The report of Straßer's resignation, which appeared in the early morning edition of the *Tägliche Rundschau*, hit Nazi party headquarters like a bombshell, particularly since it was accompanied by the comment that Straßer was the only man capable of extricating the NSDAP from the utter confusion in which it currently found itself. Hitler, who believed that Straßer's appointment as vice-chancellor and Reich labor minister was imminent, construed the entire affair as a deliberate act of betrayal and as an attempt on Straßer's part to split the party. At first he fell into a state of deep depression and talked of suicide: "If the party falls apart, I'll end it all in three minutes." Profoundly influenced by Goebbels, Hitler did not for a moment believe that Straßer was sincere. After he had regained his composure, Hitler reacted in his customary hyperbolic fashion to Straßer's action by dismissing it as a diversionary maneuver on the part of the chancellor.

While Hitler tried to minimize the party crisis by putting out the official version that Straßer had taken a three-week leave of absence for reasons of poor health, he assumed personal control of Straßer's functions as the NSDAP's Reich organization leader. At a hastily convened meeting of the state inspectors, he exacted an unambiguous declaration of loyalty from them. When he made the same request to the NSDAP Reichstag delegation shortly thereafter, his tearfully emotional rhetoric touched off quasi-Byzantine rituals of submission. The oaths of fidelity that one National Socialist functionary after another took to Hitler's leadership of the party concealed the fact that many of their peers were beginning to feel that the time had come when they should be rewarded with public offices and political power for the deprivations they had suffered during the long years of struggle. There was less and less sympathy for the course pursued by Hitler, whose insistence that he would not sacrifice the aims of the movement for a few ministerial portfolios threatened to plunge the party into disastrous new elections.

Hitler's hectic reaction obscured the fundamental character of his conflict with Straßer. Straßer, on the other hand, did not shy away from candidly addressing these differences in his letter of resignation, the draft of which has been preserved. Aside from Hitler's lack of confidence in his loyalty, Straßer lamented the party leader's resistance to his persistent efforts to centralize and hierarchically stratify the party apparatus. For his own part, Hitler preferred not to interfere with the activities of his subordinates as long as they remained personally loyal to him. From this perspective, Hitler regarded the organizational directives that Straßer had issued and that seemed inescapable in view of the rapid growth in the party membership as positively harmful.

Behind the differences concerning the principles of party organization lay an irreconcilable difference of opinion over the political goals of the Nazi movement. The party was not, as Straßer pointed out to the Führer, "a movement of Weltanschauung that had been transformed into a religion" but rather "a militant movement [Kampfbewegung] that must pursue all possibilities of gaining power so that it can use the state to implement the National Socialist program and to introduce German socialism." In speaking of the need to subordinate the party to the state and in criticizing the NSDAP's failure to assume political responsibility, Straßer was articulating ideas that were self-evident to him but that ran counter to Hitler's personalized understanding of politics. To Hitler the NSDAP was the very embodiment of the "National Socialist idea," and he felt that under no circumstances should it compromise its internal credibility by entering into tactical alliances for the conquest of power. In this respect, Hitler continued to act upon the profound conviction that only unwavering adherence to its fundamental principles would bring the NSDAP to its goal of undivided power, a view that had no basis in reality whatsoever.

Straßer was convinced that it was necessary for the NSDAP to abandon a tactic that was committed to the primacy of propaganda and that in many respects had been subversive of the NSDAP's own goals in order to rededicate it to constructive political action and the achievement of specific political goals. Straßer's repeated calls for a "German Socialism" may have lacked theoretical precision, but there was no doubt that he was as serious about this as he was about the creation of new jobs. Unlike Hitler, however, Straßer did not consider these issues to be interchangeable parts of a propaganda strategy aimed at mobilizing the masses. Furthermore, Straßer believed, in sharp contrast to his leader, that previously uncommitted industrial workers could be drawn into the Nazi fold. "Fighting Marxism by brute force," he noted to Hitler, could and should not be "the focus of domestic political activity." The task at hand was rather "to create a broad front of working men and women and to ensure their allegiance to the newly formed state."

In criticizing the terrorist methods of the party, Straßer referred to Hitler's notion of pursuing the conquest of political power by means of a violent final confrontation with "Marxism." In this respect, he warned against "thinking that chaos alone will bring the party's hour of destiny." Here Straßer was alluding to Hitler's peculiar idea that the Nazi conquest would take place in the context of a all-out confrontation with the Marxist parties. It was extremely important to Hitler that the uprising that he fully expected to take place on the Left be suppressed exclusively by the forces of the movement and without the help of the military. For only his men possessed the ruthlessness necessary to silence to Marxist adversary once and for all. The vision of a "German Saint Bartholomew's Day Massacre" could be seen after Hitler's appointment as chancellor in his demand that the Reichswehr should leave it to the NSDAP and SA "to settle accounts in the streets." To Hitler, the destruction of the "Marxist" camp was tantamount to defeating a "world view" nearly as comprehensive as his own, and it was clear to him that mere persuasion would not be able to achieve it. It was not so much the acceptance of governmental responsibility as the total and violent destruction of the organized labor movement that constituted the decisive moment in the party's attainment of political power. Straßer, on the other hand, was convinced that only a constructive sociopolitical program could wean the working masses away from the SPD. He had little faith in the ability of the NSDAP's propaganda campaign to produce the desired political breakthrough. In his opinion, it was time for the party to demonstrate that it was capable of positive political work. No longer could it refuse to cooperate with other national forces.

Straßer had numerous followers, particularly in the various administrative agencies that he had created within the party. By contrast, he could not count on the support of NSDAP district leaders, a group that had regarded his efforts to streamline the Nazi party organization with great skepticism. Within the party's inner leadership clique, only Wilhelm Frick, Gottfried Feder, and Alfred Rosenberg rose to Straßer's defense. But their voices did not carry much weight with Hitler. Straßer's declared enemies, on the other hand, included Goebbels, Göring, and Röhm, who otherwise had very little in common. Goebbels, who committed himself early on to Hitler's "all-or-nothing" strategy, had been Straßer's main antagonist since 1926. Göring, who had served as Hitler's principal liaison to important public figures and prominent businessmen, considered Straßer a serious rival, particularly with regard to the realization of his own ambitions in Prussia. Göring's aloofness from the party apparatus explains why Straßer paid relatively little attention to him. Ernst Röhm, on the other hand, would have had to resign his positions in the party if Straßer, who felt that his homosexual tendencies were a serious liability for the party, had had anything to say about it. In view of this constellation of personnel around Hitler, there was never much of a chance that Straßer would succeed in winning Hitler's support for his ideas.

Although Straßer made no attempt to coerce his supporters into supporting his political strategy, Hitler responded to the resignation of his offices within the Nazi party organization by issuing comprehensive organizational directives that confirmed the fundamental conflict of strategies that the former Reich organization leader had outlined in his letter to Hitler from 8 December 1932. With the appointment of Robert Ley, until then a high-ranking inspector within the Reich organization leadership of the NSDAP, as Hitler's special deputy in charge of the party's national organization, Hitler effectively decoupled this office from the party's central leadership organs. At the same time, Hitler decreed the abolition of the national inspectors, while the state inspectors lost their character as an intermediary agency within the party organization insofar as they henceforth functioned with the rank of NSDAP district leader and could deal with other district leaders only with special authorization from the party's national headquarters. With one stroke of the pen, Hitler effectively dismantled the hierarchical organizational structure that Straßer had worked so diligently to build up in favor of the party's district leaders, who now reported directly to Hitler himself.

The reorganization of the NSDAP took place in a totally unsystematic fashion that reflected Hitler's personalized notion of political action. Certain departments of the party's national organization were placed under Hitler's direct control and thus became autonomous elements of the party apparatus, while those that were not abolished outright were transferred to the NSDAP's Reich propaganda leadership. The net effect of these changes was to weaken seriously the NSDAP's Reich organization leadership, which Hitler handed over to Ley as soon as he had stripped it of many of its most important responsibilities. At the same time, Hitler created a Central Political Commission (Politische Zentralkommission) that was responsible for monitoring the work of the NSDAP's parliamentary delegations as well as the party's press and economic policies. Under the direction of Rudolf Heß, a man who was uncritically devoted to Hitler but utterly lacking in initiative and personality, this body was condemned to insignificance from the very outset. This meant that not only Straßer's goal of a tightly organized party apparatus but any constructive political planning had become impossible. The NSDAP was now divided into thirty-two compartmentalized district organizations, while the party's national leadership existed in name only.

Hitler explained the reasons for restructuring the NSDAP apparatus in an internal memorandum to party leaders that was characteristic of his political self-understanding. In it Hitler argued that bureaucratic structures must not prevent the movement from fulfilling its tasks as "custodian of the National Socialist idea." The movement as a political community dedicated to an idea must be insulated from contact with the mundane realities of everyday life that are only partly capable of redeeming the movement's visionary goals. There was no need, Hitler continued, for any special planning boards such as those that Straßer had wanted to establish in anticipation of the NSDAP's entry into the government: "Research institutes for the study of more or less obscure subjects have no place in a political organization." The net effect of Hitler's arguments was to block the efforts of Straßer and his supporters to divert the party from its obsession with propagandistic mobilization down the path of constructive political work.

Having completely demolished the centralized leadership structure that Straßer had tried to create, Hitler did not hesitate to attack and defame Straßer's personal reputation. He took advantage of a meeting of Nazi party district leaders that convened in Weimar on 16 January 1933 to "settle scores with Straßer" once and for all without, however, going so far as to demand his expulsion from the party. Such a step was in fact superfluous, for in spite of the high esteem in which many party functionaries and sympathizers continued to hold Straßer, neither a split within the party nor major protest actions in support of Straßer had materialized. Still, Straßer was unable to prevent the internal opposition that had crystallized in certain sections of the party and that established short-lived emergency action groups, or *Notgemeinschaften,*

from invoking his name. At the same time, he was held personally responsible
for everything that was wrong with the movement before being finally branded
as a traitor to the movement.

Just forty years old at the time of his resignation, Straßer was deeply hurt
by the acrimony and ruthlessness of Hitler's attacks. He responded to what he
later called — and not without a certain degree of justification — the destruction
of his life's work with profound depression, which was compounded by his advanced diabetes. The net result was that this unusually active and enterprising
party activist turned into a resigned and tentative private citizen who was dependent on the advice of those around him and who lacked the inner strength
to defend himself against the smear campaign that Goebbels mounted with a
cynicism inspired by hatred. Neither his friends nor his enemies believed that
it was possible that Straßer would go ahead with his announced intention of
retiring from active political life. Goebbels feared, though without any foundation whatsoever, that Straßer would resume the fight by organizing a slate of
deputies in the Reichstag under the slogan "Against Goebbels and Göring." By
the same token, Schleicher believed as late as 16 January 1933 that Straßer, who
had not declined the request to call on the Reich president on 3 January, was
still available for the post of vice-chancellor. Independently of whatever might
materialize on this front, many of Straßer's closest associates were hoping that,
despite the pledge of loyalty Hitler had extorted from them, their man would
take on Hitler himself. There were even scattered rumors to the effect that
Straßer was waiting for the appropriate moment to take over the reins of power
from Schleicher. Yet Straßer held fast to his decision to keep away from politics. His request for an interview with Hitler was granted in January, but was
subsequently withdrawn since the Nazi party leader did not want to see him.
Although Straßer had repeatedly affirmed his loyalty to Hitler in conversations
with Heß and Frick, Göring and Himmler used the liquidation of the SA command on 30 June 1934 to have their former rival assassinated. The official cause
of death was suicide. With the seditious activities of the conspirators in the
Papen vice-chancery Straßer had had nothing whatsoever to do.

The Straßer crisis obscured the fact that the NSDAP had become completely
isolated as a result of Hitler's intransigence and his refusal to back down from
his demand that he be allowed to form a presidential cabinet under his leadership. In the meantime, the party's relations to Schleicher had deteriorated in
connection with Straßer's fall from power, since many Nazi leaders believed
that the two were involved in a full-fledged conspiracy against Hitler At the
same time, Schleicher came under sharp criticism from the extreme Right. In
a commentary in *Der Ring*, the cabinet was attacked for having "harnessed
the same old party horses to the carriage of state." It was symptomatic of the
chancellor's increasingly difficult situation that, in a speech before the German
Lords' Club on 16 December 1932 in which he called for "the creation of a socio-

logically new leadership elite" and in this context declared Hitler's inclusion in the national government indispensable, Franz von Papen also demanded Schleicher's resignation. Although Papen's advocacy of the NSDAP did not reflect the official attitude of the Lord's Club, this "stab in the back" of General Schleicher—in the words of Theodor Eschenburg, who was present on the occasion—was the first step in a complicated maneuver by which the former chancellor intended to include the NSDAP in an authoritarian government under his own leadership.

On the occasion of the dinner at the Lord's Club, the Cologne banker Kurt von Schröder, who had been actively working for the NSDAP for some time, offered to arrange a meeting between Hitler and Papen. Only a few weeks earlier, such a contact would have been unthinkable. But now it offered a chance to pull the rug out from under "Straßerism" by politically eliminating Schleicher. In this case, the desire for revenge was stronger than Hitler's fear of being duped once again by the arch-reactionaries in Hindenburg's entourage. It was also significant that this somewhat unorthodox initiative for establishing contact with Hitler came from relatively second-rank representatives of industry and agriculture. Over the course of the preceding months, both groups had gone to great lengths to bring the NSDAP into the government and to commit it to a "reasonable" economic policy. It was their contention that Hitler must not be excluded from political responsibility in the state, if only because this would make it possible for him to purge his movement of its socially revolutionary and quasi-Communistic elements. Straßer's resignation provided a psychological lift for those spokesmen of the German business community who were trying to increase their influence within the NSDAP.

Kurt von Schröder, whose Cologne banking house enjoyed a certain reputation but was not in the same category as the major German banks, had been among the signatories of a petition that a group of industrialists had sent to Hindenburg on 19 November 1932. The petition called on the Reich president to overcome his reservations about entrusting Hitler with the chancellorship and to "hand over responsibility for a presidential cabinet staffed with individuals of the highest technical and personal qualifications to the leader of the largest national group," in short, to Adolf Hitler. Aside from a number of middle-sized entrepreneurs, the largest group among the signatories of the petition were representatives of large-scale agriculture, who as a result of R. Walter Darré's highly successful Agrarian Political Apparatus were for the most part already under Nazi influence. The petition was hardly representative of the German economic community as a whole. Heavy industry was conspicuous by its self-restraint. Neither Albert Vögler, who after Fritz Thyssen sympathized most strongly with the NSDAP, nor Paul Reusch signed the petition, although in principle they agreed with its content. Paul Silverberg, who had advocated placing Hitler at the head of the presidential cabinet for some time, had not been approached because of his family origins. The reticence of the German business community was prompted not so much by hostility to Hitler as by the desire to see Papen and the NSDAP reach an accommodation of their own.

Since the summer of 1932, the *Deutsche Führerbriefe*, a newsletter for influential leaders in politics and business that reflected the views of industrialist Paul Silverberg, had been particularly outspoken in advocating the "integration of National Socialism" into the national cabinet. Like August Heinrichsbauer, the editor of the *Rheinisch-Westfälischer Wirtschaftsdienst* who was in close contact with Gregor Straßer and his chief economic advisor Otto Wagener, Silverberg was primarily interested in preventing an alliance between the NSDAP and Center and in strengthening those within the NSDAP who advocated moderation in the area of economic policy. This appeal was directed to both Hitler and Straßer, although the latter was particularly important because of his discretion in matters of economic policy and his presumed ability to win the confidence of the working masses and to liberate them from the grip of the political Left. In Hitler, on the other hand, one saw a guarantee that the NSDAP would not fall back into the obsolete democratic and parliamentary structures that had just been overthrown. Indeed, Hitler was the "strongest hope" against the danger "that we will succumb to the intoxication of the masses and that there will be a renaissance of Weimar with all of its democracy, parliamentarism, legality, and the whole ideology of the last one hundred fifty years." For that reason, it was vitally important to "strengthen [Hitler's] ideological goals, which are greater than the parliamentary-political aims of the party."

In the meantime, the leaders of German heavy industry continued their efforts on behalf of closer cooperation between the forces of the German bourgeoisie and the NSDAP with a view toward isolating the latter's "more radical elements." An essential precondition for this, however, was the creation of a homogeneous bourgeois bloc. As a result, Germany's industrial leadership sought to force Hugenberg from the DNVP party leadership on the assumption that he constituted the most serious obstacle to the consolidation of Germany's bourgeois Right. At the same time, the Ruhrlade sought to intensify its contacts with the NSDAP through the establishment of a special office known as the Arbeitsstelle Schacht under the direction of the former Reichsbank president Hjalmar Schacht. Schacht, who had become increasingly identified with the Nazi program for economic self-sufficiency, had realized that heavy industry had begun to lose interest in his efforts ever since the fall of 1932 in the wake of its unconditional support for Papen. Ever since Schleicher's cabinet had come into being, heavy industry had felt the need to combat the new governments "cryptoparliamentary" tendencies. It therefore supported Papen's efforts to bring Hitler into the government on terms that effectively limited the latter's freedom of movement but remained skeptical about the prospect of a Hitler chancellorship. The plan to bring Hitler into the cabinet with a strong bourgeois counterweight, however, did not originate with German big business but rather with the group that had organized the November petition for Hindenburg, namely, the so-called Keppler Circle (Keppler-Kreis).

Wilhelm Keppler came from the ranks of Germany's middle-sized entrepreneurs and had been trying to make a name for himself as Hitler's economic advisor ever since 1931. In contrast to Gottfried Feder and Otto Wagener, Keppler was interested in bringing about a rapprochement between the ideas of big business and those of the NSDAP. With the founding of the Keppler circle he outdid Schacht himself. For the time being, however, the Ruhrlade continued to support the Arbeitsstelle Schacht, which had now set itself to the task of influencing the economic thinking of the NSDAP in a probusiness direction. His close personal relations notwithstanding, Schacht was not all that successful, particularly since the Arbeitsstelle Schacht did not enjoy as much support within the German business community as the former Reichsbank president had expected. In the final analysis, Schacht felt obliged to join the Keppler Circle, which was not any more successful in its efforts to enlist the support of German big business. Aside from the purely nominal membership of Albert Vögler from the United Steelworks (Vereinigte Stahlwerke) and the participation of the highly respected potash entrepreneur August Rostberg, the large industrial firms were not represented. The composition of the Keppler Circle was thus limited to smaller manufacturers and businessmen. For his own part, Hitler attended a ceremonial reception for the members of the Keppler Circle in Berlin's fashionable Hotel Kaiserhof in June 1932 but afterward ceased to pay attention to the group. At the very end of 1932, however, the Keppler Circle moved to the center of the political stage as a bridge between Hitler and Papen.

After his conversation with Papen in the German Lords' Club, Schröder passed the idea of a meeting with Hitler on to Keppler, who in turn transmitted it to the Nazi party leadership. Unaware that Papen was operating on his own, the national leadership of the NSDAP was convinced that the former chancellor was acting as a special emissary for the Reich president and was therefore most receptive to the proposal for the establishment of political contact between Hitler and Papen. In this respect, they were motivated primarily by the desire to change the Reich president's negative, if not insulting, reaction to Hitler's proposals from the previous November and to reverse the bitter defeat that Hitler had suffered on 13 August. A letter that Keppler wrote to Schröder on 26 December, no doubt after having cleared it with Hitler, was carefully drafted with this in mind. "What I envision as the political objective of the interview," it read in part, "is a reorganization of the government without new elections beforehand and without a presidential crisis." After this had been accomplished, the letter continued, one could consider the possibility of a "governmental election" (*Regierungswahl*) behind the slogan "Hindenburg-Hitler."

This was tantamount to restating the proposals that had been contained in the November petition. The only new feature was the suggestion that the cabinet should seek to create a parliamentary majority for itself by elections that would take place after it had taken office. By convincing the "old gentleman" of the necessity of forming a presidential cabinet under Hitler's leadership, the letter concluded, "Herr von Papen could fulfill a great historical mission." Obviously the author of this letter considered Papen a simple errand boy without political ambitions of his own.

The meeting was arranged in utmost secrecy. Both Hitler and Papen came to Schröder's private residence in Cologne by complicated detours. The NSDAP leader was intent on avoiding a renewed loss of prestige. Papen, on the other hand, was acting behind the chancellor's back and without authorization from the Reich president. Neither of them, however, realized that a photographer for the *Tägliche Rundschau*, which had somehow found out about the meeting, was secretly taking pictures of the visitors to Schröder's villa. Even before the meeting, the paper's editor in chief, Hans Zehrer, had warned the incredulous chancellor of the machinations of his predecessor. Summoned to the Reich Chancery to explain himself, Papen trivialized the content of his conversation with Hitler, which had given rise to widespread speculation in the press. Schleicher complained to the Reich president about Papen's disloyalty without being fully aware of the consequences of what was taking place. Hindenburg, however, had little sympathy for Schleicher's understandable request to "forbid him [Papen] to engage in such political activities in the future and to receive him only in his [the chancellor's] presence." On the occasion of Papen's next visit, Hindenburg not only told him what Schleicher had said, but also formally authorized him to maintain "personal and confidential" contacts with Hitler on the basis of their conversation in Cologne. In this respect, Hindenburg seems to have thought that Hitler could somehow be persuaded to set aside his party ties and cooperate directly with the government. This was only one of the many self-deceptions to which German conservatives succumbed in these weeks.

At his first meeting with Papen, Hitler had come armed with a catalog of demands, whereas the former chancellor had been interested in little more than exploring the possibilities of a rapprochement. In an attempt to placate Hitler, Papen suggested the idea of a vice-chancellorship in the existing cabinet, perhaps in the form of a duumvirate with Schleicher. Sensing Hitler's disappointment at this suggestion, Papen hastened to add that this would only be a transitional solution until the time when Hitler could claim the chancellorship for himself. Papen then revealed his own agenda and indicated that the chancellor was no longer persona grata with the Reich president. It was therefore necessary, Papen continued, to explore the possibility that the two of them might jointly assume the leadership of a cabinet "composed of other national politicians and experts" more or less along the lines that Keppler had suggested in the first place.

In a press communiqué that he drafted in consultation with Hitler—this had become necessary after the indiscretion of the *Tägliche Rundschau*—Papen tried to downplay the significance of the meeting. He claimed that the discussion had focused exclusively on the formation of a broad "national front" and had dealt with the present cabinet. In point of fact, however, the former chancellor had made it clear that he was determined to force the chancellor from office, particularly since the latter, as Goebbels learned from Hitler on the following day, would not be receiving authority to dissolve the Reichstag. To be sure, other alternatives to the formation of a presidential cabinet under Hitler's chancellorship had also been discussed. But, as Goebbels noted: "Arrangement with us being prepared. Either chancellorship or the power ministries. Defense and interior." No doubt Schleicher must have found out about this in one way or another. In late January he sneered at Hitler's interest in the Defense Ministry, which Hindenburg would never hand over to him, and concluded from this interest that Hitler was no longer pursuing the chancellorship.

For Papen the immediate objective was to forge a united front against Schleicher without having to wait for a definitive solution to the question of his successor as chancellor. It was with this in mind, therefore, that Papen mobilized his good relations with German heavy industry, whose attitude toward Schleicher spanned the gamut from cautious to frigid. In this respect, Papen sought to use to his own advantage the uneasiness that Germany's industrial elite, but most of all the circle around Paul Reusch, felt about the danger of a relapse into parliamentarism under Schleicher. In a meeting the former chancellor had with a small group of leading Ruhr industrialists, including Reusch, Vögler, and Krupp, at the home of Fritz Springorum on 7 January 1933 the main topic of discussion was not so much Papen's meeting with Hitler three days earlier but how one could pressure Hugenberg into resigning as DNVP party chairman—perhaps in favor of Papen—so that the "long-awaited concentration of bourgeois political forces" might begin. While it does not appear that Papen initiated this discussion, what the industrialists had in mind certainly fit in with his own plans to strengthen the bourgeois Right as a counterweight to the NSDAP. In the face of Hugenberg's adamant refusal to step down, all of these considerations remained purely theoretical.

For the NSDAP, Papen's overtures, insofar as they could be trusted, offered indirect encouragement to intensify its political pressure on the Schleicher cabinet. The NSDAP, however, was not directly involved in the violent attacks that the National Rural League (Reichs-Landbund or RLB) launched against the chancellor on 11 January in the form of a resolution castigating the "plunder of agriculture on behalf of the all-powerful moneybags in the international export business and their sycophants." It is nevertheless interesting in this context that the Nazi press fully concurred with the charges of "agrarian Bolshevism" that were being leveled against the chancellor. The chancellor responded to the embarrassing fact that the National Rural League published this resolution just as its leaders were meeting with the Reich president by breaking off all contact. The RLB's attacks backfired insofar as the leading industrial interest organizations protested sharply against polemics of this sort and vigorously opposed the agrarian lobby's demand for a freeze on mortgage interest rates and for general protection for agriculture against the threat of foreclosure.

Schleicher suddenly found himself in the same predicament that had faced Heinrich Brüning and Hermann Müller. Once again the agrarian lobby had enlisted the support of the president and his entourage for economically ridiculous demands and had extorted concessions that were incapable of being fulfilled. The cabinet, for instance, was forced to pass a highly unpopular regulation mandating the use of a certain percentage of butter in the manufacture of margarine, which only compounded the existing controversy over agricultural tariffs and quotas on the import of agricultural commodities. Far more damaging to Schleicher's position, however, was the counteroffensive launched by the Center, which raised questions in the Reichstag about the use of subsidies to the east and thus gave new fodder to the widespread rumors about corruption in the administration of the government's agrarian relief programs. In a much discussed publication, Erich Ludendorff had already voiced the suspicion that Hindenburg's neighbor and fellow landowner Elard von Oldenburg-Januschau had illegally profited from government agricultural subsidies. Now the Hindenburg family itself came under suspicion of corruption, although charges to this effect had little substance and were eventually proved unfounded. In Hindenburg's mind, the debate over the scandal in the Eastern Aid Program served as a telling reminder that Schleicher's return to parliamentary methods would have disastrous consequences.

Hugenberg, who was well aware of the precarious situation in which the cabinet found itself, had already registered his demands with the chancellor and had called for the creation of a "cabinet of national concentration" that included the DNVP. When Hugenberg proceeded to demand for himself the Ministries of Economics and of Agriculture, Schleicher rejected these demands rather bluntly. In the course of their discussion, Hugenberg suggested presenting the Reichstag with the alternative between adjournment for at least six months or immediate dissolution with no new elections. In the meantime, parallel negotiations that Hugenberg had initiated with Hitler without first discussing the matter with Papen ended in futility. At this point Hugenberg was not yet ready to cede control of the Prussian Ministry of the Interior to the NSDAP. At most he might be willing to negotiate for the neutralization of the Prussian police force, a proposal that Hitler indignantly rejected. With respect to the DNVP, Hitler adhered rigidly to his maximal demands and proved to be anything by conciliatory. Nevertheless rumors about the formation of a new Harzburg Front began to circulate widely after 17 January 1933.

By far the factor that was most difficult to assess in the intrigue-ridden weeks of January 1933 was the attitude of Hitler, whose prima donna affectations were disturbing even to his closest associates. In an interview with Otto Dietrich, the head of the Nazi press office, on 10 January 1933, Hitler made it clear that he remained committed to the terms of the offer he had submitted to the Reich president on 24 November. This must have created the impression that the will to compromise and reach an agreement was lacking, particularly since Papen, with whom Hitler was to meet on the same evening through the good offices of Joachim von Ribbentrop, was by no means authorized to negotiate with Hitler on the chancellorship. Papen's tactical retreat prompted Hitler to temporarily postpone the negotiations, particularly since he expected that the outcome of the Lippe provincial elections on 15 January 1933 would greatly improve his party's position. In comparison with the November Reichstag elections, the NSDAP managed to gain an additional 5 percent share of the popular vote but still remained behind the 39.6 percent it had received the previous July. This, however, did not prevent Goebbels from celebrating the election victory as a triumphal sign of the continued growth of the Nazi movement, a maneuver that had a decided effect on Hitler's conservative negotiating partners.

When the discussions resumed on 18 January with the participation of Heinrich Himmler and Ernst Röhm, Papen found himself at a distinct disadvantage because there was not yet any sign that Hindenburg was willing to consider Hitler for the chancellorship. At the insistence of Hitler, who repeatedly threatened to break off negotiations, the participants agreed to invite Oskar von Hindenburg to the next meeting. The Reich president, apparently deluded into believing that the discussion would focus on a Papen chancellorship, consented to a meeting in Papen's presence between his son Oskar, State Secretary Otto Meißner, and Hitler. This encounter took place in the strictest secrecy in Ribbentrop's villa in Dahlem, and Hitler used the opportunity to meet privately with the Reich president's son and to convince him of the absolute necessity of his appointment as chancellor.

As far as the details of an agreement were concerned, no progress was made that night. For while Papen challenged the Nazis to participate in either the existing cabinet or in a new government by assuming responsibility for several cabinet portfolios, Hitler continued to demand the chancellorship for himself, a demand that he tried, as he had done the previous November, to sweeten by agreeing to include a broad spectrum of "bourgeois" ministers in his cabinet. The decisive point in all of this was that Hitler was determined to adhere to the form of a presidential cabinet, whereas Papen thought in terms of renewing the Harzburg Front. Nevertheless, Papen agreed to support the idea of a Hitler chancellorship in his next conversation with the Reich president. In this respect, he was supported by Oskar von Hindenburg, who remarked to Meißner on the return trip home: "I fear there's no way around this Hitler."

The negotiations that took place behind Schleicher's back in the second half of January 1933 produced two opposing models for a resolution of the deepening crisis in which the government found itself. The first called for the renewal of the Harzburg Front with either the participation or toleration of the Center. In practical terms, this meant a government under Hitler's leadership that commanded a virtual majority in the Reichstag. The other model called for the creation of a *Kampfkabinett* behind Papen, Hugenberg, and the Stahlhelm's Franz Seldte. The second of these options appeared necessary in the event that efforts to unite the nationalist Right once again foundered on Hitler's excessive demands. The most important obstacle to the first of the two options, on the other hand, lay in Hindenburg's stipulation that Hitler would be acceptable only as the head of a cabinet that possessed a majority in parliament. This was also the general thrust of public discussion on the possibility of a Hitler chancellorship. While the Pan-German monthly *Deutschlands Erneuerung* found it preposterous that the Nazi party leader had to invoke the principles of parliamentary government "to achieve the position to which the sheer number of his followers entitled him," *Vorwärts* insisted that a Hitler chancellorship was tolerable only in the context of a majority cabinet that included the Center.

In point of fact, the presidential entourage had as early as the previous November considered asking Hitler to form a cabinet that rested on the support of a parliamentary majority in the expectation that he would fail because of the intransigence of the DNVP. The hope that the NSDAP would be somewhat more amenable to compromise after such a failure revealed a fundamental misreading of Hitler's basic frame of mind. Once again Papen found himself faced with the fact that Hitler refused to go along with such an experiment. The negotiations therefore quickly reached an impasse. Hitler, who was focused almost exclusively on filling key positions in a presidential cabinet, was fully prepared to leave all other personnel decisions to Papen. But in the end, he always returned to his original demand that the question of the chancellorship must be decided before the composition of the cabinet could be negotiated. The nagging fear that he might lose face once again prompted Hitler to withdraw from the negotiations, to entrust Göring with responsibility for their continuation, and to threaten to return to Munich if things did not go his way. Hitler's decision to withdraw from all further negotiations, however, proved to be something of an advantage, for Göring was much more flexible in his negotiating style than the increasingly rigid Nazi party leader. In a subsequent discussion with Papen, Ribbentrop, and Frick, Göring initiated a momentous change of direction by proposing the formation of a cabinet of the "national front" in which the NSDAP would hold a key position and that would be able to mobilize the parliamentary support necessary to secure the passage of a special enabling law. In the meantime, the question of whether new elections were to be held would be left open for the time being.

The prospect of a government of national concentration operating under the terms of special enabling legislation that had been approved by the Reichstag was particularly attractive to Hindenburg because it would free him from the onerous burden of having to use his good name and reputation to buttress the presidential regime. At the same time, Hindenburg also indicated his willingness to grant special presidential powers to a government in which the DNVP and Center constituted an effective counterweight to Hitler. Hindenburg might, Meißner informed his negotiating partners, "drop the requirement of a parliamentary majority if the cabinet had the support of the Stahlhelm, the Rural League, and the [right-wing] parties and could therefore present itself as a cabinet of the entire national movement." Even then, there would still have to be safeguards to make it impossible "for one party to rape the others." In the final analysis, all of this was tantamount to a revival of the ill-fated Harzburg Front.

Within this constellation the DNVP finally became involved in the negotiations to form a new government, even though Hugenberg's meeting with Hitler just a few days earlier had produced little in the way of concrete results. Hugenberg proceeded to burn all bridges that might have led to a compromise with the Schleicher cabinet. In a resolution drafted on 21 January the DNVP Reichstag delegation charged that "the present government [was] intent on nothing less than liquidating the idea of authoritarian government that had guided the Reich president in forming the Papen government and on returning German politics to the course that it had appeared to leave behind thanks to the strengthening of the national movement." This amounted to a virtual declaration of war against the Schleicher cabinet and reflected the last-minute fears of the conservative Right that the progress toward the establishment of a truly authoritarian state might suddenly be reversed. The net effect of these fears was to reduce whatever inhibitions Germany's bourgeois camp might have felt about the NSDAP's participation in the national cabinet.

At first Schleicher was only vaguely aware of the conspiracy against his cabinet. As late as 16 January 1933 Schleicher still believed that he could make use of the Straßer gambit. And even after this failed to work out, he still nourished the hope that he could bring about an alliance of party leaders along the lines originally proposed by Kaas. Neither Hitler's rigidity nor Hugenberg's intransigence, however, augured particularly well for the realization of such a hope. The chancellor's lackadaisical negotiations with individual party leaders and his willingness to let the Reichstag committees do their work earned him nothing but the reproach that he desired a return to the basic forms of parliamentary government. When Meißner warned him that his proposal for reorganizing the cabinet implied a rejection of the principle of the presidential cabinet, Schlei-cher brushed him aside with the accurate but unexpected observation that in the final analysis one was still dependent upon the support of a parliamentary majority. Such an insight came rather late.

After authorizing a series of short delays, the Reichstag's Council of Elders finally set the convocation of the Reichstag for 31 January, in part because of pressure from the Center. Schleicher thus found himself forced to make up his own mind about the future direction of his cabinet. In his view, a minority government of the "national front" without the NSDAP was never an option. Hitler's participation or the formation of a cabinet with National Socialist tol-eration, on the other hand, could not be achieved. Nor was another adjourn-ment of the Reichstag likely. The only way out of the current impasse seemed to lie in a continuation of the present cabinet and the dissolution of the Reich-stag with the understanding that new elections would be postponed until the following fall. The constitutionally mandated limit of sixty days between the dissolution of parliament and new elections would have to be extended on the grounds of a "state emergency." Schleicher, who continued to entertain plans for reorganizing the cabinet even after he had reached this conclusion, was hoping that a dramatic improvement in the overall economic situation, particularly in the area of unemployment, would lead to a relaxation of politi-cal tensions and undercut the appeal of the NSDAP. This, however, would not have meant an end to the chronic government crisis.

When the chancellor called on Hindenburg on 23 January to inform him of the political constellation that had arisen, he must have realized that he no longer enjoyed the president's support. The Reich president agreed to go along with the chancellor's request for the "forced adjournment" of the Reichstag subject to the stipulation that the party leaders did not object to the decla-ration of a "state emergency." It was clear from the outset, however, that the consent of the parties to such an unusual procedure would not be forthcoming. It must have been humiliating to Schleicher to be constantly reminded that in a similar context on 2 December it was he who had pleaded with the Reich president to avoid an open violation of the constitution. His arguments that since then there had been a relaxation of domestic political tensions and that a general strike by the SPD and socialist labor unions was no longer likely had little effect upon Hindenburg, who feared a constitutional conflict. While it is true that the ADGB was indeed wary of the consequences of a general strike, Peter Graßmann nevertheless issued a declaration several days later to the effect that labor opposed the proclamation of a state emergency in any form what-soever. By the same token, the Center also made it clear that it saw no ground for deviating from the constitution. The *Völkischer Beobachter* also attacked Schleicher in the sharpest possible terms, no doubt taking advantage of the ammunition that Papen's indiscretions had furnished.

Only a week and a half earlier, the Reich president had seriously considered the possibility of postponing new elections. Now, however, he began to sever his psychological ties to the old regimental comrade with whom he had worked so closely for years on end. Given Schleicher's extraordinary tactical agility, the chancellor proved unexpectedly vulnerable to Papen's intrigues. It was finally clear to him that his days as chancellor were numbered. He ascribed the president's change of heart primarily to the machinations of his rival Papen, whose influence he had obviously underestimated. Yet Hindenburg had every reason to blame the hopeless situation in which the cabinet currently found itself on Schleicher's indecipherable maneuvers. The debate on the Eastern Aid Program in the Reichstag's budget committee proved deeply embarrassing to the aging Reich president, who found himself under increasingly heavy pressure from his fellow East Elbian aristocrats to get rid of Schleicher.

Papen took immediate advantage of the crisis in which the Schleicher chancellorship found itself to recommend Hitler's appointment as the head of a presidential cabinet. Up until this point, Papen had allowed Hindenburg to believe that the discussions with Hitler focused exclusively on the possibility of a cabinet under his leadership. Now he was under pressure from Hitler, who, following his party's dramatic victory in the Lippe state elections, was less inclined than ever to settle for the vice-chancellorship. Papen as much as acknowledged this on 20 January in a letter to industrialist Fritz Springorum and accepted the demand of an enabling law for "a government with Hitler." Should that come to pass, Papen added, "a concentration of all bourgeois forces as a counterweight to Hitler was most urgently needed." The fact of the matter was that Papen no longer had any room to maneuver as long as he refused to admit the complete failure of the negotiations he had conducted behind the chancellor's back. Over the course of the preceding weeks, Papen had allowed himself to become so deeply compromised by his contacts with the Nazi party leadership that he was vulnerable to extortion. Having thus been outmaneuvered, he could only hope that Hindenburg would veto a Hitler chancellorship and that the Nazi party leader would then give in to his own demands. As expected, Hindenburg rejected this proposal and, since there was no alternative, temporarily retained Schleicher as chancellor.

Hindenburg refused to allow the arguments of his fellow conservatives to moderate his negative attitude toward Hitler. Thus the former court official (*Kammerherr*) Elard von Oldenburg-Januschau tried in vain to dispel the president's prejudices against the "crude and violent manners of the Nazis" and to convince him that the Reichswehr and the various organizations on the bourgeois Right could easily keep Hitler under control. By the same token, the commander of the East Prussian Military District I, Lieutenant General Werner von Blomberg, glossed over the facts when he threw the full weight of his office behind the formation of a cabinet of the "National Front" under Hitler as chancellor. Nor did Göring's earlier assurances that as chancellor Hitler would remain strictly within the bounds of constitutionality—whatever that was supposed to mean—reassure the president about the choice of Hitler to succeed Schleicher. In the same context Göring hinted that the National Socialists might work for the restoration of the Hohenzollern monarchy once they were in control of the government. Göring's spectacular visits to the exiled Kaiser in Doorn in January 1931 and May 1932 gave this claim the semblance of credibility.

Hindenburg's refusal to grant presidential powers to a Hitler cabinet was consistent with the position that he had always taken and seemed to destroy whatever basis there might have been for further negotiations with the NSDAP. When Papen met with Göring and Frick at Ribbentrop's house once again on 24 January, the participants agreed to call the proposed cabinet a united front of all national parties, with Hitler as chancellor and Papen as vice-chancellor in what was admittedly a transparent effort to accommodate Hindenburg's long-standing desire for the unification of all nationalist parties and associations. That this cabinet would subsequently make every effort to secure the passage of enabling legislation that would free Hindenburg from the increasingly onerous task of having to issue emergency decrees was bound to meet with the Reich president's approval. Göring, however, went one step further and called for the immediate dissolution of the Reichstag and new elections, a demand to which Papen did not immediately respond.

The next task was to persuade the increasingly impatient, suspicious, and obstinate Hitler to go along with the new label. The problem was that the very notion of "national concentration" afforded Hugenberg a more important position than he would have otherwise had and that encouraged the DNVP party leader to make additional stipulations of his own. More strongly than anyone else at the negotiating table, the Nationalist leader rejected Hitler's demand for new Reichstag elections so emphatically that there was no basis for a compromise. Nor had Hindenburg's misgivings been altogether dispelled. The Reich president continued to cling to the idea of Papen's return to the chancellorship. But Papen was upset by reports from the NSDAP that it would embark on a course of all-out opposition if he should take over as chancellor. To the public it appeared that the only alternative lay between a presidential cabinet under Papen and a government of national concentration under Hitler. The former was certain to revive the Reichswehr's fears of being torn apart in a virtual civil war, with the result that Kurt von Hammerstein, the chief of military operations, spoke out forcefully to both Meißner and Hindenburg, though without having informed the chancellor of his intentions, against a second Papen government. If necessary, Hammerstein indicated, a Hitler chancellorship would be preferable, to which the old field marshal promptly responded:

"You can't possibly think, gentlemen, that I would make this Austrian corporal chancellor."

Like Hammerstein, Schleicher was inclined to go with Hitler, since he expected that a Papen-Hugenberg *Kampfkabinett* would produce the very "governmental and presidential crisis" he had sought to avoid. By this time, however, he had already abandoned the fight to keep his cabinet in office. When on 28 January 1933 he asked with the full support of his cabinet officers for a simple order authorizing dissolution of the Reichstag, without which he was unwilling to appear in parliament, Hindenburg categorically refused this request and then spoke of Schleicher's failure to form a parliamentary majority, as if he had given the chancellor a completely free hand to try his own luck at forming such a coalition. A complete and open exchange of ideas between the chancellor and president had not taken place during their brief fifteen-minute conversation any more than it had at the time of the collapse of the Brüning cabinet. Schleicher fell from power, as Count Schwerin von Krosigk so aptly put it, "through the withdrawal of the confidence of the Reich president," who refused to honor the request of cabinet officers for an audience before he announced his decision.

Schleicher was deeply embittered over the attitude of Hindenburg, a man with whom he had been in close contact for many years. The president had, he reported to the cabinet, "not even responded to his arguments and simply rattled off a spiel he had learned by heart." Unlike Brüning, Schleicher made no secret of his conviction that the president had deceived him. He regarded it as a breach of loyalty that Hindenburg had negotiated behind his back with his successor. While this was certainly true, it was no different from what had happened to his predecessors and from the role that he had played in their demise. From the very beginning, Schleicher underestimated the extent of the intrigues against him. Having requested that the Reich president not appoint a Nazi sympathizer to the Defense Ministry, he misread Hindenburg's willingness to go along with him on this point as confirmation of his belief that he would remain on in a Hitler cabinet as the minister of defense. In point of fact, Papen was already working on the appointment of a new defense minister and at the moment favored Joachim von Stülpnagel.

The resignation of the Schleicher cabinet on 28 January 1933 gave Papen a free hand to play his role as kingmaker and only further strengthened his already overdeveloped sense of self-confidence. At long last he could engage in a high-stakes game of chance by presenting the Reich president with the choice between a cabinet of the national front with Hitler as chancellor or a Papen-Hugenberg *Kampfkabinett*. It was a choice between what he described to Schwerin von Krosigk as the "big" and the "small solution." Hindenburg had expressed a certain sense of relief over the fact that it would not be necessary to break with the constitution. In abandoning his opposition to a cabinet of the "national" majority, he also agreed to consider Hitler as chancellor as long as his influence in the cabinet was held in check by the presence of a strong conservative counterweight.

There is considerable evidence to suggest that Papen, his public endorsements of a cabinet of "national concentration" notwithstanding, deliberately ran the risk that negotiations between Hitler and the bourgeois Right would end in failure, in which case it would become immediately necessary to form a Papen-Hugenberg *Kampfkabinett*. In any event, Papen negotiated with both options in mind. In a cabinet of the bourgeois Right with Papen as chancellor, Ewald von Kleist-Schmenzin would become minister of the interior, while other cabinet appointments were still the subject of considerable controversy within the DNVP. For a time, Carl Goerdeler was even being considered. Whatever the outcome, Papen and Hugenberg were in essential agreement that if it came to an alliance with Hitler, his "powers should be limited as much as possible." According to this scenario, the Nationalist nucleus of the cabinet would be supplemented by a few National Socialists. It was on the basis of this assumption that parallel negotiations with the NSDAP went ahead. The outcome of the negotiations, however, was threatened by a sudden reversal on the part of Hitler, who on 28 January resurrected his earlier demand for a presidential cabinet free from ties to the various political parties. Göring and Ribbentrop moved quickly to talk Hitler out of this position.

A far greater obstacle to the formation of a cabinet of national concentration lay in the person of Hugenberg, who on the previous day had had a fierce altercation with Hitler that had not been resolved and that had prompted the Nazi party leader to break off negotiations and leave town. Hugenberg favored the idea of a *Kampfkabinett* but encountered strong opposition from Franz Bracht, the Reich commissar in Prussia and the Reich minister of the interior, and Hans Helferich, the president of the Prussian Central Cooperative Bank (Preußische Zentralgenossenschaftskasse) and a man whom Hugenberg had hoped would assume the post of finance minister in the new cabinet. Fearful that he might be left out altogether, Hugenberg indicated his willingness to participate in a government of national concentration on the afternoon of 29 January over the strenuous objections of Kleist-Schmenzin and DNVP Reichstag Deputy Otto Schmidt-Hannover. At this point Franz Seldte indicated on behalf of the Stahlhelm leadership that he also was willing to join such a cabinet. But the organization's second-in-command, Theodor Duesterberg, made his consent contingent upon a meeting with Hitler, which took place on the morning of 30 January in Papen's Berlin residence and during which Hitler solemnly assured the Stahlhelm leader that he would no longer be attacked in the Nazi press on account of his Jewish origins. As far as specific issues were concerned, a provisional consensus quickly emerged. Hitler agreed that the Reich commissariat in Prussia should be placed in Papen's hands while Göring would be promoted to the post of deputy commissar and would assume responsibility for the Prussian Ministry of the Interior. Hugenberg would be assigned the economics and agriculture portfolios in both the Reich and Prussian governments in the expectation that they would all be combined in a special "crisis ministry."

Beguiled by the influence that he expected to wield in the new cabinet, Hugenberg ignored the warnings of his associates in the DNVP. In this respect, he failed to pay sufficient attention to Göring's relentless calls for new elections. When Göring arrived at Papen's house to seal the agreement, any reference to this question was deliberately left out. Although Kleist issued a warning, Hugenberg claimed that it would be to his advantage to deal with this problem at a later point in time. Aside from this, there was essential agreement to ask the Reichstag for an enabling law that would make the cabinet temporarily independent of a parliamentary majority in the Reichstag. In short, the fundamental decision in favor of the "big solution" had already been made. On the afternoon of 29 January, Göring reported that a cabinet with Hitler as chancellor, Papen as vice-chancellor and Reich commissar for Prussia, Frick as minister of the interior, and himself as Prussian minister of the interior was all in place. To be sure, Papen had deliberately set aside the question of the participation of the Center, without whose cooperation a majority in the Reichstag could not be attained. He did this in the knowledge that both Hugenberg and Hitler were adamantly opposed to an understanding with the Center.

The cabinet might not have been formed so quickly had not the Reich president, motivated by a deep and in many respects unjustified distrust of Schleicher, decided at the last moment to appoint a new defense minister. Since Hindenburg placed particular emphasis on the appointment of a general without political ambitions, this automatically excluded Joachim von Stülpnagel from further consideration. His choice, therefore, fell upon Lieutenant General Werner von Blomberg, who was a member of the German delegation at the Geneva Disarmament Conference. The Reich president, however, was not aware of the fact that he had chosen an outspoken Nazi sympathizer. Blomberg was summoned to Berlin by telegraph so that he could take part in the formal installation of the cabinet on the morning of 30 January. Neither Schleicher nor the leadership of the Reichswehr had been consulted about this appointment, and their attempt to bring Blomberg to the Defense Ministry for consultation before he called upon the Reich president was thwarted by Papen.

In the meantime, the impression that a Hitler cabinet was no longer under serious consideration seemed to gain strength at the upper echelons of the Reichswehr leadership. A second Papen cabinet would not only be interpreted by the military as an open affront to Schleicher but also as a return to the untenable situation of the previous December. Under these circumstances, Germany's military leaders felt that the only tolerable solution would be a Hitler chancellorship. There were numerous signs — Hindenburg's continued hesitation to appoint Hitler, the still unresolved objections of Hugenberg (above all on the question of new elections), the simultaneous hectic debate about a Papen cabinet in DNVP circles, and the growing opposition to Hitler's appointment within the bourgeois camp — that led the Bendlerstraße to believe that a new edition of the Papen cabinet was imminent. This actually prompted the chief of military operations to call on Hitler and to ask him point-blank whether he was certain that Papen had not negotiated with him for the sake of external appearances alone.

This admittedly timid diversion, which was undertaken in ignorance of the current state of negotiations and which made Schleicher's total isolation painfully apparent, was complemented by a highly dubious attempt by the Reichswehr to get Werner von Alvensleben, a self-styled master of intrigue, to sow suspicion about Papen within the Nazi party leadership in the hope that this might drive it into the arms of the Reichswehr. Since Hitler and his entourage had already learned of Schleicher's dismissal, the offer of an alliance that Alvensleben made to Goebbels assumed the character of an open act of rebellion by the Reichswehr against the Reich president. It was not all that difficult for the Nazi party leadership to conclude from Alvensleben's unsubstantiated innuendos that the Reichswehr was about to carry out a military coup d'état and that it meant to use the NSDAP for its purposes. In any event, Hitler and Goebbels immediately persuaded themselves that the Potsdam garrison was about to be ordered into action and alerted not only Meißner and Papen but also the Berlin SA under the command of Count Wolf Heinrich von Helldorf as well as Major Walther Wecke, a Nazi sympathizer in the Berlin police force. Göring instructed the latter to prepare for an "instantaneous occupation of the Wilhelmstraße by police units."

Although the presidential palace gave no credence to the rumors of a putsch, the reports that those concerned received during the night of 29 January only confirmed their conviction that the new cabinet would have to be formed without delay. Rumors circulating after midnight that Schleicher had ordered the arrest of the Reich president, his son Oskar von Hindenburg, and State Secretary Otto Meißner made Werner von Blomberg look like the man of the hour. Whisked from the railroad station on his arrival, the general was immediately taken to Hindenburg, who administered the oath of office. The president stressed once again that the Reichswehr must eschew political activities of any kind and that the "methods of Schleicher" must come to an end. In the meantime, Papen had begun to telephone the future members of the national cabinet to summon them to an urgent meeting. He then announced, although he certainly knew better, that the new government must be formed by eleven o'clock at the latest since otherwise the Reichswehr would march and a "Schleicher-Hammerstein" military dictatorship would be established.

The preparations for the new cabinet were thus less than adequate. Konstantin von Neurath and Schwerin von Krosigk, both of whom still assumed that the "small solution" of a presidential cabinet under Papen was about to materialize, had substantive reasons of their own for opposing such a solution. It was only immediately before he took the oath of office that Schwerin von Krosigk extracted a few commitments about the future course of financial policy from Hitler. When the designated cabinet led by Papen arrived in Meißner's suite of offices, the sharp opposition between the DNVP and NSDAP suddenly flared up anew. While Hitler reiterated his claim to the post of Reich commissar for Prussia in spite of the fact that he had already renounced it a day earlier, Hugenberg took a strong stand against Hitler's call for the dissolution of the Reichstag and refused to be mollified by assurances from the chancellor-designate that the composition of the cabinet would remain unchanged regardless of the outcome of the elections. It was only when Meißner pointed out that the Reich president really could not be asked to wait any longer that Hugenberg decided to yield for the time being.

Hindenburg administered the oath of office to the cabinet of national concentration in his characteristically terse manner. Upon taking the oath of office, Hitler stressed in a short address that he would make every effort to win a parliamentary majority for the cabinet. This was a response to the president's condition that the Center and BVP must be included in the cabinet. In the process of forming the new government, Hitler had assumed an essentially passive posture. From the ranks of the NSDAP he proceeded to chose Wilhelm Frick for minister of the interior and Göring for the multiple posts of commissar for Prussian internal affairs, Reich commissar for aviation, and Reich minister without portfolio. Goebbels was not included in the cabinet, although Hitler held out the prospect of his appointment to a future Reich Propaganda Ministry that would arch over all the other ministries. The other members of the cabinet—Baron von Neurath as foreign minister, Count Schwerin von Krosigk as finance minister, Franz Seldte as labor minister, Baron Paul Eltz von Rübenach as transport minister—had been "hired" by Papen. The president himself had appointed Werner von Blomberg. Hugenberg, as he had requested, received the post of a "crisis minister." Gereke, the Reich commissar for job creation, was a holdover from the Schleicher cabinet. The Ministry of Justice was for the moment left in the hands of Franz Gürtner, who had served in both the Papen and Schleicher cabinets. No one had been appointed to this post in order not to reveal that the negotiations with the Center were a farce from the outset. Papen also obtained an agreement whereby Hitler could report to the president only in his presence on the assumption that this would be an effective device for "keeping tabs" on Hitler.

The circumstances under which the cabinet had been formed relieved Hitler of the necessity of developing a comprehensive government program. Any attempt to deal with specific problems would have led to the collapse of the fragile compromise with Hugenberg. Moreover, Hitler always gave absolute priority to tactical exigencies. The Reich president had been led to believe that the Center's inclusion in the cabinet of "national concentration" would provide the government with a clear parliamentary majority and that the enabling legislation it would request from the Reichstag would dispense with the need for future emergency decrees. Contemporaries remembered that when Hermann Müller had formed his cabinet, the Center had also joined the coalition somewhat belatedly. For his own part, however, Hitler was determined from the very outset to keep the Center and BVP from becoming part of his government.

Even before they called on Hindenburg, Papen had extracted from Hitler the promise that he would negotiate with the Center about its participation despite the fact that he was no more interested in an accommodation with the Center than was the Nazi party leader. Ludwig Perlitius and Johannes Bell had contacted Göring on behalf of the Center even before the cabinet meeting of 30 January with the complaint that they had been excluded from the coalition negotiations. They failed to realize that Papen's offer to negotiate with the Center was purely cosmetic in nature, particularly since Hugenberg was adamantly opposed to the Center's participation in light of his agrarian and social policies. Hitler seized upon this as an opportunity to entrap the Nationalist party leader by making the Center's exclusion from the cabinet contingent upon new elections.

To be sure, Hitler avoided an open break with the Center Party—although the outward forms were barely civil—so as not to jeopardize its support for the enabling law that he planned to introduce in the Reichstag once the elections had taken place. He thus used the list of questions that the Center submitted for written answers to help it decide whether it should join the government to break off negotiations on the pretext that responding to all the questions would require too much time. At the same time, Hitler demanded that the Center agree to a year-long adjournment of the Reichstag, knowing full well that it would not authorize an adjournment of more than two months. He then used the Center's reluctance to accept his conditions in their entirety to portray the dissolution of the Reichstag as the only possible alternative.

The exchange of letters between Kaas and Hitler that was published after the negotiations had been broken off only reinforced the public perception that Papen and Hugenberg were primarily responsible for this turn of events.

The *Frankfurter Zeitung*, for instance, expressed the opinion that the dissolution of the Reichstag was primarily directed against the Center. In fact, the episode constituted a severe defeat for Hugenberg, who, against his better judgment and over the objections of the DNVP notables, had been obliged to go along with new elections. He could derive little consolation from the fact that Hitler had once again assured him that the outcome of the election would not change the composition of the cabinet and that these would be the last elections for some time to come since a return to the parliamentary system was to be avoided at all costs.

If there had ever been a conservative plan to "tame" Hitler, it fell by the wayside in the very first meeting of the Hitler cabinet. While Papen nurtured the illusion that his influence over the Reich president would make it possible for him to keep Hitler in a state of permanent dependence, Hitler and his associates were hard at work drafting the enabling legislation that would eventually free them from the fetters of presidential control. Hugenberg, in the meantime, was fighting a somewhat unconvincing rear-guard action with Meißner's support by proposing a ban against the KPD and the abolition of its Reichstag seats in the hope that this would give the government a parliamentary majority without having to resort to new elections. Hitler and Göring spoke against this proposal as a team and with great eloquence. Banning the KPD, they said, would trigger a general strike and domestic unrest. By comparison, new elections would cause far less disruption in economic life. Moreover, it would be quite impossible to eliminate the ideology of the Communist movement by simply proscribing the party. For the most part, Hitler's and Göring's arguments were spurious. The immediate suppression of the KPD would have deprived the NSDAP propaganda of it most effective campaign weapon, namely, the claim that its mission was to save the nation from the Bolshevist menace. It was therefore not in Hitler's immediate interest to replace the direct fight with the "Marxist parties," which was to be carried out by the NSDAP, by a spectacular police action. Such an action would, after all, carry the added risk of having to call in the Reichswehr should Communist resistance prove too effective. There was never any doubt in Hitler's mind that a violent confrontation with the Left would occur if not before, then certainly after the elections.

At its first meeting Hitler thus forced the new cabinet to agree to the dissolution of the Reichstag. This took place by presidential emergency decree on the following day and was justified by the explanation that the "formation of a viable parliamentary majority has proved impossible" and that the German people must therefore be given an opportunity to express its opinion on the newly formed government. Since the conservative members of Hitler's cabinet had registered no protest against this reversal of the relationship between elections and the formation of a government, the Reich president could not be held primarily responsible for this decision. The NSDAP pressed for an early date, with the result that elections were scheduled for 5 March 1933. Many contemporaries felt that this was the beginning of the dreaded relapse into parliamentarism. Ewald von Kleist-Schmenzin, an incorrigible monarchist who despised everything associated with Weimar democracy, registered his protest with Hugenberg by resigning from the DNVP. Yet what was happening was precisely the opposite, namely, the elimination of the last vestiges of the parliamentary system of government. Only the trappings of parliamentary procedure and pseudolegal methods remained in place, so that the hopes of the SPD that a visible break with the existing constitution would provide it with the justification for taking up open resistance went unfulfilled.

To the general public, the formation of the government of national concentration did not represent a fundamental political turning point in Germany's postwar historical development. There was widespread agreement extending deep into the ranks of the Center that the KPD would be eliminated and that the influence of the SPD would be drastically curtailed. Most observers felt that the new government could not possibly last for very long. In the face of these attitudes, the NSDAP endeavored to recast Hitler's appointment as an event of secular importance. The transformation of what was essentially a change of cabinets into the long-expected "national revolution" was systematically staged by Joseph Goebbels and determined the tenor of Nazi propaganda right up until the Potsdam demonstration immediately before the passage of the enabling law of 23 March 1933. Celebrating 30 January as the "Day of the National Revolution" allowed the Nazi propaganda chief to gloss over the fact that the governing coalition could only operate on the basis of presidential emergency decrees.

Immediately after receiving the news of Hitler's appointment as chancellor, Goebbels issued detailed instructions for mass demonstrations in the capital and all large cities. Their purpose was to present Hitler's chancellorship as the final victory of the National Socialist movement and anticipated in the realm of propaganda the exclusive claim to power for which the NSDAP had been striving. The new minister of the interior, Wilhelm Frick, promptly lifted the restrictions on demonstrations in the immediate vicinity of the government quarter to allow the SA, the SS, and the Stahlhelm to offer their salute to the chancellor and Reich president in the Wilhelmstraße. The SA torch parades that under Goebbels's careful staging wound their way through masses of spectators did not end until midnight. Hindenburg watched the marching columns from the window of his office in the Wilhelmstraße while Hitler, Göring, and Frick received homage on the balcony of the Reich Chancery. Observing the frenzy of enthusiasm that seized the Nazi supporters, Count Harry Keßler sarcastically remarked that Berlin was "in a regular carnival mood tonight." To those who did not share this enthusiasm for Hitler and the NSDAP, the outbreak of national fervor was nothing more than a bonfire that distracted the nation from its true problems.

Many apolitical Germans, relieved that the long-drawn-out government crisis was over, no doubt greeted its resolution with hopeful expectations. In the working-class neighborhoods and among the few remaining bourgeois republicans, however, depression was rampant. Theodor Wolff, editor in chief of the *Berliner Tageblatt*, pointed out that Hitler's chancellorship was fraught with great dangers. The *Frankfurter Zeitung* reminded its readers of Hitler's threats on the occasion of the Potempa murder case and expressed doubts that he had the statesmanlike qualities for which most of his conservative allies had given him credit. All in all, however, the press tended to be focused much more closely on Alfred Hugenberg, whose position seemed to be much more powerful than that of the chancellor. As a result, Hitler's demand for an enabling law that would remain in effect for four years received relatively little attention, even though there was no precedent for such long-term enabling legislation.

From a tactical point of view, it was a masterstroke of Nazi propaganda to center the election campaign that began with the demonstrations on the night of 30 January on the demand for enabling legislation. This left the NSDAP's coalition partners with very little room to maneuver. Hitler's presentation of his government program, carried live on all of Germany's radio stations on 1 February, was a thinly disguised campaign speech despite the fact that Papen had cosigned its text. In his "Appeal to the German People" Hitler clearly dissociated the new government from the preceding fourteen years of "Marxist rule," a phrase that included the era of the presidential cabinets in its blanket rejection of the republic. He further pledged that the national government would do everything in its power to put an end to the "erosion of the nation's unity of spirit and will" for which the parties of the November Revolution were to be held responsible and to create a truly classless society based on the principle of the *Volksgemeinschaft*. Nor did Hitler fail to invoke the values of Christianity and the family and to pay special homage to Hindenburg as the "aged leader of the World War." He then announced two parallel four-year plans to remedy the plight of German agriculture and end unemployment, against which Papen had protested on the grounds that they were too reminiscent of Stalinist terminology. With his appeal "Now, German people, give us four years' time, then judge for yourself and judge us!" Hitler alluded to the enabling legislation that he and his cabinet were demanding. By approving this appeal, the conservative members of the new cabinet had effectively tied their hands with respect to Hitler.

Goebbels was quick to appreciate the significance of the state radio monopoly, which the NSDAP proceeded to mobilize for its own purposes in spite of protests from the south German states. In the meantime, whatever worries the Nazi party leadership had had about financing the campaign had resolved themselves. To be sure, the finance minister had more or less casually dismissed Göring's suggestion that the campaigns of the government parties should be financed out of public funds. But the government apparatus, including the Reich Central Office for Home Affairs (Reichszentrale für Heimatdienst) and the state-controlled radio system, was still available for use in the campaign even before Göring and Schacht were able to tap the resources of German big business in a meeting on 20 February. Even more important was the success with which the government was able to restrict the opposition's freedom of movement with decrees such as the Emergency Decree for the Protection of the German People of 4 February. The decree had already been prepared by Schleicher for use in the event that the government's general amnesty for political criminals ignited a new wave of violence. It was now used as the legal basis for far-reaching restrictions on the freedom of the press and for the imposition of heavy penalties on those who incited strikes in essential industries, whatever that was supposed to mean.

The bourgeois Right considered the election campaign to be superfluous, particularly since it feared that it would afford the parties on the Left an opportunity to catch their breath. The *Deutsche Allgemeine Zeitung*, for instance, wrote as late as 12 February that "Hitler's campaign to conquer the people" could not forever avoid "a frontal attack on the workers' parties." Hitler's bourgeois allies had assigned him the task of winning over the industrial workers to the national movement and therefore often interpreted his statements as radical rhetoric necessary to prevent the masses from sliding into communism. Hitler proved to be a far more skillful tactician than Hugenberg, who on 28 January had already obtained Meißner's approval for a ban against the KPD. Hitler, on the other hand, wanted to reverse the sequence of events and, as Goebbels noted, "let the red terror flare up" so that he could saddle the workers' parties with the odium of unlawful conduct. The coming elections, he hoped, would provide his movement with the strength it needed for the final battle against "Marxism." In the speech he delivered before a group of prominent industrialists who had been summoned by Göring and Schacht to a confidential meeting in the offices of the Reichstag president on 20 February 1933, Hitler made it clear that in his mind it was important to lay hands on "all the means of power" through elections before initiating the "second action against communism." For all practical purposes, Hitler's coalition partners had paid for this with their own freedom of action.

In connection with its efforts to crush the organized labor movement, the NSDAP took decisive measures to seize control of the state's administrative apparatus. In Prussia the motion that the NSDAP and DNVP had introduced in an attempt to force the dissolution of the Landtag had failed to obtain a majority. On this occasion, the Social Democratic delegation to the Prussian

Landtag did not follow the instructions of the SPD executive committee, which felt that new elections offered the only solution to the current crisis. A motion to the same effect that the NSDAP's Hans Kerrl submitted to the three-man collegium that presided over the affairs of Prussia's parliamentary institutions was subsequently defeated by the negative votes of Adenauer and Braun. On the advice of Papen and Meißner, the cabinet prepared a clearly unconstitutional Emergency Decree for the Restoration of Orderly Government in Prussia that was officially promulgated on 6 February. The decree transferred the powers that still resided with the Prussian government following the ruling of the State Court of Appeals in October 1932 to the Reich commissariat. The only possible way in which the Prussian ministers could protest the action of the national government was by initiating a suit in the State Court. The court, however, failed to respond, since the body that was responsible for dealing with the complaint came under heavy pressure from the national government to delay a decision until court action had been rendered unnecessary by the outcome of the March elections. In similar fashion, the protest of Bavarian Minister President Heinrich Held was also ignored. With the publication of the emergency decree Göring had a free hand to proceed with his own plans for the conquest of total power in Prussia. The three-man collegium, with Papen now in Braun's place, proceeded to approve the dissolution of the Prussian Landtag and scheduled new state elections for 5 March. At the same time, Göring decreed the reorganization of municipal administrative bodies.

Within a few short days the NSDAP had shed the fetters that had bound it to its conservative coalition partners. Hitler found it easy to turn down the request of the bourgeois Right for a national unity ticket in the Reichstag elections that had also been set for 5 March. Hitler's promise to preserve the current composition of the cabinet regardless of the outcome of the election made it impossible for the DNVP and Stahlhelm to extricate themselves from the uncomfortable situation in which they found themselves. At Papen's insistence, the DNVP and Stahlhelm joined forces in the Combat Front Black-Red-White (Kampffront Schwarz-Weiß-Rot) on 11 February. But neither the various splinter parties on the bourgeois Right nor the DVP were allowed to become part of this alliance in as much as Hugenberg refused to place their candidates on the joint ticket. Papen's plan to create "a conservative Christian *Sammlungsbewegung*" was a failure from the very outset. The Combat Front was no match for the NSDAP because it was committed to support the government program in all its essential elements. Attempts by the Combat Front to dissociate itself from the NSDAP by warning against "socialist experiments" and rejecting the "spirit of partisanship" were hardly suited to appeal to large segments of the German voting public. The situation within the Combat Front was further complicated by growing tensions between the DNVP party organization and Hugenberg, who upon his appointment to the Hitler cabinet had begun to neglect his own party. The widely held view of Hugenberg as the strong man in the Hitler cabinet, found in newspapers running the gamut from the *Frankfurter Zeitung* to *Die Rote Fahne*, did not correspond to facts. While the leadership of the DNVP and the Stahlhelm were largely helpless in the face of the NSDAP's high-handed assault, Papen still tried to gloss over the differences that separated the NSDAP from its more conservative coalition partners. At the same time, the German press seems to have been taken aback by Hitler's moderate demeanor, which was motivated by the tactical need to win the allegiance of Germany's conservative professional elites.

In the first weeks of his tenure as chancellor, Hitler was so overawed by the Reich president that he arrived at the Reich Chancery in the early morning hours. Hitler fumbled around for a way to overcome a deep-seated sense of insecurity that stemmed from his complete lack of experience with the conduct of governmental business. Immediately after his appointment Hitler established contact with the Reichswehr garrisons, which he visited without prior notice. This, in turn, encouraged Defense Minister Werner von Blomberg to invite Hitler to a banquet for the Reichswehr's group and district commanders in the home of Baron Kurt von Hammerstein-Equord, the Reichswehr's chief of military operations, to celebrate Neurath's sixtieth birthday on 3 February 1933. In unfamiliar surroundings such as these, Hitler seemed awkward and subdued. It was only after the meal that he shed his shyness and surprised his hosts with a two-hour speech in which he outlined his political program. In the course of his remarks, Hitler assured the military commanders of his commitment to the reinstatement of universal military service in the not-too-distant future and to the preservation of the nonpartisan status of the Reichswehr.

In his speech Hitler also called for the "complete reversal of the present political conditions" and for the "eradication of Marxism root and branch [*mit Stumpf und Stiel*]." A somewhat novel aspect of Hitler's speech, however, was his close identification with the aims of Germany's military leadership and his pledge that the Reichswehr would remain "nonpartisan" and "nonpolitical." The sections of the speech that dealt with foreign policy left the option between the development of a colonial empire and the "conquest of new living space [*Lebensraum*] in the East" temporarily open. Hitler's remarks on domestic politics created the impression that the NSDAP still found itself engaged in the struggle for political power. "The struggle on the domestic front," read Lieutenant General Curt Liebmann's notes on the meeting, "is not its [i.e., the Reichswehr's] concern but [that of] the Nazi organizations." Here Hitler alluded to the neutrality of the armed forces in the NSDAP's violent confrontation with organized labor. Somewhat later Colonel Walter von Reichenau, a calculating and politically astute military expert who had succeeded Bredow as chief of staff in the Ministry of Defense, summarized the essence of Hitler's remarks in a somewhat more pointed fashion when he wrote: "Need to realize that we are in a revolution. The rot within the state must be expunged, can only be done through terror. The party will proceed against Marxism. Task of the armed forces: stand by, arms at the ready."

These comments reflected Hitler's continuing obsession with the notion of a terroristic "settling of scores" with the parties of the German Left, which he expected could be provoked into a violent reaction by National Socialist provocations. The attacks the SA and SS began to launch against the basic institutions of the KPD, SPD, and socialist labor unions and that soon led to the establishment of torture chambers and unauthorized concentration camps were an essential part of this strategy. Göring added a new twist to all of this when he placed the Prussian police at the heart of the domestic struggle for power and expressly directed them in the notorious "order to shoot" (*Schießerlaß*) to work closely with the organization of the nationalist Right and to make full use of their firepower in combating Communist actions. His order of 24 February designating the SA and the Stahlhelm as auxiliary police was a step in the same direction in spite of the fact that it ran counter to Hitler's original plan of having the NSDAP's paramilitary units suppress the Left without relying upon the assistance of the state police. Whereas Hitler's conservative partners thought that the period of revolutionary upheaval was essentially over, the activists within the SA and NSDAP had just begun the fight.

With a remarkably accurate assessment of the propagandistic effect of its general strategy, the NSDAP focused its campaign for the March 1933 elections on the struggle against communism and thereby mobilized the rabid anti-Communist hysteria of the bourgeois middle classes and the peasantry positively for its own partisan purposes. In this respect, the NSDAP was assisted by the verbal radicalism of the KPD. The appearance of militant Communist groups in rural areas, sometimes in response to the actions of the SA, contributed in no small measure to the fear of a Bolshevik revolution that the parties on the extreme Right did their best to fuel. The anticollectivist phobia of the upper bourgeoisie that expressed itself in lamentations about the supposed spread of "cultural Bolshevism" and the rise of the masses would have been virulent enough without the excessively radical language of the Communists around Ernst Thälmann.

In sharp contradiction to the claims of its propaganda, the KPD had never developed a realistic revolutionary concept. There was no chance whatsoever of a proletarian uprising. The KPD's attacks against the "social fascism" of the SPD was designed to conceal this deficit from the party faithful. In point of fact, however, the KPD's reaction to the Nazi conquest of power was not fundamentally different from that of the SPD. In the first place, the KPD was caught completely off guard by the formation of the Hitler cabinet. Although for several months the KPD had been making preparations for the creation of an underground network, it was never successful in evading police surveillance.

The KPD's continued involvement in semilegal activities and its participation in the election campaign reflected a high degree of carelessness and an underestimation of its Nazi adversary. At the same time, the Prussian political police used the information that it had systematically collected for a good number of years to take effective action against the Communist Party whenever the slightest opportunity presented itself. Despite the unbroken fighting spirit of the party's rank and file, the KPD's freedom of movement was soon severely curtailed. On 22 January—a full week before the installation of the Hitler cabinet—the SA had gone so far as to hold, albeit with the benefit of police protection, a demonstration directly across from the KPD's national headquarters on the Bülowplatz while the Communist forces were being kept at bay in the adjacent side streets. Three days later, when the KPD responded with a mass demonstration in the same place that elicited the praise of Friedrich Stampfer, editor in chief of the Social Democratic *Vorwärts*, little did it know that this would be the last Communist demonstration that was not immediately broken up by the police. By early February the KPD had been pushed completely onto the defensive. A systematic ban against all party publications and meetings, search-and-seizure operations against local party headquarters, and the widespread arrest of party functionaries had rendered the KPD incapable of action. The persecution to which the KPD was subjected after the Reichstag fire on the night of 28 February led to the virtual destruction of a party apparatus that had never created an adequate underground network to which the Communists could turn under conditions of extreme repression.

Under these circumstances, the KPD's continued commitment to a "united front from below" was utopian. Yet as late as 29 January *Die Rote Fahne* published a joint appeal from the KPD and RGO calling for a "united front to take action against the general assault of fascism." On 2 February the KPD's central headquarters reaffirmed its adherence to the party line that the party's immediate objective was to crush the "social fascism" of the SPD. In doing so, it criticized the SPD for its "lamentable capitulation" to the fascist counterrevolution, as manifested in the Social Democrats' failure to respond to the KPD's call for a general strike on 30 January. An even more egregious distortion of the actual situation was to be found in a commentary *Pravda* published on events in Germany. The principal organ of the Communist International denounced the German bourgeoisie for attempting "to resolve its own internal contradictions by mounting a frontal attack against the working masses and their vanguard, the KPD." This may have been true of Hugenberg but was certainly not applicable to Hitler, and it was a grotesque misrepresentation of the situation for *Pravda* to continue to depict the SPD and the socialist labor unions as "a major pillar of social support for the [German] bourgeoisie" after the KPD had begun to feel the full weight of the regime's repressive measures.

In the face of irreconcilable differences between the SPD and KPD, Stampfer again propagated the idea of a "nonaggression pact" as the lowest common denominator upon which the two parties could unite but failed to elicit the slightest sign of interest from the leaders of the KPD. Whatever chances of effective political action the SPD still possessed were severely curtailed by its exposed flank on the left. For even if the Social Democrats had at the last moment come out in support of Schleicher, they would not have changed the course of events. Its isolation reduced the SPD to a mere observer of the political scene. On the morning of 30 January the SPD executive committee and Reichstag delegation met to discuss the situation to be created by the formation of a Hitler cabinet. Rudolf Breitscheid, who presented a fairly accurate report about the ongoing negotiations between Hitler and Papen, was honest enough to admit that it was no longer possible to keep the fascists from coming to power and that the task at hand was to "drive them from power," however difficult that might be. Even then, the news of Hitler's appointment that arrived toward the end of the meeting came as something of a surprise.

More than just a handful of high-ranking Social Democrats urged immediate action. Siegfried Aufhäuser, who functioned as their spokesman vis-à-vis the party leadership, opposed a wait-and-see attitude for fear that the opportunity for active resistance to the newly established dictatorship would be lost. This was also the sentiment of the Iron Front, which had already begun to collect arms in a number of localities throughout the country. But what Social Democratic militants lacked was an issue by which they could galvanize the party into active resistance. Resistance had been planned as a response to the unconstitutional formation of a presidential cabinet that would suspend or abolish the rights of parliament but not for a situation in which no open breach of the constitution had taken place. Moreover, some segments of the party were still operating under the erroneous impression that Schleicher had been forced out of office because he favored new elections that, according to Vorwärts, had to be prevented in order to save Hitler from another electoral defeat. Even then, many Social Democrats continued to hope that new elections would help relax domestic political tensions. The same miscalculation lay at the heart of the strong protests the leaders of the SPD and ADGB voiced with respect to Schleicher's plans for declaring a state of emergency. Similarly, Otto Braun had registered his opposition to any deviation from the constitution in an open letter to the chancellor. In doing so, however, the leaders of the SPD had psychologically tied their own hands. Even if it came to the formation of a Hitler cabinet that lacked the support of a parliamentary majority, the Social Democrats were still in essential agreement that all energies should be concentrated first and foremost on the upcoming Reichstag elections.

Hitler's appointment as chancellor only strengthened the SPD's resolve to abide by the concept of legality it had formulated under the impact of the coup against Prussia. The lead article in the 31 January issue of Vorwärts contained the essential elements of an analysis of the situation that Rudolf Breitscheid would present to the party council and that the party executive committee would subsequently publish as a brochure for mass consumption under the title of *Bereitsein ist alles!* The official party newspaper warned against precipitous action by individual workers' organizations that would only play into the hands of the NSDAP. In doing so, the paper also appealed for unconditional discipline by the party rank and file and reminded its readers that "extreme preparedness and absolute unity" were the order of the day. This appeal came not only from the SPD's notorious retreat into organizational fetishism but also from the mistaken notion that the organized labor movement would have to wait until the adversary committed an actual breach of legality before it could take action. "In contrast to a government that operates by the threat of coup d'état," *Vorwärts* declared, "the Social Democratic Party and the entire Iron Front have both feet on the ground of constitutional and legal principle. They will not take the first step away from this ground." A similar note was struck in a simultaneous appeal by the SPD executive committee, which, among other things, signaled its intention of introducing a motion of no confidence against the new cabinet.

In his address to the SPD party council and representatives of the SPD Reichstag delegation, Breitscheid advocated a wait-and-see attitude with respect to the newly formed Hitler cabinet. To be sure, he warned the party against placing its hopes on the early demise of the new cabinet. Its fall, he argued, would mean the definitive collapse of all authoritarian experiments directed against the German working class. Consequently, all of the elements in German society that were opposed to the German worker would defend the new government tooth and nail. Having asked for patience, Breitscheid then proceeded to argue that despite the party's uncompromising opposition to the new government any comprehensive extraparliamentary initiative would have to wait until after Hitler had formally violated the constitution. This conclusion, however, was not altogether consistent with Breitscheid's observation that Mussolini had managed to neutralize the Italian parliament without ever triggering an open constitutional crisis. At any rate, Breitscheid rejected any thought of immediate militant measures. A short-term general strike, he continued, was impossible if for no other reason than the fact that the KPD would demand its indefinite continuation and that this would lead to its bloody suppression by the SA and the Reichswehr. As long as the Communists were not prepared to change their political course, an alliance with the KPD was totally out of the question.

Breitscheid's position received strong support from representatives of the ADGB, who not only argued that a general strike stood no chance of success in view of persistent mass unemployment but claimed that such an expedient should be adopted as a last resort. All of this was no more than tactical window dressing for the benefit of the party's left wing. Unlike some of its local chapters, the ADGB executive committee had made no preparations whatsoever for a protest action against the new government. Leipart summarized the ADGB's official line when he said: "Organization not demonstration, that is the password of the hour." Most party and union leaders agreed with this point of view and categorically opposed any link with the KPD. Only Friedrich Stampfer and the head of the SPD's Berlin district organization, Franz Künstler, supported the idea of negotiations with the KPD and argued that, in view of the increasing number of provocations and attacks against the local KPD organization, more and more workers were ready to fight, particularly since Stampfer's offer of a nonaggression pact had been taken as a sign of Social Democratic willingness to cooperate with the KPD. The main reason why the leaders of the socialist labor unions supported an offense initiative against the new cabinet was their fear of losing membership. While in a few isolated instances the KPD and SPD cooperated in organizing protest strikes against the Hitler cabinet, these actions were in sharp contrast to the inflated rhetoric with which the Communist party press had called for a general strike.

Although the SPD had no illusions whatsoever about the ruthlessness of its Nazi opponents, it underestimated the extent to which the new government was prepared to resort to chicanery and repression in order to accomplish its political objectives. The principal target of Nazi hostility, however, was not the SPD but the KPD, most of whose party newspapers were no longer available on the streets. At this point, the SPD and KPD were still hoping to derail the formation of a Hitler cabinet in the plenary session of the Reichstag. But as president of the Reichstag, Göring was able to prevent the Reichstag from meeting before the motion providing for its dissolution could be introduced. In the meantime, the KPD had become so totally absorbed in the preparations for its semiclandestine election campaign that it neglected to provide adequate protection for its underground network. The SPD, on the other hand, still clung to the illusion that the elections would put Hitler in his place. But this could have happened only if Hitler had been forced to conduct the campaign without the advantages of the chancellorship and without access to the resources of the state, which he used without compunction to further the cause of his own party. Organized labor's preoccupation with the election campaign proved to be fatal in that it diverted attention away from the task of developing an illegal underground network before it was too late.

Unlike the parties of the bourgeois center and moderate Right, the Left recognized the NSDAP as its most formidable opponent. Those elements within the ADGB that had advocated an accommodation with the new national government were in a distinct minority. The belief that the organization could be preserved more or less intact until after the dictatorship had run its course and had fallen from power stemmed from a fundamental miscalculation of the means the fascists had at their disposal once they had gained control of the governmental apparatus. Even then, it was still difficult to judge in the first weeks after 30 January just how long the cabinet of national concentration might remain in power. To be sure, no one on the Left shared the naiveté of one of Hugenberg's closest associates when he confided to his diary on 1 February: "It all depends on whether Hitler assumes the role of a statesman or continues to base himself entirely in the party." Still, the NSDAP's left-wing critics were no different from their bourgeois counterparts in believing that Hitler's distinctive combination of paranoid fanaticism, a Catilinarian will to power, and cynical amorality was in the long run incompatible with the successful conduct of governmental affairs. Time and time again Germany's left-wing intelligentsia stressed Hitler's dangerous propaganda skills and tactical finesse, but under no circumstances could they imagine that a man who had neither sufficient practical expertise nor any sense of political responsibility could win the unconditional respect of influential bourgeois groups. Herein lay their "underestimation" of Hitler. For even if Germany's left-wing parties had anticipated the full extent of Hitler's cynical use of force that robbed them of their freedom of movement, they were no longer in a position to influence the course of events to any significant degree.

There was no shortage of early self-criticism within the ranks of the Left. In early February Carl von Ossietzky wrote in the *Weltbühne* that the republic had lost the battle because it lacked the necessary will to live. The political Right, he claimed, was superior to the Socialists and Communists by dint of its "cold, hard will to power and its feel for the issues that really matter." It had therefore "conquered the high ground without having to fire a shot." The complete suppression of the organized labor movement was the expressed goal of the new rulers. Indeed, this was the only cement that held together the coalition of heterogeneous political forces that Papen had managed to forge. For the vast majority of Germany's bourgeois parties and the professional elites that supported them, the government's explicit turn away from the Weimar Republic was a foregone conclusion.

Only a few isolated voices in what still remained of the republican camp warned that Hitler would break his oath to uphold the constitution and escape from the institutional control of the Reich presidency. In the middle of February 1933, the famed historian Friedrich Meinecke, a member of the German State Party, issued an election appeal urging that "the fight against the fascist dictatorship be borne not only by the workers but also by the bourgeoisie" so that "even a pseudolegal liquidation of our constitutional foundations" could be averted. For Meinecke the only possibility of avoiding disaster presupposed the survival of Germany's democratic forces in the upcoming elections in the hope that they would be able to assert themselves when the inevitable conflict within the governmental coalition erupted. At the same time, Meinecke expressed concern that the "emergency brake of presidential authority" might no longer function. In the final analysis, Meinecke and the handful of Germans committed to the republican form of government were fighting for a lost cause.

By the first days of February it had become apparent that the Reichstag elections of 5 March 1933 would, regardless of their outcome, result in sweeping parliamentary authorization for the government to embark upon an authoritarian revision of the German constitution. Hitler's coalition partner did not hesitate to refer publicly to Hitler's assurances that this would be the last election for some time to come. Within the DNVP Hugenberg was repeatedly criticized for having agreed to elections that from the Nationalist perspective were superfluous. Without ever being aware of the constitutional implications, the leaders of the DNVP succumbed to the illusion that the party state, including the NSDAP, would disappear with the destruction of the organized working-class movement. This was the dubious assumption that lay at the heart of the conservative strategy to "tame" the NSDAP and that prompted Papen's rash statement: "Within two months we will have squeezed Hitler so hard that he will sit in the corner and squeal." The overwhelming numerical advantage that the conservatives enjoyed in the composition of the cabinet, however, proved to little avail, for aside from the political incompetence of Papen and Hugenberg, Hitler could always invoke the populist impulse embodied in the NSDAP against his conservative coalition partners.

It is difficult to understand why Papen, as well as many representatives of the bourgeois middle parties, had placed their hopes on the Reich president as a counterweight to Hitler's independent initiatives. At the very beginning Papen, Hugenberg, and Seldte had given their support to Hitler's demand that the government should gain its independence from the Reichstag by means of special enabling legislation and therefore regarded new elections as superfluous. They overlooked or suppressed the fact that if the government received these powers, it would no longer require the support of the Reich president. No less illusory was the idea that the conservative members of the cabinet could count on the support of the Reichswehr as a politically neutral force. By the same token, the dream of a strong bourgeois counterweight to the NSDAP that had informed Papen's negotiations with right-wing industrialists and politicians in January 1933 remained a fiction despite the fact that the vice-chancellor assumed the chairmanship of the "Black-White-Red Combat Front." From the outset, Hitler's bourgeois partners were no match for the Nazi party leader's methods of bluff, blackmail, and faits accomplis. In the end, their only hope was that Hitler could be strengthened against the more radical elements in his party through a policy of goodwill and conciliation. In this respect, the charade of playing off the impetuous demands of certain Nazi party leaders against Hitler's moderation had been essentially forced upon the Nazi party leader by Hitler's coalition partners. In point of fact, however, the bourgeois Right had no alternative to its uneven alliance with Hitler. For an end to the coalition would have meant a return to the very parliamentary system that it had sought to destroy through its alliance with Hitler.

In the fever of a campaign dominated almost exclusively by the National Socialist propaganda machine, the question of what might take the place of the much maligned republic retreated into the background. Not only the KPD and SPD but also the Center and German State Party found themselves the targets of increasing harassment that ranged from a ban against newspapers and public meetings to the dismissal of their supporters from the civil bureaucracy. Even the Stahlhelm and the DNVP were subjected to interference of this kind. Protests addressed to the Reich president had no effect whatsoever. It was only in the decisions of the German Supreme Court that the arbitrary abuse of power by the new Nazi rulers was temporarily curbed. What the bourgeois Right had originally greeted as a fundamental new beginning for the state had degenerated into repression and terror. In taking leave of Weimar's republican order, the Right unwittingly left behind the legal guarantees this order had afforded.

The fire that destroyed the Reichstag on the night of 27–28 February 1933 seemed to herald the beginning of the long-awaited Communist counterattack. In point of fact, it was the work of a lone arsonist, Martinus van der Lubbe. Nevertheless, the event moved Hitler, Göring, and Frick to seek a confrontation with the Left before the Reichstag elections and without waiting for the passage of enabling legislation. The Emergency Decree for the Protection of the People and State that the Reich president issued on 28 February abolished the fundamental rights to which a citizen was entitled under the provisions of the constitution and legalized extensive repressive measures against organized labor and various republican groups. It also gave the national government the legal grounds it needed to interfere with the sovereignty of the individual German states. Blinded by their fear of an imaginary Communist uprising, neither Papen nor Hugenberg had anything to say, aside from marginal corrections, about the comprehensive powers this decree conferred upon the national government. The Reich president, who had retired to his Neudeck estate, saw no reason for not approving the contents of the decree.

Before the Nazi party leadership could claim to have won a majority in open elections, it had already established itself in power with the help of its conservative coalition partners by virtue of the Emergency Decree for the Protection of the People and State. This decree constituted the informal basic law, or *Grundgesetz*, upon which the emerging dictatorial regime was based and took the place of the Weimar Constitution that from a purely formal point of view remained in effect for the duration of the Third Reich. The civilian state of emergency authorized by the decree corresponded in every essential detail, with the exception that in the earlier version executive power was to be placed in the hands of the Reichswehr, to the so-called *Planspiel* Ott for a government coup d'état that the Defense Ministry had drafted for the Papen cabinet for use in the event of a civil war caused by the workers' parties. On his way to becoming a dictator, Hitler had simply availed himself of the instruments that the bourgeois "gravediggers of the republic" had already fashioned, whether it was special laws for the repression of the Left, the notion of protective custody, or the creation of special tribunals. It was not the instruments themselves but the ruthlessness with which they were used that distinguished the new regime of violence from the dictatorial aspirations of the bourgeois Right.

Even before the Reichstag elections of 5 March 1933 took place, the political initiative had already passed into the hands of the NSDAP. During the course of the campaign, organized labor struggled desperately against the repressive measures of the government, while the Center and German State Party tried to salvage something from the republican constitutional order. But everywhere resignation prevailed. It extended even to the DNVP and the Stahlhelm, which began to realize that their alliance with Hitler was turning to their disadvantage. The Reichstag fire made it possible for the Nazi party leadership to patch over incipient rifts within the coalition by mounting a major propaganda campaign against alleged plans for a Communist uprising. In order not to be overwhelmed by the anti-Marxist tide, the Center quietly went along with the measures that had been proposed for the elimination of not merely the KPD but the SPD as well. Even before 23 March when the government's enabling legislation had been introduced in the Reichstag, Germany's bourgeois parties sought desperately to avoid a partly real and a partly imagined Nazi reign of terror through accommodation and passivity. When the decisive vote took place, they no longer possessed the moral courage to withstand Hitler's extortion. Hopes that by going along they might be able to avert something even worse played a major role in their acquiescence, as did the illusion that they could avoid open civil war by preserving the facade of legality.

If it was not already clear, then it certainly became clear in the first weeks of February 1933 that the consensus between Germany's conservative elites and the Nazi movement was purely negative and that it never went beyond the unconditional rejection of Weimar's republican order, the destruction of the organized labor movement, and Germany's liberation from the chains of Versailles. The conservative experiment of trying to use the National Socialist movement to gain plebiscitarian support for an authoritarian regime had sealed the fate of the republic, upon whose ruins Hitler proceeded to erect his absolute rule. His bourgeois-conservative allies and the social interests they represented continued to make a fundamental contribution to the stabilization of the Nazi dictatorship even after they had been formally stripped of power.

By far the most ominous aspect of all this, however, was the notion that one stood on the threshold of a new era in German history. Translated into the myth of national revival, this notion spawned not only political blindness and a flight from political reality but also the moral indifference and naked opportunism without which National Socialist politics would have collapsed under the sheer weight of its own excesses and contradictions.

Select Bibliography

THE following bibliography lists the most important primary sources and secondary studies without claiming to be exhaustive. The arrangement according to topic is designed to facilitate clarity, but since individual titles have been listed only once, this mode of classification necessarily leaves something to be desired. In the case of essay collections, references to individual contributions have for the most part been omitted, as well as the vast majority of important contributions that have appeared in various scholarly journals. What follows, therefore, is a selective rather than a comprehensive list of the most important publications on the history of the Weimar Republic.

ABBREVIATIONS

AfS = Archiv für Sozialgeschichte
GWU = Geschichte in Wissenschaft und Unterricht
GuG = Geschichte und Gesellschaft
HZ = Historische Zeitschrift
VfZ = Vierteljahrshefte für Zeitgeschichte

BIBLIOGRAPHICAL AIDS

Bibliographie zur Zeitgeschichte. Beilage der Vierteljahreshefte zur Zeitgeschichte. Stuttgart, 1953–84; Munich, 1985–.

Bibliographie zur Zeitgeschichte 1953–1980. Edited by Thilo Vogelsang and Hans Auerbach with assistance from Ursula van Laak. 2 vols. Munich, New York, London, and Paris, 1982.

Jahresbibliographie. Bibliothek für Zeitgeschichte. Weltkriegsbücherei Stuttgart. Neue Folge der Bücherschau der Weltkriegsbücherei. Koblenz, 1988–.

Meyer, Georg P. *Bibliographie zur deutschen Revolution 1918/19.* Arbeitsbücher zur modernen Geschichte, 5. Göttingen, 1977.

Schumacher, Martin. *Wahlen und Abstimmungen 1918–1933. Eine Bibliographie zur Statistik und Analyse der politischen Wahlen in der Weimarer Republik.* Bibliographien zur Geschichte des Parlamentarismus und der politischen Parteien, 7. Düsseldorf, 1976.

Stachura, Peter D. *The Weimar Era and Hitler 1918–1933: A Critical Bibliography.* Oxford, 1977.

Ullmann, Hans-Peter. *Bibliographie zur Geschichte der deutschen Parteien und Interessenverbände.* Arbeitsbücher zur modernen Geschichte, 6. Göttingen, 1978.

Wehler, Hans Ulrich. *Bibliographie zur modernen deutschen Sozialgeschichte, 18. bis 20. Jahrhundert.* Arbeitsbücher zur modernen Geschichte, 1. Göttingen, 1976.

————. *Bibliographie zur modernen deutschen Wirtschaftsgeschichte, 18. bis 20. Jahrhundert.* Arbeitsbücher zur modernen Geschichte, 2. Göttingen, 1976.

DOCUMENT COLLECTIONS AND DOCUMENTARY SOURCES

Akten der Reichskanzlei. Weimarer Republik. Edited by Karl-Dietrich Erdmann and Hans Booms.

Das Kabinett Scheidemann. 13. Februar bis 20. Juni 1919. Edited by Hagen Schulze. Boppard, 1971.

Das Kabinett Bauer. 21 Juni 1919 bis 27 März 1920. Edited by Anton Golecki. Boppard, 1980.

Das Kabinett Müller I. 27 März bis 21. Juni 1920. Edited by Martin Vogt. Boppard, 1971.

Das Kabinett Fehrenbach. 25. Juni 1920 bis 4. Mai 1921. Edited by Peter Wulf. Boppard, 1972.

Die Kabinette Wirth I u. II. 10. Mai 1921 bis 26. Oktober 1921. 26. Oktober 1921 bis 22. November 1922. Edited by Ingrid Schulze-Bidlingmaier. 2 vols. Boppard, 1973.

Das Kabinett Cuno. 22 November 1922 bis 12. August 1923. Edited by Karl-Heinz Harbeck. Boppard, 1978.

Die Kabinette Stresemann I und II. 13. August 1923 bis 6. Oktober 1923. 6. Oktober 1923 bis 30. November 1923. Edited by Karl Dietrich Erdmann und Martin Vogt. 2 vols. Boppard, 1978.

Die Kabinette Marx I und II. 30. November 1923 bis 3. Juni 1924. 3. Juni 1924 bis 15. Januar 1925. Edited by Günter Abramowski. 2 vols. Boppard, 1973.

Die Kabinette Luther I und II. 15. Januar 1925 bis 20. Januar 1926. 20. Januar 1926 bis 17. Mai 1926. Edited by Karl-Heinz Minuth. 2 vols. Boppard, 1977.

Die Kabinette Marx III und IV. 17. Mai 1926 bis 29. Januar 1927. 29. Januar 1927 bis 28. Juni 1928. Edited by Günter Abramowski. 2 vols. Boppard, 1987.

Das Kabinett Müller II. 28. Juni 1928 bis 27. März 1930. Edited by Martin Vogt. 2 vols. Boppard, 1970.

Die Kabinette Brüning I u. II. 30. März 1930 bis 10. Oktober 1931. 10. Oktober 1931 bis 1. Juni 1932. Edited by Tilman Koops. 3 vols. Boppard, 1985, 1989.

Das Kabinett von Papen. 1. Juni bis 3. Dezember 1932. Edited by Karl-Heinz Minuth. 2 vols. Boppard, 1989.

Das Kabinett von Schleicher. 3. Dezember 1932 bis 30. Januar 1933. Edited by Anton Golecki. Boppard, 1986.

Die Regierung Hitler. 30. Januar bis 31. August 1933. Edited by Karl-Heinz Minuth. 2 vols. Boppard, 1983.

Akten zur Deutschen Auswärtigen Politik 1918–1945. Aus dem Archiv des Auswärtigen Amtes.

Series A. *1918–1925. 9 November 1918 bis 31. Dezember 1924.* Göttingen, 1982–93.

Series B. *1925–1933. 1 Dezember 1925 bis 29. Januar 1933.* Göttingen, 1966–93.

Horkenbach, Cuno. *Das Deutsche Reich von 1918 bis Heute.* 4 vols. Berlin, n.d. [1930–35].

Huber, Ernst Rudolf, ed. *Dokumente zur deutschen Verfassungsgeschichte.* Vol. 3, *Dokumente der Novemberrevolution und der Weimarer Republik 1918–1933.* Stuttgart, 1966.

Die Protokolle der Reichstagsfraktion und des Fraktionsvorstandes der Deutschen Zentrumspartei 1926–1933. Edited by Rudolf Morsey. Veröffentlichungen der Kommission für Zeitgeschichte. Reihe A, Quellen, Bd. 9. Mainz, 1969.

Quellen zur Geschichte der Deutschen Gewerkschaftsbewegung im 20. Jahrhundert. Edited by Klaus Tenfelde, Klaus Schönhoven, and Hermann Weber.

Vol. 1. *Die Gewerkschaften in Weltkrieg und Revolution 1914–1919.* Edited by Klaus Schönhoven. Cologne, 1985.

Vol. 2. *Die Gewerkschaften in den Anfangsjahren der Republik 1919–1923.* Edited by Michael Ruck. Cologne, 1985.

Vol. 3. *Die Gewerkschaften von der Stabilisierung bis zur Weltwirtschaftskrise 1924–1930.* Edited by Horst A. Kukuck and Dieter Schiffmann. Cologne, 1986.

Vol. 4. *Die Gewerkschaften in der Endphase der Republik 1930–1933.* Edited by Peter Jahn. Cologne, 1987.

Quellen zur Geschichte des Parlamentarismus und der politischen Parteien.

Series 1: Von der konstitutionellen Monarchie zur parlamentarischen Republik.

Vol. 1. *Der interfraktionelle Ausschuß.* Edited by Erich Matthias and Rudolf Morsey. Düsseldorf, 1962.

Vol. 2. *Die Regierung des Prinzen Max von Baden.* Edited by Erich Matthias and Rudolf Morsey. Düsseldorf, 1962.

Vol. 3. *Die Reichstagsfraktion der deutschen Sozialdemokratie 1898 bis 1918.* Edited by Erich Matthias and Eberhard Pikart. 2 vols. Düsseldorf, 1966.

Vol. 4. *Die Regierung der Volksbeauftragten von 1918/19.* Edited by Susanne Miller and Heinrich Potthoff. 2 vols. Düsseldorf, 1969.

Vol. 10. *Die Regierung Eisner 1918/19. Ministerratsprotokolle und Dokumente.* Edited by Franz V. Bauer. Düsseldorf, 1987.

Series 2: Militär und Politik.

Vol. 1. *Militär und Innenpolitik im Weltkrieg 1914–1918.* Edited by Wilhelm Deist. 2 vols. Düsseldorf, 1970.

Vol. 2. *Zwischen Revolution und Kapp-Putsch. Militär und Innenpolitik 1918–1920.* Edited by Heinz Hürten. Düsseldorf, 1977.

Vol. 3. *Die Anfänge der Ära Seeckt. Militär und Innenpolitik 1920–1922.* Edited by Heinz Hürten. Düsseldorf, 1979.

Vol. 4. *Das Krisenjahr 1923. Militär und Innenpolitik 1923–1924.* Edited by Heinz Hürten. Düsseldorf, 1980.

Series 3: Die Weimarer Republik.

Vol. 1. *Erinnerungen und Dokumente von Joh. Victor Bredt 1914 bis 1933.* Edited by Martin Schumacher. Düsseldorf, 1970.

Vol. 3. *Staat und NSDAP 1930–1932. Quellen zur Ära Brüning.* Edited by Ilse Maurer and Udo Wengst. Düsseldorf, 1977.

Vol. 4. *Politik und Wirtschaft in der Krise 1930–1932. Quellen zur Ära Brüning.* Edited by Ilse Maurer and Udo Wengst. Düsseldorf, 1980.

Vol. 5. *Linksliberalismus in der Weimarer Republik. Die Führungsgremien der Deutschen Demokratischen Partei und der Deutschen Staatspartei 1918–1933.* Edited by Lothar Albertin and Konstanze Wegner. Düsseldorf, 1972.

Vol. 6. *Die Generallinie. Rundschreiben des Zentralkomitees der KPD an die Bezirke 1929–1933.* Edited by Hermann Weber. Düsseldorf, 1981.

Vol. 7. *Die SPD-Fraktion in der Nationalversammlung 1919–1920.* Edited by Heinrich Potthoff and Hermann Weber. Düsseldorf, 1986.

Quellen zur Geschichte der Rätebewegung in Deutschland 1918/19.

Vol. 1. *Der Zentralrat der deutschen sozialistischen Republik, 19.12.1918–8.4.1919. Vom ersten zum zweiten Rätekongreß.* Edited by Eberhard Kolb. Leiden, 1968.

Vol. 2. *Regionale und lokale Räteorganisationen in Württemberg 1918/19.* Edited by Eberhard Kolb and Klaus Schönhoven. Düsseldorf, 1976.

Vol. 3. *Arbeiter-, Soldaten- und Volksräte in Baden 1918/19.* Edited by Peter Brandt and Reinhard Rürup. Düsseldorf, 1980.

Ursachen und Folgen. Vom deutschen Zusammenbruch 1918 und 1945 bis zur staatlichen Neuordnung Deutschlands in der Gegenwart. Eine Urkunden- und Dokumentensammlung zur Zeitgeschichte. Edited by Herbert Michaelis and Ernst Schraepler. 9 vols. Berlin, 1958–64.

Weber, Hermann, ed. *Der deutsche Kommunismus. Dokumente 1915–1945.* Cologne, 1973.

MEMOIRS AND BIOGRAPHICAL STUDIES

Adolph, Hans J. *Otto Wels und die Politik der deutschen Sozialdemokratie 1894–1939. Eine politische Bibliographie.* Berlin, 1971.

Arns, Günter. "Friedrich Ebert als Reichspräsident." In *Beiträge zur Geschichte der Weimarer Republik,* edited by Theodor Schieder, pp. 1–30. HZ, Beiheft 1. Munich, 1971.

Bach, Jürgen A. *Franz von Papen in der Weimarer Republik. Aktivitäten in Politik und Presse 1918–1932.* Düsseldorf, 1977.

Beck, Dorothea. *Julius Leber. Sozialdemokrat zwischen Reform und Widerstand.* Berlin, 1983.

Berglar, Peter. *Walther Rathenau. Seine Zeit, sein Werk, seine Persönlichkeit.* Bremen, 1970.

Braun, Otto. *Von Weimar zu Hitler.* Hamburg, 1949.

Brecht, Arnold. *The Political Education of Arnold Brecht: An Autobiography, 1884–1970.* Princeton, N.J., 1970.

Brüning, Heinrich. *Briefe 1946–1960.* Edited by Claire Nix and assisted by Reginald Phelps and George Pettee. Stuttgart, 1974.

———. *Briefe und Gespräche 1934–1945.* Edited by Claire Nix and assisted by Reginald Phelps and George Pettee. Stuttgart, 1974.

———. *Memoiren 1918–1934.* Stuttgart, 1970.

———. *Reden und Aufsätze eines deutschen Staatsmanns.* Edited by Wilhelm
    Vernekohl and assisted by Rudolf Morsey. Münster, 1968.
Curtius, Julius. *Sechs Jahre Minister der deutschen Republik.* Heidelberg, 1948.
Czisnik, Ulrich. *Gustav Noske. Ein sozialdemokratischer Staatsmann.* Frankfurt am
    Main, 1969.
Dieckmann, Hildemarie. *Johannes Popitz. Entwicklung und Wirksamkeit in der Zeit der
    Weimarer Republik bis 1933.* Berlin, 1960.
Dorpalen, Andreas. *Hindenburg and the Weimar Republic.* Princeton, N.J., 1964.
Duesterberg, Theodor. *Der Stahlhelm und Hitler.* Wolffenbüttel, 1949.
Eksteins, Modris. *Theodor Heuß und die Weimarer Republik. Ein Beitrag zur Geschichte
    des deutschen Liberalismus.* Stuttgart, 1969.
Epstein, Klaus. *Matthias Erzberger and the Dilemma of German Democracy.* Princeton,
    N.J., 1959.
Fabian, Kurt. *Kein Parteisoldat. Lebensbericht eines Sozialdemokraten.* Frankfurt am
    Main, 1981.
Felken, Detlef. *Oswald Spengler. Konservativer Denker zwischen Kaiserreich und
    Diktatur.* Munich, 1988.
Fest, Joachim C. *Hitler. Eine Biographie.* Frankfurt am Main and Berlin, 1973.
Gereke, Günther. *Ich war königlich-preußischer Landrat.* Berlin, n.d.
Geßler, Otto. *Reichswehrpolitik in der Weimarer Zeit.* Stuttgart, 1958.
Goebbels, Joseph. *Die Tagebücher von Joseph Goebbels. Sämtliche Fragmente.* Edited by
    Elke Fröhlich. 4 vols. Munich, New York, London, and Paris, 1987.
Groener-Geyer, Dorothea. *General Groener. Soldat und Staatsmann.* Frankfurt am
    Main, 1955.
Hamburger, Ernest. "Betrachtungen über Heinrich Brünings Memoiren."
    *Internationale wissenschaftliche Korrespondenz zur Geschichte der deutschen
    Arbeiterbewegung* 15 (1972): 18–39.
Hehl, Ulrich von. *Wilhelm Marx 1863–1946. Eine politische Biographie.* Mainz, 1987.
Heß, Jürgen C. *Theodor Heuß vor 1933. Ein Beitrag zur Geschichte des demokratischen
    Denkens in Deutschland.* Stuttgart, 1973.
Hitler, Adolf. *Hitlers zweites Buch. Ein Dokument aus dem Jahre 1928.* Edited by
    Gerhard L. Weinberg. Quellen und Darstellungen zur Zeitgeschichte, 7.
    Stuttgart, 1961.
———. *Reden, Schriften, Anordnungen. Februar 1925–Januar 1933.* Edited by the
    Institut für Zeitgeschichte. Munich, 1992.
———. *Sämtliche Aufzeichnungen 1905–1924.* Edited by Eberhard Jäckel and Axel
    Kühn. Stuttgart, 1980.
Hoegner, Wilhelm. *Flucht vor Hitler. Erinnerungen an die Kapitulation der ersten
    deutschen Republik 1933.* Munich, 1977.
———. *Der schwierige Außenseiter. Erinnerungen eines Abgeordneten, Emigranten und
    Ministerpräsidenten.* Munich, 1959.
Hubatsch, Walther. *Hindenburg und der Staat. Aus den Papieren des
    Generalfeldmarschalls und Reichspräsidenten von 1878 bis 1934.* Göttingen, 1966.
Jansen, Christian. *Emil Julius Gumbel. Portrait eines Zivilisten.* Heidelberg, 1991.

Jenschke, Bernhard. *Zur Kritik der konservativ-revolutionären Ideologie in der Weimarer Republik. Weltanschauung und Politik bei Edgar Julius Jung.* Munich, 1971.

Kabermann, Friedrich. *Widerstand und Entscheidung eines deutschen Revolutionärs. Leben und Denken von Ernst Niekisch.* Cologne, 1973.

Kaufmann, Arthur. *Gustav Radbruch. Rechtsdenker, Philosoph, Sozialdemokrat.* Munich, 1987.

Keil, Wilhelm. *Erlebnisse eines Sozialdemokraten.* 2 vols. Stuttgart, 1947–48.

Kellenbenz, Hermann. "Paul Silverberg." *Rheinisch-Westfälische Wirtschaftsbiographien* 9 (1967): 103–32.

Kessler, Harry. *In the Twenties: The Diaries of Harry Kessler.* Translated by Charles Kessler. New York, 1971.

Klas, Gert von. *Albert Vögler. Einer der Großen des Ruhrreviers.* Tübingen, 1957.

Krebs, Albert. *Tendenzen und Gestalten der NSDAP. Erinnerungen an die Frühzeit der Partei.* Quellen und Darstellungen zur Zeitgeschichte, 6. Stuttgart, 1960.

Krosigk, Luther Graf Schwerin von. *Es geschah in Deutschland.* Tübingen, 1951.

———. *Memoiren.* Stuttgart, 1977.

Lange, Helmut. "Julius Curtis 1877–1948. Aspekte einer Politikerbiographie." Ph.D. diss., Universität Kiel, 1970.

Leopold, John A. *Alfred Hugenberg: The Radical Nationalist Campaign against the Weimar Republic.* New Haven, 1978.

Lerner, Warren. *Karl Radek: The Last Internationalist.* Stanford, Calif., 1970.

Löwenstein, Hubertus zu. *Die Tragödie eines Volkes. Deutschland 1918–1934.* Amsterdam, 1934.

Luther, Hans. *Politiker ohne Partei. Erinnerungen.* Stuttgart, 1960.

———. *Vor dem Abgrund 1930–33. Reichsbankpräsident in Krisenzeiten.* Berlin, 1964.

Meier-Welcker, Hans. *Seeckt.* Frankfurt am Main, 1967.

Meinecke, Friedrich. *Politische Schriften und Reden.* Vol. 2. Edited by Georg Kotowski. Düsseldorf, 1977.

Meißner, Otto. *Staatssekretär unter Ebert, Hindenburg, Hitler. Der Schicksalsweg des deutschen Volkes von 1918–1945. Wie ich ihn erlebte.* Hamburg, 1950.

Mockenhaupt, Hubert. *Weg und Wirken des geistlichen Sozialpolitikers Heinrich Brauns.* Munich, 1977.

Mommsen, Hans. "Betrachtungen zu den Memoiren Heinrich Brünings." *Jahrbuch für die Geschichte Mittel- und Ostdeutschlands* 22 (1973): 270–80.

Mommsen, Wolfgang J. *Max Weber and German Politics, 1890–1920.* Translated by Michael S. Steinberg. Chicago, 1984.

Morsey, Rudolf. *Zur Entstehung, Authentizität und Kritik von Brünings "Memoiren 1918–1934."* Rheinisch-Westfälische Akademie der Wissenschaft, Vorträge G 202. Opladen, 1975.

Nowak, Johann Rudolf. "Kurt von Schleicher. Soldaten zwischen den Fronten." Ph.D. diss., Universität Würzburg, 1971.

Pentzlin, Heinz. *Hjalmar Schacht. Leben und Wirken einer umstrittenen Persönlichkeit.* Berlin, Frankfurt am Main, and Vienna, 1980.

Papen, Franz von. *Memoirs.* Translated by Brian Connell. New York, 1953.

———. *Vom Scheitern einer Demokratie.* Mainz, 1968.

Papke, Gerhard. *Der liberale Politiker Erich Koch-Weser in der Weimarer Republik.* Baden-Baden, 1989.

Plehwe, Friedrich Karl von. *Reichskanzler Kurt von Schleicher. Weimars letzte Chance gegen Hitler.* Eßlingen, 1983.

Pünder, Hermann. *Politik in der Reichskanzlei. Aufzeichnungen aus den Jahren 1919–1932.* Schriftenreihe der *VfZ*, 3. Stuttgart, 1961.

———. *Von Preußen nach Europa. Lebenserinnerungen.* Stuttgart, 1968.

Quaatz, Reinhold. *Die Deutschnationalen und die Zerstörung der Weimarer Republik. Aus dem Tagebuch von Reinhold Quaatz 1928–1933.* Edited by Herman Weiß and Paul Hoser. Schriftenreihe der *VfZ*, 59. Munich, 1989.

Rathenau, Walther. *Walther-Rathenau-Gesamtausgabe.* Edited by Hans Dieter Hellige and Ernst Schulin. Vol. 2, *Hauptwerke und Gespräche.* Edited by Ernst Schulin. Munich, 1977.

Reichwein, Adolf. *1889–1944. Erinnerungen, Forschungen, Impulse.* Edited by Wolfgang Hubner and Albert Krebs. Paderborn, 1981.

Reitter, Ekkehard. *Franz Gürtner. Politische Biographie eines deutschen Juristen 1881–1941.* Berlin, 1976.

Ribbentrop, Joachim von. *Zwischen London und Moskau. Erinnerungen und eigene Aufzeichnungen. Aus dem Nachlaß.* Edited by Annelies von Ribbentrop. Leoni, 1953.

Saldern, Adelheid von. *Hermann Dietrich. Ein Staatsmann der Weimarer Republik.* Schriftenreihe des Bundesarchivs, 13. Boppard, 1966.

Schacht, Hjalmar. *My First Seventy-Six Years: The Autobiography of Hjalmar Schacht.* Translated by Diana Pyke. London, 1955.

Scheurig, Bodo. *Ewald von Kleist-Schmenzin. Ein Konservativer gegen Hitler.* Oldenburg, 1968.

Schlange-Schöningen, Hans. *The Morning After.* Translated by Edward Fitzgerald. London, 1948.

Schmidt-Pauli, Edgar von. *Hitlers Kampf um die Macht. Der Nationalsozialismus und die Ereignisse des Jahres 1932.* Berlin, n.d. [1933].

Schueler, Hermann. *Auf der Flucht erschossen. Felix Fechenbach 1894–1933. Eine Biographie.* Cologne, 1981.

Schulin, Ernst. *Walther Rathenau. Repräsentant, Kritiker und Opfer seiner Zeit.* Göttingen, 1979.

Schulze, Hagen. *Otto Braun oder Preußens demokratische Sendung. Eine Biographie.* Veröffentlichungen der Stiftung Preußischer Kulturbesitz. Frankfurt am Main, Berlin, and Vienna, 1977.

Schwarz, Hans-Peter. *Adenauer. Der Aufstieg 1876–1952.* Stuttgart, 1986.

Severing, Carl. *Mein Lebensweg.* 2 vols. Cologne, 1950.

Simpson, Amos E. *Hjalmar Schacht in Perspective.* Studies in European History, 18. The Hague, 1969.

Stampfer, Friedrich. *Erfahrungen und Erkenntnisse. Aufzeichnungen aus meinem Leben.* Cologne, 1957.

Stern, J. P. *Hitler: The Führer and the People.* Berkeley, Calif., 1975.

Stresemann, Gustav. *Vermächtnis. Der Nachlaß in drei Bänden.* Edited by Henry Bernhard. 3 vols. Berlin, 1932–33.

Treviranus, Gottfried R. *Das Ende von Weimar. Heinrich Brüning und seine Zeit.* Düsseldorf and Vienna, 1968.

Turner, Henry A., Jr. *Stresemann and the Politics of the Weimar Republic.* Princeton, N.J., 1963.

Vogelsang, Thilo. *Kurt von Schleicher. Ein General als Politiker.* Persönlichkeit und Geschichte, 39. Göttingen, 1965.

Wandel, Eckhard. *Hans Schäffer. Steuermann in wirtschaftlichen und politischen Krisen.* Stuttgart, 1974.

Wernecke, Klaus, and Peter Heller. *Der vergessene Führer Alfred Hugenberg. Pressemacht und Nationalsozialismus.* Hamburg, 1982.

Wette, Wolfram. *Gustav Noske. Eine politische Biographie.* Düsseldorf, 1987.

Williamson, John G. *Karl Helfferich, 1872–1924: Economist, Financier, Politician.* Princeton, N.J., 1971.

Witt, Peter-Christian. *Friedrich Ebert. Parteiführer, Reichskanzler, Volksbeauftragter, Reichspräsident.* Bonn, 1982.

Wulf, Peter. *Hugo Stinnes. Wirtschaft und Politik 1918–1924.* Stuttgart, 1979.

GENERAL HISTORIES OF THE PERIOD

Bracher, Karl Dietrich. *Die Auflösung der Weimarer Republik. Eine Studie zum Problem des Machtverfalls in der Demokratie.* Villingen, 1971.

———. *Deutschland zwischen Demokratie und Diktatur. Beiträge zur neueren Politik und Geschichte.* Munich, 1964.

Bracher, Karl Dietrich, Wolfgang Sauer, and Gerhard Schulz. *Die nationalsozialistische Machtergreifung. Studien zur Errichtung des totalitären Herrschaftssystem in Deutschland.* Berlin, 1974.

Brecht, Arnold. *Prelude to Silence: The End of the German Republic.* New York, 1944.

Erdmann, Karl Dietrich. "Die Weimarer Republik." In *Handbuch der deutschen Geschichte,* 8th rev. ed., edited by Herbert Grundmann, pp. 82–180. Stuttgart, 1959.

Eschenburg, Theodor. *Die Republik von Weimar. Beiträge zur Geschichte einer improvisierten Republik.* Munich, 1984.

Eyck, Erich. *Geschichte der Weimarer Republik.* 2 vols. Erlenbach-Zurich and Stuttgart, 1973.

Fischer, Fritz. *From Kaiserreich to Third Reich: Elements of Continuity in German History.* Translated by Roger Fletcher. Boston, 1986.

Flemming, Jens, Claus-Dieter Krohn, Dirk Stegmann, and Peter-Christian Witt, eds. *Die Republik von Weimar.* 2 vols. Düsseldorf, 1979.

Hillgruber, Andreas. *Die gescheiterte Großmacht. Eine Skizze des Deutschen Reiches 1871–1945.* Düsseldorf, 1982.

Huber, Ernst Rudolf. *Deutsche Verfassungsgeschichte seit 1789.* Vol. 5, *Weltkrieg, Revolution und Reichserneuerung 1914–1919.* Stuttgart, Berlin, Cologne, and Mainz, 1978. Vol. 6, *Die Weimarer Reichsverfassung.* Stuttgart, Berlin, Cologne, and Mainz, 1981. Vol. 7, *Ausbau, Schutz und Untergang der Weimarer Republik.* Stuttgart, Berlin, Cologne, and Mainz, 1984.

Jasper, Gotthard. *Die gescheiterte Zähmung. Wege zur Machtergreifung Hitlers 1930–1934*. Frankfurt am Main, 1986.

Kolb, Eberhard. *Die Weimarer Republik*. Grundriß der Geschichte, 16. Munich and Vienna, 1988.

Matthias, Erich, and Anthony Nicholls, eds. *German Democracy and the Triumph of Hitler*. London, 1971.

Nolte, Ernst. *Three Faces of Fascism: Action Française, Italian Fascism, National Socialism*. Translated by Leila Vennewitz. New York, 1966.

Peukert, Detlev J. K. *The Weimar Republic: The Crisis of Classical Modernity*. Translated by Richard Deveson. New York, 1992.

Rosenberg, Arthur. *A History of the Weimar Republic*. Translated by Ian F. D. Morrow and Marie Sieveking. New York, 1965.

Ruge, Wolfgang. *Weimar. Republik auf Zeit*. Cologne, 1980.

Schulz, Gerhard. *Deutschland seit dem Ersten Weltkrieg, 1918–1945*. Deutsche Geschichte, 10. Göttingen, 1982.

————. *Das Zeitalter der Gesellschaft. Aufsätze zur politischen Sozialgeschichte der Neuzeit*. Munich, 1969.

————. *Zwischen Demokratie und Diktatur. Verfassungspolitik und Reichsreform in der Weimarer Republik*. Vol. 1, *Die Periode der Konsolidierung und der Revision des Bismarckschen Reichsaufbaus*. 2nd rev. ed. Berlin and New York, 1987. Vol. 2, *Deutschland am Vorabend der großen Krise*. Berlin and New York, 1987. Vol. 3, *Von Brüning zu Hitler. Der Wandel des politischen Systems in Deutschland 1930–1933*. Berlin and New York, 1992.

————, ed. *Weimarer Republik*. Freiburg and Würzburg, 1987.

Schulze, Hagen. *Weimar. Deutschland 1917–1933*. Berlin, 1982.

Winkler, Heinrich August. *Weimar 1918–1933. Die Geschichte der ersten deutschen Demokratie*. Munich, 1993.

ESSAY COLLECTIONS AND STATISTICAL OVERVIEWS

Albertin, Lothar, and Werner Link, eds. *Politische Parteien auf dem Weg zur parlamentarischen Demokratie in Deutschland. Entwicklungslinien bis zur Gegenwart. Erich Matthias zum 60. Geburtstag gewidmet*. Düsseldorf, 1981.

Bessel, Richard, and E. J. Feuchtwanger, eds. *Social Change and Political Development in Weimar Germany*. London, 1981.

Bracher, Karl Dietrich, Manfred Funke, and Hans Adolf Jacobsen, eds. *Die Weimarer Republik 1918–1933. Politik, Wirtschaft, Gesellschaft*. Düsseldorf, 1987.

Erdmann, Karl Dietrich, and Hagen Schulze, eds. *Weimar. Selbstpreisgabe einer Demokratie. Eine Bilanz heute*. Düsseldorf, 1984.

Falter, Jürgen, Thomas Lindenberger, and Siegfried Schumann. *Wahlen und Abstimmung in der Weimarer Republik. Materialien zum Wahlverhalten 1919–1933*. Statistische Arbeitsbücher zur neueren deutschen Geschichte. Munich, 1986.

Hermens, Ferdinand A., and Theodor Schieder, eds. *Staat, Wirtschaft und Politik in der Weimarer Republik. Festschrift für Heinrich Brüning*. Berlin, 1967.

Hoffmann, Walter G., Franz Grumbach, and Helmut Hesse. *Das Wachstum der deutschen Wirtschaft seit der Mitte des 19. Jahrhunderts.* Berlin, Heidelberg, and New York, 1965.

Jasper, Gotthard, ed. *Von Weimar zu Hitler 1930–1933.* Neue wissenschaftliche Bibliothek, 25. Cologne, 1968.

Kershaw, Ian. *Weimar: Why Did German Democracy Fail?* New York, 1990.

Kolb, Eberhard, ed. *Vom Kaiserreich zur Weimarer Republik.* Neue wissenschaftliche Bibliothek, 49. Cologne, 1972.

Kruedener, Jürgen, ed. *Economic Crisis and Political Collapse: The Weimar Republik, 1924–1933.* New York, 1990.

Michalka, Wolfgang, ed. *Die nationalsozialistische Machtergreifung.* Paderborn, Munich, Vienna, and Zurich, 1984.

Michalka, Wolfgang, and Marshall M. Lee, eds. *Gustav Stresemann.* Wege der Forschung, 539. Darmstadt, 1982.

Petzina, Dietmar, Werner Abelhauser, and Anselm Faust. *Sozialgeschichtliches Arbeitsbuch.* Vol. 3, *Materialien zur Statistik des Deutschen Reiches 1914–1945.* Munich, 1978.

Ritter, Gerhard A., ed. *Gesellschaft, Parlament und Regierung. Zur Geschichte des Parlamentarismus in Deutschland.* Düsseldorf, 1974.

Stachura, Peter D., ed. *The Nazi Machtergreifung.* London, 1983.

Stern, Carola, and Heinrich August Winkler, eds. *Wendepunkte deutscher Geschichte 1848–1945.* Frankfurt am Main, 1979.

Stürmer, Michael, ed. *Die Weimarer Republik. Belagerte Civitas.* Neue wissenschaftliche Bibliothek, 112. Königstein, 1985.

THE GERMAN REVOLUTION

Bieber, Horst J. *Bürgertum in der Revolution. Bürgerräte und Bürgerstreiks in Deutschland 1918–1920.* Hamburger Beiträge zur Sozial- und Zeitgeschichte, 28. Hamburg, 1992.

———. *Gewerkschaften in Krieg und Revolution. Arbeiterbewegung, Industrie, Staat und Militär in Deutschland 1914–1920.* 2 vols. Hamburg, 1981.

Bermbach, Udo. *Vorformen parlamentarischer Kabinettsbildung in Deutschland. Der interfraktionelle Ausschuß 1917/18 und die Parlamentarisierung der Reichsregierung.* Cologne and Opladen, 1967.

Bosl, Karl, ed. *Bayern im Umbruch. Die Revolution von 1918, ihre Voraussetzungen, ihr Verlauf und ihre Folgen.* Munich, 1969.

Carsten, Francis L. *Revolution in Central Europe, 1918–1919.* Berkeley, Calif., 1972.

Comfort, Richard A. *Revolutionary Hamburg. Labor Politics in the Early Weimar Republic.* Stanford, Calif., 1966.

Deist, Wilhelm. "Die Politik der Seekriegsleitung und die Rebellion der Flotte Ende Oktober 1918." *VfZ* 14 (1966): 341–68.

Elben, Wolfgang. *Das Problem der Kontinuität in der deutschen Revolution. Die Politik der Staatssekretäre und der militärischen Führung vom November 1918 bis Februar*

1919. Beiträge zur Geschichte des Parlamentarismus und der politischen Parteien, 31. Düsseldorf, 1965.

Eliasberg, George. *Der Ruhrkrieg von 1920*. Schriftenreihe des Forschungsinstituts der Friedrich-Ebert-Stiftung, 100. Bonn-Bad Godesberg, 1974.

Erdmann, Karl Dietrich. *Rätestaat oder parlamentarische Demokratie*. Copenhagen, 1979.

Erger, Johannes. *Der Kapp-Lüttwitz-Putsch. Ein Beitrag zur deutschen Innenpolitik 1919/20*. Beiträge zur Geschichte des Parlamentarismus und der politischen Parteien, 35. Düsseldorf, 1967.

Hock, Klaus. *Die Gesetzgebung des Rates der Volksbeauftragten*. Pfaffenweiler, 1987.

Hürten, Heinz. *Die Kirchen in der Novemberrevolution. Eine Untersuchung zur Geschichte der Deutschen Revolution 1918/19*. Regensburg, 1984.

Hunt, Richard N. "Friedrich Ebert and the German Revolution of 1918." In *The Responsibility of Power: Historical Essays in Honor of Hajo Holborn*, edited by Leonard Krieger and Fritz Stern, pp. 315–34. Garden City, N.Y., 1967.

Kluge, Ulrich. *Die deutsche Revolution 1918/19. Staat, Politik und Gesellschaft zwischen Weltkrieg und Kapp-Putsch*. Frankfurt am Main, 1985.

———. *Soldatenräte und Revolution. Studien zur Militärpolitik 1918/19*. Göttingen, 1975.

Könnemann, Erwin, and Hans-Joachim Krusch. *Aktionseinheit Contra Kapp-Putsch. Der Kapp-Putsch im März 1920 und der Kampf der deutschen Arbeiterklasse gegen die Errichtung der Militärdiktatur und für demokratische Verhältnisse*. Berlin (DDR), 1972.

Kolb, Eberhard. *Arbeiterräte in der deutschen Innenpolitik 1918–1919*. Beiträge zur Geschichte des Parlamentarismus und der politischen Parteien, 23. Berlin, 1978.

Kukuck, Peter. *Bremen in der Revolution 1918–1919*. Bremen, 1986.

Lucas, Erhard. "Ursachen und Verlauf der Bergarbeiterbewegung in Herborn und im westlichen Ruhrgebiet." *Duisburger Forschungen* 15 (1971): 1–119.

Ludewig, Hans-Ulrich. *Arbeiterbewegung und Aufstand. Eine Untersuchung zum Verhalten der Arbeiterparteien in den Aufstandsbewegungen der frühen Weimarer Republik 1920–1923*. Husum, 1973.

Malanowski, Wolfgang. *November-Revolution 1918. Die Rolle der SPD*. Frankfurt am Main, 1969.

Matthias, Erich. *Zwischen Räten und Geheimräten. Die deutsche Revolutionsregierung 1918/19*. Düsseldorf, 1970.

Mitchell, Allan. *The Revolution in Bavaria, 1918–1919: The Eisner Regime and the Soviet Republic*. Princeton, N.J., 1965.

Mommsen, Wolfgang J. "Die deutsche Revolution 1918–1920. Politische Revolution und soziale Protestbewegung." *GuG* 4 (1978): 362–91.

Muth, Heinrich. "Die Entstehung der Bauern- und Landarbeiterräte im November 1918 und die Politik des Bundes der Landwirte." *VfZ* 21 (1973): 1–38.

Oeckel, Heinz. *Die revolutionäre Volkswehr 1918/19. Die deutsche Arbeiterklasse im Kampf um die revolutionäre Volkswehr (November 1918 bis Mai 1919)*. Berlin (DDR), 1968.

Patemann, Reinhard. *Der Kampf um die preußische Wahlreform im Ersten Weltkrieg.* Beiträge zur Geschichte des Parlamentarismus und der politischen Parteien, 26. Düsseldorf, 1964.

Rakenius, Gerhard W. *Wilhelm Groener als Erster Generalquartiermeister. Die Politik der Obersten Heeresleitung 1918/19.* Boppard, 1977.

Ritter, Gerhard A., and Susanne Miller, eds. *Die deutsche Revolution 1918/19. Dokumente.* 2nd ed. Hamburg, 1975.

Rürup, Reinhard. *Arbeiter- und Soldatenräte im rheinisch-westfälischen Industriegebiet. Studien zur Geschichte der Revolution 1918/19.* Wuppertal, 1975.

──────. *Probleme der Revolution in Deutschland 1918/19.* Wiesbaden, 1968.

Ryder, A. J. *The German Revolution of 1918: A Study of German Socialism in War and Revolt.* Cambridge, 1967.

Schmidt, Ernst-Heinrich. *Heimatheer und Revolution 1918. Die militärischen Gewalten im Heimatgebiet zwischen Oktoberreform und Novemberrevolution.* Stuttgart, 1981.

Schneider, Dieter, and Rudolf F. Kuda. *Arbeiterräte in der Novemberrevolution. Ideen, Wirkungen, Dokumente.* Frankfurt am Main, 1968.

Watt, Richard M. *The Kings Depart. The Tragedy of Germany: Versailles and the German Revolution.* New York, 1969.

Winkler, Heinrich August. *Die Sozialdemokratie und die Revolution von 1918/19. Ein Rückblick nach sechzig Jahren.* Bonn, 1979.

Zunkel, Friedrich. *Industrie und Staatssozialismus. Der Kampf um die Wirtschaftsordnung in Deutschland 1914–1918.* Düsseldorf, 1974.

ARMISTICE AND VERSAILLES PEACE TREATY

Dickmann, Fritz. *Die Kriegsschuldfrage auf der Friedenskonferenz von Paris 1919.* Munich, 1974.

Haupts, Leo. *Deutsche Friedenspolitik 1918/19. Eine Alternative zur Machtpolitik des Ersten Weltkrieges.* Düsseldorf, 1976.

Hehn, Jürgen von, Hans von Rimscha, and Hellmuth Weiß, eds. *Von den baltischen Provinzen zu den baltischen Staaten. Beiträge zur Entstehungsgeschichte der Republik Estland und Lettland 1917/18.* Marburg, 1971.

Heideking, Jürgen. "Vom Versailler Vertrag zur Genfer Abrüstungskonferenz. Das Scheitern der alliierten Militärkontrollpolitik gegenüber Deutschland nach dem Ersten Weltkrieg." *Militärgeschichtliche Mitteilungen* 28 (1980): 45–68.

Mayer, Arno J. *Politics and Diplomacy of Peacekeeping: Containment and Counterrevolution at Versailles, 1918–1919.* New York, 1968.

Schulz, Gerhard. *Revolutionen und Friedensschlüsse 1917–1920.* Weltgeschichte des 20. Jahrhunderts, 2. Munich, 1985.

Schwabe, Klaus. *Woodrow Wilson, Revolutionary Germany, and Peacemaking, 1918–1919: Missionary Diplomacy and the Realities of Power.* Translated by Rita Kimber and Robert Kimber. Chapel Hill, N.C., 1985.

Schwengler, Walter. *Völkerrecht, Versailler Vertrag und Auslieferungsfrage. Die Strafverfolgung wegen Kriegsverbrechen als Problem des Friedensschlusses 1919/20.* Stuttgart, 1982.

Thompson, John M. *Russia, Bolshevism and the Versailles Peace*. Princeton, N.J., 1966.

Wuest, Erich. *Der Vertrag von Versailles in Licht und Schatten der Kritik. Die Kontroverse um seine wirtschaftlichen Auswirkungen*. Zurich, 1962.

THE WEIMAR CONSTITUTION, FEDERALISM, AND DOMESTIC POLICY

Apelt, Willibalt. *Geschichte der Weimarer Verfassung*. 2nd ed. Munich, 1964.

Benz, Wolfgang. *Süddeutschland in der Weimarer Republik. Ein Beitrag zur deutschen Innenpolitik 1918–1923*. Berlin, 1970.

Bessel, Richard. *Germany after the First World War*. Oxford, 1993.

Besson, Waldemar. *Württemberg und die deutsche Staatskrise 1928–1933. Eine Studie zur Auflösung der Weimarer Republik*. Stuttgart, 1959.

Biewer, Ludwig. *Reichsreformbestrebungen in der Weimarer Republik. Fragen zur Funktionalreform und zur Neugliederung im Südwesten des Deutschen Reiches*. Frankfurt am Main and Bern, 1980.

Bremme, Gabriele. *Die politische Rolle der Frau in Deutschland. Eine Untersuchung über den Einfluß der Frauen bei Wahlen und ihre Teilnahme in Partei und Parlament*. Göttingen, 1956.

Büttner, Ursula. *Hamburg in der Staats- und Wirtschaftskrise 1928–1931*. Hamburg, 1982.

Caplan, Jane. *Government without Administration: State and Civil Service in Weimar and Nazi Germany*. Oxford, 1988.

Deutsche Verwaltungsgeschichte. Edited by Kurt G. A. Jeserich, Hans Pohl, and Georg Christoph von Unruh. Vol. 4, *Das Reich als Republik und in der Zeit des Nationalsozialismus*. Stuttgart, 1985.

Ehni, Hans-Peter. *Bollwerk Preußen. Preußen-Regierung, Reich-Länder-Problem und Sozialdemokratie 1928–1932*. Schriftenreihe des Forschungsinstituts der Friedrich-Ebert-Stiftung, 3. Bonn-Bad Godesberg, 1975.

Fenske, Hans. *Bürokratie in Deutschland. Vom späten Kaiserreich bis zur Gegenwart*. Berlin, 1985.

———. "Monarchisches Beamtentum und demokratischer Staat. Zum Problem der Bürokratie in der Weimarer Republik." In *Demokratie und Verwaltung. 25 Jahre Hochschule der Verwaltungswissenschaften Speyer*. Schriftenreihe der Hochschule Speyer, 50. Berlin, 1972.

Fritzsche, Peter. *Rehearsals for Fascism: Populism and Political Mobilization in Weimar Germany*. Oxford, 1990.

Führ, Christoph. *Zur Schulpolitik der Weimarer Republik. Die Zusammenarbeit von Reich und Ländern im Reichsschulausschuß, 1919–1923, und im Ausschuß für das Unterrichtswesen, 1924–1933. Darstellungen und Quellen*. Weinheim, 1970.

Graßmann, Siegfried. *Hugo Preuß und die deutsche Selbstverwaltung*. Lübeck, 1965.

Grund, Henning. *"Preußenschlag" und Staatsgerichtshof im Jahre 1932*. Baden-Baden, 1976.

Hannover, Heinrich, and Elisabeth Hannover-Brück. *Politische Justiz 1918 bis 1933*. New ed. Bornheim-Merten, 1987.

Haungs, Peter. *Reichspräsident und parlamentarische Kabinettsregierung. Eine Studie zum Regierungssystem der Weimarer Republik in den Jahren 1924 bis 1929.* Cologne, 1968.

Hofmann, Wolfgang. *Zwischen Rathaus und Reichskanzlei. Die Oberbürgermeister in der Kommunal- und Staatspolitik des Deutschen Reiches von 1890 bis 1933.* Berlin, Cologne, and Mainz, 1974.

Huber, Ernst Rudolf. "Zur Lehre vom Verfassungsnotstand in der Staatstheorie der Weimarer Zeit." In *Im Dienst an Recht und Staat. Festschrift für Werner Weber zum 70. Geburtstag,* edited by H. Schneider and V. Götz, pp. 31–52. Berlin, 1974.

Hürten, Heinz. *Reichswehr und Ausnahmezustand. Ein Beitrag zur Verfassungsproblematik der Weimarer Republik in ihrem ersten Jahrfünft.* Opladen, 1977.

Jasper, Gotthard. "Justiz und Politik in der Weimarer Republik." *VfZ* 30 (1982): 167–205.

———. *Der Schutz der Republik. Studien zur staatlichen Sicherung der Demokratie in der Weimarer Republik.* Tübingen, 1963.

Jung, Otmar. *Direkte Demokratie in der Weimarer Republik. Die Fälle "Aufwertung," "Fürstenenteignung," "Panzerkreuzverbot" und "Youngplan."* Frankfurt am Main, 1989.

Kirchheimer, Otto. *Von der Weimarer Republik zum Faschismus. Die Auflösung der demokratischen Rechtsordnung.* Edited by Wolfgang Luthardt. Frankfurt am Main, 1976.

Kuhn, Robert. *Die Vertrauenskrise der Justiz 1926–1928. Der Kampf um die "Republikanisierung" der Rechtspflege in der Weimarer Republik.* Cologne, 1983.

Kunz, Andreas. *Civil Servants and the Politics of Inflation in Germany 1914–1924.* Berlin, 1986.

Laubach, Ernst. *Die Politik der Kabinette Wirth 1921/22.* Lübeck, 1968.

Leßmann, Peter. *Die preußische Schutzpolizei in der Weimarer Republik. Streifendienst und Straßenkampf.* Düsseldorf, 1989.

Luthardt, Wolfgang. *Sozialdemokratische Verfassungstheorie in der Weimarer Republik.* Opladen, 1986.

Meinck, Jürgen. *Weimarer Staatslehre und Nationalsozialismus. Eine Studie zum Problem der Kontinuität im staatsrechtlichen Denken in Deutschland 1928 bis 1936.* Frankfurt am Main, 1978.

Menges, Franz. *Reichsreform und Finanzpolitik. Die Aushöhlung der Eigenstaatlichkeit Bayerns auf finanzpolitischem Wege in der Zeit der Weimarer Republik.* Berlin, 1971.

Möller, Horst. *Parlamentarismus in Preußen 1919–1932.* Düsseldorf, 1985.

Morsey, Rudolf. "Der Beginn der 'Gleichschaltung' in Preußen. Adenauers Haltung in der Sitzung des 'Dreimännerkollegiums' am 6. Februar 1933. Dokumentation." *VfZ* 11 (1963): 85–97.

———. "Zur Geschichte des 'Preußenschlags' am 20. Juli 1932." *VfZ* 9 (1961): 430–39.

Muth, Heinrich. "Carl Schmitt in der deutschen Innenpolitik des Sommers 1932." *HZ,* Beiheft 1 (1971), pp. 75–147.

Orlow, Dietrich J. *Weimar Prussia, 1918–1925: The Unlikely Rock of Democracy.* Pittsburgh, Pa., 1986.

————. *Weimar Prussia, 1925–1933: The Illusion of Strength.* Pittsburgh, Pa., 1991.

Poetzsch-Heffter, Fritz. "Vom Staatsleben unter der Weimarer Verfassung." *Jahrbuch des öffentlichen Rechts der Gegenwart* 21 (1933–34): 1–204.

Revermann, Klaus. *Die stufenweise Durchbrechung des Verfassungssystems der Weimarer Republik in den Jahren 1930–1933. Eine staatsrechtliche und historisch-politische Analyse.* Münster, 1959.

Runge, Wolfgang. *Politik und Beamtentum im Parteienstaat. Die Demokratisierung der politischen Beamten in Preußen zwischen 1918 und 1933.* Stuttgart, 1965.

Schaap, Klaus. *Die Endphase der Weimarer Republik im Freistaat Oldenburg 1928–1932.* Beiträge zur Geschichte des Parlamentarismus und der politischen Parteien, 61. Düsseldorf, 1978.

Schanbacher, Eberhard. *Parlamentarische Wahlen und Wahlsystem in der Weimarer Republik. Wahlgesetzgebung und Wahlreform im Reich und in den Ländern.* Beiträge zur Geschichte des Parlamentarismus und der politischen Parteien, 69. Düsseldorf, 1982.

Schiffers, Reinhard. *Elemente direkter Demokratie im Weimarer Regierungssystem.* Beiträge zur Geschichte des Parlamentarismus und der politischen Parteien, 40. Düsseldorf, 1971.

Schnabel, Thomas, ed. *Die Machtergreifung in Südwestdeutschland. Das Ende der Weimarer Republik in Baden und Württemberg 1928–1933.* Stuttgart, Berlin, Cologne, and Mainz, 1982.

Schüren, Ulrich. *Der Volksentscheid zur Fürstenenteignung 1926. Die Vermögensauseinandersetzung mit den depossedierten Landesherrn als Problem der deutschen Innenpolitik unter besonderer Berücksichtigung der Verhältnisse in Preußen.* Beiträge zur Geschichte des Parlamentarismus und der politischen Parteien, 64. Düsseldorf, 1978.

Schulz, Gerhard. "Der Artikel 48 in historisch-politischer Sicht." In *Staatsnotstand,* edited by E. Fraenkel, pp. 39–71. Berlin, 1965.

————. " 'Preußenschlag' oder Staatsstreich? Neues zum 20. Juli 1932." *Der Staat* 17 (1978): 553–81.

Steger, Bernd. "Der Hitlerprozeß und Bayerns Verhältnis zum Reich 1923/24." *VfZ* 25 (1977): 441–66.

Stürmer, Michael. *Koalition und Opposition in der Weimarer Republik 1924–1928.* Beiträge zur Geschichte des Parlamentarismus und der politischen Parteien, 36. Düsseldorf, 1967.

Trumpp, Thomas. "Franz von Papen, der preußisch-deutsche Dualismus und die NSDAP in Preußen. Ein Beitrag zur Vorgeschichte des 20. Juli 1932." Ph.D. diss., Universität Marburg, 1963.

Wiesemann, Falk. *Die Vorgeschichte der nationalsozialistischen Machtübernahme in Bayern 1932/33.* Berlin, 1975.

Witt, Peter-Christian. "Konservatismus als 'Überparteilichkeit.' Die Beamten der Reichskanzlei zwischen Kaiserreich und Weimarer Republik." In *Deutscher Konservatismus im 19. und 20. Jahrhundert. Festschrift für Fritz Fischer,* edited by Dirk Stegmann, Bernd-Jürgen Wendt, and Peter-Christian Witt, pp. 231–80. Bonn, 1983.

————. "Reichsfinanzminister und Reichsfinanzverwaltung. Zum Problem des Verhältnisses von politischer Führung und bürokratischer Herrschaft in den Anfangsjahren der Weimarer Republik, 1918/19–1924." *VfZ* 23 (1975): 1–61.

Wright, J. R. C. *"Above Parties": The Political Attitudes of the German Protestant Church Leadership, 1918–1933.* Oxford, 1974.

Ziegler, Wilhelm. *Die deutsche Nationalversammlung 1919/1920 und ihr Verfassungswerk.* Berlin, 1932.

POLITICAL PARTIES AND INTEREST ORGANIZATIONS

Arns, Günter. *Regierungsbildung und Koalitionspolitik in der Weimarer Republik 1919–1924.* Clausthal-Zellerfeld, 1971.

Lepsius, Rainer M. "Parteiensystem und Sozialstruktur. Zum Problem der Demokratisierung der deutschen Gesellschaft." In *Deutsche Parteien vor 1918,* edited by Gerhard A. Ritter, pp. 56–80. Cologne, 1973.

Matthias, Erich, and Rudolf Morsey, eds. *Das Ende der Parteien. Darstellung und Dokumente.* Düsseldorf, 1960.

Neumann, Sigmund. *Die Parteien der Weimarer Republik.* 4th ed. Stuttgart, 1977.

Nowak, Kurt. *Evangelische Kirche und Weimarer Republik. Zum politischen Weg des deutschen Protestantismus zwischen 1918 und 1932.* Göttingen, 1981.

Ritter, Gerhard A. "Kontinuität und Umformung des deutschen Parteiensystems 1918–1920." In *Entstehung und Wandel der modernen Gesellschaft. Festschrift für Hans Rosenberg zum 65. Geburtstag,* edited by Gerhard A. Ritter, pp. 342–76. Berlin, 1970.

Scheer, Friedrich-Karl. *Die Deutsche Friedensgesellschaft 1892–1933.* Frankfurt am Main, 1981.

Scholder, Klaus. *Die Kirchen und das Dritte Reich.* Vol. 1, *Vorgeschichte und Zeit der Illusionen 1918–1934.* Frankfurt am Main, Berlin, and Vienna, 1977.

Schulz, Gerhard. "Räte, Wirtschaftsverbände und die Transformation des industriellen Verbandswesens am Anfang der Weimarer Republik." In *Gesellschaft, Parlament und Regierung,* edited by Gerhard A. Ritter, pp. 355–66. Düsseldorf, 1974.

ORGANIZED WORKERS' MOVEMENTS

Angress, Werner T. *Stillborn Revolution: The Communist Bid for Power in Germany, 1921–23.* Princeton, N.J., 1963.

Bahne, Siegfried. *Die KPD und das Ende von Weimar. Das Scheitern einer Politik 1932–1935.* Frankfurt am Main and New York, 1976.

Blau, Joachim. *Sozialdemokratische Staatslehre in der Weimarer Republik. Darstellung und Untersuchung der staatstheoretischen Konzeption von Hermann Heller, Ernst Fraenkel und Otto Kirchheimer.* Schriftenreihe für Sozialgeschichte und Arbeiterbewegung, 21. Marburg, 1980.

Bock, Hans Manfred. *Syndikalismus und Linkskommunismus von 1918–1923. Zur Geschichte und Soziologie der Freien Arbeiter-Union Deutschlands (Syndikalisten), der Allgemeinen Arbeiter-Union Deutschlands und der Kommunistischen Arbeiter-Partei Deutschlands.* Meisenheim, 1969.

Drechsler, Hanno. *Die Sozialistische Arbeiterpartei Deutschlands, SAPD. Ein Beitrag zur Geschichte der deutschen Arbeiterbewegung am Ende der Weimarer Republik.* Meisenheim, 1965.

Fischer, Conan. *The German Communists and the Rise of Nazism.* Basingstoke, 1991.

Flechtheim, Ossip K. *Die KPD in der Weimarer Republik.* New ed. Hamburg, 1986.

Fülberth, Georg. *Die Beziehungen zwischen SPD und KPD in der Kommunalpolitik der Weimarer Periode 1918/19 bis 1933.* Cologne, 1985.

Harsch, Donna. *German Social Democracy and the Rise of Nazism.* Chapel Hill, N.C., 1993.

Heimann, Horst, and Thomas Meyer, eds. *Reformsozialismus und Sozialdemokratie. Zur Theoriediskussion des Demokratischen Sozialismus in der Weimarer Republik. Bericht zum wissenschaftlichen Kongreß der Friedrich-Ebert-Stiftung "Beiträge zur reformistischen Sozialismustheorie in der Weimarer Republik" vom 9. bis 12. Oktober 1980.* Bonn, 1982.

Heupel, Eberhard. *Reformismus und Krise. Zur Theorie und Praxis von SPD, ADGB und Afa-Bund in der Weltwirtschaftskrise 1929-1932/33.* Frankfurt am Main, 1981.

Högl, Günther. "Gewerkschaften und USPD von 1916 bis 1922. Ein Beitrag zur Geschichte der deutschen Arbeiterbewegung unter besonderer Berücksichtigung des Deutschen Metallarbeiter-, Textilarbeiter- und Schumacherverbandes." Ph.D. diss., Universität München, 1982.

Huber, Wolfgang, and Johannes Schwerdtfeger, eds. *Frieden, Gewalt, Sozialismus. Studien zur Geschichte der sozialistischen Arbeiterbewegung.* Forschungen und Berichte der Evangelischen Studiengemeinschaft, 32. Stuttgart, 1976.

Hüllbüsch, Ursula. "Die deutschen Gewerkschaften in der Weltwirtschaftskrise." In *Die Staats- und Wirtschaftskrise des Deutschen Reiches 1929/33*, edited by Werner Conze and Hans Raupach, pp. 126-54. Stuttgart, 1967.

Hunt, Richard N. *German Social Democracy, 1918-1933.* Chicago, 1970.

Klenke, Dietmar. *Die SPD-Linke in der Weimarer Republik. Eine Untersuchung zu den regionalen organisatorischen Grundlagen und zur politischen Praxis und Theoriebildung des linken Flügels der SPD in den Jahren 1922-1932.* 2 vols. Münster, 1983.

Koch-Baumgarten, Sigrid. *Aufstand der Avantgarde. Die Märzaktion der KPD 1921.* Frankfurt am Main and New York, 1986.

Könke, Günter. *Organisierter Kapitalismus, Sozialdemokratie und Staat. Eine Studie zur Ideologie der sozialdemokratischen Arbeiterbewegung in der Weimarer Republik (1924-1932).* Studien zur modernen Geschichte, 37. Stuttgart, 1987.

Krause, Hartfried. *USPD. Zur Geschichte der Unabhängigen Sozialdemokratischen Partei Deutschlands.* Frankfurt am Main, 1975.

Lehnert, Detlef. *Sozialdemokratie und Novemberrevolution. Die Neuordnungsdebatte 1918/19 in der politischen Publizistik von SPD und USPD.* Frankfurt am Main and New York, 1983.

Loesche, Peter. *Der Bolschevismus im Urteil der deutschen Sozialdemokratie 1903-1920.* Berlin, 1967.

Luthardt, Wolfgang, ed. *Sozialdemokratische Arbeiterbewegung und Weimarer Republik. Materialien zur gesellschaftlichen Entwicklung 1927–1933*. 2 vols. Frankfurt am Main, 1978.

Maehl, William H. *The German Socialist Party: Champion of the First Republic, 1918–1933*. Lawrence, Kans., 1986.

Martiny, Martin. "Die Entstehung und politische Bedeutung der 'Neuen Blätter für den Sozialismus' und ihres Freundeskreises. Dokumentation." *VfZ* 25 (1977): 373–419.

———. *Integration oder Konfrontation? Studien zur sozialdemokratischen Rechts- und Verfassungspolitik*. Bonn-Bad Godesberg, 1976.

Miller, Susanne. *Die Bürde der Macht. Die deutsche Sozialdemokratie 1918–1920*. Beiträge zur Geschichte des Parlamentarismus und der politischen Parteien, 63. Düsseldorf, 1978.

Mommsen, Hans. *Sozialdemokratie zwischen Klassenbewegung und Volkspartei*. Frankfurt am Main, 1974.

Morgan, David W. *The Socialist Left and the German Revolution: A History of the Independent Social Democratic Party, 1917–1922*. Ithaca, N.Y., 1975.

Potthoff, Heinrich. *Freie Gewerkschaften 1918–1933. Der Allgemeine Deutsche Gewerkschaftsbund in der Weimarer Republik*. Beiträge zur Geschichte des Parlamentarismus und der politischen Parteien, 82. Düsseldorf, 1987.

———. *Gewerkschaften und Politik zwischen Revolution und Inflation*. Beiträge zur Geschichte des Parlamentarismus und der politischen Parteien, 66. Düsseldorf, 1979.

Pyta, Wolfram. *Gegen Hitler und für die Republik. Die Auseinandersetzung der deutschen Sozialdemokratie mit der NSDAP in der Weimarer Republik*. Beiträge zur Geschichte des Parlamentarismus und der politischen Parteien, 87. Düsseldorf, 1989.

Reulecke, Jürgen, ed. *Arbeiterbewegung an Rhein und Ruhr*. Wuppertal, 1974.

Ruck, Michael. *Die freien Gewerkschaften im Ruhrkampf 1923*. Cologne, 1986.

Schaefer, Rainer. *Die SPD in der Ära Brüning. Tolerierung oder Mobilisation? Handlungsspielräume und Strategien sozialdemokratischer Politik 1930–1932*. Frankfurt am Main and New York, 1990.

Schneider, Michael. *Das Arbeitsbeschaffungsprogramm des ADGB. Zur gewerkschaftlichen Politik in der Endphase der Weimarer Republik*. Bonn-Bad Godesberg, 1975.

Schulze, Hagen. *Anpassung oder Widerstand? Aus den Akten des Parteivorstands der deutschen Sozialdemokratie 1932/33*. Bonn-Bad Godesberg, 1975.

Sühl, Klaus. *SPD und Öffentlicher Dienst in der Weimarer Republik. Die öffentlichen Bediensteten in der SPD und ihre Bedeutung für die sozialdemokratische Politik 1918–1933*. Opladen, 1988.

Vestring, Sigrid. *Die Mehrheitssozialdemokratie und die Entstehung der Reichsverfassung von Weimar 1918/19*. Münster, 1987.

Wachtler, Johann. *Hauptfeind Sozialdemokratie. Strategie und Taktik der KPD 1929–1933*. Düsseldorf, 1982.

———. *Zwischen Revolutionserwartung und Untergang. Die Vorbereitung der KPD auf die Illegalität in den Jahren 1929–1933*. Frankfurt am Main, 1969.

Wheeler, Robert F. "Die '21 Bedingungen' und die Spaltung der USPD im Herbst 1920. Zur Meinungsbildung der Basis." *VfZ* 23 (1975): 117–154.

———. *USPD und Internationale. Sozialistischer Internationalismus in der Zeit der Revolution*. Frankfurt am Main, 1975.

Winkler, Heinrich August. *Arbeiter und Arbeiterbewegung in der Weimarer Republik*. Vol. 1, *Von der Revolution zur Stabilisierung 1918–1924*. Berlin, 1984. Vol. 2, *Der Schein der Normalität 1924–1930*. Berlin, 1985. Vol. 3, *Der Weg in die Katastrophe 1930–1933*. Berlin, 1987.

———. "Klassenbewegung oder Volkspartei? Zur Programmdiskussion in der Weimarer Sozialdemokratie 1920–1925." *GuG* 8 (1982): 9–54.

Wittwer, Wolfgang W. *Die sozialdemokratische Schulpolitik in der Weimarer Republik. Ein Beitrag zur Schulgeschichte im Reich und in Preußen*. Berlin, 1980.

POLITICAL CATHOLICISM

Becker, Josef. "Joseph Wirth und die Krise des Zentrums während des 4. Kabinetts Marx 1927–1928. Darstellung und Dokumente." *Zeitschrift für die Geschichte des Oberrheins* 109 (1962): 361–482.

———. "Prälat Kaas und das Problem der Regierungsbeteiligung der NSDAP 1930–1932." *HZ* 196 (1963): 74–111.

Grünthal, Günther. *Reichsschulgesetz und Zentrumspartei in der Weimarer Republik*. Beiträge zur Geschichte des Parlamentarismus und der politischen Parteien, 39. Düsseldorf, 1968.

Hömig, Herbert. *Das preußische Zentrum in der Weimarer Republik*. Veröffentlichungen der Kommission für Zeitgeschichte, Reihe B, Forschungen, 28. Mainz, 1979.

Junker, Detlev. *Die Deutsche Zentrumspartei und Hitler 1932/33. Ein Beitrag zur Problematik des politischen Katholizismus in Deutschland*. Stuttgart, 1969.

Morsey, Rudolf. *Die Deutsche Zentrumspartei 1917–1923*. Beiträge zur Geschichte des Parlamentarismus und der politischen Parteien, 32. Düsseldorf, 1966.

———. "Hitlers Verhandlungen mit der Zentrumsführung am 31. Januar 1933. Dokumentation." *VfZ* 9 (1961): 182–94.

———. *Der Untergang des politischen Katholizismus. Die Zentrumspartei zwischen christlichem Selbstverständnis und "Nationaler Erhebung" 1932/1933*. Stuttgart and Zurich, 1977.

Patch, William L. *Christian Trade Unions in the Weimar Republic, 1918–1933: The Failure of "Corporate Pluralism."* New Haven, Conn., 1985.

Roder, Hartmut. *Der christlich-nationale Deutsche Gewerkschaftsbund (DGB) im politisch-ökonomischen Kräftefeld der Weimarer Republik. Ein Beitrag zur Funktion und Praxis der bürgerlichen Arbeitnehmerbewegung vom Kaiserreich bis zur faschistischen Diktatur*. Frankfurt am Main, Bern, and New York, 1986.

Ruppert, Karsten. *Im Dienst am Staat von Weimar. Das Zentrum als regierende Partei in der Weimarer Demokratie 1923–1930.* Beiträge zur Geschichte des Parlamentarismus und der politischen Parteien, 96. Düsseldorf, 1992.

Schneider, Michael. *Die christlichen Gewerkschaften 1894–1933.* Bonn, 1982.

Schönhoven, Klaus. *Die Bayerische Volkspartei 1924–1932.* Beiträge zur Geschichte des Parlamentarismus und der politischen Parteien, 46. Düsseldorf, 1972.

———. "Zwischen Anpassung und Ausschaltung. Die Bayerische Volkspartei in der Endphase der Weimarer Republik 1932/33." *HZ* 224 (1977): 340–78.

Schumacher, Martin. "Zwischen 'Einschaltung' und 'Gleichschaltung.' Zum Untergang der Deutschen Zentrumspartei 1932/33." *Historisches Jahrbuch* 99 (1979): 268–303.

BOURGEOIS PARTIES AND INTEREST ORGANIZATIONS

Berghahn, Volker R. "Harzburger Front und die Kandidatur Hindenburgs für die Präsidentschaftswahlen 1932." *VfZ* 13 (1965): 64–82.

Diehl, James M. "Von der 'Vaterlandspartei' zur 'Nationalen Revolution.' Die 'Vereinigten Vaterländischen Verbände Deutschlands (VVVD)' 1922–1932." *VfZ* 33 (1985): 617–39.

Döhn, Lothar. *Politik und Interesse. Die Interessenstruktur der Deutschen Volkspartei.* Meisenheim, 1970.

Fenske, Hans. *Konservatismus und Rechtsradikalismus in Bayern nach 1918.* Bad Homburg, 1969.

Grathwol, Robert P. *Stresemann and the DNVP: Reconciliation or Revenge in German Foreign Policy, 1924–1928.* Lawrence, Kans., 1980.

Hamel, Iris. *Völkischer Verband und nationale Gewerkschaft. Der Deutschnationale Handlungsgehilfen-Verband 1893–1933.* Frankfurt am Main, 1967.

Heinemann, Ulrich. *Die verdrängte Niederlage. Politische Öffentlichkeit und Kriegsschuldfrage in der Weimarer Republik.* Kritische Studien zur Geschichtswissenschaft, 59. Göttingen, 1988.

Hertzmann, Lewis. *DNVP: Right-Wing Opposition in the Weimar Republik 1918–1924.* Lincoln, Neb., 1963.

Heß, Jürgen C. *"Das Ganze Deutschland soll es sein." Demokratischer Nationalismus in der Weimarer Republik am Beispiel der Deutschen Demokratischen Partei.* Stuttgart, 1978.

Hoepke, Klaus-Peter. *Die deutsche Rechte und der italienische Faschismus. Ein Beitrag zum Selbstverständnis und zur Politik von Gruppen und Verbänden der deutschen Rechten.* Beiträge zur Geschichte des Parlamentarismus und der politischen Parteien, 38. Düsseldorf, 1968.

Holzbach, Heidrun. *Das "System Hugenberg." Die Organisation bürgerlicher Sammlungspolitik vor dem Aufstieg der NSDAP 1918–1928.* Stuttgart, 1981.

Hornung, Klaus. *Der Jungdeutsche Orden.* Beiträge zur Geschichte des Parlamentarismus und der politischen Parteien, 14. Düsseldorf, 1958.

Jonas, Erasmus. *Die Volkskonservativen 1928–1933. Entwicklung, Struktur, Standort und staatspolitische Zielsetzung.* Beiträge zur Geschichte des Parlamentarismus und der politischen Parteien, 30. Düsseldorf, 1965.

Jones, Larry Eugene. " 'The Dying Middle': Weimar Germany and the Fragmentation of Bourgeois Politics." *Central European History* 5 (1972): 23–54.

————. *German Liberalism and the Dissolution of the Weimar Party System, 1918–1933.* Chapel Hill, N.C., 1988.

————. "Sammlung oder Zersplitterung? Die Bestrebungen zur Bildung einer neuen Mittelpartei in der Endphase der Weimarer Republik 1930–1933." *VfZ* 25 (1977): 265–304.

Kessler, Alexander. *Der Jungdeutsche Orden in den Jahren der Entscheidung.* 2 vols. Munich, 1974, 1976.

Kruck, Alfred. *Geschichte des Alldeutschen Verbandes 1890–1939.* Wiesbaden, 1954.

Liebe, Werner. *Die Deutschnationale Volkspartei 1918–1924.* Beiträge zur Geschichte des Parlamentarismus und der politischen Parteien, 8. Düsseldorf, 1956.

Lohalm, Uwe. *Völkischer Radikalismus. Die Geschichte des Deutschvölkischen Schutz- und Trutz-Bundes 1919–1923.* Hamburg, 1970.

Opitz, Günter. *Der Christlich-soziale Volksdienst. Versuch einer protestantischen Partei in der Weimarer Republik.* Beiträge zur Geschichte des Parlamentarismus und der politischen Parteien, 37. Düsseldorf, 1969.

Opitz, Reinhard. *Der deutsche Sozialliberalismus 1917–1933.* Cologne, 1973.

Portner, Ernst. *Die Verfassungspolitik der Liberalen. Ein Beitrag zur Deutung der Weimarer Reichsverfassung.* Bonn, 1973.

Schneider, Werner. *Die Deutsche Demokratische Partei in der Weimarer Republik 1924–1930.* Munich, 1978.

Schorr, Helmut J. *Adam Stegerwald. Gewerkschaftler und Politiker der ersten deutschen Republik. Ein Beitrag zur Geschichte der christlich-sozialen Bewegung in Deutschland.* Recklinghausen, 1966.

Schumacher, Martin. *Mittelstandsfront und Republik. Die Wirtschaftspartei— Reichspartei des deutschen Mittelstandes 1919–1933.* Beiträge zur Geschichte des Parlamentarismus und der politischen Parteien, 44. Düsseldorf, 1972.

Schustereit, Heinz. *Linksliberalismus und Sozialdemokratie in der Weimarer Republik. Eine vergleichende Betrachtung der DDP und SPD 1919–1933.* Düsseldorf, 1975.

Stephan, Werner. *Aufstieg und Verfall des Linksliberalismus 1918–1933. Geschichte der Deutschen Demokratischen Partei.* Göttingen, 1973.

Streisow, Jan. *Die Deutschnationale Volkspartei und die Völkisch-Radikalen 1918–1922.* 2 vols. Frankfurt am Main, 1981.

Stupperich, Amrei. *Volksgemeinschaft oder Arbeitersolidarität. Studien zur Arbeitnehmerpolitik in der Deutschnationalen Volkspartei 1918–1933.* Göttingen and Zurich, 1982.

Thimme, Anneliese. *Flucht in den Mythos. Die Deutschnationale Volkspartei und die Niederlage von 1918.* Göttingen, 1969.

Walker, Daniel P. "The German Nationalist People's Party: The Conservative Dilemma in the Weimar Republic." *Journal of Contemporary History* 14 (1979): 627–47.

Wulf, Peter. *Die politische Haltung des schleswig-holsteinischen Handwerks 1928–1933.* Cologne and Opladen, 1969.

PARAMILITARY AND PATRIOTIC ASSOCIATIONS

Berghahn, Volker R. *Der Stahlhelm. Bund der Frontsoldaten 1918–1935.* Beiträge zur Geschichte des Parlamentarismus und der politischen Parteien, 33. Düsseldorf, 1966.

Diehl, James M. *Paramilitary Politics in Weimar Germany.* Bloomington, Ind., 1977.

Klotzbücher, Alois. "Der Politische Weg des Stahlhelm. Bund der Frontsoldaten in der Weimarer Republik. Ein Beitrag zur Geschichte der 'Nationalen Opposition' 1918–1933." Ph.D. diss., Universität Erlangen, 1965.

Könnemann, Erwin. *Einwohnerwehren und Zeitfreiwilligenverbände. Ihre Funktion beim Aufbau eines neuen imperialistischen Militärsystems.* Berlin (DDR), 1971.

Mauch, Hans-Joachim. *Nationalistische Wehrorganisationen in der Weimarer Republik. Zur Entwicklung des "Paramilitarismus."* Frankfurt am Main, 1982.

Rohe, Karl. *Das Reichsbanner Schwarz-Rot-Gold. Ein Beitrag zur Geschichte und Struktur der politischen Kampfverbände zur Zeit der Weimarer Republik.* Beiträge zur Geschichte des Parlamentarismus und der politischen Parteien, 34. Düsseldorf, 1966.

Rosenhaft, Eve. *Beating the Fascists? The German Communists and Political Violence 1929–1933.* Cambridge, 1983.

Schulze, Hagen. *Freikorps und Republik 1918–1920.* Boppard, 1969.

Schuster, Kurt G. P. *Der Rote Frontkämpferbund 1924–1929. Beiträge zur Geschichte und Organisationsstruktur eines politischen Kampfbundes.* Beiträge zur Geschichte des Parlamentarismus und der politischen Parteien, 55. Düsseldorf, 1975.

SOCIAL POLICY AND INDUSTRIAL RELATIONS

Abelhauser, Werner, ed. *Die Weimarer Republik als Wohlfahrtsstaat. Zum Verhältnis von Wirtschafts- und Sozialpolitik in der Industriegesellschaft.* Vierteljahreshefte für Sozial- und Wirtschaftsgeschichte, Beiheft 81. Wiesbaden, 1987.

Bähr, Johannes. *Staatliche Schlichtung in der Weimarer Republik. Tarifpolitik, Korporatismus und industrieller Konflikt zwischen Inflation und Deflation 1919–1932.* Einzelveröffentlichungen der Historischen Kommission zu Berlin, 68. Berlin, 1989.

Brakelmann, Günter. *Evangelische Kirche in sozialen Konflikten der Weimarer Zeit. Das Beispiel des Ruhreisenstreits.* Schriften zur politischen und sozialen Geschichte des neuzeitlichen Christentums, 1. Bochum, 1986.

Dudek, Peter. *Erziehung durch Arbeit. Arbeitslagerbewegung und freiwilliger Arbeitsdienst 1920–1935.* Opladen, 1988.

Evans, Richard J., and Dick Geary, eds. *The German Unemployed. Experiences and Consequences of Unemployment from the Weimar Republic to the Third Reich.* London, 1987.

Feldman, Gerald D., in collaboration with Irmgard Steinisch. "The Origins of the Stinnes-Legien Agreement." *Internationale Wissenschaftliche Korrespondenz zur Geschichte der deutschen Arbeiterbewegung* 9 (1973) Heft 19/20: 45–103.

Feldman, Gerald D., and Irmgard Steinisch. "Die Weimarer Republik, zwischen

Sozial- und Wirtschaftsstaat. Die Entscheidung gegen den Achtstundentag. Hans
Rosenberg zum kommenden 75. Geburtstag gewidmet." *AfS* 18 (1978): 353–439.
————. *Industrie und Gewerkschaften 1918–1924. Die überforderte*
Zentralarbeitsgemeinschaft. Schriftenreihe der *VfZ*, 50. Stuttgart, 1985.
Freyberg, Thomas von. *Industrielle Rationalisierung in der Weimarer Republik.*
Untersucht an Beispielen aus dem Maschinenbau und der Elektroindustrie. Frankfurt
am Main, 1989.
Geiger, Theodor. *Die soziale Schichtung des deutschen Volkes. Soziographischer Versuch*
auf statistischer Grundlage. Reprint, Stuttgart, 1967.
Gerschenkron, Alexander. *Bread and Democracy in Germany.* 2nd ed. New York, 1966.
Lewek, Peter. *Arbeitslosigkeit und Arbeitslosenversicherung in der Weimarer Republik*
1918–1927. Vierteljahrschrift für Sozial- und Wirtschaftsgeschichte, Beiheft 104.
Stuttgart, 1992.
Mommsen, Hans. *Klassenkampf oder Mitbestimmung. Zum Problem der Kontrolle*
wirtschaftlicher Macht in der Weimarer Republik. Cologne and Frankfurt am
Main, 1978.
————, ed. *Arbeiterbewegung und industrieller Wandel. Studien zu gewerkschaftlichen*
Organisationsproblemen im Reich und an der Ruhr 1905–1924. Wuppertal, 1980.
Mommsen, Hans, Dietmar Petzina, and Bernd Weisbrod, eds. *Industrielles System und*
politische Entwicklung in der Weimarer Republik. Verhandlungen des Internationalen
Symposiums in Bochum von 12.–17. Juni 1973. 2 vols. Düsseldorf, 1977.
Preller, Ludwig. *Sozialpolitik in der Weimarer Republik.* New ed. Düsseldorf, 1978.
Schneider, Michael. *Unternehmer und Demokratie. Die freien Gewerkschaften in der*
unternehmerischen Ideologie der Jahre 1918 bis 1933. Schriftenreihe des
Forschungsinstituts der Friedrich-Ebert-Stiftung, 116. Bonn-Bad Godesberg, 1975.
Stachura, Peter D., ed. *Unemployment and the Great Depression in Weimar Germany.*
Houndmills and London, 1986.
Stegmann, Dirk, Bernd-Jürgen Wendt, and Peter-Christian Witt, eds. *Industrielle*
Gesellschaft und politisches System. Beiträge zur politischen Sozialgeschichte.
Festschrift für Fritz Fischer zum 70. Geburtstag. Schriftenreihe des
Forschungsinstituts der Friedrich-Ebert-Stiftung, 137. Bonn, 1978.
Steinisch, Irmgard. *Arbeitszeitverkürzung und sozialer Wandel. Der Kampf um die*
Achtstundenschicht in der deutschen und amerikanischen Eisen- und Stahlindustrie
1880–1929. Berlin, 1986.
Timm, Helga. *Die deutsche Sozialpolitik und der Bruch der großen Koalition im März*
1930. Beiträge zur Geschichte des Parlamentarismus und der politischen Parteien, 1.
2nd ed. Düsseldorf, 1982.
Tschirbs, Rudolf. *Tarifpolitik im Ruhrbergbau 1918–1933.* Beiträge zu Inflation und
Wiederaufbau in Deutschland und Europa 1914–1924, 5, and Veröffentlichungen
der Historischen Kommission zu Berlin, 64. Berlin, 1986.
Wengst, Udo. "Unternehmerverbände und Gewerkschaften in Deutschland im Jahre
1930." *VfZ* 25 (1977): 99–119.
Zollitsch, Wolfgang. *Arbeiter zwischen Weltwirtschaftskrise und Nationalsozialismus.*
Ein Beitrag zur Sozialgeschichte der Jahre 1928 bis 1936. Kritische Studien zur
Geschichtswissenschaft, 88. Göttingen, 1990.

ECONOMIC AND FINANCIAL POLICY

Abraham, David. *The Collapse of the Weimar Republic: Political Economy and Crisis.* 2nd rev. ed. New York, 1986.

Balderston, Theo. *The Origins and Course of the German Economic Crisis. November 1923 to May 1932.* Schriften der Historischen Kommission zu Berlin, 2. Berlin, 1993.

Blaich, Fritz. *Die Wirtschaftskrise 1925/26 und die Reichsregierung. Von der ersten Erwerbslosenfürsorge zur Konjunkturpolitik.* Kallmünz, 1977.

Böhret, Carl. *Aktionen gegen die "kalte Sozialisierung" 1926–1930. Ein Beitrag zum Wirken ökonomischer Einflußverbände in der Weimarer Republik.* Berlin, 1966.

Borchardt, Knut. *Wachstum, Krisen, Handlungsspielräume der Wirtschaftspolitik. Studien zur Wirtschaftsgeschichte des 19. und 20. Jahrhunderts.* Kritische Studien zur Geschichtswissenschaft, 50. Göttingen, 1982.

———. "Zwangslagen und Handlungsspielräume in der Großen Wirtschaftskrise der frühen dreißiger Jahre: Zur Revision des überlieferten Geschichtsbildes." In *Die Weimarer Republik. Belagerte Civitas*, edited by Michael Stürmer, pp. 318–39. 2nd ed. Königstein, 1985.

Born, Karl E. *Die deutsche Bankenkrise 1931. Finanzen und Politik.* Munich, 1967.

Büsch, Otto, and Gerald D. Feldman, eds. *Historische Prozesse der deutschen Inflation 1914 bis 1924. Ein Tagungsbericht.* Einzelveröffentlichungen der Historischen Kommission zu Berlin, 21. Berlin, 1978.

Ehlert, Herald G. *Die wirtschaftliche Zentralbehörde des Deutschen Reiches 1914 bis 1919. Das Problem der "Gemeinwirtschaft" in Krieg und Frieden.* Wiesbaden, 1982.

Feldman, Gerald D. *The Great Disorder: Politics, Economics, and Society in the German Inflation, 1914–1924.* New York and Oxford, 1993.

———. *Iron and Steel in the German Inflation, 1916–1923.* Princeton, N.J., 1977.

———. *Vom Weltkrieg zur Weltwirtschaftskrise. Studien zur deutschen Wirtschafts- und Sozialgeschichte 1914–1932.* Kritische Studien zur Geschichtswissenschaft, 60. Göttingen, 1984.

———, ed., with the collaboration of Elisabeth Müller-Luckner. *Die Nachwirkungen der Inflation auf die deutsche Geschichte 1924–1933.* Munich, 1985.

Feldman, Gerald D., Carl-Ludwig Holtfrerich, Gerhard A. Ritter, and Peter-Christian Witt, eds. *The Adaptation to Inflation.* Beiträge zu Inflation und Wiederaufbau in Deutschland und Europa 1914–1924, 8, and Veröffentlichungen der Historischen Kommission zu Berlin, 67. Berlin and New York, 1986.

———. *Consequences of Inflation.* Beiträge zu Inflation und Wiederaufbau in Deutschland und Europa 1914–1924, and Einzelveröffentlichungen der Historischen Kommission zu Berlin, 67. Berlin, 1989.

———. *The Experience of Inflation: International and Comparative Studies.* Beiträge zu Inflation und Wiederaufbau in Deutschland und Europa 1914–1924, 2, and Veröffentlichungen der Historischen Kommission zu Berlin, 57. Berlin and New York, 1984.

———. *The German Inflation Reconsidered: A Preliminary Balance.* Beiträge zu Inflation und Wiederaufbau in Deutschland und Europa 1914–1924, 1, and

Veröffentlichungen der Historischen Kommission zu Berlin, 54. Berlin and New York, 1982.

Feldman, Gerald D., and Heidrun Homburg. *Industrie und Inflation. Studien und Dokumente zur Politik der deutschen Unternehmer 1916–1923.* Hamburg, 1977.

Fischer, Wolfram. *Deutsche Wirtschaftspolitik 1918–1945.* 3rd ed. Opladen, 1968.

Gossweiler, Kurt. *Kapital, Reichswehr und NSDAP 1919–1924.* Cologne, 1982.

Grübler, Michael. *Die Spitzenverbände der Wirtschaft und das erste Kabinett Brüning. Vom Ende der großen Koalition 1929/30 bis zum Vorabend der Bankenkrise 1931. Eine Quellenstudie.* Beiträge zur Geschichte des Parlamentarismus und der politischen Parteien, 70. Düsseldorf, 1982.

Hallgarten, Georg F. W. *Hitler, Reichswehr und Industrie. Zur Geschichte der Jahre 1918–1933.* Frankfurt am Main, 1955.

Hansmeyer, Karl-Heinrich, ed. *Kommunale Finanzpolitik in der Weimarer Republik.* Schriften des Vereins für Kommunalwissenschaft, 36. Stuttgart, 1973.

Hardach, Gerd. "Reichsbankpolitik und wirtschaftliche Entwicklung 1924–1931." *Schmollers Jahrbuch für Wirtschafts- und Sozialwissenschaften* 90 (1970): 562–92.

———. *Weltmarktorientierung und relative Stagnation. Währungspolitik in Deutschland 1924–1931.* Berlin, 1976.

Hartwich, Hans-Hermann. *Arbeitsmarkt, Verbände und Staat 1918–1933. Die öffentliche Bindung unternehmerischer Funktionen in der Weimarer Republik.* Berlin, 1967.

Hertz-Eichenrode, Dieter. *Wirtschaftskrise und Arbeitsbeschaffung. Konjunkturpolitik 1925/26 und die Grundlagen der Krisenpolitik Brünings.* Frankfurt am Main and New York, 1982.

Holtfrerich, Carl-Ludwig. "Alternativen zu Brünings Wirtschaftspolitik in der Weltwirtschaftskrise." *HZ* 235 (1982): 605–31.

———. *Die deutsche Inflation 1914–1923. Ursachen und Folgen in internationaler Perspektive.* Berlin and New York, 1980.

James, Harold. *The German Slump: Politics and Economics, 1924–1936.* Oxford, 1986.

———. *The Reichsbank and Public Finance in Germany 1924–1933: A Study of the Politics of Economics during the Great Depression.* Schriftenreihe des Instituts für Bankhistorische Forschung, 5. Frankfurt am Main, 1985.

Kindleberger, Charles P. *The World in Depression.* London, 1973.

Koszyk, Kurt. "Paul Reusch and the 'Münchner Neuesten Nachrichten.' Zum Problem Industrie und Presse in der Endphase der Weimarer Republik." *VfZ* 19 (1971): 75–103.

Krohn, Claus-Dieter. *Stabilisierung und ökonomische Interessen. Die Finanzpolitik des Deutschen Reiches 1923–1927.* Düsseldorf, 1974.

Kroll, Gerhard. *Von der Weltwirtschaftskrise zur Staatskonjunktur.* Berlin, 1958.

Krosigk, Lutz Graf Schwerin von. *Staatsbankrott. Die Geschichte des Deutschen Reiches von 1920–1945. Geschrieben vom letzten Reichsfinanzminister.* Göttingen, Frankfurt am Main, and Zurich, 1974.

Leuschen-Seppel, Rosemarie. *Zwischen Staatsverantwortung und Klasseninteresse. Die Wirtschafts- und Finanzpolitik der SPD zur Zeit der Weimarer Republik unter besonderer Berücksichtigung der Mittelphase 1924–1928/29.* Politik und Gesellschaftsgeschichte, 9. Bonn, 1981.

Lüke, Rolf E. *Von der Stabilisierung zur Krise*. Zurich, 1958.

McNeil, William C. *American Money in the Weimar Republic: Economics and Politics on the Eve of the Great Depression*. New York, 1986.

Maier, Charles S. *Recasting Bourgeois Europe: Stabilization in France, Germany and Italy in the Decade after World War I*. Princeton, N.J., 1975.

Marcon, Helmut. *Arbeitsbeschaffungspolitik der Regierungen Papen und Schleicher. Grundsteinlegung für die Beschäftigungspolitik im Dritten Reich*. Moderne Geschichte und Politik, 3. Bern and Frankfurt am Main, 1974.

Maurer, Ilse. *Reichsfinanzen und große Koalition. Zur Geschichte des Reichskabinetts Müller 1928–1930*. Moderne Geschichte und Politik, 1. Bern and Frankfurt am Main, 1973.

Meister, Rainer. *Die große Depression. Zwangslage und Handlungsspielräume der Wirtschafts- und Finanzpolitik in Deutschland 1929–1932*. Kölner Schriften zur Sozial- und Wirtschaftspolitik, 11. Regensburg, 1991.

Möller, Alex. *Reichsfinanzminister Matthias Erzberger und sein Reformwerk*. Bonn, 1971.

Morsey, Rudolf. "Brünings Kritik an der Reichsfinanzpolitik 1919–1929." In *Geschichte, Wirtschaft, Gesellschaft. Festschrift für Clemens Bauer zum 75. Geburtstag*, edited by Erich Hassinger, J. Heinz Müller, and Hugo Ott, pp. 359–73. Berlin, 1974.

Müller, Helmut. *Die Zentralbank—eine Nebenregierung, Reichsbankpräsident Hjalmar Schacht als Politiker der Weimarer Republik*. Opladen, 1973.

Neebe, Reinhard. *Großindustrie, Staat und NSDAP 1930–1933. Paul Silverberg und der Reichsverband der Deutschen Industrie in der Krise der Weimarer Republik*. Kritische Studien zur Geschichtswissenschaft, 45. Göttingen, 1981.

Petzina, Dietmar. *Die deutsche Wirtschaft in der Zwischenkriegszeit*. Wiesbaden, 1977.

Pohl, Karl Heinrich. *Weimars Wirtschaft und die Außenpolitik der Republik 1924–1926. Vom Dawes-Plan zum Internationalen Eisenpakt*. Düsseldorf, 1979.

Sanmann, Horst. "Daten und Alternativen in der deutschen Wirtschafts- und Finanzpolitik in der Ära Brüning." *Hamburger Jahrbuch für Wirtschafts- und Gesellschaftspolitik* 10 (1965): 109–40.

Sörgel, Werner. *Metallindustrie und Nationalsozialismus. Eine Untersuchung über Struktur und Funktion industrieller Organisationen in Deutschland 1929 bis 1939*. Frankfurt am Main, 1965.

Turner, Henry A. "The Ruhrlade: Secret Cabinet of Heavy Industry in the Weimar Republic." *Central European History* 3 (1970): 195–228.

Weisbrod, Bernd. *Schwerindustrie in der Weimarer Republik. Interessenpolitik zwischen Stabilisierung und Krise*. Wuppertal, 1978.

Wengst, Udo. "Der Reichsverband der Deutschen Industrie in den ersten Monaten des Dritten Reiches. Ein Beitrag zum Verhältnis von Großindustrie und Nationalsozialismus." *VfZ* 28 (1980): 94–110.

Winkler, Heinrich August. *Mittelstand, Demokratie und Nationalsozialismus. Die politische Entwicklung von Handwerk und Kleinhandel in der Weimarer Republik*. Cologne, 1972.

———, ed. *Organisierter Kapitalismus. Voraussetzungen und Anfänge*. Kritische Studien zur Geschichtswissenschaft, 9. Göttingen, 1974.

Witt, Peter-Christian. "Finanzpolitik als Verfassungs- und Gesellschaftspolitik. Überlegungen zur Finanzpolitik des Deutschen Reiches 1930 bis 1932." *GuG* 8 (1982): 386–414.

———. "Inflation, Wohnungszwangswirtschaft und Hauszinssteuer. Zur Regelung von Wohnungsbau und Wohnungsmarkt in der Weimarer Republik." In *Wohnen im Wandel. Beiträge zur Geschichte des Alltags in der bürgerlichen Gesellschaft,* edited by Lutz Niethammer, pp. 385–407. Wuppertal, 1979.

AGRARIAN POLICY AND EASTERN RELIEF

Barmeyer, Heide. *Andreas Hermes und die Organisation der deutschen Landwirtschaft. Christliche Bauernvereine, Reichslandbund, Grüne Front, Reichsnährstand 1928 bis 1933.* Quellen und Forschungen zur Agrargeschichte, 24. Stuttgart, 1971.

Buchta, Bruno. *Die Junker und die Weimarer Republik. Charakter und Bedeutung der Osthilfe in den Jahren 1928–1933.* Berlin (DDR), 1959.

Flemming, Jens. *Landwirtschaftliche Interessen und Demokratie. Ländliche Gesellschaft, Agrarverbände und Staat 1890–1925.* Bonn, 1978.

Gessner, Dieter. *Agrardepression und Präsidialregierungen in Deutschland 1930 bis 1933. Probleme des Agrarprotektionismus am Ende der Weimarer Republik.* Düsseldorf, 1977.

———. *Agrarverbände in der Weimarer Republik. Wirtschaftliche und soziale Voraussetzungen agrarkonservativer Politik vor 1933.* Düsseldorf, 1976.

———. " 'Grüne Front' oder 'Harzburger Front.' Der Reichs-Landbund in der letzten Phase der Weimarer Republik zwischen wirtschaftlicher Interessenpolitik und nationalistischem Revisionsanspruch. Dokumentation." *VfZ* 29 (1981): 110–23.

Gies, Horst. "R. Walter Darré und die nationalsozialistische Bauernpolitik in den Jahren 1930 bis 1933." Ph.D. diss., Universität Frankfurt, 1966.

Hertz-Eichenrode, Dieter. *Politik und Landwirtschaft in Ostpreußen 1919–1930. Untersuchung eines Strukturproblems in der Weimarer Republik.* Cologne and Opladen, 1969.

Moeller, Robert G. *German Peasants and Agrarian Politics, 1914–1924: The Rhineland and Westphalia.* Chapel Hill, N.C., 1986.

Panzer, Arno. *Das Ringen um die deutsche Agrarpolitik von der Währungsstabilisierung bis zur Agrardebatte im Reichstag im Dezember 1928.* Kiel, 1970.

Schulz, Gerhard. "Staatliche Stützungsmaßnahmen in den deutschen Ostgebieten." In *Staat, Wirtschaft und Politik in der Weimarer Republik,* edited by Ferdinand Hermens and Theodor Schieder, pp. 141–204. Berlin, 1967.

Schumacher, Martin. *Land und Politik. Eine Untersuchung über politische Parteien und agrarische Interessen 1914–1923.* Beiträge zur Geschichte des Parlamentarismus und der politischen Parteien, 65. Düsseldorf, 1979.

Stoltenberg, Gerhard. *Politische Strömungen im schleswig-holsteinischen Landvolk 1918–1933. Ein Beitrag zur politischen Meinungsbildung in der Weimarer Republik.* Beiträge zur Geschichte des Parlamentarismus und der politischen Parteien, 24. Düsseldorf, 1962.

FOREIGN POLICY AND THE REPARATIONS QUESTION

Bariéty, Jacques. *Les relations franco-allemandes après la première guerre mondiale, 10 novembre 1918–10 janvier 1925, de l'exécution à la négociation.* Paris, 1977.

Baumgart, Winfried. *Deutsche Ostpolitik 1918. Von Brest-Litowsk bis zum Ende des Ersten Weltkriegs.* Vienna and Munich, 1966.

Becker, Josef, and Klaus Hildebrand, eds. *Internationale Beziehungen in der Weltwirtschaftskrise 1929 bis 1933. Referate und Diskussionsbeiträge eines Augsburger Symposions. 29. März bis 1. April 1979.* Munich, 1980.

Bennett, Eduard W. *Germany and the Diplomacy of the Financial Crisis 1931.* Cambridge, Mass., 1962.

Bertram-Libal, Gisela. *Aspekte der britischen Deutschlandpolitik 1919 bis 1922.* Göppingen, 1972.

Carr, E. H. *Berlin-Moskau. Deutschland und Rußland zwischen den beiden Weltkriegen.* Stuttgart, 1954.

Dyck, Harvey L. *Weimar Germany and Soviet Russia, 1926–1933: A Study in Diplomatic Instability.* London, 1966.

Enssle, Manfred J. *Stresemann's Territorial Revisionism: Germany, Belgium, and the Eupen-Malmédy Question, 1919–1929.* Wiesbaden, 1980.

Erdmann, Karl Dietrich. *Adenauer in der Rheinlandpolitik nach dem Ersten Weltkrieg.* Stuttgart, 1966.

———. "Der Europaplan Briands im Licht der englischen Akten." *GWU* 1 (1950): 16–32.

Felix, David. *Walther Rathenau and the Weimar Republic: The Politics of Reparation.* Baltimore, 1971.

Fink, Carole. *The Genoa Conference: European Diplomacy, 1919–1922.* Chapel Hill, N.C., 1984.

Fink, Carole, Axel Frohn, and Jürgen Heideking, eds. *Genoa, Rapallo, and European Reconstruction in 1922.* Washington, D.C., 1991.

Frommelt, Reinhard. "Paneuropa oder Mitteleuropa. Einigungsbestrebungen im Kalkül deutscher Wirtschaft und Politik 1925–1933." Schriftenreihe der *VfZ*, 34. Stuttgart, 1977.

Gatzke, Hans W. *Stresemann and the Rearmament of Germany.* Baltimore, 1954.

Gottwald, Robert. *Die deutsch-amerikanischen Beziehungen in der Ära Stresemann.* Berlin, 1965.

Graml, Hermann. *Europa zwischen den Kriegen.* Weltgeschichte des 20. Jahrhunderts, 5. 5th ed. Munich, 1982.

———. "Die Rapallo-Politik im Urteil der westdeutschen Forschung." *VfZ* 18 (1970): 366–91.

Hauser, Oswald. "Der Plan einer deutsch-österreichischen Zollunion von 1931 und die europäische Föderation." *HZ* 179 (1955): 45–92.

Heideking, Jürgen. *Aeropag der Diplomaten. Die Pariser Botschafterkonferenz der alliierten Hauptmächte und die Probleme der europäischen Politik 1920–1931.* Husum, 1979.

Helbich, Wolfgang J. *Die Reparationen in der Ära Brüning. Zur Bedeutung des Young-Plans für die deutsche Politik 1930 bis 1932.* Berlin, 1962.

Helbig, Herbert. *Die Träger der Rapallo-Politik.* Göttingen, 1958.

Hildebrand, Klaus. *Das Deutsche Reich und die Sowjetunion im internationalen System 1918–1932. Legitimität oder Revolution?* Wiesbaden, 1977.

Hillgruber, Andreas. *Großmachtpolitik und Militarismus im 20. Jahrhundert. Drei Beiträge zum Kontinuitätsproblem.* Düsseldorf, 1974.

————. *Kontinuität und Diskontinuität in der deutschen Außenpolitik von Bismarck bis Hitler.* Düsseldorf, 1969.

Höltje, Christian. *Über den Weimarer Staat und "Ost-Locarno" 1919–1934. Revision oder Garantie der deutschen Ostgrenze von 1919.* Würzburg, 1958.

Jacobson, Jon. *Locarno Diplomacy: Germany and the West, 1925–1929.* Princeton, N.J., 1972.

Jacobson, Jon, and John T. Walker. "The Impulse for a Franco-German Entente: The Origins of the Thoiry Conference, 1926." *Journal of Contemporary History* 10 (1975): 157–81.

Kellermann, Volkmar. *Schwarzer Adler, Weißer Adler. Die Polenpolitik der Weimarer Republik.* Cologne, 1970.

Kent, Bruce. *The Spoils of War: The Politics, Economics, and Diplomacy of Reparations, 1918–1932.* Oxford, 1989.

Krekeler, Norbert. *Revisionsanspruch und geheime Ostpolitik der Weimarer Republik. Die Subventionierung der deutschen Minderheit in Polen.* Schriftenreihe der *VfZ*, 27. Stuttgart, 1973.

Krüger, Peter. *Die Außenpolitik der Republik von Weimar.* Darmstadt, 1985.

————. *Deutschland und die Reparationen 1918/19. Die Genesis des Reparationsproblems in Deutschland zwischen Waffenstillstand und Versailler Friedensschluß.* Schriftenreihe der *VfZ*, 25. Stuttgart, 1973.

————. "Die Reparationen und das Scheitern einer deutschen Verständigungspolitik auf der Pariser Friedenskonferenz im Jahre 1919." *HZ* 221 (1975): 326–72.

Krummacher, Friedrich A., and Helmut Lange. *Krieg und Frieden. Geschichte der deutsch-sowjetischen Beziehungen. Von Brest-Litowsk bis zum Unternehmen Barbarossa.* Munich, 1970.

Leffler, Melvyn P. *The Elusive Quest: America's Pursuit of European Stability and French Security, 1919–1933.* Chapel Hill, N.C., 1979.

Link, Werner. *Die amerikanische Stabilisierungspolitik in Deutschland 1921–32.* Düsseldorf, 1970.

Linke, Horst Günther. *Deutsch-sowjetische Beziehungen bis Rapallo.* Cologne, 1970.

Lipgens, Walter. "Europäische Einigungsidee 1923–1930 und Briands Europaplan im Urteil der deutschen Akten." *HZ* 203 (1966): 46–89, 316–63.

McDougall, Walter A. *France's Rhineland Diplomacy, 1914–1924: The Last Bid for a Balance of Power in Europe.* Princeton, N.J., 1978.

Maxelon, Michael-Olaf. *Stresemann und Frankreich 1914–1929. Deutsche Politik der Ost-West-Balance.* Düsseldorf, 1972.

Megerle, Klaus. *Deutsche Außenpolitik 1925. Ansatz zu aktivem Revisionismus.* Frankfurt am Main, 1974.

Nadolny, Sten. *Abrüstungsdiplomatie 1932/33. Deutschland auf der Genfer Konferenz im Übergang von Weimar zu Hitler*. Munich, 1978.

Nelson, Keith L. *Victors Divided: America and the Allies in Germany, 1918–1923*. Berkeley, Calif., 1975.

Niclauß, Karlheinz. *Die Sowjetunion und Hitlers Machtergreifung. Eine Studie über die deutsch-russischen Beziehungen der Jahre 1929 bis 1935*. Bonn, 1966.

Pieper, Helmut. *Die Minderheitenfrage und das Deutsche Reich, 1919–1933/34*. Frankfurt am Main, 1974.

Pogge von Strandmann, Hartmut. "Rapallo-Strategy in Preventive Diplomacy: New Sources and New Interpretations." In *Germany in the Age of Total War: Essays in Honour of Francis Carsten*, edited by Volker R. Berghahn and Martin Kitchen, pp. 123–46. London, 1981.

Post, Gaines. *The Civil-Military Fabric of Weimar Foreign Policy*. Princeton, N.J., 1973.

Riekhoff, Harald von. *German-Polish Relations, 1918–33*. Baltimore, 1971.

Rößler, Hellmuth, ed., in collaboration with Erwin Hölzle. *Locarno und die Weltpolitik 1924–1932*. Göttingen, Zurich, and Frankfurt am Main, 1969.

Roos, Hans. *Polen und Europa. Studien zur polnischen Außenpolitik 1931–1939*. Tübingen, 1957.

Rosenfeld, Günter. *Sowjet-Rußland und Deutschland 1917–1922*. Cologne, 1984.

———. *Sowjetunion und Deutschland 1922–1933*. Cologne, 1984.

Rupieper, Hermann J. *The Cuno Government and Reparations, 1922–1923: Politics and Economics*. The Hague, Boston, and London, 1979.

Schieder, Theodor. "Die Entstehungsgeschichte des Rapallo-Vertrags." *HZ* 204 (1967): 545–609.

Schmidt, Royal J. *Versailles and the Ruhr: Seedbed of World War II*. The Hague, 1968.

Schröder, Hans-Jürgen, ed. *Südosteuropa im Spannungsfeld der Großmächte 1919–1939*. Wiesbaden, 1984.

Schuker, Stephen A. *American "Reparations" to Germany, 1919–33: Implications for the Third-World Debt Crisis*. Princeton, N.J., 1988.

———. *The End of French Predominance in Europe: The Financial Crisis of 1924 and the Adoption of the Dawes Plan*. Chapel Hill, N.C., 1976.

Schwabe, Klaus, ed. *Die Ruhrkrise 1923. Wendepunkt der internationalen Beziehungen nach dem Ersten Weltkrieg*. Paderborn, 1985.

Soutou, Georges. "Die deutschen Reparationen und das Seydoux-Projekt 1920/21." *VfZ* 23 (1975): 237–70.

Spenz, Jürgen. *Die diplomatische Vorgeschichte des Beitritts Deutschlands zum Völkerbund 1924–1926. Ein Beitrag zur Außenpolitik der Weimarer Republik*. Göttingen, 1966.

Stamm, Christoph. *Lloyd George zwischen Innen- und Außenpolitik. Die britische Deutschlandpolitik 1921/22*. Cologne, 1977.

Trachtenberg, Marc. *Reparations in World Politics: France and European Economic Diplomacy, 1916–1923*. New York, 1980.

Vogelsang, Thilo. "Papen und das außenpolitische Erbe Brünings. Die Lausanner Konferenz 1932." In *Neue Perspektiven aus Wirtschaft und Recht. Festschrift für Hans*

Schäffer zum 80. Geburtstag am 11. April 1966, edited by Carsten Peter Claussen, pp. 487–507. Berlin, 1966.

Walsdorff, Martin. *Westorientierung und Ostpolitik. Stresemanns Rußlandpolitik in der Locarno-Ära*. Bremen, 1971.

Wandel, Eckhard. *Die Bedeutung der Vereinigten Staaten von Amerika für das deutsche Reparationsproblem 1924–1929*. Tübingen, 1971.

Weidenfeld, Werner. *Die Englandpolitik Gustav Stresemanns. Theoretische und praktische Aspekte der Außenpolitik*. Mainz, 1982.

Weingartner, Thomas. *Stalin und der Aufstieg Hitlers. Die Deutschlandpolitik der Sowjetunion und der Kommunistischen Internationale 1929–1934*. Berlin, 1970.

Wengst, Udo. *Graf Brockdorff-Rantzau und die außenpolitischen Anfänge der Weimarer Republik*. Berlin and Frankfurt am Main, 1973.

Wollstein, Günter. *Vom Weimarer Revisionismus zu Hitler. Das Deutsche Reich und die Großmächte in der Anfangsphase der nationalsozialistischen Herrschaft in Deutschland*. Bonn, 1973.

Wurm, Clemens A. *Die französische Sicherheitspolitik in der Phase der Umorientierung, 1924–1926*. Frankfurt am Main, 1979.

MILITARY AND ARMAMENT POLICIES

Bucher, Peter. *Der Reichswehrprozeß. Der Hochverrat der Ulmer Reichswehroffiziere 1929/30*. Wehrwissenschaftliche Forschungen, Abteilung Militärgeschichtliche Studien, 4. Boppard, 1967.

Carsten, Francis L. *The Reichswehr and Politics, 1918–1933*. Oxford, 1966.

Deist, Wilhelm, Manfred Messerschmidt, Hans-Erich Volkmann, and Wolfram Wette. *Germany and the Second World War*. Edited by the Militärgeschichtliches Forschungsamt. Translated by P. S. Falla, Dean S. McMurry, and Ewald Osers. Vol. 1, *The Build-Up of German Aggression*. Oxford, 1990.

Dülffer, Jost. *Weimar, Hitler und die Marine. Reichspolitik und Flottenbau 1920–1939*. Düsseldorf, 1973.

Geyer, Michael. *Aufrüstung oder Sicherheit. Die Reichswehr in der Krise der Machtpolitik, 1924–1936*. Wiesbaden, 1980.

———. *Deutsche Rüstungspolitik 1860–1980*. Frankfurt am Main, 1984.

———. "Das Zweite Rüstungsprogramm 1930–1934." *Militärgeschichtliche Mitteilungen* 17 (1975): 125–72.

Gordon, Harold J. *The Reichswehr and the German Republic, 1919–1926*. Princeton, N.J., 1957.

Hansen, Ernst Willi. *Reichswehr und Industrie. Rüstungswirtschaftliche Zusammenarbeit und wirtschaftliche Mobilmachungsvorbereitungen 1923–1932*. Boppard, 1978.

Hürter, Johannes. *Wilhelm Groener. Reichswehrminister am Ende der Weimarer Republik (1928–1932)*. Schriftenreihe des Militärgeschichtlichen Forschungsamts, 39. Munich, 1993.

Müller, Klaus-Jürgen, and Eckardt Opitz, eds. *Militär und Militarismus in der*

Weimarer Republik. Beiträge eines internationalen Symposiums an der Hochschule der Bundeswehr Hamburg am 5. und 6. Mai 1977. Düsseldorf, 1978.

Salewsky, Michael. *Entwaffnung und Militärkontrolle in Deutschland 1919–1927.* Munich, 1966.

Schüddekopf, Otto Ernst. *Das Heer und die Republik. Quellen zur Politik der Reichswehrführung 1918 bis 1933.* Hanover and Frankfurt am Main, 1955.

Vogelsang, Thilo. "Neue Dokumente zur Geschichte der Reichswehr 1930–1933." *VfZ* 2 (1954): 397–436.

————. *Reichswehr, Staat und NSDAP. Beiträge zur deutschen Geschichte 1930–1932.* Stuttgart, 1962.

Wacker, Wolfgang. *Der Bau des Panzerschiffs "A" und der Reichstag.* Tübingen, 1959.

CULTURAL LIFE AND POLITICAL CULTURE

Becker, Werner. *Demokratie des sozialen Rechts. Die politische Haltung der Frankfurter Zeitung, der Vossischen Zeitung und des Berliner Tageblatts 1918–1924.* Göttingen, 1971.

Bergmann, Klaus. *Agrarromantik und Großstadtfeindschaft.* Meisenheim, 1970.

Bleuel, Hans P. *Deutschlands Bekenner. Professoren zwischen Kaiserreich und Diktatur.* Munich, 1968.

Breuning, Klaus. *Die Vision des Reiches. Deutscher Katholizismus zwischen Demokratie und Diktatur, 1929 bis 1934.* Munich, 1969.

Bridenthal, Renate, Atina Grossmann, and Marion Kaplan, eds. *When Biology Became Destiny: Women in Weimar and Nazi Germany.* New York, 1984.

Bullivant, Keith, ed. *Das literarische Leben in der Weimarer Republik.* Königstein, 1978.

Campbell, Joan. *The German Werkbund: The Politics of Reform in the Applied Arts.* Princeton, N.J., 1978.

————. *Joy in Work, German Work: The National Debate, 1800–1945.* Princeton, N.J., 1989.

Cancik, Hubert, ed. *Religions- und Geistesgeschichte der Weimarer Republik.* Düsseldorf, 1982.

Deak, Istvan. *Weimar Germany's Left-Wing Intellectuals: A Political History of the Weltbühne and Its Circle.* Berkeley, Calif., 1968.

Döring, Herbert. *Der Weimarer Kreis. Studien zum politischen Bewußtsein verfassungstreuer Hochschullehrer in der Weimarer Republik.* Meisenheim, 1975.

Dudek, Peter. *Erziehung durch Arbeit. Arbeitslagerbewegung und freiwilliger Arbeitsdienst 1920–1935.* Opladen, 1988.

Dupeux, Louis. *"Nationalbolschewismus" in Deutschland 1919–1933. Kommunistische Strategie und konservative Dynamik.* Munich, 1985.

Faulenbach, Bernd. *Ideologie des deutschen Weges. Die deutsche Geschichte in der Historiographie zwischen Kaiserreich und Nationalsozialismus.* Munich, 1980.

Fritzsche, Klaus. *Politische Romantik und Gegenrevolution. Fluchtwege in der Krise der bürgerlichen Gesellschaft. Das Beispiel des "Tat"-Kreises.* Frankfurt am Main, 1976.

Gay, Peter. *Weimar Culture: The Outsider as Insider.* New York, 1968.

Gerstenberger, Heide. *Der revolutionäre Konservativismus. Ein Beitrag zur Analyse des Liberalismus*. Berlin, 1969.

Götz von Olenhusen, Irmtraud. *Jugendreich, Gottes Reich, Deutsches Reich. Junge Generation, Religion und Politik 1928–1933*. Cologne, 1987.

Herf, Jeffrey. *Reactionary Modernism: Technology, Culture and Politics in Weimar and the Third Reich*. Cambridge, 1984.

Hermand, Jost, and Frank Trommler. *Die Kultur der Weimarer Republik*. 2nd ed. Frankfurt am Main, 1988.

Hiller von Gaertringen, Friedrich. " 'Dolchstoß'-Diskussion und 'Dolchstoßlegende' im Wandel von vier Jahrzehnte." In *Geschichte und Gegenwartsbewußtsein. Historische Betrachtungen und Untersuchungen. Festschrift für Hans Rothfels zum 70. Geburtstag*, edited by Waldemar Besson und Friedrich Hiller von Gaertringen, pp. 122–60. Göttingen, 1963.

———. "Zur Beurteilung des 'Monarchismus' in der Weimarer Republik." In *Tradition und Reform in der deutschen Politik. Gedenkschrift für Waldemar Besson*, edited by Gotthard Jasper, pp. 138–86. Berlin, 1976.

Holl, Karl, and Wolfram Wette, eds. *Pazifismus in der Weimarer Republik. Beiträge zur historischen Friedensforschung*. Paderborn, 1981.

Ishida, Yuji. *Jungkonservative in der Weimarer Republik. Der Ring-Kreis 1928–1933*. Frankfurt am Main, 1988.

Jansen, Christian. *Professoren und Politik. Politisches Denken und Handeln der Heidelberger Hochschullehrer 1914–1935*. Kritische Studien zur Geschichtswissenschaft, 99. Göttingen, 1992.

Kaes, Anton, ed. *Weimarer Republik. Manifeste und Dokumente zur deutschen Literatur 1918–1933*. Stuttgart, 1983.

Kater, Michael H. "Die Artamanen. Völkische Jugend in der Weimarer Republik." *HZ* 213 (1971): 577–638.

———. *Studentenschaft und Rechtsradikalismus in Deutschland 1918–1933. Eine sozialgeschichtliche Studie zur Bildungskrise in der Weimarer Republik*. Hamburg, 1975.

Kindt, Werner, ed. *Die deutsche Jugendbewegung 1920–1933. Die bündische Zeit: Quellenschriften*. Düsseldorf, 1974.

Koebner, Thomas, ed. *Weimars Ende. Prognosen und Diagnosen in der deutschen Literatur und Publizistik 1930–1933*. Frankfurt am Main, 1982.

Koebner, Thomas, Rolf-Peter Janz, and Frank Trommler, eds. *"Mit uns zieht die neue Zeit." Der Mythos Jugend*. Frankfurt am Main, 1985.

Langewiesche, Dieter. "Politik, Gesellschaft, Kultur. Zur Problematik von Arbeiterkultur und kulturellen Arbeiterorganisationen in Deutschland nach dem 1. Weltkrieg." *AfS* 22 (1982): 359–402.

Laqueur, Walter. *Weimar: A Cultural History, 1918–1933*. New York, 1974.

Lebovics, Hermann. *Social Conservatism and the Middle Classes in Germany, 1914–1933*. Princeton, N.J., 1969.

Lepsius, M. Rainer. *Extremer Nationalismus. Strukturbedingungen vor der nationalsozialistischen Machtergreifung*. Stuttgart, 1966.

Linse, Ulrich. *Barfüßige Propheten. Erlöser der zwanziger Jahre.* Berlin, 1983.

Lutzhöft, Hans-Jürgen. *Der nordische Gedanke in Deutschland 1920–1940.* Stuttgart, 1971.

Miller-Lane, Barbara. *Architecture and Politics in Germany, 1918–1945.* Cambridge, Mass., 1968.

Mohler, Armin. *Die konservative Revolution in Deutschland, 1918–1932. Ein Handbuch.* 3rd rev. ed. Darmstadt, 1989.

Mommsen, Hans. "Der Mythos des nationalen Aufbruchs und die Haltung der deutschen intellektuellen und funktionalen Eliten." In *1933 in Gesellschaft und Wissenschaft. Ringvorlesung im Wintersemester 1982/83,* 1:127–41. Hamburg, 1983.

Mosse, George L. *The Crisis of German Ideology: Intellectual Origins of the Third Reich.* New York, 1964.

Müller, Hans-Harald. *Der Krieg und die Schriftsteller. Der Kriegsroman in der Weimarer Republik.* Stuttgart, 1986.

Petzold, Joachim. *Wegbereiter des deutschen Faschismus. Die Jungkonservativen in der Weimarer Republik.* Cologne, 1978.

Peukert, Detlev J. K. *Jugend zwischen Krieg und Krise. Lebenswelten von Arbeiterjungen in der Weimarer Republik.* Cologne, 1987.

Prümm, Karl. *Die Literatur des soldatischen Nationalismus der 20er Jahre 1918–1933. Gruppenideologie und Epochenproblematik.* 2 vols. Kronberg, 1974.

Rabbe, Felix. *Die bündische Jugend. Ein Beitrag zur Geschichte der Weimarer Republik.* Stuttgart, 1961.

Ringer, Fritz K. *The Decline of the German Mandarins: The German Academic Community, 1890–1933.* Cambridge, Mass., 1969.

Schmuhl, Hans-Walter. *Rassenhygiene, Nationalsozialismus, Euthanasie. Von der Verhütung zur Vernichtung "lebensunwerten Lebens" 1880–1945.* Kritische Studien zur Geschichtswissenschaft, 75. Göttingen, 1987.

Schueller, Martin. *Zwischen Romantik und Faschismus. Der Beitrag Othmar Spanns zum Konservatismus in der Weimarer Republik.* Stuttgart, 1970.

Schulz, Gerhard. "Der 'Nationale Klub von 1919' zu Berlin. Zum politischen Zerfall einer Gesellschaft." *Jahrbuch für die Geschichte Mittel- und Ostdeutschlands* 11 (1962): 207–23.

Schwarz, Hans-Peter. *Der konservative Anarchist. Politik und Zeitkritik Ernst Jüngers.* Freiburg im Breisgau, 1962.

Schwarz, Jürgen. *Studenten in der Weimarer Republik. Die deutsche Studentenschaft in der Zeit von 1918 bis 1923 und ihre Stellung zur Politik.* Berlin, 1971.

Schwierskott, Hans Joachim. *Arthur Moeller van den Bruck und der revolutionäre Nationalismus in der Weimarer Republik.* Göttingen, 1962.

Seiterich-Kreuzkamp, Thomas. *Links, frei und katholisch — Walter Dirks. Ein Beitrag zur Geschichte des Katholizismus der Weimarer Republik. Mit einem Nachwort von Walter Dirks.* Frankfurt am Main, Bern, and New York, 1986.

Siegfried, Klaus-Jörg. *Universalismus und Faschismus. Das Gesellschaftsbild Othmar Spanns. Zur politischen Funktion seiner Gesellschaftslehre und Ständestaatskonzeption.* Vienna, 1974.

Sösemann, Bernd. *Das Ende der Weimarer Republik in der Kritik demokratischer*

Publizisten Theodor Wolff, Ernst Feder, Julius Elbau, Leopold Schwarzschild. Berlin, 1976.

Sontheimer, Kurt. *Antidemokratisches Denken in der Weimarer Republik. Die politischen Ideen des deutschen Nationalismus zwischen 1918 und 1933.* 2nd ed. Munich, 1968.

Stambolis, Barbara. *Der Mythos der jungen Generation. Ein Beitrag zur politischen Kultur der Weimarer Republik.* Bochum, 1984.

Stark, Gary D. *Entrepreneurs of Ideology: Neoconservative Publishers in Germany, 1890–1933.* Chapel Hill, N.C., 1981.

Stark, Michael, ed. *Deutsche Intellektuelle 1910–1933. Aufrufe, Pamphlete, Betrachtungen.* Heidelberg, 1984.

Stern, Fritz. *The Failure of Illiberalism: Essays on the Political Culture of Modern Germany.* New York, 1972.

———. *The Politics of Cultural Despair: A Study in the Rise of Germanic Ideology.* Berkeley, Calif., 1961.

Struve, Walter. *Elites against Democracy: Leadership Ideals in Bourgeois Political Thought in Germany, 1890–1933.* Princeton, N.J., 1973.

Thoss, Bruno. *Der Ludendorff-Kreis 1919–1923. München als Zentrum der mitteleuropäischen Gegenrevolution zwischen Revolution und Hitlerputsch.* Munich, 1978.

Von Klemperer, Klemens. *Germany's New Conservatism: Its History and Dilemma in the Twentieth Century.* Princeton, N.J., 1968.

Weisbrod, Bernd. "Gewalt in der Politik. Zur politischen Kultur in Deutschland zwischen den beiden Weltkriegen." *GWU* 43 (1992): 391–404.

Willet, John. *Art and Politics in the Weimar Republic: The New Sobriety, 1917–1933.* New York, 1978.

———. *The Weimar Years: A Culture Cut Short.* New York and London, 1984.

Wippermann, Klaus W. *Politische Propaganda und staatsbürgerliche Bildung. Die Reichszentrale für Heimatdienst in der Weimarer Republik.* Bonn, 1976.

Wohl, Robert. *The Generation of 1914.* London, 1980.

THE JEWISH POPULATION AND ANTI-SEMITISM

Gay, Peter. *Freud, Jews, and Other Germans: Masters and Victims in Modernist Culture.* New York, 1978.

———. "In Deutschland zu Hause. Die Juden der Weimarer Zeit." In *The Jews in Nazi Germany 1933–1945,* edited by Arnold Paucker, Sylvia Gilchrist, and Barbara Suchy, pp. 31–43. Schriftenreihe wissenschaftlicher Abhandlungen des Leo Baeck Instituts, 45. Tübingen, 1986.

Grab, Walter, and Julius H. Schoeps, eds. *Juden in der Weimarer Republik.* Stuttgart and Bonn, 1986.

Küttner, Hans-Helmuth. *Die Juden und die deutsche Linke in der Weimarer Republik 1918–1933.* Düsseldorf, 1971.

Maurer, Trude. *Ostjuden in Deutschland, 1918–1933.* Hamburger Beiträge zur Geschichte der deutschen Juden, 12. Hamburg, 1986.

Michalski, Gabrielle. *Der Antisemitismus im deutschen akademischen Leben in der Zeit nach dem 1. Weltkrieg.* Frankfurt am Main, Bern, and Cirencester, 1980.

Mosse, Werner E., ed. *Deutsches Judentum in Krieg und Revolution 1916–1923.* Schriftenreihe wissenschaftlicher Abhandlungen des Leo Baeck Instituts, 25. Tübingen, 1971.

———. *Entscheidungsjahr 1932. Zur Judenfrage in der Endphase der Weimarer Republik.* Schriftenreihe wissenschaftlicher Abhandlungen des Leo Baeck Instituts, 13. 2nd ed. Tübingen, 1966.

Niewyk, Donald L. *The Jews in Weimar Germany.* Baton Rouge, La., 1980.

Paucker, Arnold. *Der jüdische Abwehrkampf gegen Antisemitismus und Nationalsozialismus in den letzten Jahren der Weimarer Republik.* Hamburg, 1968.

Richarz, Monika. *Jüdisches Leben in Deutschland. Selbstzeugnisse zur Sozialgeschichte.* Vol. 3. Stuttgart, 1982.

RISE OF THE NSDAP

Allen, William Sheridan. *The Nazi Seizure of Power: The Experience of a Single German Town, 1922–1945.* Rev. ed. New York, 1984.

Böhnke, Wilfried. *Die NSDAP im Ruhrgebiet 1920–1933.* Bonn-Bad Godesberg, 1974.

Broszat, Martin. *Hitler and the Collapse of Weimar Germany.* Translated and with a foreword by Volker R. Berghahn. New York, 1987.

———. "Soziale Motivation und Führer-Bindung des Nationalsozialismus." *VFZ* 18 (1970): 392–409.

Childers, Thomas. *The Nazi Voter: The Social Foundations of Fascism in Germany, 1919–1933.* Chapel Hill, N.C., 1983.

———, ed. *The Formation of the Nazi Constituency, 1919–1933.* London and Sydney, 1986.

Deuerlein, Ernst. *Der Aufstieg der NSDAP in Augenzeugenberichten.* Düsseldorf, 1968.

———, ed. *Der Hitler-Putsch. Bayerische Dokumente zum 8./9. November 1923.* Stuttgart, 1962.

Dickmann, Fritz. "Die Regierungsbildungen in Thüringen als Modell der Machtergreifung. Ein Brief Hitlers aus dem Jahre 1930." *VfZ* 14 (1966): 454–64.

Falter, Jürgen W. *Hitlers Wähler.* Munich, 1991.

———. "Wer verhalf der NSDAP zum Sieg?" *Aus Politik und Zeitgeschichte*, B 28–29/79 (14 July 1979): 3–21.

Falter, Jürgen W., and Dirk Hänisch. "Die Anfälligkeit von Arbeitern gegenüber der NSDAP bei den Reichstagswahlen 1928–1933." *AfS* 26 (1986): 179–216.

Farquharson, John E. *The Plough and the Swastika: The NSDAP and Agriculture in Germany, 1928–1945.* London, 1976.

Faust, Anselm. *Der Nationalsozialistische Deutsche Studentenbund. Studenten und Nationalsozialismus in der Weimarer Republik.* 2 vols. Düsseldorf, 1973.

Fischer, Conan. *Stormtroopers: A Social, Economic and Ideological Analysis, 1929–35.* London, Boston, and Sydney, 1983.

Franz-Willing, Georg. *Die Hitlerbewegung. Der Ursprung 1919 bis 1922.* New ed. Preußisch Oldendorf, 1974.

Gies, Horst. "NSDAP und landwirtschaftliche Organisationen in der Endphase der Weimarer Republik." *VfZ* 15 (1967): 341–76.

Gordon, Harold J. *Hitler and the Beer Hall Putsch.* Princeton, N.J., 1972.

Grieswelle, Detlef. *Propaganda der Friedlosigkeit. Eine Studie zu Hitlers Rhetorik 1920–1933.* Stuttgart, 1972.

Hamilton, Richard F. *Who Voted for Hitler?* Princeton, N.J., 1982.

Heberle, Rudolf. *Landbevölkerung und Nationalsozialismus. Eine soziologische Untersuchung der politischen Willensbildung in Schleswig-Holstein 1918–1932.* Schriftenreihe der *VfZ*, 6. Stuttgart, 1963.

Hennig, Eike, ed. *Hessen unterm Hakenkreuz. Studien zur Durchsetzung der NSDAP in Hessen.* 2nd ed. Frankfurt am Main, 1984.

Hofmann, Hanns Hubert. *Der Hitlerputsch. Krisenjahre deutscher Geschichte 1920–1924.* Munich, 1961.

Horn, Wolfgang. *Der Marsch zur Machtergreifung. Die NSDAP bis 1933.* Königstein and Düsseldorf, 1980.

Hüttenberger, Peter. *Die Gauleiter. Studie zum Wandel des Machtgefüges in der NSDAP.* Schriftenreihe der *VfZ*, 19. Stuttgart, 1969.

Jäckel, Eberhard. *Hitler's Weltanschauung: A Blueprint for Power.* Translated by Herbert Arnold. Middletown, Conn., 1972.

Jamin, Mathilde. *Zwischen den Klassen. Zur Sozialstruktur der SA-Führerschaft.* Wuppertal, 1984.

Jochmann, Werner. *Im Kampf um die Macht. Hitlers Rede vor dem Hamburger Nationalclub von 1919.* Veröffentlichungen der Forschungsstelle für die Geschichte des Nationalsozialismus in Hamburg, 1. Frankfurt am Main, 1960.

———. *Nationalsozialismus und Revolution. Ursprung und Geschichte der NSDAP in Hamburg 1922–1933. Dokumente.* Frankfurt am Main, 1963.

Kater, Michael H. *The Nazi Party: A Social Profile of Members and Leaders 1919–1945.* Cambridge, Mass., 1983.

Kele, Max H. *Nazis and Workers: National Socialist Appeals to German Labor, 1919–1933.* Chapel Hill, N.C., 1972.

Kershaw, Ian. *Der Hitler-Mythos. Volksmeinung und Propaganda im Dritten Reich.* Schriftenreihe der *VfZ*, 41. Stuttgart, 1980.

Kissenkoetter, Udo. *Gregor Straßer und die NSDAP.* Schriftenreihe der *VfZ*, 37. Stuttgart, 1978.

Koehl, Robert L. *The Black Corps: The Structure and Power Struggles of the Nazi SS.* London, 1983.

Koshar, Rudy. *Social Life, Local Politics, and Nazism: Marburg, 1880–1935.* Chapel Hill, N.C., 1986.

Kratzenberg, Volker. *Arbeiter auf dem Weg zu Hitler? Die Nationalsozialistische Betriebszellen-Organization. Ihre Entstehung, ihre Programmatik, ihr Scheitern 1927–1937.* Frankfurt am Main, Bern, and New York, 1987.

Kuhn, Axel. *Hitlers außenpolitisches Programm. Entstehung und Entwicklung 1919–1939.* Stuttgart, 1970.

Longerich, Peter. *Die braunen Bataillone. Geschichte der SA.* Munich, 1989.

Manstein, Peter. *Die Mitglieder und Wähler der NSDAP 1919–1933. Untersuchungen zu ihrer schichtmäßigen Zusammensetzung.* Frankfurt am Main, 1990.

Maser, Werner. *Die Frühgeschichte der NSDAP. Hitlers Weg bis 1924.* Frankfurt am Main, 1965.

Matzerath, Horst, and Henry A. Turner. "Die Selbstfinanzierung der NSDAP 1930–1932." *GuG* 3 (1977): 59–92.

Mommsen, Hans. "Zur Verschränkung traditioneller und faschistischer Führungsgruppen in Deutschland beim Übergang von der Bewegungs- zur Systemphase." In *Faschismus als soziale Bewegung. Deutschland und Italien im Vergleich,* edited by Wolfgang Schieder, pp. 157–81. 2nd ed. Göttingen, 1982.

Mühlberger, Detlef. *Hitler's Followers: Studies in the Sociology of the Nazi Movement.* London, 1991.

Noakes, Jeremy. *The Nazi Party in Lower Saxony, 1921–1933.* London, 1971.

Nyomarkay, Joseph. *Charisma and Factionalism in the Nazi Party.* Minneapolis, 1967.

Orlow, Dietrich J. *The History of the Nazi Party, 1919–1933.* Pittsburgh, 1969.

Pridham, Geoffrey. *Hitler's Rise to Power: The Nazi Movement in Bavaria 1923–1933.* London, 1973.

Prinz, Michael. *Vom neuen Mittelstand zum Volksgenossen. Die Entwicklung des sozialen Status der Angestellten von der Weimarer Republik bis zum Ende der NS-Zeit.* Munich, 1986.

Roloff, Ernst-August. *Bürgertum und Nationalsozialismus 1930–1933. Braunschweigs Weg ins Dritte Reich.* Hanover, 1961.

Schulz, Gerhard. *Aufstieg des Nationalsozialismus. Krise und Revolution in Deutschland.* Frankfurt am Main, Berlin, and Vienna, 1975.

———. *Faschismus—Nationalsozialismus. Versionen und theoretische Kontroversen 1922–1972.* Frankfurt am Main, 1974.

Speier, Hans. *Die Angestellten vor dem Nationalsozialismus. Ein Beitrag zum Verständnis der deutschen Sozialstruktur 1918–1933.* Göttingen, 1977.

Stachura, Peter D. *Gregor Strasser and the Rise of Nazism.* London, 1983.

———. "Der kritische Wendepunkt? Die NSDAP und die Reichstagswahlen vom 20. Mai 1928." *VfZ* 26 (1978): 66–99.

———, ed. *The Shaping of the Nazi State.* London, 1978.

Stegmann, Dirk. "Zum Verhältnis von Großindustrie und Nationalsozialismus 1930 bis 1933. Ein Beitrag zur Geschichte der sog. Machtergreifung." *AfS* 13 (1973): 399–482.

———. "Zwischen Repression und Manipulation. Konservative Machteliten und Arbeiter- und Angestelltenbewegung 1910–1918. Ein Beitrag zur Vorgeschichte von DAP/NSDAP." *AfS* 12 (1972): 351–432.

Steinberg, Michael S. *Sabers and Brown Shirts: The German Students' Path to National Socialism, 1918–1935.* Chicago, 1977.

Stokes, Larry D. *Kleinstadt und Nationalsozialismus. Ausgewählte Dokumente zur Geschichte von Eutin 1918–1945.* Neumünster, 1984.

Turner, Henry A. *Faschismus und Kapitalismus in Deutschland. Studien zum Verhältnis zwischen Nationalsozialismus und Wirtschaft.* Göttingen, 1972.

———. *German Big Business and the Rise of Hitler.* New York, 1985.

————, ed. *Hitler aus nächster Nähe. Aufzeichnungen eines Vertrauten 1920 bis 1932.* Frankfurt am Main, Berlin, and Vienna, 1978.

Tyrell, August. *Führer befiehl . . . Selbstzeugnisse aus der "Kampfzeit" der NSDAP. Dokumentation und Analyse.* Düsseldorf, 1969.

————. *Vom Trommler zum Führer. Der Wandel von Hitlers Selbstverständnis zwischen 1919 und 1924 und die Entwicklung der NSDAP.* Munich, 1975.

Werner, Andreas. "SA und NSDAP. SA: 'Wehrverband,' 'Parteitruppe' oder 'Revolutionsarmee'? Studien zur Geschichte der SA und der NSDAP 1920 bis 1933." Ph.D. diss., Universität Erlangen, 1964.

POLITICS OF THE PRESIDENTIAL REGIME

Becker, Josef. "Heinrich Brüning in den Krisenjahren der Weimarer Republik." *GWU* 17 (1966): 291–319.

Bennecke, Heinrich. *Wirtschaftliche Depression und politischer Radikalismus. Die Lehre von Weimar.* Munich, 1968.

Bracher, Karl Dietrich. "Brünings unpolitische Politik und die Auflösung der Weimarer Republik." *VfZ* 19 (1971): 113–23.

Bühler, Karl. *Die pädagogische Problematik des Freiwilligen Arbeitsdienstes.* Aachen, 1978.

Conze, Werner. "Brünings Politik unter dem Druck der großen Krise." *HZ* 199 (1964): 529–50.

Conze, Werner, and Hans Raupach, eds. *Die Staats- und Wirtschaftskrise des Deutschen Reiches 1929/33. Sechs Beiträge.* Stuttgart, 1967.

Hentschel, Volker. *Weimars letzte Monate. Hitler und der Untergang der Republik.* Düsseldorf, 1978.

Höhne, Heinz. *Die Machtergreifung. Deutschlands Weg in die Hitler-Diktatur.* Reinbek, 1983.

Höner, Sabine. *Der nationalsozialistische Zugriff auf Preußen. Preußischer Staat und nationalsozialistische Machteroberungsstrategie 1928–1934.* Bochum, 1984.

Hörster-Philipps, Ulrike. *Konservative Politik in der Endphase der Weimarer Republik. Die Regierung Franz von Papen.* Cologne, 1982.

Holl, Karl, ed. *Wirtschaftskrise und liberale Demokratie. Das Ende der Weimarer Republik und die gegenwärtige Situation.* Göttingen, 1978.

Janssen, Karl-Heinz. *Der 30. Januar. Ein Report über den Tag, der die Welt veränderte.* Frankfurt am Main, 1983.

Köhler, Henning. *Arbeitsdienst in Deutschland. Pläne und Verwirklichungsformen bis zur Einführung der Arbeitsdienstpflicht im Jahre 1935.* Berlin, 1967.

Mommsen, Hans. "Staat und Bürokratie in der Ära Brüning." In *Tradition und Reform in der deutschen Politik. Gedenkschrift für Waldemar Besson,* edited by Gotthard Jasper, pp. 81–137. Berlin, 1976.

Schildt, Axel. *Militärdiktatur mit Massenbasis? Die Querfrontkonzeption der Reichswehrführung um General von Schleicher am Ende der Weimarer Republik.* Frankfurt am Main, 1981.

Schulz, Gerhard, ed. *Die Große Krise der dreißiger Jahre. Vom Niedergang der Weltwirtschaft zum Zweiten Weltkrieg.* Göttingen, 1985.

Stürmer, Michael. "Der unvollendete Parteienstaat. Zur Vorgeschichte des Präsidialregimes am Ende der Weimarer Republik." *VfZ* 21 (1973): 119–26.

Vierhaus, Rudolf. "Auswirkungen der Krise um 1930 in Deutschland. Beiträge zu einer historisch-psychologischen Analyse." In *Die Staats- und Wirtschaftskrise des deutschen Reiches 1929/33*, edited by Werner Conze and Hans Raupach, pp. 155–75. Stuttgart, 1967.

Vogelsang, Thilo. "Zur Politik Schleichers gegenüber der NSDAP 1932. Dokumentation." *VfZ* 6 (1958): 86–118.

Weßling, Wolfgang. "Hindenburg, Neudeck und die deutsche Wirtschaft." *Vierteljahreshefte für Sozial- und Wirtschaftsgeschichte* 64 (1977): 41–73.

Winkler, Heinrich August, ed. *Die deutsche Staatskrise 1930–1933. Handlungsspielräume und Alternativen.* Schriften des Historischen Kollegs, Kolloquien 26. Munich, 1992.

Index